THE IRISH BOOK LOVER
An Irish Studies Reader

based on the proceedings of a symposium held
at
The Princess Grace Irish Library in Monaco
on 4th–7th October 2002

THE PRINCESS GRACE IRISH LIBRARY SERIES
(ISSN 0269-2619)

1. C. George Sandulescu & Clive Hart, eds., *Assessing the 1984 "Ulysses"*.
2. Princess Grace Irish Library, ed., *Irishness in a Changing Society*.
3. A. Norman Jeffares, ed., *Yeats the European*.
4. Philip Gaskell & Clive Hart, eds., *Ulysses: a Review of Three Texts*.
5. John W. Purser, ed., *The Literary Works of Jack B. Yeats*.
6. Glanville Price, ed., *The Celtic Connection*.
7. Hubert McDermott, ed., [Anon.,] *Vertue Rewarded or The Irish Princess*.
8. C. George Sandulescu, ed., *Rediscovering Oscar Wilde*.
9. Bruce Stewart, ed., *Beckett and Beyond*.
10. Joseph Donohue with Ruth Berggren, eds., *Oscar Wilde's "The Importance of Being Earnest"*: *The First Production*.
11. Clive Hart, C. George Sandulescu, Bonnie K. Scott & Fritz Senn, eds., *Images of Joyce* [2 vols.].
12. Bruce Stewart, ed., *That Other World: The Supernatural and Fantastic in Irish Literature and Its Contexts* [2 vols.].
13. Bruce Stewart, ed., *Hearts and Minds: Irish Culture and Society under the Act of Union*.
14. Bruce Stewart, ed., *The Irish Book Lover: An Irish Studies Reader*.

THE PRINCESS GRACE IRISH LIBRARY LECTURES
(ISSN 0950-5121)

1. A. N. Jeffares, *Parameters of Irish Literature in English*.
2. Clive Hart, *Language and Structure in Beckett's Plays*; with C. George Sandulescu, *A Beckett Synopsis*.
3. Charles Peake, *Jonathan Swift and the Art of Raillery*.
4. Glanville Price, Ireland *and the Celtic Connection*; with Morfydd E. Owen, *A Celtic Bibliography*.
5. Clive Hart, *Joyce, Huston, and the Making of "The Dead"*.
6. Morris Beja, *Joyce, the Artist Manqué, and Indeterminacy*.
7. Monique Gallagher, *Flann O'Brien, Myles from Dublin*; with Marc Poitou, *Bernard Shaw & the Comedy of Approval*.
8. Arnold Goldman, *Synge's "The Aran Islands"*: '*A World of Grey*'; with C. George Sandulescu, *Joyce & Vico & Linguistic Theory*
9. Denis Donoghue, *Who Says What,* and *The Question of Voice*.

THE IRISH BOOK LOVER
An Irish Studies Reader

Taken from issues of

The Irish Book Lover
(1909–1957)

Edited with an Integrated Index
by Bruce Stewart

&

An Introductory Lecture
by Nicholas Allen

PRINCESS GRACE IRISH LIBRARY : 14

This collection copyright © 2004 by
The Princess Grace Irish Library, Monaco

Contributions copyright © 2004 by the individual contributors as listed on the Contents pages and their rights to be identified as authors of their articles are hereby asserted in accordance with the Copyright, Designs and Patents Act, 1988

First published in 2004 by Colin Smythe Limited, Gerrards Cross, Buckinghamshire SL9 8XA, UK
www.colinsmythe.co.uk

Distributed in North America by Oxford University Press
198 Madison Avenue, New York, NY 10016, USA

British Library Cataloguing in Publication Data
A catalogue record for this book is available
from the British Library

ISBN ISBN 0-86140-455-6

All rights reserved. Apart from any fair dealing for the purposes of research or private study, or criticism or review, as permitted under the Copyright, Designs and Patents Act, 1988, this publication may be reproduced, stored or transmitted, in any forms or by any means, only with the prior permission in writing of the publishers, or in the case of reprographic reproduction in accordance with the terms of licences issued by the Copyright Licensing Agency. Enquiries concerning reproduction outside these terms should be sent to the publishers at the above-mentioned address.

Acknowledgements are made to the editors and contributors of *The Irish Book Lover* (1909–1957). Every practical attempt has been made to contact the holders of any copyright entitlements attaching to articles reproduced here, all of which are copied within the meaning of the term 'fair dealing' as defined by the Copyright, Design and Patents Act, 1988. If any holders of rights in works quoted herein consider this interpretation to be incorrect, they should communicate with this company.

Produced in Great Britain
Printed and bound by T. J. International Ltd.,
Trecerus Industrial Estate, Padstow, Cornwall PL28 8RW

Contents

Editor's Preface	xi
Nicholas Allen: Introductory Lecture	1
The Irish Book Lover: An Irish Studies Reader	19
The Irish Book Lover: An Integrated Index	223
Bruce Stewart: Afterword	371
Appendix I: Chronology of Issues	385
Appendix II: Participants & Programme	389

The Irish Book Lover

Volume I (Aug. 1909 to July 1910)

John S. Crone, "Foreword: Our Forerunner"	19
E. R. McClintock Dix, "The Beaufoy Sale"	22
John S. Crone, "Honours For Irish Scholars"	23
"Forthcoming: *Robert Emmet* by Stephen Gwynn"	24
"Reviews: Julie Bredon & Lynn Doyle"	24
J. J. Marshall, "Notes From The North"	25
E. R. McClintock Dix, "Henry Bradshaw on Printing in Ireland"	26
"Forthcoming Book: *Life of W. E. H. Lecky*"	28
"Reviews: *Insurrection* by James Stephens"	29
"Post Bag: Jeremiah. King on County Histories"	30
E. R. McClintock Dix, "Keating's History of Ireland"	30
Henry R. Plomer, "Ireland and Secret Printing"	31
John S. Crone, "Reviews: *The Mountainy Singer* by Seosamh MacCathmhaoil"	32
"John [Millington] Synge's Future Fame"	33
R. S. Maffett, "The Roundwood Press"	33
E. M. McC. Dix, "Eighteenth-century Newspapers" .	35
F. J. Bigger, "John Bernard Trotter"	37
"Reviews: *Journal and Reminiscences of R. Denny Urlin*"	38
"Post Bag: Sir William Petty & The Book of Surveys"	39
"Post Bag: *Keating's History of Ireland*"	39
"Book Auctions in Cork" (1909)	40
"Reviews: *Robert Emmet: A Historical Romance*"	40
"Post Bag: John Bernard Trotter"	41
E. R. McClintock Dix, "The Roundwood Press"	41
James Tuite, "J. C. Lyons and the Ledeston Press"	42
E. R. McClintock Dix, "Rare Ephemeral Magazines of the Eighteenth Century"	44
Stephen J. Brown, S.J., "A Guide to Books on Ireland"	46
E. R. McClintock Dix, "Printing in the Town of Cavan"	47
Sean Ghall [pseud.], "A Dictionary of Irish Biography"	48
Seamus Ua Casaide, "J. B. Trotter"	50
"Miscellaneous: Lord Kelvin's *Early Home*"	51
"Post Bag: Charles Wilson's *Irish Poems with English Translations*"	51
"Replies: *Ulster As It Is* by Thomas McKnight"	51

The Irish Book Lover vii

"Queries: Phillip Harwood & John Rutherford"	52
F. J. Bigger, "Henry Montgomery"	52
D. J. O'Donoghue, "Henry Montgomery (a reply)"	53
"Reviews: *The Dublin Book of Verse*, ed. John Cooke"	53
"Queries: W. H. Maxwell & J. D. Herbert"	54
"Recent Book Auctions" (March 1910)	54
"Irish Literary Society: *The Troth* by Rutherford Mayne"	55
A. P. Graves, "Ferguson Centenary Address"	56
James Hayes, "Smith O'Brien's Pamphlets"	59
James Coleman, "Death of Capt. Dunne"	60
"Book Auctions" (April 1910)	60
"Ferguson Centenary Address" (Francis Joseph Bigger)	61
"Reviews: *Cambridge University Library Bulletin* (Bradshaw Catalogue)"	64
John S. Crone, "An Interesting Volume: *The Trial of Archibald Hamilton Rowan*"	65
John S. Crone "Replies: John Rutherford"	65
[John S. Crone], "John Rutherford"	66
"Reviews: *The Hunger* […] *Realities of the Famine Years in Ireland*, by Andrew Merry"	68
"Notes: Ireland and Secret Printing"	68
"Queries: Daniel Maclise, Peter Burrowes, et al."	69
"Replies: Dictionary of National Biography"	70
W. J. Lawrence "Replies: Amyas Griffith"	70
"Book Auction" (June 1910)	71
"Irish Literary Society: The Wild Geese of Literature	71
"Some Recent Opinions of the Press"	72
J. J. Marshall, "Irish Chap Books"	72
"Sir William Butler" (Obituary)	75
"Eva of *The Nation*" (Obituary)	75
"Gossip: Alfred Nutt" (Obituary)	76
"Reviews: *History of Kerry* by Jeremiah King"	77
"Post Bag: Dictionary of Irish Biography"	77
John S. Crone, "Afterword"	78

Vols. VII & VIII (Jan. 1916 to Oct. 1917)

Feature Article: "Selina Bunbury"	79
"Great Irish Book Collectors (V): Canon Jeremiah Murphy"	79
Stouppe McCance, "Some Old Ulster Song Books"	81
"Editor's Gossip: W. B. Yeats (Abbey Theatre Finance)"	82

E. R. McC. Dix, "The Charles Halliday Pamphets"	82
"Great Irish Book Collectors (VI): William Monck Mason"	82
E. V. Lucas, "The Two Ladies (Somerville & Ross)"	83
"Irish Literary Society: Emily Lawless Night"	83
"Notice of New Books: *An Alphabet of Irish Saints*"	84
"Queries and Replies: Thomas Church, 'Bard of Clanmaurice'"	85
"Post Bag: Standish Hayes O'Grady, A.B. (T.C.D)"	85
"Obituaries: James Collins & Emma Crawford"	85
John S. Crone, "Sir Charles Gavan Duffy"	86
Thomas Roche, "Canon Murphy: Life, Labours & Library"	88
Colm Ó Lochlainn, "Bibliography of Oscar Wilde"	89
"Editor's Gossip: Cuttings on *The Irish Book Lover*"	90
"Obituary: Stopford Augustus Brooke"	92
D. Boyle, "The Irish Genius of the Brontës" [Part I]	92
Eleanor Hull, "*Eriu* (Vol. VIII, Part 1) Reviewed"	94
"Great Irish Book Collectors (VII): Most Rev. Dr. Sheehan"	96
"Post Bag: William Marcus Thompson of The Standard"	97
E. R. McC. Dix, "Some Rare Dublin Magazines of the Eighteenth Century"	98
D. Boyle, "The Irish Genius of the Brontës" [Part II]	100
T. F. O'Rahilly, "Peter O'Connell: *Irish-English Dictionary* (MS Egerton 83)"	103
John S. Crone, "Dean Butler's *Notices of the Castle and* [...] *Abbies* [...] *at Trim*"	104
"Editor's Gossip: Easter Rising and the Book Trade"	104
"Notices of New Books: *The Irish Rebellion of 1916* by John H. Boyle"	106
"Post Bag: Bibliography of Gavan Duffy"	107
"Obituaries: Francis Sheehy Skeffington and the 1916 Leaders"	107
E. R. McC. Dix, "Some Rare Dublin Magazines of the Nineteenth Century (concluded)"	108
D. J. O'Donoghue, "Literature and the Late Rebellion"	109
Randell McDonnell, "Remembrance (Lieutenant Thomas Kettle)" [poem]	111
P. S. O'Hegarty, "Post Bag: The Dead Leaders"	111
David James O'Donoghue "Obituary: Roger David Casement"	112
"The Blind Girl of Donegal"	112
David James O'Donoghue, "*The Dublin and London Magazine*"	113
"Some Old Derry Ephemera"	113
"Post Bag: Charles O'Driscoll"	114

"Reviews: "W. B. Yeats's *Reveries* and *Responsibilities*"	114
"Notice of New Books: *Insurrection in Dublin* by James Stephens"	115
Edmund Downey, "An Editor's Reminiscences"	116
John S. Crone, "Editor's Gossip"	116
Séamus Ó Casaide, "Post Bag: O'Donovan's Supplement"	117
David Kennedy, "Queries and Replies: Edmund Getty"	118
John S. Crone, "A Rogue's Memoirs"	118
John S. Crone, "Editor's Gossip"	119
"Notice of New Books: *Lord Edward—A Study in Romance*, by Katherine Tynan"	119
"Denis Florence McCarthy"	120
"Some Interesting Manuscripts"	121
"Maginn and *Blackwood*"	121
John Francis MacEntee, "The Tramp" [poem]	123

Volume XVI (Jan. & Feb. 1928 to Nov. & Dec. 1928)

Séamus Ó Casaide, "Editorial"	125
John S. Crone, "Sgéala ó Chathair na gCeó"	125
Séamus Ó Casaide, "Three Irish Scribes of County Cork"	127
Séamus Ó Casaide "The Anonymous Prefacer, 1722"	128
Séamus Ó Casaide "The Last Irish Scribe"	130
Stephen J. Brown, S.J., "The *Book Lover* and the Libraries"	131
Colm Ó Lochlainn, "A Printer's Device"	132
Séamus Ó Casaide, "John D'Alton's Manuscripts"	132
John S. Crone, "Sgéala Ó Cathair na gCeó"	135
"*Irish Book Lover* Vols. I-XV: Note & List of Plates"	136
Séamus Ó Casaide, "Newbery's Irish Accidence: 1562–63"	138
Colm Ó Lochlainn, "The Printer on Gaelic Printing"	139
"Half-Yearly Bibliography" (May-June 1928)	139
U. D'A., "Padraic Ó Conaire"	142
John S. Crone, "Sgéala ó Cathair na gCeó"	143
Séamus Ó Casaide, "The Speche of an Irishe man in the yere 1542"	144
"Reviews: Sean O'Casey & Frank Gallagher"	145
"Half-Yearly Bibliography" (July-Dec. 1928)	148
Séamus Ó Casaide, "An O'Connell 500 Years Ago!"	151

Vol. XVIII (Jan. & Feb. 1930 to Nov. & Dec. 1930)

Colm Ó Lochlainn, "Editorial (Jan. & Feb. 1930)"	153
John S. Crone, "Sgéala ó Chathair na gCeó"	153
E. Hogan, S.J., "Father Francis O Molloy & Lucerna Fidelium"	155
Gregory Cleary, O.F.M., "Father Francis O'Molloy"	158
"Bibliographical Society of Ireland (A.G.M.)"	160
"Half-Yearly Bibliography to Dec. 30 1929"	161
Colm Ó Lochlainn, "Editorial: *The Irish Statesman*"	165
R. J. Kelly, "Anthony Trollope and Ireland"	166
Séamus Ó Donnabháin, "Commentary (Duanaire Finn, &c.)	169
Colm Ó Lochlainn, "Literature of the Conflict"	170
Séamus Ó Donnabháin, "Commentary (Carleton's *Traits & Stories*, &c.)"	172
"Reviews: Bibliography of Standish J. O'Grady"	174
Colm Ó Lochlainn, "Editorial" (July & Aug. 1930)	174
John S. Crone, "Sgéala ó Chathair na gCeó"	175
Séamus Ó Donnabháin, "A Current Commentary"	177
Séamus Ó Casaide, "Oliver Goldsmith"	178
Séamus Ó Donnabháin, "Oliver Goldsmith & the Arms Race"	179
John S. Crone, "Sgéala ó Chathair na gCeó"	179
[Colm Ó Lochlainn], "A Current Commentary"	181
Séamus Ó Casaide, "Rev. Bernard Callan"	182
Colm Ó Lochlainn, "Editorial (Nov. & Dec. 1930)"	183
John S. Crone, "Sgéala ó Chathair na gCeó"	183
E. R. McC. Dix, "Miss D. A. Ferguson" (Obituary)	185
M. J. McManus, "A Forgotten Goldsmith Poem"	186
"How James Duffy Rose to Fame" (*Sunday Independent*)	187

Miscellaneous Issues (Aug. 1912 to Sept. 1957)

J. M. Hone, "Yeats, Synge and *The Playboy*", Vol. IV, No. 1 (Aug. 1912)	191
Stephen Gwynn M.P., "Irish Book Lovers", Vol. IV, No. 8 (March 1913)	191
"George William Russell (Æ)", Vol. VII, No. 3 (Oct. 1915)	192
"Reviews: *A Portrait of the Artist as a Young Man* by James Joyce", Vol. VIII, No. 9 & 10 (April & May 1917)	193
"Irish Poetry", Vol. XII, No. 3 (Oct. 1921)	193
"Editor's Gossip", Vol. XIII, No. 3 (Oct. 1921)	195
The Nation, "Pen Portraits", Vol. XIII, No. 3 (Oct. 1921)	195
The Observer, "Pen Portraits", Vol. XIII, No. 3 (Oct. 1921)	197

Robert Lynd, "More or Less about Irish Literature", Vol. XIII, Nos. 9 & 10, (April and May 1922) 197
John S. Crone, "Sgéala ó Chathair na gCeó", Vol. XIV, No. 1 (Jan. 1924) 198
John S. Crone, "Vale", Vol. XV [Index] (1925) 199
L. M., "*More Pricks Than Kicks* by Samuel Beckett", Vol. XXII, No. 4 (July & Aug. 1934) 199
P. C. Trimble, "*Selected Poems* by Æ", Vol. XXIII, No. 6 (Nov. & Dec. 1935) 199
P. C. Trimble, "Reviews: *Finnegans Wake* by James Joyce", Vol. XXVII, No. 1 (Jan. 1940) 200
P. C. Trimble, "Reviews: *Last Poems and Plays* by W. B. Yeats", Vol. XXVII, No. 4 (July 1940) 201
John S. Crone, "Willie Yeats and John O'Leary", Vol. XXVII, No. 5 (Nov. 1940) 203
"In Memoriam John Smyth Crone, 1858-1945", Vol. XXX, No. 1 (Oct. 1946) 208
P. S. O'Hegarty, "Some Memories of Dr. Crone", Vol. XXX, No. 1 (Oct. 1946) 209
W. B. Luke, "More Memories of Dr. Crone", Vol. XXX, No. 2 (Feb. 1947) 210
Kevin Faller, "Reviews: *Yeats: The Man and the Masks*, by Richard Ellmann", Vol. XXXI, No. 4 (April 1950) 212
Austin Clarke, "Notes and Queries: Yeats and 'The Sally Gardens'", Vol. XXXI, No. 6 (Nov. 1951) .. 212
Colm Ó Lochlainn, "Editorial: P. S. O'Hegarty", Vol. XXXII, No. 5 (July 1956) 213
Patrick Henchy, "Reviews: James Joyce's 'Araby'", Vol. XXXII, No. 5 (July 1956), 107 215
"A Letter from Oliver Goldsmith", Vol. XXXII, No. 6 (Sep. 1957) 215
F. Carroll, "Clarence Mangan's Age Complex", Vol. XXXII, No. 6 (Sept. 1957) 218
F. Carroll, "'The Dream of Macdonnell Claragh': An Anonymous Poem by Clarence Mangan", Vol. XXXII, No. 6 (Sept. 1957) 220
Colm Ó Lochlainn, "Farewell", Vol. XXXII, No. 6 (Sept. 1957) 221

Editor's Preface

The present selection of articles from *The Irish Book Lover* (1909-1957) had its origins in a symposium of the same name held at the Princess Grace Irish Library in Monaco over the days of Oct. 4th–7th 2002. Conceived primarily as a tribute to that journal, the symposium brought together fifteen Irish librarians, publishers, booksellers, scholars, and web innovators to reflect on the present state of print-culture, its prospects of development and the potential for transferring Irish booklore from printed sources to an internet environment—a development already heralded on the PGIL EIRData website and several others. Part commemoration and part emulation of the enthusiasm of the original *Irish Book Lover* contributors, our namesake symposium was, above all else, a colloquy of Irish book lovers.

The academic programme revolved around keynote lectures delivered by Nicholas Allen, Clare Hutton and Christina Hunt Mahony. Dr. Allen's well-crafted lecture shared its title with the symposium itself and was commissioned from the outset to serve as an introduction to the present compilation. Clare Hutton provided an authoritative overview of the strange case of Joyce's *Dubliners* under the title 'Chapters of Moral History: Failing to Publish *Dubliners*'. In so doing she demonstrated the use to which the Maunsel publishers' archive can be put while drawing effectively on the pages of *The Irish Book Lover* to illustrate the Irish response to Joyce, using reviews which are reprinted here. Her paper has since appeared in the *Transactions of the Bibliographical Society of America* with the permission of this Library.[1] Tina Mahony gave a brilliant account of the present state of Irish studies in America which was soon taken up by *The Irish Times* where it was printed in an abbreviated form in Spring 2003, likewise with acknowledgement to the Library. A longer version is shortly to appear in a collection on Irish studies edited for Pluto Press by Liam Harte and Irene Whelan.[2] For the rest, participants were invited to make reports on their professional bailiwicks within the Irish book world—libraries, publishing houses and internet domains—while Anthony Hutton undertook the specialist task of analysising the PGIL EIRData website using an overhead digital projector to demonstrate a technological make-over for the grant-driven future.

The "Irish Book Lover" symposium broke from precedent at the Library in that its publishing outcome was conceived from the outset as an anthology based on the original series. In making a selection, the method first adopted was to gather articles from similar sections under headings provided by the editors themselves. In practice neither were these headings sufficiently stable from volume to volume—still less from editorship to editorship—nor were the materials susceptible of ready organisation under any other set of conventional headings such as Bibliography, Biography, Reviews, Notes and Queries that could be devised for them instead. Even obituary notices defied easy classification inasmuch as articles of this kind were as likely to fall under "Editor's Gossip" as under any more definite heading—though an "Obituaries" column ran to some length in later issues. More significantly, perhaps, the stranding of topics from one issue to another (even between mutually remote volumes) seemed to call for some equivalent of the original sequencing of materials to suggest both proximity and distance and this implied that the integrity of the original issues should be largely preserved if possible. From this standpoint it appeared most plausible to reproduce a single issue from each editorial session on the grounds that each editor had his own style as regards leaders and selection of materials, and this is essentially the plan adopted. Hence it is that the present compilation show-cases the editorial work of John S. Crone (Vol. I, No. 1, 1909), Séamus Ó Casaide (Vol. XVI, No. 1, 1928), and Colm Ó Lochlainn (Vol. XVIII, No. 1, 1930).

Issues of *The Irish Book Lover* nevertheless exhibit a marked degree of uniformity in character and style from editor to editor, and in this sense they amount to proof that John Crone 'founded a school', as P. S. O'Hegarty put it in his obituary-memoir (Oct. 1946). At the same time, a number of patent changes wrought by the growth of Irish literature and alterations in the social and political context in which successive volumes were published is also discernible. Many of these arise from the ideological success of the Irish-Ireland movement, though the cultural accent of that movement as represented in these pages remains opaque and even problematic from the standpoint of discursive analysis today. Some Foucaultian reflection on 'discourse as power' is doubtless appropriate here. It might be added that the analysis of that accent—by which I mean the way in which Irish critics have *talked* and *written* about Irish writing in English during the post-independence period—has never been systematically conducted in spite of numerous post-colonial interventions more concerned with ideology than critical style and the forms of literary-critical pleading involved in it. To adequately engage with such a matter would require a symposium devoted to Irish criticism—and it is just such a meeting that the Princess Grace Irish Library next convened under the title of "Speaking of the Nation: Critical Discourse in Modern Ireland" during the weekend of 3rd–4th October 2004.

Events between 1916 and 1923, when the Irish world was shaken up

The Irish Book Lover

by the Easter Rising, the War of Independence and the Civil War, triggered a series of contributions which are among the pieces that most obviously invite republication: these include, signally, the short obituaries of 1916 leaders. Likewise, the reviews of major writers such as W. B. Yeats, James Joyce and Samuel Beckett retain their interest. These are among the few sections of the series occasionally quoted by critics, if only to illustrate the lack of sympathy among Irish literary contemporaries for what James Joyce was doing to Irish literature in *Dubliners*, *A Portrait* and *Ulysses*. Taking these various factors together, it seemed wisest to base the present selection around the editorial seasons and to add in a section illustrating the historically-interesting 1916-17 issues, together with a miscellany of pieces from sundry issues dealing with those major writers. The result is the present compilation. The hope, then, is that our selection will give a 'feel' of the original issues while embracing some of the most representative and interesting material, however unlike modern commentary in style and focus this may seem. Rather more than that: I hope that the literary mentality of early contributors, as well as the changing of the bibliographical guard will be revealed by less obviously quotable portions of this compilation such as "Post Bag" items and reports of "Book Sales". Yet whatever interest is found in these items it cannot be sufficiently stressed how much interesting material has been unavoidably left behind.

A large factor in shaping this edition relates to the electronic methods by which it has been compiled and the editorial work involved. To recuperate any significant sample of the 32-volume 'run' of *The Irish Book Lover* from the bound volumes sold by Colm Ó Lochlainn's Three Candles Press necessarily involved digitising a considerable amount of text from its often acid-scarred pages. Given a combination of scanning and copy-typing as the methods in use, the question then arises: how much of the entire series to copy and what to do with text found surplus to the present publishing requirement? An answer to these questions is to be found in the context of the PGIL EIRData Project, funded by the Ireland Fund of Monaco and conducted at the University of Ulster under the direction of the editor of this volume. Within the scheduled aims and objectives of that Project it proved possible to assign a considerable portion of working time to *The Irish Book Lover* over a three-month spell. The first result of this was a wide sample of the articles in editable form. The second was an integrated index of all issues drawn from the separate indexes compiled for each volume, initially by the printers Salmond & Co. and afterwards by Ó

Lochlainn following the journal's removal from London to Dublin under Ó Casaide's editorship in 1928. Once reduced to digital text, a series of editorial sweeps through the original material were made before the final selection was arrived at. Not alone were the original issues revisited to effect corrections and additions, but the alphabetisation of the original indexes was reorganised in keeping with a more sensible system. This involved grouping similar items under logical headings since the originals were, perhaps inevitably, laden with peculiarities arising from their disparate origin, volume by volume and decade by decade. Successive editors had different notions too as to how the headwords should be chosen: whether from the literal titles of articles or references enclosed in them, book-titles, reviewers names or those of authors reviewed by them or, finally, the names of topic understood to be of categorical importance, e.g., 'the DNB corrected' in the absence of any article of that title—in practice the most unstable element of all. In hundreds of cases a given personage was listed under variant forms of his or her name, or listed by title of work only. The listing method was at times extremely happenstance—consider, for instance, an entry for "David Comyn, A Pioneer of the Language Movement, by Máire Ní Dhubhghaill" given thus under the letter "D" in Vol. XXXI. No corresponding reference appears under 'Comyn' yet the same title is listed in respect of its author, given here as 'Dhubhghaill, Máire Ní'. The rationale for this eccentric method is stated in a rubric attached to indexes after 1928 where Séamus Ó Casaide lays it down that Irish-language Macs and Ó's should be listed according to this rule:

> Surnames in Irish are arranged in the alphabetical order of the portion following the prefix. e.g., O Briain will be found under "B", O hUiginn under "H".

A degree of alphabetical unease may well have been experienced by Ó Casaide at the 'misfit' between Irish tribal lineages and the taxonomy of modern British 'surnames'—reputedly stemming from a law of Edward II at the time of the Book of Domesday—which rules everything from classroom roll-calls to telephone books today. Plainly, if all Irish names were listed by their actual initials, the Gaelic telephone book would consist of three letters only: M, N and O (with U for archaic Ua/Uí's). Faced in his turn with this quandary, Colm Ó Lochlainn retained Ó Casaide's rule up to 1946 after which he espoused the listing method familiar from other Irish reference works (fronting Mac, Ó, and Ní), though reverting to Ó Casaide's rule after 1952. Taking these variants and vagaries all in all, the attempt to integrate the

The Irish Book Lover

indexes provided by the original editors of *The Irish Book Lover* inevitably involves a considerable degree of reindexing from individual issues of the journal, though it would be waste the labour of the original editors and misrepresent the character of their creation to reindex the whole series *tabula rasa*. Some compromise between the two processes needed to be made and the present index is the result.

In view of the central role of scanning in the making of the present volume, readers are invited to regard it as a stepping-stone towards the complete digitisation of an Irish literary journal rather than a reprint selection in the familiar sense. Throughout, the development of teamwork has been paramount since what is attempted, at bottom, is not so much the republication of a single Irish journal as the trialing of a method which can be applied to *any* Irish journal in the context of a funded project connected to the EIRData website. Approximately four hundred pages of digitised text have been extracted from *The Irish Book Lover* at this stage. These have been placed in a holding area of the PGIL EIRData website, where they join a full copy of the integrated index in its initial state (i.e, the form in which the original editors compiled it). At some future date this electronic archive will become the target of a specific undertaking aimed at putting a complete edition of the *Irish Book Lover* online. Already the first volume has been launched on internet as a token of this intention. Besides the integrated index, the website version currently holds a series of shorter listings by author and topic arising from a survey of the series conducted by the present editor while serving as assistant editor on *The Oxford Companion to Irish Literature*, edited by Robert Welch (1996). All of this can be found in the "Bibliography" region of the EIRData website at:—

http://www.pgil-eirdata.org.

I am most grateful to William E. Murphy who, while acting as Research Assistant on the EIRData Project in the spring of 2004, carried out the initial task of scanning and first-proofing upon which all the subsequent work is based. I am equally grateful to Raymond Mullen who served as my assistant during August and September for his perspicacious and quite tireless attention to the series—so much so that he has constituted himself as an almost scriptural authority on its thirty-two volumes while ensuring the fidelity of this edition to the original text. A special word of thanks is due to Mr. Keith Beckett who served EIRData steadily and with great brilliance as a maestro of all things electronic over several years. The greatest debt, together with any apologies, are owing to the editors and contributors of *The Irish Book Lover* itself. If any entitlement has been overlooked I will be happy to make acknowledgement without deviating from the belief that the return of these names to living memory is the most important form of recompense.

Bruce Stewart, MA PhD/Conseiller Littéraire
Princess Grace Irish Library (Monaco)

---

[1] Clare Hutton, 'Chapters of Moral History: Failing to Publish *Dubliners*', in *Papers of the Bibliographical Society of America*, 97 (2003), pp.495–519.

[2] Christina Hunt Mahony, 'Changing Transatlantic Contexts and Contours: Irish Studies in the United States', in Liam Harte & Irene Whelan, eds*., Ireland Beyond Boundaries: Mapping Irish Studies in the 21st Century* (London: Pluto Press 2005).

The Irish Book Lover: An Introductory Lecture

Nicholas Allen

Good morning. I would like to talk to you today about *The Irish Book Lover* and its place in the cultural history of Ireland, Britain and beyond, of the first half of the twentieth century. To do this, I will take you through its development over six decades as a serial publication of bibliographic commentary and record, a storehouse of information and opinion un-rivalled by any of its contemporaries. *The Irish Book Lover*, I hope to show, is a treasure worthy of consideration by the scholar, student, book seller or enthusiast, by anyone, in fact, who cares for the currency of text, of the pleasure of the printed word. More than that, it opens, by its relentless collection of ephemera, marginalia, new insight to a period we think we know well, from the end of the nineteenth century and disorder post-Parnell, to the middle of the twentieth, with independence, the emergency and an evolving public sphere.

The first issue of *The Irish Book Lover* was published in London in August 1909. It might seem strange to us that a title such as *The Irish Book Lover* should issue from the imperial capital at a time when, we are sometimes given to think, Ireland was engaged in a decades-long cultural, political then guerilla struggle to win its independence. But *The Irish Book Lover*, informative in such a range of things, from bibliography to the book trade, early printed books, first editions, biographies, book-sellers and catalogues, offers us an important lesson in the complex, ecumenical structures of Irish identity of the diaspora, a subject doubly important as we gather here in Monaco, under the generous auspices of the Princess Grace Irish Library. For *The Irish Book Lover* forged connection beyond Ireland and England to South Africa (W. J. O'Brien wrote from Natal in February 1916 to request materials for a lecture on the Irish literary revival) and Canada (*The Irish Book Lover* identifying and positively reviewing the Irish born poets, including Father James Dollard of Kilkenny and author of "The Haunted Hazel", in John Garvin's 1918 collection *Canadian Poets*).

The Irish Book Lover's editor, John Crone, born in Belfast in 1858 and educated at what is now the Royal Belfast Academical Institution and Queen's University Belfast, belonged to a generation of Irish subjects who combined employment in Britain with imagination of the country they left behind, his employment as a doctor in Willesden, after a short spell in a London hospital, his service as High Sheriff and coroner, in the area of Kensal Green in London, providing for summer holidays in Ireland where he cultivated a range of contributors, including Frances Joseph Bigger, a nationalist, independent scholar and member of the Royal Irish Academy, Dr. W. H. Grattan-Flood, the author of *A History of Irish Music*, Dr. McCaffrey, author of a history of the church in the nineteenth century, Mr. Arthur Clery, a lawyer, and David James O'Donoghue, librarian by 1909 of University College Dublin and a man previously involved in an early phase of the cultural revival outside Ireland as a member of the Southwark Irish Literary Society in the late 1880s.

Crone's creation of *The Irish Book Lover* as a bibliographical work of commentary and record is one of the great labours of Irish culture in the twentieth century, until now pitifully neglected. Much is made in Irish literature of its multiple traditions. But *The Irish Book Lover* occupies a place in a tradition of publishing as important as any, the ephemeral journals of previous ages, the *Reformer*, the *Dublin Joker* and the brilliantly named *Trifler* of the eighteenth-century, predecessors to the *Dublin University Magazine* and the *Nation* of the nineteenth and the *Irish Homestead*, *Irish Review* and *Sinn Féin* of the twentieth. Crone was an editor modest and aware of his place among his peers. His first editorial introduced *The Irish Book Lover* as 'a connecting link between all lovers of Irish books and books relating to Ireland, wherever published; to indicate where these latter may be procured, and to assist readers in securing them.' The journal would deal with 'Irish Typography, Bibliography, and kindred subjects, while noticing briefly, or at length, all new works, the product of the pens of Irish men and women'. Immediately however, Crone gave some indication of the personal knowledge of Ireland that he possessed, a knowledge that transformed *The Irish Book Lover* into a treasure house of fact and fancy (we learn from it that the nationalist Monaghan volunteers of the 1780s marched under the standard of a Roman eagle, their motto *Pro aris et focis*—'for [our] hearths and homes'). It is a resource of scholarship but also wit, eccentricity and communion between its contributors and their readers. Modestly, Crone admitted that

> Our little venture in the field of Irish Bibliography cannot claim to be a Pioneer. That honour must be accorded to a small publication entitled *The Irish Literary Inquirer*, issued in London by John Power, 'formerly of Belle-Vue, Youghal', as he states on his title-page. Of this only four numbers saw the light, and as it as now become a 'desideratum' among book-lovers, and as little or nothing is now known of its editor and main contributor, a few notes regarding it, and him, may prove interesting to our readers. Of Power himself, little save the dates of his birth and death (1820-1872), can be ascertained, as all his contemporaries

have disappeared from he scene, and none of the usual bibliographical works even mention his name. Admiration for his work induced me many years ago to make some enquiries regarding him, which came to nought, and later when I took up the subject again, the difficulties had by no means lessened. The older officials of the Reading-Room of the British Museum remembered, and described him to me as 'a tall, thin, gray man with a bad cough'.

We are gathered this weekend in Monaco to recover *The Irish Book Lover* from like obscurity, Crone's work the stimulus to our own consideration of Ireland in the twentieth century and after, remembering always the motto of the journal, as reproduced from a traditional ballad, that 'A jollie good booke, whereon to looke | Is better to me than golde'. Such bibliographic enthusiasm attracted a varied audience to *The Irish Book Lover*. The *Freeman's Journal*, the *Irish Times* and the *Contemporary Review* all welcomed *The Irish Book Lover*, much to satisfaction of its editor. As Crone remarked on the close of the third volume, the journal 'enters upon another year with a greatly extended circulation—with subscribers in every part of the globe—its exclusive information and Reviews quoted far and wide, and nothing but praise from its contemporaries'. "Sean Ghall" (P. J. Kenney), writing in *Sinn Féin*, welcomed the new journal as a positive addition to Irish self-expression. This might surprise us when we consider that *The Irish Book Lover* was a publication self-consciously in avoidance of political controversy. But *Sinn Féin* understood the project as a necessary building block of a national literature, comparable to its calls for a Dictionary of National Biography, a project only now under way under the auspices of the Royal Irish Academy and soon due for completion.

It is fitting to think, as I know from my own experience of working on the Dictionary, that *The Irish Book Lover* is now a major resource for biographical information. We can find informative pen portraits of the neglected novelist Katherine Cecil Thurston, born in Cork and found dead there in suspicious circumstances on 6 September 1911. The daughter of Paul Madden, former Lord Mayor of the city, her second novel, *John Chilcote, MP*, sold in excess of 200,000 copies in the United States of America. We can also find Bram Stoker, whose passing makes the May 1912 issue, his fame not yet as author of *Dracula* but still as a student of Trinity College Dublin, 'silver medallist, auditor of the Historical Society, champion athlete, honourman and MA', the 'private secretary to Sir Henry Irving [...] for 27 years, it being freely admitted in Bohemian circles that the academic addresses delivered by the great actor owed much, if not all, to that clever, genial, all-round Irishman'. This wilful delight in the social ephemera of Irish culture is *The Irish Book Lover*'s gift to its readers. Take the following of April 1920.

At a tea table talk on 31st January Mr. H. Brougham Leech, Doctor of Law, related many interesting and amusing 'Reminiscences of Trinity College', which he entered in 1861 and rose to be Regius professor of law therein. At that time Dr MacDonnell, who had been connected with the college for sixty years, was provost. His son, Hercules, was the last to engage in a duel in Dublin. His opponent was Napoleon Bonaparte Finn, and the scene was the Bull in 1835, and the wits made great fun out of the combat between men bearing such valiant names. Dr Wall, the then vice-provost, had in his youth known the eccentric Jackie Barrett, of whom Lever has left such an amusing account in *Charles O'Malley*. He possessed a dry wit and always declared that the portrait of "Jacky" in the Hall grew liker the original, as it got dirtier every day.

(All of which reminds me of the Irish scientist John Tyndall's response when asked for his opinion of a dubious clerical book. 'I prefer', he replied, 'my blasphemy with grammar'.)

The general format of *The Irish Book Lover* consisted of an introductory article or editorial comment followed by bibliographical notes, queries from readers, selections from contemporary serials such as the *Pall Mall Gazette* or the *New Quarterly*, reviews and notices of forthcoming books. This makes the journal a mine of information for the enthusiast, as any issue contains rare book prices, examples of bookmarks, histories of obscure presses (who would imagine for example that the Carogh orphanage in Naas ran its own private press for the betterment of its pupils in the 1870s?) and notes on authors and their works. It also possessed a regional awareness unrivalled by any of its contemporaries, conducting a crucially important Bibliography of local printing from Armagh to Youghal in the August 1910 edition. It was fascinated by the variety of local dialect, conscious that '"Time and change are busy ever", as the poet sings' and knew it was 'well to place even [...] trivial things on permanent record before they disappear for ever'. To this end it reproduced the Ulster rhyme,

> Lisnaskea for drinking tea,
> Maguiresbridge for brandy,
> Lisbellaw the dirty claw,
> Enniskillen the dandy.

Particularly fruitful are the accounts of meetings of the Irish Literary Society in London, with which Crone was closely involved, serving as president from 1918 to 1925. Records of this expatriate community's interests give us an important sense of how Irish culture in the early twentieth century was disseminated, and to a degree created, by societies peripheral to what we might have considered previously to be the centre of Dublin (though Roy Foster's biography of Yeats's has done much to disabuse us of this conceit). We can learn for example that the night of 5 February 1910, saw production of Rutherford Mayne's play *The Troth* 'to great success, the different parts being played by Joseph Campbell, Alice O'Dea, Whitford Kane, and A. E. Morrow. The acting was very realistic, the County Down atmosphere being admirably rendered. [...] In addition, an excellent musical programme was gone through, and Miss Wheeler recited some poems of her own, suggested by a visit to the Aran Islands'. In 1911, we find a society thriving on a mix of media to which scholars still aspire, with

> Mrs Alicia Adelaide Needham, delivering one of her new Song-Lectures. This consisted of an interesting survey of Irish music from an historical point of view, interspersed with illustrations from her own Irish songs and from old Irish melodies, which were rendered by four well-known singers, namely: Miss Maud Hardy, Miss Margaret Balfour, Mr. Hubert Baker, and Mr. Owen Colyer, Mrs. Needham's Irish song-cycle, "A Bunch of Shamrock" was sung, as well as many of her cradle songs, boat songs, spinning songs and war songs.

The star of these gatherings was William Butler Yeats, the poet a regular speaker and guest at their functions, the Irish Literary Society a convenient forum for this transient between Ireland and England to gauge the evolving opinion of London society. Yeats presided over the twenty first anniversary meeting of the society on 10 June 1913, *The Irish Book Lover* recording the invaluable details of his involvement. After a speech by T. W. Rolleston on the subject of 'Irish thought and art for twenty-one years':

> Mr. Yeats recalled how, in the dark winter of 1891-92, Ireland, its high hopes dashed and its outlook darkened, was rent and torn with dissension. That, he felt, was an appropriate time to attempt to turn men's thoughts from the fierce field of politics to the higher realms of literature, where all could again unite on a common basis. He was told it was the wrong time, but he held it was the right, and in spite of many rebuffs succeeded, as the gathering there that day proved.

Yeats, of course, knew how to play to a crowd. But *The Irish Book Lover* contains surprises which the poet's published work might hide from us. The disillusion of "September 1913" and Yeats's distance from the rising generation in retrospect of "Easter 1916" is questioned two years before the rebellion in a speech of 20 November 1914 at the

Ancient Concert Rooms in Dublin to mark the centenary of the birth of Thomas Davis. In the course of the address, Yeats

> said that Davis had no practical achievements to his credit, but his influence was wholly good. He gave them the first great example of toleration. He did not attack O'Connell. It was O'Connell who broke with him, and it almost broke Davis's heart that he who worked for the unity of Ireland should be involved in its disunion. Prof. Kettle moved, and Mr. P. H. Pearse seconded, a vote of thanks to the lecturer, the latter eulogising Davis's work as a poet, patriot and teacher.

So *The Irish Book Lover* proves its worth, Pearse's support for Yeats in 1914 otherwise lost without its testimony. This is important I think because the journal offers us a history of Irish letters and society alternative to that we might presuppose from our own knowledge of book editions. Whoever heard for example of an argument between, of all people, Ezra Pound, the American poet, high modernist and one time secretary of Yeats, and James Stephens, the *protégé* of Yeats's lifetime rival George Russell and author of the fantastical *Crock of Gold*? *The Irish Book Lover* reproduced their spat from the now rare *New Age*, a weekly then edited by the occultist A. R. Orage, in May 1915. In truly independent style, it reprinted only Stephens' side of the case, which revolved around his objection to Pound's representation of the art collector Hugh Lane from a conversation held with Yeats and a claim that Stephens had deserted Ireland. 'I have written', Stephens lamented,

> Mr. Pound's name. I am going to fumigate my pen:
>
> 'Tis God can do all things He will, and will all things He do;
> He can make an ape, an ox, a fox, or a lively kangaroo,
> For God, who made all things, has made the world and made it round,
> And He made policemen's feet to beat in the verse of Ezra Pound.

This polemical world took real and disturbing form with the Easter Rising of 1916. It also posed *The Irish Book Lover* serious problems. First, the journal was based in London and reliant on newspaper report and gossip for any sense of the upset. Second, many of those connected to the journal, including Crone and the increasingly radical nationalist P. S. O'Hegarty, held official positions. O'Hegarty, a Cork-born civil servant, was an important contributor to *The Irish Book Lover*; his love of books and political acumen a potent combination. Third, *The Irish Book Lover* had attempted over the previous nine years to create in its pages a civic space dedicated to literature and avoiding controversy. This does not mean that *The Irish Book Lover* was without politics, or an idealistic retreat from the real changes its readers' experienced, as the Easter Rising does figure in its pages, quixotically, and perhaps uniquely, with reference to its effects on the sale of books. The "Editor's gossip" of August to September 1916 observes that:

> One result of the recent 'rising' in Dublin is that the Sinn Fein pamphlets and propagandist papers which were issued in such large numbers during the past year or two, having naturally become scarce, so many having been confiscated and destroyed, are being eagerly sought for by collectors ... Thomas MacDonagh's last volume of verse, *Lyrical Poems*, was offered to me in Charing Cross Road for a couple of shillings, and I found, on reaching Dublin, that it was being sold at twenty-five!

The Rising was, as *The Irish Book Lover* records, highly disruptive of the Dublin book trade, the stereotype plates of *Thom's Directory* destroyed along with plates and stock of Father Dineen's Irish-English dictionary, then in possession of the Irish Texts' Society. There was personal tragedy too. The literary critic of *New Ireland*, Crawford Neill, was shot dead and John Crone was amazed to find 'no fewer than fifteen editors suffered whether execution or imprisonment as a result of the recent troubles!' *The Irish Book Lover* offered its own quiet sympathy to the dead rebels with obituaries for Frances Sheehy Skeffington, James Connolly, Thomas MacDonagh, Patrick Pearse and Joseph Mary Plunkett, each carefully descriptive but without comment. D. J. O'Donoghue found James Connolly the intelligence of the rebellion, with Plunkett the most promising poet. As often in *The Irish Book Lover* we find an author lost but for its insight, when O'Donoghue laments the death of 'Michael O'Hanrahan [...] executed on May 4th at Kilmainham. A native of New Ross, he had written various short stories and one rather successful novel, *A Swordsman of the Brigade*, published in London in 1914'. Political violence of the next five years went unreported in *The Irish Book Lover* save for one isolated incident, the destruction of the Cork Carnegie library in 1921, a loss that Crone promised personally to repair by a donation of one hundred volumes of standard works and his collection of Cork-printed books and pamphlets. Remembering the destruction of the First World War, Crone prompted that 'English scholars are busy replacing the lost treasures of Louvain. Let us Irishmen not be behind-hand, but show the world that though we love our books much, we love our country and its intellectual development more'.

Irish book scholars of the nineteenth century had already restored lost treasure. Edward Dowden, Professor of English at Trinity College, Dublin, and a negative figure, unfairly, in Yeats's *Autobiographies*, was a world-famous Shelley scholar and obsessive bibliophile. *The Irish Book Lover* took great pleasure in remembering his profitable adventures. In December 1914 it recalled Dowden's 'search for rare books'.

Every Dublin book-buyer will remember Michael Hickie, 'the most interesting, most profane, clever, blackguardly-shrewd, mad secondhand book-seller on the Dublin quays', from whom Dowden made many of his purchases. But his greatest find was made in 1883 from a cart of books on O'Connell Bridge. '"All books on the back of the car, twopence each" was sung out by a small vendor. I saw, but could not believe I saw, a volume in calf, lettered *Refutation of Deism*. This is the lost book of Shelley, of which no copy was known until I sold one to the British Museum in 1874, and no other has since turned up'. It proved to be a copy which Shelley presented to Mary Godwin in 1814, with her name printed on the cover, and the errata written by Shelley himself.'

Such treasures were rare. But *The Irish Book Lover* remains testament to the genesis of Irish writing as a commercial trade within the global book market, providing the historian of the book, and indeed the seller of contemporary books, much information as to previous prices, through mention of auctions and records of sale. For example, the manuscript of Yeats's poem "The Lake Isle of Innisfree" sold for £5 15s. 6d. at Sothebys in late 1919, forming part of the collection of Mr. J. Nicol Dunn, one time assistant editor of the *National Observer*, the paper in which the poem first appeared in print in 1891. The first catalogue of the Irish Book Shop of 45 Dawson Street, Dublin, owned by Edward MacLysaght and made an institution by P. S. O'Hegarty, advertised full first edition sets of Synge for £75, of Padraic Colum for £60 and of Seumas O'Sullivan for £65 in October 1920. The profitability of Irish writing was confirmed in October 1921 when *The Irish Book Lover* reported the offer by a London publishing house to Michael Collins of £10,000 to write his memoirs, an offer, unfortunately, never to be taken up. Finally, the library of John Quinn, the New York lawyer and financial support of the literary revival realised in excess of £50,000 at sale in September 1924.

The Irish Book Lover too looked like coming to a premature end in the early 1920s. Pressure of finance and work on its long-serving editor John Crone, combined with the uncertain security of a new state whose traditions were yet to be set, affected the journal's circulation as it disappeared completely from 1925 until its quarterly reintroduction in 1928 for three issues of that year. It took a new source of editorial input and funding to restore the journal to its earlier vitality, an energy derived from Séamus Ó Casaide as editor and Colm Ó Lochlainn as publisher from At The Sign of The Three Candles press. Ó Lochlainn took over altogether from 1930. The title of his business came from an old Irish saying, the 'Three candles that light up every darkness: Truth, Nature and Knowledge'. Its list reflected Ó Lochlainn's national credentials; he was a volunteer during the Easter Rising, stranded in Belfast. He had informed his fellows from there that the rebellion was cancelled, a mistake for which, he claimed, Patrick Pearse never forgave him. Pearse had little enough time, one might think, for reconsideration. Ó Lochlainn won the bronze medal for book-binding and decorative leather work in the 1924 *Aonach Tailteann* exhibition of Irish Art and founded At the Sign of the Three Candles two years later at 6 Fleet Street, Dublin, having operated a predecessor, the Candle Press, from the winter of 1916 with Seán MacGiollarna. His premises had a shop that doubled as a reception area for the printing works behind, and two cramped offices. There were forty employees by the 1930s, including Andrew Devereux, a co-director, Chalmers Trench, at first a proofreader and then general manager, and two lithographic artists, Michael Ó Briain and Karl Uhlemann.

This activity took place before a reading public transformed by the evolution of the new state after independence. The Free State was founded on a Treaty whose form of words caused Civil War, while the north of Ireland grew from signature to the 1912 solemn league and covenant. The major legislative reform of Fianna Fáil's first administration was the 1937 constitution. Ireland was awash, north and south, with pamphlets, periodicals, posters and books that argued for and against the new state, the Republic, the British, and the Empire. This variety of media, including, in time, cinema and the radio, continually addressed interpretive communities fragmented by economic, educational, individual or religious inclination. Irish readers voraciously consumed daily and weekly newspapers throughout the 1920s and '30s. Many read novels, of a certain type, westerns or romance, bought for sixpence or borrowed from libraries. Reading, under both *régimes*, north and south, was a fluid activity dammed by varieties of official control, from school curricula to state censorship, from church orthodoxy to public liability. *The Irish Book Lover* transformed itself in this changing environment, developing from its genesis as a journal of record to become a serial of opinion and debate.

The new *Irish Book Lover* had a definite sense of its national responsibility, as outlined by the Jesuit intellectual and bibliographer Stephen Brown, long associated with the journal and author of the seminal *Ireland in Fiction*, first published in 1916. Brown, now heavily involved with the establishment of the Central Catholic Library in Dublin, a library meant to provide Catholic doctrine for lay readers, argued that

> Irish libraries and other organisations concerned with books have their own particular problems which are not quite those of England, and the Irish public is or ought to be particularly interested in certain classes of books—books in the Irish language and books of peculiar Irish interest, ethnographical, archaeological, social, historical, or literary.
>
> With our limited public and its general indifference about books, it may be actually a better thing that public and publisher, librarian, bibliographer, bookseller and reviewer should meet, as it were, in *one* periodical and establish points of contact.

Such was *The Irish Book Lover*. It is refreshing however that such talk of separatism, of the particular problems of Ireland, did not mean that the journal forgot its roots in the London revival of two decades previous. John Crone continued to contribute to *The Irish Book Lover* as a reviewer of books and collector of literary ephemera; 'Miss Pamela Hinkson', Crone noted in March 1928, 'made a hit with her first novel last year and now the daughter of Mrs Skrine—better known by her pen name of Moira O'Neill—has published her first, an Anglo-Irish sporting novel, *Young Entry* over the pseudonym of "M. J. Farrell", which has had the rare advantage of being warmly praised by a critic on the wireless'. Book reviews increased enormously in number and quality under Ó Casaide's editorship. Many of these works, including Frank Gallagher's record of hunger strike in Mountjoy prison, *Days of Fear*, and Dan Breen's *My Fight for Irish Freedom* (ghost written, by the way, by a Mrs. O'Doherty whom Breen refused to pay the agreed sum of £20 even after the book's great success), concerned the recent troubles. But many too were topographies of the new state as if the decolonising moment required the Irish reader to gather a new sense of his or her landscape post-independence, the familiar Ireland of the nineteenth century carefully redrawn by popular editions such as D. J. Kelleher's *The Glamour of the West*, M. J. MacManus's *So This Is Dublin*, condemned by *The Irish Book Lover* as a guide book for Americans, and Louis J Walsh's, the author himself of a wonderful account of his time on the run in 1920, *On My Keeping*. Partition of course had its own geography with the Reverend Canon Hugh Forde's *Round the Coast of Northern Ireland*, a short enough book we might think.

The Irish Book Lover meanwhile maintained its tradition as a textual resource with its publication of a half yearly bibliography of Irish books, an invaluable resource to the modern researcher. To literary scholars conditioned to appreciate the benefits of Yeats and Joyce above others it is instructive to read lists of the popular books of, say, January 1930, including Denis Gwynn's *Daniel O'Connell*, Annie Smithson's *Sheila of the O'Byrnes* and Liam O'Flaherty's *House of Gold*. For the historian of the 1920s the same issue includes a hand list of Irish periodicals relating to the civil war, unavailable elsewhere. *The Irish Book Lover* was also consistently conscious of itself as a journal among journals, an active agent of literary knowledge in a culture of ephemeral controversy. It took notice of the ending of George Russell, the Lurgan-born, Dublin-based journalist, economist, poet and painter's final editorial project, the *Irish Statesman*, in April 1930. The *Irish Statesman* was published in a second series from 1923 with the help of generous American funding. It aimed to focus the revival generation's support of the newly independent state. It ceased publication due, in part, to financial collapse as a result of the Wall Street Crash. *The Irish Book Lover* was generous, but critical in its estimation.

> The passing of *The Irish Statesman* will be regretted by many who were not 'constant readers'. Heir to a journalistic tradition begun in *The Irish Homestead* thirty years ago, and edited through its various phases [...] by Æ, it was always a fearless champion of free speech. This alone, in a country where freedom is more spoken of than understood made for a certain unpopularity, as also did Æ's lack of understanding of the Irish language or Gaelic cultural activities. [...] Independent of political parties it had yet a considerable influence which would have been far greater had it been more Gaelic.

A fair charge in the end as Russell was unable, by temperament or inclination, to adapt himself to an independence increasingly antagonistic to his influence. Perhaps more surprising is the evidence *The Irish Book Lover* gives us throughout the 1930s of a relatively vigorous book trade, despite world-wide economic difficulty. The secret of successful publishing was scale and a number of houses survived by identifying key markets, not just At the Sign of the Three Candles, but also the Quota Press of Larne, producer of many quality children's books, the Dundalgan Press, responsible for many fine historical reprints and, largest of all due to its parentage in the Educational Company of Ireland, the Talbot Press. This last is particularly interesting as it thrived in a period of censorship when the selling of books is now understood to have been a fraught, potentially ruinous, moral and financial project. Talbot's intelligence was to discover the best-selling Annie Smithson, a writer popular with Irish readers at home and abroad, her publisher offering serial rights to her books to newspapers in Australia, Britain and the United States. Smithson, so explicitly pious, explored territory forbidden to other writers less orthodox, of affairs, infidelity and revolutionary violence.

The Irish Book Lover gave every opportunity to the Irish presses to promote their products but was conscious nonetheless that serious difficulties remained in their path. It reported with some melancholy on the 1930 Dublin conference of the Associated Booksellers of Great Britain and Ireland, which

> brings home to all interested in books the very dependent position occupied by Ireland in the publishing world. Almost 97 per cent of the books available through the book trade in Ireland is the product of English Publishing Houses, and is printed in England or Scotland. Even that rare bird—the successful Irish author—is for the most part printed and published abroad. Surely, it is time that a definitely Irish Publishing Syndicate be formed with the dual object of keeping in Ireland a fair percentage of the publishing and printing of books by Irish authors, and of securing proper distribution in other countries of books printed and published in Ireland.

Competition, of course, remained strong between Irish publishers and *The Irish Book Lover*, so closely associated with the Three Candles, could not resist a little criticism of its competitors. Macmillan became the 'sweet retir'd ground' of established Irish writers, Ó Casaide expressing his surprise when it employed the talents of the young Frank O'Connor. The Catholic Truth Society was savaged for its presentation of *St. Patrick*, with 'good material for a 60-page booklet, expanded, padded, bloated, gorged, stuffed, farced, blown-out and puffed up to almost an inch in thickness, sandwiched, wedged, or interlarded between two stout slices of advertisements extorted from the unfortunate traders and manufacturers of Ireland, at whose expense this overfed monster is launched upon the reading public'. The frustration of business competition with religious authority is evident here. *The Irish Book Lover*'s antagonism to now foreign English presses hid a real anxiety that reading publics outside Ireland were dictating the representation of recent Irish history. In October 1936 it welcomed an editorial of the *Irish Independent* that criticised a modern tendency to graphic realism. The *Irish Independent* had

> endorsed what our reviewers have been saying for a few years past regarding the content of novels purporting to deal with Ireland of 1916-1923. Indeed in some instance *The Irish Book Lover* has returned to the publishers review copies of unpleasant novels without giving them the publicity of any notice. Unfortunately, following in the muddy wake of Joyce and O'Flaherty, many of our younger Irish writers, even when

not dealing with times of trouble and stress, are at pains to introduce into their stories that strong meat which seems always to open the door of the English publisher, and the purse of the English book-buyer. At one time 'the dirty Irish' was a phrase earned by our people by the squalor into which the brutality of English overlords had driven them. Soon we shall have attained the same noble title once more through the anxiety of our 'literary gents' to prove that as long as Englishmen will pay for the spectacle, Irishmen will be ready to foul their nest.

In face of this, the journal found that—

> Censorship has its virtues despite all the yelping against it. [...] When patriotism is exploited for the enjoyment of its mockers, and the poor are exploited to provide sordid sex incidents; when the decent and clean things in life are trailed in the gutters of literature to rouse malicious delight in surreptitious minds, then it is time to intervene and to outlaw what is nothing short of quackery in the world of fiction.

Samuel Beckett was a prime offender, his first novel, *More Pricks than Kicks*, reviewed in 1934 with absolute distaste. Beckett may, according to his reviewer, have 'read James Joyce with loving care' but '[u]nfortunately, no one has told him that violence and obscurity, even assisted by a considerable dash of the indecent, are, when uninformed by any real passion or direction, merely dull'. The author's skill did not hide the 'fact that Mr. Beckett has nothing to say'. This might be true, but it is the manner of Beckett's speaking that still arrests us. But it should not surprise us that the young writer should receive such a negative welcome in *The Irish Book Lover*, a journal with consistently high-church taste in literature throughout its career. For insightful book reviews we turn with more profit to its contemporary, the *Dublin Magazine*, edited for a comparable period by Seumas O'Sullivan, the poet and eventual husband of the painter Estelle Solomons.

The Irish Book Lover's strength remained its commitment to books as objects, its near fetishisation of the printed text. It is an unerring guide to the collections of Ireland, from the library of St Columb's College in Derry, with its three thousand volumes, including classics and Hebrew, an illuminated edition of the Koran and crucifixes of the Penal era, to the dispersal by auction in February 1935 of the library of Lord Monteagle, Mount Trenchard, Co Limerick, at Hodgson's in London's Chancery Lane, a collection originally founded by Spring Rice, the English Chancellor of the Exchequer in the mid 1800s. The same year saw report in October 1934 of the largest sale to date of Irish books in New York with the auction of the library of Thomas Hughes Kelly, founder of the School of Irish Learning in Paris. *The Irish Book Lover* found the 'catalogue poor and prices low', the discerning able to find 'sleepers (or unacknowledged valuables) if one had time among the bundles'. 'In one bundle', the excited correspondent told, 'was found a copy of O'Mahony's edition of Keating, with a note in his own handwriting; in another was the Book of Fenagh, full-tooled morocco with three sonnets by Sir Samuel Ferguson addressed to Denis Kelly and the latter's reply laid in'. Delights indeed.

By 1940, *The Irish Book Lover* had cultivated an influential readership, if the published list of members of the Bibliographical Society of Ireland, who subscribed to the journal, is anything to go by. They included, as institutions, Trinity College Dublin, the British Museum, Columbia University Library, the Royal Irish Academy, the Library of Congress, the National Library of Ireland, five Dublin public libraries and one each from Cork, Limerick and Tipperary. Individual members included Ethna Carberry, Richard Hayes, Lennox Robinson, the Archdeacon of Thurles and, finally, J. O'Reilly of the Garda Síochána, Phoenix Park. O'Reilly, perhaps, scanned the pages for notice of works contrary to the public good (though I may do him a disservice to suggest so). If he did, he would have been relieved to read the 1940 review of James Joyce's *Finnegans Wake*, which *The Irish Book Lover* found to contain 'a world of language which seems to have the strange minuteness, the cloying consistency and the rapacious spread of duckweed'.

> Stephen Dedalus has kept his word and his silence, exile and cunning has, in *Finnegan's Wake* [sic], produced what must be regarded as one of the most extraordinary books ever produced in any language. [...] for the moment we wonder why so great a talent, gifted with prodigious memory, a mastery of English and of other languages, a poet's ear for the beauty of vowel, and an artist's fastidiousness in form, should bend itself to a task in which no mind save its own can enjoy or appreciate the grotesque output of its labour?

Opinion was also offered of the recently dead Yeats's *Last Poems and Plays*, a collection that found 'a pathway into the inner places of the Irish character'. The journal continued to commit itself to the development of intellectual enquiry in Ireland, reviewing Richard Ellmann's *Yeats, The Man and the Masks* and T. S. Eliot's *Notes Towards the Definition of Culture* in March 1949—a work that drove the book lover to exclaim: 'For God's sake let us start with ourselves; remaking from the materials best suited to our needs—work, religion, art—that sense which we lack more than any other generation—a sense of the future, in life and in death'. Such *angst* was matched only by continuing complaint over the behavior of Dublin book-sellers, a breed that '[w]ith one or two shining exceptions [...] do not bother their heads on the point of giving value for money. They just want the money'. The profit, it considered, on books sold from lots originally bought at blind auction, was 'something fantastic—about ten thousand per cent, let us say. How can we book buyers restore sanity to the trade? Only by organising ourselves and applying the boycott. The strike weapon would work in time!'

Such revolutionary fervour is hardly the preserve of the reading classes; no strike, needless to say, followed. But the enthusiasm of such contributors could not sustain *The Irish Book Lover* in what was now its final, irregular period. From 1952 until its final edition in 1957, the journal managed only six issues, its editor and contributors aging. There is still evidence of serious scholarship, P. S. O'Hegarty reproducing a research paper into Irish editions of Shakespeare, which included an *Othello* of 1751 for Peter Wilson of Dame Street and a *Romeo and Juliet* of 1763 for Elizabeth Watts of Skinner Row, and some wit, a review of a reprint of Giraldus Cambrensis' *Topography of Ireland* remarking that 'Giraldus de Barri, called Cambrensis after his native Cambria had for mother the sister of Maurice Fitzgerald, a principal leader of the Norman invasion of Ireland; so that, considering much of the matter of this work, we may consider that this country has suffered overmuch from one family'. But the final sense is of fatigue at the end of a long venture. Seumas O'Sullivan caught the mood with his "*Quoi dono... libellum*?", dedicated to M. J. MacManus.

> To whom then, will I give you, little book,
> Now he has gone? Come make your home with me.
> It may be that the touch of your brown coat,
> Your untrimmed leaves, will sometimes bring to mind
> Old great occasions, help me to forget
> Awhile, Glasnevin and the open grave.

September 1957 saw the last issue of a journal that had lasted the almost impossible length of forty-eight years, an eternity in periodical publishing. Which leaves us make final consideration of *The Irish Book Lover*, of its significance to the culture of its day and to ours. We might look first at what *The Irish Book Lover* did not achieve; it never enjoyed a mass readership; it never gained extensive advertising; it rarely engaged in direct controversy; it did not encourage a new generation, as did the *Irish Statesman, Dublin Magazine* and *Bell*, to write. But it did achieve significance; it did maintain publication for five decades; it did restore Irish bibliography to the status of orderly science; it did connect two generations and more of book lovers, collectors and traders to their business not just in Ireland, but in Europe, the United States of America and in the colonies, current and former, of the British Empire; most importantly of all, it maintained a space for reading through a difficult period, its promotion of books a point of contact that remained open between all sides in dispute, whatever the circumstances. To this we owe the imagination of Crone, Ó Casaide and Ó Lochlainn. To the modern reader, *The Irish Book Lover* makes other promises, of a subterranean culture brought to light in its pages, of a Dublin and London in concert through personal and professional associations now lost to time, circumstance and the changing readers' tastes. To acknowledge these links, as we have here today, is to glimpse, if briefly, those possibilities of concord between cultures that make our own gathering on the southern edge of Europe so necessary. It is for this we remember *The Irish Book Lover* today, as a record of knowledge and an instrument of civic discourse. Thank you.

The Irish Book Lover (1909–1957)

An Anthology & Selection

Vol. I (Aug. 1909 to July 1910)   19

Vols. VII & VIII (Jan. 1916 to Oct. 1917)   79

Vol. XVI (Jan. & Feb. 1928 to Nov. & Dec. 1928)   125

Vol. XVIII (Jan. & Feb. 1930 to Nov. & Dec. 1930)   153

Miscellaneous Issues (Aug. 1912 to Sept. 1957)   191

The Irish Book Lover
Vol. I (Aug. 1909 to July 1910)

J. S. Crone, "Foreword", Vol. I, No. 1 (Aug. 1909), 1.

The aim and scope of this little venture will be apparent from a perusal of this. our first number. We hope to form a connecting link between all lovers of Irish Books and books relating to Ireland, wherever published; to indicate where these latter may be procured, and to assist readers in securing them. We shall deal with Irish Typography, Bibliography, and kindred subjects, whilst noticing briefly or at length, all new works, the product of the pens of Irish men and women. We have been promised the co-operation and. assistance of many well known in the world of letters, and we shall spare no pains to make '*The Irish Book Lover*' interesting and useful.

OUR FORERUNNER
Our little venture in the field of Irish Bibliography cannot claim to be a pioneer. That honour must be accorded to a small publication entitled *The Irish Literary Inquirer*, issued in London by John Power, 'formerly of Belle-Vue, Youghal', as he states on his title-page. Of this only four numbers saw the light, and as it has now become a *desideratum* amongst book-lovers, and as little or nothing is now known of its editor and main contributor, a few notes regarding it; and him, may prove interesting to our readers. Of Power himself, little save the dates of his birth and death (1820-1872), can be ascertained, as all his contemporaries have disappeared from the scene, and none of the usual biographical works even mention his name. Admiration for his work induced me many years ago to make some inquiries regarding him, which came to nought, and later when I took up the subject again, the difficulties had by no means lessened. The older officials of the Reading Room of the British Museum remembered, and described him to me as 'a tall, thin, grey man with a bad cough.' But it is possible to trace his movements during the last seven years of his life from his printed works. Thus, we know that from Monday, July 17th 1865, until Monday, April 16th 1866, he lived at No. 3, Grove Terrace, St. John's Wood. In July 1866, he dates a preface from 3, Cambridge Road, London, W., whilst that of his last work, issued in 1870, is dated from 3, College Terrace, Cambridge Road, Hammersmith, the same house. The only reference to him I have come across is contained in a letter

from Bishop Reeves to Sir John T. Gilbert, which says: 'Mr. Power writes to me that he is busy compiling his *Bibliotheca Hibernica*, and that his materials have grown to great dimensions.' This was previous to October, 1865.

An incidental reference in *Notes and Queries*, 1st August 1908, from the pen of Ralph Thomas (Olphar Hamst), the well-known bibliographer—to the 'Handy Book', states: 'For years before, and while this book was going through the press, Power was ill, and quite unfit to do the work he had undertaken.' This induced me to ask Mr. Thomas if he knew anything regarding Power and his MSS to which he replied as follows, under date 11th August 1908: 'I am sorry I know nothing more about John Power. If anybody offered me any of his MSS. I should refuse them! They were absolutely unreadable, and (the) material collected required so much verification as to be more trouble than they were worth.' Such a pronouncement from such an authority partly reconciles one to the loss.

Power has left only three works to his credit, but each is of value in its way. *The Irish Literary Inquirer, or Notes on Authors, Books and Printing in Ireland, Biographical and Bibliographical, Notices of Rare Books, Memorandum of Printing in Ireland, Biographical Notes of Irish Writers, &c., conducted by John Power*, to give its full and comprehensive title, is an octavo of 12 pages, the first number, price 2d., bearing date 17th July, 1865. It contains a long introduction foreshadowing the scope of the work, followed by a reprint of a unique copy of a prospectus of a *Bibliotheca Hibernicana* by Rev. Edward Groves, author of *The Warden of Galway*, an article on Ware's *Irish Writers* and *Antiquities* and an able sketch of the "History of Printing in Ireland". Then follow "Queries and Miscellaneous Notes of an Interesting Character", and a few advertisements, the most interesting of which is an abridged prospectus of Power's own *Bibliotheca Hibernica* to be published at one guinea by subscription, a work which unfortunately the author never lived to complete. The second number appeared 'semi-occasionally', as Power puts it on the 23rd September, 1865. It contains a scholarly article on De Burgo's *Hibernica Dominicana* 'from the pen of a gentleman at Cambridge, well-known for his intimate knowledge of Irish Books', whom we venture to name as the late lamented Henry Bradshaw, ever helpful in matters pertaining to bibliography; who also contributes over his initials an interesting notice of a rare volume recounting a bogus 'gunpowder plot' in Ireland. It concludes with some literary notes, and a reference to recent Sales. No. 3 did not appear until 16th December. It contains a review of Gilbert's "Irish Archivist's

Letters", an article by Rev. T. Gimlette on "Waterford Clerical Authors", an amusing account of John Dunton and his early Dublin Book Auctions, a continuation of the History of Printing and another letter from Henry Bradshaw on McBrudine's works and early printing in Kilkenny. A short list of subscribers given here is interesting, containing as it does several well-known names, such as Father Meehan, John D'Alton, George Benn, and Classon Porter, the only survivor of whom is the present Sir Charles Brett, of Belfast. The 4th and last number which was increased in size and price, made its appearance on 16th April, 1866. Amongst its more notable contents are a list of privately printed Irish books from Martin's Catalogue, with promised additions by Power. This is interesting, as it contains a reference to an edition of *What Passed at Killala* (Bath 1799). A verbatim reprint of *The Irish Mercury*, No. 1 (Corke 1649) follows, and the number concludes with the first issue of the list of Irish periodicals, which afterwards grew into Power's second work. It was Power's intention to issue eight numbers of the Inquirer, but owing to the poor reception accorded it, his subscribers never reached a hundred, and he said it required at least 350 to defray expense, he stopped short at the 4th, bound up the unsold copies in a green paper wrapper, which were sold at 10d. each, by, amongst others, John Camden Hotten, Piccadilly, and John O'Daly, of Dublin.

His second compilation [was] "List of Irish Periodical Publications (chiefly literary) from 1729 to the present time, reprinted from *Notes and Queries* (March & April 1866)" in *The Irish Literary Inquirer*, No. 4, with additions and corrections, by John Power, formerly of Belle-Vue, Youghal, printed for private distribution only (London, A.D. 2000-14)' [sic]. Of this the printer, James Martin, Lisson Grove, certifies that '250 copies were printed, of which 20 were on tinted paper.' It is small quarto printed in single column, on one side of paper only, thus leaving ample margin for additions, and printed from type 'listed' from *Notes and Queries.* It was dedicated to the Rev. Samuel Hayman, the well-known Cork antiquarian, and contains interesting details of nearly 300 ventures in Irish periodical literature, not more than two or three of which survive today.

The work by which Power is most generally known is his *Handy Book about Books* (London 1870), 8vo., xviii, 218, 18pp. It is a beautiful specimen of typography, the covers being facsimile reproductions of two ancient bindings, one French the other Italian, and altogether is a complete *vade mecum* for bibliophiles. In it the author has by his researches advanced the history of Irish printing beyond the point reached by Archdeacon Cotton, and his chronology is the connecting link between that divine's and the most accomplished Irish bibliographer of the present day, Mr. E. R. McClintock Dix.

In the issue of *Notes and Queries* for May 18th, 1872, the one following his death, we find this allusion from the pen of W. J. Thorns, the then editor. 'A valuable contributor to this journal from its commencement, Mr. John Power, the well-known bibliographer, died at St. Leonard's-on-Sea, on the 13th inst., in the fifty-second year of his age. Mr. Power fulfilled his articles in the office of Sir John Rennie, but forsaking his profession of civil engineer for the more congenial pursuit of literature he has done good service by his *Irish Literary Inquirer*, the *Bibliotheca Hibernica*, and more recently by his *Handy Book about Books*, which he dedicated to readers of *Notes and Queries*. Mr. Power for some years resided in Panama, where he projected the successful paper, *The Panama Star and Herald*, but an attack of paralysis obliged him to relinquish the editorship and return to England, where he lingered in a more or less enfeebled state till his death.'

E. R. McClintock Dix, "The Beaufoy Sale", Vol. I, No. 1 (Aug. 1909), 4.

The Irish portion of this fine library was disposed of at Christie's on Thursday, 10th June. The books were all in fine condition, bearing the book-plate; many beautifully bound, and, as was expected, realised high prices. Amongst the most noteworthy items were the following. A collection of upwards of 500 historical and political tracts covering the period between 1704 and 1824, bound up in 42 8vo. volumes with one MS. index volume, originally formed, I take it, by C. Watkin Williams-Wynn, as many of them bear his autograph. They contain the first issues of Swift's *Drapier Letters*, pamphlets relating to the Volunteers, the Union, the Veto, and the Catholic Question. They were bought by Quaritch for £20, who also got Hugh Reilly's *Ireland's Case Briefly Stated* (1695), a beautiful little 12mo. for 38s. For Sir James Caldwell's *Report of the Debates*, 2 vols. (1766), contemporary red morocco, Rimell paid £2 12s. For a parcel of 7 vols., by no means scarce, containing Lodge's *Desiderata*, Vallency [sic] on the *Antiquity of Irish Language*', and O'Brien's *Grammar*, £4 10s. was paid, which to my mind was the dearest item of the day, as several of them have been picked up cheaply. Mauritius Morison's *Threnodia Hiberno-Catholica* (1659), purple morocco, a rare account of the Richardson's *Great Folly and Superstition of Pilgrimages*, and Hewson's *St. Patrick's Purgatory*, fetched 18s. Two 8vo. vols., of Dublin printed pamphlets 1782-1799, realised £2 17s. 6d. Amongst them being *The Trial of Hurdy-Gurdy* (written by Counsellor Sampson), Duigenan's *Answer to Grattan*, and a *Collection of Loyal Songs Sung in Orange Lodges*, in 2 parts (1798). One of the songs in this collection was the well-known one commencing 'July the first in Oldbridge Town', and I single it out for special mention for this reason. When the late Canon Hume and David Herbison, the "Bard of Dunclug", were engaged collecting the scattered fragments of the original ballad, "The Boyne Water", supposed to be written by an eye-witness, probably a Williamite trooper, and commencing 'July the first of a morning clear', they found the original ballad had been almost superseded in popularity by this later version, which they could not trace earlier than 1814. Indeed the father of the late William Johnston, of Ballykilbeg, M.P., stated it was composed in July of that year. (See *Ulster Journal of Archaeology*, 1854.) Yet here we have it printed sixteen years' earlier.

A fine copy of Vallency's *Collectanea* (1770-1804), six vols. in five, went for £7. Amongst the quartos—Edwards gave £2 for *An Account of the Transactions in the North of Ireland* (1692), old blue morocco, and Harding bought Archdall's *Monasticon* for £2 4s. Edwards gave 3 guineas for Thomas Carve's *Lyra Sive Anacephalaeosis Hibernica* (Sulzbacii, 1666), and Tregaskis secured Nicholas French's *Settlement and Sale of Ireland* (Louvain, 1668) for 34s. Gookin's *Author and Case of Transplanting the Irish Vindicated* (1665), went for two guineas, whilst for James Howell's *Mercurius Hibernicus* (Bristol, 1644), together with (Phillip's *Interest of England in Ireland*, 1689), Quaritch gave £7 10s.

J. S. Crone, "Honours For Irish Scholars" Vol. I, No. 1 (Aug. 1909), 8.

The birthday honours list announcing the fact that knighthoods had been conferred upon two Irish Scholars—in widely different spheres of intellectual development—was certain of appreciation. The first, Sir Samuel Dill, comes of a family whose name has been a household word in Ulster for nearly two centuries. He is the eldest son of the Rev. S. M. Dill, first president of Magee College, Derry, a scholar and pulpit orator of high attainments. The new knight was born in 1844, and had a brilliant scholastic career in Belfast and at Oxford University. He is the author of several standard works dealing with life and society in Rome and Greece in the days of their magnificence. For interesting particulars of the family whence he sprung, see *Autobiography of a Country Parson*, by the Rev. James R. Dill, M.A. (Belfast 1888), 8vo., and *The*

Dill Worthies, by the same, 2nd edition (Belfast 1892), 8vo. The other recipient of the well-deserved honour, Sir Joseph Larmor, fills the high position of secretary to the Royal Society an office which was first filled two centuries ago by a fellow countryman, Sir Hans Sloane. Sir Joseph was born at Magharagall, Co. Antrim, in 1857, and brought up in the city of Belfast by a widowed mother. He was educated at the Institution and Q.C.B., and I remember him both as schoolboy and student, a very quiet studious youth, with an intense thirst for knowledge. Needless to say, he carried off all before him in the way of prizes, and it was with no surprise we found him after a few years at Cambridge coming out as Senior Wrangler, an honour which had been secured a few years earlier by another schoolfellow of his now Rev. A. J. C. Allen. As is to be expected his literary contributions consist of various memoirs on mathematics and physics.

"Forthcoming Books", Vol. I, No. 1 (Aug. 1909), 8.

ROBERT EMMET: AN HISTORICAL NOVEL, by Stephen Gwynn, M.P., 8vo., 6s. We are highly privileged in being the first literary organ in a position to announce that Messrs. Macmillan have in hand a new novel by Mr. Stephen Gwynn, M.P., the subject being one of perennial interest, viz., *The Life and Times of Robert Emmet.* It will be published during the forthcoming Autumn season, and those acquainted with Mr. Gwynn's work, who anticipate a sympathetic and masterly treatment of that romantic and fascinating period, will not be disappointed.

Sealey [sic] Bryars announce the appearance shortly of F. J. Bigger's *Land War in Ulster*, a book that we predict will cause a stir. We have been privileged by a perusal of some proof sheets, and so speak with some degree of knowledge. It will be an 'eye-opener' to many to find that a hundred years ago prosperous, peaceful Ulster set the example to other parts of Ireland of boycotting, cattle-houghing, and moonlighting.

"Reviews", Vol. I, No. 1 (Aug. 1909), 10.

If you want a book you can read in a couple of hours, and find more interesting than any novel, try *Sir Robert Hart: The Romance of a Great Career*, told by his niece, Juliet Bredon (Hutchinson, London). This well-written account of how a little Irish boy, born in Portadown, and brought up in Hillsborough, without powerful friends or political influence—but by his own innate genius, rose to be the friend and counsellor of Emperors, the most powerful European in the East, and succeeded as he prophesied in his boyish enthusiasm in 'buying back

Kilmoriarty and winning a title!', is intensely interesting from the first page to the last. There is only one point missing; the author tells us Sir Robert 'was a great reader', but omits to mention the—from our point of view—most interesting fact, that despite his manifold engagements, he kept himself abreast of all that was best and brightest in Irish literature during the past half-century.

The present writer had evidence of this upon one occasion when in the course of an after-dinner speech, Sir Robert quoted with wonderful pathos those lines from John Stevenson's fine poem, "The Wee Grey Man" commencing 'When ower [sic] the Antrim Hills, the lark has sung me his last sweet sang', which he must have learnt during his long and trying stay in Peking. For a book of quite another description let me recommend *Ballygullion*, by Lyn [sic] Doyle (Maunsel, Dublin), the funniest, in the real sense of the word, I have read for many a day. It is one long laugh, and yet these everyday characters of an Irish district are drawn to the life without exaggeration. If this be a first book, as it seems, the author who knows his rural Ulster like ABC, will, unless I am greatly mistaken, make a name for himself in the literary world.

J. J. Marshall, "Notes From The North", in *The Irish Book Lover*, , Vol. I, No. 1 (Aug. 1909), 11.

ULSTER DIALECT—An interesting little pamphlet of twenty-two pages has recently been published by the Ulster Association of New South Wales, entitled: *The People and Language of Ulster*, being a 'Discoorse' delivered at Sydney, on 17th March 1909, by Charles Russell, B.A., Q.U.I. The first six pages are devoted to a summary of Ulster history, and the remainder deals in an interesting and chatty fashion with the idioms and turns of speech of the Ulster peasantry.

An interesting little Tyrone book that is not likely to be very plentiful is: *The History of Paddy Blake and Kathleen O'Moore*, a tale into which are introduced observations on agriculture, chemistry, and various subjects, compiled and written for the instruction and amusement of the Farmers of Tyrone, by a Country Gentleman (Dungannon: printed by William Douglas, 1847). The rustic Admirable Crichton, by whom this comprehensive manual was written, was evidently Edward Houston Caulfield, of Drumcairn, Stewartstown. Cloth 8vo., 101 pages. [...]

E. R. McClintock Dix, "Henry Bradshaw on Printing in Ireland", Vol. I, No. 2 (Aug. 1909), 13.

Henry Bradshaw was the pre-eminent bibliographer of his day in England, and the only one who took a real and a deep interest in Irish bibliography. His research and knowledge were amazing; therefore anything that can be gleaned from his words or writings upon Printing in Ireland is of great value and utility and should be preserved. For this reason, I think, to reproduce the report in the *Freeman's Journal* of October the 3rd, 1884, of his speech on Printing in Ireland delivered at Trinity College Dublin, before the Library Association, in that year, is desirable. (E. R. Mc C. Dix.)

'Mr. Henry Bradshaw, Librarian of the University of Cambridge, made a communication on the subject of Printing in Ireland—what he desired to do was to appeal to them to assist him in getting materials for a history of Printing in Ireland. He suggested that in every chief library of the provinces, a collection or museum should be formed in order to show everything that had been printed or published in that locality. If an entire room could not be devoted to the purpose, a book case might, at all events a record might be made. The task might be assigned to a subordinate officer connected with the library who would have an aptitude for it. The collection would perhaps include rubbish, but for their purpose, rubbish ceased to be such, when put in order. Every newspaper or scrap of information illustrative of their object should be included. His interest in the question arose from the circumstance that his father and mother were natives of the North of Ireland, and he had been always interested in everything connected with Irish books. The catalogue should embrace books of Irish affairs, books produced by Irish writers, and books produced by Irish presses. With respect to books on Irish affairs, there was not much difficulty in finding them anywhere. The great object was to get at those sources of information which were subsidiary to the writing of history; and this was more essential than ever at, present, when the study of History was being more than ever placed on a scientific—or at, all events a methodical basis. Where each author lived and printed his book should be taken into account. The utility of what he proposed was illustrated by what had occurred in the past. Bale, Bishop of Ossory, in the reign of Edward VI, was a man unpopular in some quarters at, the time, in consequence of his, having a free, tongue—as free perhaps as some of those they had heard—but he had an intense love of literature, and he lamented the destruction of the earlier literature of that reign, that had taken place in consequence of the prejudice against what was called

Popish. Shortly before the end of his life he brought out a *Catalogue of Writers* during a period of 1400 years, the last two centuries being assigned to Scottish and, Irish, writers. In 1639 Sir James Ware produced a book on the writers of Ireland in which he included not only natives of Ireland who had written books, but also foreigners who had made Ireland their home. His work came down to 1600. In 1746 was published Harris's *History*, which included every writer of Ireland who had printed the merest pamphlet down to 1700. That history was sometimes spoken lightly of by those who use it, but it contains a mass of information which could be found nowhere else. Although a strong Protestant, he was softened by the nature of his pursuits and corresponded with Irish Catholics on the Continent, including the Franciscans of Louvain. He (Mr. Bradshaw) did not know of any other work of a similar kind down to Dr. Madden's *Periodical Literature* published in 1867, and containing a sketch of printing in Ireland down to that time. Very little had been done towards forming a history of the Irish Printing Press. In the course of his remarks, Mr. Bradshaw mentioned that the first Irish newspaper he had ever found any mention of was one called *The Irish Monthly Mercury*, published at Cork, in 1649. In 1659 there was a *Newsletter* published in Dublin, which had leading articles like those of the *Daily Telegraph*, besides news, letters, and advertisements. Mr. Gilbert's *History of Dublin* was a valuable source of information. The author told him that he was only twenty four years of age when he wrote it, and that it was full of mistakes, but it and other works should be estimated according to the positive information contained rather than any errors that occurred in them. A distinctly Irish library had been made by Mr. Evelyn P. Shirley, of the County of Monaghan.'

Henry Bradshaw (1831-1886), the father of modern bibliography, was descended from a Quaker family long settled at Milecross, in County Down, his, mother being one of the Stewarts of Ballintoy, Co. Antrim. His father bequeathed him a large collection of Irish books, to which he owed the foundation of his bibliographical studies, and to these he went on adding all his life. Educated at Eton and King's College, Cambridge, where he graduated B.A., Bradshaw for a while became a master at St. Columba's College, Dublin. Returning to Cambridge, he was appointed assistant librarian to the University Library in 1856. Here his future life-work lay, and what that work was is well known to all latter day students of bibliography, which he raised to the rank of an exact science. In 1870 he presented to the library the whole of his Irish collection, which is described in the Library Report as 'a collection of books and papers, pamphlets and broadsides either (1) printed in Ireland, or (2) written by Irish authors, or (3) relating generally to Irish affairs, about 5,000 in number.' In his letter to the Vice-Chancellor, offering the gift, Bradshaw writes: 'I have a considerable collection of books, pamphlets and other printed papers relating to Ireland. The basis of it is the Irish portion of my father's library, that portion of it in which, as coming from the North of Ireland, he took most interest, and which at his death in 1845, he left to me. For several years I did a good deal to increase the collection, especially in the matter of pamphlets. ... More than forty years ago when public libraries were less plentifully supplied than they are now, literary men used to come to my father's house to work at these books, when engaged in writing upon Irish affairs, and from the time that I was a child, they have had a particular interest for me. There are about 1,000 bound volumes, and of the pamphlets and other printed papers, there are roughly speaking, about 2,700 in octavo, 700 in quarto, and 500 in folio, including proclamations, broadsides, and flysheets.' The collection was enlarged at his death by the addition of such Irish books as he had acquired since 1870. The University authorities have never been able to afford to print a catalogue of this splendid legacy, although a card index may be consulted on the premises. His love for his Irish books ended only with his life, and one of his last letters, written only four days before his death, was to Mr. John Anderson, then engaged upon his *Catalogue of Early Belfast Printed Books*, sending him numerous titles from his own and other collections. On the morning of the 11th February, 1886, he was found dead 'sitting in his arm chair, at the table in his inner room, a little Irish book, closed, lay on the table in front of him.' The ruling passion strong in death. His life, by G. W. Prothero, has been published (London 1888), 8vo., and the Henry Bradshaw Society founded to commemorate his name and services to bibliography. (Ed.)

John S. Crone, "Forthcoming Books", Vol. I, No. 2 (Aug. 1909), p.17.

Messrs. Longman have in the press and will issue during the Autumn a *Life of W. E. H. Lecky*, by his widow. Mr. Lecky, whose bust in his alma mater T.C.D was recently unveiled, was a man whose fine modest qualities endeared him to many friends. Although he entered politics late in life, and made some little mark therein, yet it is as a literary man he will be best remembered, and it is with this aspect of him that the memoir chiefly deals. If one dare venture into the shadowy realms of prophecy, it might be said that Lecky will be best know to future generations by his *Leaders of Public Opinion*, and his *History of Ireland in the Eighteenth Century*. The career of the first work, his maiden effort, was curiously varied. It was originally published anonymously in 1861, when the author was in his twenty-third year, by Saunders of Otley, the "If you are Saunders then d— Otley, and if you are Otley then d— Saunders" of Count D'Orsay's story. It fell still-born from the press, only three copies, as he afterwards confessed, having been genuinely sold, and the critics ignored it. The only exception to the general indifference, he wrote in 1895, 'was an article from the pen of W. J. O'Neill Daunt which appeared in the a Cork newspaper, and which was equally remarkable for its kindness towards myself, and for its ample knowledge of the period I had treated. It was the first public recognition that there was some real merit in my writing, the first confident prediction that some future lay before me in literature.' Ten years passed before a new, greatly enlarged and revised edition appeared, and it really seemed as if a similar fate awaited this one. But suddenly Mr. Gladstone became converted to Home Rule and in one of his innumerable letters or speeches at the period advised a correspondent to read and ponder over Lecky's *Leaders*. Then the remainder which had been as drugs in the bookseller's hands became much sought after, and in some cases realised as much as two pounds and upwards per copy.

[...] Little requires to be said of his *History of Ireland*. It has long since taken rank as a classic, and makes one regret that the whole history of the country had not been written in the same calm, judicial style. Although possessed of a thorough knowledge of almost every work dealing with "Ninety-eight", the present writer, after reading Lecky, came to the conclusion that his was the most thorough and impartial account yet penned. The writer was privileged to meet Mr. Lecky on one occasion only, and carried away the impression of him as 'an incarnation of sweetness and light—one of Nature's noblemen. Needless to say, we predict a warm welcome to the book, which will contain many interesting letters and portraits, and will form a notable addition to the long and increasing list of Irish biographies. The same publishers also announce a new novel *The Blindness of Dr. Grey*, from the pen of Canon Sheehan, the author of those well-known novels *My New Curate, Glenanaar*, &c.

"Reviews", Vol. I, No. 2 (Sept. 1909) 19.

It was a 'happy thought'—nay, an inspiration—to entitle a volume of verse by JAMES STEPHENS, *INSURRECTIONS* (Maunsel and Co., Dublin, 1s.

net), and indeed no other word could have described the note of the book so comprehensively. Take for example the powerful opening poem, the indignant revolt against her surroundings, of "The Dancer", deprived by death of her lover; or "The Red-Haired Man's Wife". No shrieking suffragette could better voice the rebellious feelings of the woman against the whilom relations of the wedded pair, than the heroine of these forceful verses. The author is a master of rythmical effects, and to our way of thinking, "Nature" is the finest poem in the book, whose general sombreness is relieved by one little gem of humour. ("SEUMAS BEG"). [...]

"The Post Bag", Vol. I, No. 2 (Sept. 1909), 22.

Dear Sir—During the past few years I have taken special interest in the history of my native county of Kerry. My researches appear serially in the weekly *Kerry People*, of Tralee. So far I have published in book form two volumes of the *History of Kerry*, and hope to issue a third volume next year. This will consist mainly of family history, and the annals of British rule in Kerry. My correspondents now number several hundreds of natives of Kerry, resident in various parts of the world. I cannot see any end in view for the completion of my Kerry researches.

It would be very useful to bring into touch the various workers in this department with a view of securing the issue of a complete and uniform set of "Irish County Histories". I believe there are in Ireland and abroad now 32 competent Irish people prepared to compile such a set of books, provided they got the co-operation of native of each county. From my own practical experience I believe it would pay any leading publisher to issue shilling country histories similar to my books on Kerry. There is no demand for costly books on Ireland, but I am confident a set of county histories at a popular price would be an immediate success. [...] (JEREMIAH KING.)

E. R. McClintock Dix, "Keating's History of Ireland", Vol. I, No. 3 (Oct. 1909), 26.

This valuable work existed long in MS copies before it was printed. Subjoined is a very brief list of the printed editions prior to 1870, giving only the place of publication, size and year. Nos. 9 and 11 I have never seen nor even traced in any library. If any of our readers can report copies of these editions, and give further particulars of them, I hope they will do so. Also I would like cleared up the correct date of the 1st edition, was it 1722 or 1723? I think the latter is correct and the former an error, but I have seen it given. No doubt some of these 'editions' are merely re-issues or reprints of the first edition, in which the translation was by Dermot O'Connor. No. 7 was a new translation by William Halliday. In most of these editions only the English translations are given. There may be some other editions or issues prior to 1870, and if so, I would be glad to hear of them. A complete bibliography of an important and standard work, such as this, is desirable. Of course the recent edition published by the Irish Texts Society, begun by the late David Comyn and completed by Father Dineen, will be henceforth the standard edition of this great work.

Short List of Editions: Dublin, fol. 1723 (?1722); 2: London, fol. 1723; 3: Westminster, fol. 1726; 4: London, fol. 1732 (called '2nd edition with appendix'); 5: London, fol. 1738 (called '3rd edition with appendix'); 6: Dublin, 8vo. 1809; 7: Dublin, 8vo. 1811 (1 vol. only); 8: Newry, 8vo. 1817 (2 vols.); 9: Dublin, – 1847; 10: Dublin, 8vo. 1854; 11: New York – 1856; 12: New York, 8vo. 1857 (J. O'Mahony); 13: New York, 8vo. 1866.

Henry R. Plomer, "Ireland and Secret Printing", Vol. I, No. 3 (Oct. 1909), 26.

Two statements made in connection with secret presses in England towards the close of the reign of Elizabeth, make mention of Ireland, in a way that sets one thinking. The first of these occurs in the examination of the men who were found printing the notorious Marprelate tracts in 1588-89. After a prolonged and. exciting chase the press was finally captured at Manchester on August 14th 1588, and the printer and his two assistants were carried to London. On their way the printer, John Hodgkins, tried to cheer up his companions, and amongst other things, said: 'That after they were delivered he would again set them to print in Ireland.' (William Pierce, *An Historical Introduction to the Marprelate Tracts*, p.338.)

The second statement is found in certain evidence put forward in 1603, by a London printer named William Jones, to prove the existence of a Jesuit press. (See *Library*, April 1907.) He declared that a printer named Henry Oven escaped from the White Lyon prison in Southwark and went into Staffordshire, where he continued printing until some of his accomplices were captured, when he again fled, but was captured 'as he was flying with his press and letter, so it is said, into Ireland.'

Here then we have two statements, suggesting Ireland as a place where secret printing might be carried on, and they further suggest the possibility, that secret presses were at work there in the sixteenth century. Yet so far as we know, there is nothing to support the suggestion. There is, it is true, in the British Museum, one book, John Olde's *Acquittal or Purgation of Edward VIth and the Church of England, of Heresy or Sedition*, which bears the imprint: 'Imprinted at Waterford 7th November 1555', but this has generally been received by bibliographers as a fictitious imprint.

A glance at Mr. Arber's *Transcript* will show that there were more anonymous books, some with certainly fictitious imprints printed between 1550 and 1603. The mysterious press of Hugh Singleton for example, has never been located. It certainly was not in Rome, as some of the imprints declare. It would have been much easier for him to have taken his press over to Ireland, where he might have taken refuge with Humphrey Powell, who was already there.

At any rate, when one considers (1) the nearness of Ireland to England, (2) the constant intercourse between, not only Ireland an England, but Ireland and the Continent, it seems a strange thing, that no secret presses have ever yet been traced to Ireland.

J. S. Crone, "Reviews", Vol. I, No. 3 (Oct. 1909), 28.

[...] It is a pleasant recollection of the present reviewer that he once heard the late Lord [Charles] Russell of Killowen, then in the zenith of his powers, refer to the dispossessed Celtic inhabitants of Ulster, whom he had known in his youth, in words that have clung to his memory since: 'They were called "the mountainy men", for the rich valleys and the fertile plains were not for them', and the fine voice faltered and a tear glistened in the eye. It was with such thoughts one took up this handsome volume, *The Mountainy Singer* by Seosamh MacCathmhaoil (Maunsel, Dublin). Here we have a descendant of those very men who refused to go to Connaught—or the other place—but clung to their bare hillsides and their ancient faith, and well and sweetly he sings in spirited cadences the legend, customs and superstitions that yet linger amongst his own folk. Some of these poems have appeared in earlier volumes and some set to traditional airs have delighted London drawing-rooms. This judicious selection of the cream of the author's work heretofore—long may he continue—is sufficient to place him high in the ranks of contemporary singers. The author has recently been holiday-making 'in Ould Donegal' about which he has recorded his impressions with a view to publication later on. We have been privileged to read a portion of the MS, and we can assure our readers that as word pictures by a true artist they are entitled to a place beside his poems, and that is the highest praise our humble judgment can accord.

"John Synge's Future Fame", Vol. I, No. 3 (Oct. 1909), 33.

In another hundred years from now, this year of centenaries will be celebrated for its own events. People will be saying, 'It is a hundred years today since Swinburne died, that exquisite lyric poet whose verses still sing themselves in every heart; a hundred years since Meredith died, that far-seeing writer who left us so fine a picture of nineteenth-century life ... And perhaps among them all will be some close lover of literature who will add: 'Yes, and that year, too, a hundred years ago, saw the death of a young poet named John Synge, who lived only to the age so often fatal to genius, and left behind him only a few short plays, a prose book on some desolate island off the Irish coast—at that time still subject to England—and this slim volume of verses, now very rare, which I bought for twopence on a second-hand bookstall in Park Lane.' Thereon he will produce a little grey book with canvas back, under fifty pages in all, but bearing on its title page the valued mark of the "Cuala Press, Dundrum", as he will carefully point out, and containing a preface by William Yeats, with some account of the author's personality and genius. (*"THE NATION"*.)

R. S. Maffett, "The Roundwood Press", Vol. I, No. 4 (Nov. 1909), 37.

A note on Roundwood in connection with its printing may not be without interest to some of the readers of *The Irish Book Lover*, and may elicit some further information, which is desirable, with respect to the printing press in this part of the County Wicklow—a county which does not seem to have a very large output of publications to its credit. The only notice of the subject imprint which I have seen or heard of will be found at p.194 of the Second Series of Cotton's *Typographical Gazetteer*, 1866, and is as follows: 'Roundwood, a village of Ireland, situated in a beautiful part of the county of Wicklow. G. P. Bull had a printing office here in 1810.' No names of books printed at it are given. Lewis says nothing of a printing press having ever existed here, though not a usual find in a small Irish village either a century ago or at present; nor does the Rev. G. N. Wright in his *Scenes in Ireland* (London 1834), who gives an opposite account of the district encircling the village, consisting of 'a few humble cottages and two small inns', which latter he praises, while he mentions that Roundwood is in the parish of Derrylossory; 24 miles from Dublin, via Enniskerry and the Long-Hill. The name of the place is now well-known in connection with the Vartry reservoir for the water supply of the Irish metropolis. When the printing press was established, or when it came to an end, I am not aware, nor as to the amount of its output. I however have the following four items:

1. *Reports of the School of Industry, at Hofwyl, in the Canton of Berne, Switzerland*. Translated from the Bibliothèque Britannique, published at Geneva in 1814. Dublin: Sold by Martin Keene, Bookseller, College Green-Thomas Bowes, 67, Lower Gardiner Street-and at the Committee House for Charitable Societies, 16, Upper Sackville Street. 12mo. Title leaf+6+71pp. 1817.
   N. B. The title-page has a small wood-cut representing a hive of bees. On the verso is, 'Printed by G. P. Bull, Roundwood, Co. Wicklow.' The 'Reports' seem to be of the nature of a review, consisting practically of extracts, and spread over five numbers of the above periodical, i.e., from August to December, the heading of each part being the same, viz., 'Report of the Institute for the Education of the Poor at Hofwyl.' Written by M. Rengger, and published in the name of the Commission, appointed to examine the Establishment, Berne, 1814. But probably the Report itself was divided into parts.
2. *The Relations and Description of Forms, according to the Principles of Pestalozzi*. Part I. with four copperplate engravings. Dublin. Sold by Martin Keene, &c., as in No. 1. 12mo. Title leaf x, 6+[106]pp., leaf+63+36pp., and page of Errata. 1817.
   The "Description", "Relations", and an appendix have separate paginations. On the verso of the title-page is 'Entered at Station-er's Hall', and 'George P. Bull, Printer, Roundwood, Wicklow.' (Engravings wanting in my copy.)
3. *Pestalozzi's Intuitive Relations of Numbers*, Part IV: Containing the use of the Second Table of Fractions. With a large plate. Dublin. Sold by R. M. Tims, 85, Grafton Street (opposite Duke Street) 12mo. Title-leaf+192pp. 1819.
   On the verso of the title-page is 'G. P. Bull, Roundwood, Wicklow'. (Plate wanting in my copy.)
4. *The Use of the Bean Table; or an Introduction to Addition, Subtraction, and Numeration, with visible Objects. On the Principles of Pestalozzi*. Dublin. Sold by R. M. Tims, 85, Grafton Street. Bull, Printer, Roundwood, Wicklow. 12mo. Title-leaf+155pp. 1820.
   N. B. The wood cuts on the title-pages of the three last items are similar, but differ from that in No. 1.

Mr. E. R. McClintock Dix, who has also four items of Roundwood printing (one of which is identical with No. 4 of mine) told me that he had not met with any examples of this press besides the above publications, nor any mention of such except one entry in, the catalogue of the British Museum Library, which I understood made an eighth item. On looking over the catalogue the other day, however, under

'Pestalozzi', I found there No. 2 of my list, with 'By Synge?', appended to the title. As most of the above-mentioned Roundwood printing has reference to Pestalozzi's system of education, and probably emanated from the same source, it would be interesting to have this point of editorship, if possible, established and further elucidated. The ground for the suggestion would seem from the catalogue to be the fact that it has already been ascertained that 'the 'Irish Traveller' who was the author of two Dublin Pestalozzi publications of 1815, bore the above surname, which by the way is that of a County Wicklow family. With respect to the printer, there was a 'John Bull' who printed at Waterford and a Joseph Bull at Parsonstown, in the first quarter of the last century. [And Edward Bull, Bachelor's Walk, Dublin—ed. footnote]. What relationship if any, existed between these and the 'George P. Bull' of Roundwood, it would also be of some interest to know, as well as the reason of his setting up his press at this somewhat out-of-the-way village. The 'Reports' are interesting reading. The pupils of the Hofwyl school (supported by Mr. Fellenberg, 'on his landed property'), were chiefly engaged in agriculture, ten hours daily being allotted to this occupation while only three were devoted to 'instruction', in the usual meaning of this term. Religious training entered largely into the system. This the first item seems scarcely so well printed as the other three.

E. R. McClintock Dix, "Eighteenth-century Newspapers", Vol. I, No. 4 (Nov. 1909), 39.

The value of our early newspaper press is I think becoming more appreciated. The historian who wishes to get contemporary [view] of facts, the genealogist in search of his ancestors, and other enquirers, turn to the earlier newspapers as a source from which hope to derive much material for their respective studies, and no doubt if the earlier press were extant and available it would help them much. For example the student of our drama in the 18th century naturally turns to the daily press of the period to see the accounts of plays performed and the actors taking parts therein, but unfortunately very much of that daily press has vanished and is only, known by the more important journals, and even these are not to be seen in any one place in complete form. *Faulkner's Dublin Journal* (an important newspaper in its time and continued for nearly a century), is not to be found complete in any one library. It began I believe in the year 1725 and continued all through that century and on into the next, but where is the searcher for the information which it contains to see it? I will take Dublin alone. There are six principal Libraries there, viz., Trinity College, King's Inns, The Royal

Irish Academy, National Library, The Chief Secretary's Library in Dublin Castle and Marsh's Library. This latter is second in point of age to Trinity College but it is a smaller library and mainly theological, and hence I mention it last. What then would a person desiring to search through every volume of *Faulkner's Dublin Journal* have to do to that end in Ireland's Metropolis? He would find the first four volumes 1725-1728 wanting, and would have to begin for the next eight years to examine the volumes or numbers of it at the Royal Irish Academy, or, if he gets permission, in the Castle Library; for the next two years he must go to the Castle Library only; then he must, for the succeeding two years, go either to the National Library or the Castle; then for the following years he has choice between the Castle or Marsh's Library; [for] 1743 he must go either to Trinity College, the National Library or Marsh's, and so throughout the rest of the century, finding probably that the volumes in the first Library he visits are imperfect and so being obliged to visit all the Libraries in turn. It is indeed a pity that these Libraries could not, by mutual arrangement amongst themselves, and by exchange, see that at least a complete set of two or three valuable Irish newspapers or magazines should be found entire in one Library.

Pending this useful achievement being accomplished, it would be a great boon to the student of Irish history in the 18th century if there could be published in some form a return showing in what Libraries were to be found volumes of a few of our principal journals. Of course many of these volumes are imperfect; some of them lack several numbers or issues, others have the pages torn or mutilated; so that a perfectly accurate return would be very troublesome and tedious to make out without the co-operation of several workers and particularly of our Librarians.

I have made a note of the volumes of *Faulkner's Dublin Journal* existing between 1729 and 1800, but it is possible that there may be volumes of this journal either in private hands or in provincial or municipal libraries, and if anyone can give information on that point either to the Editor of this Journal or to me direct, I shall be much obliged. I think the best plan for the present would be to select say three of four leading Dublin journals of the 18th century and try to ascertain what volumes are in existence, and where they are to be found, and to publish the result. The journals I would suggest are: *The Dublin Gazette*, *Pue's Occurrences*, and the *Freeman's Journal*, besides *Faulkner's Dublin Journal*.

I might mention in this connection that the period for which existing newspapers are most sought is, I think, that from 1715 to 1740. There were several newspapers at that time, for example, *Carson's Dublin Weekly Journal*, which ran from 1726 to 1731—Query, what numbers are now in existence? Again *Reilly's Dublin Newsletter* began in 1737 and went on to 1743 at least, but I only know of four volumes now extant.

I might mention here that James Hoey published a *Dublin Journal* as a rival to Falkiner's [sic] and it must not be confounded with this latter.

What I have suggested about Dublin journals of the 18th century is equally true, of those printed in other cities and towns as for instance at Belfast, Cork, Limerick, Waterford, Galway, Clonmel, Newry, &c. In some of these cities or towns there were but few journals produced and the task would not be so great.

It is very desirable that all volumes of our 18th century journals should be deposited in Public Libraries and not kept in private hands where they are unknown or inaccessible and so lacking in usefulness.

A beginning in the direction indicated has been made by their Excellencies the Earl and Countess of Aberdeen, in presenting a large number of volumes of Irish Periodicals extending from 1783 till 1833, to the Heraldic Museum, Dublin. The value of the gift is enhanced by the fact that they are all fully indexed. (J. S. C.)

Francis Joseph Bigger, "John Bernard Trotter", Vol. I, No. 4 (Nov. 1909), 41.

This eccentric individual and clever writer was born in the County Down in 1775, and educated at the grammar school in Downpatrick, whence he proceeded to T.C.D., where he graduated in 1795. Intended for the bar, he early turned his attention to literature, and his first anti-union pamphlet brought him to the notice of Fox, who appointed him his private secretary, in which capacity he accompanied him to France. Trotter's admiration of Fox, developed into hero worship—and it is stated that the great statesman and orator breathed his last in the arms of his faithful secretary.

Living in such an atmosphere, and with his brother E. S. Ruthven, afterwards a colleague of O'Connell, it can be well believed that Trotter flung himself with ardour into the historic election of 1805 when Castlereagh was driven from Down. Thenceforth, Trotter led a chequered existence, at one time riding in a coach and four, at another pursued by duns; now dispensing profuse hospitality, to all and sundry, anon an inmate of a debtor's prison. He evinced great interest in the revival of the harp, establishing a Harp Society in Dublin. His later years were passed in poverty, and misfortunes evidently tended to unbalance his mind. He died in unspeakable destitution in Cork in 1818, tended by his young wife and a boy whom he had reared and educated from poverty. Trotter plied a busy pen. In addition to the following bibliography, for which I am indebted to Mr. E. J. Byard of the British Museum, I am inclined to attribute to him Circumstantial details of the Long Illness and Last Moments of Charles James Fox (2nd ed. London 1806, 8o., 79pp.). whilst the biography prefixed to his posthumous and best known work, *Walks Through Ireland*, mentions as either written or edited by him *Historical Register* (Lewis, Angelsea St., Dublin, c.1806), "Margaret of Waldemar", a poem entitled "The Battle of Leipsic", "The Rhine or Warrior Kings" in 24 books, and *Cork Historical Register*, but of these I can find no existing copies.

Bibliography: *An Investigation of the Legality and Validity of a Union* (Dublin 1799), 8o.

Stories for Calumniators; Interspersed with Remarks on the Disadvantages, Misfortunes, and Habits of the Irish ... &c., 2 vols. (Dublin 1809), 12o.

The Political Guardian, conducted by J. B. Trotter, No. 1 (all published.) (King, Dublin 1810), 8o.

Memoirs of the Latter Years of the Right Honourable Charles James Fox. Third edition, xxxix+152pp. R. Phillips (London 1811), 8o.

Five Letters to Sir W. C. Smith ... Catholic Relief, the affairs of Ireland, and the conduct of the new Parliament. To which are added a sixth letter, with notes on the former. The third edition. 66pp. (Dublin: C. Crookes 1813), 8o.

Walks Through Ireland, in ... 1812, 1814, and 1817; described in a serious of letters to an English Gentleman, with Biographical Memoirs of J. B. Trotter (London 1819), 8o.

"Reviews", Vol. I, No. 4 (Nov. 1909), 44.

In THE JOURNAL AND REMINISCENCES OF R.. DENNY URLIN, edited by his wife (The Arden Press, 3s. 6d. net), there are several graphic sketches of Dublin Society intermingled with descriptive accounts of excursions to the provinces. The diarist, who was a legal official for twenty-six years, embracing the eventful period of the passing of the Encumbered Estates, the Land, and Disestablishment Acts, has left on record his impressions of many of the legal luminaries of that day including O'Hagan Whiteside, Butt, Napier, and Keogh—'the latter personally the most popular judge I ever knew!'—whilst amongst clerics we obtain glimpses of Newman, lecturing in Stephen's Green, Whateley, Magee, and Trench. Socially he visited the Parnells in Temple Street, and the Wildes in Merrion Square. He had some little name as a lecturer, and edited the two vols. of *Afternoon Lectures on English Literature, 1863-64,* which were delivered by, amongst others, Ferguson, Anster, J. O'Hagan and J. K. Ingram.

"Post Bag", Vol. I, No. 4 (Nov. 1909), 45.

Dear Sir—Some time ago the Government published reproductions of the Barony Maps made by Sir William Petty for the Commonwealth in 1655-59. The maps were issued by the Ordnance Survey Department and are most interesting, but they would be doubly so if the Government went a step further and published "The Book of Surveys and Distributions", which contains the names of the original owners of the confiscated lands, and the names of the adventurers and soldiers to whom the lands were granted. On each allotment on the map there as a number and on referring to that number in "The Book", you find the name of the old proprietor, the name of the planter, and the quantity of land confiscated, the old place name, &c., &c. The original manuscript of "The Book" commonly known as the Down Survey, is in the Record Office, Dublin. There is a copy in the Royal Irish Academy.

The originals of the Down Survey Barony maps are in the Bibliothèque Royal Paris. It is a more complete set than any in Dublin, and was the personal property of Sir William Petty himself. This set has a curious history as it is related that while being conveyed from Dublin to London in 1719, it was captured on the high seas by a French privateer and brought in triumph to Paris. As the set in the Record Office was more or less injured by the fire that occurred at the Surveyor General's Office in 1711, the British Government asked permission of the French Government to have copies made from the set in their possession. This was granted and in 1907 the maps were temporarily removed from Paris to Southampton, where photographic reproductions were made. Copies are sold at 6s. and 1s. each. It is stated that the originals were used by Napoleon 1st at the time of his projected invasion of Ireland. (JAMES TUITE, MULLINGAR.)

P.S.—I think pressure should be brought to bear on the Government by the Irish members interested in history, to publish this for all Ireland, through the Record Office. In fact the Book of Surveys and Distributions is a key or counterpart of the maps.

"Post Bag", Vol. I, No. 4 (Nov. 1909), 47.

Dear Sir—With reference to Mr. Dix's request for information as to other editions of *Keating's History of Ireland*, than those named in his list [Vol. I, No. 3, p.26], I write to say that I have an edition as follows: Dublin 1841), 8vo. ('two volumes in one'). This translation (without text) is by Dermod O'Connor, and is described on the back of the volume as a "New Edition". Yours truly, R. S. Maffett (Sandymount).

"Book Auctions in Cork", Vol. I, No. 4 (Nov. 1909), 49.

A miscellaneous collection of books comprising amongst others the library of the late Father Dillon, of Kerry, was disposed of by Messrs. Scanlan on 30th July last. The catalogue included 311 lots, close on one half of which related to Ireland. The following prices were realised for a few of the Irish items:

> MacHale's Irish translation of the Holy Bible (quarto, calf extra, fine copy), Tuam (1861), £1. 7s.; A. Griffith, *Miscellaneous Tracts*, containing a curious account of the Martyrdom of Father Sheehy (portrait, calf), Dublin, 1788. 5s. 3d.; Monaghan's *Records of Ardagh and Clonmacnoise* (with author's autograph), 5s.; MacHale's Translation of Moore's *Melodies*, fine copy, cloth (Dublin 1871), 7s.; Dunlevy's *Christian Doctrine*, [in] English (Dublin 1848), 6s. Webb's *Irish Biography*, £1. 9s.; Irish Pamphlets, 11 vols., 7s.; Ditto, 16 vols., 7s. ; Brady's *McGillycuddy Papers* (fine copy, cloth), 6s.; A fine copy of the last volume of Bunting's *Irish Music*, £1. 5s.; *Leabhar Breac* (published by R.I.A.), £2 10s.; Two Irish MSS, were included in the sale, one of which consisting of 34 pages fetched. 6s. 6d.

"Reviews", Vol. I, No. 5 (Dec. 1909), 58.

ROBERT EMMET: A HISTORICAL ROMANCE (MACMILLAN). We venture to predict that this the latest emanation from the practiced pen of Mr. Stephen Gwynn, will be one of his most popular works. It relates sympathetically, what is surely one of the saddest love stories on record, already immortalised by Washington Irving and Thomas Moore. The characters of Sarah Curran and Leonard McNally are especially well defined, whilst the description of the betrayal of Emmet's hiding-place by the latter is well conceived, and in face of the evidence adduced in the appendix, founded on a stratum of strong probability. The author has no need to apologise for the shortcomings of the work, for none can be found, from its opening lines to its brilliant close. 'Sundered head and body lie today, no man knows where: to trace them has baffled many searchers. But the spirit and the life which moved them are abroad upon the world, and have been for a hundred years, defying the violence of power, the authority of dominion. Not yet can the epitaph be written; but till it be, Robert Emmet the defeated, the deceived, the undismayed and undespairing, animates for ever the hope in which he died: and she, that tender one, crazed and shattered, moves sadly in his orbit, quickening all hearts with an eternal truth for love forgone.'

"Post Bag", Vol. I, No. 5 (Dec. 1909), 59.

Dear Sir—I read with interest Mr. Bigger's note upon (John Bernard Trotter), and wish to add two or three items, now in my library, to the bibliography.

> 1808—*Address to the County of Down*, 8vo., printed by H. Fitzpatrick, Dublin.
> 1810—*The Political Guardian*, Nos. II & III (July & August), printed by J. King.
> 1812—*A Few Thoughts on the 'New Era' and Veto in Ireland*, 8vo., 72pp., printed by James Byrne, Dublin.

It will be seen from above that the *Political Guardian* was not confined to one number, as stated by Mr. Byard on the authority of the British Museum catalogue and Power's 'List', but that it reached at least to three. I am a good deal interested in J. B. Trotter. The best authority about him is, I think, the Editor of *Sinn Féin*, who some time ago published an interesting account of him and some of his writings. (E. R. Mc C. Dix.)

E. R. McClintock Dix, "The Roundwood Press", Vol. I, No. 5 (Dec. 1909), 61.

I have read Mr. Maffett's interesting article on this press in the November issue, and desire to add to his list of the works printed there the following items:

> 1817—Pestalozzi's *Intuitive Relations of Numbers*, part I. (G. P. Bull), 12mo., title-leaf + (2)pp. + 240pp. (I have a copy of this work.)
> 1818—*Letters to a Friend by the late Mrs. E. M. Maturin*, 12mo., title + 80pp. + Epitaph, 2pp., size, 7 by 4½ . Note: No printer is given. This book is in the British Museum and the Shelf reference is 4411 C 42.
> 1818—*The Communicants Companion; or Instructions and Helps for the right-receiving of The Lord's Supper*, printed by George P. Bull, 12mo., 2 leaves+6pp., folds in sixes. (I have a copy of this work..)
> 1818—*Pestalozzi's Intuitive Relations of Numbers, Part III, containing the use of the First Table of Fractions* (with a large plate), printed by G. P.Bull, 12mo., 188pp. + paper cover, folds in sixes. (I have a copy of this work..)

It will be seen from the above and his article that eight items of Bull's printing at Roundwood are extant as mentioned by Rev. Mr. Maffett, but there were probably some other works printed. For example, while Parts I, III, and IV of Pestalozzi's *Intuitive Relations of Numbers* are forthcoming, Part II is not, and there must have been a Part II. This would have made nine items, unless the item No. 2 in Mr. Maffett's list could possibly have taken its place.

The fact that there was more than one printer in Ireland of the name of 'Bull', recalls to my recollection that I have similarly found families of printers printing in different places, such as the Lindsay's, Goggin's, Park's, &c., in some of our provincial towns, besides the Grierson family and others in Dublin. I hope some day to contribute an article on this subject. I regret that I have no evidence as to why this press was set up in Roundwood, but hope that some of our readers may be able to throw light on the subject.

James Tuite, "J. C. Lyons and the Ledeston Press", Vol. I, No. 6 (Jan. 1910), 69.

The memory of John Charles Lyons and the Ledeston Press, one of the very few private presses in Ireland has almost died out of existence. Yet he was a man of really unique character and ability, well-deserving of remembrance. The son of Capt. C. J. Lyons, by Mary Anne, daughter of Sir Richard Levinge, he was born on 22nd August 1792, at Ledeston on the western shore of historic Ennel, near Mullingar, and, as he him-self states in his *Grand Juries of Westmeath*, descended from an old Protestant, or as they were denominated 'Huguenot race', he entered Pembroke College, Oxford, 25th May 1810. Leaving the University after a rather uneventful course, he entered into possession of the family estates which he inherited seven years before, on the death of his grandfather. He always had a passion for collecting records, especially those relating to county families, and John O'Donovan in his Ordnance Survey letters on Westmeath refers to him as an authority on local topography.

He was a practical working gardener and also a skilled mechanician, self-taught; in fact he might be called a born genius in that respect. The press with which he printed some of his books, and the machine with which be bound them, were his own handiwork. He made several clocks, all of them of excellent workmanship, and good timekeepers. Indeed the only relics of this remarkable man at present in the family mansion at Ledeston are four or five of his clocks, and the remains of his library. A clock presented by him to the Mullingar Board of Guardians, of which body he was chairman for about 25 years, still remains in a prominent position in the board room. It bears the following inscription: 'Made and presented by J. C. Lyons, Chairman to the Board of Guardians of the Mullingar Union, 1850.' He was the last of the old Seneschals of Mullingar and religiously presided every Saturday at the Manor Court, until its abolition in 1837. Both in the Board Room and in the Manor Court, he was always guided by a fair and honest spirit, but he had a dreadfully sarcastic tongue with which he lashed friend and foe alike. He also served as High Sheriff of Westmeath during the year 1816. He was twice married and left issue by both wives, and died on the 3rd September 1874, aged 82, and was buried in Mullingar Churchyard.

In Cotton's *Typographical Gazetteer*, 2nd series (p.114), it is stated that Mr. Lyons began printing privately in 1820, that in that year he purchased a small press at Edinburgh and transferred it to his own house, that in 1827 he himself constructed a larger one on a new plan and continued using that press for over thirty years. This press is still in existence and in excellent condition. It is worked with a lever and an eccentric [wheel]. On the socket is engraved the name 'J. C. Lyons.'

Of the works printed by him, the editions were limited, and are now difficult to acquire or to trace. However, from personal knowledge and research, and the assistance of Mr. Dix, of Dublin—to whom no bibliographical inquirer appeals in vain, I have succeeded in compiling the following list:

Cotton states that Lyons wrote some law books and *A Treatise on Feeding Cattle with Steamed Foods* (with wood cuts), and *On Orchidaceous Plants* (two editions), for the latter of which he obtained the gold medal of the Horticultural Society in Dublin in 1845. In 1852 he issued his *Book of Surveys and Distribution of Estates Forfeited in Co. Westmeath in 1641*, with a historical preface. It is demy 8vo., printed in clear black type on thick paper. The title-page is in colour and the volume is bound in cloth, nicely gilt. Under the title are the following words: 'No country in Europe has suffered like Ireland, and were not the accounts authentic beyond question, the facts would be incredible.' It is said that most of Lyons's fellow landlords in Westmeath were very sore over the publication of this book (which is mainly a copy of the "Down Survey") they being the descendants of the adventurers and soldiers of Cromwell, whose names were given in the book as having received grants of the confiscated lands. They would have preferred that the information given by him should have remained locked up as a state paper in the Record Office. All Lyons's own estates were purchased for cash by his ancestors. I am told he produced only about 40 copies of this work. It is now very scarce. A Mullingar collector, a few years ago, thought himself lucky in securing a copy at £5.

His *Grand Juries of Westmeath, from 1727-1853, with Historical Appendix*, demy 8vo., appeared in 1853, and is turned out in equally good style. The "Historical Appendix" contains a vast amount of quaint and interesting information relating to persons and places in Westmeath. No one writing a history of the county could do without delving into its pages. Both books bear the imprint at foot of title-page 'Lediston, printed by J. C. Lyons', and the dates. I cannot find out how many copies were printed, probably not more than 60. A copy was sold about five years ago for £10! and I have seen one advertised by a Dublin firm in their current catalogue for £6. 6s. The lowest price I ever saw one sold at by auction was £3. 18s.

Anecdotes, &c., from the Historical Appendix to the Grand Juries of Westmeath. This is a 12mo., of 126pp., and appeared in the same year, 1853. Mr. Lyons' full name is given to it. There is a copy in the National Library (Joly Collection).

Historical Sketch of the family of Nugent, 8vo., 28pp., paper cover. This appeared in 1853. The only copy I know of was in the possession of Sir Arthur Vicars, late Ulster King at Arms.

Historical Notes of the Levinge Family, Baronets of Ireland from the Saxon Chronicles, A.D., 1005 to 853. It was issued in 1853 and is 8vo., containing pages 18+26+14. There is a copy in the British Museum.

This year, 1853, seems to have been the busiest as it was, according to present knowledge, the last of the Ledeston Press, Mullingar.

E. R. McClintock Dix, "Rare Ephemeral Magazines of the Eighteenth Century", Vol. I, No. 6 (Jan. 1910), 71.

Besides the regular periodic press, or newspapers, there appears to have been periods in Dublin in which weekly magazines of a very ephemeral character flourished. In an old volume of such literature belonging to the Deputy-Keeper of the Public Record Office, Dublin, there are many such, all Dublin-printed, and through his courtesy I have taken some bibliographical notes of them, and now to put them on record, I give their titles, many of which are curious, and their dates. The first is called *The Reformer*. About a dozen numbers are in his possession, and it apparently lasted from January to April, 1748. There is an odd number of a magazine in the same year called *The Inspector*. Both these, of course, had some political significance and object. In 1750, we come on *The Mirror*, of which two numbers are extant, and appeared in

November of that year. It must have lasted taut, and appeared in November of that year. It must have lasted some months as it provoked a rival journal called *A Looking-glass for the Mirror*, No. 1 of which appeared in July, 1751. There are only two numbers of it in the collection.

The following year and running into 1753, there was a magazine called *The Covent Garden Journal*, perhaps a reprint of the London publication of the same name. Then we have *The Dublin Spy*, that started in August 1753, which used to appear on Fridays, and the first number of which (August 13th) was published by Thomas Hutchinson at the Reindeer in Charles Street, opposite Mountrath Street, while the third number was printed by James Byrne, of Thomas Street, for James Eyre Weeks, who was the original author and proprietor. *The Dublin Spy* went on for several months, the last date on the extant numbers being the 27th of May, 1754 and was No. LV.

Next in 1753 we have *The Dublin Joker*, which appeared in September of that year. In the following October appeared *The Censor*. It had a longer career evidently than some of the others, as the extant issue is No. 95 of Vol. II. In January 1754, appeared *The Trifler*, and in the following June, *The City Watchman*. The last in the collection is called *Every Man's Journal*, and it appeared in October 1765, and was printed by James Byrne, of Cook Street. Five numbers are forthcoming. Most of these magazines are large 4to or small folio in size, and consist of 4pp. only, and generally contain two columns in each page.

There is one other item which is very curious in title and appearance and which I kept for mention till the last. It is entitled *A Morsel from the Wolf in Bloudy Sheep's Clothing*. It appeared on the 6th of September, 1753, and was printed by Thomas Hutchinson. It contains the usual 4pp. of two columns each, but the entire is printed in red ink, which gives it a strange appearance.

This is but a very bare mention of the existence of these journals. Still it records them and may awaken interest and lead to other copies being reported, or similar journals. It would require an abler and more learned pen than mine to deal properly with these strange and rare magazines, to do justice to their contents or to fully set forth their value and importance from a historical point of view. I hope it may be done some time. It is indeed lamentable to think of the number of our magazines of the kind which have been lost.

Stephen J. Brown, S.J., "A Guide to Books on Ireland", Vol. I, No. 7 (Feb. 1910), 81.

I should like to call the attention of those interested in Irish books to a project on which I have been engaged for some time past, viz., the compilation of a Reader's *Guide to Books on Ireland*. Before explaining the nature of this undertaking, I should wish to forestall wrong impressions by saying at once what it is not. In the first place it does not lay claim to be a bibliography. By this I do not mean that I am content to be inaccurate or haphazard, but simply that my aim is not exhaustive completeness. Secondly, I do not include merely books by Irish writers, and thirdly, not merely books printed in Ireland. My idea was this, to get together in a handy workable form a carefully classified list of books dealing with Ireland and the Irish, each title included to be accompanied by a descriptive note, brief, but not too scanty.

Such a list, it seems to me, would be useful in the first place to the general reader, who wishes to study Ireland. It might also be of much assistance to those who have to prepare lectures, or speeches, or articles, and in particular the members of various national propagandist organisations, political and literary. Again, it might help such as have to select books whether for libraries or for prizes. I have been assured that publishers and booksellers might find it useful in various ways.

From a consideration of the public aimed at, it may be judged with tolerable accuracy what books should be included in my list and what omitted. I do not think a hard and fast rule can be made, but I shall be guided in my choice by the following principles. In the first place, I should wish to include all books at present, or till very recently, in print. It would take up too much of this valuable space to explain my reasons for this. Secondly, it would seem well to include all such books as because of their valuable matter or because of their form are likely to be reprinted. Thirdly, there are a number of important works which, though not likely to reprinted, have not yet been superseded and remain standard works on the subject. What of the large mass of books that would be excluded by a selection confined to the above classes? Ought their titles at least to be mentioned, perhaps in small print? It is a point on which I should be glad of the advice of Irish book lovers.

It will be asked, how much of this work has already been done? In the first place the portion of the work that deals with Irish fiction, containing about 520 titles with descriptive notes, is already complete, has been approved by competent critics and is being examined by a publishes. As to the rest, a list of titles, in the, compilation of which, most, I believe, of the available bibliographical sources have been ransacked, has been got together and alphabetically arranged. Between two and three hundred descriptive notes have been written. The work was begun in June 1908.

Of course I have not attempted this single-handed. I have had valuable help from many quarters, notably from Mr. D. J. O'Donoghue, Librarian of the National University, Mr. F. J. Bigger, M.R.I.A., of Belfast, Dr. W. H. Grattan-Flood, author of *A History of Irish Music*, Dr. McCaffrey, author of *A History of the Church in the Nineteenth Century*, and Mr. Arthur E. Clery, B.L. It is to solicit further help and suggestions that I am bringing this matter before the readers of the *I.B.L.* Any reader who has access to a good library could help in a very practical way and without considerable expenditure of time. I appeal therefore to such readers as consider this Guide to Books on Ireland a useful undertaking to send me their names and addresses with an offer of literary help. I shall not take undue advantage of their kindness.

Lest any should be indisposed to offer their help owing to the impression that the work will be done in an amateurish and unscientific way, I may add that I am endeavouring to carry it out on the lines laid down in E. A. Savage's *Manual of Descriptive Annotation* (Library Supply Company 1906), which, I understand, to be the best treatise on the subject. I shall, moreover, send to anyone who kindly offers assistance, a form which will explain definitely the points to be mentioned in the annotation, thus rendering much easier the task of composing it.

E. R. McClintock Dix, "Printing in the Town of Cavan", Vol. I, No. 7 (Feb. 1910), 83.

Having been recently asked a question as to printing in Cavan by Mr. Charles Sayle, of University Library, Cambridge, who is at present engaged cataloguing the very valuable collection of books relating to Ireland gathered by the late Henry Bradshaw and by him bestowed on that Library, it occurs to me to put on record in this magazine some particulars as to the printing in that town.

In the first place I might mention that the earliest item of printing that I have seen at Cavan was a pamphlet entitled *A List of the Several Baronies and Parishes in the County of Cavan, together with all the Denominations of Land in each Parish, alphabetically arranged, together with Carvaghs contained in each Denomination*. It is a 4to containing title leaf and 66 numbered pages. The date is so uncertain that it might be 1709, or, as I think more likely, 1790. It refers to certain Irish 'Road' Acts which, as far as I have been able to ascertain, must have been passed in the latter half of the 18th century. The name of the printer of this work is given as Henry Ireland.

The next item of printing in Cavan that I have met with is a volume of poems by James Martin. A 12mo. of 164pp.+1 leaf of errata. The printers were 'Wm. Ireland and Son', and it appeared in the year 1813. There is a copy in the Royal Irish Academy (Halliday Pamph-lets). The printer's surname, being the same as that of the previous item, suggests a family of printers, possibly of three generations, but if so it is strange that only two items of their press are extant.

Then in 1816 there was a second edition of Martin's *Poems* printed in Cavan, the printer this time being 'James O'Brien', and the volume had increased to 200 pages. James O'Brien continued as printer in Cavan down at all events to 1846, and he printed some little 'Song Books', an *Explanation of the Church Catechism*, 2 editions (1816 and 1826); *Memoirs of Mrs. Dorothy Johnston, of Lisburn* (1818); Some religious works, such as *An Exhortation to a Devout, &c., Observance of Family Worship*', which appeared in 1818, and *Leger Lessons*, which appeared in 1827.

I will not now refer to his later printing which included the *County Presentments* in 1837.

There was also printed in Cavan a newspaper called the *Cavan Herald*, which was bi-weekly, and appears to have been started in the year 1818. The proprietor in 1820 was George N. Busteed. There is one copy extant dated 19th December, 1820 and another dated 2nd January, 1821. Both are in the National Library, Dublin.

In 1828 we find a third printer at work, named Wm. Johnston, who, as late as 1850, printed *The Royal Descents of Henry Maxwell, K.P., Seventh Lord Farnham*, 8vo., and in 1860 Thomas J. Smyth printed *The Farnham Descents from Henry III*, 3 parts folio, a well-known genealogical work.

If any of our readers can supply particulars of any Cavan printed works prior to 1820, I will be very glad to receive the information.

P.S.—There is in the University Library, Cambridge, a printed copy of the *Co. Cavan Presentments* for 1820. It has no imprint, and Mr. Sayle asks where it was printed and by whom. If anyone can satisfy him on the point we will both be obliged.

Sean Ghall [pseud.], "A Dictionary of Irish Biography", Vol. I, No. 7 (Feb. 1910), 84.

Mr. Buckley's interesting letter, in the fifth number [Vol. I, No. 5, pp.60-61], is a welcome contribution. Besides Ryan and Webb the volumes of Will's *Illustrious Irishmen* should have been named, in spite of their imperfections, in spite of their animus. Humbly I suggest that the plan adopted by the projectors of the Dictionary of Distinguished Anglo-Indians would meet some of the needs of a revised edition of Webb, or better still, a wholly new work. This plan consisted of publishing, with dates, the names of the men whose life-stories had been written, and a separate list of those who needed such an antidote to oblivion. If the biographies in the *Dictionary of National Biography* and those in Webb were named alphabetically, in these columns, and readers afforded opportunity to supply *lacunae* a beginning would be made in an effective manner. Many excellent biographies of Irish Gaels and Sean Ghalls have appeared in the Irish, American, and Australian Press, but have not been included in any of the above-named works. Where suggestions are made readers would greatly help by naming, as accurately as possible, the sources. No Irishman has criticised the arbitrary manner in which some of our dead found record in the *D.N.B.* and others equally great were excluded. Why, for instance, Ferguson, who wrote a few archaeological articles of no particular significance was chronicled and John Savage, poet, historian, essayist, journalist, and politician was ignored. Why a Dowdall was selected, and a Tirlough O'Donnelly (Terence Daniel) who played a much more prominent part in Tudor Ireland, was not. These are typical of many scores of puzzles. The method adopted by the *D.N.B.* could not be improved upon—obtaining the aid of writers skilled in various departments to contribute articles on their respective notables. D. J. O'Donoghue in his able work *Irish Ability* has dotted each province with its great names, and yet has escaped the 'taint' of provincialism. The breaking up of the work, by provinces, would be most inconvenient to the student or enquirer, the alphabetical method, almost universally adapted by nations, is the wisest. With such an able general editor as Mr. O'Donoghue, whose talent for research is only equalled by his gluttony for toil (O rare gift!), the suggested work would be an honour to Ireland, for he, Pompey-like, would create an army of aiders, by a mere 'stamp of his foot', since his knowledge of contemporary bibliog-raphy is as deep and as wide as his acquaintance with that of the eighteenth century. A bibliography of works like Blackburne's *Illustrious Irishmen*, Gerard's *Some Fair Hibernians*, *Some Celebrated Irish Beauties*, Hogan's *Distinguished Irishmen of the Sixteenth Century*, O'Hanlon's *Lives of the Irish Saints*, O'Daly's *Poets and Poetry of Munster*, *Worthies of the Irish Church*, Cruikshank's *History of Methodism in Ireland*, *Six Generations of Friends in Ireland*,

O'Donoghue's *Dictionary of Irish Poets*, Appleton's *American Dictionary of Biography*, Madden's *United Irishmen, Dictionary of Famous Australasians, Dictionary of Famous Anglo-Indians*, and so on—such a bibliography would make roads and paths through the jungle. There are hundreds of illustrious Irish dead who have no niche in the Temple of Irish Biography. These crude suggestions may help the methodical-minded to formulate a definite plan. One thing is beyond dispute—we need, sorely need, a successor, even a supplanter of Webb, Ryan, Wills, and the *D.N.B.*

Seamus Ua Casaide, "J. B. Trotter", Vol. I, No. 7 (Feb. 1910), 86.

The following supplementary list of Trotter's works contains some items not included in the lists published in Nos. IV. and V. of this Journal:

1. *Circumstantial Details of the Illness of C. J. Fox*. London. 1806.
2. *Memoirs of the Life of C. J. Fox* (London 1806). The above two works do not give the author's name, and perhaps should not be included.
3. Letter to Lord Southwell on the Nomination of Catholic Bishops (Dublin 1808) There is a copy of this work in the Chief Secretary's Library, and also in National Library.
4. *Letter to Lord Grenville on the Veto* (Dublin 1810).
5. *The Harp: A Poem* (Dublin 1810). Advertised in 'Dublin Correspondent', 17th April, 1810, as published on that day by Wm Figgis, 37, Nassau Street.
6. *Poems Containing Several on Illness and Death of Fox* (Belfast 1810), Advertised in *Dublin Evening Post*, 24th July, 1810, for speedy publication by subscription.
7. *Statements Relative to the Arrest of J. B. Trotter, Esq., and Family in the County of Wexford, Ireland* (Dublin: Printed by James Byrne, 74, Fleet Street 1812).
8. *Five Letters to an Eminent Character on Catholic Relief* (Dublin 1812).
9. *Five Letters to an Eminent Character on Catholic Relief* (Dublin 1813).
10. *Five (Six) Letters to Sir W. C. Smith on Catholic Relief*. Second Edition (Dublin 1813). Third Edition in National Library.
11. *Leipsick; or, Germany Restored: A Poem* (Dublin 1813).
12. *The Progress of Music: A Poem*, 16pp. (sl. or a.) In National Library.

The Halliday collection of Pamphlets in the Royal Irish Academy has copies of Nos. 1, 2, 4, 7, 8, 9, 10, and 11 in above list, 5 in Mr. Bigger's List, No. 3 in Mr. Dix's list and possibly others.

"Miscellaneous", Vol. I, No. 7 (Feb. 1910), 90.

LORD KELVIN'S *EARLY HOME* (MACMILLAN). This interesting well written, well illustrated work comprising the recollections of Mrs. King, the eldest sister of Lord Kelvin, describes the beautiful associations amidst which the gifted Thomson family were brought up in Belfast and Glasgow. It will, we are assured, be of more than ordinary interest to readers in the former city introducing as it does anecdotes concerning the remarkable men who a century ago gained for her the title of 'The Northern Athens', and indeed throughout Ulster where 'Thomson' and his 'Arithmetic' were household words. As showing the leanings of the sturdy yeomen from whom Kelvin sprung, his sister says, her father was taught to read from handkerchiefs on which were printed mottoes and verses composed by the patriots of '98. And again before the battle of Ballynahinch, the rebel army was 'camping near my grandfather's house, and his daughters secretly carried food to the insurgents, their little brother helping them. Long after these times he wrote an account of the battle to read to the Belfast Literary Society, which was afterwards published in a magazine, and, we may add, republished in 1904 in the *Irish Presbyterian.*

"The Post Bag", Vol. I, No. 7 (Feb. 1910), 90.

In reply to a query by my friend Seamus ua Casaide, in No. III, I have much pleasure in informing him that I once possessed a copy of Charles Wilson's *Irish Poems with English Translations*, and the year of publication was 1782 not 1792. Unfortunately the volume disappeared some fourteen years ago, but I am certain as to the date. A reference to Walker's *Irish Bards*, published in 1786, will also corroborate the year as 1782. Walker highly praises Charles Wilson and quotes his *Irish Poems*. I also find that Sir Walter Scott had a copy of Wilson's verses, as he quotes his version of O'Carolan's song in praise of O'Rourke in his edition of Swift's works. (W. H. GRATTAN-FLOOD, ENNISCORTHY.)

"Replies", Vol. I, No. 7 (Feb. 1910), 91.

ULSTER AS IT IS, 2 VOLS. (MACMILLAN 1896) was written by Thomas MacKnight, who was, for nearly thirty years, editor of the Belfast *Northern Whig*. Therein he sets down his recollections and impressions of the varying political problems in Ulster, from the standpoint of the old Ulster Liberals who fought for Tenant Right and Disestablishment against the combined influence of the Church and Landlord interests in the days before the Ballot. The book is in a great measure composed of extracts from his 'leaders', generally prefaced by 'It was said in Ulster next morning', &c.; 'the comment of the Whig was', &c., or 'I took occasion to remark', &c. As the seasoned opinion of a leading Liberal Unionist journalist possessing great opportunities of learning the views of both. peer and peasant on the burning questions of the last quarter of the nineteenth century it is well worth study. (REV. FATHER BROWN, S.J.)

"Queries", in Vol. I, No. 7 (Feb. 1910), 93.

Who were Phillip Harwood, who wrote *History of the Irish Rebellion of 1798* (London 1844), 8vo.., and John Rutherford, author of *The Secret History of the Fenian Conspiracy*, 2 vols. (London 1877), 8vo.?

You will find the biography of the first in the D.N.B., Vol. XXV, page 104. It was suggested to me, long ago, that the second was an assumed name, but I must leave the answer to our readers. [—Ed.]

F. J. Bigger, M.R.I.A., "Henry R. Montgomery", Vol. I, No. 8 (March 1910), 100.

We would like to know more of this writer. There is a meagre note in O'Donoghue dealing with his *Early Native Poetry*, published by James McGlashan (Dublin, 1846), a new edition of which, largely augmented, was published by Hodges and Figgis in 1892. He was evidently deeply affected by the Young Ireland movement. The preface is dated from Belfast and the editor describes himself as a member of the Dublin University Philosophical Society. The volume contains an excellent selection of translations from the Irish highly favouring the Northern poets, Charlotte Brooke and Samuel Ferguson. The biographical notes are concise and instructive. There is, however, an earlier little book of Montgomery's, not so well known, *An Essay Towards Investigating the Causes that Have Retarded the Progress of Literature in Ireland* (Belfast, G. Phillips, 2, Bridge Street, MDCCCXL [1840])

The information contained in this brochure is most valuable and we believe equally reliable. Its data concerning Irish literature, periodicals and literary societies is perhaps unique, and was utilised to the full by John Power in his works. For instance, he refers to a *School Master's Magazine*, published in Armagh about 1840. Who can tell of it? He gives a short account of the Ulster Gaelic Society in 1830, of which Lord Downshire was president. This was Ferguson's stimulant. He deplores the neglect of Irish literature quoting Byron's verse:

> For happy are they now reposing afar
> Thy Grattan, thy Curran, thy Sheridan, all

Who for years were the chiefs in the eloquent war,
And redeemed, if they have not retarded thy fall
Yes, happy are they in their cold English graves.

He notes the *Belfast Magazine* of 1808-14, initiated by Dr. Drennan and John Templeton. John Lawless *Ulster Register* of 1816 is mentioned, as is the *Belfast Magazine and Literary Journal* of Professor Cairn's (1825), and Charles H. Teeling's short lived *Ulster Magazine* of 1830, and the *New Belfast Magazine*, run by the Institution youths in 1833-34.

We only accentuate the Northern productions, but other centres are equally noted by the writer.

D. J. O'Donoghue "A Reply: Henry R. Montgomery", Vol. I, No. 8 (March 1910).

Mr. Bigger's note on this writer is full of interest, as everything he writes always is, and it gives me, for one, a curious bit of information as to the authorship of an anonymous brochure that I have often seen. I daresay that Mr. Bigger is aware that Montgomery wrote other books, including *A Short Life of Thomas Moore*. I regret to say that I do not know where or when Mr. Montgomery was born or it he is still alive. I am inclined to think he is still to the fore. He called on me some years ago and I found him a very interesting old (but ever young), gentleman. He gave me some reminiscences of Carleton, Mangan, McGlashan, the publisher, and other Irish notables, whom he knew in Dublin in the 'forties. As I fully expected to see him again I did not ask his address or make any note, except a mental one, of what he said, things I now regret. When I published the first edition of *The Poets of Ireland*, I knew nothing of him, except that his excellent specimens of the *Early Native Poetry of Ireland* contained pieces specially written for him by Mangan and others.

"Reviews", Vol. I, No. 8 (March 1910), 106.

The Dublin Book of Irish Verse (Hodges, Figgis), is a carefully compiled anthology of poems written from the middle of the 18th Century to the present day, in which the editor, Mr. John Cooke, has had the advice and assistance of many well-known Irish critics and scholars. One Irish anthology is of necessity so much like another that little requires to be said. But what strikes one most is the evidence afforded of the great wealth of verse that has been poured out during the last decade by our younger singers. If we compare this with the last similar work issued, Messrs. Stopford Brooke and Rolleston's *Treasury*

(1900), we find upwards of thirty names that have no place therein, and these are responsible for over a third of the total number of selections; and not to judge by quantity alone, much of the newer verse will bear comparison with the older, and not suffer. The book itself is a thing of beauty, fitting cage for such a flock of singing birds!

"Queries", Vol. I, No. 8 (March 1910), 110.

In *The Native*, a Belfast weekly paper, for 22nd January 1910, two poems are given: "The Triumphs of O'Neill" and "The Spellbound Chiefs of Clannaboy". It is there stated that the poems were written by W. H. Maxwell, rector of Balla, author of *Wild Sports of the West*. Is there any corroboration for this statement?

In the preface to *Irish Varieties*, by J. D. Herbert (London 1836), there is a statement: 'Should this volume prove worthy of public favour, another series can be prepared for the press, events and occurrences nearer the present time such as the Rebellion, Insurrection, the Londonderry family and some northern anecdotes.' Did this second volume ever appear—if not, what became of the writer's MSS and notes? (FRANCIS JOSEPH BIGGER.)

"Recent Book Auctions", Vol. I, No. 8 (March 1910), 110.

On 19th December, Marsh and Sons, of South Mall, Cork, disposed of a collection, some of which realised the following prices: Lenihan's *Limerick*, 24s; another copy, 23s.; a presentation copy of Caulfield's *Council Book of Youghal*, 6s.; Petrie's *Round Towers*, £2 5s.; Stoke's *Christian Architecture* and Brash's *Ecclesiastical Architecture*, together 35s.; Cusack's *Cork*, 3s. 6d.; Brash's *Ecclesiastical Architecture*, and *Ogham Inscribed Monuments*, together 18s.; O'Curry's *Manners and Customs*, 3 vols., 35s.; Bunting's *Ancient Music*, 20s.; Bennett's *History of Bandon*, 7s. 6d.; O'Hart's *Irish Pedigrees*, 8s. 6d.; O'Curry's *Manuscript Materials* 19s.; Smith's *Cork*, 2 vols. (1774), 6s.; *Pacata Hibernia*, 2 vols. (1810), 17s. 6d.; Smith's *Kerry*, 34s.; another copy with maps, 14s.; Sainthill's *Olla Podrida*, 9s.; Dalton's *Drogheda*, 13s.; Betham's *Antiquarian Researches*, 2 in 1, 22s. 6d.; Dalton's *History and Annals of Boyle*, 2 vols., 4s. 6d.; Cox's *History*, 2 vols. (1689), ills.; Croker's *Researches*, ills.; *Anthologia*, 4 vols., 7s.; Walker's *Irish Bards* and *Armour and Weapons*, together, 21s.; Fitzgerald's *Cork Remembrancer*, 1783, 12s.; Smith's *Waterford*, with maps, 12s.; Stuart's *Armagh* (1819), 4s.; Weld's *Killarney*, 1s.; Pendergast's *Cromwellian Settlement* (1875), and Trotter's *Walks*, 3 vols., together, 28s.; 4 vols. *Transactions of Ossianic Society*, 25s.; Gibson's *Cork*, 2 vols.,

7s.; Caulfield's *Council Books of Cork, Kinsale and Youghal*, fetched [ills.], 8s., and 7s., respectively; Murphy's *Annals of Clonmacnoise*, 7s.; Hardiman's *Minstrelsy*, 21s.; Holenshed [sic] and Stanihurst's *Historie Black Letter* (1577), 17s.

On Monday, 7th February, Messrs. Sotheby disposed of the library .of the late Rev. J. Duncan Craig, D.D., of Glengeary, the author of *Real Pictures of Clerical Life in Ireland, Bruce Reynell*, and other works. The Irish portion, not in very good condition, was made up in lots, and went cheap. O'Conor's *Columbanos ad Hibernos*, 4 vols., and Boulter's *Letters*, 2 vols., 9s.; *Trials of Smith O'Brien* (1849), and at Cork and Limerick (1867), and 3 others, 4s.; O'Curry's *Manuscript Materials*, Miss Hickson's *Ireland in the 17th Century*, 2 vols., and two others, 25s.; account of Mrs. Ireland (1745); the Chevalier's Hope; Henry's *Oration Against the Pretender's Son, and other Tracts on Rebellion of '45*, by Irish writers, and five others, £2 8s.; Donlevy's *Catechism*, O'Donovan's *Grammar*, Neilson's *Introduction*, and Bible and Testament in Irish £2 6s.; ten vols. of pamphlets on Emancipation, Repeal, Education, Orangism, 15s.; Smith's *Waterford*, Watkinson's *South of Ireland* and Young's *Tour*, 8 in all, 17s.; Gordon's *Rebellion*, Taylor's, H.B.C.'s *Insurrection of 1803*, Madden's *Reflections, Repeal Discussion* and five others, 13s.; Ferrer's *Limerick, Rebellion of 1641*, and eight others, 22s.

"Irish Literary Society", Vol. I, No. 8 (March 1910), 112.

An Original Night was held on February 5th, when Rutherford Mayne's play *The Troth* was presented with great success, the different parts being played by Joseph Campbell, Alice O'Dea, Whitford Kane, and A. E. Morrow.

The acting was very realistic, the County Down atmosphere being admirably rendered. The play, a fine spirited piece of work, was greatly appreciated by the audience, which was one of the largest seen recently. In addition, an excellent musical programme was gone through, and Miss Wheeler recited some poems of her own, suggested by a visit to the Aran Islands. [...]

On the 17th February there was a Literary Tea-Table, at which Miss Eleanor Hull introduced the subject of "Irish Folk-Lore Collecting", and gave an interesting account of the folk-lore of different parts of Ireland, and of its connection with that of other Celtic countries [...]

On the 19th, Mr. Graves lectured on "Music in Irish Life". Mr. Stephen Gwynn was in the chair and made an amusing speech as to the connection between music and politics in Ireland. Mr. Graves traced the history of Irish music from the earliest times, and showed the immense influence it has exercised on the music of other countries, though he declared that "The Wearing of the Green" was originally Scottish. He dealt with the collecting work done by Petrie and Bunting, and more recently by Dr. Joyce. Mr. Graves had got together a number of talented artistes, and vocal and instrumental items were rendered, illustrating Irish music in the heroic and mediæval periods, in the 18th and 19th centuries, and at present. among those who helped with the evening's success were Mrs. Milligan-Fox, Miss Georgina McDonald (harpist), Miss May Coleman, Mrs. Harry Bedford, Miss Cecilia Kemp, Madame Betty Brooke, Miss Mays, and Mr. Owen Coyler. ("H. T.")

A. P. Graves, "Ferguson Centenary Address", Vol. I, No. 9 (April 1910), 113.

The Centenary of Sir Samuel Ferguson was celebrated with much enthusiasm in Belfast, the city of his birth. The proceedings commenced on Wednesday, 9th of March, when Miss E. Alexander opened in the Art Gallery, an exhibition of relics and mementoes of Ferguson and his illustrious fellow workers in art, literature, music and archaeology, and gave a delightful address. This was followed by a reception by the Lord Mayor, McMordie. Sir John Byers delivered an interesting lecture on Ferguson's life and work to the students of Victoria College, and the Ulster Literary Theatre produced his dramatic scene "The Naming of Cuchullain". On Thursday 10th, Mr. F. J. Bigger placed a wreath of bay upon the graves of Ferguson and his wife in Donegore, and after a memorial service in the church, delivered a glowing eulogium on their beautiful lives. In the evening Mr. Percival Graves interested a crowded audience with the following centenary address:

'The relation in which Sir Samuel Ferguson stood towards Irish music and poetry was remarkable. As a poet, born both before and after his time, he was the only modern Irish epic writer of commanding genius who united in his personality the three requirements of the old Irish bard:

> Lips free from satire's poisonous flow,
> Knowledge that nothing base doth know,
> And love unsullied as the snow.

Yet, while the three ancient sorrows of Irish story telling—the fate of the Children of Lir, the fate of the Sons of Tuireann, and the fate of the Sons of Uisneach—are written in stately Gaelic prose, Ferguson modelled himself upon Homer, but in the metre of Chapman's great translation when he gave himself over to his *magnum opus* "Congal". This great epic records the final struggle between paganism and Christianity, in which the legions of the Cross ultimately prevail on the field of Maigh Rath. This poem abounds with great passages, and whilst, as Roden Noel remarks, Ferguson frequently makes use of the sonorous native names they are sometimes almost too thickly strewn over his pages, but the interest on the whole is sustained throughout, and the development of the action is conducted with the utmost artistic skill; the chariot of song thunders majestically to its goal with burning axle in direct impetuous course. But Ferguson is even greater in the epopee than in the epic. The "Tain Quest", written in rhymed trochaics, had the sublime and impetuous power and a mystical grandeur unequalled in any modern poem written upon an heroic supernatural subject. For splendid savagery Ferguson's "Welshmen of Tirawley" has excited the admiration of Swinburne, and for a calm beauty of an old world character "Aideen's Grave" furnished a beautiful contrast. Indeed, the modes of Ferguson's Heroic Lyric were many and wonderful; but he achieved his highest excellence in his great dramatic poem of "Conary", which Mr. W. B. Yeats placed even before his vivid and haunting "Deirdre".

Ferguson did not, like some of his successors, reproduce the verse technique of the old Irish bards exhibited by Dr. Douglas Hyde and others in their works on Irish Gaelic metres. He struck out a line of his own, and a strong and significant one, of which perhaps the most original was to be found in the "Welshman of Tirawley". It was only when he was translating from the Irish that Ferguson felt himself constrained to adopt Gaelic measures. Ferguson had made up his mind to turn his back upon modern themes, or at any rate only to give them a by-the-way attention. He was persuaded of the nobility of heroic Irish subjects. He was equally persuaded that at the time they had no public behind them. A generation before, they would have had the support of a cultured and unprovincialised upper class; a generation later they would have claimed attention in his hands as the noblest outcome of the Irish literary revival. He was therefore both before and after his time, and he realised his position to the full.'

'Indeed', said the lecturer, 'when I once spoke to him, with regret, of the neglect of all but Irish political literature, he acknowledged it but with a quiet expression of confidence that his time would come. It has come today! Quite apart; from the beautiful addresses delivered on the previous day by the literary daughter of famous literary parents, Miss

Alexander, there appears in the March number of the *Irish Monthly* a masterly review of Ferguson's poetry, which was delivered in the form of a lecture for the Irish Literary Society of London by the Hon. Roden Noel—Irish on his mother's side and a poet who had yet to win the fuller recognition due to his genius. This appreciation was followed by a charming poetic tribute to Ferguson by Miss Emily Hickey, in whose hands the manuscript of this lecture had been left.

He (the lecturer) did not think the characteristics of Ferguson's genius could be more ably summed up than in this fine passage from that criticism by Roden Noel: "But the poetry of Ferguson is the very reverse of what may be described as popular; it is human, unaffected, sincere, without mannerism, remarkable for economy of power and parsimony of epithet—concentrated, firm in outline, with a strong grip upon the chosen theme; vivid and graphic in delineation; constructed with the utmost artistic skill, symmetrical proportion of parts, and general unity of effect; now and again moving us profoundly by a touch of unforced and thrilling pathos all the more telling for this economy of power and use of the simplest means to produce the effect intended. A touch does it, a master touch as in Byron's "Gladiator" or Wordsworth's "Michael", or a song of Burns's, or one of the old ballads such as the "Twa Corbies". Sometimes profoundly tragic, and again instinct with the fairy glamour or shadowy sublimities of the early Celtsmythopoetic genius, interpreting the mystic scenes and sounds of nature, primeval forest, wild craggy mountain or stormy ocean." Miss Alexander and Miss Hickey had shown the fine appreciation of Irishwomen's literary insight into Ferguson's position as an Irish poet.

To the testimony of Professor Dowden that Ferguson was the only true epic poet of the Victorian age, he wished to add the following appreciation which he had received that morning from Stopford Brooke, the foremost living literary critic who wrote in the English language: "I have not only a great admiration for Sir Samuel Ferguson's poems, but I consider him as the first and perhaps the best of all those who have striven to bring into recognition, light, and beauty the ancient poetic sagas and tales of Ireland. The scholars have done much to make them known; he struck home to their poetry, and fired into importance their national essence, and great has been the use and the results of this to the Irish people and to the literature of the world. What he did so well, and with such fire and passion has had a life in it which has grown and will continue in the work of others.' (TO BE CONTINUED.)

James Hayes, M.R.S.A.I, "Smith O'Brien's Pamphlets", Vol. I, No. 9 (April 1910), 118.

I knew William Smith O'Brien. My first interview with him was at 107, Stephen's Green, where he called upon me, the day he returned to Ireland, from his exile, to discuss some educational subject. He collected Irish pamphlets, but only the best—those referring to the progress of Ireland, or to religious subjects of the pure, generous, and exalted tendency, which his mother loved and taught him. He had some of them bound up in three vols. for presentation to her. Nearly all of them bore an inscription, such as 'To my beloved mother, W. S. O'B.' His handwriting in these pamphlets and in his letters was beautiful. A few days after his arrest and incarceration in Richmond Prison, he received a present of a box of Burren oysters from a lady admirer. I have his letter of thanks to the sender. It is beautiful, and will be sold with my collection of autographs, at Sotheby's shortly.

One of the presentation pamphlets was entitled *Nirvana, or A Dream*, a very rare and beautiful production, originally written by Q. Q. (Jane Taylor), and dealing with Eastern ideas of the Supreme Being. Another was the rarest pamphlet I have seen on the Irish Famine. It is entitled, *Narrative of a Journey from Oxford to Skibbereen during the Irish Famine* (Oxford 1847), 28pp., 8vo. It was written by the late Lord Dufferin when he was only twenty years old. He asked for fourteen days' leave from Oxford and, having got it, proceeded to Dublin with his friend the Hon. George Boyle, afterwards Earl of Glasgow. He borrowed and begged amongst his friends and relations, and walked with Boyle to Athy, and then took coach to Skibbereen. I was a boy at the time, and well remember being sent to Skibbereen on business, and well remember seeing Dufferin and Boyle, with the Doctor, priest, the parson and his wife, all working hard in burying the dead! They stayed a few days and got back to Oxford on the evening of the fourteenth day. They stayed up all night whilst the pamphlet was being printed. Copies were sent to the Prime Minister and members of the Cabinet; to the rich and charitable, and money poured in, which was at once transmitted to Skibbereen. After this good act, Lord Dufferin was recognised as one of the best of men. I lent my unique copy inscribed as above 'To my beloved mother. W. S. O'B.' to Sir Alfred Lyall when he was writing the *Life of Lord Dufferin*.

His eighteenth-century pamphlets dealing with Irish parliamentary affairs I would think very good, and very rare, as I was only able to get two volumes of them [...]

We print Mr. Hayes' very interesting communication with much pleasure, and trust he will favour us with further recollections. (—Ed.)

James Coleman, "Death of Capt. Dunne", Vol. I, No. 9 (April 1910).

The death occurred in February of Capt.. John Joseph Dunne, the wellknown author, artist, sportsman and soldier. Born in Queen's Co. in 1837 and educated at Clongowes and on the continent, he entered the army and served all over the world, being wounded in the Maori War. On his retirement he became secretary to Isaac Butt, for whom he evinced the warmest admiration, and who humorously described him as 'a walking encyclopedia of useless knowledge'. He was subsequently appointed governor of Castlebar gaol, but the last years of his life were spent in the vicinity of London. An ardent Nationalist, he was nursed by O'Connell and lived to be intimate with Parnell. An accomplished fly-fisher, he published *How and Where to Fish in Ireland* (London [1886]), 8vo., viii.+183pp., under the pen-name of "Hi Regan", which has gone through seven editions. He also, wrote *Here and There Memories, by H.R.N.* (London 1896), 8vo., x-xi+411pp. which contains many racy stories of sport, politics and adventure. It is dedicated to the memory of Butt, of whom it relates interesting reminiscences. His eldest daughter is Mrs. Golding Bright, better known as "George Egerton", author of *Keynotes* (1893), and many other works of fiction.

"Book Auctions", Vol. I, No. 9 (April 1910), 122.

Mr. P. F. Scanlan, of the firm of Messrs. Scanlan & Sons, auctioneers, Cork, sold the extensive Library of the late Mr. C. G. Doran, on February 15th and following days. There was keen competition for the books, notably for the Irish collection. Appended are some of the prices obtained:

The Irishman, £7 10s.; *The United Irishman*, 'Thomas Francis Meagher's copy, £6 6s.; MS Pedigrees from Windele's Library, £5 10s.; *The Irish People*, Vols. 1 & 2, £3 17s. 6d. *The Statutes of the Irish Parliament*, £3; Madden's *United Irishman*, £2 16s.; Irish Pamphlets, £7; O'Reilly's *Irish Writers*, £2 1s.; *The Annals of Ireland* (1 vol.), £1 15s.; *The Citizen*, Vol. 1, £1 12s. 6d.;. *The Dublin Penny Journal*, 2 vols., £1 14s.; Irish MS, £1 15s.; Ruskin's *Works*, £2 4s.; Petrie's *Ecclesiastical Architecture*, £1 12s.; Stokes' *Christian Architecture*, £1 12s.; Keating's *History of Ireland*, £1 11s.; *Celtic Illuminative Art*, £1 10s.; *Transactions of The Ossianic Society*, 1855-58, £1 11s.; Brady's *Records of Cork*, £1 12s.; O'Byrne's *Queen's County*, £1 10s Tandy's *Appeal* and O'Flaherty's *Ogygia*, £1 7s.; Gimlette's *Huguenot Settlers*,

£1 6s.; Walker's *Dress of Ancient Irish*, £1 2s.; Walker's *Irish Bards*, £1 1s.; Bunting's *Music of Ireland*, £1; Ferguson's *Cromleach on Howth*, £1 1s.; Cronnelly's *Irish Family History*, &c., £1 7s.; *The United Irishman*, (Vol. 1), £1 4s.; Keogh's *Hibernica*, £1 4s.; *The Irishman,* Vol. 1, £1 1s.; Taffe's *History of Ireland*, £1 2s.; *Scotichronicon*, £1; Mulloly's *St. Clement*, £1; O'Donovan's *Dun Na Gedh*, £1 2s.; Mason's *Survey of Ireland*, £1 1s.; *Bulletins of the Campaign* (1798), £1; O'Curry's *Ancient Irish History*, £1 2s.; *The Earls of Kildare*, 7s. 6d.; O'Donoghue's *Memoir of the O'Brien's* (auto. of Smith O'Brien), 12s.; MS "Trial of Francis Arthur of Limerick", 1804, 12s.; *Life of Thomas Reynolds*, 8s. 6d.; "Trial of Quigley and Others", 1798, 4s.

F. J. Bigger, "Ferguson Centenary Address", Vol. I, No. 10 (May 1910), 125 [continued].

> Hold not lightly home, nor yet
> The graves on Donegore forget,

—sang Samuel Ferguson whilst contemplating the resting-places of England's illustrious dead in Westminster Abbey. His admonition was not disregarded during the Centenary celebrations, for there, on the 10th March, his natal day, Francis Joseph Bigger, before placing a wreath of Irish Bay upon the grave, delivered the following oration:

'They were assembled in Donegore that day, in that holy house and on that equally holy hill in their own beloved land, to place a wreath— an Irish wreath—upon the graves of Sir Samuel and Lady Ferguson, and the honour had been put upon him of being asked to say a few words at that time. The grave was robbed of its sadness on the present occasion: There was a spring in the earth and a brightness in the sky, telling of hope and resurrection. Amongst the Gaels was an old belief in heroes slumbering in the hilltops in great caverns awaiting the times for them to ride forth, a mighty host, to right the wrongs of the people. Their heroes slumbered on the hilltops beside the massive moat, but in consecrated ground, and every pagan bitterness had been taken away, as it was in the lives of those who lived so gently, so humanly, so lovingly. To Ferguson was given the privilege of opening the closed gates of the past, calling forth the dead heroes from the mountains of suppression and ignorance, and they had ridden forth, and no one could stay their progress. The heroes of Ireland were brought forth from their caverns by the Fergusons, who marshalled and formed their ranks, speeding them on their way to conquest and renown, crowning them for all time with haloes of valour and truth and strident manliness, placing high names upon their breasts that future generations might know and so recognise them as their own. To the Fergusons the hills of holy Ireland were bedewed with such a spirituality, such a fulness of life and adventure as must appeal to all lovers of our country in every or any aspect of her life. The carn-crowned mountain, the *cromleach* on the hillside, the cavern by the river bed, the deep crimson of the setting sun across the Shannon wave from the storied cross of Clonmacnoise, the lone wave-beaten islands of Arran [sic], each had its own tale to tell. The rugged path from slope to slope did to them resound with the tread of heavy armed warriors, tracking their way from dun to dun, their bronze shields and spears glancing in the sun's rays, or seemed to level itself to the wearied feet of the learned scholar or pious pilgrim treading his road from school to school in the acquisition, of a fuller knowledge, to be again spread abroad to other lands and other peoples. The bards of old chronicled the daring actions of their clan, in order that a due and proper pride of race might be given to the rising youth, and their mantle fell on the shoulders of Samuel Ferguson. Did they not say, did he not urge this in the most vehement of all his verses?

> Oh, brave young men, my love, my pride, my promise,
> 'Tis on you my hopes are set,
> In manliness, in kindliness, in justice,
> To make Erin a nation yet.
> Self-relying, self-respecting, self-advancing,
> In union or in severance, free and strong.

The clear morality, the unfeigned rectitude, the splendid principle of every word that ever proceeded from mouth or pen of Samuel Ferguson were indeed evident to the most casual student of his life and works. There was never any stepping aside to meet contingencies, his duty was plain to him; his honour fitted him as a well-made garment without seam or rent in any part of it; a truly Irish mantle that he ever wore by day, and it was his covering at night, aye, and his burial cloak. His friends and neighbours, and those who knew and valued him in other places, and a newer race that knew him not in the fleet, but loved and, acknowledged his worth all the same, were assembled there that day to do honour to his name and memory. They might stand there on the Moat of Donegore and look over the many scenes so dear to him, and so familiar to his earthly eyes—the rich valley of the Sixmilewater, over Templepatrick and past Lyle, and away to Divis or over Carnmoney to the ransomed hill of Down, or across the woods of Farranshane and Antrim, past the historic Rathmore of Moylinney and the Grange of

Mucamore to the shimmering waters of Lough Neagh. Far across the lake, the hills of Tir Eoghan rose to view. the fair land of the princely O'Neills, and, as they looked around, they must, if there was one drop of Irish blood in their veins, have some thoughts akin to those which surged so often through the hearts of the slumberers there beside them. There was an old Gaelic proverb which reads 'man is like the waves of the sea, which are here today and tomorrow are hence.' Erin of old had three great sounding waves of the sea, which, when any danger menaced the nation, resounded through the whole land, thus acting like a great protecting trinity. The past, the present, and the future—these were the three great waves affecting every one of them now, individually and nationally. Let them know the past as fully and as conscientiously as Ferguson knew it—nought extenuating and nought set down in malice—and if they did they would bear a conscious pride in their breast, and a fuller loyalty would be theirs to their own beloved land.

> 'Tis she shall have the golden throne,
> 'Tis she shall reign and reign alone,
> My dark Rosaleen,
> My own Rosaleen.

With a knowledge of the past and such a line of conduct in the present, they could walk assured as to the future. The gates had been thrown open to them, and hitherto hidden forces were riding forth over our land. In most unexpected places, from most unanticipated quarters influences have generated all tending the one way—the regeneration of our country. God grant that the future might be as full of fruit as the present was full of promise. In placing that wreath on the Ferguson tomb, they were only acting as good citizens, and like mercy they were blessed in the giving. Might the soil of Ireland lie light upon the sleepers—might the people of Ireland know and love them, and follow their good example, and might all assembled there that day be the better Irishmen and Irishwomen for having stepped aside for a little while from the ordinary duties of every-day life to pause at the grave of a sweet Gaelic poet, a learned Irish antiquary, a loving husband and wife, and, above and beyond all, a true patriotic and tenderhearted Antrim man, Ulsterman, Irishman.'

Both before and after the eulogy which was delivered from the lectern in the chancel of the church to a crowded audience, the usual invocations on such occasions were delivered in the Gaelic tongue, of which Ferguson was such an ardent student.

"Reviews", Vol. I, No. 10 (May 1910).

CAMBRIDGE UNIVERSITY LIBRARY BULLETIN. The Henry Bradshaw Irish Collection, presented in 1870 and 1886. We welcome this, the first instalment of the long looked-for catalogue of this celebrated collection. It contains upwards of seven thousand titles-exclusive of variants and duplicates—of works varying from a folio to a single leaf broadsides, proclamations, chap-books and street ballads extending from 1601 until 1906, all are here enough to gladden the heart of *The Irish Book Lover*. The titles are given as prepared for the General Catalogue, and a very full index renders the finding of any work easy. We are promised 'a full catalogue' of the collection at no distant date, and until that appears, this bulletin is a decided gain to the bibliographer. We have submitted it to many searching tests and can only submit a few suggestions—not in any spirit of carping criticism, but, merely with a view to render the full catalogue more complete. At p.139, Manzon, fl.1823, should be Manson fl.1792, as at 1001. At p.541, *A Narrative, ... &c., An Eye-Witness* [i.e., S. McSkimin], delete 'i.e., &c.'—for, as the author was not born until 1775, he could hardly have been an 'eyewitness' of events occurring in 1711. At p.694, *Veridicus* was Sir Richard Musgrave, the historian. As regards the Patriotic Miscellany Co., Down Election, 1805, at p.710, the title-page undoubtedly bears the London imprint, and no printer's name, but we have seen a copy bearing a MS. note 'Printed by Smith and Lyons, Belfast', which we believe to be correct, and the cartoons therein are the acknowledged work of John Thomson, the Belfast engraver. *Harlequin and the Eagle* (p.766), is by Crofton Croker, "H.G.C." (p.784), was most probably Henry Grattan Curran, and "Kilmore" (p.885), is better known to history as Culmore. But these are only trifling spots on the sun, and still leave us with feelings of gratitude to the very capable compiler and the Syndics of the University Press.

REV. J. IRWIN BROWN, *IRELAND: ITS HUMOUR AND PATHOS*. Truly we are a ubiquitous people, and the farther afield we travel, the warmer, our hearts grow towards the Motherland, and the louder we sound her praises, in song or story, as we have had abundant evidence in our pages, and now from Rotterdam comes a most interesting study, entitled *Ireland: Its Humour and Pathos*, from the pen of the Rev. J. Irwin Brown, minister of the Scotch Church in that city. The book contains some racy stories and is bright and readable throughout. It is dedicated to the author's father, Rev. Dr. Brown, of Drumachose, Co. Derry, in his prime a famous platform orator and gallant defender of the rights of the Irish tenant farmers.

J. S. Crone, "An Interesting Volume", Vol. I, No. 10 (May 1910), 135.

TRIAL OF ARCHIBALD HAMILTON ROWAN (1794). There has lately come into my possession, a volume, of more than ordinary interest to the student of Irish history, as well' as the book lover. It is a copy of the *Report of the Trial of Archibald Hamilton Rowan, Esq. for the Distribution of a Libel ... &c.*, &c. Dublin, printed for Archibald Hamilton Rowan, Esquire, and sold by Byrne, Grafton Street, 1794, 8vo., title-page & 152pp., bound in contemporary red morocco with gold tooling. It bears the armorial book-plate of Leonard MacNally, Barrister, with his autograph on title-page, and half portraits of Curran and Hamilton Rowan inserted. On the fly-leaf is written 'To his worthy friend Leonard MacNally, Esq., from Archb. Hamilton Rowan, March 25th 1794, Newgate.' But the word 'worthy' was obliterated and 'steady' written above it. Throughout the book there, are several MS notes, some by MacNally, signed "M.", and others by Rowan, who with his pen fills up 'an hiatus, the printer having refused to print this part', but the most interesting addition is a piece of paper six inches by seven and a half, containing some notes hastily jotted down. It is headed 'J. P. Curran's Notes from which he spoke on Rowan's defence in his own hand-writing. Leo. MacNally.' They are as follows:

> Lambert, Muir, character of R. Furnace, &c. To Arms, 2nd Reform, 3rd Catholic Emancipation, 4th Convention—now unlawful. Consequence of conviction, trials before revolution, drowned, &c.

Here is the framework on which the consummate orator built up than magnificent specimen of forensic eloquence, which will live for all time. The volume possesses yet an additional interest, for Thomas Davis, in an introductory note to the defence of Rowan, in his edition of Curran's speeches, says: 'The back of Curran's brief (I saw it a few years ago, in a copy of this trial sold at an auction), contained these catch-words', as above, but he does not state that it had once been the property of that modern Iscariot Leonard MacNally.

"Replies", Vol. I, No. 10 (May 1910), 136.

JOHN RUTHERFORD (Vol. I, No. VII, p.93.) In *Recollections of Fenians and Fenianism* by John O'Leary (1896, Vol. 1, p.67), there is a note about Rutherford's *Secret History of the Fenian Conspiracy.* O'Leary says: 'This history is, on the whole, as vile a book as I have ever read.

"John Rutherford" is of course, a false name, and I cannot make out that anyone can give even a probable guess at the ruffian who used it.' (Frederick Boase. St. Leonard's-on-Sea.)

Has not the secret been recently disclosed? Sir Robert Anderson, who has admitted the authorship of some of the famous articles on. *Parnellism and Crime*, says in *Blackwood's* for March: 'Forty years ago I published the secret history of the Fenian movement up to date'. (J. S. CRONE.)

[John S. Crone], "John Rutherford", Vol. I, No. 11 (June 1910), 141.

In our last number we suggested in an editorial note, basing our opinion upon a paragraph in the March number of *Blackwood's Magazine*, that Sir Robert Anderson was the author of the *Secret History of the Fenian Conspiracy*, a work whose authorship has baffled inquiry for a generation, and on which we have published communications from two gentlemen well known in the world of letters, one a valued contributor to the *Dictionary of National Biography,* the other the author of *Modern English Biography*. In a notice of that issue, the *Daily News* on the 6th inst. said: 'Sir Robert Anderson is connected by *The Irish Book Lover* for May with yet another anti-Irish publication whose authorship has hitherto been a matter of conjecture. This is *The Secret History of the Fenian Conspiracy*, published about forty years ago, with the name of "John Rutherford" on the title-page. Sir Robert Anderson's statement in *Blackwood'* for March—'Forty years ago I published the secret history of the Fenian movement up to date'—certainly seems to justify *The Irish Book Lover* in identifying him with John Rutherford.

On the same evening *The Star* had the following leading article 'Sir Robert Anderson is in danger just now of being credited with the authorship of every anonymous or pseudonymous attack on his native country. The latest suggestion comes from *The Irish Book Lover* that Sir Robert is the author of the *Secret History of the Fenian Conspiracy*, a work which bore the name of John Rutherford on the title-page. In *Blackwood's* for March Sir Robert Anderson wrote: 'Forty years ago I published the secret history of the Fenian movement up to date', and the *Daily News* thinks that this seems to justify the *Irish Book Lover* in identifying this with John Rutherford's work. But in this our contemporaries have done Sir Robert an injustice. He stated some weeks ago to an interviewer that in 1868-69 he wrote the history of the Fenian Conspiracy, and a *Star* representative called on him to learn whether this was to be taken as admitting his identity with the mysterious "John Rutherford". Sir Robert replied that the history in question consisted of articles in the *Contemporary Review*, and denied that he was "John Rutherford", or had any connection with his "history". As that work was published in 1877 and Sir Robert's articles in 1868-69, it seems that he is entitled to be acquitted of being "John Rutherford". As Mr. John O'Leary, the Fenian leader, wrote that the latter's "history" was 'as vile a book as I have ever read', and that he was unable even to guess at the 'ruffian' who used the name of "John Rutherford", Sir Robert Anderson may well wish this made clear. At the same time, one of the minor mysteries of nineteenth-century authorship still remains unsolved.'

This explanation, coupled with the fact that Sir Robert, in a letter to Mr. A. A. Campbell, of Belfast, whose query in our February number had first caused the investigation, directly denied the suggestion, left us no other course but to make an *amende honorable*, which we at once did in the *Star*, as follows:

> Being most unwilling that the slightest appearance of injustice should be done Sir Robert Anderson, I take this, the earliest opportunity of expressing my regret in your columns that the suggestion in *The Irish Book Lover* should have appeared, and shall insert a note to that effect in the next number. I may say that the editorial note in question was the outcome of a correspondence that has been going on in our pages since February as to the identity of "John Rutherford", and had no connection with the recent revelations.

And now comes the curious and interesting termination to the story. A gentleman who read our letter in *The Star*, at once wrote us, saying he was the son of the John Rutherford in question, and could produce material evidence of his statement. We accepted an invitation to call upon him at his residence, were kindly received, and introduced to the mother of our correspondent—the widow of the author, a pleasant, well-preserved old lady, of eighty-two, in full possession of her faculties, who answered all our questions readily and freely. From her we gathered the following facts which should, once for all, dispel the mystery that has so long hung around the name of John Rutherford. He was born in the West of Ireland (Galway?) in 1829, and as a lad came with his parents to Liverpool, where her father was a professor of music. They were married in 1862 at the pro-cathedral in Liverpool, and two years afterwards came to London, where her husband underwent all the difficulties incidental to a literary man, friendless and unknown in the Metropolis. But by dint of hard and unremitting endeavour, he slowly made his way, his first patron being the late

Frederick Greenwood, who employed him on the *Pall Mall* and *Cornhill Magazine*. His most successful book was *Sketches from Shady Places*, issued under the pen-name of "Thor Fredur", an anagram of his own name and published by Smith, Elder, the proprietors of the two organs mentioned. These had originally appeared in the *Pall Mall*, and from a number of criticisms still piously preserved along with the MS. by the widow, we judge it met with a very favourable reception. He published other works under his own, and his pen-name, but in the case of his *Secret History*, he boldly placed his name on the title-page, and took full responsibility for every statement, contained therein. And this very boldness misled all enquirers! Nor did he cease here to place on record his knowledge of Fenians and Fenianism, often gained, as he told his wife, who acted as his amanuensis, at the risk of his own life, for in the *Whitehall Review* for 29th November 1879, he commenced over his pseudonym "Thor Fredur", a series of articles entitled "Passages in the Career of a Fenian Conspirator", dealing with the romantic side of that great movement. These have never been republished. He died on Advent Sunday, 1889. His widow describes him as kindly and home-loving, fond of his only child, his one fault— an uncertain temper, which we comforted her by saying, was a hereditary defect, derived from his ancestors, the 'hot and hasty Rutherfords', as Scott called them.

"Reviews", Vol. I, No. 11 (June 1910), 150.

THE HUNGER—BEING REALITIES OF THE FAMINE YEARS IN IRELAND, 1845 TO 1848, BY ANDREW MERRY (ANDREW MELROSE [1910]). The inhabitants of a typical barony named Torrabegh—landlord and agent, priest and parson, peasant and 'driver' are here faithfully and graphically sketched by a practiced pen, and the effects of the appalling famine on each painfully pictured. In reading the pages one feels as if the writer had been an eye-witness of the scenes so vividly described, so well is the atmosphere, as painters say, conveyed. The characters are painted to the life. The "People's Larry" which in a measure recalls the Fintan Lalor of real life; Tony O'Donoghue the shop-keeper, with the great heart in the puny body; the searing parson, Jimmy Murray, kindest of muscular Christians, and the hedge—schoolmaster, live in these pages. A sympathetic study of a painful period—a book that will live.

"Notes", Vol. I, No. 11 (June 1910), 150

IRELAND AND SECRET PRINTING: Henry R. Plomer's article induces reference to the secrecy that attended the publication, and in some cases the printing of early Belfast tracts. Bern, the historian, says: 'The printing business being thus fairly launched in the town was entered into with commendable activity, so much so as to attract the notice of the Church party.' He then quotes Archbishop King as writing to the Archbishop of Canterbury in terms implying secret printing of 'the Covenant' and the 'Catechism' and such works. (J. W. K.)

"Queries", Vol. I, No. 11 (June 1910), 151.

DANIEL MACLISE: I have almost ready a biography of Harrison Ainsworth which will be published shortly by Mr. John Lane. For the purposes of this book it is desired to trace the present representatives of Daniel Maclise the painter, who was an intimate friend of Ainsworth's. Any one knowing the address of Miss Rhoda Banks or other member of the family of Mrs. Percival Weldon Banks (Maclise's sister) will much oblige by communicating with Mr. Lane, or directly to: Yours faithfully (S. M. ELLIS, HILL HOUSE, SOUTHWOLD, SUFFOLK.)

PETER BURROWES: Can any of your readers supply me with particulars as to the family of Peter Burrows the famous barrister and judge of the Insolvent Debtors' Court in Dublin, who died in London in1841? His nephew (also Peter Burrows) was clerk of the same Court, and what I want to arrive at is, who were the nephew's father and mother? Please reply direct. 44, Crownhill Road, Willesden. (HENRY R. PLOMER.)

BELFAST HISTORIC SOCIETY: Of this Society I never heard, till the other day I came across an Address delivered to the Belfast Historic Society, on the evening of the 9th September 1830, being the opening of the Fifth Revived Session. By B[artholomew] T[eeling] Stannus, Lecturer On Elocution, Belfast College, Belfast: Printed by Joseph Smyth, Highstreet (1830), 36pp. Nothing distinctive about the aims of the Society can be learned from the address. It encouraged debate; rejoiced that 'the tocsin of freedom is ringing the knell of despotism', and numbered 'Drennan, Tennent, and Templeton', among its 'distinguished founders'. Is the career of this Historic Society generally known? (A. G., MANCHESTER.)

According to the Belfast Almanack for 1817, this Society was founded in September 1811, by 'a few young men for their improvement in the knowledge of general history and of the British laws and constitution.' Amongst its presidents, whose addresses have been published, were Sheridan Knowles, the dramatist, Prof. Cairns, and R. J. Tennant, M.P. It ceased about 1819, for it does not appear amongst the institutions of Belfast mentioned in the Almanack for the years 1820-22. The title-page of your pamphlet would imply that it was revived in 1825. We have a copy of the address delivered by James Hirst, President in 1831. Perhaps some of our Belfast readers could supply additional information. (J. S. CRONE.)

Who wrote *The Orientalist, or Electioneering in Ireland; A Tale by Myself,* 2 vols. (London, 1820)? I have seen it stated somewhere that the writer was a 'Mrs. Purcell.' Who was Mrs. Purcell? (X.Y.Z.)

HYACINTH O'GARA: Who wrote this tale? (A.A.C.)

Mr. O'Donoghue in an article on Irish Novelists, which we hope to publish shortly, refers to 'Rev. George Brittain[e], who wrote *Hyacinth O'Gara*, and other religious tracts disguised as novels.' (J. S. CRONE.)

CORRECTION: I find from the *Bulletin of the Henry Bradshaw Collection* that a copy of *Parthenissa* is in the University Library, Cambridge. I was not aware of this when writing *A Cork Bibliographical Puzzle*, and wish to correct my erroneous statement on the point (No. X, p.129.) The imprint gives 'London', but Bradshaw considered it was printed in Waterford. (E. R. McCLINTOCK DIX.)

"Replies", Vol. I, No. 11 (June 1910), 154.

DICTIONARY OF IRISH BIOGRAPHY—Such a publication properly edited should meet with general approval, but there is one important feature which is clearly in danger of being overlooked. So far it has not been even mentioned, and it is obvious to those who suggested the names of editors were entirely unmindful of its importance. I refer to biographies of those Irishmen who work in Irish, the language of their own nation. Keating, for instance, never wrote a line of English. There were hundreds, one might even say thousands, of Irish scholars who could not have written or spoken a sentence of English to save their lives. What interest could the writings of such men have for editors unacquainted with the native language of Ireland, or what consideration could they reasonably be expected to received at their hands? [...] ("FEARGAL")

"Replies", Vol. I, No. 11 (June 1910), 154.

AMYAS GRIFFITH (Vol. X, p.136): Benn errs in saying he was co-author ' of the *Series of Genuine Letters between Henry and Frances*. These letters were written by Richard Griffith (for whom see the *DNB*), and his future wife, Elizabeth Griffith, the playwright and novelist. There is a memoir and portrait of Amyas Griffith in *Exshaw's Magazine* (i.e., the Dublin reprint of *The London Magazine*) for December, 1785. An earlier account of him had appeared in *The Hibernian Magazine* for January, 1773. He was born in Roscrea, Co. Tipperary, in 1746. An exemplar of his comedy, *The Swaddler* (1771), in which he is said to have lampooned his own mother is in the Halliday Collection of pamphlets, Vol. 362, R.I.A. It was apparently never acted. I have other details concerning him among my voluminous notes on the old Irish stage, and I should be glad to look these up on your correspondent's behalf if he is writing any account of that forgotten notoriety. 32, Shelbourne Road, Dublin. (W. J. LAWRENCE.)

"Book Auction", Vol. I, No. 11 (June 1910), p.155.

On Friday 29th April, Messrs. Hodgson, of Chancery Lane, London, sold by auction the fine library of the late Professor Percival Wright, T.C.D. The bulk of the books were scientific, but there were about fifty lots of valuable works relating to Ireland. The following are some of the prices realised: O'Curry's *Manners and Customs*, 3 vols., 50s.; His *Lectures on MSS Materials*, 28s.; Petrie's *Ecclesiastical Architecture*, 38s.; *His Christian Inscriptions in Irish*, 46s.; Lord Dunraven's *Notes on Irish Architecture*, £8 15s.; a collection of 258 photographs of monuments, stone crosses, &c., by R. Welch, Belfast, in 3 portfolios, £5; Brash's *Ogam Inscribed Monuments*, 12s.; Borlases's *Dolmens*, 3 vols., 38s.; a complete set of *Kilkenny Archæological Society Transactions*, £20 10; *Ulster Journal of Archaeology*, old series, £7s; a complete set of the *Cork Historical and Archæological Journal*, 18 vols., cloth, £6 15s; the *Galway* and *Louth Archæological Journal*, all the published parts, 32 12s; Madden's *Periodical Literature* (a shabby copy), 8s.; Ball's *History of Dublin*, 4 parts, 12s.; 7 vols.; *Dublin Parish Register Society*, 26s.; Young's *Town Book and Historical Notices of Old Belfast*, 20s.; Hore's *Wexford*, 4 vols. 42s.; Carrigan's *Diocese of Ossory*, 4 vols., 17s.; Grave's and Prim's *St. Canice, Kilkenny*, 14s.; and Smith's *Cork*, 2 vols., 1815, 16s.

"Irish Literary Society", Vol. I, No. 11 (June 1910), 156.

A Literary Tea-Table was held on Thursday, April 28th, when Mr. Graves opened the discussion, the subject being "The wild Geese in Literature" [...] Mr. Graves gave a very interesting account of the Irish exiles who attained fame and fortune on the continent in the troubled years of the eighteenth century, tracing the motives which actuated them, and giving many interesting quotations from the prose and poetry of which they had been the subject. The poems of Miss Lawless, two of which were recited by Miss Leishman, and the brilliant essay "A

Great People, Sir", by Sir William Butler, were especially noteworthy. A hearty vote of thanks was passed on the motion of Mrs. Samuel Royse, seconded by Miss Eleanor Hull. (p.156).

"Some Recent Opinions of the Press", Vol. I, No. 11 (June 1910), 156.

THE DUBLIN EVENING TELEGRAPH says: 'The Ferguson Centenary has pride of place in the May number of *The Irish Book Lover*, which publishes the eloquent oration spoken by Mr. F. J. Bigger at the poet's grave in Donegore on the occasion of Ferguson's 100th birthday. It is an eloquent tribute, worthy of both the orator and his theme. *A Cork Bibliographical Puzzle* contains some conundrums for those interested in the early printing presses in Ireland. "An Old Book Lover" contributes some notes on the historians of County Clare. Not a little mild amusement will be caused by the modest literary joke which a jury of London clubmen are said to have pronounced to be 'the best sample of humour and instantaneous Irish wit on record'. At any rate it seems to have been instantaneous. Amongst forthcoming works our contemporary mentions a volume of John Redmond's *Speeches on Home Rule*, covering the period from 1883 to 1909. It will be edited and provided with an introduction by Barry O'Brien, and will be published by Fisher Unwin. Amongst the books reviewed is F. J. Bigger's history of the Hearts of Steel in his *The Ulster Land War of 1770*, published by Sealey, Bryers' and Walker. One is tempted to chuckle to find an omniscient pamphleteer who recently assailed Parnell being taught how to spell John Mitchel's name, being corrected as to Mr. Bryce's nationality, and being gravely assured that he was wrong in his description of Douglas Hyde as 'a Protestant clergyman from the West', apparently confusing him with "George Birmingham".

J. J. Marshall, "Irish Chap Books", Vol. I, No. 12 (July 1910), 157.

In the eighteenth century Ireland did not possess the boon of Education Commissioners to prepare interesting and useful school books, nor a Kildare-place Society to issue cheap works of a harmless and edifying character. However, as the mass of the peasantry wished to give their children the only education they could command, namely, that afforded by the hedge schools, and as young and old liked reading stories and popular histories, or at least hearing them read, some enterprising Dublin, Cork, and Limerick printers assumed the duties neglected by churchmen and senators, and published "Primers", "Reading-made-easys", "Child's-new-plaything", and the widely diffused "Universal Spelling Book" of the magisterial Daniel Fenning, for educational purposes. These were 'adorned with cuts', but the transition from stage to stage was too abrupt, and the concluding portions of the early books were as difficult as that of the "Universal Spelling Book" itself, which the author in order to render it less practically useful, had encumbered with a dry and difficult grammar placed in the centre of the volume.

Two Dublin publishers, Pat Wogan, of Merchants' Quay, and William, Jones, 75, Thomas Street, were the educational and miscellaneous Alduses of the day, and considered themselves as lights burning in a dark place for the literary guidance of their countrymen and countrywomen of the shopkeeping, farmer, and peasant classes. In the frontispiece of some editions of the spelling book grew a tree of knowledge laden with fruit, each marked with some letter, and ardent climbers plucking away. Beneath was placed this doggerel inscription: 'The tree of knowledge here you see, / The fruit of which is ABC. / But if you neglect it like idle drones, / You'll not be respected by William Jones.' ... We cannot leave the school books, without mention of the really valuable treatise on arithmetic composed by Elias Vorster, a Dutchman, naturalised in Cork, and subsequently improved by John Gough, of Meath Street, one of the Society of Friends. *Book-keeping by Double Entry*, written by Dowling and Jackson was so judiciously arranged that it was until recent years looked upon as a standard work.

The same followers *longo intervalla* of Stephens and Elzevir published, besides prayer, and other devout books, a series of stories, histories, and literary treatises, such as they were, printed with worn type, on bad grey paper, cheaply bound in sheepskin, and sold by the pedlars throughout the country at a tester (6½d.) each. Of history, voyages, &c., the pedlar's pack was provided with Hugh Reilly's *History of Ireland*, *Adventures of Sir Francis* Drake, *The Battle of Aughrim and Siege of Londonderry*, the two latter being dramas, one the composition of Robert Ashton a graduate of Trinity, and the other generally attributed to Col. John Mitchellburne [sic], a defender of Derry; *Life and Adventures of James Freney the Robber*, *The Irish Rogues and Rapparees*, *The Trojan Wars*, *Troy's Destruction*, *The Life of Baron Trenck*, and *The Nine Worthies—Three Jews, Three Heathens, and Three Christians*. Every reader is familiar with Thackeray's description in the *Irish Sketch Book* of the pleasure he derived from the perusal of some of these when storm-stayed in Galway. The fictional department embraced, chiefly, in an abridged state, *The Arabian Nights*,

The History of Don Quixote, Gulliver's Travels, Æsop's Fables, Adventures of Robinson Crusoe, Robin Hood's Garland, The Seven Champions', Seven Wise Masters and Mistresses of Rome, Royal Fairy Tales, Tales of the Fairies, The Noble Slaves, The Garland of Love or Royal Flower of Fidelity, The Fortunate and Unfortunate Lovers, Montelion the Knight of the Oracle, Guy, Earl of Warwick, Parismus and Parismenos, Don Belianus of Greece, The Death of Abel, The Hibernian Tales, Life of Jeremiah Grant', Reynard the Fox, and the collection called *Laugh and Grow Fat*—the last two being decidedly objectionable both in. manner and matter.

The celebrated Dr. Cooke has left it on record that some of these, were the books he was given to study at his first school in Co. Derry. about the time of the Dungannon Convention; and Dr. Adam Clarke, the famous commentator and Oriental scholar, who was born about the same time and place, states in his *Life* that these formed the foundation of his once-famous library.

In the department of belles lettres may be classed *Lord Chesterfield's Letters to his Son, The Academy of Compliments, The Fashionable Letter Writer, Hocus Pocus, or the Whole Art of Legerdemain*, Joe *Miller's Jest Book*, &c.

The list would not be complete without mention of the garlands and books of ballads. These were printed in Waterford, Monaghan, and other provincial towns, and sold in sheets, each forming 8 pages, 18mo., and adorned with cuts, seldom germane to the subject. Some of these sheets contained only one production; as the "Yarmouth Tragedy", or some other early English ballad, others contained a selection.

The purchasers of these sheets sewed them as well as they could in book form, but they were so thumbed and used, that it is at this date, nearly impossible to procure one of these repertoires of song, printed towards the close of the 18th or beginning of the 19th century. The British Museum fortunately possesses a large collection of them.

The following, up till forty years ago formed portion of the pedlar's stock: *The Academy of Compliments, The Arabian Nights, The Battle of Aughrim, Æsop, Gulliver, O'Reilly's Ireland, The Cottagers of Glenburnie, Hocus Pocus, Irish Rogues, James Freney, Robin Hood's Garland, Seven Champions, Tales of the Fairies, The Trojan War, Valentine and Orson, The Seven Wise Masters and Mistresses of Rome*, some of them absolutely harmless, whilst forty years before Joseph Smyth, of Belfast, issued a catalogue of no less than 70 similar works.

These little books still continue to be printed In Dublin, but even chap books are progressive, and *The Fortunate and Unfortunate Lovers*, *Montelion*, *Guy of Warwick*, *Don Belianus*, others of that ilk, have disappeared, to leave room for more modern celebrities such as *Burns*, *Captain Cook*, *Napoleon Buonaparte*, *Lord Edward Fitzgerald*, *Robert Emmet*, and *General Jackson*, whilst in the department, of fiction and belles lettres we have *The Accomplished Gentleman*, *Cabinet of Arts*, *Children of the Abbey*, in 5 vols. (a weighty undertaking), *Modern Irish Tales*, *Susan Gray*, &c. The *Cabinet of Arts*, it should be stated according to the writer's recollection—he has not seen it for over thirty years—was the mechanical arts and had for sub-title: *or Ingenious Man's Companion*. There is also in the list a *Complete Farrier*, and *Domestic Cookery, with the Art of Carving*, so that all tastes whether aesthetic or utilitarian were catered for *In the Poor Man's Library*.

"Sir William Butler", Vol. I No. 12 (July 1910), 162.

It is with feelings of the deepest regret that we chronicle the death of this distinguished soldier and big-hearted Irish gentleman, which occurred in his 72nd year, at Bansha Castle, Tipperary, on 7th June. After an army service of almost half a century, in almost every part of the globe, which brought him many well-merited rewards, he retired to his native country and devoted himself to literary work, to which he had always been inclined, as witness the many glowing descriptions of the campaigns he had undertaken, and the perils he had endured, which he had amassed a collection of books amounting to a library in itself. It is stated that he had left complete for publication, his memoirs, 'The battles, sieges, fortunes he had passed'—which are certain to make interesting reading, for he possessed a fine literary style, and was equally at home on lecture platform, the study and the tented field. As is well known his wife was the famous painter of "The Roll Call". The following is a list of his books: *The Great Lone Land* (1872); *The Wild North Land* (1873); *Akim-Foo* (1875); *Far Out* (1880); *Red Cloud, the Solitary Sioux* (1882); *The Campaign of the Cataracts*(1887); *Life of Genial Gordon* (1889); *Sir Charles Napier* (1890); *Life of Sir G. Pomeroy Colley* (1899); *From Naboth's Vineyard* (1907); *The Light of the West* (1909). Sir William was a vice-president of the Irish Literary Society before which he had frequently lectured.

"'Eva' of *The Nation*", Vol. I No. 12 (July 1910), 163.

We regret to announce the death in May, at Brisbane, of Mrs. Kevin Izod O'Doherty, who gained fame by her poetic contributions under the pseudonym of "Eva" to *The Nation*, the organ of the Young Ireland movement in 1848. She was Eva Mary Kelly, the daughter of a Galway gentleman, and when quite a young girl, contributed poems to the *Nation* which attracted wide attention. Among the admirers of Eva's poetry was Kevin Izod O'Doherty, a young medical student who was also engaged in the patriotic movement. From a literary admirer, O'Doherty, advanced to the position of Eva's lover. As registered proprietor of the *Tribune*, another Dublin paper of rebellious tendencies, he was arrested and tried for seditious writing, and transported, but being allowed out on parole in Australia he was able to finish his medical studies and take out his degree. Years passed, and he returned to Ireland, where "Eva", awaited him. Two days after his return to Dublin they were married and O'Doherty, with his bride, returned to Australia as a voluntary exile. In 1885 O'Doherty came back to the Old Land, and entered the House of Commons as member for North Meath. He quickly tired of Parliamentary life, however, and once more returned to Australia, where he survived until a few years ago. Mrs. O'Doherty was the last survivor of the brilliant band of writers who in *The Nation* put 'a new soul into Ireland'. A volume of her poems was published at San Francisco in 1877 and republished later in Dublin by Messrs. Gill.

"Gossip", Vol. I No. 12 (July 1910), 166.

ALFRED NUTT. One can hardly allow the tragic death of Mr. Alfred Nutt to pass unnoticed in a journal devoted to Irish literature, for no English publisher has done so much as he to popularise the Celtic classics. He assisted in founding the Irish Texts Society, all of whose works he published, and was one of the leading authorities on our legends and folk lore. Among his own works may be mentioned, *Cuchulain, the Irish Achilles*, *The Irish Vision of the Happy Other World*, *The Voyage of Bran*, *The Holy grail and Its Celtic Origin*, and *The Influence of the Celtic upon National Romances*. A man of engaging popularity and an accomplished scholar, his heroic end is deeply regretted by a wide circle of friends.

MR. JAMES HAYES. [...] In the town of Ennis, the capital of Clare, lives Mr. James Hayes, a well-known bookseller, who we can imagine a George Falkiner [sic], the friend of Swift and the publisher of his books, or Grierson, to have been in Dublin—a man steeped to the lips in the literature he vended; able to tell of every work all that one cared to know of it, and familiar with every phase of the life-history of almost every one of the books on his shelves. To meet such a man is, indeed, an education.

Mrs. Hayes writes to me that his large collection of autographs will come under the hammer at Sotheby's this month [...]

"Reviews", Vol. I No. 12 (July 1910), 168.

MR. J. KING pursues his patriotic way, undaunted, and we have come to look upon the parts of his *History of Kerry* as welcome hardy annuals. The third, just published, fully bears out his reputation as a careful and painstaking chronicler, and the topographer and genealogist will find therein a rich mine. He gives the names of the settlers in Tralee at the Plantation and deals fully with the families of Fuller, Stokes, O'Halloran, McCarthy, Denny and Moriarty. He throws out the suggestion that the now ennobled families of Iveagh and Ardilaun may have sprung from the Ginnisses of Tralee and not the Magenisses of Down. We have noticed only two slight slips: at p.231 'Nicholas Madgett born 1799 (sic), was a French-Irish official known to Wolfe Tone, and at p.226 a reference is made to Robert Holmes, Q.C. Now, it is a well-known fact that Mr. Holmes refused the silk gown offered him by successive governments and died a stuff gowns-man. He was the father of the North-East Bar and cornmony called "Bitter Bab". By the way, do any of our readers know where he was buried?

"Post Bag", Vol. I No. 12 (July 1910), 169.

IRISH BIOGRAPHY. In regard to that dictionary so much to be wished for, I came across a prospectus of a similar work, issued by Dr. Dennis Dowling Mulcahy in Newark. New Jersey, in the 'eighties which you may think worth reprinting in part. "Dictionary of Irish Biography and Bibliography of Irish and Anglo-Irish authors and literature; of Irish and Anglo-Irishmen, living and dead, Famous and Infamous; of Recreant Patriots and Repentant Rebels, who have acknowledged the right of England to rule Ireland". Appended is the following 'stand and deliver form', which was hardly calculated to stimulate assistance: 'I am preparing a Brief Biographical Dictionary of Famous and Infamous Irishmen, &c., in which I may insert your name, I will therefore take it as a favour if you will be so good as to fill the subjoined form at your earliest convenience and return it with your photograph to your very obedient servant. P.S.—If the party receiving this circular should decline to give the desired information, the author will avail himself of the most reliable at his disposal.'

Mulcahy was a Young Irelander and a Fenian. I remember him on a lecturing tour of Ireland in the 'seventies.

"Afterword", Vol. I, No. 12 (July 1910), 173.

This number of *The Irish Book Lover* concludes the first volume, and we think we can safely say we have carried out the promises contained in our foreward [sic] to our readers. That there is great room for improvement, no one will admit more readily than ourselves; and it shall be our constant endeavour to render our pages brighter and more interesting. We have many ideas for the betterment of the journal in the coming year, but in order to effect this we require the cordial assistance of every reader and subscriber in making our journal known in their respective districts and to the local press. The annual subscription being small (2s.) brings it within the reach of all book lovers. As several postal orders went astray last year, we ask subscribers to cross them and make them payable to the publishers.

An index and title-page for Vol. I is in preparation, and can be obtained for three penny stamps, which for safety can be attached to the postal orders.

The Irish Book Lover
Vols. VII & VIII
(Jan. 1916 to Oct. 1917)

[John S. Crone,] "Selina Bunbury", Vol. VII, No. 6 (Jan. 1916), 105-07.

The founder of the Bunbury family was a follower of the Norman conqueror, named St. Pierre, who eventually settled at Bunbury, in Cheshire. In the reign of Elizabeth a scion of the house migrated to Carlow. Some of his descendants have frequently represented that county in Parliament, and one of them, Isabella Bunbury, became the mother of Lord Roberts. Another, Rev. Henry Bunbury, B.A., T.C.D., was rector of Mansfieldstown, Co. Louth, from 1793 till 1815. He married in 1791 Henrietta Eleanor, daughter of Hon. and Rev. Walter Shirley, a brother of Earl Ferrers, and rector of Loughrea, and became the father of Selina Bunbury, a voluminous writer and traveller in foreign parts at a time when it was considered that women shone best at home. Selina, named after her relative, Lady Selina Shirley, afterwards the celebrated Countess of Huntingdon was born at Kilsaran House, Co. Louth, in 1802, one of a family of fifteen children. Two of her brothers entered the church, and a third, Molesworth, the navy, and served as a volunteer of the first class on H.M.S. *Undaunted*, when conveying Napoleon to Elbe in May, 1814. Retiring from, the navy, he obtained a commission in the army and fell fighting in the American campaign. He was heir favourite brother, and in her *Smuggler's Cave* she describes a narrow escape they both had from drowning whilst boating at the mouth of the Boyne; and she has depicted him as the "Allen Ruthven" of her first story. [...]

"Great Irish Book Collectors (V): Canon Jeremiah Murphy", Vol. VII, No. 6 (Jan. 1916), 107.

The valuable and extensive library of the worthy P.P. of Macroom, who, it will be remembered, died last August, came under the hammer at Messrs. Woodward's mart in Cork on 7th December and two following days. The catalogue, a neat publication of some 80 pages, printed by Messrs. Guy, enumerates over twelve hundred lots, and some of these include eight, ten, and more volumes. The three incunabula which he was known to possess do not appear. They, perhaps, if not already disposed of privately, are reserved for the foreign market. The purely Irish portion runs to about 300 lots, occupying nearly twenty pages of the catalogue. Here are some of the prices obtained with the purchaser's names as far as could be ascertained. *The Journal of R.S.A.I.*, hf. calf, 21 vols. 1849-92, £15; *The Journal of Cork Arch. Society*, all published, in original wrappers, £2 10s.; *The Cork Southern Reporter*, 1827, '29, and '30, 37s. 6d.; *Bennett's History of Bandon*, 1869, 10s.; Beling's *Vindication*, 1674, *A View of Ireland*, 1809, Boulger's *Boyne*, and two of Litton Falkiner's, £8; *The Tribes and Customs of Hy Many*, *The Down Survey*, and two other vols. of the *Irish Arch. Society*, £5 15s; Madden's *United Irishmen*, 4 vols., 1860, £3 10s.; *The Castlereagh Memoirs and Correspondence*, 4 vols., 1848, 25s.; *The Council Books of Cork, Youghal and Kinsale*, edited by R. Caulfield, 15s., 17s., and 12s. 6d. respectively; Mazière Brady's *Records of Cork*, English State Church, and Reformation in Ireland, five in all, £3; O'Hanlon's *Lives of Irish Saints*, £3 2s. 6d.; Smith's *Kerry* 1756, £2 2s.; Smith's *Waterford*, 1787, and Ryland's, together, 21s. (Massey, Dublin); Story's *Narrative of the War in Ireland*, 1693, 23s. (Neale); *The Book of Leinster*, 1880, £5 (Mr. John O'Connell, Cork); *The Book of Ballymote*, 1887, £3 15s. (O'Connell); *Leabhar Breac*, 2 vols., 1876, £2 15s. (O'Connell); O'Curry's *Manners and Customs*, 3 vols., £3; Gilbert's *History of the Confederation*, 7 voles., 1882, &c., £6; *The Ancient Laws of Ireland*, £5 15s. (The Bishop of Cloyne); *Tripartite Life of St. Patrick*, 1887, £2 10s.; *Hibernia Dominicana*, 1762, £5 10s.; *The Calendar of Papal Registers*, £2 10s. (Fr. Roche, Fermoy); *Calendar of Irish State Papers*, 21 vols., £12 (ditto.); Lord Dunraven's *Irish Architecture*, £4 15s. (Massey); *The Nation*, 6 vols., 1842-48, £4 10s.; *List of Claims Entered at Chichester House*, 1700, with MS entries, £10 10s.; *The Irish Statutes*, 20 vols., £2; *The Journals of the Irish House of Commons*, 1661-1751, £4 (Bishop of Cloyne). There were also six Irish MSS, three of them written by Father Matt. Horgan, the famous P.P. of Blarney. These were purchased by Rev. Canon O'Riordan, of Macroom, and Rev. T. Roche, of Fermoy. Seamus O'Casaide, M.R.I.A., bought the other three, which were *Ceisniomh Inghine Ghoil*, &c., 68pp., 4to., c. 1770, 10s; A copy of Keating's *Eochair Sgiath an Aifrinn*, 108pp., 4to., 18s., and one of over 200pp., 4to., written like the latter by Seadhan O'Murchada, about 1752, 22s. 6d. Amongst the other purchasers were Rev. P. Power, M.R.I.A., Sir John O'Connell and the President of St. Colman's College, Fermoy.

The total sum realised was well over £800.

Stouppe McCance, "Some Old Ulster Song Books", Vol. VII, No. 6 (Jan. 1916), 108.

In the valuable paper on "Irish Song Books", read before the Royal Irish Academy by Mr. Dix, and subsequently printed in *I.B.L.*, Volume III, page 81, he dealt exhaustively with the specimens preserved in that library. I have been fortunate enough to secure recently a small collection of these scarce little products of the printing press, entirely of Ulster origin, and all over a century old. A few notes on them may be of interest. They all conform to the eight page size, are all of the same rude type of printing, with, in many cases, the same rough wood-cut, little germane to the subject matter, and doing duty over and over again. To save space, I only give the title of the principal song, but in one or two instances quote the quaint imprint:

Armagh

1. "The Wounded Hussar", (No name 1803).
2. "The Irish Phantasmagoria", (Young & Stephenson 1804).
3. "The Dear Whiskey", (ditto).
4. "Sally Roy", (ditto).
5. "Burns' Farewell" (ditto).
6. "Kate of Aberdeen", (Young 1805).
7. "The Sailor's Farewell", ('William Young, Market Street, where Chapmen and Dealers can be well assorted with Pictures, Pamphlets, School-Books and Stationery 1805').
8. "Paddy O'Rafferty's Courtship", (ditto).
9. "England's Glory", (Young 1805).
10. "The Habit Shirt", (Young [No Date])
11. "Luke Caffrey's Kilmainham Mint", (Young [n/d]).

Belfast

12. "Jane Shore's Garland", (At the Public Printing Office)
13. "The Tragical Garland of Jemmy and Nancy", (ditto 1804).
14. "The Old Ballad of William and Margaret", (ditto [n/d]).

London-Derry

15. "The Unhappy Hunting in Chevy Chase", (John Buchanan, Bishop Street, 1804).
16. "The Banks of the Dee", (John Buchanan, Lurgan 1804).
17. "The Bacchanalian Toper", (R. Crawford 1805).
18. "Cupid's Revenge", (ditto).
19. "William and Margaret", (ditto)
20. "Omnia Vincit Amor", (ditto).

[Also Newry, &c]

"Editor's Gossip", Vol. VII, No. 6 (Jan. 1916), 111.
[...] I am glad to see that Mr. Yeats has succeeded in wiping off a debt of £1,200 incurred by the Abbey Theatre Company—no mean achievement in these days of enforced economy. He made the announcement in the course of an address at Sunderland House on 6th December, in which he descanted interestingly on "The Irish Theatre and Other matters" before a distinguished audience. [...]

E. R. McClintock Dix, "The Haliday Pamphlets", Vol. VII, Nos. 7 & 8 (Feb. & March 1916), 121.
Our readers will be interested to learn that these, the finest collection of pamphlets and tracts relating to the history, topography, political economy, &c., of Ireland ever formed, is at last being catalogued. As is well known, the collection is housed in the Royal Irish Academy, Dawson Street, Dublin, and the work has been entrusted to the Library Clerk, Mr. J. J. O'Neill, a careful and competent bibliographer, and we hope that the catalogue will be printed without any undue delay. An idea of the magnitude of the task may be formed from the fact that the collection, according to Prendergast, originally consisted of twenty-nine thousand individual items [...]
   Charles Haliday (1789-1866) who formed this noble collection, was a Dublin merchant of literary tastes and a younger brother of that precocious scholar William Haliday, who, at the age of 19, published *A Grammar of the Gaelic Language* by E. O'C[urry]. (Dublin 1807).

"Great Irish Book Collectors (VI): William Monck Mason", Vol. VII, Nos. 7 & 8 (Feb. & March 1916), 125.
WILLIAM MONCK MASON (1775-1895), on attaining his majority, was, by family interest, appointed land waiter for exports at Dublin, one of the numerous sinecures that then existed. This enabled him to pursue his favourite studies in philology and history. He is best remembered by his monumental work on *The History and Antiquities of St. Patrick's Cathedral* (4to. 1820), in compiling which he amassed a large number of MSS. He also published a pamphlet, *Suggestions Relative to a Survey of Ireland* (1825) and had intended writing the history of his country. But it is as a collector we deal with him here. He had three sales during has lifetime. The first took place at Sotheby's on Thursday, 30th January, 1834, and continued for five days. It consisted entirely of books collected during his residence on the Continent, all in the choicest condition There were 1,259 lots, and they realized a total of

£633 10s. His second sale, at the same mart, commenced on Friday, 4th June, 1852, and lasted for six days. It consisted of a unique collection of books in all the languages and dialects of Europe, and many of those of Asia. The catalogue contained 1,698 entries, and the sum realised was £1,373. His third and last sale commenced at the same place and lasted three days, 29th-31st March 1858. This was his great Irish library, and his fine collection of MSS formed towards a *History of Ireland*, 'the results of many years labour and research, which the increasing infirmities of age precluded him from completing'. His collection of *Tracts* numbered upwards of 2,300, and were all arranged in chronological order from 1641 till 1836, and in sets of from ten to a hundred, each in cases. Their titles and places of printing, other than London, being fully set out in tale catalogue, one of the best arranged we have ever seen. Of broadsides there were 900, and of dead and gone newspapers 90 volumes, besides 300 maps and plans But the gems of the Collection were undoubtedly the writings in 'the Irish character, some on vellum of unusual antiquity, of many of which no other copies were existent'. [...]

E. V. Lucas , "The Two Ladies" [reproduced from *The Spectator*], Vol. VII, Nos. 7 & 8 (Feb. & March 1916), 127.

It chanced that I was engaged, in another connection, with some criticism, or, rather, with an appreciation, of "The Two Ladies" (as I always think of Martin Ross and E. Œ. Somerville) at the very moment that the sad news of Martin Ross's illness reached me. Two days later she died, and now part of that eulogium all suddenly and tragically becomes an elegy.

I had been reading aloud some of the sketches, and in particular "The House of Fahy", which I have always held was one of the best short stories ever written, with a last sentence that no one but a professional elocutionist with nerves of steel could possibly compass; and afterwards it had amused me to imagine a room filled with devotees of the *Irish R.M.*, capping quotations from that and its companion books and finding pleasure in expressing admiration in the warmest terms and in minute detail; and there are not many pleasures greater than that. [...]

"Irish Literary Society", Vol. VII, Nos. 7 & 8 (Feb. & March 1916), 129.

On Saturday, 15th January, we had an 'Emily Lawless Night', and a triple bill. Mr. A. Perceval Graves delivered an interesting and lucid critical address on that lady's two volumes of verse, *With the Wild Geese* and *The Inalienable Heritage*. The first was given to the world in 1902, at the earnest solicitation of Mr. Stopford Brooke, who accidentally discovered a privately printed copy, and recognised its value. He wrote an interesting preface to the volume. The second was privately printed after the death of the gifted author by another literary friend, Miss Edith Sichel, now also departed. Mr. Graves, as a literary critic, has a world-wide reputation, and as a reader of poetry has few equals. As a student of Trinity, he used to take part in the famous readings held in the home of Sir Samuel Ferguson, in which many distinguished men joined, many a year ago, and has ever since continued the practice and encouraged it in others. Therefore it was no small intellectual treat to listen to his fine delivery of the poems quoted and commented on. He fairly thrilled has audience with the fine lines "After Fontenoy":

> Jesus save you, gentry! Why are ye so white,
> Sitting all so straight and still in the morning light?'
> 'Nothing ails! us, brother; joyous souls are we,
> Sailing hoarse together, on the morning sea.
> Cousins, friends, and kinsfolk, children of the land,
> Here we come together, a merry, rousing band;
> Sailing home together from the last great fight
> Home to Clare from Fontenoy, in the morning light.

[...]

"Notice of New Books", Vol. VII, Nos. 7 & 8 (Feb. & March 1916), 135.

AN ALPHABET OF IRISH SAINTS. (DUNDALGAN PRESS, DUNDALK.) 1s. The composition of this unique and interesting work is the joint effort of several scholarly men and women. Miss Charlotte Dease supplies a versified account of the principal incidents in the lives of nineteen Irish saints; "Torna" deals with them in Gaelic; and Lucas Rooney supplies some capital sketches. Dr. Douglas Hyde writes an interesting foreword in the old tongue, and Sir Henry Bellingham does the same in English. The whole forms a remarkable volume, excellently turned out by the Dundalgan Press, which seems to excel in this particular class of work. In closing it one can only echo the opinion of Sir Henry Bellingham that 'those who have co-operated in this new rhymed alphabet of Ireland's leading Saints are to be heartily congratulated'.

"Queries and Replies", Vol. VII, Nos. 7 & 8 (Feb. & March 1916), 138.

THOMAS CHURCH. In a recent issue of "Notes and Queries" there is a reference to this gentleman who was assistant to his father, the schoolmaster at Causeway, Co. Kerry. The son was a voluminous contributor both in prose and verse to the *Tralee Chronicle*, under the pen name of "De Cantillon", and known as "the Bard of Clanmaurice". He eventually emigrated to the States, and died in New York several years ago. His half sister, Miss H. Church, is said to be still living in the village of Causeway, and to possess a large collection of her brother's manuscripts. Could any reader supply further biographical facts? (BIBLIO.)

"Post Bag", Vol. VII, Nos. 7 & 8 (Feb. & March 1916), 139.

STANDISH H. O'GRADY (Vol. VII., p. 81). In the interesting sketch of this great Irish scholar it is stated that he did not graduate at T.C.D. This is not correct. I see A.B. after his name in the list of officers and members of the Ossianic Society for 1858. Moreover, in *T.C.D. Calendar* for 1896, at p.299, I find that 'Mr. O'Grady, Standish H.', graduated as a respondent in April, 1854. (O.O'B., RATHMINES)

"Obituaries", Vol. VII, Nos. 7 & 8 (Feb. & March 1916), 140

JAMES COLLINS died suddenly at his residence, Drumcondra, on 13th January. He was born in Dublin about 1840, and entered the service of Isaac Butt at an early age, and to the end retained a great love and veneration for that leader. He thus became acquainted with Parnell, for whom he formed a library of Irish books which fetched fancy prices at the Avondale sale; and with James Stephens, the Fenian chief, whose MS diary was presented to him by another close friend, Michael Davitt. Mr. Collins was a born book lover and an untiring collector, and has left a fine Irish library, particularly rich in works relating to his native city and the United Irishmen. He published in 1913 a most interesting volume, *Life in old Dublin* (Duffy), handsomely illustrated. A man of marked personality, his genial presence will be greatly missed in the haunts of the Dublin book lovers. A portrait and lengthy appreciation of him appeared in the Dublin *Evening Telegraph* on the day of his death. […] (D. J.O'D.)

EMILY CRAWFORD, for over thirty year, one of the most distinguished.

figures in journalism, died at Bristol on 30th December, aged 84. She was born in Dublin, her father being Robt. A. Johnstone, and her mother one of the Connemara Martins On the death of her father, her mother went to live in Paris, and whilst still in her teens, Emily wrote some private letters descriptive of the French Court, which were shown to a London editor, who was so struck with them that he asked for regular contributions. In 1864 she married Geo. M. Crawford, the Paris correspondent of the *Daily News* and the original of 'George Warrington' in *Pendennis*. When Paris was in the hands of communists she made her way at night and alone through the barricaded city on 23rd March 1871, and actually interviewed the communist leaders as they sat in council. On the death of her husband in 1885, she became the Paris correspondent of the *Daily News*, *Truth*, and *New York Tribune*, and as such did some brilliant work, until her retirement in 1907. She was acquainted with every celebrity of the time, and President Carnot offered her the Legion of Honour. Her only publication in volume form was *Victoria, Queen and Ruler* (1903). She wrote much under pseudonyms, but, as she said: 'History thus written is like snow falling on the sea'. Her son, Robert, writing in *Truth*, said, 'The proudest distinction of my mother's life was when she was made an honorary member of the Irish Literary Society of London'.

[John S. Crone], "Sir Charles Gavan Duffy", Vol. VII, Nos. 9 & 10 (April & May 1916), 145.

On Good Friday, the 12th of April, a hundred years ago, in a small shop in Monaghan town, was born Charles Gavan Duffy, sprung from the old stock, and destined in his long career to play many parts, and to influence the course of public events in two hemispheres. To his education at a classical seminary conducted by a Presbyterian minister, may be attributed his breadth of view, and that belief in a real union of has countrymen that never failed. He early became an omnivorous reader, and remained so all his life, for even when Premier of Victoria, he devoted three hours a day to the practice. His boyhood's friends were Henry McManus, the painter, and T. B. McManus, of '48 fame, and his first patron was C. H. Teeling, the historian of the Rebellion, who invited him to contribute to his newspaper, *The Northern Herald*. In his twentieth year Duffy was apprenticed to M. Staunton, of the Dublin *Morning Register*, and he tells us the society into which he was then introduced 'swarmed with the gypsies of literature. The editors of the three peculiarly Catholic papers at that time were all protestants, and the co-editors of a pre-eminently Protestant organ had been born and bred Catholics'. The pleasant dream he had of journalism had a rude awakening, but he found solace in the hitherto unattainable books now at his command in the libraries, and his soul rose above his sordid surroundings and cynical colleagues. He was soon appointed sub-editor of the *Register*, became a leader writer on the *Pilot*, and correspondent of the London *True Sun*. When only 23 he was invited to Belfast to edit a new national bi-weekly journal, *The Vindicator*, which first appeared on 1st May, 1839. In this he made a feature of including national verse, old and now, and amongst his contributors was Clarence Mangan, whose friendship he had already cultivated. Whilst in Belfast he attended the Philosophy Course in the Royal Academical Institution, and wooed and won his bride.

Desiring a wider scope for his talents than that afforded by a provincial town, at the end of two years Duffy returned to the metropolis to found *The Nation*, the journal that brought a new soul into Ireland. The story of that newspaper is familiar to our readers, and the fact that its proprietor was arraigned for treason felony no less than five times, and always escaped, belongs to the realms of history. He projected and carried out Duffy's *Library of Ireland*, without doubt the finest popular publishing enterprise ever initiated in Ireland, which came to an untimely end, through the famine, when only about half completed. To the pages of *The Nation* he contributed many poems, of which T. W. Rolleston says, 'None of the Young Irelanders wrote in rhyme and metre with more sinewy force than Duffy. His lines smite home, like the axe of an Irish gallowglass; and though his mind, as his whole career shows, was eminently that of a statesman, he clearly thought and felt as a reckless fighter when he faced the enemies of his cause with the keen blade of verse in his hand'.

On the failure of Young Ireland, Duffy formed a Tenants' League, uniting North and South on a common platform, which for a time almost carried the country with it and returned him M.P. for New Ross. Three years in Parliament, sweetened only by his close communion with Carlyle, convinced him of the venality of some of his colleagues, and the open defection of Keogh and Sadleir, and its condonation by the hierarchy, disgusted him, and he withdrew from politics. After twenty years of storm, strife and suffering for his country, he lost heart, health, and hope, and, disposing of his newspaper, sailed. for Australia on the eve of his fortieth year to begin life anew. Settling in Melbourne, he was called to the bar, entered Parliament, quickly rose to the premier-ship and the K.C.M.G. On his return, after a pleasant visit to Europe, he was unanimously elected speaker. After another quarter of a century's public service, and oh! how different the reward! he retired and settled at a pleasant villa at Nice. There he occupied himself with the writing of those entrancing volumes in which he tells so fully and charmingly the thrilling story of his early manhood's years. He refused all offers to re-enter political life, but true to his first low, the spread of knowledge and enlightenment of his people, he founded the Irish Literary Society, and edited the *New Irish Library*. His visits home in connection with these projects always found him the centre of devoted friends and earnest admirers. After a full life extended far beyond the usual span, in which he mingled with the most memorable men of the age, he passed away peacefully in his home by the tideless sea, on 9th February, 1903, and his remains, honoured with a public funeral, were deposited in Glasnevin, where slumber his youth's compeers.

Thomas Roche, "Canon Murphy: His Life; his Labours; his Library", Vol. VII, Nos. 9 & 10 (April & May 1916), 148.

CANON MURPHY, D.D., P.P. Macroom, was born at Lisladeen, Innis-carra, Co. Cork. He received his early education at the local school, such as it was, and thence went to Donoughmore, to a classical school kept by a Mr. Golden. As the young scholar was anxious to enter the church, he was sent to the diocesan seminary in Fermoy, St. Colman's College, qualifying for the class of logic. He was ordained priest in 1871, and in 1872 was appointed to the staff of St. Colman's College. His first appointment on the mission was to the curacy of Ballyclough, and after a few months there he was transferred to Queenstown. On the death of Father Barry, he was appointed Administrator of the Parish, and hold the position for 22 years. In 1897 he was appointed P.P. of Macroom, and later was made a Canon of Cloyne. He died about 9.45p.m. on Sunday, August 1st, 1915. He is buried in the churchyard at Macroom, in a place selected by himself a day or two before he died, close to the grave of another Cloyne priest, a great Celtic scholar, Very Rev. Dr. B. McCarthy. R.I.P.

Canon Murphy was a fluent speaker of Irish, but he did not write it. I don't think there is any article in Irish from his pen, for he used to say he detested Irish articles printed in Roman type. He was a lifelong abstainer, as he took the total abstinence pledge at two years of age from Father Mathew himself, and kept it to the end. His old housekeeper, 'Ellen', was his great friend; looked after him and ruled his household during the time he was in Queenstown, and for some years in Macroom. Readers of *My New Curate*, by Canon Sheehan, will be interested to know that Ellen has been there immortalised as the housekeeper of the Parish Priest in the story.

The Canon travelled extensively, both over Ireland and on the Continent, and was always full of stories and reminiscences. His knowledge of Theology was remarkable, but has familiarity with History, especially Irish History, was marvellous. He was a fine priest, a great man, who spent himself for his people, and as Cardinal Logue said, 'his death was a loss to the whole Irish Church'. [...]

"Bibliography of Oscar Wilde", Vol. VII, Nos. 9 & 10 (April & May 1916), 151.

It has been our fortune to make use of many a bibliography, upon many a subject, for many a year; but we can safely say that for width of research, comprehensiveness of scope, excellence of arrangement, in short, everything that goes to the making of the perfect work, we have never come across anything in the least approaching this remarkable volume, which we owe to the unwearying assiduity of Mr. Stuart Mason, and represents the labours of ten years. Nothing printed or in manuscript relating to his subject seems to have escaped his omniscient eye. The veriest parody in an ephemeral magazine, or the slightest reference in the newspapers of two continents would seem to be chronicled here. Not only that, but we have reproductions of title pages and covers of the principal magazines to which Wilde contributed, and not unfrequently interesting notes on their history. One of the most striking facts, to one reader at least, is that, whilst Wilde was posing as the curled darling of society, the entertainer of Royalty itself, behind the scenes he was slaving away at the eeriest hack work, wasting his genius in reviewing the worthless fiction of his day for third and fourth rate journals. The whole literary life of Wilde is here laid bare, and beyond this, nowadays, when he has taken his rightful rank in the world of letters, no right-minded person seeks to pry. This is a finer monument to his genius than any work, so far fashioned, be it in printed page or chiselled stone.

It will be of greatest interest to Irish readers to learn that Wilde's earliest known effort in verse appeared in the *Dublin University Magazine* for November 1875. This was followed by another in *Kottabos* for Trinity Term 1876, and another in September, In the *Irish Monthly*, then, edited by Father Matthew Russell, one of whose letters is printed here, as well as one from Keningale Cook, then editing *D.U.M.* To all these, as also to *The Monitor*, he continued to contribute during the next two or three years, in fact, until he woke and found himself famous. Whilst travelling with Dr. (now Provost) Mahaffy, in Italy, they visited Ravenna, and here Wilde found the material for his famous Newdigate prize poem on that subject in 1878, and 'made improve-ments and corrections' in his senior's work on Greece. It is interesting to find that in Wilde's unsigned reviews he dealt *inter alia* with such Irish works as Froude's *Two Chiefs of Dunboy*, Mr. Graves' *Father O'Flynn*, and Willy Yeats's "Wanderings of Oisin". To the long defunct *Saunder's News Letter*, which is here stated to date from 1688 (it should really be 1755), he contributed a notice of the Grosvenor Gallery. Since this volume was published Mr. D. J. O'Donoghue has traced another article of his in the same journal. It was an appeal on behalf of Henry O'Neill, the author of *Sculptured Crosses in Ireland* and *Fine Arts of Ancient Ireland*, then in a state of distress. But one might go on picking fruit from such a prolific garden intermittently. Suffice it now to say that the work is published by T. Werner Laurie in two editions, one at 25s. net and another, the edition de luxe, at three guineas.

"Editor's Gossip", Vol. VII, Nos. 9 & 10 (April & May 1916), 156.

Will my readers acquit me of the almost unpardonable sin of 'blowing my own trumpet', if I inflict upon them a couple of compliments out of many paid me by the Press, on a recent appointment. I quote these, as I owe them entirely to my congenial labours on *I.B.L.*, and as the spontaneous and unsought-for opinions of two journals, wide as the poles asunder on other points, but evidently at one on this—the Belfast *Northern Whig* and the Dublin *Freeman's Journal*.

'His many friends—and few men are richer in friendship, that 'sweet'ner of life and solder of society'—will be glad to learn that Dr, J. S. Crone, J.P., has been appointed deputy-coroner for Middlesex. A native of Castlereagh district, Dr. Crone has been in practice in Willesden for over thirty years. Here he lives on the Harrow Road, and one is rather taken aback (writes A. R.) if he does as I did start at one end to walk to the Doctor's house, for the road is something like a score of miles long, but the welcome one gets were payment for two-score. In his long residence in this London suburb Dr. Crone has done good service both on the District Council and on the County Council, and without doubt he is one of the most popular men in Willesden. But he is more than a painstaking king physician and a busy publicist, as those who are readers of the *Northern Whig* know. He is proud of his County

Down, and his series of histories of *Distinguished Downshiremen* which appeared in our columns several years ago meant, as anyone knows who has tried apprentice hand at the same style of work, an infinity of pains, research, and balanced judgment. His *Irish Book Lover* is, too, one of the best things of the kind we know, history as it might be written with the pen of Father O'Flynn, with learning and gaiety. To those who approach him for aid in their study Dr. Crone is the most cordial, ready, and sympathetic of helpers, giving the contents of his library, his mind, his research, his knowledge with the freest and kindliest of generosity. And one at least—why should we say one?—all of those he has helped are as "proud as Punch" of any honour that may come his way.

'Few publications dealing with Ireland have a more distinctive and enduring place in the esteem of Irish litterateurs than the dainty little green-covered *Irish Book Lover*. Strange, to say, this magazine, which is so peculiarly, and we might say intensely, Irish emanates from London. That, however, has been entirely due to the fact that its editor, whose genial personality seems to exude from almost every page, though an Irishman, has his lot cast, as a medical doctor in a London suburb. For thirty years, Dr. J. S. Crone, J.P., to whose patriotism, unwearied pains, wide research and literary taste and judgment, we are indebted for *The Irish Book Lover*, has practised his profession in Willesden. Here he has, besides ministering medicinally to the needs of a large and populous area, interested himself in municipal problems, both as County Council or and Chairman of the Willesden District Council. Moreover, as a Justice of the Peace, he also takes an active share in public life. His numerous friends will hear with pleasure that he has just been appointed Deputy Coroner for Middlesex. A native of Belfast, Dr. Crone is by temperament much more allied to the Southern Irishman. He is full of enthusiasms, of most of which his native land is the inspiring theme. A charming conversationalist, he has a rare fund of anecdote, which he delights to retail. No one takes greater pleasure than he in putting at the disposal of his friends his extensive store of knowledge, wide reading and ripe experience, and his annual holiday to Ireland, when he renews old acquaintances, North and South, is a particular pleasure to both to himself and to those who are favoured with his acquaintance.'

This being what I might almost call a "Gavan Duffy number", reminds me of the first occasion on which I met that veteran, at a garden party given by Henry Holiday, the artist, at his charming home at Hampstead, one summer Saturday afternoon in 1892. I gazed with absorbed admiration at one who seemed to have returned from another century, another world than, ours, and thought as I grasped his hand how that hand had once held those of Davis, Mangan, O'Connell, Mitchel, Carleton, Smith O'Brien, Carlyle and Thackeray, those great ones gone, as well as several of the survivors of '98. [...]

"Obituary", Vol. VII, Nos. 9 & 10 (April & May 1916), 165.

REV. STOPFORD AUGUSTUS BROOKE, M.A., LL.D., poet, preacher, and critic, died suddenly at his home, The Four Winds, Ewhurst, Surrey, on 18th March, in his 84th year. He was born at Glendoen, Letterkenny, on 14th November, 1832, the son of Rev. R. S. Brooke, a voluminous writer and descendant of Henry Brooke, the famous 18th century author and publicist. He was educated at Kingston, whither his father had been transferred, and T.C.D., where he won the Downes Divinity Prize and the Vice-Chancellor's Prize for English Verse, and graduated a B.A., in 1856, M.A., 1862.

[...]

He entered warmly into the project for establishing the Irish Literary Society, and delivered the inaugural lecture on "The Need and Use of Getting Irish Literature into the English Tongue". In the preface to this he characteristically writes: 'I was so interested in the Society; I was so delighted to think that we should perhaps induce England to look more fully into Irish literature, and espeically Irish heroic literature; I was so entirely at one with the aims of the Society; I was so glad to meet more of my countrymen, and Ireland was so dear to me, that I forgot my own unfitness for the work, and only thought of the work itself.' He was elected President in 1889, and so continued until failing health compelled his retirement. [...]

D. Boyle, "The Irish Genius of the Brontës" [Pt. I], Vol. VII, Nos. 11 & 12 (June & July 1916), 169.

At the present time, when the literary world has been celebrating the centenary of the birth of Charlotte Brontë, it may be interesting to recall her Irish origin, so frequently overlooked, and its influence on her work. The genius of the three sisters, Charlotte, Emily and Anne, has presented a fascinating study to those interested in heredity. Rarely, if ever, has a whole family been individually endowed with such intellectual gifts as distinguished all the children of the Rev. Patrick Brontë, the County Down farmer's son.

Many theories have been advanced in explanation of what appears a phenomenon, namely, that all the children of a country rector should in their early youth betake themselves to writing romances (characterised by wild moods and fierce passions strangely out of harmony with the sober, conventional upbringing of a rural parsonage. Some writers maintain that the remarkable literary bent of the Brontës was inherited from their mother, a native of Cornwall. This supposition is based on the alleged excellence in style of letters written by the lady during the period of her engagement to Patrick Brontë.

But Mr. Shorter, who is the greatest authority on all matters relating to the Brontës, after a perusal of all the letters and also a MS article, written for a Church magazine, says that the good lady's compositions abounded in the obvious; and that no editor would have any desire to publish the article. Natives of Yorkshire who wish to make the most of the literary associations of that county boldly assert that the desolate moors and wild scenery of the district where the children were born and reared were powerful factors in inspiring and moulding the peculiarly romantic strain noticeable in the writings of the sisters. The Brontës figure largely in Yorkshire guide books, and in books relating to 'the North' generally. They have made that region classic ground, and have proved a valuable asset. So it is but natural that those who wish to make capital out of the Brontës' connection with their county should deprecate all attempts to trace the source, of the genius of this Celtic family back to their Irish forbears, and this feeling may account for the animus which some biographers display towards the father of the novelists and his Irish connections. In her *Life of Emily Brontë*, Miss Robinson says of Mrs. Brontë: 'She was, indeed, a well-educated young lady; a very Phoenix she must have seemed in the eyes of a lover conscious of a background of Pruntyism and potatoes'. Potatoes loom large in the book. She says Patrick's father owned 'a few scant acres of potato growing soil'; 'the Rev. Patrick Brontë, B.A., had grown to heroic proportions on potatoes', and so forth. Wishing to emphasise the progress which Patrick had made in the social scale during a decade in his career, she exclaims: 'At twenty, a hedge-school master at Drumgooland, he was at thirty a respectable clergyman of the Church of England!' Mr. Brontë had no need to have recourse to hedge-school mastering. The hedge-school masters were Catholics, who, because of their religion, were debarred from giving instruction in any of the State-supported Protestant schools, or in any building whatever. One more extract which is characteristic but in part inaccurate, as we shall see: 'When he [Patrick] left Cambridge he had dropped his Irish accent and taken his B.A.' If possible, Mrs. Gaskell, in her *Life of Charlotte Brontë*, is still mere contemptuous of the Irish Brontës. Wishing to show that the Brontë sisters could have received no influence from their Irish relatives, she says: 'The father having settled in England kept up no intercourse with his Irish connections ... Mr. Brontë has now no trace of his Irish origin remaining in his speech; he never could have shown his Celtic descent in the straight Greek lines and long oval face; but at five-and-twenty, fresh from the only life he had ever known [in Ireland], to present himself at the gates of St. John's, Cambridge, proved no little determination of will and scorn of ridicule'. We shall see that the statements that he at any time dropped his Irish connections or his Irish accent is incorrect, and that, on the contrary, he was in constant communication with his brothers and sisters up to the time of his death. (To BE CONTINUED.)

Eleanor Hull, *"Eriu"*, Vol. VII, Nos. 11 & 12 (June & July 1916), 173.

There is much valuable material in the new part of *Eriu* (Vol. VIII, Part 1), especially the opening article by Mr. J. Fraser on the "First Battle of Moytura", which occupies sixty pages. It is now twenty-five years since Dr. Whitley Stokes edited in *Revue Celtique* (XII) the famous story of the Second or Northern Battle of Moytura, in which the Tuatha De Danann are represented as defeating the Fomorians in a place identified with the present barony of Tirerril, in Co. Sligo. Thirty years were supposed to have elapsed between this event and the date of the earlier Battle of Moytuma Cong, in Mayo, and we have been nearly as long awaiting an edition of the first Moytura Battle, in which the Tuatha De Danann are in conflict with and victors over the Fir Bolg, with whom they disputed the kingship and supreme rule of Ireland. Whoever actually fought these great primeval contests, it is certain that on these spots ancient battles of great extent were fought, for their cairns remain to this day. Keating, who is too much occupied with the genealogy of the personages concerned in the conflict and in the meaning of their names to give more than a passing mention to either battle, sums up the whole matter in a neatly-turned phrase. He says: 'It is they [the Tuatha De Danann] who won the battle of Moytura (Magh Tuireadh) North on the Fomorians, and the battle of Moytura South on the Firbolg. It is in the first battle his hand was cut off Nuada, and his head in the last battle'. (*History of Ireland*, Bk. I).

It seems unlikely that be could have known the fine romantic tales of which he gives so brief a summary, or he might have been tempted to add some further details. O'Curry gave a resume of the text now published by Mr. Fraser in his *Lectures on the Manuscript Materials* from this, the only MS which contains a copy of it, a Trinity College MS (H.2.17); even this copy being, unfortunately, imperfect. It seems likely that the idea of two battles of Moytura is not a very ancient one. The Battle of Moytura Cong is not mentioned in the earliest lists, and the fact that only a single copy exists points to it not having been a popular story. It is, however, mentioned in the *Book of Invasions* (*Leabhar Gabhala*) in the *Book of Leinster*, but it holds a curious, uncertain position, and Keating's brief mention of it seems to show that he accepted it doubtfully. It opens abruptly, the earlier portions having possibly been lost. It describes the wanderings of the Fir Bolg and of the Tuatha De Danann in a way which seems to show that two separate tales have been pieced together, and then recounts the arrival of the latter in Ireland and the defeat of the Fir Bolg after a great battle, fought in the West of Ireland, after which the Fir Bolg settled in Connaught. The story, thus patched together, has not the cohesion of the tale of the "Second Battle of Moytura", neither has the piece the same wild archaic flavour. Nor is there any passage so grotesque as the description of Balor, whose 'Evil Eye' in the middle of his forehead needed four men to lift the lid with a polished rod that passed through it, and who, when Lugh encountered him on the field of battle, called to his servant, 'Lift up my eyelid, lad, that I may see this babbler who is talking to me'.

The tale before us is partly in prose and partly in poetry, and is addressed, like all matters dealing with remote antiquity, to the venerable and erudite Fintan who had survived all the changes in Ireland for the sole purpose of handing down the story of them to posterity. Even the most ancient accounts of battles have a certain modern flavour; here we have both parties entrenching before the fight, and arranging hospital relief, in the form of a 'Well of Healing', for the wounded. They use something very like poisonous gases and liquid fire in the 'compact clouds of mist' and 'furious rain of fire' with which the Morrigan supports the invaders, and they burn their boats behind them. They even give the six weeks' (or month's) delay which Lord Haldane confidently expected from the Germans after the declaration of war, for our preparation. 'Some delay is called for', said the Fir Bolg nobles, 'for we shall have to prepare our spears, to mend our mail, to shape our helmets, to sharpen our swords, and to make suitable attire'. The Tuatha, more considerate than the Teuton, readily consented to such just demands. We may note that Danann is here, as in Keating, spoken of as 'a female chief', and she and Bechuille are spoken of as foster-mothers of the three Tuatha chiefs. Keating, in his desire to complete the triad, the common form in Ireland, adds 'Brigid the poetess'. They are slain in the battle. He equates Danann with the goddess who gives her name to the mountains called 'the Paps', the *Dá Chích Danann*, near Killarney, but this is probably only a southern tradition. It shows how local cults were drawn into the general scheme of the Irish mythology. The three chieftainesses are a triad representing a single personage, as the Badb, Macha, and Morrigan are forms of the war-goddess, and Éire, Fodhla, and Banba represent Ireland.

Among the other contents of this number are a valuable catalogue of the first lines of the poems contained in *The O'Conor Don's Book*, drawn up by Dr. Douglas Hyde, dealing with poems by 85 bards, and an important grammatical tract, the first of a series of such which Prof. Osborn Bergin proposes to edit from Middle Irish material. These treatises were drawn up by the Irish teachers and bards for the instruction of their pupils and for their own guidance. They expound in great detail the rules of prosody followed by the bards in the construction of their verse, such as what rhymes were allowed and what to be avoided, what spellings were acceptable, with explanations of the metrical systems permitted, and paradigms of the irregular verbs, declensions, and so on. These tracts, when complete, will afford a guide in reconstructing difficult or ill-spelled texts, especially of poetry; it will be possible to know what the bards themselves considered to be correct.

"Great Irish Book Collectors (VII): Most Rev. Dr. Sheehan, Bishop of Waterford", Vol. VII, Nos. 11 & 12 (June & July 1916), 180.

Much local interest centred in the sale by Messrs. Bennett and Son, 8, Upper Ormond Quay, in April, of the splendid library of the late Bishop of Waterford, Most Rev. Dr. Sheehan. The collection was a very representative one, its chief feature being the comprehensive and valuable selection of works dealing with Irish subjects. Civil and ecclesiastical history, antiquities, archaeology, biography, polemics, and general literature were all embraced in this section, and not only was the collection practically an exhaustive one so far as standard and recognised authorities are concerned, bit it included many scarce and rare works of famous Irish refugee ecclesiastics of penal times, several of them in the original and early Continental editions. Bidding was brisk, and some high figures were reached. For a fine edition of the

Four Masters in seven volumes, with supplementary index volume, 10 guineas was paid. A fine set of the 45 volumes of *The Journal of the Royal Society of Antiquaries, Ireland*, from 1849 down to last year, fetched £19 10s. *The Irish Ecclesiastical Record* from October, 1864, to June, 1915, sold at 16 guineas, and *The Journal of the Waterford Archaeological Society*, 16 vols. and 8 parts, at £5, while *The Journal of the Cork Archaeological Society* (21 vols.), with Smith's *Cork* in two vols., fetched £6. *The Lismore Papers* (Grosart), in 10 volumes, £8 8s; Hardiman's *History of Galway*, £3 12s. 6d; Monck Mason's *History and Antiquities of St. Patrick's Church*, £2 5s; Reeves' *Ecclesiastical History of Down and Connor*, £1 2s; O'Laverty's *History of the Diocese of Down and Connor*, £1 6s.; *Hibernia Dominicana*, De Burgo, £4 7s. 6d; *Fasti Ecclesiae Hibernicae*, Cotton, £4 7s. 6d; *Manners and Customs of the Ancient Irish*, and *Manuscript Materials of Irish History* (O'Curry), £4 15s; *Annals of Lough Cé*, £2 2s; Sir J. T. Gilbert's *History of Irish Confederation and War*, £5; Madder's *United Irishmen*, 3 series, 7 volumes, £3; O'Hanlon's *Lives of the Irish Saints*, £3 5; £20 was paid for a complete set of *The Dublin Review*, in four series, comprising 156 vols., tastefully bound. A copy of the *Annals of the Four Masters* Irish Text, with translation and notes by O'Donovan, fetched £13. For an edition of Malton's *Views of Dublin*, coloured copy (uncut), the bidding reached to ten guineas, and other figures recorded were: Montalembert's *Monks of the West*, 42s; *Irish Monthly*, 43 vols., £3 10s; *Irish Texts Society*, vols. 1 to 15, and second edition of vol. 3, £5 10s; O'Donovan's *Tribes and Customs of Hy-Many*, £2 15s.; O'Flaherty's *Tribes of Iar-Connaught*, edited by Hardiman, £1 5s; *Calendar of the Ancient Records of Dublin*, Gilbert, 1889-1909, 16 vols., £2; and Vols. I. to VII., £1.

"Post Bag", Vol. VII, Nos. 11 & 12 (June & July 1916), 190.

THE STANDARD (Vol. VII., p159). In gossiping on the Irish writers on the staff of this journal, you have overlooked one of the best, the late Wm. Marcus Thompson, a well-known advocate, politician, and journalist. He was a Derry boy, and in his teens contributed verse to his friend William Roddy's *Derry Journal*. (FLEET STREET)

E. R. McClintock Dix, "Some Rare Dublin Magazines of the Eighteenth Century", Vol. VIII, Nos. 1 & 2 (Aug. & Sept. 1916), 1.

Some time ago I acquired at the auction of the library of the late James D. Latouche two volumes, one of old newspapers, both English and Irish, and the other containing the magazines I am about to mention. As they are the only copies known, I will deal with them fully in their order of date. The first is called *The Reformer*. There are thirteen numbers of it following each other weekly, and appearing every Thursday. The date of No. 1 is Thursday, the 28th of January. The year is given 1747-48. This shows that the change in the beginning of the New Year to the 1st of January had not yet become law, and therefore the date belongs to what is called the 'Old Style', but according to our dates this magazine appeared first on the 28th January 1748. Each copy of the magazine consists of four pages (10 inches x 7½ inches), and each page is divided into two columns each two and five-eighths inches broad. There are ample margins, and the type, ink, and paper are all good. The title is at the top of the first page, then the date, next a quotation from a poem in English or Latin, and then follows an article or essay similar in fashion to the essays that appeared in the earlier English magazines edited by Addison, Steele, and others—*The Spectator*, *The Tatler*, &c. This essay extends to the third page, but the last, part of it consists of some humorous stanzas. Then in the second column of the third page is a humorous advertisement by Hackball, the well-known mendicant of that period. The fourth page consists of three advertisements, one of some humorous publications, another by a draper of a sale, of all sorts of Irish woolen drapery, and lastly proposals for printing a book by an author whose initials only are given. Then comes the imprint, as follows: 'Dublin. Printed for and Sold by J. Cotter, under Dick's Coffee House, Skinner Row'. The essay in this number is signed with capital letter "B". The subject of it is to combat the dullness alleged against Ireland and to restore Taste to its long usurped rights. The second number of *The Reformer* contains an essay dealing specially with the stage, admits the improvements already effected here, and then deals with some of the leading dramatists including Shakespeare. It also is signed "B", and so lengthy is it that there is only room left for one short advertisement at the end of the second column of page 4. The article in the third number is signed "Æ". It also deals with the stage, and criticises certain practices on it to which it takes exception, and the article extends into the fourth page. The rest of this number is taken up with proposals for printing a book entitled *An Essay Towards an*

Historical Account of Irish Coins, &c. by James Simon, of Dublin, Merchant. There was in Dublin at that time a Society called 'The Physico-Historical Society', and it strongly recommended the publication. The book was published and is still an authority on its subject. It might be here mentioned that each essay in each number has a motto, sometimes in English, sometimes in Latin. These latter are from such classical authors as Horace, Terence, Tully, &c. The fourth number has an article signed "U." It tries to awaken a more public spirit and interest in home affairs. Following the articles are two stanzas of a poem, and the rest of the number filled with advertisements. One short one informs the public that the Old Cold Bath in Crown Alley, near Temple Bar, was rebuilt and in good order.

The essay in the fifth number of the magazine is again by "B" who relates his experiences in visiting several coffee houses in the City, and the remarks he overheard on the subject of *The Reformer*. There are also three advertisements.

In No. 6 "Æ" has an article shorter than usual. It is followed by a short poem called "Apollo's Decree", of a satirical nature. Amongst the advertisements, on page 4 is one, that Mr. Foote intended to make a short stay in Dublin, and would treat the nobility and gentry with his *Chocolate* at the Theatre in Capel Street, the hour for raising the curtain being 12 o'clock noon. A note follows: 'This polite entertainment ran upwards of eighty times at the Opera House, &c., in London.'

In No. 7 there is a very long essay by "Æ", of over three pages, drawing attention to the wretched condition of the people in the country, where he divides the inhabitants into three classes exclusive of the gentry. One class was the Labourers, the second the Cottiers, and the and the Graziers, and he instances a land owner who acted differently to the majority of the class, who lowered his rents instead of raising them, and lived with his people and saved his money. The writer's pleas are similar to those of Swift, who wrote to the like effect more strongly at an earlier period. In this number Mr. Foote's entertainment is altered to begin at seven in the evening, by desire, it is stated, of several persons of quality. There is a Proposal to print a volume of Poems, but the author's name is not given.

In No. 8, "B" contributes the leading article, and it also contains a short letter pressing the Editor to see Mr. Foote's entertainment. The writer of this letter signs it "S.S." Nearly the whole of No. 9 is taken up with two letters, one signed "Constant Reader", and the other unsigned, the former against Laziness, and dealing with beggars and robbers, the latter with the stage. There is one small advertisement.

No. 10 has an article unsigned also dealing with the stage and plays. Besides the usual advertisements it has one of *The Irish Theatre*, by W. R. Chetwood, which is still an authority on this subject.

In No. 11 the article, a short one, is signed "U." and deals with virtue and religion, followed by a poem by an author signed "A.C." It is called "Retirement", and is said to be in imitation of Mr. Pope. I might mention that the essay in this paper is the only one without a motto. The other advertisements are the same as before.

No. 12 contains an essay by "Æ" and is partly on the subject of good writing and criticism. Amongst its advertisements is an amusing one, a proposal to print a book with the title of *The Foolish Miscellany*, that reads as if it were only a joke. There is an advertisement in it also of the acting of a play in the Theatre in Capel Street for the setting free of the young man who got into trouble at the Smock Alley Play House some two years previous. Whether this was a joke or not I cannot say.

The last number of the magazine, the thirteenth, has a short leading article unsigned on "The Foolish Miscellany". It also contains two letters, a short satirical poem on the Rev. Dr. Henly, and an epigram. It is then announced that the thinness of the town for the ensuing summer obliged the proprietor of the paper to discontinue it until the following winter. I fancy that it is unlikely that it was revived. The imprint to each number is the same. The pagination of each number is separate. The value of such a small periodical consists mainly in its local allusions and the light it throwers on the social and dramatic life of Dublin at the time.

D. Boyle, "The Irish Genius of the Brontës" [Part II], Vol. VIII, Nos. 1 & 2 (Aug. & Sept. 1916), 4.

We also find Mr. Birrell surmising that Mr. Brontë's first love affair was nipped in the bud, because the stern guardian of the lady made inquiries in this disagreeable fashion: 'Who is this Patrick Brontë? Where does he come from? An Irishman is he? What are his chances of carrying his brogue into an English rectory?' Patrick attained to the English rectory, notwithstanding his brogue, which owing to the prejudices of his times would undoubtedly handicap him in the race for ecclesiastical preferment.

Perhaps the most fatuous of all Mrs. Gaskell's statements regarding Mr. Brontë is her reference to his scorn of ridicule in presenting himself, as she phrases it, at the gates of St. John's, Cambridge. As St. John's was then a college at which the least opulent of students were educated at a comparatively trifling cost, and as Patrick Brontë, before presenting himself, had for five years occupied the position of tutor to the Rev. Mr. Tighe's children, as well as maintaining a school of his own, we fail to see any occasion for fear of scorn or ridicule.

I shall now give some particulars of the remarkable Irish family to which Patrick Brontë belonged, and we shall see incidentally that the literary gifts as well as the intense, force and passion which characterise the writings of the Brontë sisters were inherited from their Irish progenitors and that it is to them, and not to the wild, gloomy moors of Yorkshire, nor to the respectable but sickly nonentities of Cornwall, from whom the mother sprung, that we must look for the origin and source of the peculiar genius of the Brontës. Patrick Brontë was one of a family of ten—five sons and five daughters. The father of this large family, all remarkable for strength, good looks, and fierce dispositions, was Hugh Prunty (for so he spelt his name), a native of the south of Ireland, who, going north in early manhood, took a farm, married a Catholic girl named Alice McClory, settled down in the parish of Drumballyroney, Co. Down, and here all his children were born, and all, except Patrick, died. The surname was spelt differently by different members of the family. [Prof. Alex. Macalister, Fellow of St. John's, told me recently that the original signature in the books of the College, still extant, is Patrick Pranty!—Ed.] Little importance was attached in those days to the spelling of surnames, and the public records of births, deaths, &c. give the name variously as Prunty, Bronte, and Brunty. The Pruntys (adhering to Hugh's spelling) were a literary stock. In the *Story of Early Gaelic Literature*, Douglas Hyde gives a translation from a manuscript, dated 1763, by a romance writer named Patrick O'Prunty, and Mr. Shorter, who has investigated all the records of the family, says that this Patrick was a brother to Patrick Brontë's father. This early romance is called *The Adventures of the Son of Ice Counsil*—and has an inscription on the last page in Irish, translated thus: 'I pray the blessing of each reader in honour of the Trinity of the Virgin Mary on the writer, that is Patrick O'Prunty, son of Niall, son of Seathan, &c. April ye 20, 1763'.

Hugh, notwithstanding the large family he had to maintain, found time to dabble in literature. One of his published poems contains an expression which his granddaughter put into the mouth of Jane Eyre in one of her vehement declarations to Rochester—'the finest fibre of my soul'!

The eldest of Hugh's children was William, a prominent United Irishman who fought at the battle of Ballinahinch, and Hugh, the second son, was locally known as 'the giant'. James was a musician, and is described as 'very smart and active with his tongue'. He visited his brother Patrick at Haworth. Charlotte refers in one of her letters to his visit and describes him as a 'substantial yeoman'. He described Charlotte as 'tarrible, sharp and inquisitive'. Walsh was described as 'a fine-looking man, gentlemanly though uneducated, with a sensible way of expressing himself, and a quick sharp utterance'.

The five sisters of Patrick Brontë are said to have been 'tall, red-cheeked, fair haired, handsome women, with dark eye-lashes, strong minds and massive frames'.

Patrick was born on St. Patrick's Day, 1777. He was a schoolmaster at the age of sixteen. When twenty-five years of age he had saved £100, with which, acting on the advice of the Rev. Mr. Tighe, he set out for Cambridge, where he obtained his degree after four years' residence. When Charlotte Brontë, in her sixteenth year, and twenty-five years after the date at which we are told her father rid himself of his Irish accent, went to a boarding school, her teacher describes her thus: 'She was very shy and, nervous, and spoke with a strong Irish accent'.

Regarding Emily, whom some critics acclaim the greatest of the three, a recent writer says in reference to her exquisite poem, 'Tell me, tell me, smiling child', she 'seemed to know by more than an hereditary memory and feeling the mode of her kinsman, Patrick O'Prunty'.

Now, regarding Mrs. Gaskell's assertion that Patrick kept up no intercourse with his Irish connections after he became 'a respectable English clergyman', an extract from Mr. Brontë's will disposes of the assertion: 'I leave forty pounds to be equally divided amongst my brothers and sisters to whom I have given considerable sums of money in times past'. Mr. Brontë was a voluminous writer in prose and verse. Most of these have been collected and published by Mr. J. H. Turner (Bingley, 1898), who thinks that the origin of the Brontë genius can be revealed by English investigation, without having recourse to Irish legends. Patrick had often to withstand the bigotry of the time against his countrymen. In one of his controversial pamphlets he writes, 'You break some of your jokes on Irishmen. Do you know an Irishman is your lord and master? You ate under the King's ministry, and are not they under O'Connell? And is not the Duke of Wellington the greatest of living heroes, an Irishman?'

His writings in prose and verse, such as "The Maid of Killarney", "The Irish Cabin", and "The Harper of Erin", show a kindly sympathy for the lowly and pious peasantry of his native country.

We have now seen something of the Irish Brontës, and I think we may fairly conclude they were the main factors in producing the three geniuses, Charlotte, Emily, and Anne. (CONCLUDED.)

T. F. O'Rahilly, "Peter O'Connell", Vol. VIII, Nos. 1 & 2 (Aug. & Sept. 1916), 6.

The name of Peter O'Connell (Peadar Ó Conaill), the best Irish scholar in the Ireland of a century ago, deserves to be much better known than it is. His great work, an *Irish-English Dictionary*, which unfortunately was never printed is still consulted with profit by editors of Irish texts. The autograph of the *Dictionary* now constitutes the 'MS Egerton 83' in the British Museum; and three transcripts exist, namely one in the British Museum (by John O'Donovan), one in Trinity College, Dublin, and one in the Royal Irish Academy. Some information concerning the history of the *Dictionary* and its author will be found in the *Catalogue of Irish MSS* in the British Museum, pp.161-63, where O'Grady prints a memorandum on the subject written by Eugene O'Curry in 1849. Some years earlier (about 1840) when cataloguing the Royal Irish Academy MSS O'Curry wrote on the same topic a note which, so far as I know, has not hitherto been printed. Speaking of the MS "23B34" he says (Hodges & Smith Catalogue, p.42):

> It was transcribed in the year 1806 by Mr. Malachy Curry (brother to the compiler of this Catalogue), who was then pupil to the justly celebrated Irish scholar, Peter O'Connell. At the period of making this transcript Mr. Curry was living in his native village Dunaha, in the west of the County of Clare, and Mr. O'Connell kept a respectable English and Irish school at Cares (now Money-point), about five miles to the east of Kilrush in the same county. Shortly after this period both left that part of the country—Mr. O'Connell on his itinerary to collect materials for his English-Irish Dictionary, and Mr. Curry to fill a confidential situation in a respectable mercantile house in the city of Limerick, where he still resides. After the lapse of some years Mr. O'Connell returned to his native country, and set about the compilation of his Dictionary under the patronage and in the house of the late much-lamented and highly-esteemed Doctor Reardon, of Limerick. To that compilation Mr. Curry lent great and useful assistance (an assistance that would be honourably and gratefully acknowledged, had the patron and compiler lived to see the work published), and he had been just engaged to make a new transcript of it for the press at the time that Doctor Reardon died. The doctor's death put all chance of publishing the work out of the question, and poor O'Connell was constrained once more to seek an oblivious (sic) and solitary refuge in the humble but hospitable cottage of his brother, Mr. Patrick O'Connell, in his native village of Carne; where, after a few years of comparative privation and entire seclusion, he died in the year 1824, forgotten and neglected by a nation of un-Irish Irishmen, for the advancement of whose national

literature he spent a long and laborious life. Peace be to thy venerated shade, O'Connell—so say I, though nobody should join me! [...]

J. S. Crone, "Dean Butler's *Trim*", Vol. VIII, Nos. 1 & 2 (Aug. & Sept. 1916), 9.

In an article on "Printing in Trim", in your first volume, p.77, Mr. Dix mentions several editions of this scarce little book, but was 'not certain if they were correct'. I have recently had an opportunity off inspecting and collating copies of all the editions issued, so perhaps a description of them may be of interest, and settle the matter once for all.

1. *Some Notices of The Castle and of the Abbies and other Religious Houses at Trim*. Collected from Various Authorities. Trim. Printed by Henry Griffith, 1835. 6¾ x 4 cut down, t.p. + 1 blank + 1 frontispiece. Plan of part of Town + 1 preface, + hlf. t. + 1 to 64 + 1 engraved plate of coins. In fours, 39 lines to a page. Bound up with this is: *Some Notices of the Church of St. Patrick, Trim*. Collected from various authorities. Trim: Printed by H. Griffith, 1837. T.p.+ hlf. t. + 3 to 38, in fours. This copy bears an inscription, 'From the Editor', and the book-plates of James Maidment, the Scottish antiquary, and Sir John Whittaker Ellis, one time Lord Mayor of London and Governor of the Irish Society, whose bust adorns the vestibule of the new Guildhall in Derry.
2. *Some Notices of the Castle of Trim, collected from Various Sources*. Second edition enlarged. Trim: Printed by H. Griffith, 1840. 7 1/8 + 4¼. 1 hf. title + 1 title p. + 1 preface + Contents × frontispiece, as above, + 1 to 143 + plate of coins. In fours, 37 lines to a page. Inscribed 'Owen Blayney Cole from Rev. R. Butler, in remembrance of a pleasant visit from him, September 23, 1841'. For O. B. Cole, see O'Donoghue's *Poets of Ireland*.
3. *Some Notices of the Castle and of the Ecclesiastical Buildings of Trim*. Compiled from Various Authorities by Richard Butler, Dean of Clommacnoise. Third Edition. Trim: W. H. Griffith, Printer, 1854. 6 ¾ × 4½, cut down. 1 t.p. + 1 quotation, + 1 contents, + 1 contents of appendix, + 1 to 312. In fours, 35 lines to a page. Notice of Castle ends at p.143. This edition also contains two plates, different from the previous ones, one taken from the *Dublin Penny Journal* and one from the *Gentleman's Magazine*.
4. Same title as No. 3. Fourth edition. Dublin: Hodges, Smith and Co., 104, Grafton Street, 1861. 8vo., 6½ × 4, 1 t.p. + 1 quotation + 1 contents + 1 contents of Appendix, + 9 to 312, 30 lines to a page. No plates.

"Editor's Gossip", Vol. VIII, Nos. 1 & 2 (Aug. & Sept. 1916), 12.

One result of the recent 'Rising' in Dublin is that the Sinn Féin pamphlets and propagandist papers which were issued in such numbers during the past year or two, having naturally become scarce, so many having been confiscated and destroyed, are being eagerly sought for by collectors. Some booksellers more alive than their fellows have made corners in them, and are disposing at fancy prices the literature that but yesterday was being given away. The same thing applies to the published works of the unfortunate leaders. Thomas MacDonagh's last volume of verse, *Lyrical Poems*, was offered to me in Charing Cross Road for a couple of shillings, and I found, on reaching Dublin, that it was being sold at twenty-five!

Another result is that some books are bound to become scarce shortly owing to so many having been consumed in the fires that raged during the Easter week. The publishing trade suffered severely, for of such large establishments as Eason's and Sealy, Bryers, hardly a vestige remains, and Maunsel's premises are an empty shell. In Sealy, Bryers the stereotype plates of the well-known *Thom's Directory* were reduced to a molten mass of metal, and it is doubtful if it will ever appear again. A similar fate befell the plates (and stock) of Father Dineen's great *Irish English Dictionary*, the property of the Irish Texts Society, valued at a thousand pounds. I hear the same firm have lost a MS *History of the Diocese of Raphoe*, of which no copy exits, whilst almost the entire stock of Father Brown's excellent work, *Ireland in Fiction*, was destroyed in Maunsel's. [...]

In the thirty years that have sped so swiftly since Mr. Yeats's maiden, and now much sought after, publishing venture, *Mosada*—an off-print from the *Dublin University Review*, then edited by his friend Rolleston—issued from the house of Sealy, Bryers, he has had many publishers at home and abroad. Now, I am told, he has finally transferred all his copyrights to the great firm of Macmillan, who will henceforth be solely responsible for his future works. I should not be a bit surprised but that when normal conditions return the outcome of this might be an additional bay in the chaplet of our bard, viz., a *Globe Edition of Yeats*! [...]

As was to be expected, the 'Rising' in Easter week occupies a good deal of space in the English magazines for June. Thus, in *Blackwood*, Moira O'Neill, who apparently has ceased to sing altogether, graphically relates her experiences, 'during the Rebellion in Wexford'. Rev. Dr. Murray describes the outbreak and what led up to it fully and with strict impartiality in *The Nineteenth Century*, whilst in the *English Review* a Major Stuart Stephens discloses in a hardly credible narrative how he foretold the Rebellion, and follows it up in the July number with another entitled "The Secret Constitution of Shinn Fane" (sic).

As regards the July magazines: In *The Nineteenth Century*, Rev. R. H.

Murray concludes his account of "Humbert's Invasion of Ireland in 1798", and acknowledges his indebtedness to Lady Ardilaun for the loan of the valuable papers of her grandfather the first Lord Bantry, who was particularly active at that period; and Mr. D. C. Lathbury indicates several "Ways out of the Irish Labyrinth". *Blackwood* contains an ably written account of the doings "In Trinity College During the Rebellion", by "One of the Garrison"; and "The Protest" of "A Southern Loyalist", somewhat out in its dates. *The Edinburgh Review* has an article on "Sinn Féin" noticeable by its anonymity, whilst Mr. Swift MacNeill deals with the cognate subject "The Breakdown of Dublin Castle Regime" in *The Contemporary Review*. [...]

James Stephens contributes a touching elegy entitled "Spring in Ireland, 1916" to *The Nation* of 6th July, from which I quote a stanza:

> Be green upon their graves, O happy Spring,
> For they were young and eager who are dead;
> Of all things that are young and quivering
> With eager life be they remembered.
> They move not here, they have gone to clay,
> They cannot die again for liberty;
> Be they remembered of their land for aye;
> A garland of the flow'rs you gatherèd.

"Notices of New Books", Vol. VIII, Nos. 1 & 2 (Aug. & Sept. 1916), 16.

THE IRISH REBELLION OF 1916: A BRIEF HISTORY OF THE REVOLT AND ITS SUPPRESSION. BY JOHN F. BOYLE. (CONSTABLE AND CO.) 4s. 6d. net. It is, of course, too soon yet to expect 'the full, true and faithful account' of the terrible outbreak that drenched the streets of Dublin in blood during the Black Easter week. But Mr. Boyle, who is first in the field with a connective narrative of the sad events, wields a skilful pen and presents a graphic and, on the whole, impartial picture of what occurred, with pen portraits of the unfortunate leaders; and painful reading it makes. It is mainly based, as he admits, on contemporaneous newspaper reports, nothing apparently being set down from personal observation. Two good maps will assist the reader unacquainted with the scenes of the outbreaks in Dublin and the provinces, to follow the course of events, and the book will serve a useful purpose until some future Madden arises to tell the whole truth.

"Post Bag", Vol. VIII, Nos. 1 & 2 (Aug. & Sept. 1916), 17.

BIBLIOGRAPHY OF GAVAN DUFFY. (Vol. VII., p.177.) I miss from this otherwise exhaustive list two articles that also appeared in *The Contemporary Review*, Vol. 72, under the heading "The House of Commons Half a Century Ago: A Chapter from My Autobiography". Though the gist of these, somewhat altered in arrangement, appeared in *My Life*, yet there are a few interesting passages that do not. (X.)

"Obituaries", Vol. VIII, Nos. 1 & 2 (Aug. & Sept. 1916), 20.

FRANCIS SHEEHY SKEFFINGTON was born in Bailieborough, Co. Cavan, in 1878, the only child of John Skeffington, J.P., of Co. Down, some-time inspector of schools. He was educated at home, and won many honours in his university career, amongst them the Chancellor's gold medal for a prose essay on Henry Grattan in 1903. He became known as a free lance journalist and as editor or co-editor of various journals such as *The Nationist* and *The National Democrat*, but was perhaps most successful in the witty "Dialogues of the Day", a weekly commentary on current events in Ireland. In 1908 his *Life of Michael Davitt* appeared, and in 1913 he took over the editorship of *The Irish Citizen*. He was arrested on the evening of the 25th April, when returning home after attempts to stop looting, and on the next morning, at Portobello Barracks, he was shot without trial at the command of an officer subsequently found to be insane.

JAMES CONNOLLY was born in Monaghan and is said to have imbibed socialistic doctrines whilst working in England and Scotland. He was the author of two books, *Labour in Irish History* (Maunsel 1914) and *The Re-Conquest of Ireland* (Liberty Hall 1915). He was Commander-in-chief of the rebel forces, and was wounded during the rebellion. He was executed on 12th May, aged forty.

THOMAS MACDONAGH, one of the signatories of the Republican proclamation and in command at Jacob's factory, was shot in Kilmainham on 3rd May. He was born at Cloughjordan, Tipperary, in 1878, the son of a school master, and was a teacher at St. Enda's College. He graduated M.A. in the National University, and was appointed Lecturer in English at University College. He was a frequent contributor to *The Irish Review*, and a play by him, *When the Dawn is Come*, was produced at the Abbey Theatre in October, 1908. His published works are: *Through the Ivory Gate* (12mo., 1903); *April and May* (12mo.,

1904); *The Golden Joy* (8vo., 1906); *Songs of Myself* (8vo., 1910); *Thomas Campion and the Art of English Poetry* (8vo. 1913); *Lyrical Poems* (4to., 1913); and posthumously, *Literature in Ireland: Studies in Irish and Anglo-Irish* (8vo., port 1916).

PATRICK H. PEARSE, President of the Republican Provisional Government, was born in Dublin in 1880, of English parents. A fine Gaelic scholar and a notable orator, he graduated B.A. and was called to the Bar. He was the founder and headmaster of St. Enda's College, Rathfarnham, established to inculcate Irish-Ireland principles, and wrote miracle plays in Gaelic for the scholars. For a time he edited *An Claidheamh Soluis*, and contributed original Gaelic verse and translations to *The Irish Review*. He published a small collection of these, entitled *Suantraidhe agus Goltraidhe* in 1914, and one of prose, *An Máthair agus Sgéala Eile* (1915). He wrote a touching poem, "A Mother Speaks", immediately before his execution at Kilmainham on 3rd May.

JOSEPH MARY PLUNKETT, eldest son of Count Plunkett, was born in 1887, and educated at Stonyhurst. He published a volume of verse, *The Circle and the Sword* in 1911, and subsequently edited *The Irish Review*. An active member of Sinn Féin, he signed the Proclamation, was condemned to death, and shot on 4th May. A few hours previously he was married in his cell to Miss Grace Gifford, a clever artist.

E. R. McClintock Dix, "Some Rare Dublin Magazines of the Nineteenth Century (concluded)", Vol. VIII, Nos. 3 & 4 (Oct. & Nov. 1916), 25.

II. The next magazine (taking them chronologically), is called *The Inspector*. There is only one number of it. It consists of four pages of one column each, that is, the full page is printed across. It is smaller in size than *The Reformer*, and has a poorer or inferior appearance in every respect. The date is 1748.

III. I now turn to another magazine called *The Mirror*. There are only two numbers of it. It is about the same size as *The Reformer*, but not so well printed, nor is the paper so good. This magazine consists of four pages, but the advertisements in it are printed mostly in small type and so take up less room than those in *The Reformer*. Half of page 4 is blank. The date of No. 1 is Thursday, Nov. 8th, 1750. It is therefore more than two years later than *The Reformer*. Each page is divided into two columns. Immediately under the date there is printed a short quotation from Ben Jonson. [...]

IV. The next journal which I have to describe is called *The Covent Garden Journal* and is simply a reprint of the London journal bearing that name, with the addition of a few advertisements put in by James Hoey, the Dublin printer. It is, of course, well known that there was no copyright law at that time between England and Ireland, and the Dublin printers used to publish pirated editions of English authors for the reading of the Dublin public. [...]

V. We now come to a totally different journal, one purely local. It is called *The Dublin Spy*, by Roger Spy, Esq. And deals entirely with local matters.

D. J. O'Donoghue, "Literature and the Late Rebellion", Vol. VIII, Nos. 3 & 4 (Oct. & Nov. 1916), 28.

I.B.L. has already given the chief facts in the lives of most of the writers and enthusiasts who were executed as a result of the recent rebellion, and it is lamentable to think how many promising literary careers have been sacrificed. The present writer knew several of the insurgents quite well. Connolly, whose age is given as forty, but must have been much more than that, was perhaps the ablest member of the whole group, but he had not the surface brilliancy of some of his younger associates. No one can read his *Labour in Irish History* without recognising its argumentative force and skill. He had not the oratorical gifts of his quandom [sic] leader, James Larkin (whom he led), but his were the brains behind the Irish labour movement of the past dozen years. As a talker and writer, Thomas MacDonagh was beyond question the most distinguished of the insurgents. His last three or four books showed so great an advance on his earlier work that his friends had high hopes for his future. It came as a shock and surprise to most of them that he had involved himself in the wild scheme of an armed rebellion. It was quite clear to them, notwithstanding, that his ambition and self-confidence were rather abnormal. Though personally most amiable and charming, he lost no opportunity of expressing his supreme belief in his literary work. The writer had a long and interesting correspondence with him on the all-engrossing subject of himself (the poet) about ten years ago, and every emphasis was placed upon this point by MacDonagh. His correspondent did not take the same view, naturally, but he was charmed with the naïveté and earnestness of the poet, and had no doubt that had he lived MacDonagh would have been a, powerful literary personality in the days to come. A cleverer or more stimulating talker it would have been difficult to meet. Subtle and logical, if sometimes discursive, and saturated with a literary sense, it was a pleasant intellectual event to have a conversational tussle with so bright a thinker. If his friends little suspected his revolutionary tendencies, a look through his writings in the light of subsequent happenings, does not fail to show that the germ was in his mind. His play, *When the Dawn is Come*, written for the Abbey Theatre eight years ago, reads curiously now. As one of those who was present when it was produced (I fancy it was performed only once or twice), the writer had the unique experience (after many years of play-going) of noticing that the piece was played right through, and the curtain fell without one single hint of applause or encouragement for the author. Yet many of the author's friends were present, sincerely anxious to applaud. One remembers nothing like it on the stage. There was no disapprobation, either, from the ordinary public. The thing was simply incomprehensible. Yet there was 'something' in it, which emerges after close study of the work and its author, who was disconcerted, but not discouraged, by his experiment. He wrote other plays, it is known, but nothing seems to have come of them. His later work, especially in prose, has high merit, and altogether it is a sad pity that so bright a personality should have been extinguished so early. But ambition and intellectual vanity are often very deadly in their results. P. H. Pearse was not so essentially literary as MacDonagh, and I confess I have never been able to see his merits as a writer. But he was certainly a remarkable speaker and would probably have achieved fame in that direction rather than in literature. He published several Gaelic texts for the Gaelic League, several pamphlets, I think, a couple of English essays on Irish subjects in a small volume. He wrote a certain number of articles for various Sinn Féin papers, but there is nothing very striking about them. A bibliography of the writings of all the insurgents would be interesting. It would include not only the books of Connolly, Pearse, MacDonagh and Plunkett (the latter had the real poetical faculty, and his *Circle and the Sword* contains some of the best verse written in recent years), but also the most interesting and indeed valuable account of his prison life written by T. J. Clarke in *Irish Freedom*. I have read nothing quite as good of its kind. It would also find a niche for Michael O'Hanrahan, who was executed on May 4th at Kilmainham. A native of New Ross, he had written various short stories and one rather successful novel, *A Swordsman of the Brigade*, published in London in 1914.

Randall McDonnell, "Remebrance", Vol. VIII, Nos. 3 & 4 (Oct. & Nov. 1916), 34

Remembrance
(LIEUTENANT THOMAS KETTLE)

He took the dreary themes of earth
And made them sparkle with his mirth;
An epigram went flashing forth,
   A pointed hit:
Of Sheridan's immortal birth,
   A brother wit.

A poet of the faultless line,
Who laid his gift on Ireland's shrine,
Who soared from earth to the divine
   Free-winged and bold:
And leaden words, translated, shine,
   Touched into gold!

Deep in the blood-stained soil of France,
Where thunders of the great advance
Ruffle within their iron trance
   The stars above.
Sleep Satire, Poetry, Romance
   And fadeless Love.

      RANDAL MCDONNELL

"Post Bag", Vol. VIII, Nos. 3 & 4 (Oct. & Nov. 1916), 44.

THE DEAD LEADERS (Vol. VIII., p.21). In your obituary notices there are a few omissions which might be supplied as follows: James Connolly, who was Commander of the Dublin Division of the Republican Army only, edited and wrote most of *The Harp*, an Irish-American journal, and wrote the best of *The Irish Worker*. He edited *The Worker*, printed in Glasgow, which succeeded *The Irish Worker* and had a short run, only three, or four numbers appearing. On its seizure, a press was established in Liberty Hall from which issued *The Worker's Republic*, also edited by him. P. H. Pearse edited and wrote much in *An Bárr Buadh*, a weekly nationalist paper written altogether in Irish and published in Dublin in 1912; edited and wrote much in *An Maeaomh*, an occasional magazine issued from St. Enda's College. He edited for the Gaelic League, with notes and vocabulary, the Ossianic tales: *Bruidhéan Chaorthainn* and *Bodach an Chóta Lachtna* (1906). As a young man of 18, he published *Three Lectures on Gaelic Topics* (1898), and more recently *Póll an Phíobaire*, boy's adventure story, and *Iosagán agus Sgéalta Eile*, Connacht child studies. He was, besides, the author of the following pamphlets: *From A Hermitage*, reprinted from *Irish Freedom*; *The Murder Machine*; *Ghosts*; *The National Idea*; *The Spiritual Nation*; and *The Sovereign People*. (P. S. O'HEGARTY).

"Obituary", Vol. VIII, Nos. 3 & 4 (Oct. & Nov. 1916), 45.

ROGER DAVID CASEMENT was born near Ballymena, Co. Antrim, 1st September 1864. He entered the Consular Service in 1892, and gained world-wide fame by his Reports on the condition of the, natives in the Congo district, and afterwards in Putumayo. He was knighted for his services in 1911, and retired in 1913. He contributed verse to the *Review of Reviews*, prose and verse to *The Irish Review*, chiefly anonymously, to *The Fortnightly Review*, and *The Irish Volunteer*. He was executed for high treason at Pentonville Prison on 3rd August, 1916. (D.J.O'D.)

"The Blind Girl of Donegal", Vol. VIII, Nos. 5 & 6 (Dec. & Jan. 1916-17), 49.

The centenary of the birth of Frances Brown, once known far and wide as "The Blind Girl of Donegal", which occurred on 16th January last, did not elicit, a single line in any journal, as far as I am aware, showing, alas! how transient a thing is a literary reputation. Yet our northern province is not so rich in women writers that it can afford to neglect one, who, in her day, brought to it some degree of fame, as much by her widely acknowledged abilities as her heroic struggle to overcome the results of her early affliction. Her name is to be sought in vain in the *Dictionary of National Biography*, though many less deserving appear there; so the following facts pieced together from many sources may help to keep her name in memory.

Frances Brown, born in Stranorlar, Co. Donegal, the seventh child of the dozen that filled the quiver of the local post-master, was rendered sightless by an attack of small pox when eighteen months old. Though thus afflicted, she attended the village school kept by a Mr. McGranahan, and had as fellow pupils Isaac Butt and. William Mac Arthur, afterwards M.P. and Lord Mayor of London (*Sir William Mac-Arthur: A Biography*, London 1891). In the preface to her first published volume, she tells us how she listened to the lessons which her brothers and sisters nightly conned aloud and invariably knew them better than the others. Later, she bribed them by doing their share of the household work, as well as her own, to read to her the 'Burton books' like *Robinson Crusoe* and *Park's Travels*, the only literature, Butt tells us, that ever reached the village in those days. Every available book she borrowed and had read to her to quench the thirst for knowledge that grew with her growth, and she committed to memory long passages from Scott, Byron, and Pope's "Homer". As a child of seven, she turned the Lord's prayer into verse, reams of which she wrote and destroyed. [...]

D. J. O'Donoghue, "*The Dublin and London Magazine*", Vol. VIII, Nos. 5 & 6 (Dec. & Jan. 1916-17), 53.

To the list of Irish periodicals already commented upon in these pages should be added the above excellent magazine, one of the best, as it was one of the earliest periodicals of the modern type. It was a monthly, published by J. Robins, of London, at a shilling, and was wholly Nationalist and Catholic in tone. It commenced in March 1825, and each number contained 48 closely-printed pages in double column, generally embellished with a steel engraving of an eminent Irish contemporary, and the best Irish pens of the day were at its service. From an annotated copy in the Royal Irish Academy and from information in my possession, I am able to give a detailed account of the authorship of all the important contributions, most of which were anonymous or pseudonymous.

Its editor and chief writer was Michael James Whitty (1795-1873), who, under numerous disguises and anonymously, wrote the greater part of many numbers. For example, in the first number he was responsible for the opening article, "Ireland", and a slashing attack on the "Letters from the Irish Highlands", as well as a contribution signed "Z.Z." He never signed his name to anything, and was "Rory O'Rourke", "Z.Z.", "Geoffrey K—n", "O'Sullivan Bear", and various other veiled personalities. [...]

"Some Old Derry Ephemera", Vol. VIII, Nos. 5 & 6 (Dec. & Jan. 1916-17), 56.

At the sale of the library of the late Robert Day, of Cork, Mr. Séamus Ó Casaide, B.L., secured a miscellaneous parcel of locally printed pamphlets, &c. and amongst them discovered some of Derry origin. These he has kindly forwarded for inspection and perhaps a few notes on them may be of interest to our northern readers, at least. The first is a broadside, a requisition to the sheriffs, dated 9th March, 1831, to call a meeting of the inhabitants to support the Reform Bill then engaging the attention of Parliament. This was printed at *The Sentinel* office, and is of note because one of the sheriffs was Joshua Gillespie, who wrote a *History of the Siege of Derry* (1823). The next in order of time is an eight-page pamphlet, *A Seed in the Teeth or the Juror Unmasked, By a New Zealander.* (Printed at the Moon Office, Blue Bell Hill, November, 1832.) It is a bitter attack on Sir Robt. A. Ferguson, who long represented the city, for his actions as a grand juror of the three counties, and his alleged 'road jobbing'. The next two items are single sheets, both dated March 1837, and refer to the general election then threatening. One is the address of Geo. R. Dawson, and bears no imprint; the other that of Francis Horner, who dates from Rossville Street, and offers himself as a candidate in the reform interest. This bears the imprint of 'Wm. H. Buchanan, Richmond Street'. The election did not take place until 2nd August, when Horner did not go to the poll, and Dawson was defeated by Sir R. Ferguson, who henceforth represented the city unchallenged, until his death in 1860, and his statue now adorns the Diamond. [...]

"Post Bag", Vol. VIII, Nos. 5 & 6 (Dec. & Jan. 1916–17), 49.

CHARLES DRISCOLL. In Newton Crosland's *Rambles Round My Life* (London 1898), I came across this interesting reminiscence: 'Among the acquaintances whom I made about the year 1840 was the Rev. Charles Driscoll, a clever Irishman, and at that time curate of St. Clement Dane's Church. He possessed a wonderful gift of improvisation. He would undertake to write fifty lines of poetry in fifteen minutes on any subject given to him, the verses to be sensible, metrical, grammatical, and the rhymes correct. I tested him with surprising results'. He was probably Charles Driscoll, B.A., T.C.D., 1825, M.A. 1842. I should like to find out if he ever published anything. (BIBLIO.)

"Reviews: *Reveries* and *Responsibilities*", Vol. VIII, Nos. 5 & 6 (Dec. & Jan. 1916–17), 59.

Mr. Yeats signalizes his change of publishers by the re-issue of his two latest books, one in prose the other in verse, both burned out in the elegant style that marks the output of the house of Macmillan. Somehow one always regards Mr. Yeats as endowed with perpetual youth, and few consider that half a century has passed over his head, so lightly does time touch him. Yet such is the fact, and now having gained, fame, well deserved and not altogether undreamt of, he sits down to pen these *Reveries Over Childhood and Youth* (6s.). It is a remarkable self-revelation, and though dealing with early formative influences and boyish adventures, can hardly be called an autobiography—there isn't a date in it. He tells us of his early trials at school, trials common to all shy boys as well as misunderstood geniuses; his recollections of the artistic circles in which his father moved; his own predilections towards Art; his associations with the stern ship-owning grandfather in his well-loved Sligo, and the mystic influences of the lake island of Innisfree. [...]

Responsibilities (6s.) exhibits the poet in many moods, satirical, mystical, musical. It is, in a measure, the complement of the *Reveries*, for, from the "Introductory Rhymes", which deal with doings of his ancestors, 'traders or soldiers', old Butlers, who 'took to horse and stood beside the brackish waters of the Boyne', to that Pollexfen who 'leaped overboard after a ragged hat in Biscay Bay', to the final note, we find many person reflections of the author on recent happenings. Thus he ventilates his opinions on those who disturbed performance of *The Playboy*, and addresses the shade of Parnell on the treatment meted out to Sir Hugh Lane by the same 'old foul mouth that slandered you'. He admits that when in September 1913, he wrote "Romantic Ireland's dead and gone / It's with O'Leary in the grave" he could not foresee Easter week 1916, and the heroism of those who 'weighed so lightly what they gave'. As is his wont of recent years, Mr. Yeats continues to revise and polish up his earlier work, so the volume ends with a very fine poetic version of "The Hour Glass", first published in 1904. Taken altogether, it will enhance the poet's fame.

"Notices of New Books", Vol. VIII, Nos. 5 & 6 (Dec. & Jan. 1916–17), 64.

THE INSURRECTION IN DUBLIN. BY JAMES STEPHENS. (MAUNSEL). 2S. 6D. This is not a history of the outbreak, but rather the fresh and vivid impressions of an eye-witness endowed with the seeing eye, and as the reading world knows, the master of a fine style, 'written day by day' during the black Easter week. Nightly, from a point of vantage, Mr. Stephens watched the red glare over the city, and listened to the pitiless rifle and machine gun, and daily mingled with the crowd, and listened to the rumours of the many alarmists, one of whom he depicts as 'a wild individual who spat rumours as though his mouth were a machine gun or linotype machine'. The utter unexpectedness of the whole thing, the popular feeling varying with each speaker, the hopelessness of the attempt, and the numerous 'effective' incidents, are all portrayed with the skill of the practised writer, and oh! the pity of it. The book contains a graceful eulogy on Sheehy Skeffington and a terrible attack on John Redmond; some recollections and estimates of the late leaders, and concludes with wise words for the future guidance that men of all parties should lay to heart.

Edmund Downey, "An Editor's Reminiscences", Vol. VIII, Nos. 7 & 8 (Feb. & March 1917), 73.

When I was entrusted by the late William Tinsley, in 1880, with the Editorship of his magazine—*Tinsleys'*—a task which (owing to multifarious other duties) had to be performed by me in a perfunctory manner, the principal warning given to me was to avoid as far as possible the introduction of anything Irish. Not that Mr. Tinsley had any antipathy to Ireland or Irishmen, but as a London publisher of books and magazines, he could detect no 'business' in the distressful country. The leading serial for the year 1880 was written by an Irishman, for whom William Tinsley had the highest regard Richard Fowling—but "Under St. Paul's" was manifestly not an Irish tale, and had no Irish characters in it.

Looking through *Tinsleys'* for the year 1880, I find that notwithstanding the warning about Irish contributions, some Irish 'matter' crept into the magazine. In the February number there was a sketch entitled "The Cab I Got at Tussaud's", bearing the signature "Pater Mendaciorum", a pseudonym which Richard Dowling occasionally employed. In the March number there is a short piece of verse, "My Lady of Dreams", written by my brother, Richard Downey, and an article, "Havelock in Afghanistan", by John Augustus O'Shea. "Honeymooning", by "Pater Mendaciorum", appeared in the April number; also an essay by the same author entitled "The Decay of the Sublime", republished in his *Ignorant Essays* (1887). [...]

"Editor's Gossip", Vol. VIII, Nos. 7 & 8 (Feb. & March 1917), 82.

The death, in his 72nd year, of Mr. J. J. O'Kelly, M.P., which occurred at the residence of his cousin, the well-known sculptor, Mr. Michael Lawlor, removes the last of the famous war correspondents of the Victorian era. Curiously enough these were nearly all of Irish origin—

Russell, MacGahan, O'Shea, O'Donovan, and O'Kelly. The latter had the most eventful life of all, for he had fought as well as written in three continents. Of his work in America I cannot speak, but I remember his wonderfully full and vivid dispatches from the Soudan in *The Daily News* in the 'eighties. He sat for Roscommon since 1880, challenged a fellow M.P. to fight a duel, the last such challenge on record, and once on his return from the Soudan, 'bearded like the pard', was denied admission by the Commons doorkeeper.

M. J. WHITTY. Sir Edward Russell, the veteran editor of *The Liverpool Daily Post*, founded by M. J. Whitty, and the first penny daily paper published in the provinces, kindly writes me: 'I thank you very much for sending me your periodical. All that is in it about Michael James Whitty has interested me very deeply. He often talked to me about *The Dublin and London Magazine*, though he never went into particulars. The associate of his at that time of whom he thought most, and most frequently spoke, was James Bacon, who, as you know, eventually became Vice Chancellor'. I remember Sir James Bacon well. He hung on to the Bench until he was 88, in spite of the clamour of a section of the Press, which stated that he was always asleep, and lived to be 97. I wonder had he any Irish connection?

"Post Bag", Vol. VIII, Nos. 7 & 8 (Feb. & March 1917), 87.

O'DONOVAN'S SUPPLEMENT (Vol. VII., p.163). My extract from Rev. Dr. Todd's Catalogue (1869) should have read:

> 1433. A fair copy of the unpublished portion of O'Donovan's Irish Glossary. The *Supplement* to O'Reilly's *Irish Dictionary*, published by Mr. Duffy, contains only those words which were found in Dr. O'Donovan's copy of O'Reilly on the blank sheets with which it was interleaved.. But a large number of words and additions were written by Dr. O'Donovan on the printed pages of O'Reilly, which are omitted in Duffy's edition. These are collected in the present volume. Folio.

This MS appears to have been bought by Mr. Figgis [from] Messrs. Hodges, Foster and Co. for £2 5s. Perhaps this MS or its original is in the Royal Irish Academy or Trinity College Library, Dublin. Edward O'Reilly's *Irish Dictionary* first appeared in 1817. A new edition was published in 1821. Duffy's edition, containing John O'Donovan's *Supplement*, first appeared in 1864, and I think the preliminary advertisements stated that the Irish type had been specially designed by George Petrie. The editor's name has not yet been traced. Duffy's edition was re-issued in 1877, and (without date) in later years. (SEÁMUS

Ó CASAIDE).

"Queries and Replies", Vol. VIII, Nos. 7 & 8 (Feb. & March 1917), 88.

EDMUND GETTY. I acquired lately a thick quarto MS volume consisting of papers read before a learned society which met in the Belfast Institution in 1822-23. They deal with the principal vegetable productions used in manufactures and for other useful purposes. Appended are beautifully executed coloured drawings of various plants. The author was Edmund Getty (1799-1857), for some time Secretary of the Belfast Harbour Board, and a frequent contributor to *The Ulster Journal of Archeology*, 1st series. [...] (DAVID KENNEDY).

J. S. Crone, "A Rogue's Memoirs", Vol. VIII, Nos. 9 & 10 (April & May 1917), 105.

The name and ill-fame of RICHARD PIGOTT, journalist, forger, and perjurer, are fast fading into a well-deserved oblivion. But the historical delver of future ages, when he comes to deal with the Ireland of the last half-century, may, perhaps, display some curiosity concerning him, even as they do today, regarding, say—Titus Oates. As some correspondence of his with Mr. Figgis, once head of the well-known publishing firm of Hodges and Figgis, Dublin, relative to his book *Recollection of an Irish Nationalist Journalist*, has recently come into my possession, a few notes thereon may not be without some interest to some readers, as, in my opinion, they afford, as nearly all letters do, some indication of the character of the man. Writing from 17 Vesey Place, Kingstown, under date 3rd February 1882, he says: 'I propose calling upon you about a book I have some intention of publishing, and meantime I would be obliged if you would look into the matter so that you may be able to give me an accurate idea of how much it would cost to bring it out and advertise it. I would not undertake it at all unless I could calculate on making something out of it, as I have other work on hand, with which the writing of it would interfere to some extent, so that I want to be in a position to decide whether to go on with it or not'. The reply was evidently satisfactory and the MS delivered. On 16th April he writes: 'I send proofs by this post. I have been obliged to make considerable additions to the last few chapters, but it was necessary. I send the Preface enclosed. The printers can, of course, make out the contents. They have only to set up the chapter headings. I think it would be wise not to put my name on the title page. Personal Recollections by a person looks bad. I have put my name at the foot of the preface, and that will do just as well as if it were on the Title [...]'

"Editor's Gossip", Vol. VIII, Nos. 9 & 10 (April & May 1917), 110.

Mr. James Carson is engaged in collating and arranging the voluminous literature relating to Lisburn and district, and publishing it in *The Lisburn Standard* under the title "Some Extracts from the Records of Old Lisburn and the Manor of Killutagh". The articles commenced in October 1916, and are expected to run till the end of this year. The Notes appearing in January and February deal with local literary men. In 1909 he published in collaboration with his wife, Sara Coburn Carson, B.A. [...] a *History of the Carsons of Monanton, Co. Monaghan*. This volume, in addition to the family history, contains a large amount of information relating to the County of Monaghan. In 1914 they published in *The Irish Presbyterian* a series of articles entitled "The Cahans Exodus", dealing with the emigration of practically an entire Presbyterian Congregation of some 300 souls to America. Henry Ford, of Princeton University, refers to these articles in his book, *The Scotch-Irish in America* (London 1915), and quotes largely from them.

In the issue of *An Claidheamh Soluis* for 20th January 1917, our scholarly correspondent, Mr. Seamus O'Casaide, B.L. published some very interesting notes on Peadar O'Conaill, including S. H. O'Grady's description of the autograph MS (Egerton 83) of the *Dictionary* in the British Museum, and also gave extracts from a printed (Limerick 1813) prospectus of the *Dictionary*.

"Notice of New Books", Vol. VIII, Nos. 9 & 10 (April & May 1917), 112.

LORD EDWARD: A STUDY IN ROMANCE, BY KATHARINE TYNAN (SMITH, ELDER). Readers of Mrs. Hinkson's autobiographical writings need not be to be told of the love and veneration in which she holds Lord Edward Fitzgerald, the rebel chieftain of '98, and his descendants, even to the fifth generation. For the materials of this present volume she selected telling passages from family memoirs and biographies. With entire sympathy, exquisite skill and cunning workmanship, she has deftly woven them into a continuous and thrilling narrative, supplying where necessary connecting links. It was a happy thought incited her to do so. For in the telling she brings out all that was best in that most remarkable family, of which 'Eddy' was the merriest member. But was it wise to revive the long dead rumour that his step-father Ogilvie acted as his betrayer? Even Sam Neilson, true as steel, was at one time so accused, as well as others, until the researches of Dr. Madden and W. J. Fitzpatrick revealed the real traitor.[...]

A PORTRAIT OF THE ARTIST AS A YOUNG MAN. BY JAMES JOYCE (The Egoist, Ltd.) In spite of the serious drawbacks to be mentioned later, truth compels one to admit that this pseudo autobiography of Stephen Dedalus, a weakling and a dreamer makes fascinating reading. We read it at a single sitting. The hero's schooldays at Clongowes Wood, and later at Belvedere, are graphically and doubtless, faithfully portrayed, as is the visit to Cork in company with his father, a clever ne'er-do-well, gradually sinking in the social scale. One of the strongest scenes in the book is the description of the Christmas dinner party during the black year of 1891, when Nationalist Ireland was riven to the centre over the Parnell 'split'. Mr. Joyce is unsparing in his realism, and his violent contrasts—the brothel, the confessional—jar on one's finer feelings. So do the quips and jeers of the students, in language unprinted in literature since the days of Swift and Sterne, following on some eloquent and orthodox sermons! That Mr. Joyce is a master of a brilliant descriptive style and handles his dialogue as ably as any living writer is conceded on all hands, and, oh! the pity of it. In writing thus is he just to his fine gifts? Is it even wise, from a worldly point of view—mercenary, if you will—to dissipate one's talents on a book which can only attain a limited circulation?—for no clean-minded person—could possibly allow it to remain within reach of his wife, his sons or daughters. Above all, is it Art? We doubt it.

"Denis Florence McCarthy", Vol. VIII, Nos. 9 & 10 (June & July 1917), 121.

On 26th May, 1817, at 24 Lower Sackville Street, Dublin, a house which occupied the site of the erstwhile Imperial Hotel, Denis Florence the only son of John McCarthy, a descendant of the old Clan Macaura, was born. Intended for the priesthood, the boy, after preliminary schooling in Dublin, where he showed his interest in Spanish, which later bore such abundant fruit, was sent to Maynooth, where he had as class-fellow the late Cardinal McCabe. Very early McCarthy showed a decided taste towards literature, and ere he reached his seventeenth birthday had published some poems in *The Dublin Satirist*, and continued his contributions in prose and verse for a couple of years. He then formed a connection with *The Evening Packet*, a journal to which he felt 'deeply indebted for many acts of literary courtesy and kindness'. When *The Nation* was exactly one year old he was welcomed to its pages by Gavan Duffy as 'a young recruit', and there for the next six years appeared many, a stirring ballad and scholarly review, mainly pseudonymously. [...]

"Some Interesting Manuscripts", Vol. VIII, Nos. 9 & 10 (June & July 1917), 125.

Messrs. Sotheran, of the Strand and Piccadilly, having purchased the correspondence of the one-time Premier, Earl Russell (1792-1878), which covers a period of seventy years, have issued a most interesting catalogue. The various letters and documents therein, cast a flood of light upon the politics of the time, in which Ireland played no inconspicuous part, and are of much literary interest, also, for "Lord John", as well as writing a play, a novel and a history, was the literary executor and biographer of Thomas Moore. A verse from an unfinished poem of 21 pages shows his youthful enthusiasm for Lord Edward Fitzgerald:

> Erect and firm Lord Edward stood,
> His glorious aim his country's good;
> And tho' the scornful lip, may style
> His cause insane, his comrades vile,
> His name shall long endure.

Another fragment of 12 lines entitled "The Irish" was enclosed in a note to Moore in 1833.

"Maginn and *Blackwood*", Vol. VIII, Nos. 9 & 10 (June & July 1917), 127.

In the Centenary Number of *Blackwood's Magazine*, (April, 1917) the following appreciation appears from the pen of Charles Whibley.

'At the outset, then, the weight of conducting the *Magazine* fell upon Wilson and Lockhart. And then suddenly there burst upon Prince's Street a new contributor, who came nowhither, who gave no address of his own, and who for a long while refused even to reveal his name. He wrote from Minerva Rooms, Cork, and signed his letters with the mystic initials "R.T.S.", which he pretended stood for Ralph Tuckett Scott. Presently he declared that he was called James Higginson, and only after a long interval wrote himself down as William Maginn, of Trinity College, Dublin. His name and address mattered not a jot. What was of importance is that he fell at once into the ways and thoughts of "Maga". He assumed to himself all the loves and hates of Wilson and Lockhart. He outdid them both in attacking the stronghold of Cockney-dom, and those that took shelter therein. Thus a firm alliance was founded on sympathy, not on sycophancy, for Maginn was a born Tory, with a rollicking humour, which none of his contemporaries surpassed. And he was to boot a finished scholar. A man whose versions of Homer were edited by John Conington and praised by Matthew Arnold, need not fear to face the sternest criticism. And all that he knew, all his Irish wit, all his infinite skill in burlesque, were freely given to the cause of the *Magazine*. "Christopher says it is quite astonishing", wrote Blackwood to Maginn, "how you enter so completely into the very essence and spirit of "Maga", just as if you had all along been seated with me at Ambrose's, where the highest of our fun was concocted". So he was admitted instantly into the inner circle. He is found capping verses with Wordsworth, receiving complacently the praises of Coleridge, daring to lay a hand on the "Noctes" themselves, and doing and saying all that became a friend and ally of the Professor. For the *Magazine* he created the famous O'Doherty, sketched the famous duel of Ensign Brady, and (incidentally) wrote the article which Edgar Poe parodied from *Blackwood's*. His activity and adaptability were alike remarkable, but he was not born for the success which comes only from sustained effort. He beat the pavement of London for many a year, fell into debt, and into the Fleet prison, lived to be befriended by Thackeray, and to make a second reputation for himself in the pages of *Fraser's Magazine*. If now and again, in the stress of life, he forgot that he was a gentleman, he never forgot that he was a scholar, and two admirable volumes of prose and verse remain to attest his skill and fancy. Such are the three whose names are most closely knit with the early fortunes of *Blackwood's Magazine*.'

"Penguin", writing in *The Nation* on the same subject says:

'Everybody knows how Lockhart and Wilson set *Blackwood's* upon its legs. But while Lockhart and Wilson are remembered, their chief ally, Dr. Maginn, has dropped out of notice. Yet Maginn would form a capital peg for an account of the periodical literature of the first part of the nineteenth century. The original of Thackeray's Captain Shandon, he was a man of varied learning and brilliant gifts, who never did himself justice. The late Dr. Garnett describes him as "a perfectly ideal magazinist", and he was that and something more. He shares with Lockhart and Wilson the credit for the success of *Blackwood's Magazine*. He was one of the founders of *Fraser's*, and neither Thack-eray nor Carlyle did so much to make it popular. He helped to conduct *The Standard*, and he was one of the contributors to John Murray's newspaper, *The Representative*, with which Disraeli was connected. In addition to the part he played in journalism, Maginn deserves to be remembered for other qualities. He was a wit as well as a scholar, and a parodist as well as a poet. He was an admirable story teller who with a little more industry, might have made his name as a novelist. And his critical writings, if abusive and libellous, were so lively and learned that Dr. Saintsbury declares in his *History of Criticism* that if Maginn "could have only kept his hand from the glass and his pen from mere gambols or worse, he not only might, but would have been one of the most considerable of English critics". Surely here is a subject for a biography that would be a welcome addition to the world of books.'

John Francis MacEntee, "The Tranp" Vol. VIII, Nos. 9 & 10 (June & July 1917), 129.

The Tramp

The lonely road, the open road,
    And the wind swept in from the sea,
The swinging trees and bending own
    And the fight with the rain for me.
The long dim road, the dim wet road,
    Stretching out to hills, afar,
With the massed cities of Dawn in the East,
    And the shuddering Morning Star.
With the moorcock's cry and the herd bull's roar
    All the voices that wake the morn,
And out in the silent and sleeping west
    The reveille call of a horn.
Give wives to fools, give gold to knaves,
    To breed and to bear misery
The long dim road, the open road,
    And the freedom of God give me.
              JOHN FRANCIS MACENTEE.

NOTE. John Francis MacEntee, the author of the above verses, was one of the commanders of the Louth contingent of the Sinn Féin Volunteers during the Irish Rebellion 1916. Having surrendered with P. H. Pearse and others, he was deported to Stafford. He was afterwards brought back to Dublin, tried by court martial, and sentenced to death. The death sentence was, however, commuted to that of penal servitude for life, which he is now undergoing in Dartmoor Convict Prison. The poem is published by permission of the author's literary executor, Mr. Padraic Gregory, who is at present preparing a complete volume of Mr. MacEntee's poems for the Press.

The Irish Book Lover
Vol. XVI
(Jan. & Feb. 1928 to July–Dec. 1928)

Séamus Ó Casaide, "Editorial", Vol. XVI, No. 1 (Jan. & Feb. 1928), 1.

Founded in 1909 by Doctor J. S. Crone, M.R.I.A., *The Irish Book Lover* was conducted for many years by its original founder and editor, who by his splendid example of wide and accurate knowledge conveyed in an agreeable manner attracted the contributions of the best authorities on Irish literature and biography.

Owing to his continued exile from Éire, Doctor Crone found himself unable to retain the editorship of *The Irish Book Lover* and it is now reestablished under a new editor with the full approval and the very welcome assistance of its predecessor.

It is proposed to issue *The Irish Book Lover* on every alternate month during the year 1928 and to re-consider at the close of the year the advisability of monthly publication.

The new editor trusts that *The Irish Book Lover* will acquire an ever-widening circle of readers and that it will continue to develop as a medium by which students engaged in research on work on various Irish subjects may be brought into contact with a view to mutual aid and encouragement.

Notes on forthcoming books of Irish interest will be welcomed from publishers and books sent to the editor will be placed in the hands of those best fitted to appreciate their worth. In the advertising columns may be inserted notices regarding books for sale or books wanted and through this section devoted to the technique of book production it is hoped that some appreciation of the aesthetics of bibliography will gradually become general.

Readers will help materially towards the success of the *Book Lover* by sending the editor the names of friends likely to be interested.

Iarraim ar mhuinntir na Gaedhilge breis eolais do sholátar dhúinn ar litridheacht na hÉireann agus ar daoinibh do shaothraigh an Ghaedhealg agus rinne a ndícheall cum í do choimeád beó.

J. S. Crone, "Sgéala ó Chathair na gCeó", Vol. XVI, No. 1 (Jan. & Feb. 1928), 2.

In the first place, allow me to offer you my best wishes and hearty congratulations on your assuming the editorial control of a new series of *The Irish Book Lover.* May you never find a thorn in the cushion of your editorial chair, your occupancy of it be as long and happy as mine was, your contributors as able and generous, and your subscribers as loyal.

On the 8th ult. I attended a meeting of the British Academy. The occasion being the delivery of the John Rhys Memorial Lecture. The president, the Earl of Balfour, being unavoidably absent, the chair was taken by Professor Tout, who, in a few appropriate words introduced the chosen lecture, Mr. Robin Flower is lecture of the Department of MSS, British Museum. Mr. Flower is lecturer in Gaelic in the University of London, chairman of scholars of the day, whose new volume of the *Catalogue of the Irish MSS in the British Museum* is a marvellous piece of scholarship, and a great advance on Standish [Hayes] O'Grady's epoch making volume. Mr. Flower chose for his subject 'Medieval Ireland', which he placed between 1172 and the beginning of the 19th century; indeed, in some respects it still existed in the Blasket Islands, about which he has a book in preparation. His racy translations of some Gaelic poems were well received by a large and enthusiastic audience.

Isn't it surprising how that old grand come-all-ye "Cowld Kilmainham Jail" crops up in the most unexpected places? Here it is in this month on the leader page of *The Times* no less! It appears that Sir John Ross, the last Lord Chancellor of Ireland, in his recently published *Pilgrim Scrip* tells how he and Percy French composed the song—two more claimants to the honour, mark you—that makes five I have known. But Mr. Fletcher, the literary executor of A. D. Godley, the late Public orator at Oxford, denies the statement, gives the date of its first appearance, and says the original MS is still in the possession of Godley's sister. The fact is: when the ballad first appeared in an English periodical, it was doubtless 'touched up' doubtless by several persons, real names introduced, and local colour added. It was printed as a ballad slip, and sung through the streets of Dublin. St. John Ervine in his *Parnell*, quotes it in full, and the curious can compare it with the original in *Lyra Frivola* (London 1900). So far, St. John has not replied to the charge.

Two Irish novels have been much talked of here this month. One, *Soldier Born* (Collins) from the pen of Conal O'Riordan, is the best that has yet appeared from the pen of that prolific and able writer. The story opens in the Dublin of George III, with the hanging of Dr John Esmond on Carlisle Bridge, and afterwards shifts to the London of the Regency.

There is one scene in Charlemont House that is equal to anything in Thackeray. The other, *Hanging Johnny* (Murray) is one of the shortest and most original works of fiction I have ever read. There are practically only three characters: the hangman, his wife, and a half-mad priest, and the attention is gripped in the first paragraph, and held enthralled to the last. Yet I am told the author, Myrtle Johnson, is only eighteen years old. If this be so, she is a genius.

Séamus Ó Casaide, "Three Irish Scribes of County Cork", Vol. XVI, No. 1 (Jan. & Feb. 1928), 4.

The following obituary notices taken from scraps of old Cork newspapers dated May 1837, April 1840 (?) and August 1845 (?) may have been written by John Windele, who, like Dr. John Murphy, Bishop of Cork, and Father Mat. Horgan of Blarney, was a good friend to Irish scholars:

MICHEAL ÓGE Ó LONGAIN. 'On the 17th inst. at Cnocbuidhe, in the North Liberties of this city, Michael Óge Ó Longain, aged 72 years. From the early age of 18 he devoted himself in a particular manner to the study and culture of his Native Language. He composed several pieces and transcribed nearly 300 volumes of Irish MSS thus rescuing from destruction several rare and curious specimens of the ancient literature of Ireland. During the troubles of 1798, he had some providential escapes from falling a victim to that persecution and unjust suspicion which pursued every ardent lover of his country, and from which his quietness and simplicity of character could not altogether protect him. A few hours before his death, still calm and confiding in a future hope, he breathed into the ear of an affectionate son, a short and expressive Irish stanza, which he wished to have inscribed on his tomb, showing that even at the last hour the strong and ruling passion of his life—the perpetuation of the language "of his own loved island of sorrow", was not entirely forgotten.'

Ó Longain died on 17th May, 1837, in the parish of Carrignavar near Cork city. A portrait and biography of this poet, scribe and United Irishman was published by Tadhg Ó Donnchadha, D.Litt., in the *Ivernian Journal*, 1909. Three generations of the family were distin-guished as Irish scribes, and specimens of their work are to be found in most of the important collections of Irish MSS.

SEÁN Ó DREADA. 'On Sunday, 23d ultimo, at Evergreen, aged seventy years, Mr. John Draddy, stone cutter, one of the most zealous, correct and indefatigable Irish copyists of the present day. For the last thirty years of his useful and meritorious life his leisure hours were mostly employed in rescuing from ruin and oblivion, by beautiful and correct transcripts, the various Irish Manuscripts, prose and verse, that he could possibly collect, or in instructing through the medium of their native language his poorer brethren in the principles of Religion and morality. Many tombstones in different parts of the County were epitaphed by him in the Irish character, among which, that erected to the memory of the late Thomas Sheahan, in the cemetery of St. Joseph, is not the least conspicuous. He died as he lived, calmly resigned and confiding in the mercies of his Redeemer.'

Ó Dreada died 23rd March, 1840 (?) at Evergreen, a suburb of Cork city. A MS. written by Ó Dreada in 1820 and now in the possession of Risteard Ó Foghludha has been used by two editors of Munster poets.

ÉAMONN Ó MATHGHAMHNA: 'On the 18th inst., in the 70th year of his age, Edmund O'Mahony, one of the last, and certainly the best of the Irish scribes of modern times. He was well versed in the ancient literature of his country which he cultivated with affectionate zeal and an enthusiastic perseverance. To the few collectors of Irish manuscript works in Cork city and county, who gave him employment in transcribing, his loss will be much felt, as he has not left many of equal ability, fidelity and honesty as a copyist, to represent him. His funeral was attended by the Rev. M. Horgan, and others of the local antiquaries; and the interment took place in the ancient and romantically situated cemetery of St. Senan, at Iniscarra—"the loved island"—near the confluence of the rivers Bride and Lee.'

Ó Mathghamhna died 18th August, 1845 (?) in or near Cork city. I have some of his Irish MSS, including one written by him at Fathadh for Donnchadh Ó Fionnagain in 1828 and describing the medical properties of various herbs (*An Lochrann*, 1927).

Séamus Ó Casaide, "The Anonymous Prefacer, 1722", Vol. XVI, No. 1 (Jan. & Feb. 1928), 10.

An important work on the history of Ireland, in the middle of the 17th century is the—

> *Memoirs of ... The Marquis of Clanrickarde, ... To which is Prefix'd, A Dissertation* ... London: Printed for James Woodman, at Camden's Head, under Wills's Coffee-House, in Bow-Street, Covent-Garden. MDCCXXII.

The *Memoirs* occupying 259 (8vo.) pages are preceded by eight pages of one hundred and fifty-three subscribers' names (including some notable Irish and foreign personages) and the most interesting part (pp.i-clxxxiv) of the volume which consists of "A Dissertation, Wherein several Passages of these Memoirs are illustrated With a Digression containing an Account of the Education and Studies of the ancient Irish

Fillim, or Poets, and of their Works; out of which Dr. Keating has chiefly compiled his Historical Collections relating to Ireland. To which are added some Particulars of Dr. Keating's Life, and the Occasion of his making those Collections". The *Memoirs* with the Dissertation were again issued over twenty years later with the imprint:

> Dublin: Printed by S. Powell, For C. Connor, at Pope's Head on the Blind-Key, near Essex-Gate, MDCCXLIV.

The author of the Dissertation had occasion to indicate the limitations of Keating's *Foras Feasa Ar Eirinn* as an authority on early Irish history, and commented several on the assertions in certain recent Advertisements of an English Version, 'which is getting ready for the Press'. This criticism was apparently directed against Dermod O'Connor (*I.B.L.*, III, pp.125, 155) whose translation of Keating was published early in 1723 with a rejoinder accusing 'this Prefacer' of having only an elementary knowledge of the Irish language, and of having for some years past promised the public a *History of Ireland*, which he had never produced. The controversy was continued in the *Post Boy* of January 1723, in which the Prefacer stated that he had 'in Foreign Universities taken all the Degrees in the Civil Law, and resided in one of our Inns of Court these last twelve years', and that as to his knowledge of Irish he was prepared to 'submit to a trial with the modest Mr. O'Connor, who thought he had Irish enough when he applied to him for assistance, and offered him a share in the profits of the Edition'.

The Prefacer's identity was not revealed by O'Connor and for over two centuries it has remained a problem. The British Museum cataloguer's authority for assigning them to Robert Lindsay, a Puisne Judge in Dublin and a subscriber to O'Connor's work (1723) is unknown according to Henry R. Plomer (*I.B.L.*, III, 127).

William Nicholson, Bishop of Derry, in his *Irish Historical Library* (Dublin 1724) judged from the tone of the Dissertation that the writer was not of his view in politics or religion, and said 'The Anonymous Publisher has indeed prefix'd a Dissertation of his own, wherein he pretends to illustrate some dark Passages in these *Memoirs*. But, keeping himself in the Shades, we want to be better inform'd how far his Conjectures may be rely'd on'.

The Very Rev. W. Canon Burke, P.P. of Lismore, the greatest authority on the Ireland of the *Penal Days*, informed me some time ago that the author of the *Dissertation* of 1722 was Silvester Lloyd, the Franciscan, who was regarded by his contemporaries as the ablest man in Ireland, whether of native or foreign extraction.

While Guardian of the Franciscan Friars in Dublin, Silvester Lloyd was instrumental in rebuilding their chapel; which had fallen down one Sunday and killed many who were waiting to hear him preach. When George the First's Dublin Parliament and local Privy Council were engaged in drafting a Bill of peculiar ferocity against the Catholic clergy, the latter body deputed Lloyd to wait on the Duke of Orleans, Regent of France, to use his influence with England, then anxious for peace with France, to prevent the Bill from becoming law. Lloyd who appears to have had powerful friends in France was successful. Lloyd was appointed Bishop of Killaloe on 25th September 1729. In 1733 he was in Brussels in ill health, and by Papal Brief dated 29th May 1739, he was translated to the see of Waterford and Lismore. In his will dated 9th August 1743, (published by Canon Carrigan in the *Waterford Archeological Journal* (1897) Lloyd mentioned his two half-sisters, Jane and Rebecca Lockington. He was then 'weak in body' and on 20th August 1743, Jacobus Rex, dating from Rome, recommended Thomas Stritch, D.D., (a native of Clonmel) to be Lloyd's coadjutor and the Papal Brief was dated 18th December, 1743, It is stated (Power's *Waterford and Lismore*, 1912) that symptoms of acute mental trouble, prevented Stritch's consecration. Lloyd, who had been active in the Jacobite movement in Paris, in Clare and in Tipperary, fled to the Continent in 1744, and a vain search was made for him in Waterford by the Hanoverian authorities. Peter Creagh, Dean of Limerick, was appointed Lloyd's coadjutor in 1745, and Lloyd died in Paris in 1747, but his will was not proved until August 1748.

Joseph Gillow (*Bibliographical Dictionary of the English Catholics*) relying apparently on the Rev. John Kirk's *Biographical Collections* (MS in the archives of Westminster diocese?) stated that Silvester Lewis Lloyd was a Welshman and was professed at the English Franciscan Convent at Douay, but at present I cannot say whether either of Gillow's statements is correct, or whether the person mentioned by Gillow was identical with or related to Bishop Lloyd.

I must hold over a note on the editions (in Irish or English) of the catechetical works published by Lloyd over his initials "S. Ll."

Séamus Ó Casaide, "The Last Irish Scribe", Vol. XVI, No. 1 (Jan & Feb. 1928), 13.

A familiar and venerable figure is missing from the great Dublin libraries. The Rev. Patrick M. MacSweeney in his fine study *A Group of Nation Builders: O'Donovan-O'Curry-Petrie* (C.T.S.I. 1913) commented on the attraction which the Summer Hill district of Dublin city appears, to have possessed for the Irish scholars who settled in Dublin about ninety years ago. After his return from the United States, Seán Ó Faircheallaigh was a resident in that district for about fifty years, and during that long period was a faithful supporter of the various movements for the preservation of the Irish language and for the cultivation of traditional Irish music—notably that of the Union pipes.

For many years he was engaged on research work in the Record Office and other depositories of manuscripts for Irish-Americans and others interested in genealogical or historical inquiries, and his classical education stood him in good stead while employed in calendaring and transcribing historical documents in connection with the process for canonising some of the Irish martyrs. It was while engaged on this latter work on 11th November 1927, in the Franciscan Library, Merchant's Quay, Dublin, that he was unexpectedly seized with the illness which terminated fatally before he reached his home.

On the 15th he was buried in the family grave at Rathmore, Co. Meath, not far distant from Telltown—the historic Tailte where he was born about eighty years ago—the, son of Séamus Ó Faircheallaigh and Jane Boland. The surviving relatives include his widow (Mary Anne Flynn) and a younger brother (Criostdóir of Edenderry) as well as several nephews and nieces. The death of his nonagenarian brother (Séamus of Tatestown) about six months previously had affected Seán very much.

With this simple, kind and courtly scholar an interesting link with the past is gone. Seán was the last person employed officially in Trinity College, Dublin, and in the Royal Irish Academy on the transcription of documents in the Irish language. *Solus na bhflaitheas d'a anam.*

Stephen J. Brown, S.J., "The *Book Lover* and the Libraries", Vol. XVI, No. 1 (Jan. & Feb. 1928), 14.

[...] Irish libraries and other organizations concerned with books have their own particular problems which are not quite those of England, and the Irish public is or ought to be particularly interested in certain classes of books—books in the Irish language and books of peculiar Irish interest, ethnographical, archaeological, social, historical, or literary.

With our limited public and its general indifference about books, it may be actually a better thing that public and publisher, librarian, bibliographer, bookseller and reviewer should meet, as it were, in one periodical and establish points of contact. [...]

Colm Ó Lochlainn, "A Printer's Device",Volume 16, No. 1 (Jan. & Feb. 1928), 15.

In *The Irish Book Lover* for August-September, 1924 appeared a query regarding Thomas Brown, who had a workshop in High Street, Dublin 'at the Sign of the Three Candlesticks' and in the following number I mentioned that I had also discovered a little Latin Grammar with a similar imprint. As I had for some years previous to 1924 been issuing booklets of prose and poetry 'at the Candle Press' some interest attached to this discovery.

In the winter of 1916 Seán Mac Giollarna (then editor of *An Claidheamh* [*Soluis*] and now District Justice for the County of Galway) and myself formed the idea of getting suitable material and publishing a series of booklets of Irish interest. Casting around for a suitable style or title, it struck me that the triad (from the volume edited in the Todd Lecture Series, R.I.A. by Kuno Meyer) *Tri caindle forosnat cach ndorcha*: *fir, aicned, ecna* ('Three candles that light up every darkness: Truth, Nature and Knowledge') was very suitable as a legend for the sort of book we meant to issue, and so the name of The Candle Press was chosen. I myself, in common with the public, thought the title rather new and original and it was many years before I realised that I was not the ori-ginator but rather the reviver of the Sign of the Three Candles.

In 1926 when I decided to set up my printing press in Fleet Street, it gave me great joy to find that a large sign board hung outside the premises. This I took down and painted with the Sign of the Three Candles which—as Katisha says—has been much admired.

In October last I read before the Bibliographical Society a few notes on the books known to have been issued by Brown. These notes I hope to print in a future issue, and I shall be very grateful if readers who may know anything further on the subject will write to me.

It is a strange and interesting development that here—centrally situated between Anglesea Street (where John O'Daly and Kennedy flourished in the middle of the 19th century) and Aston's Lane where the second-hand book merchants most do congregate—the device of the Three Candles should once again, after two hundred years hang over a bookshop as it did of old '*in vico vulgo vocato* High St.'

Séamus Ó Casaide, "John D'Alton's Manuscripts", Vol. XVI, No. 1, (Jan. & Feb. 1928), 16.

The following is a copy of a report made by me in December 1926, after an examination of the documents referred to, and prior to their acquisition by the University of Chicago:

'John D'Alton (1792-1867) barrister, poet and historian, who achieved fame by his histories of Drogheda, Boyle and Co. Dublin and other published works, had accumulated from the manuscripts and printed works in the chief libraries and public offices in Ireland and England a great collection of material bearing on the topography, genealogies and general history of Ireland—'the result of upwards of thirty years devoted application of study, time and income'. D'Alton's manuscript indexes and compilations were contained in some 200 volumes, 'all of the compiler's own collecting and handwriting'.

D'Alton made frequent private and public appeals for financial assistance, to publish from his manuscript collection Irish county histories and similar works, but his appeals were not responded to, and most of his materials remained in the possession of his family after his death.

Some of his, collections for county histories were sold to Sir T. Esmonde (Wexford) Mr. O'Connor (Sligo) the Marquis of Kildare (Kildare) Major Armstrong McDonnell (Clare) and Maurice Lenihan (Limerick and Tipperary). Two of the volumes relating to Tipperary became the property of Canon Power, M.R.I.A., of University College, Cork, a few years ago.

In recent years enquiries have been made through *The Irish Book Lover* and elsewhere relative to the present location of the D'Alton manuscripts, and a few years ago a grand-daughter of John D'Alton presented the surviving D'Alton manuscripts to the Rev. Patrick Dinneen [sic], D.Litt., the celebrated Irish scholar.

The manuscripts which passed into Dr. Dinneen's possession consist of some 153 volumes mostly of 8vo. size and practically all of them relate exclusively to Ireland. The extent to which the volumes are occupied with the small and compact script of the compiler varies considerably. Many of the volumes might be described as notebooks and in some cases they are made up of indexes to printed and manuscript sources, which D'Alton intended to use in preparing works for the press. Numerous letters from prominent Irishmen of the last century are loosely inserted in the notebooks. It is possible to identify most of the surviving volumes from the descriptive catalogue which D'Alton published with his *Annals of Boyle* (1845) and a special effort should be made to trace the volumes which have not passed into Dr. Dinneen's possession, as they would probably throw light on some of the rather cryptic references in the notebooks. The collection is of considerable interest and prior to the publications of O'Donovan, O'Curry, Petrie, Reeves and their successors must undoubtedly have been of great value. To estimate the value of the collection at the present day would necessitate a prolonged study of the manuscripts themselves, and of the numerous important publications on Irish history, topography and genealogy, which have appeared since the manuscripts were compiled. Undoubtedly the whole collection will well repay careful investigation by students of any phase of Ireland's history, and probably it will be found that the information relating to the history of Irish and Anglo-Irish families is not the least valuable portion of the fruits of D'Alton's labours. Included in the collection are a few books which are not in D'Alton's handwriting and the most valuable and interesting of these are three quarto volumes written in Irish, probably in the earlier part of the 18th century. The first of the three Irish MSS contains the *History of Ireland* (*Foras Feasa ar Eirinn*), by Seuthrun Keitinn in the handwriting of two different scribes. The *Dionbhrollach* and the *Liber Primus*, and a leaf of the *Liber Secundus* in a good early 18th century (or possibly late 17th century) hand occupies nearly half the volume, and a later scribe using a stronger paper has continued the History (from the opening of *An Dara Leabhor*) in the latter part of the volume, which appears to have belonged at one time to a Rev. Mr. Marron. The second Irish MS written in a good hand contains Keating's *Eochuir Sciath an Aifrinn*, and also another religious treatise (beginning with *Feria Secunda*) in Irish prose on the Life of Christ. Both tracts were transcribed in 1703 by Henri Ó Caiside (macConnla) for Brian Maguidhir (mac Conchubhair mhodharrdha mhic Briain mhic Seaain). The following names (of owners?) have been written in the volume at different periods: Semus [sic] Ó Colladhtane (1771) John, Mary, Judy and Bridget Henegan, Thos. Woods, Rev. Mr. Bennett (?) of Killucan (?) and (Rev.?) Shemus A. Marron. Loosely inserted in the preceding volume is a sheet folded to form sixteen pages (8vo) on which Labhras Ó Connghadh (Conway?) transcribed inter alia circa 1780 without giving the author's name Donnchadh Ruadh MacConmara's poem *Eachtra an Sgolaire*. The third Irish MS consists of various pieces in prose and verse in the handwriting of Feidhlim O'Neill including an abridgment of Irish Grammar, various Litanies in Irish, *Agallamh idir Dochtuir Thaleu*; *us agus Fior-Bhochtan*, another religious dialogue (after Dionysius Sicanus) in nine chapters and partly in verse, entitled *Agallamh an Anma agus an Carp*, and some poems including "*An Siogaidh Romhanach*", "*A nuair caoinabh air saoithibh na hearionn*" (Seadhan Ó Conuill cct) "A dhaoinne caoinabh ar do crioca deighnach", *Maible sheimh Ni Chealluighe* (without Carolan's name) *"Tearc aon maith aca da bhfuil, Laoidh na mBuadhi"* (Colum Cille cct) *"Do chaill Éire a ceile fire"* (Cathal Magruaraidh an sagart Ulltach cct) and *"Mo cheille mo chead searc mo leannan ruin"* (Cathal Magruaraidh cct). This MS belonged to James Bermingham in Galway in 1736 and 1737.'

J. S. Crone, "Sgéala Ó Cathair na gCeó", Vol. XVI, No. 2 (March & April 1928), 26.

It is a pleasure to note that the fine literary gifts of two well-known woman writers have descended to their daughters. Miss Pamela Hinkson made a hit with her first novel last year and now the daughter of Mrs. Skrine—better known by her pen name of Moira O'Neill—has published her first, an Anglo-Irish sporting novel, *Young Entry* (Elkin Mathews) over the pseudonym of "M. J. Farrell", which has had the rare advantage of being warmly praised by a critic on the wireless.

On the 18th March, the Irish Literary Society gave a complimentary dinner to one of its original members Mr. Michael MacDonagh of *The Times*, the doyen of the press gallery in the British Parliament. Mr. MacDonagh, a Limerick man and one of the pleasantest personalities possible to meet, came to London to report the unhappy proceedings in Committee Room XV, for the old *Freeman* in 1891, the time of the 'Parnell Split', joined *The Times* staff in 1894 and has since continuously served it. Though such a busy journalist he has found time to contribute to all the leading monthlies and write some admirable works. These fall into two sections, one dealing with his political experiences in the House, such as *The Book of Parliament*; *Parliament: Its Romance, Comedy and Pathos*; and *The Reporter's Gallery*. The other—and from our point of view the better because of its Irish associations—comprises *Irish Graves in England*; *Bishop Doyle*; *The Viceroy's Postbag*; *Ireland at the Front*, and *The Home Rule Movement*. He inherited the papers of that one time great orator but unstable politician O'Connor Power and now he has been appointed literary executor and biographer of his life-long friend William O'Brien.

Writing of Irish biography reminds me that his brother Frank MacDonagh, also a capable journalist, has almost ready a *Life of Isaac Butt*. I understand that Capt. Harrison of *Irish Truth* is engaged on a work dealing with the later years of his old leader, Parnell. I hear that Monsignor Walsh of Glasthule has written a biography of Archbishop Walsh, which is to appear in autumn, and that the Rev. Dr. Toner is engaged on a similar work dealing with Cardinal Logue, whilst a full and much needed life of John O'Donovan is also being prepared. In addition, it is stated that Mr. Healy completed his reminiscences before leaving the Vice-Regal Lodge, which should act as a counterpoise to Liam O'Flaherty's so-called biography, and the long looked for reminiscences of "T.P." are announced in two volumes by a London publisher.

This all points to a rich crop of what generally proves to be 'best-sellers', yet not without risk, for a friend of mine was asked by an insurance company to read and advise upon a recent book of reminiscences by an Irish lawyer, whose publisher was anxious to insure against the risk of an action for libel or libels. The lesson taught a whilom Dublin journalist had not been forgotten.

Mr. James Stephens' latest work *Etched in Moonlight* (Macmillan) which by the way includes his pseudonymous booklet, *Hunger*, first issued from the Sign of the Three Candles, has met with a chorus of praise from all the critics with one notable exception. He gave a Poetry Recital on 27th March under the auspices of the English Association at the Central Hall, Westminster, and the great building was packed with an enthusiastic audience. Mr. Stephens is an elocutionist of rare power, in addition to his remarkable gift of humour, and literally held his hearers enthralled, as only a great orator can. He chose amongst others "The Golden Bird"; "The Fur Coat"; "The Main Deep"; "Nora Criona"; "To the Queen of the Bees" and "Peggy Mitchell", and added to their beauty and understanding by his faultless delivery.

"A Note on the First Fifteen Volumes of *The Irish Book Lover*", Vol. XVI, No. 2 (March & April 1928), 34.

The first number of *The Irish Book Lover* was dated August, 1909, and a new volume was begun each August down to and including August, 1921 (Vol. XIII). It was published in monthly parts but after Volume VII, No. 6 (Jan. 1916) the monthly publication became more or less nominal by the unavoidable necessity of publishing frequent double numbers and, in three instances, triple numbers. Nevertheless the numbers and dates are consecutive down to and including Volume XIII, Nos. 9-10 (April-May 1922) when publication was interrupted. Whyte and Salmond, London—with a change in title to Salmon & Co. in April 1911—printed the first twelve volumes and the first part (Nos. 1-2) of Volume XIII. The rest of Volume XIII. was printed by Cahill & Co., Ltd., Dublin. From the completion of Volume I until Messrs. Cahill took over the printing, the parts bore the following supple-mentary imprints, in addition to that of the printers: Hanna & Neale, Dublin (to

Vol. VI, No. 2); F. Hanna, Dublin (Vol. VI ,No. 3 to Vol. VIII, Nos. 1-2); W. G. Neale, Dublin (from Vol. VI, No. 3); and Hugh Greer, Belfast (from Vol. XII, Nos. 1-2).

Publication was resumed in January, 1924, with Volume XIV No. 1. This volume consisted of six monthly parts and three double numbers, completing the year. It was printed for subscribers by Delmege Trimble, Armagh, and the title page of the volume bears the imprint 'Armagh: The Armagh Guardian Office, 1924'. Numbers 5, 6 and 7, 8 of this volume were issued without wrappers, tables of contents or printer's name.

Volume XV (1925) was published as a quarterly by the Talbot Press Ltd., Dublin, and in a different format, foolscap quarto, whereas the earlier volumes were, like the current one, demy octavos. The four parts for the year were issued. No numbers were published in 1926 and 1927.

A separate title page and index was printed for each of the fifteen volumes.

THE PLATES: From time to time half-tone plates were issued as supplements to *The Book Lover*. They were simply 'laid in' and their absence from a volume can seldom be detected since there were no lists of plates printed with the title pages, and they are not mentioned in the tables of contents and seldom even in the articles which they illustrate. Moreover, some of the plates bear neither the name of the periodical nor the date of issue. It is thought, therefore, that the following list of these plates will be useful to librarians and others, including bookbinders. Considerable pains have been taken to make it complete but there may be omissions, as no official record of the plates has been preserved. The editor would he grateful for information of such omissions.

LIST OF PLATES ISSUED WITH *THE IRISH BOOK LOVER*, VOLS. I-XV.

Vol. No.	Issue No.	Subject
I	9	Sir Samuel Ferguson
II	3	J. D'Arcy Sirr
	4	William Sampson
III	3	Facsimile title page (Carrick-on-Suir 1796)
IV	1	Facsimile title page (Drogheda 1802)
	2	Patrick MacGill
	3	Facsimile title page (Clonmel 1811)

	6	James Stephens
	8	Rev. Edward MacCoy
	10	William Blacker
V	1	Alfred Perceval Graves
	2	Isaac Butt
	6	Edward Dowden
	7	P. W. Joyce
	10	T. D. Sullivan
	11	Joseph Brenan
	12	Padric Gregory
VI	3	Thomas Davis
	4	Statue of ThomasDavis
	10	Fragment *New Testament* (Belfast 1700)
	1	Rev. W. T. Latimer
VII	1	Bishop Murphy's book-plate
	3	George W. Russell
	4	John Mitchel
	6	Selina Bunbury
IX	1-2	Richard Dowling
XII	1-2	James Montgomery
	6-7	"Barney Maglone"
	10-12	Thomas Stott
XIV	2	John Anderson
	4	William Allingham (intended for binding in No.3)

Séamus Ó Casaide, "Newbery's Irish Accidence: 1562-63", Vol. XVI, No. 3 (May & June 1928), 61.

No copy of any book printed in the Irish language before 1571 has yet been traced, though Irish phrases occur in a book printed as early as 1542. Edward Arber's *Transcript of the Registers of the Company of Stationers of London, 1554-1640*, (5 vols., Birmingham 1875-94) gives the following entry in the receipts from London stationers for the period from 22nd July 1562, to 22nd July 1563: 'Recevyd [of] Raufe Newbery for his lycense for pryntinge of an introduction or accidence in laten and Iresshe … iiij^{d}'.

Kuno Meyer (*Irisleabhar na Gaedhilge*, 1909) drew attention to the fact that it was about the same period, though perhaps later, that Baron Delvin prepared for the use of Queen Elizabeth a MS *Iryshe-Latten-Englishe Primer*, facsimiles of portions of which are given in Part IV, I (1882) of Gilbert's *Facsimiles of National Manuscripts of Ireland*. The original MS of Delvin's *Primer* from the Shirley Library (Lough Fea) was auctioned (lot 514) in July 1924 at Sotheby's (London) and acquired by Messrs. Maggs Bros., booksellers, London for £48. It subsequently figured as item 217 (but 'sold') in their Catalogue No. 456 (1924).

Colm Ó Lochlainn, "The Printer on Gaelic Printing", Vol. XVI, No. 3 (May & June 1928), 62.

The technicalities of Gaelic Printing have hitherto been given very scant attention, either by Printers, Typefounders, or Authors—the three crafts most intimately concerned.

Nothing less than a study of the problems by a group or commission representative of all three bodies would be likely to bring about any results, but for the moment it is useful to set forth the difficulties as seen by the Printer.

In the ordinary Roman Fount as used for Newspaper and book-work there are altogether 151 pieces, made up as follows:

> Capital 29; Small caps. 29; Lowercase letters (which includes the usual diphthongs and ligatures æ, œ, fi, ffi, fl, ffl, ff) 33; Points, i.e., punctuation marks and brackets, 10; Fractions, i.e., halves, quarters, thirds, and eighths, 9; Commercial signs, 8; Reference marks—i.e., asterisks, daggers, &c., 8; Braces, 3 sizes; Dashes, 3 lengths; Leaders, 1; Quads, 4 kinds; Spaces, 4 kinds.

This enumeration does not include accented letters (not often used in English Printing); italic type, which is so useful for emphasis; or the heavy black type called Clarendon, so much used for headings, subheadings, and (in school books) for important names or incidents. While Clarendon can be done without, the italic can hardly be, and a workable font of italic contains capitals, lowercase, and points—at least 72 characters, even if the figures, &c. are omitted. [...]

Half-Yearly Bibliography, Vol. XVI, No. 3 (May & June 1928), 64.

BIOGRAPHY

Viscount Bryce, O.M. 1838-1922. By H. A. L. Fisher. 8vo. 9pp. (Oxford University Press) 1/-.

David Corkey: A Life Story. By Ethel Corkey. 8vo. 288pp. (Religious Tract Society) [One of eight brothers who became Presbyterian ministers; worked in the Belfast slums, badly wounded when a chaplain in the war and died shortly after].

A Concise Dictionary Of Irish Biography. By John S. Crone, M.R.I.A. 8vo., viii + 270pp. (Talbot Press and Longmans) 10/6.

The Skull of Swift. By Shane Leslie. 8vo. (Chatto and Windus) 12/6. 'An extraordinary piece of biographic portraiture.'

Matt Talbot. By Sir Joseph Glynn. (Catholic Truth Society) 2/-.

DRAMA

The Long Road to Garranbragher. A play by J. B. MacCarthy. 8vo. 30pp (M. H. Gill) 1/6.

Original Comedies, Character Sketches, Dialogues and Recitations by Mr. and Mrs. McHardy Flint. 8vo. 96pp. (James Duffy) 2/-.

The Silver Tassie: A Tragi-Comedy in Four Acts. By Sean O'Casey 8vo. (Macmillan) 7/6.

Plays by Lennox Robinson. 8vo. (Macmillan) 10/6 Containing *The Round Table*; *Crabbed Youth*; *Portrait*; *The White Blackbird*; *The Big House*; *Give a Dog*—

The Playboy Of The Western World. By John M. Synge. Illustrated by John Keating. 4to. 112pp. (Allen and Union) 42/-.

Isolt of Ireland: A Legend in a Prologue and Three Acts. By John Todhunter. 8vo. 133pp. (Dent) 3/6.

FICTION

Kitty the Madcap. By M. McD. Bodkin. 8vo. 208pp. (Talbot Press) 2/6.

The Wayward Man. By St. John G. Ervine. 8vo. 375pp. (Collins) 7/6. 'The strongest impression left by this story is that of its little gallery of Belfast types'—*Times Literary Supplement*.

Young Entry. By M. J. Farrell. 8vo. (Elkin Mathews) 7/6. By Miss Skrine, a daughter of 'Moira O'Neill'.

Hanging Johnny. By Myrtle Johnston. 8vo. 309pp. (J. Murray) 7/6.

Irish Vignettes. By Ella MacMahon. 8vo. (The Bodley Head) 7/6.

Islanders. By Peadar O'Donnell. 8vo. (Cape) 6/- With an Introduction by Robert Lynd.

The Assassin. By Liam O'Flaherty. 8vo. (Cape) 7/6.

The Fairy Goose and Other Stories. By Liam O'Flaherty. 8vo. 58pp (Faber and Gwyer) 25/6.

Soldier Born. By Conal O'Riordan. 8vo. 292pp. (Collins) 7/6.

The Bog of Lilies. By Mrs. M. T. Pender. 8vo. 254pp. (Talbot Press) 3/6.

A Key to the Ulysses *of James Joyce.* By Paul Jordan Smith. 8vo. 89pp. (Chicago: Covici) 3 dollars.
Etched in Moonlight. By James Stephens. 8vo. (Macmillan) 7/6.
The World's Pilgrimage. By Eva Gore-Booth. 8vo. 118pp. (Longmans) 3/6.

HISTORY

The Black Book of Edgeworthstown and Other Memories, 1585-1817. By H. J. Butler and H. E. Butler. 8vo. xii + 260pp. (Faber and Gwyer) 18/-.
Spenser in Ireland. By Pauline Henley, M.A. 8vo. 231pp. (Cork University Publications and Longmans) 6/-.

MISCELLANEOUS

Hibernia, or the Future of Ireland. By Bolton C. Waller. 8vo. 96pp. (Kegan Paul) 2/6. 'A fair-minded survey of what has been done under the Free State'.
The Connaught Rangers, 2nd Batt. By Lieut.-Col. Jourdain and Edward Fraser. Vol. II. 8vo. xxiii + 545. (Royal United Service Institute) 40/-.
Songs of the Irish Gaels with English Translations. By Clandillon. (Oxford University Press) 10/-.
The Archæology of Ireland. By R. A. S. Macalister, M.A., D.Litt. 8vo. 390pp. (Methuen and Co) 16/-.

POETRY

Midsummer Eve. By Æ. 8vo. (Dulav.) 31/6.
Ad Perennis Vitae Fontem. Poems by J. L. Donaghy. 8vo. 32pp. (Dublin Minerva Press) 7/6.
The Scholar's Treasury: A Book of Irish Poetry. Selected by Stephen Gwynn. 8vo. 128pp. (Educational Company) 1/3.
Pomes Penyeach. By James Joyce. 16mo. 20pp. (Paris: Shakespear and Co) 1/-.
Poems. By S. R. Lysaght. 8vo. (Macmillan) 5/-. Comprises the author's two previous volumes, *Poems of the Known Way* and *Horizons and Landmarks.*
Ancient Irish Poetry. By Kuno Meyer. 8vo. (Constable) 3/6. A new edition.
By the Way: Songs and Fables. By Anne Page. 8vo. (Belfast: Quota Press) 1/-.
Piper's Tunes from Donegal and Antrim. By Elizabeth Shane. Illustrated. 8vo. 70pp. (Selwyn and Blount) 3/6.
Trivium Amoris and the Wooing of Artemis. By John Todhunter. 8vo.

72pp. (Dent) 3/6.
The Holy Wells of Orris and Other Poems. By R. N. D. Wilson. 8vo. 54pp. (John Lane) 6/-.

TOPOGRAPHY

Ireland. By Harrison Dale. Illustrated by A. Heaton Cooper. 8vo. xii + 208pp. (A. & C. Black) 7/6.
So This is Dublin. By M. J. MacManus. 8vo. 123pp. (Talbot Press) 2/6. 'A guide-book for Americans'.

U. D'A., "Padraic Ó Conaire", Vol. XVI, Nos. 4-6. (July–Dec. 1928), 74.

The death of Padraic Ó Conaire is a national loss, and Ireland present and future is the poorer. He went too soon, leaving great work undone, but the work he did was also great. Take the opening invitation to the highroad in *An Crann Géagach.* Here in this passage is a master of words and phrases just feeling himself, disporting himself in the wonderful medium of his art language. How at home he is, never jerky, never pausing, just flowing from the first word to the last! But later in the same book we have all the varying scenes, just a series of vignettes; the craftsman—for he is a craftsman—makes his medium vanish; words and phrases no longer dwell in the mind lost in the atmosphere the great master has created. Then (to borrow the phraseology of a sister art) we note economy of line. Ó Conaire's work is a sketch in the paucity of line and a picture in the fullness of meaning and expression; so much in so little. A sentence or two suffice. Ó Conaire simply conjures up something you onetime saw or felt, but in his happy language he supplies the warmth or light your poor observation missed. All is quickly done, but simply and calmly. There is none of the effervescence of the modern short story in his style. But has he style? Well, of course he has, but you do not see it, nor find it by comparison with other writers. Someone has likened Ó Conaire to Anatole France, and it is possible the suggestion came from a perusal of *Le Jongleur de Notre Dame. Le Jongleur* is great work with more imagination but less of pleasing fancy than *An Crann Géagach.* They resemble in their tenderness, their humanity, simplicity, playfulness. But Pádraic lets things happen and relates them while the Frenchman invents the happenings that relation may follow. So by comparison *Le Jongleur* is scintillating and dramatic whereas Ó Conaire flows, engaging, interesting, even. You observe the way that Anatole France carries you, but in Ó Conaire you see nothing of the way until he surrenders you to yourself at the end.

It is hard to say what writer, if any, he really resembles. Did he make his style or did he discover something new and old—in the native speech? In him Ireland lost her most original writer since Synge. *Ar dheis Dé go raibh a anam!*

J. S. Crone, "Sgéala ó Cathair na gCeó", Vol. XVI, Nos. 4-6 (July–Dec. 1928), 75-76.

The bicentenary of the birth of Oliver Goldsmith on 10th November was noted by almost every periodical here from the *Quarterly Review* downwards. I considered Edmund Blunden's article in *The Times* poor and perfunctory and liked best of all George Sampson's in *The Daily News* and Humbert Woolf's in *The Observer*. A number of his admirers assembled where the 'white stone flashes over Goldsmith's ashes, in a quiet cloister near Temple Bar' and duly deposited wreaths. On the following night the members of the Irish Literary Society to the number of a hundred celebrated the event by a dinner presided over by Mr. Ashe King. The veteran president now in his 90th year delivered a remarkable oration on the life and works of the poet. It is not so well known as it should be that Mr. Ashe King in his fine *Life of Goldsmith* (Methuen 1910) was the first biographer to demolish the false portrait first painted by the jealous Boswell and unhappily copied by Prior and Foster of the 'Poor Poll' Goldsmith, and showed him as he was a lovable, tender-hearted, farseeing, brilliant Irishman.

Mr. H. L. Morrow, who has been for the past four years acting as assistant to his fellow townsman Robert Lynd, the literary editor of the *Daily News* has been appointed editor of the well known and popular journal *John O'London's Weekly* and takes up duty with the New Year. Mr. Morrow is one of the second generation of the clever Belfast family 'the Seven Morrows', brothers, each of whom attained distinction as painters, modellers, playwrights or artists. The best known now of course is George Morrow, the clever member of the staff of *Punch* whose humorous sketches delight innumerable readers in all parts of the globe.

The unexpected death of Sir James Percy in his 59th year, so shortly after his departure from his native country to take up his residence in a London suburb, removes a genial humourist, a born raconteur and an admirable after dinner speaker. Born in Belfast, he was throughout his career, connected with the Dublin press, both on its literary and commercial sides. He published several entertaining volumes on *Bulls and Blunders* which had a wide circulation and ready sale. [...]

I called attention earlier in the year to the merits of that remarkable work of fiction *Hanging Johnny* (Murray) by Myrtle Johnston. I am now pleased to see that it has been awarded the *Femina-Vie Heureuse* prize at the Institut Français. The prize is an annual one of £40 awarded by a committee of French women writers for the best work of imagination in English published during the year by an author whose work has, in the opinion of the Committee not received sufficient recognition.

Séamus Ó Casaide, "The Speche of an Irishe man in the yere 1542", Vol. XVI, Nos. 4-6 (July-Dec. 1928), 80.

If there be any man the which wyll lerne some Irysh English and Irysh dothe folow here togyther.

One, Two, thre, foure, fyue, syx, seuen, eyght.
Hewen, dow, tre, kaar, quiek, seth, showght, howght.
Nyne, ten, aleuyn, twelue, thirtene, fourtene.
Nygh, deh, hewnek, dowek, tredeek, kaardeek.
fyuetene, syxtene, seuentene, eyghtene, nynetene.
quiekdeek. sehdeek. showghtdeek. howghtdeek. nythdek.
twenty, one & twenty, ii & twenty, thre & twenty.
feh, hewn feet, dowhfeet, trefeet.
Thirty, forty, fyfty, syxty, a hondred.
dehfeete, eayfeete, dewhegesdayth, trefeet, keede.
God spede you, syr! *Anoha dewh sor!*
You be welcome to the towne. *De van wely.*
How do you fare? *Kanys stato?*
I do fare well, I thanke you. *Tam agoomawh gramahogooa.*
Syr, can you speke Iryshe? *Sor, woll galow oket?*
I can speke a lytle. *Tasyn agomee.*
Mayden, come hether, and gyme som meate!
Kalyn, tarin chowh, tour dewh!
Wyfe, haue you any good meate? *Benitee, wyl beemah hagoot?*
Syr, I haue enoughe, *Sor, tha gwyler.*
Wyfe, gyue me bread! *Benytee, toor haran!*
Man, gyue me wine! *Farate, toor fyen!*
Mayden, gyue me chese! *Kalyn, tour case!*
Wyfe, gyue me fleshe! *Benyte, tour foeule!*
Gyue me some fyshe! *Toor yeske!*
Much good do it you *I Teena go sowgh!*

How far is it to Waterford? *Gath haad o showh go port Iaarg?*
It is one and twenty myle. *Myle hewryht.*
What is it a clocke? *Gaued bowleh glog?*
It is vi. a clocke. *She wylly a glog.*
When shall we go to supper? *Gahad rah moyd auer sope*
Giue me a rekenyng, wyfe. *Toor countes doyen, benitee.*
Ye shall pay iii. pens. *Yeke ke to tre pyn Iny.*
Whan shal I go to slepe, wyfe? *Gah hen rah moyd holowh?*
By an by. *Nish feene.*
God night, sir! *Ih may, sor!*
Farewel, fare wel! *Sor doyt, sor dolt!*

Thus endeth the maner and speche of Irland.

The above instruction (without the heading) form the concluding part of 'the thyrd Chapter [which] treateth of Irland' in *The fyrst of the Introduction of knowledge ... Made by Andrew Borde, of Physycke Doctor.*

The earlier (about two-thirds) part of the chapter gives in English verse and prose some quaint observations on the manners and customs of the 'wylde Irysh [...] and the Redshanks among them'.

Only two Irish cities—Dublin and Waterford—are mentioned by Borde, and possibly it was in the latter city that he obtained the phrases which he gallantly attempted to record in print—probably for the first time.

Andrew Borde or Boorde (1470?-1549), traveller, physician and quondam Carthusian monk, was a native of Sussex (England) and dedicated his book to Princess (afterwards Queen) Mary of England on 3rd May 1542. The book was printed by Copeland in London in 1547 or 1548, and again in 1562 or 1563. it was reprinted in 1814, and again by the Early English Text Society in 1870 and in 1893.

"Reviews", Vol. XVI, Nos. 4-6 (July–Dec. 1928), 109.

THE SILVER TASSIE. BY SEAN O'CASEY. MACMILLAN. 7/6 NET. Three years ago, in his book, *The New Spirit in the European Theatre*, Mr. Huntly Carter wrote: 'The workers are to be liberated to freest expression by the theatre ... some people argue that the workers have done nothing of importance as yet in the theatrical line, and therefore they may be incapable of doing anything of importance ... Against this argument is the fact that worker-authors of sterling ability have come out of the War and Revolution in different parts of Europe. Ireland can show two or three, including Sean O'Casey, a labourer whose proletarian comments on social conditions are contributions to the workers drama repertory from the proletarian point of view. Unfortunately, he has fallen into the net of middle-class conventional technique—a circumstance which fully illustrates the powerful influence of middle-class out-of-date methods'. When I read that statement for the first time in 1925 I was of the opinion that it meant little or nothing; merely an effort on Mr. Carter's part to buttress the freakish drama of such dramatists as Toller and the Capek brothers. I am still of that opinion today when the thing known as 'expressionism' has nearly faded from the theatre.

Apparently the statement was taken seriously by Sean O'Casey, so seriously that in *The Silver Tassie* he has endeavoured to satisfy the requirements of his critic-adviser. The requirements of Huntly Carter, however, were not the requirements of the Directors of the Abbey Theatre, who decided not to stage the play there, with consequences which added to the gaiety of nations if they did not add to the stature of Sean O'Casey. Proletarian drama may, or may not, be a good thing, but proletarian manners, as exhibited in the correspondence, are plainly undesirable.

Whether the Directors of the Abbey Theatre were right or wrong in rejecting the play is still a matter of dispute, and the dispute can only be decided by seeing the play on the stage. For my own part, I am satisfied that the Directors should have accepted, and produced, the play. Numbers of plays that were very much inferior to *The Silver Tassie* were staged in the Abbey Theatre before that play was rejected, and some have even been staged since. But I believe that when the Directors accepted, and staged, Sean O'Casey's own *Nannie's Night Out* and *Kathleen Listens-in* they abdicated all right to sit in judgment upon O'Casey's future work. It was an enlightening experience to see critics who had praised these two plays condemn the infinitely finer thing that is *The Silver Tassie*.

Sean O'Casey is changing: changing from a local dramatist working in Dublin materials in the technique of the Abbey Theatre, to a dramatist who thinks he is taking all the world for his materials and moulding them in the manner approved by Mr. Huntly Carter and the 'expressionists'. It may be that he will overlook the fact that in dealing with Dublin workers he dealt with the workers of the world; and that in accepting a novel technique he is accepting something that is already outmoded. Wherever Sean O'Casey goes, and whatever he may do for drama in the future, he can no more escape from his youth in Dublin than can Bernard Shaw.

I do not share Mr. O'Casey's belief that *The Silver Tassie* is his best work to date, and I am quite certain that it is not the worst as its rejection would seem to imply. It might be a very powerful thing on the stage, although I doubt that it would, but in reading it lacks that reality which can make it convincing. The first act in a Dublin tenement is the O'Casey now so well known; the inconsequence of Tchechov combined with the vivacity of the Dublin slums. The second act is a different matter; here the 'expressionism' of the Toller school takes command and the effort to fit the European War into a single act is hardly a success. The act reads more like a nightmare than anything I have read in contemporary drama; the chants are merely absurd, and the symbolism is strained beyond endurance. In the third and fourth acts events happen without cohesion, and quite inconsequentially so that people who moved in one social sphere in the first act are moving in quite another in the third. The war may have done much to level classes but it did not do so much as to bring Surgeon Forby Maxwell to the rooms of the Avondale Football Club. But even the Football Club itself changes its social tone between the first and the fourth act. In the first act it seems to be what Dubliners call a 'Phoenix Park' Club, but in the fourth act it resembles a first-class professional organisation.

But when all this has been said, and when all the technical faults have been emphasised; when it has been seen how untrue to themselves are the characters; and how unreal the chanting of the second act; it still remains to be repeated that the play should have been staged in the Abbey Theatre. Quite plainly Sean O'Casey is now endeavouring to make his appeal to the world in terms which he believes the world will understand more readily than it understands *Juno* or *The Plough and The Stars*. I believe that he is wrong in attempting such a feat, but he is as much entitled to experiment as other dramatists. *The Silver Tassie* is not calculated to inspire one with hope that he will succeed in the terms which Huntly Carter prescribed but, such as it is it is, an interesting play, infinitely greater than any other play by an Irish dramatist since his own *Plough and The Stars* was produced. That it should have been rejected by the Abbey Theatre is a calamity which will not be easily rectified. Sometime we may see it staged in Dublin by one of the several companies now producing plays. (A. E. MALONE.)

DAYS OF FEAR. BY FRANK GALLAGHER. (JOHN MURRAY, LONDON) 5/-. I think that Mr. Frank Gallagher's record of the Mountjoy Hungerstrike of 1920, *Days of Fear* [...] is the most important contribution to Irish literature of many years past. Dan Breen, in his book, *My Fight for Irish Freedom*, gave us the physical side of the war in Ireland, and now we are offered by Mr. Gallagher the spiritual side. We are more than grateful for it. A fragment of literature and life, it holds high the thing that was Irish nationalism in those days. 'Ireland is justice, is truth' makes a logical end to one of the many spiritual storms that shake this record; and to that definition one can carry for affinity much of the terrible sincerity and faith half-divine that have manifested themselves in the thought and action of those that bred revolt in Ireland. The book is governed by that definition. Yet there is no wintry monotone in it, for all its physical starvation. Rather does it remind one of a Spring day where rain and sun interchange. And I must leave the likeness to portray the quality of this strangest of all diaries; so natural and so rich is the ebb and flow of its passion; and so wholesome the prose that carries it. A great book. (P. C. T.)

"Half-Yearly Bibliography", Vol. XVI, Nos. 4-6 (July–Dec. 1928), 113.

AUTOBIOGRAPHY AND BIOGRAPHY

Letters and Leaders of my Day. By T. M. Healy. In two volumes. Vol. I.-356pp. Vol. II.-xi + 357-678pp. (Thornton Butterworth) 42/- nett.

The Life of William O'BRIEN, the Irish Nationalist: A Biographical Study of Irish Nationalism, Constitutional and Revolutionary. By Michael MacDonagh. 282pp. (Ernest Benn) 21/- nett.

William J. Walsh, Archbishop of Dublin. By the Right Rev. P. J. Walsh. xvi + 612pp. (Longmans) 21/- nett.

Young Ireland in Exile. By Rev. J. H. Cullen, BA. 136pp. (The Talbot Press) 3/6 nett.

Random Records of a Reporter. By J. B. Hall. 8vo. 240pp. (Dublin: The Fodhla Press) 6/- nett.

A McCarthy Miscellany. By Judge McCarthy. 64pp. (Dundalk: Dundalgan Press) 2/6 nett.

HISTORY

Londonderry and the London Companies, 1609-1629. Being a Survey and other Documents submitted to King Charles I. By Sir Thomas Phillips. 11 x 7¾. xiii. + 198pp. (Belfast: H.M. Stationery Office) 12/6.

Catholic Emancipation Reviewed a Century Afterwards. By Rev. T. O'Herlihy. Cr. 8vo. (M. H. Gill) 3/6.

The Poor Clares in Ireland (A.D. 1629-1929). By Mrs. Thomas Concannon, M.A. Cr. 8vo. (M. H. Gill) 6/-.

The Struggle for Catholic Emancipation (1750-1826). By Denis Gwynn. Illustrated. Demy 8vo. xxiv. + 290pp. (Longmans) 10/6 nett.

Vespasian and Some of His Contemporaries. By Christine Longford. (Hodges, Figgis and Co.) 5/- nett.

A Short History of Western Europe. By R. A. S. Macalister. 242pp. (The Talbot Press) 5/- nett.

Ireland from A.D. 900 to 1600. By Rev. John Ryan, S.J., M.A. With Illustrations and Maps. 282pp. (Browne and Nolan) 3/- nett.

LITERARY

The Collected Letters of Oliver Goldsmith. Edited by Katharine C. Balderston. li + 190pp. (Cambridge University Press) 7/6 nett.

New Essays by Oliver Goldsmith. Now first collected and edited with an Introduction and Notes. By Ronald S. Crane. xli + 147pp. (Chicago: University Press & Cambridge University Press) 12/- nett.

Early Literary Channels Between Britain and Ireland. By Clark Harris Stover. 111pp. Author (University of Texas, Austin, Texas, USA).

DRAMA

Three Last Plays. By Lady Gregory. 280pp. (Putnam's) 7/6 nett.

The Big House. Four Scenes in its Life. 113pp. *Give a Dog: A Play in Three Acts.* 102pp. By Lennox Robinson. (Macmillan) 2/- nett. each.

FICTION

The Runaways. By George A. Birmingham. 252pp. (Methuen) 7/6 nett.

Destiny Bay. By Donn Byrne. 432pp. (Sampson Low) 7/6 nett.

The Unmarried Daughter and Other Stories. By Patrick Hogan. 94pp. (George Roberts) 3/6 nett.

The Magic Inkpot: A Volume of Irish Fairy Stories. By the Marchioness of Londonderry. Illustrated by 16 coloured plates and numerous black-and-white decorations by Edmond Brock and Lady Margaret Stewart. (Macmillan) 15/- nett.

Black Bonar. By Patrick MacGill. 384pp. (Herbert Jenkins) 7/6 nett. A story of life in a Donegal village.

The Mirror in the Dusk. By Brinsley MacNamara. 278pp. (Sampson Low) 7/6 nett.

Ballymulcaghey. By Mat Mulcaghey (the Oul' Besom Man) 245pp. (Belfast: McCaw, Stevenson and Orr; London: Bank Chambers) 5/- nett.

Donovan's Island: An Original Story. By G. H. Powell. 309pp. (Hodder and Stoughton) 7/6 nett.

Yesterdays in the Green Country. By Frances Woodwright. Crown 8vo. (London: Fowler Wright) 3/6 nett.

The Story of Keth. By Lady Blanche Girouard. 7½ X 5. viii. + 216pp. (Macmillan) 7/6. 'Wanderings through a quaint Ireland of crooked roads, midnight firesides, and cold woods.'

Told to His Reverence: County Down Sketches. By Rev. W. McNeilll. With a Foreword by Robert Lynd. 9 x 6. 96pp. (Talbot Press) 3/6.

Tristram Lloyd. By Canon Sheehan (completed by Rev. H. Gaffney, O.P) 276pp. + xlviii. (Talbot Press) 7/6 nett.

Our Own Wee Town. By Louis J. Walsh. 236pp. (The Talbot Press) 3/6.

POETRY

The Poems of Shane Leslie. 96pp. (Cayme Press) 15/- nett.

Songs of the South and the Hidden Land. By M. Michael. Illustrations by M. Q. Haig. 65pp. (Talbot Press) 2/6 nett.

The Song of the Salmon-God. By W. P. Ryan. 20pp. (J. M. Watkins) 1/- nett.

An Introduction to Irish Syllabic Poetry of the Period 1200-1600. With Selections, Notes and Glossary, by Eleanor Knott. viii + 135pp. (Dublin: Educational Company of Ireland) 3/6 nett.

Sea Gulls and Mariners: Songs and Verses. By Kathleen Conyngham Green. 8vo. 13pp. (P. Allan) 1/-.

A Little Anthology of Irish Verse. Selected by Lennox Robinson. 36pp. (Cuala Press) 10/6 nett.

On the Shining Bann. By R. M. Sibbett. 207pp. (Belfast: W. & G. Baird) 3/6 nett.

TOPOGRAPHY

Round the Coast of Northern Ireland: Antrim, Derry and Down. By the Rev. Canon Hugh Forde. With a Foreword by The Right Hon. Sir John Ross, Bart. 215pp. (Belfast: R. Carswell and Son) 3/6 nett.

Ulster: Its Archæology and Antiquities. By H. C. Lawlor, M.A., M.R.I.A. Cr. 4to. xvi + 230pp. (Belfast: Carswell) 6/-.

Carrickfergus and its Contacts. By the Ven. J. T. McNeice, B.D. Illustrated. 8vo. 100pp. (Simpkin, Marshall and W. E. Mayne) 3/6.

Historical, Traditional and Descriptive Account of Island Magee. By Dixon Donaldson. Illustrated. 154pp. (Matthews, Carrickfergus) 5/-.

The Down and Connor Diocesan Archæological Magazine. No. I. (P. Quinn, Belfast) [no price].

Short History of Keady Parish (Its Church and People). 50pp. (Armagh: *Ulster Gazette Office*) 1/- nett.

The Glamour of the West. By D. L. Kelleher. 123pp. (The Talbot Press) 2/6 nett.

The Glamour of Limerick. By W. J. O'Halloran. 108pp. (The Talbot

Press) 2/6 nett.

MISCELLANEOUS

Ireland's Tribute to Saint Francis: Seven Lectures on Franciscan Subjects. Edited by the Rev. Gregory Cleary. vii + 148pp. (Dublin: M. H. Gill) 3/6 nett.

Tour of the Tipperary Hurling Team in America, 1926. By Thomas J. Kenny. x + 112pp. (George Roberts) 2/6 nett.

Ireland: A Catspaw. By Elizabeth Lazenby. 7½ x 5, 254pp. (Boswell Printing and Publishing Company) 6/- nett.

A Monetary History of Ireland. Part II: From the Anglo-Norman Invasion to the Death of Elizabeth. With an Introductory Essay on the Anglo-Saxon and Anglo-Norman Money Systems. By the Rev. Dom Patrick Nolan, O.S.B. xl + 213pp. (P. S. King) 5/- nett.

Irish Bogs: Sport and Country Life in the Irish Free State. By J. W. Seigne. xii + 249pp. (Longmans) 15/- nett.

The History of Aenach Tailtenn and the Ancient Irish Laws. By M. J. MacAuliffe, B.L. lxiv. + 120pp. (Hodges, Figgis and Co) 7/6 nett.

Trodden Gold (The Book Of The Forest). By John Mackay. 310pp. (The Talbot Press) 15/- nett.

Golden Memories: Love Letters of William O'Brien. Edited by Sophie O'Brien. Cr. 8vo. (M. H. Gill) 5/1-.

The Poor Man of Assisi. By Rev. H. Gaffney, O.P. (Dublin *Irish Rosary* Office) 2/6 nett.

Catalogue of MSS in the Public Library, Armagh. Edited by James Dean, Assistant Librarian. 44pp. (The Public Library, Armagh) [no price].

Deora Druchta Camhaoire. By Rev. M. McGrath, S.J. 100pp. (M, H. Gill and Son. Ltd) 2/- nett.

O'Connell School Centenary Record (1828-1928). Illustrated. 216pp. (Dublin: Colm O'Loughlin) 6/- nett.

Rural Science and Nature Study. By A. W. Stelfox and M. D. Stelfox. 215pp. (Educational Co. of Ireland) 3/6 nett.

Séamus Ó Casaide, "An O'Connell 500 Years Ago!", Vol. XVI, Nos. 4-6 (July-Dec. 1928), 116.

The following beautiful lines in praise of one of O'Connell's ancestors, chief of a clan then located in Kerry, was found by the eminent scholar to whose kindness we are indebted for it.

Whether the lines were part of a larger composition or not, cannot be ascertained. They are supposed to have been written in the fourteenth century:

> *Níor chaith biadh, Ó Conghuil cais,*
> *Is cliath na comluih lé na lis*
> *Níor shuig ar each bile rois,*
> *Is file da chois maraon fris.*

No meat did eat the brave O'Connell
With the gate or door of his mansion shut,
On a steed he sat not, the oak of Ross,
While a poet trudged by his side on foot.

The publication of the above article in the *Nation* of 22nd April 1843, may have been intended as a gentle reminder to the great Dan of the desirability of adopting a more national attitude (cf. *I.B.L.* VIII, 8) towards the native language.

The Irish Book Lover
Vol. XVIII
(Jan. & Feb. 1930 to Nov. & Dec. 1930)

Colm Ó Lochlainn, "Editorial", Vol. XVIII, No. 1 (Jan. & Feb. 1930), 1.

A léightneóirí fhoighdeacha, seo chugaibh anois 'an curaichín óir a tigheacht le cóir / is giolla na n-amhrán ag a stiúir.' Acht chogar mise libh, cé gur lámh Éasu a bhéas air, cluinfidh sibh glór Iacob!

Is éachtach an méad atá déanta la blianta ag seadairíbh na leabhar— an Dochtúir Ó Maolchróin, Earnán Ó Diocsa agus Séamus Ó Casaide, agus míle buideachas le Dia go bhfuilid i n-ann a dhéanta go fóill. Gura fada an bhail sin ortha! Mar is ró-chinnte gur lom bacach a bhéinn gan iad-san le tigheacht i gcabhair orm agus mé i n-éadan an Irisleabhair seo.

As a contribution to the study of what may be termed 'Early Printed Books in Irish', a particular interest attaches to the article (for which I have to thank our good friend Séamus Ó Casaide) on that very noble exile of the seventeenth century—Father Francis O'Molloy. There is still a great field for profitable study in the Gaelic books of that early (the scholars would call it modern) period.

Father Paul Walsh has kindly transcribed and translated the verse from Bonaventure O'Hussey's *Teagasg Croisduidhe*, which was reprinted in *I.B.L.* XVII, No. 6; but this, in common with "Reviews" and "Library Notes" has to be held over to next issue—notwithstanding an increase in the number of pages.

And so for the first time I make the editorial bow!

J. S. Crone, "Sgéala ó Chathair na gCeó", Vol. XVIII, No. 1 (Jan. & Feb. 1930), 2.

I am sure the younger playwrights of your good city will read this with interest. The Greenwich Village Theatre, in its prospectus, states 'that few countries in the past 25 years have contributed as formidable a list of first-rank dramatists as Ireland claims in George Bernard Shaw, W. B. Yeats, J. M. Synge, Lady Gregory, Lord Dunsany, Padraic Colum, Lennox Robinson, St. John Ervine, and Sean O'Casey.'

There is every evidence today, it is stated, that the younger Irish writers will perpetuate this insistent tradition, and continue to provide a steady and vital contribution to the spoken drama; and the function of the Irish Theatre will be to give adequate interpretation to worthy Irish plays. To this end the Irish Theatre will be greatly interested in seeing manuscripts of plays from younger Irish playwrights. These should be submitted to the Director, the Irish Theatre, Seventh Avenue and Fourth Street, New York City.

It makes one rub one's eyes to read in the pages of the ultra-Tory *Saturday Review* a question like this, recently put by its well-known contributor "Stret", who, it is an open secret is Mr. T. Earle Welby:

> What I want to know is why a ballad like Samuel Lover's delicious "Whistling Thief", which has ease, humour, character, happy sentiment, was not the rage throughout Victorian days and into our own. If ever a set of 'words' was born for honourable popularity, Lover's was; but it has never had it.

And in a review in the same periodical of Robert Graves' somewhat surprising autobiography *Good-by to All That*, I find the following reference to his family, celebrated in Anglo-Irish literature for more than a century:

> The Graves family has a long literary tradition. There was the writer who is remembered chiefly as Shenstone's friend; there were various scholars and divines, besides a scientist or so and the discoverer of the disease from which Christina Rossetti suffered; there was the author of *Father O'Flynn*; and so on. Graves is glad, he says, that his father was a poet: it saved him from any 'false reverence for poets'.

A MS with a slight Irish interest sold recently was that of Dickens's *The Schoolboy's Story* (1853), on ten 8vo. pages, written in blue ink on blue paper as was usual with him. It was given by the author to Dean Bagot of Newry, a prolific writer, and something of a translator whose memory is still green in the Frontier Town. From him it passed to Mr. Greer, a well-known bookseller and printer there and then by marriage to Mr. William A. Traill of Portrush, the well-known engineer, who formed the first electrical railway in the three Kingdoms—that leading to the Giant's Causeway.

No Irish reader can allow the old buff and blue *Edinburgh Review* to depart after a great career of 125 years without a sigh of regret, for, from the days of Sidney Smith its only and sole begetter, until the Liberal split over the policy of Home Rule in 1886, it fought and well on behalf of the rights of Ireland and her people. Even today one can re-read with shaking sides the merry onslaughts of the witty Canon on the shortcomings of the Irish Church Establishment, and his powerful pleas for Catholic Emancipation. Amongst its finest contributors in the heyday of its fame was Rev. Dr. Charles W. Russell, the president of Maynooth. Thomas Moore wrote many of the reviews a century ago, and according to Henry Reeve a former editor, Lord Clarendon, supplied material for attacking O' Connell and the Young Irelanders. Many of the articles that constitute the three volumes of the late Litton Falkiner originally appeared in its pages.

The following, which I cull from *The Daily News*, may interest readers, especially Northern ones, as Miss Helen Waddell hails from that 'airt', and is a sister of the well-known playwright 'Rutherford Mayne'.

> It is rumoured that when Miss Waddell's *Wandering Scholars* was published a regius professor at Oxford exclaimed at the book's brilliance and sanity, but protested: 'She must be wrong—this upsets all my ideas of the dark ages!' I am afraid this new volume [*Medieval Latin Lyrics*] will distress him further; for of all the lovely, delicate, poignant, robust, meditative, or splendid poems which she translates, more than five-sixths belong to the period still vulgarly known as dark, because of its intellectual, moral and imaginative stagnation. It would not be a bad thing if no one was allowed to use the expression dark ages, in reference to the years between 500 and 1200, who could not give a fair account of two people, the Irish and the Scandinavians. The Irish spread light and learning, as the Scandinavians spread slaughter and stupidity; and it is a fitting thing that it is an Irish scholar who brings back to popular knowledge and affection the treasures which Irishmen of old knew how to value, and taught men how to fashion.

Miss Waddell is announced to lecture at the Irish Literary Society on 1st March on Alcuin, the medieval scholar.

Mrs. Alfred Austin, the widow of the Poet Laureate who succeeded Tennyson, and 'dear Lami' of his poems, died recently in Kensington. She was one of the fifteen children of Thomas Homan Muloch of Bellair, Offaly, and so related to the two distinguished novelists, the author of *John Halifax, Gentleman*, and Miss M. E. Braddon, the mother of Mr. W. B. Maxwell. Mrs. Austin rendered assistance to her husband as author and journalist throughout their married life.

Edmund Hogan, S. J., "Father Francis O Molloy & *Lucerna Fidelium*", Vol. XVIII, No. 1 (Jan. & Feb. 1930), 5.

[The following notice appeared in *Irisleabhar na Gaedhilge* for Lughnasa, 1897, but I have not been able to trace any other contribution by Father

Edmund Hogan in that journal or elsewhere on the subject.]

He was born in the Diocese of Meath, since he calls himself "Medensis" in the title-page of his *Lochrann na gCreidmheach*. Furthermore, he was born in that part of the diocese called 'O'Molloy's Country', which is co-extensive with the present baronies of Ballycowan, Ballyboy and Eglish—this I gather from page 180 of his *Irish Grammar*, where he said that he 'had heard from eye-witnesses that Charles, son of Conall, Prince of the O'Molloys, and grandfather of the present illustrious head of that clan, had, in times of great scarcity during the Elizabethan wars, entertained 960 people at his own house for the space of twelve days'.

The Conall mentioned here died in 1599; as the Four Masters say (Vol. VI, 2,093) he died in spring of this year, and his son, the C[a]lbhach, took his place, being appointed by the queen (*a hucht na bainrioghna*); some of the gentlemen of his tribe vied and contended with him for that name (of Ó Maolmhuaidh), according to the custom of the Irish. That Francis was born in the country of O'Molloy, seems pretty certain from the above statement of his, coupled with Harris' assertion that he was born in King's County.

He may have been a kinsman of Conall or of the *daoini uaisli a chinidh*; there is no reliable evidence of it, though in 1793, a writer in the *Anthologia Hibernica*, Volume I, says so, and the new *Dictionary of National Biography* seems to suggest it.

I fancy, from his name and his relationship to the family of Daly, that he was a native of the barony of Ballycowan where the Molloys and Dalys still abound. The following significant trifles bear on this point. As we shall see further on, his nephew was Father John Daly; his *Grammar* bears the approbation of the Rev. John Daly, D.D., Abbot of Kilbeggan; the copy of his *Irish Grammar* in the National Library bears the names of Hugh and Francis Daly, and the date 1727.

He must have been born about the year 1615, as he was an old man in 1676, had been away from Ireland for over forty years. So he entered the Franciscan Order about 1635, as I gather from page 280 of his *Irish Grammar*, and page 12 of his *Lochrann na gCreidmheach*.

It is more than probable that he made his noviciate at the Irish Franciscan Convent at Louvain, where the archaeologists, Ward, Colgan, Brendan, O'Connor, Bonaventure, O'Docharty, and O'Sherrin were living and working in the year 1635.

In 1645 we find a trace of him at Gratz, in the Duchy of Styria, in Austria, where a 4to. book of his was printed with the title: *Disputatio Theologica de Incarnatione Verbi ad mentem Joannis Duns Scoti*;

sustinuit autem Conclusiones Paulus Budinminorbich et Antonius Molledy. This book or Thesis is quoted in De Alva et Astorga's *Militia universalis de Immaculate Conceptione*, ed. 1663, col. 440. This shows he was then Professor of Theology at Gratz.

In 1658 he seems to have been in Spain, as he then published his *Jubilatio Genethliaca in honorem Prosperi Balthasaris Phillipi Hispani Principis*.

We next meet him in Rome as Professor of Divinity at St. Isidore's, in 1666 as his *Theologia Sacra*, 8vo., was then and there published. At or before, and certainly before 1675, he was Primarius Professor of Theology at St. Isidore's, and Lector Jubilatus, as appears from the title-page of his *Lucerna*. He is said, in Harris's *Ware*, to have been 'Divine to some Cardinals and General Agent for the Irish in that city'. In the new *Dictionary of National Biography* it is stated that he was agent for the Irish Catholics. But, in fact, he was only Agent-General of the Irish Province of the Franciscan Order, as is clear from the title-page and the "Approbationes" of his *Grammar*.

1675. Before the 1st of March his *Lochrann na gCreidmheach* had been read and approved of by the Rev. Dr. Pierce Creagh; by Father Patrick Tyrell, Professor of Theology, a Father of the Provinces of Castile and Ireland, ex-Definitor-General of the Order of St. Francis; and by Father Marcus Brown, Professor of Divinity, a Father of the Irish Province, and Secretary-General of the (whole) Order. It consists of 409 pages, printed in 1676, in the bold, clear Irish type of the *Propaganda*. It ends with 44 verses, with the heading '*Soruidh ó Dhithreabhach Ruama go Clár Coinn*'. It is dedicated to Cardinal Altieri, Protector of Ireland, *Dídineoir Banbha*.

1676. His *Irish Grammar*, written in Latin, and covering 300 pages, was approved of on the 12th of April 1676, by Father Tyrell, mentioned above, by Father Michael Toner, and on December 30th, by Rev. John Daly, D.D., Abbot of Kilbeggan. It is dedicated to Camillo Massimo, 'a great Maecenas of St. Isidore's College', a member of whose princely family is now a Jesuit in Rome, and takes a keen interest in Ireland, as I know from having lived with him for some months a year or two ago. The *Grammar* was published in Rome in 1677.

At page 280 he says he was away from Ireland and its Masters for over forty years, '*a quadraginta et amplius annis*'. There are 56 Irish verses by O'Molloy at page 277 of the book; at pages 177 and 179 he has Irish and Latin verses on Father Tyrell, O.S.F.

In one of the Roman Archives I found a letter written by Father O'Molloy to the General of the Jesuits in 1677. In it he asked that

Father John Daly, a pupil of the Irish College, Rome, who was under orders to go to the Irish Mission, might be allowed to wait some time for him, that they might travel home together. Perhaps he himself was waiting to see his *Grammar* through the Press; and, if my memory does not fail me, he said in the letter that John Daly was a nephew of his. It is stated in that MS, of which I had not time to make a copy, that O'Molloy died in France, on his journey home with Daly, in 1677. Sir John T. Gilbert, the author of the biographical sketch of O'Molloy in the *Dictionary of National Biography*, says the date of his death has not been ascertained; but it is now certain that he died in the last quarter of the year 1677. I hope to have before long the precise date and place of his death. His Irish verses to be found in the *Lochrann* and the *Grammatica* would be worth inserting in the *Gaelic Journal*.

Gregory Cleary, O.F.M., "Father Francis O'Molloy", Vol. XVIII, No. 1 (Jan. & Feb. 1930), 8.

[In view of the disparity of one or two statements it may be well to republish in full the following notice from Father Cleary's *Father Luke Wadding and St. Isidore's College, Rome* (Rome 1925), as that writer may not have seen Father Hogan's article.]

Francis O'Molloy, O.F.M., was born in Meath in the early part of the seventeenth century. He entered the Order at an early age; and on completing his studies at St. Isidore's was sent, in the year 1642, as Lector of Philosophy to Klosterneuberg near Vienna, and, in 1645 was transferred to the Chair of Theology at Gratz. Here he published his work on the Incarnation, mentioned below. About 1650 he was recalled to St. Isidore's, and appointed Primary Professor of Theology. In 1662 he was deputed by the Irish Provincial and Definitory to represent the Provincial, Antony Docharty, at the General Chapter to be held in Rome, and to present the official *Relatio Status* of the Province forwarded to him to that effect. This very interesting document is still extant in the Archives of Merchants' Quay. On May 22 1670, he was appointed the official Agent or Procurator of the Irish Province in the Roman Curia. In pursuance of this trust, besides transacting with the Roman Authorities the ordinary business of the Province, he obtained two briefs from Pope Clement X (Feb. 16 1671, and Sept. 12 1672, respectively) wherein it is commanded that the system prevailing at the Franciscan Colleges of Louvain and Prague, relative to the election and appointment of the Guardians, Lectors and Vicars of these Colleges, be applied to St. Isidore's, viz., that said officials should be selected from each of the Four Provinces of Ireland alternately and in strict rotation.[1] This innovation in the constitution of our College as devised by the founder was not destined to be of long duration; it was revoked by Innocent XII by brief dated July 20 1695.[2]

In Philosophy and Theology O'Molloy was a keen, robust thinker and expressed his thoughts in clear, forcible and not inelegant language. This characteristic is particularly evident in his *Cursus Philosophiae*, to which the General of the Order gave his approval September 3 1664. Whether more than the first volume of his work was ever issued I have not been able to ascertain. Patrick Tyrell, subsequently Bishop of Clogher, who was one of the censors of the work, describes it as '*succo nervoque refertum opus mole exiguum, acumine magnum*'. And the author himself he qualifies as: '*Caelo et cedro dignus.*'[3] O'Molloy frequently indulged in verse, both Irish and Latin. But he will be principally remembered as the author of the first printed *Irish Grammar*, which came from the Propaganda Press in 1677. He wrote it, as he tells us, in holiday time, 'when free for a month from graver cares', at a time when the Irish people 'were being stripped of their every possession, even of their native language.'[4] He had been then living 'for forty years and more among foreigners, far separated from fatherland, from its monuments and its teachers.'[5] This work has attracted the attention of several Celtic scholars. Edward Lhuyd in his *Introduction to the Irish and Scottish Language* refers to it.[6] Joseph Loth in his *Le Metrique Galloise* reprints from it.[7] My valued friend, the late Tomas Ó Flannghaile, published an English translation of the part dealing with Irish Prosody.

The zeal which inspired O'Molloy to write his grammar—to counteract the heretical enemy's set programme, 'which proscribed the public and even the private use of the Irish language in order that, when the latter had been consigned to eternal oblivion, no knowledge might survive of native antiquities, of the Lives of our saints, of our Faith, of our ecclesiastical traditions'—that same zeal had inspired him the previous year to publish an Irish Catechism for the use of the Faithful in Ireland. It appeared at Rome from the Propaganda Press under a double title—Latin and Irish—and is generally known as *Lucerna Fidelium*. The exact date of his death is unknown. He died at St. Isidore's about 1684. The following are his works, so far as known to us:

1. *Tractatus de Incarnatione ad mentem Scoti*, (Gratz 1645) in 4o.
2. *Iubilatio Genethliaca in honorem Prosperi Balthasaris Philippi Hispaniarum Principis*. (Rome 1658) Latin heroic verses, in 4o.
3. *Various Latin Poems Addressed to Cardinal Altieri, Protector of*

Ireland, Composed when His Eminence Visited St. Isidore's on St. Patrick's Day: Isidorense Collegium more iam solito in solemnitate D. Patricii invisenti. (Rome 1672) in 4to., 18pp.
4. *Lucerna Fidelium.* (Rome 1676) An Irish Catechism.
5. *Grammatica Hiberno-Latina, nunc compendiata.* (Rome 1677).
6. *Cursus Philosophiae. Tomus Primus, Dialecticae Breviarum complectens.* (Rome 1666).
7. *Historia Hiberniae.* Francis Porter (*Compendium Annalium Hiberniae*, Rome 1690, p. 4) informs us that O'Molloy left this Work ready for the press, and that in it he corrects existing maps of Ireland with reference to geographical latitude.

NOTES: 1.] Archives, St. Isodore's. 2.] Idem. 3.] Tom. i. xxii. 4.] *Grammatica Latino-Hibernica*, p. 1. 5.] Ibid., p. 280. 6.] *Archaeologia Britannica*, Oxford, 1707. 7.] Tom. ii. app., pp.271-313.

"Bibliographical Society of Ireland", Vol. XVIII, No. 1 (Jan. & Feb. 1930), 19.

At the stated Annual Meeting of the Society held on Monday, 27th January 1930, the following Officers and Council were elected for the coming year:

PRESIDENT—Mr. J. de Lacy Smyth.
VICE-PRESIDENT—Mr. Séamus Ó Casaide.
HON. AUDITOR—Mr. J. H. Delargy.
COUNCIL—Dr. F. S. Bourke, Mr. E. Carberry, Mr. E. R. McC. Dix, Miss. R. Elmes, Mr. J. de W. Hinch, Dr. T. P. C. Kirkpatrick, Mr. F. O'Kelly, Dr. Lloyd Praeger and Miss R. Walsh.
HON. SECRETARY AND TREASURER—Mr. R. Phelps.

Cordial votes of thanks to the out-going President (Mr. Charles McNeill) and Secretary (Mr. V. H. Dowling) were passed by acclamation. Mr. Colm Ó Lochlainn read a note on "Some Irish Ballads and their Printers", and exhibited a number of interesting specimens.

At a meeting of the Council held on Wednesday, 12th February 1930, the president (Mr. de Lacy Smyth) in the Chair, it was decided to hold general meetings of the Society as follow:

Monday, 24th February.
Monday, 31st March.
Monday, 28th April.

Members are specially invited to communicate with the Secretary with a view to submitting papers or exhibits at the meetings. Further meetings during the session are to be arranged.

Members are asked to remember that the annual subscription (10s) is now overdue, and should be remitted to the Treasurer, Mr. Robert Phelps, without delay.

"Half-Yearly Bibliography to Dec. 30 1929", Vol. XVIII, No. 1 (January & Feb. 1930), 20.

BIBLIOGRAPHY

A Bibliography of the Works of J. B. Bury. Compiled with a memoir by Norman H. Baynes. 8vo. 184pp. (Cambridge: University Press) 10s. 6d.

Notes on the Printers in Dublin during the Seventeenth Century. By T. Percy C. Kirkpatrick. 8vo. 24pp. (Dublin University Press).

BIOGRAPHY

G. A. Studdert Kennedy. By his Friends. 8vo. 251pp. (London: Hodder & Stoughton). 5s. '"Woodbine Willie"—thoroughly Irish in spirit.'—*Times.*

Chicago May: Her Story. An autobiography. 8vo. (London: Sampson Low). 12s. 6d.

The Life of Mother Margaret Hallahan, O.S.D. By Mother Frances Raphael Drane, O.P. 8vo. New edition. (London: Longmans). 10s. 6d.

Standish O'Grady: The Man and the Writer. By Hugh Art O'Grady. 8vo. (Dublin: Talbot Press). 3s. 6d.

Daniel O'Connell: The Irish Liberator. By Denis Gwynn. (London Hutchinson). 16 illustrations.18s.

The Diaries of Mary, Countess of Meath. Edited by her Husband. Two vols. (London: Hutchinson). 21s. and 18s.

Little Nelly of Holy God. By Margaret Gibbons. 202pp. (London Sands). 3s. 6d.

Dom Columba Marmion. By Dom R. Thibaut. 555pp. (Paris: Desclée). [no price].

Edmund Burke and the Revolt against the Eighteenth Century. By A. Cobban. (London: Allen and Unwin) [no price].

Burke, the Founder of Conservatism. By A. A. B. (London: Eyre and Spottiswoode). 7s. 6d.

FICTION

The River. By Katherine Tynan. 8vo. 247pp. (London: Collins). 7s. 6d.

Every Dog. By E. and V. Pringle West. 8vo. 319pp. (London: Benn). 7s. 6d. 'The Irish scenes are done very delightfully'—*Times.*

The Rocky Road. By Bernard Duffy. 8vo. (Dublin: Talbot Press). 5s.

Sheila of the O'Beirnes. By Annie M. P. Smithson. 8vo. (same publishers). 3s. 6d.
O'Neill's Folly. By Hugh A. MacCartan. 8vo. (same publishers). 5s.
Ambushed Lovers. By Martin T. Henry. 8vo. (same publishers). 5s.
Irish Tales. By Mairead Fennessy. (London: The Mitre Press) [no price].
The Smiling Faces and Other Tales. By Brinsley MacNamara. (London: The Mandrake Press) [no price].
The Most Charming Family. By Katherine Tynan. (London: Ward Lock). 7s. 6d.
The House of Gold. By Liam O'Flaherty. 8vo. (London: J. Cape). 7s. 6d.
The Land of Let's Pretend. By Clifford Carter. 8vo. 33pp. (Belfast: Quota Press). 2s. 6d.
The Stormy Hills. By Daniel Corkery. 8vo. 260pp. (London J. Cape). 7s. 6d.
The Small Fields of Carrig. By Edward MacLysaght. 8vo. 286pp. (Heath Cranton) 7s. 6d.
The Sword in the Soul. By Roger Chauvire. (London: Longmans) [no price].
L'Incantation. Par Roger Chauvire. 293pp. (Paris: Firmin-Didot) [no price].
The Call to Arms. By Esther Graham. (Dublin: Browne and Nolan). 3s. 6d.
In a Glass Darkly. By J. Sheridan Lefanu. New edition, with numerous illustrations, by Edward Ardizzone. 382pp. (London: Peter Davies). 12s. 6d.
The Return of the Brute. By Liam O'Flaherty. (London: Mandrake Press). 5s.
Noreen. By Garrett O'Driscoll. (London: George Roberts) [no price].
Through a Glass Darkly. By Betty A. M. Byard. (London: George Roberts) [no price].
The Wasted Island. By Eimar O'Duffy. 2nd edition. (London: Macmillan) 7s. 6d.

HISTORY AND REMINISCENCES

With Michael Collins: Through The Fight for Irish Independence. By Batt O'Connor. 8vo. (London: Peter Davies). 6s.
With the Dublin Brigade. By Charles Dalton. 8vo. (same publisher). 5s.
The Irish Battalion in the Papal Army of 1860. By George F. H. Berkeley. 8vo. xxii + 254pp. (Dublin: Talbot Press). 15s.
A Page of Irish History. By Fathers of the Society of Jesus. 8vo. (same

Publishers). 21s. 'The story of the old University College, Stephen's Green'.

The Celtic Church in England after the Synod at Whitby. By J. L. Gough Meissner. Demy 8vo. xxii + 240pp. (London: Hopkinson). 10s. 6d.

Modern Research with Special Reference to Early Irish Ecclesiastical History. By Dom Louis Gougaud, O.S.B. (Dublin: Hodges, Figgis) [no price].

Agin the Governments: Memoirs and Adventures of Sir Francis Fletcher Vane, Bart. (London: Sampson Low). 16s.

Random Records of a Reporter. By J. B. Hall. (London: Simpkin Marshall). New cheap edition. 2s. 6d.

Golden Memories: Love Letters of William O'Brien. Vol. I. Edited by Sophie O'Brien. (Dublin: Gill). 5s.

More Love Letters, Prison Letters, and Others. Vol. II. xiii + 238pp. (Dublin: Gill). 5s.

White Light and Flame. By L. MacManus. 8vo. 228pp. (Dublin Talbot Press). 5s. Memories of the Irish Literary Revival and the Anglo-Irish War.

At the Court of the Eucharistic King. By Mrs. Thomas Concannon. (Dublin: Gill). The Story of the Franciscan Convent of Perpetual Adoration, Drumshambo, Co. Leitrim [no price].

TOPOGRAPHY

Clogher Clergy and Parishes. By Rev. Canon Leslie. 8vo. xii + 303pp. (The Author, Kilsaran Rectory, Co. Louth). 30s.

History of the Parish of Knockbreda. By the Very Rev. W. P. Carmody, Dean of Down.144pp. (Belfast: Carswell). 2s. 6d.

A Pictorial and Descriptive Guide to Belfast and Northern Ireland. 192pp. (London: Ward Lock). 2s.

A Pictorial and Descriptive Guide to Dublin and Its Environs. 192pp. (London: Ward Lock). 2s.

The Book of Dublin. 190pp. Edited by Bulmer Hobson. (Dublin Eason & Son., Ltd). 1s. Profusely illustrated [no price].

Dublin Civic Week Official Handbook. 4to. 142pp. (Dublin The Civic Week Council) 1s. 6d. Elaborately decorated by members of the Dublin Book Studio.

Tipperary. By the Rev. James H. Cotter. (New York: Devin Adair Co) [no price].

Ireland of the Welcomes. By D. L. Kelleher. 158pp. (Dublin: Irish Tourist Association). 1s. Illustrated.

The Abbey of Holy Cross. By Dr. M. Callanan. 48pp. (Dublin: At the

Sign of the Three Candles). 1s.

Cruach Phadraig. By P. L. O'Madden. 48pp. (Dublin: At the Sign of the Three Candles). 6d.

The Glamour of the South. By D. L. Kelleher. (Dublin: Talbot Press). 3s. 6d.

LITERARY

Ierne: An Anthology of Prose and Verse. 8vo. (Dublin: Talbot Press) [no price].

Field and Fair: Travels with a Donkey in Ireland. Translated from the Irish of Padraic O'Conaire by Cormac Breathnach, with Biography and Literary Appreciation by F. R. Higgins. (Dublin: Talbot Press). 3s. 6d. 10 illustrations.

There was Magic in Those Days. By Norreys Jephson O'Conor. 8vo. 62pp. (London: Elkin Mathews). 6s.

Stirabout: From an Ulster Pot. By Ruddick Millar. 192pp. (Belfast The Quota Press). 5s.

The Rosy Fingers. By Col. Arthur Lynch. 8vo. (London: Cecil Palmer). 7s. 6d.

Conversations with George Moore. By Geraint Goodwin. (London Benn). 10s. 6d.

Gaelic Literature Surveyed. By Aodh de Blácam. 390pp. (Dublin The Talbot Press). 12s. 6d. Illustrated by portraits.

James Clarence Mangan and the Poe-Mangan Question. By Henry E. Cain. 93pp. (Washington, DC: Catholic University of America) [no price].

The Renaissance of Irish Poetry. By David Morton. (New York: Eves Washburn). $2.50.

VERSE

Brown Earth and Green. By Michael Walsh. With a Foreword by Katharine Tynan. 8vo. 32pp. (Dublin: Talbot Press) [no price].

A Cluster of Oak Leaves and Other Poems. By Amo Nesciri. 8vo. 48pp. (Same publisher). 1s. "Sing of the Natural Beauty or the Legendary Lore of Ireland."

Poems, by W. B. Yeats; *Poems,* by "Æ"; *Poems,* by James Stephens. (London: Faber and Faber). 1s, each.

Fifty Poems. By Lord Dunsany. 8vo. ix + 57pp. (London: Putnam). 5s.

Poems of Eva Gore-Booth. Complete edition, with "The Inner Life of a Child" and a Biographical introduction by Esther Roper. (London: Longinans). 8s. 6d. Illustrated.

Selected Poems: Lyrical and Narrative. By W. B. Yeats. 8vo. x 230pp. (London: Macmillan). 7s. 6d.

Poems. By Archibald M. Close. 8vo. 96pp. (Belfast: McCaw, Stevenson and Orr). 3s. 6d.
Escape: *Poems.* By Ruth and Celia Duffin. 8vo. x + 130pp. (London: Dent). 4s. 6d.
The Winding Stair. By W. B. Yeats. (London: Grant Richards). £3 3s.
Songs of Glen na Mona. By Brian O'Higgins. 112pp. (Dublin: The Author). 2s. 6d. Printed, with decorations, by Colm Ó Lochlainn.

MISCELLANEOUS

My Countrymen. By an Irishman. 8vo. (London: Blackwood). 7s. 6d.
Party Government in the Irish Free State. By Andrew E. Malone. 8vo. 16pp. (NY: Academy of Political Science). 1s. 6d.
The Ulster Branch of the Family of Wauchope. By G. M. Wauchope. 8vo. 186pp. (London: Simpkin Marshall). 18s.
Ireland's National Theatre. By Rev. Father Dawson Byrne. 8vo. (Dublin: Talbot Press). 7s. 6d.
Handbook for Catholic Social Workers in Dublin. 78pp. (Dublin: St. Vincent de Paul Society, 30 South Anne Street) [no price].
The Ulster Book. Edited by Ruddick Millar. 48pp. (Belfast: The Quota Press). 6d. Vol. I. No. I.
A Tourist's Guide to Ireland. By Liam O'Flaherty. 13+pp. (London: The Mandrake Press). 3s. 6d.
Catholic Emancipation Centenary Record. 4to. 203pp. (Dublin: Printed by Colm Ó Lochlainn and published by the Literary Committee). Upwards of 40 full-page illustrations as well as decorations.
Le Catholicisme en Irelande. By Dom Thomas Becquet, O.S.B. (Liège La Pensée Catholique).

Colm Ó Lochlainn, "Editorial", Vol. XVIII, No. 2 (March & April 1930), 34.

[...] The passing of *The Irish Statesman* will be regretted by many who were not 'constant readers.' Heir to a journalistic tradition begun in *The Irish Homestead* thirty years ago, and edited through its various phases—it has had two reincarnations—by Æ, it was always a fearless champion of free speech. This alone, in a country where freedom is more spoken of than understood made for a certain unpopularity, as also did Æ's lack of understanding of the Irish language or Gaelic cultural activities. This latter fault sometimes led him to open his columns to the vapourings of self-styled authorities whose right to fulminate was strenuously denied by many who listened eagerly to Æ's doctrine on economics and literature. Independent of political parties it had yet a considerable influence which would have been greater far if it had been more Gaelic.

And now almost alone among the weeklies stands *The Leader*, still independent, still edited by the veteran D. P. Moran. Is it too much to hope that *The Leader*'s message—economic and National—will once more find a welcome in the minds of those Irishmen who set their country's good above the clash of contemporary political endeavour? *The Philosophy of Irish Ireland* after thirty years still rings true, and the walls of Jericho have not yet 'come atumbling down.' The re-Gaelicising of Ireland connotes the revitalising of Irish life. In the Church, in the schools, in commerce, and in sport there is a broad field for National work. If *The Leader* leads will Ireland follow?

R. J. Kelly, "Anthony Trollope and Ireland", Vol. XVIII No. 2 (March & April 1930), 46.

Anthony Trollope was undoubtedly one of the most popular authors of his day in England fifty years ago. His books, entitled the Cathedral series, were deservedly very widely read and highly appreciated. He, however, commenced his literary career by writing two novels upon Ireland, which country he knew well. These were *The MacDermots of Ballycloran*, and *The Kellys and the O'Kellys*. Both books dealt with local incidents in the West, and very fairly portrayed rural life. The first turned on incidents in Co. Leitrim. They were not a success, and were never republished. He turned his thoughts, wisely for himself, to write of English clerical life, and did so although at the time he was living in Ireland, and, as he admitted, he never moved among the circle nor met the class he so well described. Now, in the course of time his last novel was destined to be concerned with Ireland, and with the West, which he knew so well once and it was entitled *The Land Leaguers*. It, however, fell flat on the English reading public, and as the Irish reading public that could relish such a class of writing is very limited, the book was still more neglected, and it is now comparatively rare.

The scene of the story was laid in Co. Galway, and we find many familiar names of places and people turning up. It appears that a Mr. Jones purchased in 1850 the estates of Ballintubber and Morony in the Landed Estates Court. They belonged to different owners of the old stock, but lay to the right and left of the road which runs down from the little town of Headford to Lough Corrib. 'At the time of the purchase there was no quieter spot in all Ireland, one in which the lawful requirements of a landlord were more readily performed by a poor and obedient tenantry'. Such is his description. Jones had two sisters, and they left their fortune with him to take care of, and they lost every thing in the land trouble. He had a family. Frank, his eldest boy, a clever lad, and educated at the Queen's College, Galway, and two girls, and a younger boy, Florian, who became a Catholic. Father Giles, we are told, was parish priest of Headford for forty years. He was one of the old type, but Father Malaki, in the neighbouring parish of Ballintubber, was of a different class, and he had no curate 'who would interfere with his happiness'. Chapter IV deals with a Mr. Thomas Blake of Camlough, 'a gentleman living about two miles the other side of Tuam, the first Irishman whom Mr. Jones had become acquainted with, and they became very intimate'. Then we have a Gerald O'Mahony, an Irish-American, who was married and had a daughter, Rachel. He passed over frequently to America, and was a man of strong Republican views. There was a meet of the hounds one day at Ballytoungal, two miles from Clare Galway, on the road to Oranmore, where Sir Nicholas Bodkin lived. He had a rental of £5,000 and spent every penny of it in the county, where he altogether resided, and died poor as usual with spendthrifts.

We have a splendid description of "Black Daly", who was Master of the Hounds which 'used to be called the Galway Blazers, but the name had nearly dropped out of fashion a quarter of a century ago'.

'Who Black Daly was or whence he had come many men, even in Co. Galway, did not know. It was not that he had no property, but that property was so small as to make it impossible that the owner should be master of the county hounds. But in truth Black Daly lived at Daly's Bridge, in the neighbourhood of Castle Blakeney, when he was supposed to be at home. And the house in which he lived he had undoubtedly inherited from his father. But he was not often there, and kept his kennels at Ahascragh, five miles away from Daly's Bridge. Much was not therefore known of Mr. Daly in his own house. But in the field no man was better known or more popular if thorough obedience is an element of popularity. The old gentry of the county could not tell why Mr. Daly had been put into his present position five and twenty years ago, but the manner of his election was often talked about ... He had no money and very few acres of his own on which to preserve foxes ... He never borrowed a shilling from any man, and he certainly paid his way. But if he told a young man that he ought to buy a horse the young man certainly bought it. And if he told the young man that he must pay a certain price, the young man generally paid it. But if the young man were not ready with his money by the day fixed, that young man generally had a bad time of it. Young men have been known to be driven not only out of County Galway, but out of Ireland itself, by the tone of Mr. Daly's voice and by the blackness of his frown [...]'

He is thus described—a perfect picture of John Dennis—'He was tall but very thin and bony, and seemed not to have an ounce of flesh about his face or body. He had large whiskers, coarse and jet black, which did not quite meet beneath his chin. He never joked, and he knew not only every hound in his pack, but he knew their ages, their sires and their dams ... As a man to ride he was a complete master of his art. There was nothing which a horse could do with a man on his back which Daly could not make him do ... He was unmarried: his hounds were his children. He was a Protestant as opposed to a Roman Catholic; but no one had ever known him go to church or speak a word in reference to religion. He was equally civil or uncivil to priest or parson when priest or parson appeared in the field. But on no account would he speak to either if he could avoid it ... He was unmarried. No one who knew him could conceive that he should have a wife. His hounds were his children, and he could have taught no wife to assist him in looking after them with the constant attention and tender care which was given them by Barney Smith, his huntsman. A wife would have been useless ... It may be said that Black Jack filled all positions in the kennels himself. Two rooms had been prepared for him near the kennels, and Barney Smith gave him such attendance as was necessary. Black Daly wanted very little, his tastes were simple. He always dressed the same. Fox hunting was the work of his life'.

Trollope loved a horse and rode to hounds in this very county many and many a time. He followed Black Jack in many a field, and he has painted a perfect picture of him. He describes a meeting at the cross roads of Monivea and the bitter feelings of Black Jack when at that spot for the first time of his life, the hounds were prevented from hunting. He saw the surging mass of angry people, threatening and determined. Then we have Sir Nicholas Bodkin, Mr. Persse of Doneraile, Sir Jaspar Lynch of Bohemane, Mr. Blake of Letterkenny, and Lord Ardrahan. They all tried to get Black Jack to desist from hunting and rousing the anger of the angry crowd. He could not understand why they should oppose hunting, for he had no politics or prejudices. He rode on to Kilcornan intending to draw it, but there a crowd awaited them. There he sat on his horse, frowning at the world before him, a sorrowful man. He rode on to Mr. Lambert's place at Clare, but the same fate of disappointment awaited him. Hunting for him was done in that part of the county. It was his last attempt to act as master of the hounds, according to the story.

So, much for Black Jack. There are people still living in Tuam and the county who remember John Dennis of Birmingham, two miles from Tuam. There he lived and remained M.F.H. to his dying day, a lonely bachelor, but liked by every one. He never had any trouble in the field, for his day was passed before the Land League day came. That was a writer's pardonable liberty with facts. His portrait in oils was painted by a celebrated artist, and presented to him in the Town Hall in Tuam. Lithographed copies of it were given the subscribers, and few houses in County Galway were without John Dennis on his favourite horse with his three favourite dogs around him.

Under the name of Captain York Clayton, Trollope partly describes Clifford Lloyd and his pompous magisterial doings in Galway as Chief Resident Magistrate. Boycotting, murder, the Galway Court House, Ardfry Castle, the trial for the murder of Florian Jones, Cong and its surroundings, and the double murder there, are all mentioned, and then follows a long semi-political dissertation on the "State of Ireland" as Trollope thought it was when, as he says, 'a new and terrible aristocracy was growing up amongst the people—the aristocracy of hidden firearms'. It would be impossible to criticise this work and useless to do so; but it brings before one's mind under assumed names many once well-known characters in the county of Galway, men whose names alone remain with a certain halo of legend about them, men withal as unlike the present generation, whether peasant or landlord, whether in castle or in cabin; as could be conceived—so unlike that one can hardly believe that a half a century, barely fifty years, have come and gone and wrought such changes. But the men of that period of the old landlordism of the early Victorian age, these men with their ways and faults and good qualities are gone, and not one remains today who can be compared with them or considered a fit survivor, and whose action or methods of thinking and living could recall the dead past never to be reenacted.

Séamus Ó Donnabháin, "A Current Commentary", Vol. XVIII, No.2 (March & April 1930), 51.

A very notable contribution to Gaelic literature will be made by the publication now announced of the completed *Duanaire Finn*. The first volume with translation appeared in 1908 from the pen of Dr. Eoin MacNeill, and it is but fitting that the work should attain to fruition through the labours of a student of his, Mr. H. Gerard Murphy, M.A. *The Book of the Lays of Finn* is edited from a unique MS in the Merchants' Quay Franciscan library.

The successfully predatory habits of American bibliophiles has continued to cause uneasiness in England, the archives of whose institutions are every month depleted of their most valuable historical records. Recent lamentations in the English House of Commons over the sale by the Royal Institution of original Headquarters papers of the British Army during the American War of Independence, elicited from Mr. Ramsay MacDonald an appeal to the public, in fairness to the nation, to disclose always any intention to sell such records. A similar appeal in Ireland would, it is feared, go equally unheard.

An Irish poet, Mr. James Walsh, has ventured into prose with a novel of the Belfast shipyard workers entitled *The Islan' Man*. We are reminded that this interesting type has been belatedly treated of in prose, as he has already been fascinatingly delineated on canvas by William Conor, in verse by Richard Rowley, and in sculpture by Miss Praeger.

Lady Gregory's *Hyacinth Halvey* has appeared in translation in *Lectures pour tous* under the name of "The Village Saint", and has been acted on the French stage. It will be remembered that Molière's *Bourgeois Gentilhomme* was most happily adapted by Lady Gregory in her *Would-Be Gentleman*. Such interchanges are all to the good of our cultural development. [...]

"Literature of the Conflict", Vol. XVIII, No. 3 (May & June 1930), 69.

Further contributions on this interesting subject (see Vol. XVII, p.127), are here given. The Editor is very grateful to Mr. Frank Gallagher (well known as author of *Days of Fear*), to Dr. Bourke and to Mr. Mulhall, and hopes that a real bibliography will result from their joint activities. Would it not be well to begin at, say, 1913, when the *Irish Volunteer* was started—or even further back with *Irish Freedom*—or even further still with the *United Irishman*? Much remains to be done in classifying what might be called "The Literature of Revolt." (COLM Ó LOCHLAINN.)

Either as member of the staff or contributor I have been associated with many papers: *New Ireland, Old Ireland, Éire, An Saoghal Gaedhealach, Poblacht na h-Éireann*, and *The Irish Bulletin*. Others were *Freedom, Chun an Lae, The Plain People* (the last named run by the brothers Flanagan from Derry).

By far the most important of all these fugitive papers was *The Irish Bulletin*. From memory I give the following facts: *The Irish Bulletin* was the daily organ of the Irish Government during the War of Independence. It was first published (in the cyclostyled form it always kept) in November, 1919. It seems to have originated with a typewritten sheet issued to the Press about once a fortnight in the spring and summer of 1919 from the Dáil Éireann Publicity Department, giving a summary of British acts of aggression. This was first compiled under Lawrence Ginnell's Directorship of Publicity. I was then his assistant. In November 1919, Mr. Robert Brennan, then Director of Publicity for Sinn Fein, thought of a regular organ for the Government, and *The Irish Bulletin* was the result. At first it took the form of listing acts of violence and aggression by the British, and was not daily in its publication. Afterwards it became the daily organ, and published elaborate statements of the Irish case, and a full history of the contemporary growth and development of the Republican Government. Later still it published a regular weekly supplement called *The Weekly Review* which gave a running history of the Guerilla War, compiled from the official reports of the I.R.A. Commandants in the field.

The Irish Bulletin was published under the general editorship of whoever was Director of Publicity—first Desmond Fitzgerald and then Erskine Childers. In the main it was compiled by me. When Erskine Childers became Director (February 1921) *The Bulletin* was a joint work, except in the case of numerous brilliant issues which were written by him alone. At first only a few hundred copies were printed, but as the war continued and the interest in the struggle grew abroad the number increased until at the end over 2,000 copies went out daily to the British, Irish, and foreign Press, to heads of State and leading politicians in England and America, to writers everywhere who showed any sympathy at all with freedom, and to heads of Churches. It also went to all the Republic's foreign representatives, being translated into the language of the particular country, and circulated in large numbers. Its main circulation was, of course, to the Press in London, Paris, Rome, Madrid, Berlin, &c., and to every national paper in America. Most of the critics of the Black-and-Tan regime in the British Parliament, platform and Press received their information through the Bulletin. Its last number appeared about a week after the "Treaty" was signed. There is a full file of *The Bulletin* in the National Library, and I have heard of other complete files in private hands but it is now exceedingly rare and of prime historic value. In March 1921, *The Bulletin* office was discovered by the British, and its whole extensive plant and files carried off. There was a staff of seven. Dublin Castle afterwards issued forged editions to those named on lists captured in. the same raid. The genuine *Bulletin* continued without missing an issue.

The *Irish Bulletin* was succeeded by *Poblacht na h-Éireann* of which Erskine Childers was editor, and I assistant-editor. The first issues were published as under the editorship of Liam Mellowes, but Erskine Childers was always the editor. His name appears first on the issue of 21st February.

The *Poblacht* was a full-sized weekly, representing the Republican opposition to the "Treaty". It first appeared on January 3rd 1922, and in its ordinary form continued until the issue dated June 29th 1922, which was published on June 27, the day before the attack on the Four Courts. Thereafter it became a daily 'war news', printed at first on double-crown posters, and stuck up over the city, and then on single sheets 9 inches by 14, which were sold in the streets or surreptitiously distributed. I have about 140 numbers of this *War Poblacht* (as it was called) on my files. The first date is June 28th 1922, the last I have is numbered 161, and dated February 19th 1923. Like *The Bulletin* it contains war news, articles, commentaries setting forth the principles and progress of the Republican defence.

In the beginning of August or the end of July Erskine Childers was called to Republican headquarters in Munster. There he published *Poblacht na h-Eireann: Southern War Edition*. It was in its nature the same as the Dublin edition which it then fell to me to carry on, and was at first published on a smaller-sized sheet than the Dublin issue. In its third number it takes the same size. The first issue of the *Southern Poblacht* (as it was called) is dated 11th August 1922, and the last on my very much broken file is No. 35, dated 'Tuesday, January 23. Seventh Year of the Republic' (viz., 1923). I understand that after Erskine Childers' arrest it was carried on by others—amongst them Daniel Corkery. The Dublin edition was frequently captured, its machinery seized, its staff arrested. After my arrest it was edited by Mrs. Frank Kelly, after her by Mr. P. Lynch, and after this by Robert Brennan, who all this time was issuing a second Irish Bulletin. Many others were associated with its production, so that it seems unfair to name only some; but a long quest would be necessary to give a complete list of these gallant men and women. (FRANK GALLAGHER, DUBLIN.)

Séamus Ó Donnabháin, "A Current Commentary", Vol. XVIII, No. 3 (May & June 1930), 3.

Other times, other tastes. One hundred years ago Carleton's *Traits and Stories of the Irish Peasantry* was hailed as the opening-up of a new world. W. B. Yeats, in later days, wrote that with these stories 'began modern Irish literature'. Today Carleton is unread; tomorrow we shall have lost record of him.

The death of James Winder Good should not pass unrecorded in these pages. The anonymous writings of a journalist of repute mould a larger volume of opinion than often is directed by a published work. Irish journalists have penetrated every quarter of the globe, and upon the soundness of their judgment and the integrity of their interpretation of passing events, many outsiders are dependent for their knowledge of Ireland. Mr. Good had published two noteworthy works: *Ulster and Ireland and Irish Unionism.*

The unfamiliar name of John of Gaddesden, Physician to Edward II of England, acquires interest from the fact that his medical text-book *Rosa Anglica* was translated at the time from Latin into Irish, although no English version existed, and now the Irish Texts Society have published the Irish translation, under the editorship of Miss Winifred Wulff a brilliant National University graduate.

Pursuing a somewhat cognate line of thought, it has occurred to us that if no Irish bibliography of specialized scientific subjects exists, this might be undertaken by some competent person, and given shape in these pages. An instance is the numerous books on the *Fauna* and *Flora* of Ireland, such as *Cybele Hibernica*, Dickie's *Ulster Flora*; Praeger's *Flora of the West of Ireland*, &c., which are familiar even to the layman.

Mr. Herbert Wood, M.R.I.A., in a paper read before the Royal Historical Society, has dealt with the loss of Irish public records caused by the destruction of the Four Courts in 1922, which, he stated, would deprive Irish historians of a field that had received but scanty treatment.

Turning to an Irish author whose works arouse controversy in his own country, we find Sean O'Casey the subject of a critical and biographical review by Herr Harry Bergolz in the current issue of *Englische Studien*.

Among recent best-sellers we notice the names of two Irish authoresses—Miss Norah Hoult and Mrs. Monica Ewer. Miss Hoult has done well with her *Time! Gentlemen! Time!*

G. B. Shaw's latest work *The Apple Cart* has not yet been published in England. Mr. Shaw's collected works are to be issued, commencing in July, in an edition of about thirty volumes, which for the first time will include *The Apple Cart*. This astute move debars the first-edition collector of small means from possession of this volume, and at the same time ensures rapid sale of this costly set of complete works. A point of interest to us here is the binding of the set in Irish linen dyed jade green.

The operation of the Censorship of Publications Act is now in full swing; three lists of banned publications having already been issued. These concern non-Irish publications only; but it may be that an Irish author will one day attain to the doubtful distinction of being included in a subsequent list.

"Reviews", Vol. XVIII, No.3 (May & June) 1930, 95.

STANDISH JAMES O'GRADY (*I.B.L.* XII: 60). This distinguished kinsman of the great Irish scholar, Standish Hayes O'Grady, was born on 18th September 1846, at Castletownbere, Co. Cork, of which place his father the Rev. Thomas O'Grady was Protestant rector, and died on 18th May, 1926, at Shanklin in the Isle of Wight.

MR. P. S. O'HEGARTY has issued (Dublin 1930) twenty-five numbered, autographed and interleaved copies of his excellent *Bibliography of Books Written by Standish O'Grady*, beginning with the *Scintilla Shelleiana*, which O'Grady edited in 1875 over the pseudonym of "Arthur Clive". (S. Ó C.)

Colm Ó Lochlainn, "Editorial", Vol. XVIII, No. 4 (July & Aug. 1930), 97.

The Conference held in Dublin early in July of the Associated Booksellers of Great Britain and Ireland brings home to all interested in books the very dependent position occupied by Ireland in the publishing world. Almost 97 per cent of the books available through the book trade in Ireland is the product of English publishing houses, and is printed in England or Scotland. Even that rare bird—the successful Irish author—is for the most part printed and published abroad. Surely, it is time that a definitely Irish publishing syndicate be formed with the dual object of keeping in Ireland a fair percentage of the publishing and printing of books by Irish authors, and of securing proper distribution in other countries of books printed and published in Ireland. Such a body would command the confidence of Irish authors, and could have a permanent agent in London, and a traveller for the English and Scottish Provinces.

But before Dublin can reach the front rank as a publishing centre, a higher standard in book printing must prevail. Dublin-printed books as a whole cannot stand comparison with those printed in other countries. The Dublin University Press Classics of 1740-50 were perfect in type and style, in paper, presswork, and general appearance equal to anything of their period, and superior to anything of ours. To recapture the charm of such books should be the aim of all Dublin printers: the proper design and planning of bookwork will achieve it.

J. S. Crone, "Sgéala ó Chathair na gCeó", Vol. XVIII, No. 4 (May & June 1930), 99.

I have just returned from a most enjoyable holiday in the old land. Beginning with a week in Co.Wexford with the R.S.A.I., in the course of which we visited many places of historical, archæological and literary interest, from Beg-an-Bun to Graiguenamanagh, and were hospitably entertained wherever we went. From Bannow, birthplace of Mrs. S. C. Hall, to Mount Leinster, whose legends, enshrined in the pages of Patrick Kennedy, delighted our childhood, to New Ross, whose story has been sung in old Norman-French, and translated by L. E. L., every inch was redolent of memories. The best history of New Ross is contained in a biography of Bp. John Thomas O'Brien (Dublin 1875), a place where few would look for it. This biography was written by Rev. W. G. Carroll, an uncle of Bernard Shaw's. Mr. Goddard H. Orpen, the author of *The Normans in Ireland*, a few years ago published, in pamphlet form, for private circulation, a lecture, entitled *New Ross*, which he had delivered in the town for a charitable purpose.

Mr. Orpen, who was amongst our hosts, at his beautiful home, Monksgrange, possesses the finest library we saw in all our visits. It is particularly rich in historical works, as befits a historian so highly esteemed, and amongst his treasures are some half-dozen volumes from the pen of his late wife, and an *incunabulum* bearing the autograph of Jonathan Swift. I may here say that the books I found most interesting and edifying were a neat little pamphlet, *Wexford*, published by the Educational Company of Ireland at a shilling, and written by Senator Miss Browne, who proved a very useful cicerone in some of our rambles, and that quaint little work, *The Dialect of Forth and Bargy*, by Jacob Poole, a native of the district, who was an uncle of the late Alfred Webb, M.P., author of the well known *Compendium of Irish Biography*. It was edited by the great philologist, Rev. Wm. Barnes, whose statue stands in the High Street of Dorchester, is long out of print, but well deserves republication. Hore's classic *History of Wexford* is a wonderful compilation, but, of course, out of the question in travelling.

Eighteen years ago I had the pleasure of being the guest of the Associated Booksellers and Publishers of Great Britain, during their visit to Dublin, and their visit being repeated this year I was again honoured with an invitation. Representatives of the printing, bookselling and publisher's craft were much in evidence and I had the gratification of meeting many old friends and making new ones at their social board.

As far as I could see, Stephen Gwynn and myself were the only surviving penmen of the previous function present. But, of course, many new writers have come into their own since then, and Lynn Doyle, T. C. Murray, Maurice Walsh, and the delightful poetess we used to know as W. M. Letts, were there to bear testimony to the literary abilities of our countrymen and women.

In Belfast I found the Francis Joseph Bigger Memorial Library, generously presented to the city by his brother, Col. Frederick Bigger, neatly arranged in a special department in the Public Library, Royal Avenue. The catalogue slips are ready for the printer and the esteemed librarian, Mr. Goldsworthy, hopes to have the special catalogue published in the autumn. I visited the new Municipal Art Gallery in Botanic Gardens, a palatial building, admirably arranged under the skilled guidance of Mr. A. Deane, M.R.I.A., embracing all the latest improvements, even to a cinema, used for lecturing purposes. The princely donation by Sir John Lavery of his many valuable pictures, now well hung in the Gallery, is alone worth going all the way to see.

The chief event of this publishing season is the appearance of the early volumes of the complete Shaw. It is issued in sets, at 30 guineas, 'for fools and speculators', as the author characteristically says. The chief attraction of the first volume is a long, frank and humorous, autobiographical introduction, recalling his home circle and relations, like so many Dubliners of his day—his father who 'was fond of the drop' and his namesake 'Uncle Barney' who played the ophicleide, all hit off with true Shavian felicity. His early struggles in London as a 'ghost' and a 'potboiler' are told with gusto, and now, looked back on from the pinnacle of success, seem not such bad times after all. Mr. Shaw promises that all new matter in this edition will be re-published at prices to suit poorer purses.

Amongst the names in the recently issued Civil List Pensions for literary services, I am pleased to see that of my old friend, S. M. Ellis, who during the past quarter of a century has written many a biography, edited many a volume of reminiscences. No one has traversed the whole range of Victorian literature—published and unpublished—with better result than he, for he is indefatigable in research and plies a charming pen. Mr. Ellis knows and loves Ireland and has many Irish friends. He is the leading authority on the life and works of that singular genius, Sheridan Le Fanu, who, though put by discerning critics on as high a pedestal as Wilkie Collins or Edgar Poe, has never had justice done to him. Mr. Ellis's admirable "Bibliography of Le Fanu", which first appeared in these pages, has many times been reprinted but never surpassed.

His latest work, just published by Gollancz at 25s., is *The Life of Michael Kelly*, a fully annotated edition of an autobiography dictated by the subject to that arch humourist and hoaxer, Theodore Hook. Kelly (1762-1826), a Dublin boy, was the possessor of a remarkable singing voice, and sang in Milan, Vienna and other musical centres with great *éclat*. He knew Mozart, Hayden and Gluck, and on settling in London, became a favourite of the Prince Regent, sang for years at the Opera House, was familiar with all the bucks and beaux of the time— Sheridan, Kean, Kemble, Mrs. Siddons and Lady 'Hamilton'. Mr. Ellis, in this handsomely illustrated book, makes the brilliant scene live again for the edification of his readers.

Séamus Ó Donnabháin, "A Current Commentary", Vol. XVIII, No. 4 (July & Aug. 1930), 103.

Dearth of subjects fortunately enables me to treat of other matters that have for some time engaged my mind. The value of *The Book Lover* would be greatly enhanced were readers to exercise their right to make of these pages a forum wherein to gossip about books and men, and bring forth their problems in historical research and their bibliographical or genealogical enquiries.

The interest taken in the "Literature of the Conflict" has been gratifying, and it is hoped that the valuable contributions now being published will be of assistance to historians.

For those whose hobbies can take literary shape, a pleasant and useful compilation would be that of Irish magazines and periodicals of different periods. At two guineas there has recently been published the first volume of *A History of American Magazines*, by Frank Luther Mott, surveying the period ending 1850. The second volume will bring the work down to the present day. Their quaint titles and peculiar programmes, not to stress their historical value, might find a parallel here, where even recent years have evoked an *Eye-Opener*, a *Spark*, and a *Scissors and Paste*.

Another suggestion originates with Séamus Ó Casaide there is immediate scope for a record of all articles of Irish biographical, historical or topographical interest appearing in current periodicals. If a small circle of bibliophiles were to allot a particular journal, one to each member, whose responsibility it would be then to furnish a half-yearly or yearly list, much valuable ground would be permanently surveyed. As an example, the last few months of *The Irish Times* yields, among others, the following articles with their descriptive sub-titles and the

author's name or pseudonym:
> J. J. Callanan. Centenary of a Cork Poet. An Innovator in Anglo-Irish Verse. By "S.F.C."

[...]

Séamus Ó Casaide, "Oliver Goldsmith", Vol. XVIII, No. 4 (July & Aug. 1930), 118.

Amongst the depositions preserved in T.C.D. Library relative to the outrages alleged to have been committed by the Irish in 1641 is an account (F. 3, 1) by "Mr. John Gouldsmith, parson of Brashowle", of "an inhuman and barbarous massacre" at Sruell on the confines of Galway and Mayo counties in February, 1641.

The narrative was published by Lodge in his *Peerage of Ireland* (vol. ii. p. 331, first edition, and Vol. IV. p.239, Archdall's 1789 edition), but James Hardiman in the *Miscellany of the Irish Archaeological Society* (1846) mentions that Lodge omitted the following passage (Mayo volume, p. 5):

> Deponent [John Gouldsmith] having been a Romish papist [sic] and converted to the Protestant religion by the light of God's truth, and therefore more hated than any other by the Papists. The rebells coming to his house at midnight, the—— day of——, 1641, presented their sharp skeines to his throate, robbed him then and other times of all his goods, worth about £500; and forcibly expelled him from his church-living and lands, worth about £100 per annum. Having heard and being told by some of his neighbours, that he had no waye to save his life but by going to masse, he fled away, and was pursued by Edmond O'Maley McLaughlin, who besett the house whither he was fled, with about 20 of his men, saying unto him: 'Mr. Gouldsmith doe you remember how your English have served us. How they slitt our noses and scared our faces; come forth.' And was so bitter against this deponent, that, had not a friar begged for him upon his knees (as the neighbours told him) he had cut out the deponent's tongue. At length, with much difficulty, deponent escaped to the Lord of Mayo's house; and was the second man that was robbed in the county of Mayo, as he supposeth.
>
> The deponent further stated [according to Hardiman] among other matters also omitted by Lodge in the narrative, that 'he was in the county of Westmeath, as a Protestant clergyman.'

Hardiman adds that the deponent:

> was the ancestor (grandfather?) of Oliver Goldsmith, our highly-gifted poet and essayist, but superficial and prejudiced historian; for proof of which see that part of his *History of England* that treats of the affairs of Ireland in the seventeenth century. There is a tradition current in the

counties of Westmeath and Roscommon, that the poet was descended from a friar, whom the people designate by an epithet too gross to be mentioned here. That tradition is in some degree supported by the testimony above quoted. These particulars were, probably, unknown to Doctor Prior, the elegant biographer of Goldsmith.

Turning to Archdall, I find that John Gouldsmith, incumbent of Brashowle (i.e. Burrishoole in county Mayo), stated that his brother Francis Gouldsmith was 'a Romish Priest of good account, being Capilian Majore of the Castle of Antwerp in Brabant.'

Many biographies of Oliver Goldsmith have been published, of which those by Forster, Prior and Ashe King are perhaps the best known. Two Roscommon writers—Mgr. James J. Kelly (*The Haunts of Goldsmith*) and Dr. Michael F. Cox (in the National Literary Society's *Journal*, Dublin 1900)—claim the poet as a native of their county.

Séamus Ó Donnabháin, "Oliver Goldsmith", Vol. XVIII, No. 4 (July & Aug. 1930), 119.

A magazine article appearing in 1761, advocating a treaty of naval limitation with France, has been attributed to the pen of Oliver Goldsmith. It would be of some interest to verify Goldsmith's role as precursor of the present-day movement.

J. S. Crone, "Sgéala ó Chathair na gCeó", Vol. XVIII, No. 5 (Sept. & Oct. 1930), 130.

The Bodleian Library in Oxford has recently acquired a broadside copy of Tom Tickell's famous ballad of "Lucy and Colin", printed in Dublin and dated 1725. The ballad was written about 1723, and this broadside is claimed to be 'the unique copy of the first edition of the poem'.

Whilst the wealth of Irish MSS in the Bodleian has long been known to researchers like Dr. C. W. Russell and J. P. Prendergast in the past, and in our own time to Charles MacNeill, few Irish bibliographers know its great collection of Irish books, unfortunately, not separately catalogued. It contains Irish periodicals I have never seen elsewhere. It is many years since I was there, at the time Willy Yeats was working at his book on Blake under the helpful guidance of that great librarian Falconer Madan, who was so proud of his descent from the O'Maddens of Hy Many. It is interesting to recall that the two great University libraries at Oxford and Cambridge owe so much of their worth to two book lovers of Irish descent—Henry Bradshaw and Falconer Madan.

Our Irish writers are much to the fore this publishing season, and none more so than Denis Gwynn, who must surely be the busiest—but then he has the advantage of being an expert typist. Last publishing season he issued two important works dealing with the centenary of Catholic Emancipation, and his monumental work on O'Connell. This season appears his sympathetic and charming memoir of 'dear Edward' Martyn, the description of whose home-life at Tulyra recalls a pleasant day I spent there twenty golden years ago.

Mr. Gwynn's most recent publication is a pamphlet entitled *Daniel O'Connell and Ellen Courtney*, elaborating that unpleasant episode in the life of the Liberator, with some hitherto unpublished documents. Now, I see announced by Cape *The Life and Death of Roger Casement*, which should prove interesting. Mr. Gwynn who promises to be our Irish biographer par excellence, has on the stocks, his official *Life of John Redmond*. Thirty years ago the name of Frank Harris was more prominent in the world of letters than it is today, for he holds the unique record of having, at one time or another, edited such important periodicals as *Vanity Fair*, *The Saturday Review*, and *The Fortnightly Review*, as well as his own brilliant, but short-lived, venture—*The Candid Friend*. Few who knew him and valued his work as novelist, playwriter and Shakespearian scholar, ever guessed the strenuous life he had lived in his youth. Now in *On the Trail* he lifts the curtain, and reveals how he left his native Galway as a lad in his teens for U.S.A., and joining up with two cattle kings led the wild life of a cowboy in the seventies, on the Rio Grande and Mexican boundary. His astonishing adventures and exciting experiences are sufficient to fit out a wild west film, and make excellent reading.

Arnold Bennett in one of his weekly causeries in *The Evening Standard* recently makes this comment which I think worthy of preservation.

> We relatively taciturn Anglo-Saxons are apt to ignore the fact that modern imaginative English literature is dominated by three Irishmen. W. B. Yeats is the greatest living poet. Shaw is the greatest literary world-force (with the possible exception of Wells). George Moore is— in my opinion—the greatest living novelist; many would deny this, but few would deny he was one of the greatest. I might mention Synge, author of the greatest modern play, *The Playboy of the Western World*. But Synge is dead, and of late years the spirit of his masterpiece has been assassinated in performance. One could name about five plays by Irishmen with which no play by a living Englishman can advantageously compare. No mean record for a small country, and a country whose brains have been mainly devoted to politics and backchat.

The Belfast Civil Engineer, Mr. Freeman Wills Crofts, who is regarded by various experts as the greatest writer of detective fiction, has scored another great success in *Sir John Magill's Last Journey*, the scene of which is partly laid about Larne and Belfast. Mr. Crofts, I understand, is of Cork extraction, and related to the family which gave us Rev. James Wills of *Illustrious Irishmen* fame, Willie Wills, poet, painter, and playwright and Rev. Freeman Wills who so ably adapted the famous play *The Only Way*.

I hear that Edward Marjoribank, who scored such a success last year with his *Life of Marshall Hall* is engaged on an 'official' life of that whilom stormy petrel of Irish politics—Lord Carson. A true account, and unbiased (if that were possible) should make racy reading!

This month marks the centenary of the death of William Hazlitt, admittedly the second best essay-writer in the English language—the gentle "Elia" being first. They were fast friends, and it was to Lamb that Hazlitt declared with almost his last words, after a career of storm and dreg, of strife and penury: 'Well, I've had a happy life.' Hazlitt was ever a fighter—to the end, and his championing of the first Napoleon, when to do such, rendered him liable to worse pains and penalties than ever endured by a pro-German in our day. J. L. Garvin in *The Observer*, I think, touches the secret spring when he says that it was Hazlitt's Ulster blood and lineage, and his Arian upbringing that inspired him to fight against the tyranny of the classes over the masses. And now this 'disreputable quill-driver' is having his scattered writings published in twenty-one vols.

[Colm Ó Lochlainn], "A Current Commentary", Vol. XVIII, No. 5 (Sept. & Oct. 1930), 137.

Among the most interesting cases of Englishmen who have adopted with enthusiasm the country of domicile and become earnest workers for Ireland, must be numbered Rev. Euseby Digby Cleaver, M.A., who, born in Connacht in 1826, earned well the right to the name he later adopted, E. D. MacCliabhair. The account by Michael O'Mahony in *Honesty* (July 26 1930) demonstrates still further the desirability of keeping a full record of all original articles on Irish subjects appearing in current periodicals.

Elsewhere Dr. Crone reminds us that Mr. Freeman Wills Crofts whose 'thrillers' adorn so many of our public library shelves, is an Irish civil engineer. He thus joins that little band of professors and professional men—we bring to mind Dr. Stewart the Belfast professor of Chemistry ("J. J. Connington"), G. D. H. Cole, Stephen Leacock—who seek relaxation in the lighter letters. Mr. Crofts is said to survey meticulously the terrain in which his plots are woven, so that no inexactitude or impossible situation may be detected by the reader.

We notice among recent deaths the names of Maria de la Cherois-Crommelin, F.R.G.S., better known under her pen-name "May Crommelin", Patrick J. Murphy, a leading U.S.A. publisher of books relating to Ireland, and William A. Locker, a former editor of *The Irish Times*.

A biographical study of Father Gerard Manley Hopkins has been strongly featured this autumn. Interest was bound to revive in this poet, the beauty and complexity of whose imaginings demanded a new mode of expression, a fantastic imagery, that only a coined and intensely hybridized language could supply. It is possible that he was the forerunner of the vagrant moderns of like vein, although he has been universally exonerated from meaninglessness.

The fourth novel of Mr. Peadar O'Donnell, *The Knife*, is looked forward to with great interest. Mr. Maurice Walsh has not yet acceded to a wide demand for a novel located in Ireland. A new short novel of his will shortly be published by Chambers, but first only in serial form.

The censorship of books continues to operate with general satisfaction. Further lists of banned books and newspapers have been issued, and there are rumblings in the North of a demand for the adoption of some similar procedure for self-protection.

There is now an organ of the Dublin Writers' Club, *The Muse*, edited by Mr. W. A. Downes. From *The Irish Printer* we learn that the Cumann na nGaedheal organ, *The Star*, has ceased publication as a weekly; but has resumed in the form of a monthly review.

Séamus Ó Casaide, "Rev. Bernard Callan", Vol. XVIII, No. 5 (Sept. & Oct. 1930), 140.

In *The Irish Ecclesiastical Record* for November 1905, Father Matthew Russell, S.J., quotes as follows from to a letter dated 1st September, 1891, which was addressed him by Canon O'Connor, P.P., of Newtownbutler:

> In turning over some back numbers of the *I. E. Record*, I came across an interesting contribution of yours in the September number of 1883, entitled "Piscatores Hominum". At once it occurred to me that I possess a copy of that *concio ad clerum*, written about 1776, by a student of the College of Antwerp named Bernard Callan, who afterwards became P.P. of Inniskeen [near Carrickmacross] in the diocese of Clogher. From this manuscript copy you will see that the title given therein is more appropriate: *Summi Sacerdotis Jesu Christi ad Sacerdotes Alloquium*. The missing line in the second quatrain is supplied. In other respects, too, my copy appears to be more perfect; at least it is more in harmony with metre and rhythm. I have marked the points of

difference, and take the liberty of sending them to you, that you may make what use of them you deem best.

Canon O'Connor appears to have stated in the letter that Father Callan, who was a maternal relative of his, died in 1809, parish priest of the united parishes of Inniskeen and Donaghmoyne, and that in copying the *Alloquium* he signed his name in Irish characters as "Brian na Callan mac Art".

As there appears to be some mistake in the spelling of the Irish name as printed in the *Record*, it would be interesting to know if Canon O'Connor's letter to Father Russell (obit. 1912) has been preserved in any Jesuit library in Dublin, as the letter may contain further information about an t-Athair Brian Ó Colláin (mac Airt).

The Right Rev. Daniel O'Connor, Dean and Vicar-General, died parish priest of Carrickmacross on 11th November 1919, and some Clogher priest interested in the history of the former clergy of the diocese may from a search among Father O'Connor's papers or otherwise be able to throw further light on the career of Father Brian (son of Art) Callan (Ó Colláin?) [...]

Colm Ó Lochlainn, "Editorial", Vol. XVIII, No. 6 (Nov. & Dec. 1930), 153.

Deo Gratias! Felicitus explicit primum volumen meum libri quae Amator Librum Hibernicus vocatur. And I veil my sigh of relief in the most culinary of kitchen Latin lest it may sound too loud. In all seriousness—a frame of mind which only now I bring to my task as the year rounds off—it is no small thing to have collected and carried; picked and chosen; set and proofed; held up and held over [...] and otherwise projected on an unexpectant and (I'm afraid) unresponsive world 184 pages of *The Irish Book Lover*, during the year 1930.

Not alone that I can claim like the famous Dublin Merchant, 'Alone I done it', for had I not Dr. Crone and Seamus Ó Casaide as the prop and pillar of my reclining youth? With the cloak of their charity they covered my errors, they have sheltered my ignorance with the wings of their wisdom. *Ad multos annos an Bheirt aca. Agus cogar, cé bhóir an bhliann dar gcionn*?

J. S. Crone, "Sgéala ó Chathair na gCeó", Vol. XVIII, No. 6 (Nov. & Dec. 1930), 154.

The Irish Literary Society has had so far a most successful Autumn Session. The evergreen President (Mr. Ashe King) although in his 92nd year, opened the session with a brilliant discourse on his "Memorable Memories", from his boyhood in Ennis until he was contributing novels to the *Cornhill Magazine*, and of the great set which included George Meredith, James Payne, Leslie Stephen and George Du Maurier. Col. Arthur Lynch delighted a large audience with his racy account of "Irish Traits at Home and Abroad". Michael MacDonagh read "A Bunch of Anglo-Irish Verse", with Mrs. K. Tynan Hinkson in the chair, whose daughter Pamela contributed to the pleasure of the gathering by reading some of her own verse; and a dinner in honour of Stephen Gwynn, a former Honorary Secretary, was held at which a company of a hundred sat down.

Capt. Henry Harrison, who was the youngest of Parnell's Parliamentary colleagues, in a letter to the press says:

> It is a full year since my book was accepted for publication. After various vicissitudes and a change of publisher, it now exists in corrected proofs, and I may safely promise it for an early date after the New Year. The purport of my book can be gathered from its title, which is to be *Parnell Vindicated: The Lifting of the Veil*. It gives the inner story of Parnell's private life. The story of "The Split" and of Parnell's case against the Liberal Party and Mr. John Morley must come later. I had access to and read all the documents ... because I was asked to write forthwith a biography of Parnell—a task which I did not feel myself competent to undertake.

There was a very pleasant little function recently arranged by John Masefield, the Poet Laureate, at his charming house at Boor's Hill, Oxford, where he has a private theatre. He invited Mr. W. B. Yeats there, who was entertained by several young ladies with beautiful voices, who recited some of his poems. The occasion was the thirtieth anniversary of the meeting of the two poets. As a young man, Mr. Masefield wrote to W. B. submitting some of his verses and soliciting criticism. Mr. Yeats received him kindly, and gave him advice to go working at poetry—and today he is Poet Laureate. Though Mr. Yeats had forgotten the date of this event, Masefield had cherished it, and so arranged the delightful recognition. Truly there is nothing lost by kindness.

One of those delightful stories that warm the heart of the book lover has just been made public. It tells how a search for a croquet set in an attic at Malahide Castle last Summer led to the discovery of a box containing Boswell MSS of great value—literary and monetary. The most important portion of the discovery—the second in four years—was 107 pages of the original MS of the *Life of Johnson*. Hitherto it was considered that only about thirty pages had survived the damp and for these a New York dealer had (it is said) offered £16,000.

Lord Talbot de Malahide is a direct descendant of James Boswell, hence, the presence of the papers at his home. The MSS previously found were sold to Col. Isham, one of the most prominent book collectors in U.S.A., who has had them privately printed. They will now eventually run to about 15 volumes, and will cost when complete £150 a set.

As was to be expected the publication of Denis Gwynn's *Life and Death of Roger Casement* has created a commotion in official circles, and Scotland Yard is all agog at his outspoken charge against it of having 'faked' the terrible 'diary' which did so much to hang Casement. A perfect deluge of denials and interviews has appeared in the London Press, and Mr. Gwynn has boldly met his attackers in the same columns; which all needless to say, 'booms' the book, and makes good for the publisher and author.

E. R. McC. Dix, "The Late Miss D. A. Ferguson", Vol. XVIII, No. 6 (Nov. & Dec. 1930), 157.

The news of Miss Ferguson's death came unexpectedly to all who knew her, and proves a very great loss, not only to the Librarians and Staff of the National Library, of which she was one, but also to students and others like myself who made use of that Library, and benefited much by her ever ready help and knowledge.

It gives me some satisfaction, though of a melancholy and sad kind, to testify to her wonderful ability as a bibliographer particularly of Irish printed pamphlets and books. I do not recall how many years she has been in the Library; but it is many years since I made her acquaintance there, and had the benefit of her wide knowledge and hearty sympathy in the work of Irish bibliography.

One of her special tasks there, was the classification of the vast number of Pamphlets dealing with Ireland or printed there—a great collection, of which the National Library may well be proud.

For several years the late Miss Ferguson had, as her special work, the identifying and cataloguing of these pamphlets, and in the course of years she acquired a vast knowledge of that particular literature unequalled, I think, by anyone. She was most painstaking, careful and reliable in her work, as far as I am able to judge, as well as being most courteous and helpful and ready to place her knowledge at the use of any bona fide student.

All who knew her can testify to her attractive character and helpfulness. I find I have lost, more than a helper, a real friend.

M. J. McManus, "A Forgotten Goldsmith Poem", Vol. XVIII, No. 6 (Nov. & Dec. 1930), 166.

In Messrs. Sotheby's *Catalogue of Books* to be sold during the week commencing Monday, April 14, Lot 465 is described as follows:

> ... two volumes of poems edited by Joshua Edkins and published in Dublin in 1789 and 1790.

The second volume of this collection contains on pp.87-88 a poem of thirty-six lines entitled "The Fair Thief", with the name 'Oliver Goldsmith, M.D.' [sic] appended.

Now, it is a very curious thing that the Goldsmith poem mentioned has been overlooked by all the editors of Goldsmith from Prior to Austin Dobson. The book cannot be described as excessively rare, for besides the copy I am exhibiting I have seen at least two others, and I shall be surprised if it is not in our principal libraries. In a foreword to the first volume Edkins says:

> By far the greater number of the poems contained in this volume have never met the public eye, and those, will not, it is presumed, be thought unworthy of being preserved from the perishable publications, in which they made their first appearance.

From this we gather that the compiler collected the poems from manuscript sources or from fugitive periodicals. Later on in the preface he says that 'to many of his friends he is much indebted for the readiness with which they furnished him with several pieces of merit in the present volume', and again, 'that whenever he could find out an author his desire was strictly attended to, either in the publication or suppression of his poem'.

Now, it is hardly likely that he found the poem attributed to Goldsmith (at any rate with Goldsmith's name appended) in any of the literary magazines of the period. These have been so well combed out by English and American scholars within recent years that it would be almost impossible for an unrecorded poem by such an important author to escape. Other sources will have to be looked for, and we will, I am afraid, have to learn a little more about Edkins and his literary friendships before indulging in anything in the nature of a likely surmise. Underneath the title of the poem we find 'not printed in his works'. This proves, on investigation, to be quite correct.

It is not in the *Select Poems* published by Griffin in London in 1775 nor in the very different selection published in Belfast in the same year, nor in the *Miscellaneous Works*, containing all his essays and poems, also published by Griffin in that year. The only other editions published before Edkins's volume appeared were the first collected edition, Dublin 1777, and Newberry's London edition of 1780, and in neither of these does the poem appear. There is nothing surprising in this, for if my surmise is correct, the poem up to the time of Edkin's discovering it, had only existed in manuscript; but who would have thought that 140 years after Edkins had rescued it, and given it the dignity of print in a popular collection it would still be true to say that it was 'not printed in his works'? Yet, such is the case, and it is not to be found in Dobson's definitive edition.

The question will, of course, be raised, is the poem genuine Goldsmith or merely an attribution? And here we shall have to rely largely on internal evidence. The metrical form employed is the one which Goldsmith nearly always used in his longer poems of the lighter sort—the three other examples are *The Double Transformation*, and his two imitations of Swift, *A New Simile* and *The Logicians Refuted*. Technically, the poem is a little masterpiece, and betrays that perfection of form which Goldsmith even in his lightest moments always seemed able to achieve. But whether genuine or spurious it is an entirely charming piece of fantasy, and one which will take away nothing from even such a great reputation as that of Goldsmith.

The Goldsmith poem, however, is not the only point of interest in these volumes. They also contain, amongst others, poems by Samuel Johnson, Henry Grattan, Edmund Burke and Richard Brinsley Sheridan. One of the Sheridan contributions is called *Verses Left in a Grotto near Bath*. This, I find, had already appeared in the *European Magazine* for 1782, and it is noteworthy that in the version here printed there are numerous textual alterations.

The book has some pretty vignette illustrations engraved by Esdaile, and was issued with half-titles, which are present in the copies on exhibition. A third volume appeared at a much later date, 1801, and this is rather more frequently met with than its predecessors.

"How James Duffy Rose to Fame" [reprinted from *The Sunday Independent*], Vol. XVIII, No. 6 (Nov. & Dec. 1930), 168.

There is a tradition among the printers of Dublin that the first book published by James Duffy, who a hundred years ago founded the Dublin publishing firm of James Duffy and Co., was a twopenny edition of the famous old dream-book known as *Napoleon's Book of Fate*.

The tragedy of Napoleon's overthrow and death was still fresh in people's minds at the time, and his so-called *Book of Fate* had a fabulous circulation. Duffy's edition, entitled *Boney's Oraculum*, found its way into every corner of Ireland. It was a lucky venture, and set James Duffy on his feet as a publisher. The amount of solid work he accomplished in the interests of Catholicity in Ireland and Irish nationality during the next forty years can never be estimated.

James Duffy was born in County Monaghan early in the last century, and received his education at a hedge school. There he became the friend and close companion of a lad named John Donegan, who was later to win fame as a Dublin watchmaker. Donegan watches—ever suggestive of ancestral respectability—may still be seen occasionally, ticking as reliably as they did a century ago.

Donegan was the first of the two to come to Dublin, and it was through him that Duffy got a start some time later in the book-selling business in Anglesea Street. I have heard it stated that he began as an assistant with John Daly, the Celtic scholar and publisher of Mangan's and Sigerson's translations from the Munster poets. At all events, he took the flood-tide with his cheap edition of the aforesaid dream-book, and never looked back.

Until this time the price of books had been very high, prohibitive indeed, as far as the majority of the Irish people were concerned; and, except for weekly papers and cheap monthly journals, popular reading, in the sense we understand it today, did not exist. Duffy set himself to cater for the masses and his enterprise quickly justified itself.

Establishing a publishing house in Anglesea Street, he simply flooded town and country with cheap books of Catholic and of national interest, devotional works and healthy Irish fireside tales, by writers who were until then known only to the few who could afford to buy their books. Nor was there anything shoddy about the manner in which these popular volumes were produced. Pocket editions they mostly were, each volume complete in itself, well printed, and often embellished with engravings, bound in cloth with gold lettering—all for the modest sum of 6d.

He had broken new ground, and the people were not slow to prove their appreciation of his gesture. So rapidly did the business swell that its founder was obliged after a few years to move into roomier premises on Wellington Quay.

It is, however, as publisher of the remarkable output in national literature which came from the brilliant pens of the Young Irelanders that James Duffy is best remembered now. For a decade or so before the founding of the *Nation* he had, through his Popular Sixpenny Library, been unwittingly cultivating the popular taste for the mighty feast of song and story that was to be sprung upon them in the early 'forties.

Says his more famous namesake and fellow-Monaghan man, Charles Gavan Duffy, in one of his books:

> The volumes projected by the Young Irelanders were nearly all published by James Duffy. He was originally a bookseller on a small scale in an obscure street, dealing chiefly in reprints of religious publications; but enterprise and liberality carried him into a wider field, and ultimately created a trade extending to India, America and Australia. *The Spirit of the Nation* was issued in the first instance from the *Nation* office; but as the demand for them became embarrassing, I looked out for a publisher, and fixed upon James Duffy. This was the beginning of his connection with the Young Ireland Party.

And this connection led at once to such an expansion of business that Duffy had to move into still larger premises, where no fewer than 120 hands were kept constantly employed. Here all manner of books relating to Ireland were turned out at white heat—classics from the pens of Davis, Mitchel, Mangan, D'Arcy McGee, D. F. McCarthy, Gavan Duffy, Carleton, Dalton Williams, Martin Haverty, the Banims, Gerald Griffin, Father Meehan, and later, the matchless stories of Kickham, and the scholarly hagiological works of Cardinal Moran, Bishop Comerford, Canon O'Hanlon and others.

Throughout the middle decades of the century his office and bookshop were the Mecca of a daily stream of the foremost notabilities of the generation—leaders of Catholic thought, Young Ireland and Fenian 'felons' in the making, grave and reverend prelates, long-haired poets and the rest. And all honoured James Duffy for his manly character, his uprightness and steadfast loyalty to his country and the class whence he was sprung.

Like Rockfeller, he would seem to have deliberately set aside a certain proportion of his net income from year to year for charitable purposes. In his long and strenuous career he never took a regular holiday; and while in every other respect he was an ideal employer, he would not on any condition allow holidays to any of his staff. But each Christmas Eve found him going round his premises to wish each member the compliments of the season, and to hand him a sealed envelope containing his Christmas Box, varying from £3 to £20, according to the length of service and status of the worker.

He died in 1871. This is the striking epitaph inscribed on his tombstone in Glasnevin, composed by his friend, Father C. P. Meehan, the historian:

PRAY FOR HIM, O READER, FOR HE DESERVED WELL OF RELIGION AND COUNTRY. HIS DEVOTIONAL PUBLICATIONS HAVE INSTRUCTED MANY UNTO SALVATION, AND THE HISTORICAL WORKS HE PUBLISHED HAVE EXALTED THE CHARACTER OF HIS NATIVE LAND, AND SAVED ITS SAINTS AND HEROES FROM OBLIVION.

The Irish Book Lover
A Miscellany
(Aug. 1912–Sept. 1957)

J. M. Hone, "Yeats, Synge and *The Playboy*", Vol. IV, No. 1 (Aug. 1912), 7.

The remark was once made of Oscar Wilde that he might have been Parnell's successor. Of another Irishman, who is only known to the mass as a man of letters. Mr. W. B. Yeats, the biographer will probably say that an Irish leader, a Grattan perhaps rather than a Parnell—an orator—was lost in a poet. That will not be strictly true, for, in fact, Mr. Yeats has done much for Ireland, aside, I mean, from his actual literary achievement. It is not possible for an Irish writer working in Ireland to live detachedly. Synge returning home after a long absence did not realise this; the row over *The Playboy* bewildered him utterly; when he was asked what he thought of it he could only say, 'It's an extravaganza. I don't care a rap'.

For the time and energy he has had to spend in interpreting Synge to the Irish public, for his limitless patience in propaganda and generous labours when all seemed hopeless, Mr Yeats has never been sufficiently praised. In the upshot, Synge has not only been accepted as a national dramatist, but he has taken—wrongly, I think, though here I express a purely personal opinion—the place among modern Irish writers that previously belonged by popular consent to Yeats himself.

Stephen Gwynn, M.P., "Irish Book Lovers", Vol. IV, No. 8 (March 1913).

Irish people are very odd about books. They are, and every Irish writer knows it—to his cost, the best book buying of publics. We, who write of Ireland, labour like the peasant proprietor in his hayfield, under a wholesome cloudy sky, earning our diet of potatoes and buttermilk, though unhappily often in places where buttermilk, at least, is hard to be came by; and we have always leisure since the day is long from dawn to sunset, for passing the time of day with our neighbours. Our occupation is effectually shielded from the glare and glamour of commercialism, and, no doubt, so much the better for our virtue. Mr. Yeats has done more than any man living, perhaps than any man living or dead, to raise the fame off Ireland in the craft of letters; but heaven help Mr. Yeats—heaven help any of us—if existence depended on the sale of books to the Irish public. Yet Ireland is a country of booklovers: the man for whom books are a passion and a treasure is perhaps commoner there than anywhere in the world. [...]

"George William Russell (Æ)", Vol. VII, No. 3 (Oct. 1915), 37.

Mr. George W. Russell, earlier and perhaps better known as "Æ" was born in Lurgan in 1867, and began life in the forwarding department of a big Dublin firm, but has been for more than twenty years associated with the movement for agricultural co-operation organized by Sir Horace Plunkett. If a man had a separate name for each sphere of work in which he is distinguished, Mr. Russell would be entitled to at least one more alias, for besides being a poet, under those mysterious initials, and an organizer and editor under his own name, he is a painter who has worked out a style and technique of his own, and whose works distinctly count for something in the history of modern Irish art. His poetry is noticeable besides its fine qualities of rhythm, for what is commonly called its 'mysticism', by which we suppose is meant the writer's habit of seeing spiritual forces behind all material phenomena. Mr. Yeats has declared his poems to be 'the most delicate and subtle that any Irishman of our time has written'. As editor of a weekly paper, *The Irish Homestead* he has preached with an eloquence and intellectual force which are not surpassed, if they are even equalled, in British journalism, against the habit of mind which regards Ireland as a kind of parasite on the full-blooded and vigorous organism across the water. To feed the sense of power, manhood and self-reliance in Ireland is the mission of this brilliant little paper which, alone among Irish periodicals, has a distinct social ideal and a distinct conception of the way to attain it. It adds the ferment of thought to the ingredients out of which the Irish nation is being made—a necessary addition, if the words of another poet about another historical situation are to come true:

> *For queerly as the must may heave and*
> *   bubble*
> *A wine will be the outcome of the trouble.*

"Reviews", Vol. VIII, No. 9 & 10 (April & May 1917), 113.

A PORTRAIT OF THE ARTIST AS A YOUNG MAN BY JAMES JOYCE. In spite of the serious drawbacks to be mentioned later, truth compels one to admit that this pseudo autobiography of Stephen Dedalus, a weakling and a dreamer makes fascinating reading. We read it at a single sitting. The hero's schooldays at Clongowes Wood, and later at Belvedere, are graphically and doubtless, faithfully portrayed, as is the visit to Cork in company with his father, a clever ne'er-do-well, gradually sinking in the social scale. One of the strongest scenes in the book is the description of the Christmas dinner party during the black year of 1891, when Nationalist Ireland was riven to the centre over the Parnell 'split'. Mr. Joyce is unsparing in his realism, and his violent contrasts—the brothel, the confessional—jar on one's finer feelings. So do the quips and jeers of the students, in language unprinted in literature since the days of Swift and Sterne, following on some eloquent and orthodox sermons! That Mr. Joyce is a master of a brilliant descriptive style and handles his dialogue as ably as any living writer is conceded—on all hands, and, oh! the pity of it. In writing thus is he just to his fine gifts? Is it even wise, from a worldly point of view—mercenary, if you will—to dissipate one's talents on a book which can only attain a limited circulation?—for no clean-minded person could possibly allow it to remain within reach of his wife, his sons or daughters. Above all, is it Art? We doubt it.

"Irish Poetry" [extract from *Saturday Review*], Vol. XII, No. 3 (Oct. 1921), 27.

A few years ago Ireland seemed to be the greatest dreamer among nations. Its poets no longer made warlike ballads, but seemed to exist in a region of druid twilights and elfin tunes. They bathed their spirits in Connla's Well, the Irish fountain of All-Wisdom. The Gaelic League had set thousands of young men and women studying the national language and literature the tales of demi-gods, voyages to faery, and that exquisite lyric poetry revealed in translation by Hyde, Sigerson and Meyer. The National Theatre Society produced poetic drama and the countryman was peacefully building up a rural civilisation and social order by means of co-operative societies.

Only those wise folk who know that action and re-action are equal and opposite, could have foretold that the pendulum was bound to swing back from dream to action, and remote as was the dream, so would be the incredible daring of the adventure in reality. In that period of brooding Ireland was finding its way back to its ancestral self. Its poetry was becoming more and more lit by gleams from Ildathach, the many-coloured land. Even in the technique of the verse the influence, conscious or unconscious, of the Gaelic metres, was becoming apparent. William Larminie, who had written on Gaelic prosody, told the present writer he could have illustrated the Gaelic metrical system almost as well from the poetry of Yeats and Æ as by quotations from Gaelic, though neither of these were Gaelic scholars. Synge, Lady Gregory, and later on, Stephens, began to write an English in which the construction of the sentences was often really Gaelic. It is impossible for anybody to remain standing on tiptoe, says Lao-tze, the Chinese sage, and just at the time Yeats believed a spiritual tradition had been created in Anglo-Irish literature, the reaction to objectivity began in Synge, Colum and later in Stephens. These could dream, but their dreams were acquiring [a] solidity of flesh and blood, and were not the beautiful shadows as of creatures come to earth out of the Country of the Young with which Yeats had populated the Irish imagination. No doubt if literature is the shadow of life, this growing solidity and realism in poetry and drama indicates a change in the national mood; and that change, once it began, brought Ireland rapidly from its achievement of spiritual independence to a fierce struggle for economic and political freedom. The Chinese sage already quoted said, 'to see things in the germ, this I call intelligence', and we might speculate whether the imprisonment of Standish O'Grady, Yeats, Hyde, Æ, Lady Gregory, and other pioneers of the Gaelic mood in Anglo-Irish literature, once they showed tendencies to revert to ancestor worship, might not have made it unnecessary to have five thousand young Irishmen in prison today.

In the anthology *Irish Poets of To-Day*, compiled by Mrs. Walters, it would need a profound clairvoyance to discern the germs of revolution. Yeats is here, inviting us to the lake island of Innisfree. Thomas Boyd searches for the Leanan Sidhe. Padraic Colum, in one of the liveliest lyrics, of earth not of faery, hushes his world to sleep in a Cradle Song to a silence in which even a faery footfall might be heard.

James Stephens, the poet of reality, in his first volume, is here with a no less lively lyric in which the big heart of childhood seems bursting with pity over a rabbit in a snare, and the whole cavalcade of poets seems to be travelling to the Golden Age. From all that we have come in half-a-dozen years to battle, murder and sudden death; the strings of the harp are broken, or their sound cannot be heard because of the roar of bomb or machine-gun. How much of all that dream went into the insurrection, how much of all that poetry comforts the hearts of the outlawed members of the Republican Army, trysting among the mountains and rocks, and in the starry nights, we may know perhaps when some of them later write their memories.

That there is a connection is certain. We know that Padraic Pearse made his soul out of the epic tales. MacDonagh, Plunkett and other poets were with him in the rising of Easter Week. It is probable that poetry is being born somewhere in the stillness of the night when the Republican soldier looks up at the stars, or hears the rabbit rustle in the fern, a reaction which will lead him back from the physical to the spiritual once more, and so far as he risked the body, so high later may be the adventure of the soul.

"Editor's Gossip", Vol. XIII, No. 3 (Oct. 1921), 34.

[...] MR. W. B. YEATS concludes his recollections of "Four Years, 1887-1890", in the August number of *The London Mercury*. Dealing with the Rhymers' Club, he says: 'Among these men, of whom so many of the greatest talents were to live such passionate lives and die such tragic deaths, one serene man, T. W. Rolleston, seemed always out of place. It was I brought him there, intending to set him to some work in Ireland later on. I have known young Dublin working-men slip out of their workshops to see 'the second Thomas Davis' passing by, and even remember a conspiracy by some three or four to make him the leader of the Irish race at home and abroad, and all because he had regular features'. Mr. Yeats, in the July number, made an interesting confession as to the origin of the well-known "Innisfree" poem. 'I had still the ambition', he says, 'formed in Sligo in my teens, of living in imitation of Thoreau on Innisfree, a little island in Lough Gill, and when walking through Fleet Street very homesick I heard a little tinkle of water and saw a fountain in a shop-window which balanced a little ball-upon its jet, and began to remember lake water. From the sudden remembrance came my poem "Innisfree", my first lyric with anything in its rhythm of my own music'.

"Pen Portraits" [extract from *The Nation*], Vol. XIII, No. 3 (Oct. 1921), 41.

GEORGE RUSSELL, equally well known as "Æ", occupies during these years of the Terror in Ireland much the same kind of position that Tolstoy held in Russia during the last fifteen years of the Tsardom's tyranny. He belongs to no party; he is not a leader of revolt; he has no political following. To those who know, the wonder is that such a man as "Æ" is not regarded with dislike and suspicion by extremists of every party, just because he is so far removed from all extremes, except the extremes of passionate love for his country and persistent reasonableness about it. Yet as Tolstoy was honoured and beloved by all true Russians, so there is no true Irishman who does not think of "Æ" with honour and affection.

It seems difficult for English people to realise how strong is his hold. At the time of the Larkin strike in Dublin, though he is shy of public speaking, he made by far the greatest speech at a meeting in the Albert Hall; but, if we remember right, not a single English paper even mentioned his name. Very likely they had never heard of the poet, visionary painter, visionary thinker, and practical economist, who has created lyrics in the finest Anglo-Irish verse, illuminated walls with scenes from Irish fairyland and the depths of Irish reality, striven to devise the noblest lines for Irish nationality to follow, and for many years helped to restore the prosperity of Irish peasants by the scheme of co-operation which scattered creameries and farming centres throughout the country. His life and varied energies are proof that a man of fine brain and strong vitality can accomplish almost any kind of work that he sets his heart upon. By energy he has sought to save his country; by ecstasy he continually saves himself.

In the very aspect of the man there seems room for multitudinous variety. That tall and largely moulded form, the great head with its masses of dark brown hair and tawny beard, the imperturbable bearing holding in control the sensitive, and burning spirit within, those deep-set, blue-grey eyes, full of benevolence and of rage, the low Irish voice equally capable of both; all show a large and generous nature, abounding in contradictions, capable of energy and ecstasy alike. Consider his letters to *The Times* upon the misgovernment of Ireland within the last six months—their knowledge of finance and economics, their Swiftian indignation, their steady reasonableness. His *Imaginations and Reveries* are descriptions of the leading issues, spiritual and external, of Irish life during the twenty or twenty-five years that ended about 1918. We are shown once more the national value of those poets, scholars and essayists who began to infuse a new spirit into their nation about thirty years ago the men who rescued old Irish history and legend, the founders of the Gaelic League (now proscribed by our Government), the creators of the Irish drama, the singers of lyrics among the most beautiful in the world, and the originators of Sinn Féin.

"Pen Portraits" [extract from *The Observer*], Vol. XIII, No. 3 (Oct. 1921), 42.

Neither the morals nor the literary manner of JAMES JOYCE, now permanently residing in Paris, do I intend to discuss; but I must register an odd fact about his forthcoming book, *Ulysses*. The cult of James Joyce, the most original of modern Irish writers, may be restricted, but it is intense, not only in certain American and British circles, but also in French circles. The peculiar power of his psychological notations is, whether you like it or not, unquestionable. He regards, I believe, his *Dubliners* and his *Portrait of the Artist as a Young Man* as merely preparatory exercises and outgrowths of the greater work that he has been writing for more than a decade. Difficult as it was to find a publisher who would take the responsibility of issuing his earlier works, the difficulty of publication of *Ulysses* has now grown into impossib-ility. *The Little Review* of America had to suppress much of it. James Joyce was almost in despair, when an American girl, Sylvia Beach; who courageously founded a little library of English books in the Quartier Latin, at the sign of Shakespeare and Company, came to the rescue. She has undertaken to have it printed in France and to publish privately the big and strange volume. Whatever may be thought of the work, it is going to attract almost sensational attention.

Robert Lynd, "More or Less about Irish Literature", Vol. XIII, Nos. 9 & 10 (April & May 1922), 157.

[...] OSCAR WILDE ONCE SAID TO WILLIE YEATS, "We Irish are too political to be poets; we are a nation of brilliant failures, but we are the greatest talkers since the Greeks". To be a nation of talkers, as the Irish are, is not an evil but an achievement. Conversation is the traditional Irish substitute for poetry, and, to us who have heard it by the roadside and around the fire, not a bad substitute either. Mr. Yeats seems to think that conversation is the enemy of poetry. We know, however, that it is the friend of comedy. Poetry is the child of the isolated spirit: comedy is the child of the social spirit. Hence the Englishman, whose house is his castle, is more likely to write poetry than the Irishman, while the Irishman, whose house is an open house when it is not a ruin, is more likely to become a conversationalist and to cultivate comedy. Thus the Irish gift of comedy is, in a sense, the direct result of the tragedy of Irish history. The arts that could not flourish in public found a sort of private existence in the homes of the people, and as laughter is the most sociable thing on earth, the comic spirit kept alive in Ireland even in the valley of the shadow of death. [...]

J. S. Crone, "Sgéala ó Chathair na gCeó", Vol. XIV, No. 1 (Jan. 1924), 10.

I need not assure my readers of the great pleasure it gives me to resume once more our monthly gossips, on men, women. and books. Circumstances over which I had no control have kept us apart for many long months; and conditions, now, happily, in great part passed away, also contributed to the severance. Now, thanks to the generosity of book-loving friends in both North and South, I am enabled once more to place my services at the disposal of my readers and friends as in the years that are gone. In return, I promise to do my best to render our little magazine more interesting and useful in the coming year, which I trust will be a happy and prosperous one for all.

I do not remember any recent event in the literary world which has caused such widespread satisfaction as the award of the Nobel Literature Prize of £8,000 to Mr. W. B. Yeats. The announcement was greeted with a chorus of praise on every hand, so different from the 'nagging' in some quarters, when he became the recipient of a Civil List 'pension', which I was the first to announce. Here are a couple of comments I have selected:

Stephen Gwynn declares: 'Whatever is honestest in Northern Ireland will recognise and rejoice that the honour done to Mr. Yeats reflects something on every man, woman, and child in Ireland; and whatever is honestest, in the Ireland that desires to be Gaelic and Republican will recognise that Mr. Yeats and those whom he associates with him are none the less Irish because they belong to the Anglo-Irish stock. Irish nationality is a real thing, none the less real because it defies definition. The real is that which is present in sensation: a man is Irish if he feels Irish and can make others feel the same of him: or destroy the reality if you seek to attach it to a shibboleth'.

And another writer says: 'In some ways Mr. Yeats has a strange personality, but behind the frail figure, with its inevitable huge bow tie, there was always a strong character and a brilliant mind. His work is marked by the most painstaking toil, and by a rare delicacy and restraint. He has been, writing since 1886, and during that time has not ceased to give to the world books of verse, plays on Irish life, and essays. But to the "man in the street", Mr. Yeats lives as the author of lyrics such as "The Lake Isle of Innisfree".'

John S. Crone, "Vale", Vol. XV [endnote to index] (1925), iii.

With this volume of *I.B.L.* I take farewell to my readers, as circumstances render it too difficult. To the many friends at home and abroad who, either as contributors or subscribers, have assisted me in my labour of love during the past sixteen years—a long career for any periodical devoted to Anglo-Irish literature—I return my warm and heart-felt thanks.

L. M., "Reviews", Vol. XXII, No. 4 (July & Aug. 1934), 92.

MORE PRICKS THAN KICKS BY SAMUEL BECKETT. Mr. Beckett has evidently read James Joyce with loving care. Unfortunately, no one has told him that violence and obscurity, even assisted by a considerable dash of the indecent, are, when uninformed by any real passion or direction, merely dull. For that is the worst thing about *More Pricks Than Kicks*—it is appallingly dull. Joyce is one of the worst of masters for young men who would play the sedulous ape. In his own terrifying sphere he has expressed totality; he has left nothing for them to say; and it is really too much of a good thing to have a stupid pastiche such as Mr. Beckett has produced setting up to be some tremendous expression of the modern mind. All its attempts at violence, its liberal sprinkling of esoteric words and literary allusion, its cheap inversions of trite phrases, its large assumption that to write down the meaningless is somehow to invest it with meaning, do not conceal the elementary fact that Mr. Beckett has nothing to say.

P. C. T[rimble], "Reviews", Vol. XXIII, No. 6 (Nov. & Dec. 1935), 155.

SELECTED POEMS BY Æ. To a country out of tune with so many of his ideals Æ. handed the testament of his poetic life a few months before he died. This choice from forty years of verse is his own:

> All that he loved and moulded into thought
> From shape and hue, and odour and sweet sound.

In *Song and Its Foundations,* essentially a prelude to his *Selected Poems,* he says: 'I have thought it unnatural to see together in galleries pictures unrelated to each other, or taken from altars for which they were painted'. So he has grouped in this last book such verse as expressed only the philosophy of his life. In our opinion, it holds the full measure of his genius and imaginative life. To many it must surely bring that spiritual solace and joy which are the benedictions of great verse. He was a poet with a painter's eye and his love of colour transfuses thought and syllable:

> From crag to crag did Michael leap
> Until he overhung the deep;
> Saw in vast caves the waters roam
> The ceaseless ecstasy of foam,
> Whirlpools of opal, lace of light
> Strewn over quivering malachite,
> Ice-tinted mounds of water rise,
> Glinting as with a million eyes,
> Reel in and out of light and shade,
> Show depths of ivory or jade,
> New broidery every instant wear
> Spun by the magic weaver, Air.

A seer of childlike meditation, an Earth-lover to whom her moods were the substance of symbolic dream, he has the voice of a prophet crying out of the wilderness the promise of the Gates of Gold:

> If men adore It as the power
> Empires and cities tower on tower
> Are built in worship by the way
> High Babylon or Nineveh.
> Seek It as love and there may be
> A Golden Age and Arcady.
> All shadows are they of one thing
> To which all life is journeying.

In his century there are poets whose lyrical gifts are greater than Æ's; his verse was never popular, his verse-forms remained simple, almost uniform, in pattern. But few can show such steadfastness of vision, so sure a journeying. In the candelabra of poetry on the altar of time the steadfast flame of this lover of Irish earth will not be quenched.

P. C. T[rimble], "Reviews", Vol. XXVII, No. 1 (Jan. 1940), 165.

FINNEGAN'S WAKE [SIC] BY JAMES JOYCE. Maurice Hewlett, the novelist, in one of his letters relates how he searched James Joyce's *Portrait* to find what other words besides 'bloody' the author had used. He found one that he had not seen since Swift and one never before, not even in Shakespeare. Pointedly he remarks that 'nobody since Swift has been so good at urinals'.

What would Hewlett say today were he alive and faced with *Finnegan's Wake* which is written for the most part in a language foreign to Swift, Shakespeare, or the guttersnipe or the yokel? It took Joyce sixteen years to write these 600 odd pages, practically all of which must convey little or no meaning to the ordinary reader. When a dialect is transmuted to a language it produces literature; but what can be said of a language that has reverted not into the dialect of a com-munity but of one isolated mind? In Joyce, traditional structures are broken down, reset with obsolete words, with slang, dialect, with words broken and remoulded to convey allusive sound or in satire of their original meaning. The hotch-potch flows on from page to page inter-preting what appears a vast mimicry. In essence, the clear opaque surface of traditional language is broken and the oscillations are so tremendous that all that words convey: theme, mood, passion, vision, disappear in mysterious confusion. With these disappearances the surface again reappears and we see a world of language which seems to have the strange minuteness, the cloying consistency and the rapacious spread of duckweed.

Stephen Dedalus in *Portrait* says: 'I will not serve that in which I no longer believe, whether it call itself my home, my fatherland or my church and I will try to express myself in some mode of life or art, as freely as I can and as wholly as I can, using for my defence the only arms I allow myself to use-silence, exile and cunning.'

Stephen Dedalus has kept his word and his silence, exile and cunning has, in *Finnegan's Wake*, produced what must be regarded as one of the most extraordinary books ever produced in any language. We approach it mainly through interest and curiosity and our first emotions remain at the close. Perhaps, in a future time, but not in our generation, glosses may be provided and pleasure may then become the third attraction. But for the moment may we wonder why so great a talent, gifted with prodigious memory, a wide erudition, a mastery of English and of other languages, a poet's ear for the beauty of vowel, and an artist's fastidiousness in form, should bend itself to a task in which no mind save its own can enjoy or appreciate the grotesque output of its labour?

P. C. T[rimble], "Reviews", Vol. XXVII, No.4 (July 1940), 238.

LAST POEMS AND PLAYS BY W. B. YEATS. Though he wrote in English, the Irish genius of William Butler Yeats created poetry which has no kith or kin in the world of English verse. That is his triumph, and all through the long and fruitful years of his craftsmanship he strove to achieve that end by stubborn isolation of his personality. He was to English letters what Parnell (whom he admired) was to English politics, and both men were of true aristocratic mould of mind. Early Yeats sought distinctiveness through the medium of Irish folk-lore, then in the interpretation of the Irish longing for political freedom, later in political satire, later still by recession to that great period of the Irish intellect, the period of Swift, Burke, Goldsmith, Berkeley, and by gropings through many darknesses to a personal philosophy, and finally, as in this last book, by variations on old themes.

English-speaking peoples owe him much. All that he took, and he absorbed everything, from the traditions of English verse he gave back revivified. A hundred years separates "La Belle Dame Sans Merci" from "The Host of the Air", but Yeats proved that the lyric note had not dimmed in the passage of a century. When he outgrew that early spontaneous genius to become the supreme artist, he reached an eloquence in English verse that has no equal. He died sustaining it.

What is the debt which the Irish people owe to him? Chiefly, that he was the first Irish poet writing in English to state and fulfil the canon 'One's verse should hold, as in a mirror, the colour of one's own climate and scenery'. To read his verse, written from youth to the last lines in this book, is to realise how fully he saw the verities of colour and mood in the Irish scene, and by seeing them found a pathway into the inner places of the Irish character.

There are many other debts, too—his 'responsibilities', he called them. He gave to the Irish theatre, which he helped to found, its spiritual flame, and to the renascent literature of the pre-Easter week period his contribution was invaluable. In after years he subjected much of that nationalist contribution to severe personal criticism, and there are many in Ireland who cannot easily forgive him for the rancour of his satires. He knew that resentment against him was abroad:

> You think it horrible that lust and rage
> Should dance attention upon my old age;
> They were not such a plague when I was young;
> What else have I to spur me into song?

It is a poor plea, but in his last ringing ballads, by eloquence and invective; he proves a better case. Roger Casement, the O'Rahilly, Sean Connolly, Parnell: to these memories he gives his last political verse.

Here is the last of all his works, and he sustains his genius despite his medieval knees. Laying aside this book, now more than ever in the past it can be said of him, as it was said of another, that he touched nothing that he did not adorn. Some of the best ballads made by him are in this books—ballads that derive from the country fair and better their progenitors; ballads like "Colonel Martin", which turn away from the sedate and sophisticated art to the old Border ballads, with their vivid, dramatic presentation, their spoken emotion, magic and fearfulness, There is, too, the profound eloquence which, as Mr. Austin Clarke has remarked, he released when he drew the organ stops of English poetry. There is finally all the old loyalties reaffirmed: to his country, to his art, to his friends and to the Irish poets of tomorrow.

John S. Crone, "Willie Yeats and John O'Leary", Vol. XXVII, No. 5 (Nov. 1940), 245.

After the death of D. J. O'Donoghue, in 1917, his widow sent me a quantity of correspondence which he had inherited from John O'Leary, the old Fenian chief, whose literary executor he was. Much of it had been used by "D.J." in his "John O'Leary and his Friends", which ran serially through *The Weekly Independent* and *The Newcastle Weekly Chronicle.* I prepared the text of that series for re-publication in volume form, with a prefatory memoir of O'Leary. But unfortunately in transit to a Dublin publisher, the 'copy' disappeared and was never heard of again, presumably burnt in a mail train at a time when such an incident was not uncommon. Amongst the unused matter were the following letters from Willie Yeats, as he was then known to us:

3 Blenheim Rd., May 7 (1889).
Dear Mr. O'Leary,

I should have thanked you before for the Carleton's, but the day I got them I started for Oxford and only returned the day before yesterday. Down there I had no time to write letters at all, what with copying out in the Bodleian all day and dining with dull college dons—friends of York Powell with whom I stoped (sic)—in the evening. Met one or two people of interest, however—a student on the ground floor had got my book—he was of interest of course—they have it too, in the Oxford Union.

I have started reading Carleton's *Miser,* and will write to the Coffeys about what Carleton's they have as soon as I hear of their return to Dublin. My father will ask the Butts about him. They, or their father knew him well, of course. I have been busy with Blake. You complain about the mysticism. It has enabled me to make out Blake's prophetic books at any rate. My book on him will, I believe, clear up that riddle for ever. No one will call him mad again. I have evidence, by the way, to show that he was of Irish extraction—his grandfather was an O'Neal who changed his name for political reasons. Ireland takes a most important place in his mystical system. You need not be afraid of my going in for mesmerism. It interests me but slightly. No fear of Madam Blavatsky drawing me into such matter. She is very much against them, and hates spiritualism vehemently—says mediumship and insanity are the same thing.

By the way their [sic] has been a stir lately among the faithful, Madam Blavatsky expelled Mrs. Cook (Mabel Collins), a most prominent theosophist writer and daughter of Mortimer Collins, and expelled also the president of the lodge for flirtation; and expelled an American lady for gossiping about them. Madam Blavatsky is in great spirits, she is purring and hiding her claws as though she never clawed anybody. She is always happy when she has found a Theosophist out and clawed him. She thinks she is the most long suffering person. One day she said 'forty thousand theosophists are gushing away. I try to stop them, then they scratch'.

According to her there are about half-a-dozen real theosophists in the world and one of these is stupid (Olcott, I imagine). The rest she classifies under the head 'flap doodles'. Come to see her when you are in London. She is the most human person alive, is like an old peasant woman and is wholly devoted. All her life is but sitting in a great chair with a pen in her hand. For years she has written twelve hours a day. I have no theories about her, she is simply a note of interrogation. 'Olcott is much honester than I am', she said to me one day, 'he explains things. I am an old Russian savage', that is the deepest I ever got into her riddle.

I read a scene of my new play to an actress yesterday. She seemed to think it suitable in all ways for the stage. I think you will like it, it is in all things Celtic and Irish. The style is perfectly simple and I have taken great care with the construction, made two complete prose versions before writing a line of verse. Miss O'Leary wished to keep the review of my book she had. I return those of which I have duplicates. My father is delighted with Miss O'Leary's poem ["My Own Galtees"] in the *Irish Monthly* and so am I. It is most simple, delicate and tender. I shall write to her very presently. I have to go out now—have been unwell these last two days through want of exercise I suspect, but am nearly all right again now. Still do not care to write much. Forgive me all this chatter about Madame Blavatsky.

I hope Miss O'Leary's health will feel the benefit of this good spring weather.

Yours very sincerely, W. B. Yeats.

Oct. 8 (1890).

My dear Mr. O'Leary,
I quite let the acknowledgement of those forms and checks slip out of my mind. Your letter today for the first time brought them to memory. I suppose they were crowded into forgetfulness by the telegrams where with Walter Scott's printer was pelting me at the time—however, that matter is over and the book out. I send this post or next a copy to Miss O'Leary. I brought 'forms' to Keegan Paul and one of the checks—the one pound check I had to borrow for a few days but will send amount to Keegan Paul tomorrow or next day when paid for Folk Tales book. Rhys (editor of Camelot Classics) is much delighted with Folk Tale book, says it is one of the half dozen books of his series he is proud of.

The article on Allingham is all you say most likely as well as much misprinted. I find it hard not to think of somebody like Sparling when writing prose and writing at them. I have some notion of doing Todhunter for *Providence Journal,* also Professor Rhys' (not Camelot Rhys) book on ancient Celtic religion. My novel or novelette draws to a close. The first draft is complete. It is all about a curate and a young man from the country. The difficulty is to keep the characters from turning into eastern symbolic monsters of some sort which would be a curious thing to happen to a curate and a young man from the country.

There is little news: Charles Johnston is gone to Russia to get married to Madam Blavatsky's niece who is pretty and simple. Madam Blavatsky and her sister, the girl's mother, do not much like it. The sister weeps and Madame covers them with lambent railery [sic]—she likes Johnston very much, but then he was intended for a Mahatma. The lodge Blavatsky despairs. He is the last failure. Only one member of the lodge is happy-a young lady who turned up her eyes and said 'Oh that beautiful young man. How wicked of Theosophists to try and prevent people from falling in love'. We are all well. I am writing to Miss O'Leary.
Yours very sincerely, W. B. Yeats.

P.S.—Keegan Paul cannot make out enclosed three forms. No more can I. I send them in hopes you will remember the names.

P.P.S.—Thursday, I wonder how Dowden likes the crown of Martyrdom. You heard, I dare say, that he did not get the Scotch Professorship he tried for. The reason was that all the unionists wanted him so the other side ran a Scotchman named Knight. Lord somebody or other, who had the chair in his gift, said as they were both party men he would have neither and put in a young man who had not yet taken any side.

I am sorry to hear about Miss Kavanagh not being so well and glad to hear of her going to Paris. Does she write anything now? I wish she would make her Uncle Rhemus' children hunt up folk tales. She might make one or two of her weekly competitions on the matter. She got a couple or so from the children at Xmas and they were very interesting. I could give any help needful in the matter, of course.

I am taking a few days, having finished Carleton, at my play the *Countess*. When that is done I mean to write a series of Irish ballads - folk tales from Sligo set into rhyme and things out of history and so forth. You will like the *Countess*, its Irish right through.

[Rose Kavanagh died of consumption in the following February. Charles Johnston was a son of Johnston of Ballykilbeg, the Orange leader, and was educated at High School, Dublin, and T.C.D.]

*

53 Mountjoy Square, Dublin (1892).
Dear Mr. O'Leary,

We have postponed our concert until after the inaugural meeting which will, I believe, take place in the second week in August at the Ancient Concert Rooms. We hope by that time to have the program of our autumn session arranged so that we can distribute it at the meeting. The concert which will probably take place in Horse Show Week will be an item. We will have our permanent reading room taken too, I hope, by the opening of our session. We have had to postpone the concert through delays about Ludwig and other things of the kind. Next Monday—the 25th—we have a general meeting of the members to adopt rules and nominate the officers. We intend to start a 'Contemporary' of our own as soon as we have our reading room. This is, I believe, all the news concerns society. As to my suggestion about Mathews. In suggesting to you that if any advanced Nationalist was going to Paris he should see Mathews, I was acting to some extent on the advice of Quinn, to whom I showed Mathews' letter he gave me leave to show it. Quinn held the matter of some possible importance. Mathews is a specialist and might have given useful advice to any one who thinks as you do. 'He might be useful' was your own phrase. Now as to Magic. It is surely absurd to hold me 'weak' or otherwise because I chose to persist in a study which I decided deliberately four or five years ago to make, next to my poetry, the more important pursuit of my life. Whether it be, or be not bad for my health can only be decided by one who knows what magic is and not at all by any amateur [...] If I had not made magic my constant study I could not have written a single word of my Blake book, nor would *The Countess Kathleen* have ever come to exist. The mystical life is the centre of all that I do and all that I think and all that I write. It holds to my work the same relation that the philosophy of Godwin held to the work of Shelley and I have allways considered myself a voice of what I believe to be a greater renaissance—the revolt of the soul against the intellect—now beginning in the world. By all this I have, however, probably called down upon myself another reproving post card which shall be like to the other in all things. It is my own fault I daresay, for I sometimes forget that the word 'magic' which sounds so familiar to my ears has a very outlandish sound to other ears.

Miss Gonne has given up her rooms in Paris—which means, I imagine, that she intends to live more constantly in Ireland and devote herself to the work here. She is now with her sister, 25 Hans Place, but returns next week, I believe. When do you return? Duffy comes over, I believe, in a week or two. I have [G. F. Savage-]Armstrong's collected works—nine volumes, to review for *Bookman,* and have given them a preliminary notice, mainly hostile, in this week's *United Ireland,* also like treatment to Larminie. Does Barry O'Brien want that 'causerie'? He was to write me and has not. Hyde has settled with Unwin about his translations of Gaelic sagas and got very good terms. I am writing this post to Duffy.

Yours very sincerely, W. B. Yeats.

*

3 Blenheim Rd., June 26, (1894).
Dear Mr. O'Leary,

I fear I never sent you a copy of my play. I now do so. The edition is quite exausted (sic). An edition has been arranged for in America, and Unwin is considering the wisdom of a new edition here. George Russell has, as I dare say you know, published a little book of verse, which is exceedingly wonderful. I think we will be able to organize a reception for it here. It is about the best piece of poetical work done by any Irishman this good while back. It is the kind of book which inevitably lives down big histories and long novels and the like. It is full of sweetness and subtlety and may well prove to have three or four immortal pages. I send you *The Second Book of the Rhymers Club* in which everybody is tolerably good except the Trinity Collegemen— Rolleston, Hillier, Todhunter and Greene, who are intolerably bad as was to be expected—Todhunter is of course good and skilful enough with more matter of fact themes and quite admits the dreadful burden of the T.C.D. tradition—and some are exceedingly good, notably Plar (sic) Dawson Johnson and Le Galliene.

I should have gone to Dublin before this, even though it were but to return in the autumn for the performance of my new play but for sheer [illegible] which I am about to clear off and soon extend by an Irish Anthology which is nearly finished. Do you remember getting from me a little green paper covered book called, I think, *Irish Ballad Poetry* and containing work by Kickham and De Vere, and some rebels? If you have it by you I wish you could send it me as it would save me a very great deal of trouble. I have tried to buy a copy (but neither Gill's or Duffy's agent here knows anything of it. It cost sixpence when I bought it). I have written a severe article on "The New Irish Library" which will appear in the August *Bookman*. An inevitable re-organization of the scheme is at hand, and therefore it seems better to speak out and I believe my article will only make patent the latent convictions of all the people here. Surely this world has not seen a more absurd 'popular series' than this one and the sale has very properly fallen steadily. I have no information about the Library Committee or the Nat. Lit. Society itself, though D. has written twice for it—the last time to Kelly. Dora Sigerson is here and she and Miss Piatt came with me to see Bernard Shaw's play at the Avenue and were, I think, well pleased. Any news of your book? I saw a passing allusion to its approaching publication in the *Pall Mall* or *Westminster.*

Yours ever, W. B. Yeats.

P.S.—I find I was mistaken. The book has just turned up.

"In Memoriam John Smyth Crone, 1858-1945", Vol. XXX, No. 1 (Oct. 1946), 1.

Dr. Crone, to whom our little magazine owes its existence, led a full, a useful, a long and honourable life. His eighty-seven years spanned the time from the Indian Mutiny to the second World War. We will miss him sadly.

Son of John and Isobel Crone, Belfast, he was educated at the Royal Academical Institution and Queen's College, Belfast. London Hospital experience was followed by medical practice in Willesden for 40 years. Many were his honours: Chairman, Willesden District Council, 1900-1903; Member Middlesex County Council from 1906 to 1916, Deputy Coroner for the County from 1917; High Sheriff from 1933-34; J.P. in

1907; President Irish Literary Society (London) from 1918 to 1925; President Willesden Medical Society.

His first wife was Mary Smith who died in 1890. One son of this marriage is Mr. J. W. S. Crone, Local Government official, Middlesex Co. Council. In 1897 he married Nina Gertrude, who died 1933, daughter of Peter Roe, a well known Dublin printer. Of this marriage there are three sons living: Gerald Roe Crone, Librarian and Map Curator, Royal Geographical Society, London; Desmond R. Cronc, O.B.E., Colonel, R.E. Indian Survey; James K. Crone, Capt., Melbourne Port Authority, Australia.

To all of them *The Irish Book Lover* offers sincere regrets.

P. S. O'Hegarty, "Some Memories of Dr. Crone", Vol. XXX, No. 1 (Oct. 1946), 1.

I first met Dr. Crone shortly after the start of *The Irish Book Lover* in 1909. I had seen somewhere an advertisement of its forthcoming appearance, and I sent in the modest subscription which was demanded, to Whyte and Salmon, the printers. Some time afterwards, after some correspondence with the Editor, I went to see him one Sunday evening. It was the first of a few, but not many, visits. My main interest was the Irish Ireland movement, which overshadowed even my interest in books, while his was books, books alone, and mostly Irish books. I remember that first evening vividly, and the magnificent spectacle which his room presented, a magnificent spectacle of how to use all available space in a room. The room possessed a writing table, a couple of armchairs and a desk-chair, and books, and chiefly books. The shelves crept everywhere, and there was not even one inch of wallpaper to be seen. The room was, so to speak, bursting with books, and he had then a small overflow room elsewhere in the house where books were deposited temporarily, not on shelves, in a sort of Limbo. He had the true booklover's faculty. He would take out a book, a rarity, and then tell of how he got it. He had just then got a very great rarity in the shape of a book of Irish historical interest, of which only a few copies were printed, with copious manuscript notes by the author. I do not now remember the book, but I do remember his telling me how he stood in the auction room and saw it auctioned for a sum which was beyond his means, and, after that, kept an eye on it. It changed hands a couple of times, and eventually, by persistently following it up, he was enabled to buy it at a figure within his means, and somewhat under its value.

It is difficult to think of Dr. Crone apart from *The Irish Book Lover*. They were really the same thing. To us Dr. Crone was *The Book Lover* and *The Book Lover* was Crone. His knowledge of Irish books was not in any sense a scholar's knowledge, but it was wide and catholic. He embraced everything about Ireland or written by Irishmen, and he included everything from family history to fiction. He was a pioneer in Irish letters. In his first number he refers to John Power as the pioneer in Irish Bibliography, and so he was, but Power left no school, and only a few men like Crone knew of him, whereas Crone founded a school, which has a lot of good work to its credit and still has some, perhaps unworthy, pupils. The first number contained contributions by himself, J. J. Marshall, and E. R. McC. Dix, and in the course of the first volume there was a powerful reinforcement—James Coleman, F. J. Bigger, Seamus Ó Casaide, D. J. O'Donoghue, and others. In a few years it had attracted to its pages practically everybody who had any Irish bibliographical knowledge and interest, and the volumes of *The Book Lover* to date contain the raw material of a mass of books. It is full of facts, not alone about Irish writers and Irish books, but about Irish history, and everything about Ireland which has been recorded in books or in manuscript.

Dr. Crone was wholly and entirely Irish, and wholly cheerful. You felt at ease with him in ten minutes, with his cheerful, beaming, countenance, his friendly laugh, and the way he made you at once free of his knowledge and of his books. He took no interest at all in Irish politics, beyond being a good Irishman, and I never knew, nor cared to know, where he stood upon politics. It was enough that, in Allingham's phrase, he was 'Ireland's friend' and so blood brother to everybody who was also Ireland's friend, and that he was doing more than one man's part to make her known to her children. He retained his cheerfulness, his gaiety, and his infectious good humour to the end. The last time I saw him was to meet him in College Green accidentally ten years ago, and to spend fifteen happy moments with him. He said to me then, what F. A. Fahy and W. P. Ryan had said not so long before in almost the same place, that it was most heartening and most wonderful to see how much the Treaty had changed Ireland for the better. We did not see it here, we were too close to it. But the London Irishman sees it.

Well, may the Earth lie light on him. We can, at least continue the work he began and carried on so magnificently for so many years.

W. B. [Luke], "More Memories of Dr. Crone", Vol. XXX, No. 2 (Feb. 1947), 27.

[We reprint this tribute to Dr. Crone written twenty-two years ago, by permission of the Libraries Committee and Mr. T. Gillett, F.L.A., Borough

Librarian, Willesden, from the Willesden Public Libraries Quarterly Record, Vol. I, No. 2, August, 1925.]

There is nothing novel or incongruous in the alliance of medicine and letters. Sir Thomas Browne, Arbuthnot and Oliver Goldsmith are remarkable examples of men who, trained to practice the healing art, have established their title to fame in the walks of literature; and the doctors of this present day include not a few who are as much at home in the library as in the consulting room, and wield the pen with as much facility as the lancet. Amongst these a conspicuous place must be accorded to the subject of this sketch.

Dr. Crone has had a busy professional career and has filled many important civic positions in Willesden and the County of Middlesex, but one is inclined to think that with all his varied employments—as practitioner, coroner, magistrate and councillor—he is at heart preeminently and sincerely a bookman before everything else.

The Willesden Library system owes him a heavy debt. He took part in the inception of the movement for adopting the Library Acts in 1890, and ever since he has been closely associated with every stage of progress; first in co-operation with his old friend Samuel Hutton the Harlesden Committee, and later as one of the promoters and as Chairman of the Kensal Rise Library, a position he now holds.

Every local honour that Willesden can bestow, including the chairmanship of the District Council, has been given to Dr. Crone at one time or another, and he has not lacked recognition by the outside world of letters. Since 1892 he has been a Fellow of the Royal Society of Antiquaries; he was elected a Member of the Royal Irish Academy (the highest literary distinction Ireland can confer) in 1916. For several years he was President of the Irish Literary Society of London, and for fifteen years he has acted as editor of that unique magazine *The Irish Book Lover*. Thus he has been brought in close touch with the literary celebrities of the Sister Isle of all creeds and parties, and with bibliophiles throughout the world. The crowning proof of his extensive learning and critical acumen will appear in the *Irish Biographical Dictionary* now passing through the press, a work to which he has devoted many years of research.

Of Dr. Crone as a man it is hardly necessary to speak. Every reader knows well the breezy personality, the warm heart, the quick mental activity and the jovial wit of one who for more than a third of a century has enhanced the gaiety of Willesden. In private as in public life he is a popular and attractive figure. Nobody has yet succeeded in quarrelling with him for there is no tinge of bitterness in his nature and he radiates a cheerful tolerance all too rare in these days of feverish dispute and hot antagonism. Young in everything but in years, may he long continue to shed, his genial influence on the community he has served so well.

K[evin] F[aller], "Reviews", Vol. XXXI, No.4 (April 1950), 94.

YEATS: THE MAN AND THE MASKS, BY RICHARD ELLMANN. A good many people can take an alarm-clock to pieces, but how many can out it together again? Ellmann deftly removes all-the occult balances, he hair-spring tension of father and son, the gyrating cog-wheels of body and soul— from behind the metallic and luminous dial; and—wonder of wonders—at the end of it all the Byzantine gong thrills one more than before.

Perhaps the demonstration is so effective because the manipulator gives the impression that he doesn't care tuppence whether or not the clock can be put together again. The fact is, you can tell the time of Yeats's life of this work; and appreciate, almost as much as the poet, the miracle of the time-piece itself.

"Notes and Queries", Vol. XXXI, No. 6 (Nov. 1951), 133.

YEATS AND "THE SALLY GARDENS". In his note on Yeats and "The Sally Gardens", P. S. O'H. does not seem to be aware of the fact that some lines of the original folk song were published by the late P. J. McCall. They will be found in *Feis Ceoil Collection of Irish Airs Hitherto Unpublished.* Edited by Arthur Darley and P. J. McCall. Vol. I. Published by the Feis Ceoil Association, 37 Molesworth Street, Dublin, 1914. In his note on page 43, P. J. McCall states that the song is well known in South, Leinster and gives the first stanza:

> Down by the sally gardens my own true love and I did meet,
> She passed the sally gardens a-tripping with her snow-white feet,
> She bid me take life easy, just as the leaves fall from each tree,
> But I being young and foolish with my true love would not agree.

It is interesting to compare this with the adaptation by Yeats

> Down by the salley gardens my love and I did meet;
> She passed the salley gardens with little snow-white feet.
> She bid me take love easy, as the leaves grow on the tree;
> But I, being young and foolish, with her would not agree.

An inferior version of this folk song will be found in a collection of Victorian Street Songs, published some years. Unfortunately, I have not this book to hand. (A[USTIN] C[LARKE].)

Colm Ó Lochlainn, "Editorial", Vol. XXXII, No. 5 (July 1956), 97.

P.S.

Duinne sa gcéad a bheith againn mar Phádraig Ó h-Éigearta agus is gearr go mhéadh Éire cheart againn—Éire shaor—Éire Ghaedhalach—Éire gan roinn.

I gCorcaigh a rugadh é—ceithre sgór bliann ó shoin—nó gan dhó—agus ó tháinig ciall agus réasún chuige, ní raibh lá dá shaol nár chaith sé cuid dhe ag saothrú leasa tír 'a dhúthchais. Máthair ionnraic dhícheallach bhí aige a chuir misneach 'na chroidhe agus Gaedhlachas fairis sin. Ní rófhada ó nochtuigh sé dhúinne sa mBiblio an grá bhí aige di agus chaoi ar fágadh na bainntreach í.

Is doiligh d'fhear mar mise teastas ceart a leagan amach ar a leitheidhe—ach I gcochall mo chroidhe mairrfe a chuimhne fad is beó mé.

The death of P. S. O'Hegarty on 17th December last has left a great gap; as he was for almost fifty years a notable figure in Irish affairs. His genius was many-sided, his sincerity never in doubt, his generosity and friendliness unbounded, and his love of country deep and unwavering.

Born in Cork in 1879, he was educated by the Christian Brothers at the famous 'North Mon' and, after a short time in a lawyer's office, he entered the Post Office Service in which he had a distinguished career. His high administrative capacity was mostly gained in the Secretary's Office in London from 1902 to 1913, and during these years he was a prominent figure in all Irish activities in London.

Transferred to Cobh in 1913 his stay was short. Already the British Authorities looked on him as a dangerous rebel, and when the 1914 war broke out he was moved first to Shrewsbury and then to Welshpool, and warned that he must remain there while the war lasted. In 1918 he refused to take the Oath of Allegiance to England and resigned his post.

When I first met him he had just taken charge of The Irish Book Shop in Dawson Street opposite St. Anne's Church. It had been founded some time before by E. MacLysaght, but it was P.S.'s personality which made it a Mecca for all Dublin booklovers. I had known his name for years as a contributor to *Irish Freedom, An t-Eireannach (The Irishman*—a monthly he edited for the Gaelic League in London) and to *The Irish Book Lover*, which had been founded by Dr. J. S. Crone in 1909. Indeed from that year until this hardly a number of the *I.B.L.* appeared without some contribution from him on books of Irish interest. I have published the *I.B.L.* in Dublin since 1928, and he was one of my most valued contributors.

Already in London he had amassed an enormous library, and until a few weeks before his death he kept adding to it. His first and greatest passion was books about Ireland, and books by Irish authors, both in Gaelic and in English. No man I ever met knew so much, and his orderly trained mind could sort out the facts and marshal them in a lucid and interesting way.

Another interest was boys' books. Adventure stories, *Kingston* and *Ballantyne the Brave*, G. A. Henty and even the 'bloods', and so called 'Penny Dreadfuls' appealed to him. Sunday after Sunday for many years I used to walk up Rathgar Road to borrow detective stories-of which he always had an enormous collection.

He read French easily and spoke it with fair fluency, so it was natural he should collect illustrated editions of French Classics, Shakespeare's early editions interested him, and he had many Spenser rarities also.

During the years from 1922 to 1944, while working strenuously to build up the Irish Post Office administration after the years of unrest and the establishment of the home government, he always found time to visit the bookshops and hunt for treasures.

A great work to which he devoted many years of research and patient compilation, indeed his greatest work, is *A History of Ireland Under the Union 1801-1922*. His foreword to *John Devoy's Post Bag* published in 1953 is a masterly summary of the Fenian movement, and no one was better fitted to make such an assessment as he, himself a Fenian, the son of a Fenian, and the friend of many of the old-timers now gone to rest.

A full bibliography is in preparation, but it would be difficult to include in it all the articles he contributed to *The Irish World* and *The Separatist*—a short-lived journal which sought to heal the cleavage caused by the Treaty and the Civil War. He was fearless and incisive in debate or controversy. He spoke quickly and vehemently, rarely at a loss for a word. He spoke Irish fluently and brought up all his family as Irish speakers, spending his summer holidays with them in the Gaeltacht of Donegal.

Physically he was not tall or robust, though active both in walking and cycling. He had a merry glint in his eye, and a ready smile. Of latter years he was troubled with bronchial asthma, but he never gave way to despondency; he never forsook his books, and he used to send in short papers to the Bibliographical Society of Ireland to be read by his friend Dr. F. S. Bourke.

A great Irishman, a great book collector, a great friend, has gone from us, and all Ireland is the poorer for his loss.

"Reviews", Vol. XXXII, No. 5 (July 1956), 107.

JAMES JOYCE'S "ARABY". The third story in Joyce's *Dubliners,* 1914, is "Araby" the tale of a young boy's hope and disappointment. 'the syllables of the word Araby were called to me through the silence in which my soul luxuriated and cast an eastern enchantment over me. I asked for leave to go to the bazaar'. It is late when his uncle arrives home on Saturday and gives the promised florin to the boy who travels to the bazaar by train from Westland Row. Failing to find any sixpenny entrance and fearing that the bazaar would be closed he passes in quickly through a turnstile, paying a shilling. The sadness of the situation is conveyed to us as he finds himself in an almost deserted hall listening to a girl and two young men chatting in front of Cafe Chantant. 'I lingered over her stall', he relates, 'though I knew my stay was useless'.

Students of Joyce who seek the image of reality or personal experiences in his writings may be interested in an item which the National Library has recently acquired: the official catalogue of Araby grand oriental fete at Ball's Bridge, Dublin, in aid of Jervis Street Hospital, May 14th, 15th 16th, 17th 18th and 19th, 1894. (Dublin: Browne & Nolan 1894). It is octavo size and has 80 pages. The outer cover is in colour showing an Arab on a camel, and bears the admission price-one shilling. Café Chantant is featured on page 71.

The 19th of May, 1894 was on Saturday and James Joyce was then twelve years old and living with his family at 14 Fitzgibbon Street. (PATRICK HENCHY.)

"A Letter from Oliver Goldsmith", Vol. XXXII, No. 6 (Sept. 1957), 130.

[The Goldsmith letter here printed was addressed to Richard Bryanton, and the original is deposited on loan in Trinity College Library. It is the property of Colonel W. T. Gregg, Ballypatrick, Clonmel. It has been published already in an abbreviated form, and is here republished from the original by kind permission of Colonel Gregg.]

Edinburgh, Apr. 26th 1753

My Dear Bob,

How many Good Excuses, (& you know I was ever Good at an Excuse) might I call up to vindicate my past shamefull silence, I might tell how I wrote a Long letter at my first coming hither, and seem

Vastly Angry at, my not Receiving an answer, or, I might Alledge, that
Buissness (with Buissness (you know) I was always pester'd) had never
given me time to finger a Pen, but I suppress these and twenty more
equally Plausible, and as easily invented, since they might all be
attended with a slight inconvenience of Being known to be Lies, let me
then speak truth, an Hereditary Indolence (I have it from the Mother's
Side) has hitherto prevented my writing to you, and still prevented my
writing at least twentyfive Letters more due to my friends in Ireland.
No Transport Dog gets up into his Wheels with More Reluctance than I
sit down to write, yet no Dog ever loved the roast meat he turns better
than I do him I now address. Yet What Shall I say now I'm enter'd
shall I tire you with a description of this unfruitful Country Where I
must lead you over their hills all brown with heather their Valleys
scarce able to feed a Rabbitt—Man Alone seems to be the only
Creature who has Arived to the natural Size in this poor Soil—every
part of the Country Presents The same dismal Landship—no Grove nor
Brook lend their Musik to Cheer the Stranger, or make the Inhabitants
forget their Poverty—Yet with all these disadvantages to Call him
down to Humanity A Scotch Man is one of the Proudest things alive—
the Poor have pride Ever ready to Relieve them if mankind should
happen to despise them they are masters of their own admiration and
that they can plentifully Bestow on themselves from their pride and
poverty as I take it Results one Advantage this Country Enjoys,
(namely) the Gentlemen are much Better bred than amongst us no such
Character here as our foxhunters And they've expressed great surprise
when I informed them, that some men in Ireland of a Thousand a Year
spend their Whole lives in Running after a hare, drinking to be drunk,
and getting every Girl (that will let them) with Child, and truly if such a
being equiped in his huntingdress came among a Circle of Scotch
Gentry, they would behold him with the same astonishment that a
Countryman would king George on Horseback—the men here have
generally high cheek'd bones, and are Lean and Swarthy, fond of
Action, dancing in particular Tho now I've mentioned dancing, let me
say something of their Balls, which are very frequent here, when a
Stranger enters the dancing hall he sees one end of the room taken up
with the ladies who sit dismally in a Groupe by them Selves, on the
other end stands their Pensive Partners that are to be, but no more
intercourse between the sexes, than there is between two Countrys at
War,—the ladies indeed May Ogle, and the Gentlemen Sigh, but an
Embargo is laid on any closer commerce at length to interrupt
hostilities. The Lady Directress or intendant or—what you will, Pitches

on a gentleman and Lady to Walk a minuet which they perform with a formality that aproaches despondence, after five or six Couple have thus Walked the Gauntlet all stand up to Country dances each Gentleman furnished with a Partner from the aforesaid Lady Directress; so they dance much and say nothing, and thus concludes our Assembly I told a Scotch Gentleman that such profound silence resembled the ancient procession of the Roman Matrons in Honour of Ceres, and the Scots Gentleman told me (and faith I Believe he was Right) that I was a very great Pedant for my pains, now I'm lame to the Ladies, and to shew that I love Scotland And every thing that Belongs to so Charming a Country, I insist on it, and will give him leave to break my head that denys it that the Scots Ladies are ten thousand times finer and Handsomer than the Irish—to be sure now I see your Sisters Betty and Peggy vastly surprised at my Partiality, But tell them Flattly I Don't Value them or their fine Skins, or Eyes, or Good Sence, or—a Potatoe, for I say it, and will Maintain it, and as a Convincing proof (I'm in a Very Great Passion) what I assert the scotch ladies say it themselves— But to be less serious, where will you find a Language so pretty Become a pretty mouth, as the Broad Scotch and the Women here speak it in its highest purity. For instance, teach one of the Young Ladies to pronounce Whear will I Gang, with a Becoming wideness of Mouth, and I'll Lay my life they will wound every Hearer—we have no such Character here as a Coquet But alas! have many envious Prudes— some days ago I walk'd into my Lord Kilcoubry's—dont be surprized my Lord is but a Glover, when the Dutchess of Hamilton (that fair who sacrificed her Beauty to ambition, and her inward peace to a title and Gilt Equipage) Pass'd by in her Chariot her Batter'd Husband, or more properly the Guardian of her Charms, sat by her side, Strait envy began in the shape of no less than three Ladies who sat with me, to find faults in her faultless form, For my part says the first, I think that I always thought that the dutchess has too much Red in her Complexion, Madam I'm of your Opinion says the Second and I think her face has a palish Cast, too much in the delicate order—and let me tell you adds the Third Lady) whose mouth was pucker'd up to the size of an issue, that the dutchess has fine lips but she wants a mouth, at this every Lady drew up her own mouth, as if she was going to pronounce the Letter, P, But how ill my Bob, does it become me to ridicule women, with whom I have scarce any Correspondence, there are 'tis Certain Handsome Women here and 'tis as Certain there are handsome men to keep them Company—an ugly and a poor man is Society for himself, and such Society, the World lets me enjoy in Great abundance—fortune has

given you Circumstances, and Nature A Person to look Charming in the Eyes of the fair World, Nor do I envy my Dr Bob such Blessings, while I may sit down and Laugh at the World, and at my self, the most ridiculous Object in it But I begin to Grow ———— and perhaps the fitt may continue till I Receive an answer to this—I know you cant send much news from B:mahon But such as it is send it all Every thing you write will be agreeable, and entertaining to me, has George Conway put up a Sign yet—or, Johnny Fineely left off Drinking Drams—or Tom Allen got a new Wig—But I Leave to your Choice what to write—
While
     Oliver Goldsmith lives
              know you have a friend.
PS Give my sincerest Regards not Compliments (do you mind) to your agreeable Family-And give my advice to my Mother if you see her For as you Express it in Ireland I have a sneaking kinship for her still.

Direct to me Student in Physick in Edinburgh.

F. Carroll, "Clarence Mangan's Age Complex", Vol. XXXII, No. 6 (Sept. 1957), 133.

Mangan was born on the 1st of May 1803.

(1) He writes as follows in his "Fragment of an Unfinished Autobiography" which appeared in *The Irish Monthly* for November 1882, and subsequently in the *Poets and Poetry of Munster* (3rd Edition 1883), edited by Rev. C. P. Meehan:

> I had been sent to Mr. Courtenay's Academy in Derby Square. It was the first evening of my entrance (in 1820) when I had completed my eleventh year.

He was 17 on the 1st of May 1820.

(2) He writes as follows in an extract of an 'autobiography' which James Price (*Evening Packet* 22nd September 1849) 'was confided by him to his generous publisher':

> It was when I was about fifteen years old that I awoke to a sense of the changes that had come over our household. This was in 1824.

He was 21 on 1st May 1824.

(3) His well-known poem "The Nameless One" contains the following verse:

> And lives he still, then ? Yes ! Old and hoary
> At thirty-nine, from Despair and Woe,

He lives, enduring what future Story
Will never know.

This poem appeared in *The Irishman* of 27th October 1849 four months after his death, but was probably written some months before that event took place and when he was 45 years of age. *The Irishman*, commencing with its second issue, printed 34 of Mangan's poems, and no less than 15 of these appeared after his death.

(4) His poem "Genius: A Fragment" appeared in *The Irishman* of 23rd June 1849 with the following note under the title:

> Some few of my readers may, perhaps, take an interest in the following verses, from the fact that they were penned at the age of sixteen and were the first that I ever committed to paper. I had, indeed, myself forgotten their existence, and only happened to light on them while rummaging the contents of an old chest of mine, which for twenty years had been consigned to a lumber-room.

This poem previously appeared in *The Dublin and London Magazine* for March 1826, signed "M, Dublin". He was then 22 years of age.

An examination of the four statements set out above shows that in each of them Mangan's age has been understated by 6 years! This remarkable consistency suggests that for a number of years previous similar statements must have been made, and it would, I think, be no exaggeration to say that in the last few years of his life the family believed that he was born in the year 1809.

The question now arises: When and in what circumstances did Mangan decide to adopt 1809 as the year of his birth? The expectation of life a century ago was about 60 years and any person in the forties was definitely 'middle-aged'. Mangan was 40 on the 1st of May 1843.

On the 8th of October 1843 John O'Donovan addressed a letter to the Rev. Dr. J. H. Todd which commenced as follows:

> I was born in the townland of Attatimore (Ait an Tighe Móir) on the 3rd of August 1809. My father died on the 29th of July 1817, when I was about eight years old. (*J.R.S.A.I.*, July 1884, p.348.)

The exact date of O'Donovan's birth does not appear to be known, but he was baptized on the 26th July 1806. [See "Entries relating to John O'Donovan and his Immediate Relatives", *J.R.S.A.I.*, Sept. 1915].

I now put forward the following suggestion. By October 1843, Mangan, assuming he is suffering from age complex, is worried about his age. He is frequently in touch with both John O'Donovan and Dr. Todd and presumably gets to know shortly after O'Donovan's letter was written that he (O'Donovan) has claimed to have been born in

1809. From his long acquaintance with O'Donovan he knows that statement to be incorrect. Mangan now has an example to follow and no doubt he now chooses 1809 as the year of his birth as this will give him six years' escape from 'middle age' worries.

F. Carroll, "The Dream of Macdonnell Claragh: An Anonymous Poem by Clarence Mangan", Vol. XXXII, No. 6 (Sept. 1957), 135.

This poem, which appeared in *The Dublin Penny Journal* of 22nd December 1832, with no signature attached, seems to have escaped the notice of Mangan's biographers. It is an unrhymed version of a translation from the Gaelic probably based on a literal translation furnished by Petrie or O'Curry. Hitherto, Mangan's earliest known Gaelic translation was "The Woman of Three Cows" which appeared in *The Irish Penny Journal* of 29th August 1840.

About 1943 I came to the conclusion through internal evidence that "The Dream of MacDonnell Claragh" was possibly Mangan's as it contained two words—'evanished' and 'palace-walls' and 'halls'—which he had a tendency to use. A year or two later I unexpectedly came across proof.

In the issue of *The All-Ireland Review* for 30 August 1902 Standish O'Grady, the Editor, printed a verse of Mangan's "And Then No More" and added this interesting note: 'The following lines by the same poet were discovered by me in manuscript in, I think, O'Donovan's letters, written while he was engaged on the Ordnance Survey:

> I lingered on the royal Brugh which stands
> By the dark-rolling waters of the Boyne,
> Where Angus Og magnificently dwells.

The Mangan Manuscripts in the National Library (which were not available during the war) include a rough, unrhymed, preliminary rendering which presumably was used by him as a 'working model'. The opening lines are as follows:

> One night I lay asleep
> My thoughts ran wild. Disturbed.
> A Banshee soul-subduing mild
> Lay down beside me smiled upon me,
> Small her waist—her raven locks (ebon locks)
> Waving in wanton ringlets to her heels.

Colm Ó Lochlainn, "Farewell", Vol. XXXII, No. 6 (Sept. 1957).

In bringing to a close this, the thirty second volume of *I.B.L.*, I thank all who have helped Seamus Ó Casaide and me since we took it over in 1926. I have only succeeded in printing sixteen volumes in 30 years. There were many difficulties. Lack of material: lack of money, as *The Book Lover* never paid, and never took advertisements. Many a time I had to fill a number almost unaided; but I do not regret having carried it on; it gave me a certain joy in the making. After all, 1909 to 1957 is a good spell for any Irish journal. If it is possible we may start a new series; at the moment it looks doubtful.

The Irish Book Lover
Vols. I-XXXII (1909–1957)
An Intregrated Index

A

"A.A.C." (queries), II: 47, 75, 112, 119, X: 91.
Abbey Theatre Company, III: 8, 30, 32, IV: 8, VII:111.
Abbey of Holy Cross, The (M. Callanan), XVII: 96;
Abbott, T. K., V: 105.
Abbott, Thomas, XXIV: 111, XIX: 100.
"A.B.E.H", II: 145.
Aberdeen, Earl of, I: 41.
Abraham, James Johnston, IV: 171, 187, V: 65, VI: 192, VII: 56, VIII: 84.
"A.C." (on *Michael Kavanagh*), II: 195.
"A Chara na n órd n-Eóghan S. Ó Hogáin", XXXI: 121.
Account of the Honourable Society of King's Inns, An (Gustavus Everard Hamilton), VII: 30.
Achill Press, II: 65, 110, III: 29, 38, VI: 104, 116, XIX: 101, XX: 114, XXII: 103.
Acres, William, XIV: 107.
Adair, Ivan(*Songs from Dublin City*), X:15.
Adam of Dublin (Conal O'Riordan), XII: 65-66.
Adam, [Major] W. A., II: 43.
Adams, Dick, XIII: 8.
Adams, John ("The Three B's") IX: 75; XXII: 142.
Address to Tibbot na Long (Pól Breathnach), XXVIII: 2.
Adelais (John Taffe), V: 208.
"Adieu to Belashanny" (anon.), XXXI: 97.
Adolescent (Gerald Raftery),

XXVI: 63.
Adrigoole (Peadar O'Donnell), XVII: 110-11.
Adventurer, The, (John Mitchel) IV: 161.
Adventures in the Revolution and under the Consulate (Moreau de Jonnes, trans. by Cyril Hammond), XVII: 67-68.
Adventures of Siuibhne Geilt, The (J. G. O'Keefe) IV: 183.
"Æ" (ed. *The Reformer,* 1748), VIII: 1.
"Æ", see Russell, George.
Agg, John (*MacDermot, or the Irish Chieftain*) XII: 21.
"A h-Uiscidhe Chroidhe na n-anmann/*L'Elixir de la vie*" (An Irish Drinking Song in French), XXVII: 232-33.
Aickin, Joseph ("Londeriados"), VII: 118.
Aidhleart, An t-Ath. Risteárd (S.P.), XVI: 51.
Áilleacht agus an Beitheach (Sinéad de Valéra), XXX: 46.
Ainsworth, William Harrison, II: 70.
Airchinneach, XXXII: 55.
Airteach's Western Boundary (M. J. Connellan, P.P.), XXXI: 125.
Aitchison, C., VI: 6.
Alcock, Deborah, IV: 143, 150.
Alexander, [Archb.] William, III: 35, 85, 206; (Primate Alexander) XIV: 51.
Alexander, Eleanor, V: 69.
Alexander, Miriam, III: 133.
Alexander, [Mrs.] C. F., III: 35, 85, X: 35.
Allan, John Steele (*The Young*

Angler), XXXI: 93.
Allen, Anthony (*First Songs*), X: 46-47.
Allen, J. A., XI: 64.
Allingham, H.C., XIV: 79.
Allingham, William., II: 198; (*Irish Songs and Poems*) III: 76; (*Letters to William Allingham*) III: 83; XII: 104, XIV: 35 78.
Almanacs—(Irish Almanacs) III: 128; (Early Dublin Almanac) VIII: 35; (*Early Dublin Printed Almanacs*) X: 14; (Account of the Almanacks) XVI: 22; (Early Irish Almanacs) XVIII: 38; (Almanac Compiled by a Farmer, 1587) XVIII: 38; (Old Moore's Almanacs) XVIII 156; (An Old Dublin Almanac) XXI: 81-85; (An Irish Scribe and the Almanacs) XXVI: 80.
Almoritia, Co. Westmeath (Rev. John Brady), XXIX: 92.
Alphabet of Irish Saints, VII: 135.
Alumni Dublinensis (eds. George Dames Burtchaell & Thomas Ulick Sadlier), XIV: 123.
"A.M.", XIII: 95.
Amateur Army, The (Patrick MacGill), VI: 187.
Ambrosian Codex, The, XXVI: 108.
American Irish Historical Society, XVI: 39; (*The Recorder*) XIX: 152; (Library), XXIV: 112.
American Magazines, V: 130.
American Reference Works, XXIII: 94.
Amhráin Mhuighe Scola (Mrs. Costello), XI: 8
"Amhrán Bádóra" (Tomás Mac Aoidh), XXVI: 57.
"Amhrán ó Oileán Cliara" (Canónac Mícheál Ó Conaire), XXVI: 30.
"Amhrán ó Inse an Rinnce"

(Donnchadh Mac Craith), XIX: 141.
Analecta Hibernica, XXVIII: 93; XXIX: 116; (*Guide to Irish Genealogical Collections*) XXIV: 70; XXX: 16, 22.
An bás 'nár Measc (D.), XIX: 1.
Ancestry of an Historian (Pól Breathnach), XXVII: 221.
Ancient Irish Parish, Past and Present, An (J. Davison Cowan) V: 165.
Ancient Trade Signs (Colm Ó Lochlainn), XXIX: 99.
Anderson, Avril (*Whisht! Listen a Minute*), XXIV: 45.
Anderson, J. Redwood (on *The Pursuit of Diarmuid and Grania*) XXXI: 115.
Anderson, John (bibliographer), II: 6, XIV: 19; (book catalogue), XVII: 52.
Anderson, John Crossley, X: 70.
Anderson, Paris (*Nooks and Corners of the County of Kilkenny*), VII: 102, X: 92.
Anderson, R. A. (*With Horace Plunkett in Ireland*), XXIII: 118.
Anderson, [Sir] Robert, I: 73, 137, 142, 147, 16, II: 9, 124.9; (The Cumberland Bard) III: 198; IV: 108; (Obit.) X: 44.
Andrews, [Dr.] Thomas, VI: 205.
Andrews, Thomas (shipbuider), IV: 105.
Andrews, Elizabeth, V: 65.
"An Eala Bhán" (James Stephens), XXVIII:1.
Angelus, Fr., XIII: 91.
Anglo-Irish Essays (John Eglinton), IX: 53.
Anglo-Irish Library, A (17th c.), XXX: 30-34.
Anglo-Irish Literature, see Irish Literature in English.
Anglo-Irish Literature (St. John

Drelincourt Seymour), XVII: 112.
Anglo-Irish Relations (P. S. O' Hegarty), XXXI: 9.
Annals of—(*Loch Cé*), XVIII: 68; (*Aughnacloy*) XII: 63-65; (*Boyle*) XVI: 17; (*Annals of the City and Diocese* of Limerick) XVII: 144; XVIII: 60; (*Fir Manach*) XXIII: 7; (*Innisfallen*) XXII: 25; (*Leinster*) XXIV: 58, 87; (*Four Masters*) XX: 32, 92, XXXI: 126; (*Tirconall*) XXIV: 13, XXII: 104; (Sundry) XXIV: 13, XXV: 37, XXVII: 179. Also (Curiosities from Irish Annals) XIX: 37; (Letters concerning Irish Annals) XIX, 96.
Annuaire International de l'Education et de l'Enseignement, XXIII: 23.
Anonymous Correspondent (cited in *The Minstrelsy of Ireland*), XXVII: 234.
Anonymous Prefacer 1772, The, (Preface to *Memoirs of Marquis Clanrickarde*) XVI: 10.
"An Philibin", see "Philibin, An" [pseud.].
Anson, Peter F. (*An Irish Pilgrimage*), XXIII: 21.
Anstor, John, II: 149.
An t-Europach (F. W. O' Connell), XVIII: 66.
Anthology of Contemporary Catholic Poetry, An (Cecil Leahy), XIX: 151.
Anthony, Irvin (*Raleigh and his World*), XXII: 122.
Anti-Unionist, The, VI: 208, VII: 12.
Antiquities of Ireland (James Ware), II: 11.
Antiquities of Limerick and its Neighbourhood (T. J. Westropp), VIII: 10.

Antisell, Thomas, VI: 80, 102, 118.
Antrim (Libraries), XIII: 47; (MSS) XIII: 94.
Aonach na Leabhar (editorial) XXVII: 265.
Aonach Tailteann Prize Winners, XIV: 120.
Apple Blossom, The, and Other Poems (W. J. Steenson), XIV: 46.
Appreciations and Depreciations (John Eglinton), IX: 53.
"A.R." [psued.] see Aylward, R.
"Araby" (James Joyce), XXXII: 107.
Arbuthnot, [Sir] Alexander, II: 55.
Archaelology of Ireland (R. A. S. Macalister), XVI: 37.
Archaeological Journals, III: 170.
Archaeological Society (Dublin), XIX: 142, 165.
Archbishops of Tuam, VI: 152.
Archdeacon, Matthew, III: 191.
Archer, Robert (Obit.), XXI: 15.
Archivium Hibernicum, V: 216, XVII: 49, XXIX: 119.
Ardagh and Clonmacnoise, XVII: 17; (*Antiquarian Society Journal*), XXXII: 62.
Ardagh, John, XIV: 77, 86, 93, XV: 24; (Bibliography of Irish Botany) XVIII: 143; (Bibliography of *The Shamrock*) XXI: 37; (*The Irish Emigrant*) 64; ("Zozimus") XXVI: 58, XXIX: 19; (Martin Family Cup) XXIV: 13; (Medical MSS) XXX: 67.
Arden, Francis, XIII: 116.
"Ardglass, or the Ruined Castles" (Samuel Burdy), III: 28.
Ardhill, [Rev.] John R. (*St. Patrick 180 A.D.*), XIX: 178.
"Ardrigh" [pseud.], VIII: 134.
Ards Farmer, An (James C. Rutherford), IV: 208.

Ards Penninsula, XX: 28, 140.
"Arduaree", V: 191.
Are We All Met? (Whitford Kane), XIX: 150.
Arensburg & Kimball (*Family and Community in Ireland*) XXVIII: 94.
Ár gCreach is ár gCár (C. Ó L.), XXVIII: 97.
Arlen, Charles R. (*Chart of Irish History*), V: 67.
Armagh—(Rogers' *History of*) I: 10; (with Tyrone) I: 10; (Armagh Poet) II: 92; (Irish Parliament) II: 111; (Hymnal) IV: 142; ("Barring-Out") V: 14; (Book of) V: 170, VI: 47, VII: 114; (printing in), XIV: 7, 55, XVII: 2, 4; (in 1860) XXVII: 211.
Armour, W. S. (*Armour of Ballymoney*) XXIII: 100; (*Facing the Irish Question*) XXIII: 120; (*Mankind at the Watershed*) XXIV: 141.
Armstrong, C. F. Savage, XI: 115.
Armstrong, F. C. [Capt.] (*The Cruise of the Daring*), XXIII: 17.
Armytage, Walter, XXXII: 106.
Art Competition in Repeal Days, XVII: 116.
Art Union, XVII: 116, XXIV: 84, 133.
Artane (printing in), XXVII: 259.
Arthur, [Dr.] Thomas (Bishop of Limerick), XXVI: 38.
Arthur, Mary Lucy, XI: 25.
Arthur, [Sir] George (*General Sir John Maxwell*), XX: 94.
Articles of Interest in Foreign Periodicals, XIX: 10, 57, 94, 123, XVIII: 165, XIX: 10, 94, 123, 132, XX: 27, 134, 144, XX: 27, 134, 135, XXI: 2.
Ashbourne, Lord, IV: 212, 213, V: 18; (*Grégoire and the French Revolution*), XXI: 22.
Ashton, Robert (*Battle of Aughrim*), I: 158, X: 65.
Aspects of Wilde (Vincent O' Sullivan), XXIV: 94.
Asquith, Lady Cynthia (*Beginnings*), XXIII: 96; (*New Tales of Humour*), 153.
Association Books, VI: 115, 183, 151, 204, X: 58-60, XIV: 78, 110, 126, XVIII: 145, XXX: 74-78.
Aston, W. G., III: 100, 206.
As Luck would Have It (M. P. Campbell), XXXI: 20.
Athenaeum, The, XII: 133.
"Athene" (pseud. S. M. Harris), V: 11.
Athlone—(*Athlone Herald*) XIX: 90-91; (printing in) II: 84, VI: 106, 136, XIX: 95, XXIII: 93.
Atkins, J. B., II: 130.
Atkinson, E. D., XV: 58.
Atlantic Rhymes and Rhythms (Emily Lawless) XXXII: 76.
At the Sign of the Sword, (Prof. J. Lawrence Rentoul) VII: 162.
Atthill, Lombe (*The Recollections of an Irish Doctor*), II: 177.
At Vancouver's Well, (Prof. J. Lawrence Rentoul) IX: 79.
Auctions, see Book Auctions.
Auctioneer's Hammer, The VI: 18, XVI: 71, XXVII: 230, XXI: 44,
"Auctor" (The Worm Turneth), XXXI: 54.
Austin, Alfred, IV: 105.
Author's Club, XIII: 83.
Authors wanted, III: 28, 82, 103, 138, XII: 19, 41.
Autographs, III: 69, IV: 46, XVIII: 98.
"Avoca", A History, IV: 208.
Aylward, Margaret, XVII: 48.

Aylward, R. ["A.R."] II: 158; (on Co. Kilkenny Irish Poetry) XVIII: 144; (Bibliography of Eucharistic Congress) XX: 136.
Ayscough, Anthony (*Country House Baroque*), XXVII: 282.

B

Back Lane Parliament, The, III: 213, IV: 38.
Bád Beag Glas, An (MS magazine) XXII: 144.
Bagenal, P H., VII: 55, XV: 31.
Baggot, James (of Ballingarry), XXI: 135, XXIV: 112.
Bagwell, Richard, VII: 143; (Obit.) X: 44.
Bailey, W. F., VIII: 141.
Baine, or Bayne, II: 59, 60, 94.
Báinne 'Dhubh na Féile' (Máirtín Ó Cadhain), XXVI: 30.
Baird, Beatrice M. (*Adventures in Music-Land*) XXI: 141.
Bairéad, Ciarán (*Cúirt an Mheadhon Oidhche*) XXX: 8-11; (Canon Hannay [George Birmingham]) XXXI: 87.
Bairéad, Tomás, ("Cailín Deas Chrúite na nGabhar")XXXII: 1.
Baldwin, [Dr.] (the Race of Castlebar), V: 165.
Bale, [Bishop] John, I: 14, XXI: 64.
Balfe, John Donnellan, XIV: 38.
Balfe, M. W., (biography) III: 209.
Ball, Francis Elrington, I: 48, III: 9, 12, IV: 211, VI: 155, VIII: 136, XII: 107.
Ball, Richard (*The Better Part*) XIII: 171.
Ball, [Sir] Robert, V: 105, 203, VI: 119.
Ballad—(*Historical Ballad Poetry of Ireland*) III: 168; (Ballad) VI: 199; (Irish Ballad Printers) XIV: 88; ("Ballad of Canine Proclivities, A") XXIV: 43; (*Ballads of Ballytumulty*) XIII: 90; ("Lurgan Town") XXIX: 133; ("Ballad of a Quinsical Printer") XXX: 132.
Ballinasloe (printing in) VII: 147, XVII: 9, 93; (Fair) XVIII: 175.
Ballinrobe (printing in), XVII: 9, 93.
Ballycarry Holiday, A (W. Mayne Knox) XIV: 91.
Ballyclare (printing in), V: 129, 167 185, VII: 33, XII: 42.
Ballygullion (Lynn C. Doyle), I: 9.
Ballyhullan Register, The, (old Monaghan journal) X: 30, XI: 29.
Ballykinlar, XIII: 58.
Ballymena (*Old Ballymena*) II: 30; (printing in), XII: 128, XIII: 67, 95, XV: 53.
Ballyshannon (printing in), XVII: 101-102.
Ballytubber and the Pedlars (J. G. Rhynehart), XXXI: 106.
Banba (Irish magazine) XX: 66, 115, 140.
Banbridge (History of), I: 10, 73; (printing in), XVII: 7.
Banim, John, II: 149.
Banim, Michael (*Joe Wilson's Ghost*) XIII: 140; XVI: 125.
Banking (Irish), V: 69.
"Bard of Dunover, The" (Andrew MacKenzie), III: 197.
Barántas, XXII: 40.
"Bard of Louth, The" [Peadar Ó Doirnín] XVII: 21.
Bard, Clan, VI: 3.
Bardic Poetry (ancient), II: 154.
Bardin, [Rev.] C., XIV: 41.
Barker, Ernest, VIII: 134.
Barker, I. F., IV: 105.
Barlee, Annette (*On Our Hill*), XXVIII: 96.

Barlow, Jane, IV: 46, VIII: 141.
Barlow, [Rev.], J. W., V: 15.
"Barney Maglone" (psued. of Robert Arthur Wilson), XII: 75-77.
Barony, The (Cork), XX: 137.
Barrett, John, XIII: 79.
Barrett, William Alexander (*Balfe: His Life and Work*), III: 209.
Barrington, [Sir] Jonah, IX: 107.
Barron, Philip, I: 121, II: 18, IV: 57; (Irish College Waterford) IV: 77. 77, XVII: 167, XXI: 42, XXV: 40.
Barry, [Rev.] Albert, I: 21.
Barry, Dermot (*Tom Creagan*), XIX: 149.
Barry, Lord, VII: 49.
Barry Lyndon (W. M. Thackeray), III: 3.
Barry, Michael Joseph, III: 24, 25; IX: 25, 41.
Barry, William, X: 51.
Barry, W. Whitaker (*A Walking Tour Round Ireland in 1865*), III: 173.
Bartley, J. O., (Topical Play of Ninety-Eight) XXVIII: 57-60; (Bulls and Bog Witticisms), XXX: 59-62.
Barton, [Sir] Dunbar Plunket (*Timothy Healy*) XXI: 140; XIII: 142, XV: 56.
Battle of Aughrim, The (Robert Ashton), X: 65.
Battle of Ballynahinch, The (James Bryce), XI: 85.
Battle of Carrickshock, The XXXI: 26.
Battle of Cluain Tiobraid, The XXI: 103-06.
Bauer, Robert (*Ireland*) XXVII: 186.
Baumann, A. A., (*Personalities*) XXV: 71.
Bax, Arnold [pseud. "Dermot O'Byrne"], *Red Owen*, XI: 46; (*Wrack and Other Stories*) X: 61.
Baynes, Norman H. (*Bibliography of J. B. Bury*), XVIII: 20.
"B.D.", IX: 37.
"B.E.", X: 43.
Beaconsfield, Lord, II: 31.
Beál an Uaiguis, XII: 135.
Béaslaí, Piaras (*Eigse NuaGhaedhilge*), XXII: 124.
Beatha Chríost, XXVII: 208, XXVIII: 44.
Beatty, [Sir] Chester (MSS collection) XXXII: 105.
Beaufoy Library, I: 4.
Beauties of the Boyne, The (Sir William Wilde), XXXI: 71.
Beauties of the Press, The I: 56.
Beautiful Types, XXIX: 138.
Becher, Lady, see Miss O'Neil.
Beck, J. W., VI: 32.
Beckett, Samuel (*More Pricks Than Kicks*), XXII: 96.
Bedell, [Bishop] William ("Bedell's Bible"), IV: 100; (Bedell's Old Testament) XXVIII: 67,135.
"Beggarman, The" (William Boyle), X: 99.
Beginning of Modern Ireland (Philip Wilson), IV: 70.
"Beirt Fhear" (pseud. of J. J. Doyle), XVII. 51.
Belfast—(in the 20th Century) I: 19; (Historic Society) I: 151; (Belfast Bible) II: 109; (Henry Linn, book-binder) II: 110; (Booksellers) III: 138; ("The Belfast Boy") IV: 12; (printing in) IV: 15; (*Belfast*) V: 120: VI: 151, 159, 187, 209, XI: 102, XIII: 176; (shipyard workers) V: 120, VI: 5, 25; (books in) V: 211, 214; (Belfast City) X: 14; (Early Printed Books) XI: 1, 13,

XII: 22, 137, XVII: 52; (Politics) XI: 64, 84; (N. H. & P. S. Centy) XIV: 90; (Book Auction) XXIV: 28.
Belfast Newspapers—(*Belfast Penny Punch*) III: 103; (*Belfast Morning News*) III: 69; (*Belfast Evening Star*) XI: 102; (general) XIII: 32; (Two Gaels) XIII: 3; (*Belfast Commercial Chronicle*) XIX: 90; (*Belfast Irishman*) XIX: 90; (*Belfast Mercantile*) XIX: 90; (*Belfast News-Letter*) XIX: 90.
Belgium (books on Ireland), XXXII: 16.
Bell, David Charles, VII: 103, 188, XI: 113.
Bell, H. I. (*Robin Ernest William Flower*), XXXI: 18.
Bell, John, IV: 91.
Bell, Julian (*We Did Not Fight*), XXIII: 152.
Bell, Marguerite, I: 45.
Bell, Robert, VI: 115.
Bell, Sidney (*Celts and Other Poems*), XXX: 71.
Belmore, Earl of (Obit.) IV: 176.
Beloved Man from Ulster, The (Patrick Riddell) XXX: 27-29.
Benburb: Its Battlefields and Histories (John J. Marshall), XIV: 124.
Benham, [Sir] Gurney (*Book of Quotations*), XXXI: 20.
Benn, Alfred William (Obit.), VII: 76.
Bennett, Arnold (on G. Moore, G. B. Shaw and W. B. Yeats), XVIII: 131.
Bennett Family of Forkhill, XXII: 32.
Benson, E. F., (*Edward VII*), XXII: 69.
Benson, [Rev.] Charles William (Obit.), X: 94.

Beque, Etiennette, (*L'Appel de la Race*), XXI: 93.
Beresford, [Lord] Charles XI: 25.
Bergh, G. Van den, see Van den Bergh, G.
Bergin, [Prof.] Osborn J. (*Mirror of the Sacrament of Penance*), V: 149.
Berkeley, George F. H., V: 167.
Berkeley, [Mr.] George, II: 147.
Berkeley, Grantley, IV: 28.
Berry, *[Rev.]* J. Fleetwood (*Story of St. Nicholas' Collegiate Church, The Galway*), V: 87.
Berwick, [Rev] Edward (Marginalia), XXX: 126-28.
Bernard, Bayle, III: 24.
Bernard, [Dr.] (Obit.), IV: 103.
Bernard, [Dean] J. H., III: 24; (*Cathedral Church of St. Patrick*) XXVII: 237.
Best, R[ichard]. I[irvine]., (National Library) XIV: 138, V: 146, VI: 156; (Henry Bradshaw) XIX: 54; (*Irish Philology and Literature*) XXIX: 42.
Best Short Stories of 1937, The (E. J. O'Brien), XXVI: 23.
Betham, [Sir] William, II: 149.
Betjeman, [Sir] John (*Ghastly Good Taste*), XXII: 74.
Better Part, The (Richard Ball), XIII: 171.
Betts, John (*The Story of the Irish Society*), V: 10.
Betty, [Sir] Charles (MSS collection), XXXII: 105.
Beware the Cat (Anon.), VIII: 89, 140.
Bewick, Thomas, XXXII: 146.
Beyond Soundings (R: Lloyd Praeger), XVIII: 178.
Bhagwan Shri Hamsa (*The Holy Mountain*), XXII: 150.
Bharuntacht, An, see Barony, The.
Bhrugha, Chathail (see Brugha,

Cathal).
Bhuíle Shuibhne (J. G. O'Keeffe), XIX: 182.
Bianconi, Charles (Travelling in Ireland), XXIX: 34.
Bibby, Thomas, III: 49.
Bible—(Bible Tercentenary, The) II: 109; (Blow's Bible) II: 109; ("Sin on More" II: 109); ("Bedell's Bible"), IV: 100; (Bedell's Old Testament) XXVIII: 67,135.
Bibliographical Account of Irish Theatrical Literature, A (James J. O'Neill), XII: 38-40.
Bibliographical Acquisition (Recent) I: 54.
Bibliography Quarterly VI: 15, 64, 120, 171, VII: 19, 78, 144.
Bibliographical Society of Ireland (Annual General Meetings), (1930) XVIII: 19, 124, 162, XX: 10; (1931) XIX: 62; (1932) XX: 39; XXI: 16; (1933) XXI: 27; (1935) XXIV: 11; (1936) XXIV: 33, 35, 126; (1937) XXV: 12, 31, 61; (1938) XXVI: 8, 134; (1939) XXVI: 76, 103, 134; (1940) XXVII: 176; (1943, 1944) XXIX: 6, 15; (sundry) IX: 82, 101, 132, X: 13, 20, 38, 87, XI: 44, 79, 101, XII: 87-88, 115, 140, XII: 140-41, XIII: 89, 97, 118, 166, XIV: 61, 104, XV: 23, XVII: 30, 33, XX: 10, 39, XXI: 16, 27, XXII: 28, 53, XXIII: 11, 84, XXVIII:13, 61; XXVIII: 13-14, 61, 128-30, 128. (Reports) XXIII: 11-13.
Bibliographies—I: 20, 42, 43, 50, 53, 59, 78, 85, 86, 94, 96, 98, 138, 143, 144, 164, 166; (Irish Literature) II: 15, 38, 63, 115, 119, 166; XXIX: 22; (Local Printing) II: 4, 23, 51, 66, 84, 101, 120, 151, 186; (Proclamations) II: 90; (*Irish Quarterly*) V: 11, 31, 116; (Isaac Butt) V: 54; (Family History) V: 91, 110, 151, 168, 204, 213; VI: 83; (Thomas Davis) VI: 68; (C. G. Duffy) VII: 177; (John Mitchel) VII: 86; (Frances Brown) VIII: 51; (Jane Barlow) VIII: 142; (Fielding Hall) VIII: 143; (J. S. Le Fanu) VIII: 30; XVIII: 100; XXIV: 36; (D. F. McCarthy) VIII: 123; (F. H. O'Donnell) VIII: 70; (John Todhunter) VIII: 71; (M. J. Barry) IX: 27; (*Handbook to County Bibliography*) X: 13; (E. V. Kenealy) X: 5; (W. J. Fitzpatrick) X: 29; (Edward Evans) X: 58; (J. P. Mahaffy) X: 112; (Edwin Hamilton) XI: 15; (*W. B. Yeats*) XV: 47; (Young Ireland) XV: 48; (Books of Irish Interest) XVII: 86-89; (Paul Hiffernan) XIX: 20; (T. M. Healy) XIX: 36; (Henry Bradshaw) XIX: 54; (Lafcadio Hearn) XIX: 139; (Edmund Burke) XX: 32; (Lady Wilde) XX: 60, 74; (Fr. Prout) XX: 74; (Dublin Eucharistic Congress) XX: 136; (Athletics) XXI: 18, XXII: 109; (*Shamrock*) XXI: 37; (Literature in Irish) XXII: 33, 131; (Skeffington Gibbon) XXII: 61; (Orange Society) XXV: 2, 85; (J. G. O'Keeffe) XXVI: 28; (Michael Hogan) XXVII: 276. Also (Some Unexplored Fields) XXII: 33-37; (Irish Bibliographies) XXII: 131.
Bibliographies of recent works, see *Irish Book Lover.*
Bibliotheca Hibernica, II: 196, VII: 117, 138.
Bibliotheca Phillippica, I: 164, III: 10.

Bibliotheca Putlandia, XXII: 33.
Bieler, Ludwig (Fr. Francis Nugent), XXX: 98, 99.
Big Wind of 1839 (John O'Donovan), XVIII: 77ff.
Bigger, Francis Joseph (*Land War in Ireland*) I: 9, 35; (John Bernard Trotter) I: 41; (John & William Magee) I: 47; (*The Beauties of the Press*) I: 56; (Robert Emmet) I: 63; 73; (Henry R. Montgomery) I: 101; 125, 132; (*Ulster Land War of 1770*) I: 133-134; 150, 152, 170; (Royal Academical Institution) 172, II: 12; (William Sampson) II: 49-50; 74, 130, 162; ("To F.R. Bigger") 173; (Dr. Drennan) III: 9; (Ardglass, or the Ruined Castle) III: 28, 38; (Portrait of Robert Emmet) III: 72-73; (*The Rushlight & The Irish Rushlight*) III: 115; (Andrew Mackenzie) III: 197-99; (Cumberland Monument) IV: 36; (Robert Gowdie) IV: 53-54; (Knox's Letters) IV: 124; (A Relic of '98) V: 45; (*Centenary Volume of the Royal Belfast Academical Institution*) V: 120; (John Mitchell's Books) V: 136; (Ireland in Stones and Story) V: 144 161, 167 VI: 189, 208, VII: 15, 16, 33, 54; (*Inis-Eoghain and its Crosses*) VII: 136; 167, 186, VIII: 38, 39, 43, 68, 115; ("Ardrigh") VIII: 134; IX: 28, 61, 83, X: 14, 17, 62, 95, 102, XI: 7, 63, 104, XII: 3, 10, 21, 33, 41, 56, 111, 129, XIII: 18, 32, 36, 37, 47, 94, 126, 140, 176, 178, XIV: 13, 26, 31, 40, 46, 61, 78, 98, 106, 126, XV: 11, 32, XXXII: 63.
Bigger, Gladys Singers, (*Blue Earth*) V: 182.
Bigger Memorial Library (Belfast Public Library), XVIII: 179.
Bile Buadhach ar Lár (F. É.), XVI: 44-45.
Bilingual Chap-Book, A, XXIII: 40-41.
"Billy Bluff" (James Porter), XIII: 126.
Bindon, David, III: 27, 46.
Biographical Puzzle, XV: 32, 48.
Biography [*see* Irish Biography].
Birch, James, XIV: 38.
Bird Watcher's Notebook, A (J. W. Seigne) XIX: 29.
Birds of Ardrigh, XIII: 32.
Birmingham, [Fr.] William, XXIX: 115.
Birmingham, George A. [Canon Hannay], (sundry) III: 99, IV: 10, 17, 32, 120, 127, 128, 192, V: 101; (*Connaught to Chicago*) VI: 78; (*Minnie's Bisho*), VI: 204; XI: 99, XII: 65, 141, XIII: 89, 99, 179; (*Red Hand of Ulster*) IV: 32; (*Up the, Rebels!*) XI: 99; (*Innisheeny*) XII: 65-66; (*The Lost Lawyer*) XIII: 89; (*Irish Short Stories*) XX: 22, XXXI: 47; (*Wisdom Book*) XX: 142; (*Elizabeth and the Archdeacon*) XXI: 21; (*The Silver Gilt Standard*) XXI: 21; (*General John Regan*) XXI: 139; (*The Birmingham Bus*) XXIII: 28; (*Two Fools*) XXIII: 28; (*Love and Money and Other Stories*) XXIII: 127; (*Millicent's Corner*) XXIII: 149.
Birminghams in Literature, XVIII: 121.
Birr (printing in), III: 177; (Statute of) IV: 36.
Birrell, Augustine (*Rogue's Memoirs*) VIII: 105; (*Things Past Redress*), XXV: 72.
Bishop Bale of Ossory, I: 14.

Bishop Gallagher's *Irish Sermons*, XVIII: 28.
Bishop Jeb of Limerick (Harry Vere White), XV: 15.
"Bit of Crack, A", III: 53.
Bithas' Wonderful Year (Katherine Tynan), XIII: 17.
"B.J.", V: 103, 222; VII: 35; X: 108.
"B.J.T.", XII: 22.
"Black Daly" (character in Trollope), see Dennis, John.
Black Doctor, The (Anon.), XI: 65, 86.
Black, Joseph, II: 76.
Blacker, [Rev.] Beaver Henry, II: 1, IV: 211; XIV: 3.
Blacker, [Col.] William, II: 149, IV: 163.
Blacker, [Rev.] George (*The Castle of Maynooth* and *the Castle of Kilkea*), XIII: 94-95.
Blackham, Henry Hamilton (*Bard of Clanrye*), XXI: 117.
Blackwell, P. T., XII: 87.
Blackwood's Magazine, I: 32, 143, XII: 15, 35, 60, 61, 80, 133.
Blackwood, Frederick, see Dufferin [Lord].
Blake, [Sir] Henry, IX: 110, 111.
"Blake, Robert" [Pseud. of R. H. Thompson) VIII: 14, 35, 144.
Blake-Forster, Charles Ffrench, XIII: 74, 165.
Blakes and Birminghams in Literature, XVIII: 121.
Blarney Ballads, The (Charles L. Graves) IV: 197.
Blasket[s], see Great Blasket, The.
"Blind Girl of Donegal" [Francis Brown], VIII: 49.
Bliadhain Bhreithe an Athar Maitiú Ó Riain (editorial), XXVII: 193.
Blow's Bible, II: 109.
Blow's Books and Bibles, VI: 191.

Blue Earth (Gladys Singers Bigger), V: 182.
Blue Stocking (Irish), VI: 126, 206, 207.
Bluebell, Co. Dublin (printing in), XXVII: 212.
Blyth, Oliver (*The Irishman*), XII: 66.
Boas, Guy (*An Anthology of Wit*), XXII: 97; (*Short Modern Plays*), XXIII: 151.
Boase, Frederick, I: 136.
Bob Norberry ("Captain Prout" [pseud. of John Levy]), XIV: 106.
Bockwitz, [Dr.] H. (on Henry Bradshaw), XX: 93.
Bodkin, [Fr.] M. (*The Treasure of the Mountain*), XXV: 48.
Bodkin, [Judge] M. McDonnell (*True Man and Traitor*), I: 107; XIII: 154. (*When Youth meets Youth*), XII: 135.
Bodkin, Thomas (*Hugh Lane and His Picture*), XXII: 98; (*My Uncle Frank*) XXVIII: 22.
Bodleian Library (Irish Books and Periodicals), XVIII: 130.
Bodmer, Martin (*Eine Bibliothek Der Weltliteratur*), XXXI: 22.
Bogg-Witticisms, IV: 311.
Boland, Brigid (*The Wild Geese*), XXVI: 69.
Boland, J. P., II: 80.
Bold Heroes of Hungry Hill, The (Seumas MacManus), XXXII: 48.
Bolg an t-Solair (Gaelic magazine), X: 91, XXII: 57, 102, 143.
Bolger, Bryan, XXVIII: 66.
Bonaparte Library, II: 140.
Bond, Eliza L. (*The Spirit of the Nation*), XIV: 118.
Bond, R. Warwick (*The Marlay Letters*), XXV: 72.
Bones of Contention (Frank

O'Connor), XXIV: 70.
Bonmahon Press, I: 97, 121, II: 47; (Letter) XIX: 95; (Printing House) XXXII: 79.
Book Auctions, (Canon O'Riordan) VIII: 80; (A. M. Broadley) VIII: 81; (S. F. Milligan) VIII: 111; (James Tuite) VIII: 117; (Dr. O'Hickey) VIII: 118; (Huth Library) IX: 57; (J. R. Garstin) IX: 102; (Sir J. Olphert) IX: 103; (Sundry) V: 88, 89, 107, VI: 181, XII: 16, 18, 33, 34, 129, XIII: 83, XIV: 6, 37, 91, 121; (S. T. Thompson) XXIV: 28; (Limerick) XXIV: 127; (sundry) I: 49, 67, 110, 122, 155, 171, VI: 181, XII: 16, 18, 33, 34, 120.
Book Auctions (catalogues), III: 32, 40, 48, 65, 85, 87, IV: 214; (*Book Auction Records*) V: 218. (Sundry) VI: 58, XII: 39.
Book Buyers in the Olden Time, III: 159.
Book Catalogues, IV: 214.
Book Collectors, I: 144.
Book Lover's Song, V: 29.
Book Lovers, XIII: 43.
Book of—(*Book of the O'Conor Don*/Tomás Mac Gamhradhan), II: 174; (*Armagh*) V: 170, VI: 47, XXIX: 77; (*Kells*) V: 185, VI: 29; (*This and That*) VI: 186; (*Caricatures*) VII: 50; (*Irish Verse*) VII: 61; (*Irish Poetry*) VII: 62; (*Loughscur*) VIII: 115; (*Lismore*) X: 71, 93; (*Saint Ultan*) XII: 108, 109; (Sir Edward Sullivan) XII: 108, 109; (*Book of Irish Poetry*) XIII: 27; (*Lecan*) XXVI: 62; (*Leinster*) XVIII: 60; (*Clannaboy*) XIX: 165; (*Ballymote*) XX: 17, 139; (*Ballymote*) XX: 17, 139; (*Yellow Book of Lecan*) XX:
115; (*Láimhsgribhinn Sheálin Gaillighe* [John Galwey's Book]) XXI: 28, 54, 76; (*Benham's Book of Quotations*) XXXI: 20.
Bookbinders, (Dublin) II: 152, 180; (18th c. Dublin) XXIV: 10; (Belfast) II: 110; (Irish) VII: 159; (Youghal) XVIII: 173.
Booksellers, (sources concerning) XX: 55; (Irish-speaking in Dublin) XXIV: 111, XIX: 111, 114; (Old Dublin, XX: 62).
Books—(Book Sales) IV: 126, 177, 204, VII: 137, XIII: 83; (Books in Belfast) V: 211, 214; (*Book Monthly*) XII: 33; (Book Plates) XIII: 12; (General Vallancey's Irish MSS) XVIII: 89; (Books in preparation) XXIII: 1, 73; (Books of Munster) XXVI: 6, 61; (Bookman's Bedlam) XXXI: 13; (Books of Irish interest) XXXI: 50.
"Bookworm, A." [pseud.] (Dublin Pirate Publishers), III: 47; (*The Kilrush Magazine*) 62.
Booth, Eva Gore, see Gore-Booth, Eva.
Borde, Andrew, XVI: 81.
Border Ballads, V: 140.
Borel Petrus, XXXI: 74.
Borrow, George VIII: 63.
Bossuet's Works, IV: 212, V: 15; (*Exposition* printed in Rome, 1675), XVIII: 10.
Boswell, James (MSS in Malahide Castle),XVIII [q.p.].
Bóthar Cualann (Pól Breathnach), XXVII: 170.
Bourchier, James David, V: 215; (Obit.) XII: 116; XIII: 136.
Bourke, [Dr.] F. S., (Thomas Walsh) XXVII: 275; XXXII: 17, 18, 39, 50, 73, 99, 104, 106;

(Patrick O'Kelly) XXIII: 42; (literature of Civil War, 1919-23) XVIII: 31, 69; (Rev. Edward Mangin) XXXI: 28.
Bowen, B. P. (*The Comet Newspaper*), XXVIII: 120-127; (John Guinan) XXX: 11-12.
Bowen, Elizabeth [Dorothea Cole] (*The Shelbourne*), XXXII: 45.
Bowen, Marjorie, (*Brave Employments*) XIX: 125; (*Dark Rosaleen*) XX: 67; (*Great Tales of Horror*) XXII: 75; (*William Cobbett*) XXIV: 93.
Bowers, Fredson (*Bibliographical Description*), XXXII: 19.
Boyd, Earnest A., VII: 189, VIII: 48, 85, 136; (*Appreciations and Depreciations*) IX: 53; XII: 13, XV: 64.
Boyd, [Rev.] Henry ("Dante Boyd"), III: 171, XIII: 102, XVII: 63.
Boyd's Shop (St. John Ervine), XXV: 69.
Boyle (printing in), VII: 24.
Boyle, D., (Irish Genius of the Brontës) VII: 169-170, VIII: 4-6.
Boyle, Francis (*Life of Canon Sheehan*), IX: 124.
Boyle, John (freeholder), V: 14.
Boyle, John F., (1916 Rising) VIII: 16.
Boyle, Robert, (*Sceptical Chymist*) XXIII: 12; XXXII: 84.
Boyle, Roger [Lord Broghill], II: 180, XIII: 9.
Boyle, William, VI: 9, X: 99.
Bradbrooke, Patrick (*Some Catholic Novelists*), XIX: 153.
Bradley, Dennis, XII: 108.
Bradshaw, Henry, I: 3, 13, 36, 129; (Bradshaw Collection) I: 134; II: 98, 175, 180, 186, IV: 162; (Bradshaw Catalogue) VIII: 77, 101; (*Lucerna Fidelium*) XVIII: 5; (*His Life and Work*) XIX: 41; (anon. on) XIX: 121; (Lists of Dublin Printers) XX: 19.
Brady, Cheyne, IV: 173, 197.
Brady, [Sir] Francis (Library of), I: 123.
Brady, John (Laurence O'Connor, Rebel Schoolmaster), XXVI: 61; XXX: 16, 17, 38, 39, 50, 100; (Govt. printing in Waterford) XXXI: 12.
Brady, [Rev.] John, ("Zozimus") XXVI: 16, 58; (Laurence O'Conno, Rebel Schoolmaster) XXVI: 61; (Brennan of Adamstown, Co. Westmeath) XXIX: 14, 41; (Fr. Robert Nugent, S .J.) XXIX: 17; (Juring and Non-Juring Priests) XXIX: 18; (Mosney : A Meath Place Name) XXIX: 19; (Ua Maelechlainn Kings of Meath) XXIX: 37; (Ploughing by Horses' Tails) XXIX: 40; (Fergal Ó Gara) XXIX: 78; (Nugent of Corbetstown, Co. Westmeath) XXIX: 90; (Almoritia, Co. Westmeath) XXIX: 92; (Dr. John Fergus) XXIX: 108; (Piercetown, Co. Westmeath) XXIX: 114; (Edward Lhuyd's Irish Manuscripts) XXIX: 134; (Kin of Blessed Oliver Plunket), XXIX: 135; (Genealogy) XXX: 16-17; (More about Lavalin J. Nugent) XXX: 100-02; Government Printing in Waterford XXXI: 12; (Irish Language in London in 1773) XXXI: 32. Also (sundry) XXX: 38, 39, 50, 100-102.
Brady, [Dr.] Maziere, II: 3.
Brailsford, H. N. (*Shelley*,

Goodwin and Their Circle) XXXII: 24.
Branar Magazine, XX: 66, 115.
Brave Employments (Marjorie Bowen), XIX: 125.
Breathnach, Micheál, XVI: 82; (*Fion na Filidheachta*) XIX: 146; (*Stair na hEireann*) XXII: 146.
Breathnach, Pól [Rev. Paul Walsh]—(Pól Ó huIginn, Epitaph) XVIII: 143; (Plunket Genealogies) XXVI: 16, 17, XVIII: 143; (Rival Confederate Generals) XIX: 5; (Curiosities from the Annals) XIX: 37, 96; (*Book of Clannaboy*) XIX: 165; (*Memoranda Gadelica*) XIX: 166; (David Ó Duigenan) XX: 4; (Walter Luin) XX: 12; (Four Masters, Translation) XX: 51;(Notes on the Two Mageoghegans) XX: 75; (The Four Masters) XX: 105, XXII: 128; (Tadg Ó h-Uiginn) XX: 115; (O'Reilly Family Obituaries) XX: 127; (In Conal Mageoghegan's Neighbourhood) XXI: 4; (Link with Tadhg Dall, XXI: 33; (Richard O'Connor, Scribe) XXI: 52, 112; (Eoghan Caomhánach) XXI: 66; (Battle of Cluain Tiobrad) XXI: 103; (Fragments of Meath History) XXI: 124; (Paul Higgins) XXI: 118; (Numbering of Dublin Houses) XXI: 137; (Saying of the Earl of Tyrone, XXI: 138; (Earls of Tyrone and Tyrconnell) XXII: 4, 91; (Epithalamium) XXII: 78; (Capt. Sorley MacDonnell) XXII: 81; (*Short Annals of Tirconnaill*) XXII: 104; (*Short Annals of Fir Manach*) XXIII: 7; (How the Bissets Came) XXIII: 36; (Two O'Hagans) XXIII: 46; (What We Know of Cuchoigeriche Ó Cléirigh) XXIII: 60; (Some O'Reilly Geneologies) XXIII: 85; (Convent of Donegal) XXIII: 109; (Pretty Pair of Ruffians) XXIII: 134; (Tippermessan, Co. Meath), XXVI: 15; (*Do Lionadh mBáin Oile*) XXVI: 29; (Derricke's *Image of Ireland*) XXVI: 37; (*Book of Lecan*) XXVI: 62, (Higginstown, Co.Westmeath) XXVI: 86; (Red Hugh's Sister) XXVI: 105; (Shrovetide and Inid) XXVI: 106; (Méla Mór in Co. Kilkenny) XXVI: 138; (Bothar Cualann) XXVII: 170; (Supposed Place-name) XXVII: 179; (Leacan Mic Fhirbhisigh) XXVII: 210; (Jamestown, Co. Leitrim) XXVII: 242; (Maolmórdha Mac Suibhne) XXVII: 266; (Shrine of Colman of Lynn) XXVII: 200. Also XXIV: 61, XXV: 26, 37, 50, 73, 99, 100; XXVI: 17.
Breen, Dan, XV: 12.
Brefny [Breffni], see Folk Tales of Brefny
Brenan, Joseph, V: 189, VI: 14.
Brenan, [Rev.] Martin (*Schools of Kildare and Leighlin, 1775-1835*), XXIV: 67.
Brennan of Adamstown (Rev. John Brady), XXIX: 14, 41.
Brennan, Edward John ["E. St. John Brenon"], VIII: 142.
Brennan, [Dr.] John ("The Wrastling Doctor"), VI: 42.
Brennan, John (Young Irelander), III: 81, 118.
Brennan, Martin, (trans. *Annals of Loch Cé*), XVII: 68.
Brennan [also Brenan], Michael John XXVIII: 90.

Brennan-Whitmore, W.J., IX: 80.
"Brenon, E. St. John" [see Brennan, Edward John].
Bretherton, C. H. (*Rhyme and Reason*), XIV: 74; (*The Real Ireland*) XVII: 75.
Breton Commentary on Irish Music, XXVII: 168.
Brewer's *Beauties of Ireland*, IV: 212.
Bricriu's Feast (Eimar O'Duffy), XI: 25.
Bridges, Robert (*Gregory Darley*), XIX: 66.
Bridget (B. M. Croker), X: 46.
"Brighdín Deas ní Mháille" (Pádraig Mac Amhlaoí), XXII: 63.
Brief Biographies of Irish Presbyterians, VII: 10.
Brigid, see St. Brigid.
Bringmann, Rudolf (*Geschichte Irlands*), XXVII: 166.
Bristol, Earl of, VI: 119
British Academy, The, II: 154.
British and Irish Newspapers before 1801 (W. J. Lang), XXII: 56.
British Annual of Literature, XXVI: 93.
British Empire and Other Poems, The (Hewson Cowen), XV: 46.
Brittaine, [Rev.] George, XI: 14.
Broad-Sheet Ballads (Padraic Colum), V: 101.
Broadside, The, II: 56.
Brocas, H., III: 72.
"Brógaí Kennedí" XXVI: 11.
Broken Glory (Eva Gore Booth), X: 46.
Bromage, Arthur W. (*Constitutional Developments in Saorstát Éireann*), XXVI: 89.
Brommage, A.W. & M.C., (*Irishmen like P.R., The Irish Constitution, Ireland—What now?*), XXVIII: 20.
Bronnta na Féil-Scríbhinne an Ollamh Eóin Mhic Neill, XXVII: 217.
Brontë family, II: 80; (Irish influences) VII: 169-170, VIII: 4-6, 43; (Charlotte) XVII: 62.
Brooke, Arthur St. Clair (*Occassional Verses*), IV: 158.
Brooke, [Rev.] James Mark Saurin, IX: 111.
Brooke, [Rev.] Stopford A., I: 18, II: 42, IV: 211, VII: 165 192, VIII: 10; (*Life and Letters of Stopford Brooke*) IX: 77; (Stopford Brooke on Ireland), XXX: 108-10.
Brookes family, XI: 32.
Brookfield, Co. Down (printing in), XVII: 19.
Brooks, E. St. John (Rev. Edward Mangin's Memoir of his father), XXXI: 122; XXXII: 91.
Brooks, Sydney, IV: 20.
Brophy, John (*The Rocky Road*), XXI: 21.
Brophy, Michael, X: 69.
Brotherhood (Limavady weekly paper), XI: 102.
Broughton, Rhoda, XII: 15.
Brown, A. C. L. (*Origin of Grail Legend*), XXIX: 43.
Brown Brethren, The (Patrick MacGill) IX: 33.
Brown[e], Frances ("Blind Girl of Donegal") II: 149; VIII: 49, (Bibliography) VIII: 51.
Brown, [Fr.] Francis (Collector from Ancient Archives), XVIII: 144.
Brown, J., (*Historical Ballad Poetry of Ireland*), III: 168.
Brown, J. G., IV: 213.
Brown, J. N. (J. S. Le Fanu), XXII: 91.
Brown, [Rev.] Stephen J., (*Guide*

to *Books on Ireland*) I: 81, 102, III: 150; I: 91; (*Reader's Guide to Irish Fiction*) II: 57, 161, 181, VI: 48, VI: 169; (*The Orange Society*) II: 76; II: 198; (*The Question of Irish Nationality*) IV: 143; (American magazines) V: 130 (Orange Songs) V: 166; (The Irish Bar Sinister) VI: 62; (Irish Fiction) VI: 104; (*Ireland in Fiction*) VII: 14, 134, XXI: 15; (*Irish Historical Fiction*) VII: 49; (Irish Novels) VIII: 88; (Ireland in Fiction) IX: 35, XI: 10, 12; (*The Realm of Poetry*) XII: 135; (The Book Lover and the Libraries) XVI: 14, 68; (*The Life of Margaret Aylward*) XVII: 48; (Bibliography of Dublin Euchar-ist Congress) XX: 136; (Books about Ireland Wanted) XXIII: 117; (*Novels and Tales by Catholic Writers*) XXIV: 48; (poem on Dermot Mac Murrough) XXXI: 106, XXXII: 40.

Browne, Thomas (printer), XII: 20, XVI: 15, XXXII: 8-11, 59; (*Tryal of the Roman Catholics*) XX: 59; (At the Three Candles) XXXII: 11, 59.

Brownlow, Arthur, XXII: 18; XXIV: 26, 78, 133.

Brugha, Cathal (Election Poster), XXVI: 138; (Sgéal Chathail Bhrugha) XXIII: 144-146.

"B.R.W.H.", III: 82.

Bryce, [Viscount] James, IV: 87; XIII: 137, 145.

Bryson, Samuel, XIII: 3.

"B.S.", X: 69, 92.

"B.T.C.", V: 15.

Buchan, [Earl] John (*Irish Chiefs: or The Harp of Erin*) VI: 170; (*The Poetry of Neil Munro*), XIX: 181.

Buchanan, George (*Words for Tonight*) XXIV: 72; (*Rose Forbes*) XXV: 48.

Buchanan, Robert, XII: 41, XIV: 73.

Buchanan, W. P., II: 94.

Buck, Adam (Irish Artist), V: 51.

Buckley, James, I: 61, 105, III: 180, 202, IV: 56, 83, V: 104, VI: 116, 134, VIII: 34, 127.

Buile Suibhne/*The Adventures of Suibhne Geilt* (J. G. O'Keefe), IV: 183, XX: 3.

Buitléir, Eibhlín de (*Geograif do nGhaedheal Óg*), XVIII: 61.

Buitléir, Maitiú de, XVII: 42, 61,83, 91, 108; (*Waterford Spectator*) XVIII: 133; (History of Co. Waterford; Lost MS) XXII: 64; (James St. John, M.D.) XXIV: 61, 87.

Bulkeley, [Sir] Richard (Matthew Butler). XXIX: 79.

Bull, Joseph, III: 177.

Bull, Edward & G. P. (printers), IV: 53.

Bullen A. H., XI: 96.

Bulletin of the International Institute for Social History, XXXI: 112.

Bulletin Refuses, *The* (editorial), XXV: 73.

Bullock, Shan, III: 39; (*Race of Castlebar*) V: 165; (Bullock family) VI: 32; VI: 202, VII: 130; (G. B. Shaw) XIV: 89; XV: 10; (Obit.) XXIII: 82.

Bulls and Bog Witticisms (J. O. Bartley), XXX: 59-62.

Bunbury, Selina, I: 136, III: 119, VII: 105-107.

Bunting, Edward, XVII: 31-32, 117; (*Bunting Collection of Irish Folk Music and Songs*) XVI: 23, 33, 700, 120.

Bunyan, John (Irish trans. of

Pilgrim's Progress), XVI: 118.
Búrca, de, see de Búrca.
Burch, R., I: 160.
Burdy, [Rev.] Samuel, III: 28 ("Ardglass"); VI: 185, VII: 12, 54, XI: 117, XII: 52, XIV: 142.
Burgo, [Dr.] Thomas De, [also Burke] (*Hibernia Dominicana*) XVI: 6; XVII: 9.
Burgoyne, F. J. P., II: 196, VI: 189, IX: 112.
"Burial of Sir John Moore" (Charles Wolfe), V: 3.
Burke, [Sir] Bernard, XXII: 127; (Library of) XXIII: 16.
Burke, Edmund, IV: 209, VI: 14; (*The Reformer*) VIII: 68; XX: 32-33; (*Cluster of Shamrocks*); IV: 12; (Dublin Editions of *Works*) XX: 32.
Burke, J. J. (*Last Resting Places of Notable Irishmen*), XXVII: 216.
Burke, Joseph (Matthew Butler) XXIX: 88.
Burke, Michael, see de Burca, Micheál.
Burke, [Gen.] T. F., IV: 107, 124.
Burke, [Rev.] William, see de Búrca, Liam.
Burlingham, Russell (*Forrest Reid*), XXXII: 43.
Burnt Flax (Mrs. H. H. Penrose), V: 164.
Burrows, Peter, I: 151.
Burtchaell, George Dames (*Alumni Dublinensis*), XIII: 40, 98, 138, XIV: 123.
Burton, H. B. (*Der Kaiser von Potsdam*) VI: 186.
Burton, Richard, II: 128.
Bury, John B. (*A Bibliography of J. B. Bury*), XVIII: 20.
Bury, Robert G. (*The Devil's Puzzle*), XXXI: 71.
Bushnell, G. H. (*Sir Richard Grenville*), XXIV: 143.

Busy Biographer, A, X: 27-29.
Butcher, Samuel H., II: 103.
Butler, Archer, IV: 209.
Butler, Dean, VIII: 9.
Butler, [Dr.] James, XVII: 9.
Butler, Matthew [Maitiú Butleir], XXIX: 11, 18, (*The Parnellite*) 19; 26, 30; (Obituaries of Irish Poets) XXIX: 41; XXIX: 27, 79, 81; (*Joseph Burke of Elm Hall*) 88; (*William Brawders*) XXIX: 30; (*The Waterford Flying Post & The Waterford Freeman*) 91; XXX: 4-8, 35-37, 63, 66, XXXII: 79.
Butler, [Prof.] W. F. T., V: 139; (*Confiscation in Irish History*) VIII: 137.
Butler, [Sir] William, I: 162, II: 73, 124, 156, III: 9, 206.
Butlers, The (*A Genealogical History*), V: 149.
Butt, Isaac, III: 3, 47, IV: 158, 190, 210, 211, V: 13, 21, 48, 51; (Bibliography) V: 54; (with Richard Whately), XII: 112, XIII: 19.
Byard, Edwin J., I: 166, III: 184, IV: 63 151, 187, VI: 134.
By Bog and Sea (Elizabeth Shane), XIV: 47.
Byers, James, V: 202, VI: 45, XI: 86.
Byers, [Sir] John William, I: 79; (Obit.) XII: 43; 56; (Bibliography of) XII: 56-57.
Bye-Ways of Study (Darrell Figgis), X: 61
Byrne, Donn, XIV: 14, XVI: 49, XVII: 63, 65, 111.
Byrne, Miles, XIII: 30.
Byrne, Patrick, XVIII: 89.
By the Brown Bog, (Owen Roe and Honour Urse), IV: 208.

The Irish Book Lover 239

C

Cabra, Co. Dublin (printing in), XXVII: 210.
Cadhain, M. O., XXVI: 10, 30.
"Cailín Deas Chrúite na nGabhar" (Tomás Bairéad), XXXII: 1.
"Cainneach", see Mooney, Rev. Fr. Canice (O. F. M.)
Cainnt Choitcheannta o'n Gheadhealtacht (Brighid Ní Dhochartaigh), XIII: 172.
Cairnes, J. E., XI: 70, 79-80.
Calcutta (Irish Author in, 1788), XVII: 118.
Caldwell, Robert (Obit.), XX: 26.
Caledon Private Press, IX: 5.
Calendar of State Papers, XVIII: 144.
Calendar of Wills, I: 89.
Callaghan, [Fr.] John (*Vindiciarum Catholicorum Hibernia*) II: 104, 129.
Callaghan (F. Winthrop), XIII: 15.
Callan, [Rev.] Bernard, XIX: 97; XIX: 61; (sources on) XVIII: 140ff.; (poem by) XVIII: 170, XIX: 27; XXVII: 160.
Callanan, Jeremiah Joseph, (A Current Commentary) XVII: 108-109.
Callanan, M. (*The Abbey of Holy Cross*), XVII: 96; (Pol O'hUuiginn), XVIII: 85.
Callwell, Josephine Martin (*Old Irish Life*), III: 133; (Obit.), XXIII: 83.
Calwell Collection, The, XI: 123.
Cambridge Hibernians, XIII: 113, 135.
Cambridge University Press, XX: 95.
Cambridge Medieval History (eds. C. W. Previte-Orton & Z. N. Brooke), XXV: 18.
Cameron, [Dr.] Sir Charles

Alexander, C. B., IV: 142, VII: 165, (Obit.) XII: 142-143.
Cameron, John (*Celtic Law*), XXVIII: 139.
Campbell, A. Albert, I: 93, 136, 142; (James Godkin) II: 118, XIII: 114; (*Old Irish Life*) IV: 49, 92, 109; (Hazlitt of Bandon) V: 62; 105- 106; VI: 32, 81, 135; (Rev. William Thomas Latimar) 175; VII: 7, 34; (Thomas L'Estrange) 43-45; 46, 53, 91; IX: 6; (three Tyrone presses) 8; 9, 38, 60, 62; XI: 14; (*Irish Presbyterian Magazines, Past and Present*) 26; (Belfast politics) 64, 84; XII: 20, 42, 67, 138, XIII: 16; (*Belfast Newspapers Past and Present*) 32; (Ballymena printing) 67; ("The Exiled Irishman's Lamentation") 175; (A Kilkenny *Catechism*) XX: 113; (*Belfast Naturalists' Field Club*) XXVI: 91.
Campbell, [Lady] Colin, III: 77.
Campbell, Frederick W. Groves (Obit.), VI: 114.
Campbell, J. L. (Musical Talent in Highlands and Islands), XXXI: 85.
Campbell, [Dr.] John, VI: 79.
Campbell, Joseph [Seosamh Mac Cathmhaoil], I: 28, I: 140, II: 165, XII: 13.
Campbell, Lord, II: 6.
Campbell, M. P. (*As Luck would Have It*), XXXI: 20.
Campbell, [Rev.] William, XIII: 140.
Campbell, William Bernard (Obit.), III: 57.
Campion, [Dr.] J. T., III: 2.
Campion, Thomas, XII: 32.
Candle Press, The (The Candleman) XII: 40; (origins of)

XVI: 15.
Candle and Crib (K. F. Purdon), VI: 114.
Cane, Robert (*Williamite and Jacobite Wars*), XXVI: 58, 85.
Canning, Albert Stratford George (Obit.), VII: 190.
Canon Hannay and the Gaelic League (Ciarán Bairéad), XXXI: 87.
"Cantab" (on Henry Bradshaw), II: 180.
Canty, David (Waterford Newspapers), XVIII: 133.
Canty, James (*A Class-book of Irish History*), XVIII: 64.
"Caoine an t-Athair Tadhg Mhac Carthaigh" (Fionán Mac Coluim), XXIV: 4, 6.
Caoineadh Airt Uí Laoghaire, XXIX: 12.
Caomhánach, Eoghan, XXI: 66, 113.
"Captain Prout" [pseud. of John Levy], XIV: 106.
Captain Rock in Rome (Thomas Moore), XXXII: 40, 92.
Captain Sorley MacDonnell and his Books (Fr. Paul Walsh), XXII: 81-87.
Carberry, Eugene (Articles of Interest in Foreign Periodicals) XVIII: 165; (*Journal of the Ivernian Society*) XXV: 62.
Carberry, T. A., III: 118.
Carbery, Ethna [also Eithne Carberry] (*The Four Winds of Eirinn Poems*), X: 11; X: 46; XXXII: 63.
Carbery, Lady, IX: 53.
Carey, John (Obit.), XX: 15.
Carey, Matthew, III: 203.
Carleton, William, II: 134, 149, 150, 156, III: 69, IX: 5, XII: 20, (Unread Today), XVIII: 73; (*Carleton's Country*) XVIII: 150; (Description of his Mother) XXIII: 142; XXX: 39, 66.
Carleton, William (Jnr.), IV: 145.
Carlow—(*Carlow College Magazine*) III: 69; (The *Carlovian: Annual Review*) V: 217; (printing in), XI: 75, 94, 109, 126, XII: 71; (*Carlow Morning Post*) XIX: 90-91.
Carlyle, Thomas (in Dublin), XII: 55, 56.
Carmelite Nun (*Our Eternal Vocation*), XXXI: 45.
Carnegie, Canon, VIII: 13.
Carney, James (*Poems on the Butlers*), XXX: 45.
Carogh Orphanage Private Press, IX: 7.
Carolan, Turlough (portraits), XXII: 9-10.
Carpenter, Daniel (Newry printer), VI: 17.
Carpenter, [Archbishop] John (Irish scripts of), XXII: 57, 142.
Carr, Albert (*L'influence des huguenots français en Irlande*), XXVI: 88.
Carrickfergus—(*The Carrickfergus Press*) II: 196; (printing) VII: 186.
Carrick-on-Suir—(printing in) III: 33, 60, IV: 161; (*Carrick-on-Suir Casket*) IX: 85; Carrick-on-Suir (Library of Seán Ó Floinn), XXVII: 210.
Carrick's Morning Post, XIX: 90-91.
"Carrigart" ("The rock of Arthur"), III: 27, 47.
"Carrigeenduff" (on facs. of *Book of Leinster*), XVIII: 60.
Carrignavar, XVI: 4.
Carroll, F., (18th c. Dublin Music Sellers) XXXI: 129; XXXII: 9-11; 40; (Goodman Collection of Irish Music) 41; Eugene

O'Curry's Signature) 42; 66; (A Poem by Clarence Mangan) 134-37.
Carroll, Paul Vincent (*The Things That Are Caesar's*), XXIII: 24.
Carroll, [Rev.] William George (works of), XVII: 27, 143.
Carry, Francis (*The Irish Volunteer*), XX: 70.
Carson, James (Carson's *Dublin Weekly Journal*) I: 41; VIII: 110, XII: 137.
Carte, Thomas, IV: 108.
Carter, Cornelius (printer), XVII: 84-85, 119.
Carter, William (on *Tamerlane*), XXIV: 86.
Carty, Francis, XX: 70.
Carty, John (*Bibliography of Irish History*), XXV: 106, XXVIII: 140; (*Ireland*), XXXI: 93.
Carve, Thomas, XVI: 79.
Cary, Joyce (*Castle Corner*), XXVI: 23.
Carysfort, Lord, XIV: 12.
Casement, Roger (*Sir Roger Casement*) VIII: 34, 45, IX: 59, XVIII: 155; (letters on execution of) XVII: 114, 115; (*Trial of Sir Roger Casement*) IX: 59; (*Some Poems of Roger Casement*) X: 46-47.
Casey, Daniel, VII: 53, (Obit.) VIII: 90.
Casey, John (mathematician), XVII: 8, 93; XXII: 113; (query) XXV: 63.
Casey, John K. ["Leo"], (*The Rising of the Moon*) XXI: 116; (*Poems*) XXII: 13.
Casey of the I.R.A. (A. T. Walsh), XIV: 30.
Cashel, XVIII: 79, 175; (Irish sermons in Cashel Cathedral) XVIII: 85, XIX: 144; (*Psalter of Cashel*) XXII: 39, 91; (Cashel Cathedral Chapter Library) XXII: 40; (An Old Cashel Magazine) XXII: 39, 91); (printing in Cashel) XI: 103, XVIII: 79, 175; (Private Press in Cashel) IX: 8.
Cassidy, [Rev.] James F. (*The Old Irish Love of the Blessed Virgin Mary*), XXII: 23; (*Some Noted Priests of Yesterday*), XXVIII:140.
Cassidy, Thomas E., XIV: 126.
Castlebar (printing in), IX: 47.
Castle Bran (K. F. Tegart), XXVI: 22.
Castle Conquer (Padraic Colum), XIV: 12.
Castle Martyr (anon.), XIX: 62.
Castlereagh, Lord [Robert Stewart] (*Life of*), II: 163.
Castlerosse, Viscount (*Valentine Days*), XXII: 52.
Catalogues—I: 11, 23, 36, 48.64, 79, 93, 137; (Chat on Catalogues) IV: 136; (Dublin) VI: 42; (Irish Sect., Linenhall Library) IX: 12; (Catalogue of early Belfast printing), XVII: 52; (MS Catalogue of Swift's Library) XVIII: 60; (F. J. Bigger Memorial Library) XVIII: 99; (MS Catalogue of Swift's Books in his own Handwriting) XVIII: 160; (Sir Patrick Dun's Library) XVIII: 60, 117; (Printed Sale Catalogue of Swift's Books) XVIII: 61; (Periodicals, Internat. Code) XIX: 96; (1872 Catalogue of Lough Fea Library) XXI: 12; (Irish MSS in Royal Irish Academy) XXIV: 68; (*Irish MSS in the Royal Irish Academy*) XXV: 41; (*Novels and Tales by Catholic Writers*) XXIV: 48; (Irish MSS in Maynooth) XXIX: 93; (Dr.

Plunket's Library, MS) XXXII: 106; (Early Book Catalogues) XXXII: 137.
Catechism (Bonaventure O'Hussey), XVIII: 175.
Cathach MS, VII: 8.
Cathill, Una Ní (*Tales My Father Told*), XXIX: 144.
Catholic—(Catholic Convention of 1793) III: 213; (liturgy in French edition) IV: 93; (Catholic Books) VI: 207; (*Catholic Anthology*, 1915) VII: 77; (Central Catholic Library) XIV: 121; (*Catholic Magazine*) XV: 63; (Catholic Map of Ireland) XVII: 78, XVIII: 138; (Catholic Record Society) XVII: 49; (Catholic Relief Act Centenary) XVII: 49, 108; (Catholic Writers in Penal Days) XVII: 77; ([...] *Catholic Writers*) XIX: 153; (Catholic Truth Society) XX: 71, 97; (*Catholic Juvenile Literature*) XXIV: 48; (Catholic Map of Ireland) XXVIII: 44; (Catholic Printing in Penal Days) XXXI: 63; (Catholicism Today) XXXI: 90.
Caulfeild, Hon. Mrs., II: 195.
"Causidicus" (*Freeman's Journal*), IV: 107.
Cavan—(printing in) I: 83, IV: 165, XI: 6, 22, 40; (*Cavan Herald*) XIX: 90-91.
Cavanagh, Carmen, XIII: 60.
Cavanagh, Kit (*A Dunleary Legend and Other Tales*), XXIII: 128.
Cavanagh, Maeve, (*Sheaves of Revolt*), VIII: 34, 104.
Cavanagh, Michael, VI: 14.
Caven, Stewart (*A Pair of Idols*), XI: 133.
Caxton, William, II: 4.
Cead Foghla Thug Torna Dham Féin Gan Duadh (Colm Ó Lochlainn), XXVI: 121.
Cearnacht, Connal (*The Writings on the Wall*), VII: 162.
Cecil Press (Co. Tyrone), XXIV: 55.
Ceitinn, Seathrun, see Keating, Geoffrey.
Celt and Maori (J. W. Joynt), VI: 142-43.
Celt and Saxons (Robert McKinstry), XI: 84-85.
Celtic Studies, see *Journal of Celtic Studies*.
Celt, The, III: 1; XI: 30.
Celtic Dictionary (Triglot), XXII: 12.
Celtic Memories (Norreys Jephson O'Connor), V: 68.
Celtic Moods and Memories (Joseph McGarrity), XXVII: 216.
Celtic Nature Poetry (Alfred Perceval Graves), III: 94-96.
Celtic Psaltery, A (Alfred Perceval Graves), IX: 58.
Celtic Times (and the GAA), XX: 93.
Celtic Wonder Tales (Ella Young), XV: 32.
"Celticus" (pseud. of Rev. Denis Taaffe), XVII: 5-6.
Celts and Other Poems (Sidney Bell), XXX: 71.
Censor or Covent Garden Journal, The, (Rare Dublin Periodical), XII: 104-106.
Censorship, XIV: 122.
Census of Ireland, XXIX: 21.
Century, I: 39, 71, 108.
Challenge of the Sentry, The (David Hogan), XVI: 112.
Chalmers, George, VIII: 139.
Chamberlain, [Rev.] Robert (otherwise Mac Artuir), XX: 103.

The Irish Book Lover 243

Chambers, C. Haddon, XII: 134.
Chambers, John (printer and United Irishman), XXVII: 234.
Champneys, Arthur C. (The Ecclesiastical Architecture of Ireland), I: 89.
Changing World, The (eds. Bernard Wall & Marrya Harari), XXX: 120.
Chap Books, I: 157, II: 12, 19, 33, 35, 110, 129; (Bilingual) XXIII: 40.
Chapel of Finnbarr, UCC (Rev. Professor Power), XII: 64.
Chapters in '98 History (Joseph H. Fowler), XXVI: 115, 198.
"Captain York Clayton" (character in Trollope), XVIII: 48.
Charlemont, Lord, XIII: 103; (Charlemont and Mountjoy) XIV: 59; (Charlemont Library) XIV: 121.
Charles, Dr., III: 216.
Charles, James, VII: 116, 187.
Charlestown, Co. Louth (printing in), V: 6.
Charlton, [Rev.] H. P.(Obit.), III: 77.
Chart of Irish History (Charles R. Arlen) V: 67.
Chart, [Dr.] D. A., IX: 55; (*An Economic History of Ireland*) XII: 38; XVII: 127; (*Preliminary Survey of the Ancient Monuments of Northern Ireland*) XXVII: 260.
Charwoman's Daughter, The (James Stephens), III: 169.
Chat on Christmas Books, I: 54.
Chauviré, Roger (*L'Irlande*), XXIV: 21.
Chavasse, [Mrs.] Claude [Moireen Fox] (*Midhir and Etain* & *The Fire Bringers*), XII: 9.
Cheavasa, Moirin A. (*The One Unfaithfulness of Naoise*), XVIII: 184.
"Cheerful Giver, The" (trans. of *Havamal*), XXV: 9.
Cheltenham Irish MSS (N.L.I), XX: 114.
Cherry, Andrew, VI: 190; VII: 14.
Chesterton, G. K. ("Ballad to an Irishman"), VII: 184; XIII: 141.
Childers, Erskine (*Irish Bulletin*), XII: 10, XVIII: 70.
Children of Earth (Darrell Figgis), X: 40-41.
Children of the Abbey, The (Regina Maria Roche), XI: 117.
Children of the Dead End (Patrick MacGill), V: 164.
Children of St. Columba (Rev. H. Vere White), V: 218.
Children's Books in Irish, XVI: 47-48.
Children's Games, XXVIII: 117.
Chisholm, Cecil (*Repertory*), XXIII: 122.
Choimisiún agus Cumainn Béaloideasa Éireann, XXIII: 81.
Chrétien, Douglas (*The Battle Book of the O'Donnells*), XXIII: 124.(Wheel of Fortune in), XVIII: 122; (Edward Seymour and George Street) XXII: 2; Christ Church Cathedral Dublin, (Ronan, [Rev.] Myles) XXIII: 80; (J. E. L. Oulton & Dean J. H. Bernard) XXVII: 237; (Franciscan Preacher in) XXXI: 25
Christian's Guide, The (Rev. Rankin), XI: 65.
Christina, S. M. (*Lord Clandonnell*), VI: 132.
Christmas Greeting, XIII: 114.
Christmas Rhymes and Mummers, XVI: 126.
Chronicle of Ireland, The (James Perrott), XXII: 25.
Chronicle of Jails (Darrell Figgis),

IX: 81.
Chumainn le Béaloideas Éireann, XXVI: 49.
Church, Thomas, VII: 138.
"Ciarruigheach Malluithe, An" (Eoghan Ruadh Ó Súileabháin), XXIX: 73, 97; XXXI: 134.
Ciosóg, Micheál, (*Celtic Times*), XX: 93.
Citizen (Waterford), XXX: 4-8.
City of Refuge and Other Poems (Richard Rowley), IX: 109.
City Songs and Others (Richard Rowley), X [q.p.].
Civil War, see Literature of the Conflict 1922-23.
Civil Survey (R. Dudley Edwards), XXIX: 8.
"C.J.O'T.", II: 75.
Clan system (end of), II: 184; (The Clan Bard) VI: 3..
Clancy, Basil (*Ireland Among the Nations*), XXX: 118.
Clancy, James, III: 186.
Clandillon, Mr. & Mrs. Séamus, XVI: 23.
Clannaboy, Book of, XIX: 165.
Clárach, Séan & Liam Dall (*An Irish Song*), XX: 58.
Clár Litridheacht na Nua Ghaedhilge (Risteárd de Nae & Brighid Ní Dhonnchadha), XXVI: 25.
Clare Journal (Ennis), XIX: 90-91.
Clare, [Rev.] Wallace (*Simple Guide to Irish Genealogy*), XXVI: 68.
Clare (History and Topography), I: 130; (printing in), VII: 139, XI: 104.
Clarendon, Lord, XIV: 37.
Clark, Sydney A. (*Ireland on £10*), XXVI: 69.
Clark, William Andrew (Memorial Library), XXXI: 19.

Clarke, [Dr.] Adam, I: 158.
Clarke, Austin, (*Pilgrimage and Other Poems*) XVII: 66; 113, 114; (*The Flame*) XIX: 65; (*The Bright Temptation*) XX: 70; *The Singing Men at Cashel*) XXIV: 65; (*Collected Poems*) XXIV: 140; (Yeats and "The Sally Gardens") XXXI: 133.
Clarke, Desmond (*Thomas Prior*), XXXII: 21.
Clarke, Jackson C. (*Knockinscreen Days*), V: 30.
Clarke, Marcus, IV: 6, XII: 111.
Clarke, Michael (of Whitewood), XXVI: 84.
Classics [Graeco-Roman] (Irish Medieval Translations), II: 147.
Cleary, [Rev.] Gregory, O.F.M., XVI: 70, (on Francis O'Molloy), XVIII: 8.
Cleaver, [Rev.] Euseby Digby, XVIII: 137.
Clemens, Cyril (Bibliography of Fr. Prout), XX: 74.
Clery, Anthony B., (Sean O'Clery of Dublin), XXIX: 124-28.
Cleveland, Frederick A., II: 181.
Clifford, Sigerson (*Ballads of a Bogman*), XXXII: 119.
Clime, [Rev.] George (*Christian Social Reorganisation*), XXVII: 288.
Clive, Arthur (pseud. of Standish James O'Grady), XVIII: 94.
"Clódóir i gCorcaigh" (Donnchadh Ó Donnchadha), XXX: 49.
Clongowes Centenary, V: 206.
Clongownian, The (Fr. Stephen Brown),VI: 41, X: 14, XI: 12.
Clonmacnoise (Records relating to Ardagh), XVII: 17.
Clonmel—(*Clonmel Advertiser*) IV: 72, XIX: 90-91; (*Clonmel Booklover*) XXIV: 84; (*Clonmel

Gazette) XV: 11, 24; (*Clonmel Herald*) XIX: 90-91; (printing in Clonmel) XXV: 90, XII: 40, XXII: 14, XXIV: 135, XXVI: 39; (*Clonmel Scrap Book*) XIV: 123; (*Annals of Clonmel*), VI: 134; (George Grace and Clonmel) XVII: 39-42.
Close, [Rev.] Maxwell, XXVIII: 16.
Cluain Tiobraid, Battle of, XXI: 103.
Cluster of Shamrocks, (Edmund Burke), IV: 12.
"Cn. J", see Crone, John S.
Co. Louth Archaeological Journal (Fr. L. Murray), XIV: 91, XXIV: 114, XXVII: 237.
Cochrane, Robert, VII: 189.
'Cock's Skip, A', (an expression), III: 103.
Code, Henry Brereton (poet & dramatist), XVII: 90; XIV: 76.
Coffey, George, VIII: 45.
Cogan, [Fr.] (*Diocese of Meath*), XVII: 49.
Coghill, Rhoda (*The Bright Hillside*), XXXI: 47.
Cohen, Victor (*The Nineteenth Century*), XXI: 47.
"Coilin" (*Patrick H. Pearse*), VIII: 135.
Cóimhthional Gaoidhilge (unpublished 18th c. journal), XVI: 126, XVII: 18.
Coins of the Danish Kings of Ireland (Bernard Roth), II: 107.
Cole, Owen Blaney, XIV: 139.
Coleman, J. C. (*Journeys into Muskerry*), XXXI: 118.
Coleman, James, I: 22, 121, II: 6, 19, 72, III: 46, 51, 74, VI: 61, 80, 118, IX: 68, X: 18, XI: 63, 100, XII: 40, XIII: 38, 40, XIV: 65, XV: 1, 23, 42; (Bibliography of Lady Wilde) XX: 60.

Coleraine (printing in), XXIV: 15, XXVII: 178.
Coleridge, Lord, II: 89.
Colgan, John, IV: 4, 21, 22, 23, 24.
Colgan, Nathaniel, (Obit.) XI: 66.
Colhoun, David, IV: 48.
Collar of Gold, and Other Fantasies, The (Brian Cooper), XII: 16-18.
Collected Poems (Stephen Gwynn), XIX: 155.
Collector of Irish Dance Music, A, XIX: 23.
Collectors, Great, VII: 1, 21.
"Colleen Bawn" [Ellen Hanley], V: 221, VIII: 8.
College Chorus, A (ed. Eimar O'Duffy), XI: 62.
College Magazine, The, XI: 107.
College Recollections (Rev. Mortimer O'Sullivan), XIV: 76.
Colles, Ramsey, II: 14, III: 26; (Obit.) X: 9.
Collins, James, VII: 140; (The Collins Collection) VIII: 130; (*Life of Old Dublin*) XX: 62; (Library of) XIX: 25.
Collins, Michael, XIII: 29.
Collis, J. S. (*The Sounding Cataract*), XXIV: 89.
Collis, Robert (*The Silver Fleece*), XXIV: 71.
Collisson, Dr., XI: 80.
Colman of Lynn (shrine), XXVII: 200.
Colum, Mary (*Life and the Dream*), XXX: 118.
Colum, Padraic, III: 212, IV: 20, 64, 194, V: 101, VII: 56, VIII: 65, XIV: 12, XV: 4; (*The Island of the Mighty*) XV: 46; (*Cross Roads in Ireland*) XIX: 68; (*A Half Day's Ride*) XXI: 46; (*The Legend of St. Columba*) XXIV: 117.

Columba Press, XXXII: 57, 58.
Columcille's Prophecies (Ó Cearnaigh's edition), XVIII: 171.
Comet Newspaper, The (B. P. Bowen), XXVIII: 120-127; XXX: 43.
Coming of the Earls, The (Florence M. Wilson), X: 62-63.
Commentarius Rinuccinianus Vols. III & IV (ed. Fr. Stanislaus O.M.C.), XXVIII: 137.
Commercial Restraints of Ireland, IX: 34.
Commins, Andrew (Obit.), VII: 141.
Compendium of the History of Ireland, The (John Lawless & P. B. Shelley), XVII: 3.
Compossicion Booke of Conought (M. Freeman), XXX: 22.
Compton, Piers (*Bad Queen Bess*), XXII: 69.
Comus (John Milton), XII: 21.
Comyn, David (Máire Ní Dhubhghaill), XXXI: 64.
"Conall Cearnach" (pseud. of F.W. O'Connell), XVIII: 66.
"Conán Maol", XVI: 44-45.
Concannon, Helen [Mrs. Thomas Concannon], VI: 211, X: 108, XII: 83 (*Daughters of Banba*) XIII: 153; (*St. Patrick*) XIX:178; (*Blessed Oliver Plunkett*) XXIII: 150.
Conchubhair, Padraic, XXVII: 159.
Condon, E. O'M., VII: 141.
Confederate Catholics, II: 104, 129.
Confederate Generals (Pól Breathnach), XIX: 5.
Confiscation in Irish History (W. F. T. Butler), VIII: 137.
Congregations in the Presbytery of Dungannon (Rev. W. T. Latimer), X:14.
Congreve, William, XVII: 12, 3, 5.
Conlon, Michael, III: 47.
"Conm[h]aicne", XXV: 13, 14; (*Pars Verna*) XXVII: 280; (A Gaelic Catechism) XXIX: 18.
Conmee, [Rev.] J.S., II: 8.
Connacht in Prehistoric Times, XIV: 48.
Connaught Journal, XIX: 90-91.
Connaught Literary Men, VI: 1.
Connell, James (*The Red Flag*), XIV: 45.
Connell, Philip, XIV: 75.
"Connell, Norreys" [pseud. of Conal O'Riordan], XI: 115.
Connellan, Joseph, XII: 10.
Connellan, [Rev.] M. J., (Cineál Fheichín) XXIX: 86; (Airteach's Western Boundary) XXXI: 125; XXXII: 55.
Connellan, Owen (O'Donovan's on *The Four Masters*), XXXII: 50.
Connemara Twenty Years Ago (anon.), XXII: 126.
Connolly, James, VIII: 21, 28, 44, XII: 118, XV: 13, (*Socialism and Nationalism*), XXX: 137, 138.
Connor, Elizabeth (*Dead Star's Light*), XXVI: 69.
Connaught to Chicago (George A. Birmingham), VI: 78.
Conolly, James, V: 108.
Conquests of Charlemagne, The (Douglas Hyde), XI: 60.
Conroy, [Archbishop] Florence, IV: 4.
Conroy, Patrick, XIII: 43.
Considine, Bridget, VI: 131.
Constiutional and Parliamentary History of Ireland (J.G. Swift MacNeill), IX: 109.
Constitutional Developments in

Saorstát Éireann (Arthur W. Bromage), XXVI: 89.
Contemporary Drama of Ireland (Ernest A. Boyd), VIII: 136.
Contemporary Poetry, XV: 43.
Contemporary Review, I: 142.
Conway, Agnes (*Henry VII* [...] *Scotland and Ireland*), XX: 47.
Conwell, Eugene Alfred (antiquarian), XIV: 93.
Convent of Donegal, The, (Pól Breathnach) XXIII: 109-15.
Conyngham, [Maj.] David Power (Irish-American Writer), V: 97.
Conzatti, Zachariae (Dublin printer), XVIII: 123.
Cooke, Alice, VII: 50.
Cooke, [Dr.] Henry, I: 158. [no page 158! but in original index]
Cooke, Hester (*Fallen Petals*) XXIII: 125.
Cooke, J. E., V: 185.
Cooke, Stephen, XX: 92.
Cooke, T. (composer), VI: 210; VII: 12.
Cooke-Taylor, C. R., IV: 8, VII: 182.
Cookstown (printing in), XVII: 137-138.
"Coolen, The" (Rev. Elly Hanley), XVIII: 24.
Cooney, Peter (printer), XXIV: 64.
Cooper, Brian (*The Collar of Gold and Other Fantasies*), XII: 16-18, 133.
Cootehill (printing in), XV: 53.
Corcoran, [Rev.] T. (*State Policy in Education, 1536-1816*), VIII: 66.
Cordon, E. M, VII: 41.
Cork—(Cork Bibliographical Puzzle) I: 128, 153; (Cork, Cloyne and Ross Records) II: 3; Cork (Bishop Murphy) II: 17; (Windele's Cork) II: 72, 75; (Cork Cuttings) III: 189; (*Glamour of Cork*), *The*, XI: 98; (Cork Library) XII: 80, 106, XIII: 33; (Old Cork) XIV: 27.
Cork Newspapers & Journals— (Old Cork Newspapers) II: 75; (*Cork Magazine*) VI: 125, 169, 188, VII: 103; *Cork's Own Town*, XI: 61; (*Cork Advertiser*) XIX: 90-91; (*Cork Freeholder*) XIX: 90-91, XXV: 32, XXVII: 280; (*The Cork Numismatist*) XXVIII: 134; (*Cork Mercantile Chronicle*) XIX: 90-91; (*Cork Morning Intelligencer*) XIX: 90-91; (*Cork Southern Reporter*) XIX: 90-91.
Cork Printing—(printing in Cork) IV: 12, 97, 125, VII: 45, XXI: 90; (Cork printed) XXVII: 181; (pamphlets printed) XXII: 26.
Corkery, Daniel, (*A Munster Twilight*) VIII: 138, IX: 52, XII: 82; (*Synge and Ango-Irish Literature*) XIX: 102; (*Earth out of Earth*) XXVII: 191; (*Resurrection*), XXVIII: 139.
Corkran Alice, VII: 166.
Cormenin, Louis Marie de, XXIII: 95.
Cornhill Magazine, I: 87.
Corpus Astronomise (F. W. O'Connell & R. M. Henry), VI: 119.
Corpus Inscriptionum Insularum Celticarum (ed. Prof. R. A. S. Macalister), XXIX: 141.
Corr, Elizabeth, XIII: 173.
Corrib Country, The (Richard Hayward), XIX: 44.
Coryat's *Crudities* (Presence of Irish Verse), XX: 138.
Cosgrave, [Dr.] Ephraim MacDowell, (Obit.) XV: 29.
Costello, Mrs., (*Amhráin Mhuighe Scola*) XI: 8.
Costello, [Dr.] T. B., IV: 149, VI:

152; (Obit.) XXXII: 129.
Costly Pipeful, A, XXIV: 108.
Cotter, Maire (*To Victory*), XXIV: 139.
Cotton, [Archbishop] Henry (*Typographical Gazetteer*) I: 8, 37, 70, 117, III: 141; 99; (Biog.) II: 1-4; (Achill Press) 65; (Printing in Youghal) IV: 24; (Printing in Kilkenny) XVI: 6.
Cotton, Charles Phillip, II: 3.
"Coul Goppagh" (pseud. of Dr. Gordon), II: 150.
Coulter, Henry, III: 41.
Country Postbag, XX: 9.
Country House Baroque (Anthony Ayscough), XXVII: 282.
Countryman, The, (John Cripps) XXXI: 23; (*Paddy-the-Cope* and *Memories of Connemara*) XXXII: 149.
Coupland, Reginald (*The Empire in These Days*), XXIV: 94.
Courcy, de, see de Courcy.
Cours de Littérature Celtique, XXIX: 115.
Cousins, James H., VI: 155, 186.
Covent Garden Journal, The (Rare Dublin Periodical), XII: 104-106.
Cowan, J. Davison (*Ancient Irish Parish, Past and Present*) V: 165.
Cowan, Samuel K. (*From Ulster's Hills*), V: 101; (Obit.) X: 45.
Cowen, Hewson (*The British Empire and Other Poems*) XV: 46.
Cox, Michael F., III: 109.
Cox, [Sir] Richard, VI: 151.
Cox, Watty (Cox's Ghost), V: 106. (*Irish Magazine*) XXI: 135, XXII: 50; (more about) XXVII: 228; (Publications) XXXII: 104.
"C.P.O.", XVIII: 170.
Crabbed Youth and Age: A Little Comedy (Lennox Robinson),

XIV: 124.
Crab's Irish Dictionary, XVI: 88.
Craig, E. T. (*An Irish Commune: The History Ralahine*), XII: 38.
Craig, [Rev.] J. D., I: 111, 165
Craig, Maurice James, ("Ken ye Aught o' Captain Grose?") XXX: 56-58; (*Some Way for Reason*) XXX: 119; (Edward Berwick) XXX: 126-28; (*The Legacy of Swift*) XXXI: 69.
Craig, Richard Manifold (obituary), IV: 213.
Craig, W. J., II: 8, IV: 134.
Craigan, Máirín (*Hunger Strike*), XXI: 47.
Cranley, [Archbishop] Thomas, IV: 102.
"Craoibhin, An" [Douglas Hyde] (An Siota sa Mháthair), XXIV: 134.
Crawford, Emily, VII: 141.
Crawford, Isabella Valancy, IX: 76.
Crawford, Michael G. (*Legendary Stories of the Carlingford Lough District*), VI: 11.
Crawfor, Mabel Sharman, III: 152.
Crawford, Robert, V: 219.
Crawford, William Horatio, VII: 38, 59.
Crayon, G. (pseud. of George Darley), XXXII: 75.
Creel of of Peat, A (Desmond Mountjoy), II: 10.
Crescent, L. R. (*In Old Belfast*), XIV: 141.
Crevequer, S. M., (*Leaves on the Wind*), X: 47.
Crichton, Francis Elizabeth, (*Tinker's Hollow*) IV: 69; (Obit.) X: 45.
Crickstown, (Pól Breathnach), XVII: 206.
Crioch Deigheanach Don Duine (Séamus Ó Casaide), XIX: 80.

Crilly, Daniel, II: 164, 172, III: 2, 92, 107.
Crimmins, John D., IX: 56.
Críoch Deigheanach Don Duine, XIX: 80.
Cripps, John (*The Countryman*), XXXI: 23.
Crisp, F. A. (*The Vistation of Ireland*), II: 159.
Crockett, S. R., V: 221.
Crofton, Francis Blake, III: 101.
Crofton, Morgan, VII: 35.
Croke, [Prof.] John Lacy O'Byrne, XVII: 43-44.
Croker, [Mrs.] B. M., (Obit.) XII: 68.
Croker, J. Wilson, I: 32, IV: 192, XIV: 39, XV: 49.
Croker, T. Crofton, I: 32, 135, 149, II: 149, III: 143, IV: 8, VI: 133, XV: 49; (Unpub lished Letters) XXVIII: 6-12, 27-33.
Croker, Thomas Francis Dillon (Obit.), III: 151; VI: 115.
Cromie, Helen, III: 52, 113.
Cromwell, Oliver, IV: 51.
Crone, Gerald Roe (*The Southern Patriot*), XI: 104; 136-37; (Letter from London), XXX: 122, 123.
Crone, J. S. [also "J.S.C." & "J. Cn."] (Foreword) I: 1; (Forthcoming Books) 18; (Reviews) 29; 57; (An Intersecting Volume) 136; (Archdeacon Cotton) II: 1-2; (The Bard of the Lee) 40; (Thackery and Ireland) III: 3-4; (Early Printing in Derry) 113; (Book Buyers in the Olden Time) 159-60; (J. C. Lyons) IV: 99; (unpublished history of Fermanagh) 109; (Hitherto Unknown Private Press) 113; (Battle of Ventry Harbour) V: 52; (Thomas Davis) VI: 33-35; (An Interesting Find) 160; (Unfinished Irish Books) VII: 175-77; (Dean Butler's *Trim*) VIII: 9; (A Rogue's Memoirs) 105-07; (Cashel) IX: 8; (Editor's Gossip) IX: 55, XIV: 52-53, XV: 4-5, 22-23, 40-41, 54-55; (Sir Henry Blake) IX: 111; (Association Books) X: 58; (John F. Hogan) 95; ("To Dr. Crone") XII: 37; (Bibliographies of Irish History) XIII: 73-74; (Blake-Foster) 74-76; (Randon Readings) XV: 46-47; (Sgéala Ó Cathair na gCeó) XVI: 2, 26, 67, 75, XVII: 2, 27, 50, 74, 98, 122, XVIII: 2, 35, 66, 98, 130, 154, XIX: 2, 34, 70, 106, 130, 162, XX: 2, 26, 50, 74, 98; XXI: 25, 50-51, 74, XXII: 2, 26, 50, 102, 126, XVI: 3, 28, 68, 76, 88, 127, XVII: 4, 7, 8, 19, 30, 53, 69, 75, 90, 93, 100, 125, 135, 142, 144; XVIII: 2, 35, 66, 98, 130, 154, XXIV: 49, 143, XXX: 1, 2 26, 27-29; (Henry Bradshaw) XIX: 41; (Lafcadio Hearn) XIX: 137; (Bibliography of Irish Athletics) XXI: 18; (printing in Limerick) XXI: 109; (MSS from Library of Sir Bernard Burke) XXIII: 16; Sgéala faoi) XXIV: 74; (The Orange Bibliography) XXV: 85; (William Maginn and *Blackwood's*) XXVI: 73; (Willie Yeats and John O'Leary) XXVII: 245; (Dublin periodical publications) XVIII: 66; 98, 130, 154, XIX: 2, XX: 2, 26, 50, 74, 98, XXI: 50, 74, 98, 122, XXII: 2, 26, 50, 102, 126, XXIII: 34, 82; (The Crone Collection) XXX: 29; (Sundry) I: 110; II: 47, 148; III: 30, 109, 120, 211; IV: 27, 39; V: 15, 16; IV: 45, 73, 77, 125; VII: 36, 95, 103, 120, 139, 142, 160; VIII: 109, 120;

IX: 14, 16, 28, 35, 36, 110; X: 68, 69, 92; XI: 13, 42, 85, 101, 102; XII: 61, 137, 140; XIII: 68, 176; XV: 32.
Crone, J. S. (Appreciations), (Séamus Ó Casaide) XXIX: 25; (Colm Ó Lochlainn) XXIX: 93; (Some Memories of) XXX: 2; (More Memories of Dr. Crone) XXX: 26; (The Beloved Man from Ulster) XXX: 27.
Crone, [Mrs.] J. S. (Obit.) XXI: 25.
Cronin, Mary (*Sir Redmond Intervenes*), XX: 68.
Cronin, T. B. (Obit.), VIII: 118.
Cronin, William, V: 33.
Cronnelly, Richard, VI: 118, 135.
Crook, W. M., XII: 139.
Crosbie, Bligh Talbot, IX: 16.
Crosbie, Mary, VI: 131.
Crosby (*Signification of things borne in Heraldry*), XXXII: 93.
Crosby Papers, The (Richard Sainthill), IV: 212, V: 15.
Cross, Maurice, X: 58.
Cross of Cong, XXIX: 19
Cross of Shamrock, The (Rev. Hugh Quigley), IV: 34.
Cross-Grove, Henry, V: 215.
Crossle, Philip, II: 158,III: 12, 154.
Crouch, Nathaniel, II: 128.
Crow, Gerald H. (*William Morris, Designer*), XXIII: 78.
Crowe, Eyre Evans, II: 130.
Crowley, Florence, XXI: 87-89, XXV: 105.
Crozier, [Brig.-Gen.] William (*Ireland Forever*), XXI: 48.
"Cruck-a-Leaghan" [pseud. of Dougald MacFayden] (*Lays and Legends of the North of Ireland*), III: 119, 138.
Cruise of the Daring, The (Capt. F. C. Armstrong), XXII: 115,

XXIII: 17.
Cruise, [Sir] Francis, III: 152.
Crusaders: A Play in Two Acts (J. Bernard McCarthy), X: 46,47.
Cuala Press, The, XI: 119.
Cuilean, (Mullingar), IV: 112.
Cúirt an Mhéan-Oíche, see Merriman, Brian.
"Cúirt Eigse Chorcaighe" (Tomás Tóibín), XXIX: 1.
Cuirtéis, Eamonn (Obit.) XXIX: 8.
Cuisle na h-Eigse (ed. Prof. Eamonn Curtis), XII: 130.
Cullen, [Cardinal] Paul, III: 36.
Cullen, Luke (MSS), XVII: 56-57.
Cullybackey Congregation, V: 49; IV: 207.
Cumann Bealoideasa Eireann (works of), XXIII: 81.
Cumann Léigheacht an Phobail, (P. S. O'Hegarty), XXX: 113.
Cumann na Leabharlann, XVI: 73.
Cumna Mná an Tabhairne, XX: 34.
Cuming, A. (on May Hartley Hartley), XX: 137.
Cummins, Andrew, VII: 141.
Cummins, Geraldine (*Dr. E. E. Somerville*), XXXII: 43.
Cú na gCleas (Ida Nic Neill & Seamus Ó Searcaig), VI: 78-79.
Cundun, Padraig Phiarais, XX: 120.
Cunningham, John (poet), XVII: 89.
Cunningham, John (Castle Martyr, A Tale of Old Ireland), XXXI: 105.
Cure for Sprain Throughout the Ages (Wulff, Winifred) XXIV: 129.
Curiosities from the Annals, XIX: 37, XXIV: 13, XXV: 37.
Curiosity in Book-spelling, XIV: 60.
Curran, C. P. (*The Rotunda*

Hospital), XXX: 71.
Curran, John Adye, VII: 56; (*Reminiscences*) VII: 160.
Curran, John Philpot, I: 135, XVII: 3.
Curran, Sarah (and Robert Emmet), II: 10.
Curry, [Dr.] John, XVI: 66.
Curry, John (signature), XXX: 18, 19, 44.
Curry, William, III: 137.
Curtayne, Alice, (*Patrick Sarsfield*) XXIII: 56; (*House of Cards*) XXVII: 285; (*St. Brigid of Ireland*) XXI: 141.
Curtis, Edmund, (Irish MSS in Sheffield) XXII: 91; (*Calendar of Ormond Deeds*) XXIII: 74; (unpublished letters of T. Crofton Croker) XXVIII: 6-12, 27-33,
Cusack, Mary Frances ["The Nun of Kenmare"], VI: 134.
"Cushendall", XV: 32.
"Cú Uladh" [pseud. of P. T. McGinley], XXXII: 76.

D

Daéd, Pádraic (M. Mag Ruaidhrí), XXX: 44.
Daffodil's Love Affairs (Louise M. Stackpoole Kenny), V: 11.
Daft, Eddie, VI: 41.
Daiken, Leslie H. (*Goodbye Twilight*), XXV: 43.
Daily News (Irishmen working on), V: 89.
Dall, Liam & Sean Clarac ("An Irish Song"), XX: 58.
Dalton, Charles (*With the Dublin Brigade*), XVIII: 61.
Dalton, John, II: 151.
Dalton, John Paul, IV: 198.
D'Alton, John (historian), XVI: 16-19; XXIX: 137; (MSS) VII: 101, 116, 138, 187.
D'Alton, Louis L. (*Rags and Sticks*), XXVI: 23.
Daly ("Black Daly"), XVIII: 47.
Daly, [Mrs.] De Burgh, VII: 56.
Daly, [Rt. Hon.] Denis De Burgh, III: 159, 191
Daly, J. Bowes, XXV: 9.
Daly, John, see O'Daly, John [scholar & bookseller].
"Danby, Frank" (pseud. of Mrs. Julia Frankau), VII: 167.
Dangerfield, George (*The Strange Death of Liberal England*), XXIV: 115.
Dánta Grádha: An Anthology of Irish Love Poetry (ed. Thomas F. O'Rahilly), VIII: 65.
Dante Alighieri, (An Irish Version of Dante) XIII: 19 (Ireland's Tribute to Dante) XIII: 101-105 & 162-164; XIII: 112.
Daoine Macanta: The Plain People, XVIII: 71.
Dara Óir-Chiste, An (Séamus Ó hAodha), XIX: 184.
Darby the Dodger (Capt. William F. Lynam), III: 7, 63.
Darby, Mildred, I: 133.
D'Arcy, [Dr.] C. F. (*The Adventures of a Bishop*), XXIII: 152.
Dargan, Dermot J. (Irish Bibliographies), XXII: 131.
Dargan, William, IV: 144.
Dark Mountain (David Hogan), XIX: 148.
Darley, Charles, III: 17.
Darley, George [pseud. John Lacey] II: 176; III: 17, XXXII: 75.
Darley, William, III: 17.
Darling, [Rev] J. Lindsay, III: 190.
Darlington, Joseph (*The Dilemma of John Haughton Steele*), XXII: 23.

Daughter of Donagh, The (Alice L. Milligan), XI: 134.
Daughters of Banba (Mrs. Thomas Concannon), XIII: 153.
Daunt, Alice O'Neill, VI: 63.
D'Avaus, M. Le Count, IV: 173.
Davidson, Florence (*Loan Ends*), XXII: 71.
Davies, [Sir] John (*The Poems of Sir John Davies*), XXVIII: 48.
Davies, Sydney, X: 62.
Davin, N. F., II: 68, 93.
Davis, John N. C. Atkins, XXXII: 12.
Davis, Thomas Osborne, (Pamphlets) I: 105; III: 1, IV: 210; (Library of) V: 37, XXVII: 156; XXX: 40-41; VI: 33, 49; (Davis Centenary) VI: 57, 59, 77; 61, 65; (Bibliography) VI: 68; 79, 81, 82, 85, 96, 100; (Essays) VI: 113; (Selections) VII: 61; (Davis Society) XI: 96; XIII: 36, 96; (ed. *Irish Brigade*) XIX: 58; (*Essays and Poems*) XXX: 20; (Signature) XXX: 41; XXXII: 12;
Dawn Mist, The (Frank J. H. O'Donnell), XIV: 30.
Dawson, J. G. (*Aquinas: Selected Political Writings*), XXXI: 46.
Day, Robert (Obit.), VI: 63. (The 'Day' Sale) VII: 63.
Days and Destinies (Peador MacTomais), XI: 26.
Days of Fear (Frank Gallagher), XVI: 111.
Debating Society, IV: 209.
de Bhaldraithe, Tomás (*The Irish of Cois Fairrge*), XXIX: 118.
de Bhall, Tomás (*A West-Limerick Anthology*), XXIV: 105, 131, XXV: 10, 59.
de Blácam, Aodh, X: 91, XII: 9; (*Roddy the Rover and his Aunt Louisa*) XXII: 97; XIII: 18, 87,
99, 106, 151, XVII: 69; (*The Lady of the Cromlech*) XVIII: 94; (*A First Book of Irish Literature*) XXIII: 103; (*Old Wine*) XXII: 3, 46; (*A Life of Wolfe Tone*) XXIV: 10.
de Brún, Pádraig (*Oidiopús i gCólón*), XVIII: 62.
De Burgo, Thomas (*Hibernia Dominicana*), XVI: 6, 66.
de Burca, Liam [Canon William Burke], XVI: 11, XVII: 76.
de Burca, Micheál [Micheal Burke], XVII: 130; ("Night of the Big Wind") XVIII: 77.
de Buitléir, Maithiú, see Butler, Matthew.
de Courcy, Kenneth (family history), XXII: 13, XXI: 89.
Dead Leaders, The (of 1916), VIII: 44.
Deane, Arthur, XIV: 90, XV: 43.
Deevy, Teresa (*Three Plays*), XXVII: 263.
Defenders of the Ford (Mrs. Thomas Concannon), XIX: 64.
Defoe, Daniel (*A Review*), XXI: 123.
Deirdre (James Stephens), XV: 38.
De Jean, VI: 79.
de Jubainville, Henry d'Arbois XVI: 112.
de Lacy family, XXIV: 15. See also Lacy.
de Latocnaye, Chevalier (*Frenchman's Walk Through Ireland*), IX: 59.
Delia Daly of Galloping Green (Patricia Lynch), XXXII: 120.
Delina Delaney (Amanda McKitterick Ros) XXIII: 126.
Delville, XIV: 11.
Delvin, Lord, II: 10.
Delvin's *Irish Primer*, XVI: 61.
Demi-Gods, The (James

Stephens), VI: 78.
Dempsey, [Rev.] P., IV: 69, 208.
Denham, [Sir] William, XIII: 12.
Denn, Patrick [Padraig Din], XXXII: 142.
Dennan, Joseph, XII: 131, XVI: 21.
Dennehy William Francis (Obit.), IX: 111.
Dennis, John ("Black Daly" in Trollope), XVIII: 47.
Denny, [Rev.] H. L. L., XIV: 12, 43.
Denvir, John, II: 14; (Obit.) VIII: 91; XXII: 126.De Quincey, F. H. VIII: 42.
De Pienne, Peter (Waterford printer), XXIV: 75.
De Quincey, F. H., VIII: 42.
De Quincey, James, VII: 163, VIII: 41.
De Rentsi, [Sir] M., XIII: 95.
Der Kaiser von Potsdam (H. B. Burton), VI: 186.
Dermody, Thomas, VI: 129.
d'Erm, Camille le Mercier ("*Ode aux Martyrs de 1916*"), XIX: 139.
de Etienne, Rabaude, XII: 21.
de Róiste, An t-Ath. Seamus, XXVI: 59.
Derrick, Samuel (Irish poet), XXVI: 40.
Derricke's *Image of Ireland* (Pól Breathnach), XXVI: 37.
Derry Brien, XXIX: 19.
Derry—Derry (journalism in Derry) I: 108, 161, II: 74; (Derry Cathedral Register) III: 14; (*Old Derry Ephemera*) VIII: 56; (Siege of Derry) III: 56, 214; (printing in Derry) III: 112, IV: 91, XVII: 92; (*The Derry Spy*) VIII: 57; (Derry Surveys) XIV: 98.
Description of Ards Peninsula (William Montgomery of Rosemount), XX: 28-32.
Description of Type, XVIII: 17.
Desmond, Shaw (*We Do Not Die*), XXII: 121.
de Valera, Eamon (David T. Dwane), XIV: 28.
de Valéra, Sinéad (*Forbhas Chluain Meala*), XXVIII: 139; (*Áilleacht agus an Beithidheach*) XXX: 46.
Development of Musical Talent (J. L. Campbell & Mr. Fay Shaw), XXXI: 85.
De Vere, Aubrey, II: 149, IV: 46, V: 114.
Devil's Puzzle,The (R. G. Bury), XXXI: 71.
Devoy, John (*Devoy's Post Bag*), XXX: 136, 137, XXXII: 110.
De Wil, Ernest, XXXI:104.
Dicey, A. V., IX: 55.
Dickens, Charles (gift to Dean Bagot), XVIII: 3.
Dickenson, P. L. & T. U. Sadlier (*Georgian Mansions in Ireland*), VI: 203.
Dickson family (Dublin printers), XVII: 45-47.
Dickson, Charles, XXXII: 122, 142.
Dickson, [Dr.] William Steele, V: 43, 68.
Dictionaries, see Irish Dictionaries.
Dictionaries of Irish Biography, see Irish Biographical Dictionaries.
Dictionary of National Biography, III: 205, IV: 80, 116.
Digby, Margaret (*Horace Plunkett*), XXXI: 92.
Dignified Dialogues of Peter and Paul (P. MacBrien), XIV: 75.
Dilke, [Sir] Charles, II: 157, IV: 210.

Dill, [Sir] Samuel, I: 8,
Dillon, [Dr.] Emile J., VII: 18,
Dillon, Eilís (*Midsummer Magic*), XXXI: 119.
Dillon, Fr. (Library of), I: 49.
Dillon, John B. (*The Spirit of the Nation*), II: 187; VI: 43.
Dillon, Michael, XXXII: 69.
Dillon, Myles, (*Early Irish Literature*) XXXI: 43; (*The Cycles of the Kings*) XXX: 72.
Din, Padruig, see Denn, Patrick.
Dineen, [Rev.] Patrick S. (*A Smaller Irish-English Dictionary*), II: 11; (Keating's *History*) VI: 101; XVI: 17
Dinneen, Joseph F., (*Pius XII, Pope of Peace*), XXVII: 190.
Directories in Ireland, IV: 33, 72, 91; XVI: 22. See also under Almanacs and Dublin.
Dirge of Erin, The/Tuireamh na hÉireann (Seán O'Connell), XXII: 14.
Disraeli, Benjamin, IV: 28.
Diverting Post, The, XII: 104-106.
Divided We Stand (Michael Sheehy), XXXII: 117.
Dix, Ernest R. McC[lintock] (Printing in Cavan), I: 83-84, IV: 167, IX: 6-7, 22-23, 40-41; (Bonmahon Press) 97-101; (Indexing) II: 6-7; (Printing in Sligo) 21-24, VI: 52-54, 69-71, 89-90; (Chap Books, Song Books and Ballads) II: 33-35; (Irish Song Books in the R.I.A.) II: 81-83; (Printing in Athlone) II: 84-85; (Reviews) II: 90-91; (William Reeves) II: 97-10; (Dublin publishers) II: 112; (Constantia Grierson) II: 136-137; (Printing in Loughrea) II: 151-52, VI: 175-76; 180, 196; (Facsimiles of Title Pages) III: 33, 78, 129-31; (Initials Used by a Dublin Printer) III: 59; (Printing in Birr or Parsonstown) III: 177-79; (Provincial Printing in Ireland) IV: 1-3; (Printing in Youghal) IV: 25; (Printing in Galway) IV: 59-61, IX: 130-31, X: 9-10; (Printing in Armagh) IV: 83-85; (First Irish Papers) IV: 97-98; (Printing in Strabane) IV: 114-16, 134-35, VII: 68-69; (Printing in Tralee) IV: 149-50, X: 79-81; (Printing in Dungannon) IV: 188-89, VIII: 75-76, 100-01; (Printing in Monaghan) IV: 200-02, V: 2-3, 26-27, X: 34-35, 55-56; (Printing in Dundalk) V: 46-47, 58-59, 78-80, VIII: 123-25; (*The Case of Ireland's Being Bound by Acts of Parliament in England Stated*) V: 116-18; (The Rosanna Press) V: 193, 199-200; 130; (Printing in Athlone) VI: 106-07; (The History of Irish Printing) VI: 124-25; (Printing in Mullingar) VI: 127-28, 160-61; (Earliest Belfast Printing) VI: 157-58; (Printing in Enniskillen) VII: 3-5; (Printing in Boyle) VII: 24-26; (Printing in Tuam) VII 40-41; (Irish Provincial Printing) VII: 90-91; (Earliest Printing in Irish Towns) VII: 110-11; (Printing in Portadown) VII: 123-24; (Printing in Ballinasloe) VII: 147-48; (Printing in Waterford) VII: 170; (Rare Dublin Magazines) VIII: 1-3, 25-28; (Early Dublin Occasional Journal) VIII: 51-52; (Some Private Presses) IX: 7; 14, (Printing in Castlebar) IX: 47-49; (Pamphlets—Prose and Poetry) X: 13-14; 71; (Printing in Carlow) XI: 75-76, 94, 109-11, 126-27, XII:

11-13; 103; (Printing in Letterkenny) XII: 31; (Printing in Longford) XII: 53-55; (Printing in Limavady) XXII: 78-79; (Printing in Newtownards) XXII: 101-02; (Printing in Ballymena) XXII: 128-30; (Print-ing in Lurgan) XXIII: 54-56; (Printing and Printers in Fermoy) XIII: 76-77; 97, 167; (Printing in Dungarvin) XIV: 67; (Printing in Enniscorthy) XIV: 83-84, XVII: 38-39; (Printing in Gorey) XIV: 100-01; (Who Printed *Hibernia Dominicana*?) XIV: 116-17; (Kilkenny Printing in 18th c.) XVI: 6-9, 40-41, 55-58, 89-109; (Gaelic Printing) XVI: 85-87; (Irish Provincial Printers) XVI: 121; (Printing in Banbridge) XVII: 7-8; (Printing in Ballinrobe) XVII: 9; (Dublin 17th c. Printing) XVII: 12; (W. H. Gratten Flood) XVII: 26; 35, (Plays Printed in Ireland Prior to 1701) XVII: 36-37; (Note on the Dickson Family) XVII: 45-46; (Printing in Athy) XVII: 58-59; (Government Advertise-ments in Dublin Newspapers of 1723) XVII: 80-81; (Cornelius Carter, Printer) XVII: 84; (John Cunningham, Poet) XVII: 89; (Printing in Ballyshannon) XVII: 101-02; (Printing in Cookstown) XVII: 137-38; (Printing in Limerick in the 19th c.) XVIII: 39-42, 75-76, 101-02, 135-36, XIX: 117-20, 134-36, 174, XX: 84-85, 106-08, 124-26, XXI: 7-9, 30-32, 56, 78-80; (Dublin Music Printers and Sellers) XVIII: 26-28; (Obit. of Miss D. A. Ferguson) XVIII: 157; (Office of King's Stationer in Ireland) XIX: 82-84; (Edmund Burke) XX: 32-33; (The Registry of Deeds) XX: 55-56; (Dr. Young) XX: 66; (Early Limerick Printing) XXI: 110; XXII: 30; (*The Cruise of the Daring*) XXIII: 17; (Beannacht dílis Dé ar anam uasal Earnáin Uí Dhíosca) XXIV: 49-50; (An American Appreciation) 122; (Clonmel Printing) XXV: 90; (Waterford Printing) XXVI: 128; (*Early Dublin-Printed Books*) XXVII: 184; (Printing in Wexford) 250; (Commemoration Meeting) XXIV: 125; (Sundry) I: 6, 91, 112, 137, 153, II: 43, 46, 66; III: 9, 25, 73, 157, IV: 12, 16, 32, 51, 62, 72, 91, VI: 43, VII: 116, 139, 164, VII: 35, VIII: 112, XII: 81, XV: 23, XVI: 66, 73, XVII: 61, 78, 113.

Dixon, Henry, XII: 13,
Dixon, Hepworth, III: 70.
"D.K.", I: 153, III: 56, 82, 103.
"Do Líonadh mBáin" (Tadhg Ó Neachtain), XXV: 105; XXVIII: 103.
Doak, H. A. (*The Three Rock Road*), XI: 12.
Dobbs, Margaret E., XII: 134.
Dobell, Bertram, V: 64, 99.
Dobell's Catalogue, XVII: 142.
Dobrée, Bonamy (*Modern Prose Style*), XXIII: 51.
Dod (of the *Peerage*), XI: 19.
Dodd, E. R. (*Journals and Letters of Stephen MacKenna*), XXV: 108.
Doddington, Bubb, II: 24.
Doheny, Michael, V: 181
Dolan, Francis (book sale), XIX: 99.
Dolan, Joseph T. (ed. *Louth Archæological Journal*), XIV:

91.
Dollard, James B., IX: 76.
Dolly's Brae, XIV: 39.
Domenech, Emmanuel, VIII: 140.
Donaghadee (printing in), VII: 46.
Donaghy, Lyle (*Into the Light and Other Poems*), XXII: 137.
Donahoe, Patrick, XVII: 134-135.
Donegal Christmas Annual, (ed. P. T. MacGinley) XXXII: 76.
Donegal County Historical Society, XXX: 67, 68.
Donemana Private Press, IX: 8, 63.
Donlevy's Catechism, XXI: 91, XXIV: 16.
Donnelly, Edward, III: 5.
Donnelly, [Rt. Rev.] Nicholas, XI: (Obit.) 118.
Donoghmore, Co. Down, V: 165.
Donovan, [Rev.] J., IV: 58.
Don's Book, The [the O'Conor Don], III: 7.
Doomsland (Shane Leslie), XIV: 140.
Doran, Charles G. (Library of), I: 122; (Great Irish Book Collectors) XIV: 97.
Doudney, [Rev.] D. A. (Bonmahon Press), Rev, I: 97.
Douglas, George, I: 108, 161.
Douglas, James, II: 70, XI: 24, 112.
Douglas, John M., V: 201,.220, VI: 13, 69, 80, VII: 86, 177.
Douglas, Ronald MacDonald (*The Irish Book*), XXIV: 143.
Dove in the Castle, The (Earl of Longford), XXX: 46.
Dowden, Edward, IV: 46, 167, 185; V: 41, 65, 93, 153; (Book sale) VI: 28; VI: 76, 77, XIII: 13.
Dowden, [Dr.] John, I: 105; (sale of library) V: 65, 209, VI: 28; XII: 81.

Dowling, Madge, IX: 1, XIII: 20, 117, XIV: 63.
Dowling, P. J. (*The Hedge Schools of Ireland*), XXIII: 99.
Dowling, Richard, III: 91, 106, IX: 1, 99, XI: 20, 36, 51, XIII: 117.
Down Survey, The (Sir William Petty), I: 45, 70; II: 61.
Down County Historian, A, XII: 22.
Down—II: 12, 30, III: 173, 214; (County Elections of 1790), III: 82.
Downey, Alan, VIII: 108, XIII: 154; (*The Cruise of the Daring*) XXII: 115; (*Jade House*) XXIII: 97.
Downey, Archbishop (*Critical and Constructive Essays*), XXIII: 121.
Downey, Edmund, I: 34, 45, 169, III: 100, 3, 214, VI: 10, 11, 23, 73, 77, VII: 27; (An Editor's Reminiscences) VIII: 73, 97; VIII: 73, 97, 114, 119, 135, IX: 69, 98, 123, XIV: 140; (Obit.) XXV: 38.
Downfall of Grabbum, The, (An Ulster Fable by an Ulster Clergyman) IV: 158.
Dowse, Baron, XIII: 57.
Doyle, [Rev.] A., (*The Passion and Triumph of Christ*), XXX: 143.
Doyle, [Sir] Arthur Conan, II: 55.
Doyle, Bernard, XXII: 62.
Doyle, J. J. (pseud. "Beirt Fhear"), XVII: 51.
Doyle, Lynn C.[Leslie Alexander Montgomery], VIII: 59, XXXII: 42; (*Ballygullion Ballads*) XXV: 71; (*The Spirit of Ireland*), XXIII: 123.
Doyle, Martin, II: 149.
Doyle, Richard, II: 151.
Doyle, Rev. Dr. ["J.L.K."] (Life

of), XXI: 42; (*The Clergy Vindicated*) XXIV: 61.
Doyle, W. B., I: 13, 35.
"D.P." (on printing in Cashel), XVIII: 79.
Draak, [Dr.] Maartje (*Terse Letterkunde als Toetsteen*), XXXI: 88.
Draddy, John [Seán Ó Dreada]. XVI: 5.
Dragon, The (Lady Gregory), XI: 135.
Dramatic Sketches (Sir Charles Rockingham), XIX: 26.
Drapier's Letters, The (Jonathon Swift) XXI: 110.
"Dream of Mac Donnell Claragh", (James Clarence Mangan), XXXII: 134-36.
Dream Physician (Edward Martyn), X: 46-47.
"Dreamer, The", Randal MacDonnell, IV: 199.
Drennan, Thomas, XVII: 127.
Drennan, [Dr.] William, III: 9, V: 142. 203, 209, XII: 51, XVII: 63.
Drew, Catherine, II: 40.
Drew, [Sir] Thomas, V: 10.
Driscoll, Charles, VIII: 57.
"D.R." (Graveyard at George's Hill, Dublin), XVIII: 175.
Droc Saogal, An—Penal Days ("Ardrigh") VIII: 134.
Drogheda—(*Drogheda Journal*) XIX: 90; (printing in Drogheda) IV: 1, VI: 116, XIX: 78; (*Old Moore's Almanac*) XVIII: 156; (Unrecorded Example) XX: 39; (A Drogheda, Printer) XVII: 120.
Dromore: An Ulster Doicese (E. D. Atkinson), XV: 58.
Druidean the Mysticand Other Irish Stories (Mrs. Nicholas Noble/Madge Irwin), V: 102.

Drummond, [Rev.] James., X: (Obit.) 19.
Drummond, [Rev.] Robert Blackley (Obit.), XII: 117.
Drummond, [Dr.] William Henry, V: 34, IX: 76.
Duanaire Gaedhilge (Rois Ní hÓgain), XVIII: 64.
Dublin, books on—(Gilbert's *History*) II: 6; (*Topography of Dublin*) II: 92; (Dublin Catalogues) VI: 42; (*Dublin in Irish Legend*) XI: 61; (*Dublin Directory*) XVI: 19-22; 29-32, 52-54; (*Dublin Street Names*) XVI: 77; (*History and Antiquities of Dublin*) XVI: 77; (*Dublin of Yesterday*) XVII: 29; (*Dublin Old and New*) XXVI: 43.
Dublin city—(Records of 18th c. Dublin architecture) I: 28; (Dublin Municipal Records) II: 11; (Dublin Historical Society) VI: 43; (Dublin Linen Hall) VI: 61; (Dublin Library) XIII: 119; (Dublin Pharmacopœas) XIII: 156; (Dublin Statue of Shakespeare) XV: 24; (Dublin Library Society) XIV: 112; (Dublin Street Cries) XIV: 141; (Dublin Literary Society Revival) XV: 10; (Early Alphabetical Lists of Dublin Streets) XVI: 77-79; (Dublin Society of United Irishmen) XVII: 3; (Royal Dublin Society) XVII: 5, 6; (Gaelic Society of Dublin) XVII: 6; (Dublin Fanlights) XVII: 143; (18th c. Music Printers & Music Sellers) XVIII: 26, XXXI: 129; (Dublin Coffee Houses) XXIII: 133; (Dublin City Maps) XXVI: 2.
Dublin Booksellers, bookbinder, and Book-trade—(Dublin publ-

ishers in 1720) II: 93, 112; (Book auctions in Dublin); XII: 18; (Dublin publishing firm) XIV: 40; (Jeremiah Pepyat, 1721), XIX: 82; (Lawrence, Peter, 1706) XVII: 47, 61; (18th c. Bookbinders) XXIV: 10; (Irish-Speaking Booksellers in Dublin) XXIV: 111; (John O'Daly) XXVI: 135; (Dublin Booksellers) XXXII: 8, 9, 10; (Dublin booksellers' and others' signs) XXXII: 9.

Dublin, printing in—(Dublin University Press) II: 3, 163; (Dublin Pirate Publishers) III: 47; IV: 32, XXIII: 13, 97; (17th c. Dublin printers) XVII: 12, 113; (Dublin printers' depositions) XVII: 33-35; (Graiseberry, Dublin printer) XVIII: 24; (18th c. music printers) XVIII: 26; (Zacharia Conzatti, Dublin printers) XVIII: 123; (Edwin Sandys, Dublin printer) XVIII: 123; (Cambridge list of Dublin printers) XX: 119; (Dublin printers of verse in 1841) XX: 62; (Elizabethan Dublin printing) XXI: 113; (Dublin "Song Books") XXIII: 92; (Early Dublin printing) XXIV: 44; (fictitious Dublin imprints) XXVII: 180; (Dublin printed classics) XXVII: 184; (Dublin printers in English financial records) XXVIII: 112-15; (*Lucy and Colin*, 1725) XVIII: 130.

Dublin Newspapers, Magazines & Journals—(*Dublin Penny Journal*) II: 4, 5, 6, 7, 12, 28, 149; (18th c. Newspapers) II: 43; (*Dublin University Magazine*) III: 3, V: 50, VI: 42, 81, 103, X: 75, XXV: 61; (*Dublin Review*) VII: 182, XII: 138; (18th c. Dublin magazines) VIII: 1, 25; (*The Reformer*) VIII: 1; (*Dublin and London Magazine*) VIII: 53, 83; (*Dublin Directories*) XII: 131, XIV: 84, XVI: 19; (*Dublin University Review*) XII: 89; (*Dublin Review*: index) XIII: 116; (Dublin Theatrical Journals) XIV: 115, 131; (*Dublin Magazine*) XVII: 52, 124, XXII: 120; (Govt. advertising in, 1723): XVII: 80-81; (*Dublin News*) XVIII: 31; (Dublin periodical publications) XVIII: 66; (Dublin German Newspaper) XVIII: 88; (*Dublin Magazine and Irish Literary Register*) XVIII: 146; (*Dublin Saturday Magazine*) XXVIII: 87; (Dublin daily papers) XIX: 90; (Faulkner's *Journal*) XIX: 90-91; (*Dublin Gazette*) XIX: 90-91; (*Dublin Observer*) XIX: 90-91; (*Dublin Historical Record*) XIX: 92; (Dublin Periodicals) XXII: 50; XXVII: 190; (*Dublin Weekly Register*) XIX: 90-91; (*Éigse*) XXVI: 139; (Newspapers in 1788) XXXII: 67. See also Rare Dublin Periodicals.

Dublin, Easter 1916, (Alice Furlong), XXX: 107, 108.

Dublin Society Episode, A, XVI: 118.

Dublin University Press (Classics 1740-1750), XVIII: 97.

Dubliners (James Joyce), VI: 60.

Duff, Charles, (*Ireland and the Irish*) XXXII: 44; (*This Human Nature*), XVIII: 177.

Duff, Douglas V. (*Sword for Hire*), XXIII: 50.

Dufferin, Lord [Frederick Blackwood], I: 118, XII: 34.

Duffin, Celia (with Ruth Duffin

The Irish Book Lover 259

The Secret Hill), V: 126, 142.
Duffin, E. (*The Magic Glasses*), XXIV: 45.
Duffin, Helen (*Over Here*), IX: 137.
Duffin, Ruth (with Celia Duffin The Secret Hill), V: 126, 142.
Duffy, Bernard (*Oriel*), X: 60.
Duffy, B. J. (on White, Fleet St. printer), XXX: 37.
Duffy, [Sir] Charles Gavan, II: 117, 187, 188, III: 1, 2, 4, 27, 206, IV: 26, V: 53, VI: 43, 183, VII: 54, 145 155 157, 177, VIII: 17, XI: 36, XIII: 30, XVII: 51, XXXII: 12.
Duffy, George Gavan, XXXII: 12.
Duffy, James [publisher] (*Sketch of his Life*), XVIII: 168-69.
Duffy, W. A. (*Shaded Lights*), XIV: 46.
Duffy's Fireside Magazine, IV: 41, VII: 47.
Duffy's Library of Ireland, XII: 137.
Dugan, C. W., IV: 32.
Dugan, Michael Ignatius, XXI: 136.
Dugdale, Blanche E. C. (*Arthur James Balfour*), XXV: 47.
Duilearga, Séumas [James H. Delargy] (on *Royal Hibernian Tales*), XVIII: 174.
Dun, [Sir] Patrick, (Library of) XVIII: 17, 105-117; (MS Catalogue) XVIII: 160.
Dunbar, T. J. (Obit.), VII: 104.
Duncairn Press, I: 7, 25, 91.
Duncan, James, XIX: 177.
Duncan, Ronald (*The Death of Satan: A Comedy*), XXXII: 118.
Dundalk—(*Dún Dealgan*) II: 11; (printing in) V: 46-47, 58-59, 78-80, VIII: 123-25, IX: 4; (*Dundalk Guide*) VIII: 12; (*Dundalk Annual*) VIII: 135, IX:

105, XV: 43; (Blackrock and Dundalk Visitor) IX: 105.
Dundas, [Rev.] W. H., (*Enniskillen—Parish and Town*)V: 41, 87.
Dún Dealgan: Cuchulain's Home Fort (Harry G. Tempest), II: 11.
Dungan, James, XVI: 47.
Dungannon—(printing in) IV: 188, VIII: 73, 100, 111; (*Dungannon Magazine*) V: 115, 184; (Dungannon Presbytery) X: 14; (History of Dungannon) XVII: 69.
Dungarvan (printing in), XIV: 67.
Dunlavin (history of), XVII: 16.
Dunlop, A. (*Fifty Years of Irish Journalism*), II: 159.
Dunlop, Durham, X: 14.
Dunlop, Robert, I: 88, II: 144, XII: 119, XIX: 72.
Dunluce Castle and the Route (H. C. Lawlor), XI: 26.
Dunn, Archibald J., IX: 36.
Dunn, Joseph (ed. *The Glories of Ireland* with & P. J. Lennox), VI: 149.
Dunne, [Capt.] John [father of "George Egerton"], I: 120.
Dunning, T. P., (*Piers Plowman*), XXVIII: 48.
Dunphie, C. J., XII: 53.
"Dunphy's Corner" (James Stephens), VII: 95.
Dunquel, Alfred (*Ireland and France*), VIII: 39.
Dunraven, Lord [Windam T. W. Quin], VII: 133.
Dunsany, Lord [Edward Plunkett], IV: 181, VII: 77, IX: 30, X: 61, XI: 58, XIII: 93, 112; (*The Curse of the Wise Woman*), XXII: 48; (*If I were Dictator*) XXIII: 20; (*Up the Hills*), XXIII: 154; (*Rory and Bran*) XXIV 139; (*My Ireland*) XXV:

109; (*The Man Who Ate the Phoenix*) XXXI: 118.
Durham, Lord, II: 170.
Durkan, Patrick F., II: 123.
Dust of the World: An Historical Romance of Belfast ("Athene"), V: 11-12.
Dutch Publications Relating to Ireland, XXX: 114.
Dwan, John, XIII: 114-15.
Dwane, David T. (*Life of de Valera*), XIV: 28.
Dynamite Drummer,The (Alice & W. H. Milligan), XII: 35-36.

E

Eadar, XXXI: 33.
Eagle of Garryroe, The (Charles Kickham), XI: 82.
Eakin, James H., I: 161, II: 74, IV: 91, IX: 86.
Eala Bhan, An, XXVIII: 1.
Earl, Laurence (*The Battle of Baltinglass*), XXXII: 21.
Earls of Tyrone and Tyrconnell (Fr. Paul Walsh), XXII: 4.
Early Dublin Journal, VIII: 51.
Early Irish Fairies and Fairyland, The (Norris Jephson O'Conor), XII: 108-109.
Early Limerick Printing (E. R. Mc C. Dix), XXI: 110.
Earna (magazine), XX: 66, 115.
Easter 1916 (Alice Furlong), XXX: 107, 108.
Eccles, [Miss] C. O'Conor, II: 198.
Ecclesiastical Architecture of Ireland (George Petrie), I: 89.
Economic History of Ireland, An (D. A. Chart) XII: 38-40.
"E.D.", XII: 68.
Eddystone Lighthouse, VI: 13.
Edge, John H., VI: 94, VII: 72, VIII: 46; (*An Irish Utopia*) VII: 72.
Edgeworth, Abbe, IV: 177.
Edgeworth, Henry Essex [Abbé Edgeworth], IV: 177.
Edgeworth, [Lt. Col.] K. E., (*The Industrial Crisis*) XXI: 119; (*The Trade Balance*) XXIII: 54.
Edgeworth, Maria, V: 202.
Edinburgh Review, XVIII: 3.
Editorial, XVIII: 33, 34, XIX: 104, 105, 162, XX: 1, 25, 49, 73, 97, 121, XXI: 2, 26, 49, 73, 97, 121, XXII: 1, 25, 49, XXII: 77; ("The Poor Scholar") XXII 101, 125, XXIII: 1, 33, 57, 81, 129, 105, XXV: 1, 25, 49, 73, XXVIII: 97.
Editor's Gossip, VII: 8 28, 48, 69, 96, 111, 132, 156 181, IX: 9, 81, 55,82, 104, 133, X: 15, 41, 63, 85, 104, XI: 9, 23, 43, 57, 95, 111, 128, XII: 13, 31, 59, 80, 106, 131, XIII: 11, 33, 57, 83, 112, 135, 172, XV: 4, 22, 54, 40.
Editor's Reminiscences, An (Edmund Downey), VIII: 73, 97.
Education in a Free Ireland (Michael Tierney), XI: 62.
Edward Hill, M. D. (T. Percy Kirkpatrick), XII: 110.
Edward Lhuyd's Irish Manuscripts (Rev. John Brady), XXIX: 134.
Edward O'Donnell (Jeremiah O'Donovan Rossa) VII: 27.
Edwards, R. Dudley, (Catalogue of MSS in Harris MS) XXVI: 112; (The Civil Survey) XXIX: 8.
Egan, Fr. (P. P. Deering), IV: 131.
Egerton, George, XIV: 105.
Eglinton John [pseud. of William Magee], IX: 53; (*Irish Literary Portraits*) XXIII: 122; (*A Memoir of Æ*) XXV: 111.
Eighteenth-century Limerick Printing Venture (Robert Herbert), XXVIII: 104-112.

The Irish Book Lover 261

Eighteenth Century Magazine of *Music* (W. J. Lawrence), III: 76.
Eighteenth Century Miscellany, *An* (Martin Freeman), XII: 114.
Eighteenth Century Periodicals, I: 39, 71, 108.
Éigse, XXVII: 241.
Éire: Department of Agriculture Journal, XXIX: 116.
Éire: The Irish Nation, XVIII: 71, 72.
"E.J.B.", I: 28.
Electioneering Bill of Former Days, An (P. S. O'Hegarty), XXXI: 8.
Elgee, Jane Francesca, see Lady Wilde.
"Elixir de la Vie" (John D'Alton), XXVII: 232.
Ellen Hanley: Or the True Story of the Colleen Bawn (Rev. W. Fitzgerald), V: 221.
Elliott, [Rev.] Robert (of Waterford), XXX: 66.
Elliott, Robert (Obit.), II: 40, (*The Immortal Charlatan*) II: 71.
Elliott, Thomas, XII: 53.
Ellis, [Mrs.] Havelock, IV: 85.
Ellis, Hercules, VI: 152.
Ellis, S. M., I: 151, V: 129, VI: 29, VIII: 30, X: 86, XII: 15, XV: 47; (An authority on S. Le Fanu) XVIII: 100.
Ellis, [Sir] Whittaker, IV: 177.
Ellmann, Richard, (*Yeats: The Man and the Masks*) XXXI: 94; (*The Identity of Yeats*) XXXII: 117.
Elmes, Rosalind M. ["Zachariae Conzatti"] XVIII: 123; ("Zozimus") XXVI: 58; (*Catalogue of Engraved Irish Portraits*) XXVII: 286; (*Catalogue of Irish Topographical Prints and Drawings*), XXIX: 44.
Emerald, The (monthly magazine), IX: 28.
"E.M.F.G.B.", XII: 20, 78.
Emigrants (Irish), XVI: 48.
Emmet, Robert, I: 8, 20, 58, 62, 107; (Emmet and Sarah Curran) II: 10; III: 13, 72, 191; IV: 163, 164, 209; *Emmet and his Comtemporaries* (Edmund Downey), VIII: 73; XI: 85; (Southey and Emmet) XI: 118, 137; (Emmet's Insurrectionary Movement) XX: 13; (Emmet and Thomas Moore) XXII: 8; XXIII: 34.
Emmet, Thomas Addis, X: 95, XXI: 19.
Emmets, The, VII: 66.
Empire in these Days, The (Reginald Coupland), XXIV: 94.
Enchantment (E. Temple Thurston), IX: 12.
"Encounter between the King's Troops and Peasants at Ballynahinch" (Painting by Thomas Robinson), XXXII: 142.
End of a Chapter (Shane Leslie), VIII: 38.
English as We Speak It in Ireland (P. W. Joyce), II: 25.
English Drama (Camillo Pellizzi), XXIV: 2.
English Historical Review, II: 13, 72.
English, James Russell, X: 69.
Englishman in Ireland (R. A. Scott-James), II: 106.
Ennis, (printing in) III: 158; *Ennis Chronicle.* Wednesday and Saturday. XIX: 90-91.
Enniscorthy, (printing in) XIV: 83; XVII: 138-139, XX: 43, XXVI: 64.
Enniskillen, (Inniskillin Dragoons) I: 18; (printing in) II: 186, V: 147, VII: 3, 32, 46, 92; Parish

and Town) V: 87; (*Enniskillen Chronicle*) XIX: 90.
Eochar Na bhFlathas (Leabhar Úrnatihe Caitlici), XIX: 125.
"Epithalamium" (Seán Ó Súilleabháin na mBannaoi), XXII: 78.
Equinox (R. N. D. Wilson), XXV: 119.
Erin, The XI: 118, 137.
Eriu (II: 173); XXIII: 75; XXIX: 117.
Erskine, Dean, XVII: 9.
Erskine, Ruaraidh (*King Edward VII and Some Other Figures*), XXIV: 65.
Ervine, St. John G., VI: 14, 27, 99, XI: 56, XII: 36, 139, XIII: 97, 99, XIV: 45, 139, XV: 60, XXV: 69; (*Omnibus*) XXII: 22; (*If I were Dictator*) XXIII: 20; (*People of Our Class, Boyd's Shop*) XXV: 69; (*The First Mrs. Fraser*) XIX: 156; (*The Theatre in My Time*) XXII, 21.
Escoriflaire, R. C. (*Is Ireland Hostile?*), XI: 15.
Esler, see Mrs. Rentoul-Esler.
Esler, [Dr.] Robert, XI: (Obit.) 31.
Esposito, Mario VII: 8, XIII: 86.
Essays Irish and American (John B. Yeats), X: 12.
Essays on Poetry (George O'Neill, S.J.), XI: 83.
Essays (W. B. Yeats), XIV: 89.
"Ethna Carbery" [psued. of Anna Johnston MacManus] (*The Four Winds of Erinn—Poems by Ethna Carbery*), X: 11.
"Ethne" (*Poems by Ethne of The Nation*) VI: 204.
Ettingsall, Thomas, II: 149.
Études Celtiques (J. Vendryes), XXV: 115.
Eucharistic Congress, Dublin (Bibliography), XX: 136.

Europac, An t- (J. S. Crone), XVIII: 66.
"Eva" of *The Nation* [pseud. of Eva Mary Kelly], I: 163.
Evans, A.W., XII: 60.
Evans, E. Estyn, (*Irish Heritage*) XXIX: 23; (*Irish Folk-ways*) XXXII: 149.
Evans, Edward, X: 57, XVI: 22.
Evans, Ned, XXX: 41.
Evatt, George, [Sir], XIII: 119.
Evening Chronicle, The, XII: 104-106.
Evening Herald (Dublin), XXXII: 67.
Evening Memories (William O'Brien), XII: 17.
Ever the Twain (Lennox Robinson), XIX: 30.
Every Irishman's Library, IX: 106.
Evin, Saint, III: 47, 62, 82.
Evolution of Irish Type, XIV: 81.
Ewald, William B., Jnr. (*The Newsmen of Queen Anne*), XXXII: 150.
Ewing, Thomas ("Ode to Walter Hussey"), XVIII: 67.
"E.W. L.", IV: 71, V: 13, 140.
Excursions in Thought ("Imaal"), XIII: 15.
Exhibition of illuminated western MSS at T.C.D., XXXII: 105.
"Exile of Erin, The", ("*The Exile of Erin*"—*Who Wrote it?*) XIII: 17, 38, 66.
"Exiled Irishman's Lament", XIII: 128, 175.
Exiles: A Play in Three Acts (James Joyce), X: 46-47.
Exposito, Mario, XIII: 86.
Extents of Irish Monastic Possessions (ed. Edward Mac Lysaght), XXIX: 20.

F

Fahy, Francis A. [or Frank] VI: 162, XII: 140, XIII: 169, XIV: 23; (Obit.) XXIII: 83; (*The Ould Plaid Shawl*) XXXI: 69.
Fahey, Monsignor (Gort), IV: 131.
"Failbhe Fionn" (pseud. of Tadhg Mac Coitir), XVIII: 88, XXVII: 212.
Fairy Led and Other Verses (Helen Lanyon), VII: 100.
Falkiner, Caesar-Litton, IV: 134.
Falkiner, [Sir] F. R., I: 88.
Falkiner, George, I: 167.
Falkiner, Litton ["Caesar Litton"], III: 9; (in *Edinburgh Review*) XVIII: 3.
Faller, Kevin ["K.F."], (*Lyric and Script*) XXX: 141; (*The Word and the World*) XXXI: 10; XXXII: 21-24, 43-48, 70-72, 94-96, 117-120.
Fallon, [Mrs.] E. J. (McSparran's *Norman de Borgos*), XXIII: 94.
Falloon, [Mrs.] G., VII: 53.
Falls, Cyril (*The Birth of Ulster*), XXIV: 95.
Famine (Liam O'Flaherty), XXV: 22.
Famine of 1847, I: 118, 150.
Famous Cities of Ireland (Stephen Gwynn), VII: 99.
"Faoiseamh" (poem by "An File Fannlag"), XXIX: 121.
Farewell to Garrymore ("M. A. Rathkyle"), XI: 62.
"Farewell to Murrisk", XVII: 76-77, 117, 132.
Farington's Diary, XIII: 174.
Farmer Almanac (dated 1587), XVIII: 38.
Farmer and O'Reilly Collection of Irish Music (Séamus Ó Casaide), XXVIII: 62-66.
Farquhar, George, VI: 47.

Farrell, John J. (Dublin Coffee-Houses), XXIII: 133.
Farrell, M. J. [pseud. of Molly Keane], (*Conversation Piece*) XXI: 68; (*Full House*) XXIII: 149.
Farren, Elizabeth, II: 143.
Farren, Robert (*The First Exile*), XXIX: 95.
Fasti Ecclesiae Hibernicae (Archdeacon Cotton), II: 2, 3.
"Father O'Flynn" (Alfred Perceval Graves), III: 165.
Father Ralph (Gerald O'Donovan), IV: 188.
"Faugh a Ballaugh" (regimental magazine), I: 18, 172.
Faugh-a-Ballagh—A Book of old Irish and Scotch Ballads, II: 130.
Faulkner's *Dublin Journal*, I: 40.
Fauriel, M. (Irish MS. of), XVIII: 25.
Fay, W. G. & Catherine Carswell (*The Fays at the Abbey Theatre*), XXIII: 150.
"F. de B.", X: 69.
Fea, Allen, VIII: 90.
Fea Family, VIII: 90.
"Feargal" (Call for Dictionary of Irish Biography), I: 154.
Fearon, W. R. (*Parnell of Avondale*), XXVI: 65.
"Feart-Laoi" (An t-Ath. Maitiú Ó Riain, S.P.), XXVII: 145.
"F.E.C.", V: 51.
Federalist, The (Rev. Thaddeus O'Malley), XV: 48, XVII: 144.
"Féile Thióboid" (Séan Ó h-Ógáin), XXXI: 25.
Feis Coel Collection of Irish Airs (eds. Arthur Darley & P. J.McCall), V: 198.
Felon's Track (Michael Doheny), V: 181.
Fenelly, Rev., IV: 57.

Fenianism—(Rutherford, *Secret History of Fenian Conspiracy*) I: 136, 141, 147; (History of Fenianism) IV: 108; (*History of Fenianism*, Stephens) XVIII: 146.
Fennelly, Patrick (of Moynalty), XXVII: 259.
Fenning, Daniel, I: 157.
Fenton, Seamus, (*Tradition in Co. Wexford*) XXVI: 7; (*A Great Kilkennyman—John O'Donovan*), XXVIII: 72. (*Kerry Tradition*) XXXI: 118.
Fenton, Sergeant (A Military Poet in Birr), XXVII: 231.
Fergus, John, (Rev. John Brady), XXIX: 108.
Ferguson, [Miss] D. A., (Obit.), XVIII: 157.
Ferguson, J. A. (*Bibliography of Australia*), XXIX: 93.
Ferguson, John, VI: 31.
Ferguson, [Sir] Samuel (Centenary Commemoration), I: 74 , 105, 113, 126, 132, 133, II: 149, III: 3, VI: 42; (and John T. Gilbert) XXX: 123-125.
Fermanagh, History of, IV: 109, 12t.
Fermoy (printing in), XIII: 76
Ferns (W. H. G. Flood, *History of the Diocese*), XVII: 26.
Ffrench, Yvonne (*The Amazons*), XXIII: 125.
"Fiachra Eilgeach" (O'Sullivan's Pious Miscellanny), I: 130, XVI: 44-45.
Fictitious Dublin Imprints, XXVII: 180.
Fiddler's Green (Patrick Purcell), XXXI: 95.
Fidelis (Irish pamphlet), IV: 144.
Field, [Mrs.] E. M., II: 131.
Field, John (inventor of the Nocturne), VI: 76, XVII: 26.

Fielden, Olga (*Island Story*) XXI: 143; (*Stress*) XXIV: 142.
Fielding-Hall, H. P., VIII: 43.
Fields of Heaven (Nora Tynan O'Mahony), VII: 11.
Fifty Years of Irish Journalism (A. Dunlop), II: 159.
"Figgins" Type, XIX: 78.
Figgis, Darrell, IX: 81, (*Children of Earth*) X: 40-41; (*Bye-Ways of Study*), X: 61; XIV: 26; (*Fight for Irish Freedom*) XV: 12.
Filí agus Fir Léinn (G. Ó Murchadha), XXX: 102-104, 129-132.
Finnegans Wake (James Joyce), XXVII: 165.
Fingall Mummers (description), XX: 34.
Finghín na Leamhna, (*Amhráin na nGleann*), XXVII: 213.
Finlay, J. L., VII: 185.
Finn, Edmund (Kilkenny Printer), (*Finn's Leinster Journal*) XIX: 8; XVI: 6; (will of) XXIV: 40.
Finnan, Jeremiah, J., IV: 143, 172.
Finnerty, Eugene Guilford, XVII: 23, 120, XIX: 143.
Finn's *Leinster Journal*, XIX: 8.
Fíon Na Filidheachta (Micheál Breathnach), XIX: 146.
"Fionn ag Caoineadh" (Néil Mic an Róthaich), XXVII: 169.
Fiorthairbhe na nGaoidheal: The True Interest of the Irish Nation (Unrecorded Irish Book, 1716), XXIX: 36.
Fir Manach (Annals), XXIII: 7.
First Irish Papers IV: 61, 97.
First Songs (Anthony Allen), X: 46-47.
Fisher, Joseph R., II: 190, XI: 79.
Fisher, Walter Mulrea, (Obit.) XI: 67.
Fitzgerald, [Admiral] Charles Cooper Penrose, XIII: 40.

Fitzgerald, David, XXI: 19.
Fitzgerald, Desmond (*Irish Bulletin*), XVIII: 70.
Fitzgerald, [Lord] Edward, II: 139, VIII: 112, 125, IX: 21, XIII: 174, XIV: 45.
Fitzgerald, G. B., VII: 104.
Fitzgerald, John ("Bard of the Lee"), II: 39.
Fitzgerald, Percy, I: 64, IV: 195.
Fitzgerald, [Rev.] Phillip (Irish Sermon), XIX: 144.
Fitzgerald, Professor (T.C.D.), XXXII: 144.
Fitzgerald, Professor (U.C.C.), XIV: 27.
Fitzgerald, [Rev.] T. A., (Obit.), XIII: 20.
Fitzgerald, T. D., VI: 97, 201, XIII: 167, XIV: 63.
Fitzgerald, [Rev.] W. (*Ellen Hanley: Or the True Story of the Colleen Bawn*), V: 221.
Fitzgerald, [Lord] Walter, XIV: 45.
Fitzgibbon, Philip, IX: 74, XVI: 51, 125.
Fitzpatrick, Hugh (Irish language), XXVIII: 5.
Fitzpatrick, Samuel A. Ossory (Obit.), IX: 140.
Fitzpatrick, [Dr.] Thomas, III: 134, 152, IV: 89, XXI: 90.
Fitzpatrick, William John,VI: 94; (debt to Luke Cullen), XVII: 57; (A Busy Biographer), X: 27, XXIV: 16, 63.
Fitzsimon, Elizabeth A., XII: (Obit.) 144.
Fitzsimons, [Fr.] James (on Don Jayme Nochera), XXVI: 113, 135.
"Fitzstewart, Bannside", IV: 165.
Five Young Ireland pamphlets, XVIII: 86.
Flaming Wheel, The (Sophia St. John Whitty), XV: 11.
Flannery, Thomas, (Obit.) VIII: 91.
Flannghaile, Tomás (trans. of O'Molloy's *Irish Grammar*), XVIII: 10.
Flapper, The (18th c. periodical), XVII: 61, 94-95.
Fleming, Canon, XIII: 40, 153.
Fleming, John [Irish Scribe and Scholar], (Canon Power) XXV: 77.
Fleming, J. P. (on Aubrey de Vere), XXIV: 42.
Fleming, J. S., VI: 30; (on MS on Irish Castles), XIX: 113.
Fleming, Thomas, IV: 22.
Fletcher, George, XIII: 153.
Flight of the Earls, The, VII: 52, 104, XVII: 119.
Flitter, Tatters and the Counsellor (Mrs. Hartley), XIX: 142, XX: 137.
Flood, J. M., IX: 84, XI: 61, XII: 82; (*Ireland: Its Saints and Scholars*) IX: 84; (*The Northmen in Ireland*) XXII: 24, 45;
Flood, William, XXXII: 93.
Flood, [Dr.] William Henry Gratten ["W.H.G.F."], (*Spirit of the Nation*) II: 175, 187-89; (*The Clongownian*) III: 9; (Vincent Wallace) IV: 40; (Dublin Printed Books) IV: 71; (William Todd Jones) IV: 93; V: 166; (reviews) V: 183; (Thomas Davis) VI: 62; (*Musical Opinion*) VI: 76; (*History of the Diocese of Ferns*) VI: 154, VII: 185; ("Kitty of Coleraine") VI: 168; (Apostolic Benediction) VI: 184; (*The Armagh Hymnal*) VII: 114, XII: 32; (Lewis Young) VIII: 88; (A Labour of Love) XI: 8; (*An Introductory Sketch*

of Irish Musical History) XI: 14; (*History of Enniscorthy*) XII: 64; (*John Field of Dublin*) XII: 108; (Wexford Printing) XII: 110-11; (*Ireland's Own Song Book*) XIII: 179; ("Kathleen Mavoureen") XIV: 39; (Obituary) XVII: 26; (Sundry) I: 90, II: 112, 124, 129, III: 24, 44, 47, 57, IV: 14, 53, 161, 209, VI: 119, 136, 170, VI: 190, VII: 116, 134, 188, VIII: 42, 68, IX: 32; XI: 57, 86, 137, XII: 15, 21, 144, XIII: 35, 86, 151, 166, 175, XIV: 32; 44, 76, 110, XV: 8, XVII: 30, 37.
Flower, Robin, II: 31; VIII: 65, XI: 67, 77, XVI: 2, XVII: 113; (*Poems and Translations*) XIX: 183; (*Catalogue of Irish Manuscripts in the British Museum*) XXIII: 45, XXXII: 91, 109, 148; (Obit., *The Times*) XXX: 13-14; (*The Irish Tradition*) XXX: 115.
Floyd, Michael (*The Face of Ireland*), XXV: 107.
Flying Post, The, XII: 105.
Flying Wasp, The (Seán O'Casey), XXV: 70.
"F.M.", X: 109.
Fods, John S., IV: 77.
Focal Molta, XXXI: 96.
Fogarty, Lily, X: 62.
Foghludha, Risteard ["Fiachra Eilgeach"], I: 130, XVI: 44, 45.
Fógra Polataíochta ón Naoú Aois Déag (Brian Ó Cuiv), XXXII: 33-35.
Folds, John S., IV: 77.
Foley, C. H., (*Loughrea Journal*), XXI: 13.
Folk of Furry Farm (Katherine Frances Purdon), V: 165.
Folk Song Society Journal (D. J. O'Sullivan & A. Martin Freeman), XIV: 109.

Folkliv (Internat. Journal of Ethnology & European Folklore), XXVII: 162.
Folk Tales of Brefny (B. Hunt), IV: 122.
Fond Opinions (Stephen Gwynn), XXVI: 45.
Foolish Lovers (St. John Ervine), XII: 36.
Football in Ireland (earliest reference), XVIII: 59.
For Daws to Peck At (Monk Gibbon), XVII: 67.
For Motherland (Randal McDonnell), VI: 39.
Forde, Samuel, XXIX: 137.
Fords, [Col.] Lionel, II: 144.
Foreign Periodicals, (Articles of Irish Interest), XXI: 2.
Foreman, Charles, VI: 117, 189.
Foreman, Stephen, III: 26.
Foreword to first issue of *I. B. L.*, I: 1
Forged, Anonymous and Suspect Documents (Capt. A. J. Quirke), XIX: 63.
Forgotten Irish Writers, XI: 13.
Forster, John, IV: 211.
Forthcoming Works, X: 20, XI: 14, 27, 47, 86, 104, 119, 140, XII: 23, 45, 88, 115-116, 141.
Foster, L. M. (*The Bush that Burned*), XIX: 147.
Foster, Lydia (*Tyrone Amongst Bushes*), XXII: 71.
Foucault, Roche (*Moral Maxims*), XXII: 2.
Foundation of Australia, The (Eris O'Brien), XXVI: 20.
Fountain of Magic, The (Frank O'Connor), XXVI: 144.
Four Green Fields, The (George O'Brien), XXV: 24.
Four Masters (dubious translation of), XX: 51; (Pól Breathnach); XX: 105, 106; XXII: 128;

(1450, 1454), XXIV: 31, 56.
Four Plays for Dancers (W. B. Yeats), XII.
Four Shots From Down, (Francis J. Bigger), X: 62-63.
Four Winds of Eirinn Poems, The (Ethna Carbery), X: 46-47.
Fourth Wise Man, The ("An Philibin"), XXIV: 22.
Four-line Stanza in Poem by Thomas Ewing, XVIII: 67.
Fowler, J. F., (printed pamphlet of 1861), XIX: 144.
Fowler, Joseph H., XXVI: 16, 115, 198.
Fox, Charlotte Milligan, VII: 191.
Fox, George, II: 150.
Fox, J. A., V: 85.
Fox, [Rev.] J. Spenser (*Pastoral Annals*), VII: 17.
Fox, Moireen [see "Chavasse, Claude"].
Fox, R. M. (*Rebel Irishwomen*), XXIV: 48.
Foy, [Rev.] Thomas (*Richard Crashaw, Poet and Saint*), XXIII: 30.
"F.R.R." (A Plea for Local History), XXX: 40.
Fragments of Meath History (Fr. Paul Walsh), XXI: 124.
Fragments (A. E. Green), XI: 115.
France—(Irish MSS in) I: 86; (Irish Brigade in) II: 114.
"Francis, M. E." [pseud. of Mary E. Sweetman, Mrs. Blundell], VII: 97.
"Francis McGann" (Irish song), XXVI: 29.
Franciscans—(The Franciscans' Library) IV: 3, 21; (History of Franciscans in Ireland) XVIII: 59; (facsimiles of 17th c. Franciscan Texts) XVIII: 87; (Franciscan Library, MS A30) XXVII: 4, 202; (Franciscan Library Acquisitions) XXVII: 182; (*Franciscan Preacher in Christ Church Cathedral, Dublin*) XXXI: 25.
Frankton [also Francton], John, III: 59, 109, IV: 82, 141.
Frangoch (with the Irish in), see Whitmore, W. J. Brennan.
Frankau Julia (psued. "Frank Danby"), VII: 167.
Franklin, Benjamin (visit to Ireland), XVIII: 145, XXVI: 40; (Samuel Johnson & Samuel Madden), XXVI: 98.
Fraser, Hugh, XII: 22.
Fraser, James, IV: 28.
Fraser, [Rev.] J., (*Irish Texts*), XX: 45; XXIII: 76.
Fraser's Magazine, IV: 28.
Frazer, Jean de Jean, XIII: 140.
Freedom [1922], XVIII: 31.
Freeman, A. Martin, XII: 114, XIII: 86.
Freeman's Journal, I: 13, 40, II: 2, 12, V: 77, XIX: 90-91.
French books on Irish Subjects (1801-1900), XVI: 42, 43, 59-61, 127.
French, Canon, V: 178.
French, Daniel, XIV: 32.
French, Lord, XIII: 116.
French, W. Percy, (Obit.) XI: 87, XII: 46, 118; (Poems) XIV: 47, XXIX: 20, 128.
Frenchman's Walk Through Ireland (Le Chevalier de Latocnaye), IX: 59.
Freyer, Dermot (*Not All Joy*), XXIII: 28.
Friel, Redmond (ed. *Paterson's Irish Song Book*), XXXII: 146.
Friends of the Library of T. C. D., XXX: 112.
From Far Lands—Poems of North and South ("Gervais Gage"), VI: 131.

From Prison Cells (Ben O'Hickey), XIX: 139.
From the Editor's Chair, XIV: 10, 25, 44, 56, 72, 91, 104, 121, 138.
From Ulster's Hills (Samuel K. Cowen), V: 101.
Fromme, Franz (*Irlands Kampf um die Freihheit*), XXII: 94.
Frost, James, I: 130.
"Fudge in Ireland" (Andrew Meredith Graham & Patrick Fitzpatrick), V: 81.
Fuinn na Smol—Fr.Walsh's Song Irish Books (Fr. Patrick Walsh), VII: 33.
Fuller, James Franklyn *Omniana: Autobiography of an Irish Octogenerian*), VIII: 16, XI: 97; XII: 29; XV: (Obit.) 29; XXXII: 12.
Fuller, Samuel, XVII: 48, 61.
Furlong, Alice ("Some Memories" by K. O'Brennan), XXX: 105, 106; (*Easter 1916*) XXX: 107, 108;
Furlong, [Rev.] Johnathan, IV: 57.
Furniss, Harry, III: 91, 136, XI: 27, 51.
Fyfe, Hamilton (*T. P. O'Connor*), XXII: 93.
"F.W.P.", XII: 87, 115, 140.
"F.X.B.", X: 43.

G

"G.A.", I: 109, 151, 169, III: 61, 112.
Gadelica (T. F. O'Rahilly), IV: 143, V: 124.
Gael óg ar Scoil (Antoine Ó Dochartaigh), XIV: 58.
Gael, The, IX: 110; (Edward Lysaght), XII: 16-18.
Gaelic Athletic Association (Bibliography of), XVII: 97-98; see also Athletics, Irish.
Gaelic Churchman, The, (A bilingual periodical) X: 87.
Gaelic Genealogies of the Plunkets, XXV: 50.
Gaelic League, The, II: 11.
Gaelic Literature Surveyed (Aodh de Blácam), XVII: 69.
Gaelic Manuscripts (Dr. Crone's), XXII: 27.
Gaelic Pioneer, A (Rev. Euseby Digby Cleaver), XXIX: 28.
Gaelic Pioneers, Three, XXVIII: 16.
Gaelic Poets, XV: 51.
Gaelic printing, VI: 194; (*Gaelic Books*) XV: 25; (the printer on) XVI: 62-63, 85-87; (Monotype Corporation) XVII: 38; (Type in *Lucerna fidelium*) XVIII: 17; (Earliest Gaelic type in Cork), XXXII: 144.
Gaelic Society of London, 1840 (Colm Ó Lochlainn), XXX: 80-84.
Gaeltacht in Nova Scotia, XXXII: 93.
Gaffney, [Rev.] M. H. (*The Story of St. Patrick*) XIX:153; (*Stories of Padraig Pearse*), XXIII: 149.
Gaillide, Seagan (*Láimh-scríbhinn*), XX: 82, 109, 132.
"Gairmscoile ag glaodhach na bhFilí chun Cúirt Éigse Chorcaighe" (Conchubar Ó Cuilleanáin), XXVIII: 25.
"Gairmscoile ó Chúirt Éigse Chorcaighe" (Conchubar Ó Cuilleanáin), XXVIII: 73.
Gallagher, Frank [pseud. "David Hogan"] (*The Challenge of the Sentry*) XVI: 112; (*Days of Fear*) XVI: 111; (*Literature of the Conflict, 1922-23*) XVIII: 69; (*Dark Mountain*) XIX: 148.
Gallagher, [Bishop] James, XVII:

116; (Bibliography of his *Irish Sermons*), XVIII: 28; (his Irish Sermons), XIX: 144.
Gallchubhair (Septs of Muintear), XXVII: 194.
Galligan, Peter, XIII: 5, XVII: 10-11, 23, 102.
Gallup, Donald (*T. S. Eliot: A Bibliography*), XXXII: 43.
Galway Catechism, (Nicholaus Antoinus O'Kenny) XIX: 100, 124.
"Galway, Conor" (*Towards the Dawn*), XI: 99.
Galway County Libraries (*Annual Report and Supplementary Catalogue*), XIX: 152, XX: 141.
Galway—(printing in) II: 50, IV: 69, X: 9, XIV: 76; (Trade Tokens) III: 75; (*Galway Weekly Register*) XIX: 90-91; *Galway Chronicle*, XIX: 90-91; (in Trollope) XVIII: 46.
Galwey, John (*Láimhsgribhinn Sheálin Gaillighe*), XXI: 28, 54, 76.
Gamble, [Dr.] John, I: 20, IV: 7.
Gaodhal, An (American Gaelic periodical), XX: 82, 109, 132.
Gaodhlach, Tadhg, VIII: 43.
Garahan, Isabel (trans. *In Emmet's Day*), XIX: 64.
Garden by the Sea, A (William Barry), X: 51.
Garden of the Sun (Albert Ernest Stafford Smythe), XIV: 108.
Garryowen (Henry de Vere Stacpoole), I: 106.
Garstin, John Ribton, II: 2, 4, 99, IX: 16, 102.
Garvin, J. L., XIV: 26.
Garvin, [Mrs.] J. L., XV: 8.
Gaskin, Catherine (*With Every Year*), XXXI: 47.
Gaultier, Barony of (history), IV: 208.

"Gautimozin", IV: 107.
Gavan Duffy, see Duffy, Charles Gavin.
Gavan, George, V: 63.
Gaynor, John P., VI: 75.
"G.C." (on John O'Hart), XVIII: 53.
Gealacain, Peadar, XXVI: 36.
Gearrbhaile (Eanair, 1930), XVIII: 95.
Geary, Eugene, VI: 191.
Genders, Roy (*Holiday in Dublin*), XXXI: 48.
Genealogy—(O'Reilly Family) XXIII: 85; (of Irish poet), XXV: 58; (Gaelic Plunkets) XXV: 50; (Clann Fhirbhisigh) XXVII: 227; (John Brady), XXX: 16-17; (*Simple Guide to Irish Genealogy*), XXVI: 68.
General Evening Post, XIII: 95.
General John Regan (George Birmingham), IV: 190.
General Post Office, XXXII: 67.
Geographical Society of Ireland, The (Swan, H. P.), XXX: 45, 140.
Geoghegan, A. G. ("Monks of Kilcrea"), II: 150.
George IV's Visit, XIII: 11, 38.
George, David Lloyd, see Lloyd George, David.
Georgian Mansions in Ireland (T. U. Sadlier), VI: 203.
Georgian Society, The, I: 28.
Geraldus Cambrensis, see Giraldus.
German—(*Germans in Cork*) IX: 53; (Dublin-printed German newspaper,1786) XVIII: 88; (German Script in Irish Printing) XXX: 89-91; ("German" Script in Irish Printing) XXX: 89-91; (German publications on Ireland) XXXI: 13, 87; (German Literature on Napper Tandy)

XXXI: 108, 109; (18th & 19th German translations in Dublin) XXXII: 93; (German mock catalogue of 17th c. Irish books) XXXII: 102.
"Gervais Gage" [pseud. of J. Lawrence Rentoul], VI: 131.
Geschichte Irlands (Rudolf Bringmann), XXVII: 166.
Gethin, Grace, XIII: 11.
Getty, Edmund, VIII: 88, 113, 116.
Getty, John, II: 149.
Ghost of Watty Cox, The, V: 106.
Ghost Stories (Irish), V: 90.
Ghloine Draoidheachta, An, XXIII: 156.
Gibbings, Robert (*Lovely is the Lee*) XXX: 21; (*Coconut Island*) 93. XXXI.
Gibbon, Monk, (*For Daws to Peck At*) XVII: 67; (*The Seals*) XXIII: 55.
Gibbon, Skeffington, VIII: 18; (Goldsmith Country) XXII: 58; XXXII: 18, 104.
Gibbons, John (*Tramping Through Ireland*), XVIII: 64.
Gibbons, Margaret, IV: 105.
Gibbs, J. T., XVII: 117.
Gibbs, [Sir] Philip, XIV: 64.
Gibson, [Dr.] J. Hill, II: 94.
Gibson, William, VI: 8.
Giffard, [Sir] A. H., IV: 38.
Gifford, Grace [Mrs. Joseph Plunkett], XI: 62.
Gilbert, [Sir] John (*History of Dublin*) II: 6; III: 154, 172, IV: 9, X: 54; (birthplace of Fr. O'Molloy) XVIII: 11; (Lady Gilbert) XIII: 22; (Gilbert's Facsimiles) XXII: 147.
Gildea, [Canon] William L. (Obit.), VI: 82.
Gildea, [Sir] James (Obit.), XII: 88.

Gillespie, Joshua, IX: 138.
Gillespie, [Sir] Robert Rollo, III: 173, XII: 111.
Giraldus Cambrensis, XIV: 58, XV: 25; (*Topography of Ireland*), XXXII: 23.
Girdle of Song, A (ed. Edith M. Fry), XXIX: 120.
Girouard, Lady Blanche (*The World Is For the Young*), XXIV: 23.
Given, Thomas, IX: 36.
"G.W.K.", III: 173.
Glamour of Waterford (Alan Downey), XIII: 154.
Gladstone, William, XV: 40.
Glasnevin (historic graves), VII: 50.
Glastonbury, VII: 41.
Gleeson, L. P. (whole day auction at Limerick) XXIV: 127; (*Poets of Ireland*), XXVI: 112.
Glenmore, Co. Wicklow, (printing in) XIV: 110.
Glenmornan (Patrick MacGill), X: 40.
Glensman, The (Belfast periodical), XIX: 164.
Globe, The, XII: 133.
Glories of Ireland, The (Joseph Dunn & P. J. Lennox, eds.), VI: 149.
Glover, Jimmy (*Jimmy Glover— His Book*), III: 44.
Glynn, John, VII: 119.
Glynn, W. John, IV: 147.
"Gobán Saor" (*Economics for Ourselves*), XXII: 145.
Goblet, Y. M., (*La Transformation de la géographie politique de l'Irlande au xvii siècle*) XIX:64; (*Les Noms de Lieux Irlandais dans l'oeuvre géographique de Sir W. Petty*) XIX: 64.
Godfrey, Mary D., V: 219.
Godkin, James, I: 162, II: 117,

118, 145, XI: 21, XIII: 114.
Godley, A. D. (*Lyra Frivola*), XIV: 111; (Obit.), XV: 55.
Godley, [Gen.] Alexander (*Life of an Irish Soldier*), XXVII: 167.
Goethe, Johann Wolfgang von (knowledge of Irish scientists), XXXII: 84.
Gogan, Liam S. (*Dánta agus Duanoga*), XVIII: 151.
Gogarty, Oliver St. John, XII: 33, XIV: 32, XXVI: 48; (*I Follow Saint Patrick*) XXVI: 48, XXXI: 120; XXVI: 116.
Gogarty, Thomas, V: 75, 179, VI: 12.
Goggin, Stephen (Monaghan printer), IV: 200.
Going Home (Patrick MacGill), III: 145.
Golden Barque, The (Seumas O'Kelly), XI: 59.
Golden Legends of the Gael (Maud Joynt), XV: 32.
Golden Treasury of Irish Verse (Lennox Robinson), XV: 31.
Golding (the surname), XXVII: 211.
Goldsmith, Oliver I: 167; II: 44, 45, 56, 89; IV: 194; V: 145; (Goldsmith Commemoration) V: 175-77; IX: 49; XII: 87; XV: 5; (Bicentenary) XVI: 75; XVII: 52-53, 136; (Note on Ancestors) XVIII: 118; (List of works on) XVIII: 43, 119; (Poem not Included in *Collected Works*) XVIII: 124; (A forgotten poem by) 166; (Goldsmith Country) XXII: 58; (ballad singers and) XXV: 15; ("Deserted Village" in Irish) XXXII: 49; (Letter to Richard Bryanton) XXXII: 130.
Goliardic Rime, A (Adrian Ross), XXXI: 36, 66.
Good, James Winder, IX: 31, 56,
XI: 45, 77; (*Irish Unionism*) XII: 45; XII: 84, XIV: 79; (Obit.) XVIII: 75.
Good-bye Twilight (Leslie H. Daiken), XXV: 43.
Goodman Collection of Irish Music, XXXII: 40, 137.
Goodman, [Rev.] James, XVI: 34.
Good Old Rule, the Simple Plan, The (Thomas Becher & Richard Cox), XIX: 133.
Goold, Thomas, VIII: 72.
Gordon, Alexander, VI: 112, XIX: 71.
Gordon, Eustace, VI: 136.
Gordon, Lady (*The Winds of Time*), XXII: 73.
Gordon, Seton, (*Islands of the West*) XXI: 97; (*Highways and Byways in the Western Highlands*) XXIV: 18.
Gore-Booth, Eva, VI: 111; (*Poems of*) XVIII: 182; (*The Sword of Justice*) X: 46-47.
Gorey (printing in), XIV: 100.
Gortin Private Press, IX: 8, 60.
Gossip (in *I. B. L.*), XIV: 5, 20, 37. 52, 67.
Goudy, Henry (Obit.), XII: 143.
Gough, John, I: 157; (*Tour in Ireland*) II: 48, 62, 76; (*The Topographer*) XIII: 35, 64.
Government Advertising in Dublin Newspapers, XVII: 80.
Government Printing in Waterford, XXXI: 12.
Government of Northern Ireland, The (Nicholas Mansergh), XXV: 65.
Gowdie, [Rev.] Robert, III: 197, IV: 17, 53.
Goyer, May, III: 135.
Grace, George, XVII: 39-42, 91.
Grace, Sheffield, VII: 89, 118, XIX: 175.
Grady, Thomas, VII: 188.

Graignamanagh Abbey (Patrick, William & John O'Leary), XV: 43.
Graham, [Canon] C. Irvine, III: 43.
Graham, Walter, III: 193.
Graham, William, III: 101.
Grainne Mhaol (Fulmar Petrel [Rev. W. S. Green]), XXVI: 60.
Graiseberry, Printer (libel action against), XVIII: 24.
Grammatica Latino-Hibernica [1677] (Fr. Frances O'Molloy), XXXII: 101, 141.
Grass of Parnassus ("An Philibin"), XXIV: 119.
Grattan, [Rt. Hon.] Henry, IV: 209, XII: 22, 51,
Grattan Flood, William Henry, see Flood, W. H. G.
Graves, Alfred Percival, I: 73, 74, 112, 113, 124, 132, 156; II: 73, 154, 174; III: 73; (Celtic Nature Poetry), 94-96; 137; (Father O'Flynn), III: 165; 174, IV: 10, 65, 198, 202, V: 1, 9, 196, 197, VI: 71, 73, 77, 79; (*Instructions of King Cormac—The Irish Solomon*) VI: 121; 204; VII: 62, 95, 129, 156, VIII:79, 83, 109, 132; (*A Celtic Psaltery*) IX: 58; XII: 90, XIII: 99, 168, XIV: 35, 56, 78, 94, 96, XV: 27, 55, 64, XVII: 3; *To Return to All That*) XVIII: 147; (Obit.) XX: 2; (*The Irish Fairy Book*) XXIII: 124.
Graves, Arnold, VI: 212, VII: 30.
Graves at Kilmorna, The (Canon Sheehan), VI: 148.
Graves, Charles L., II: 54; (*The Blarney Ballads*) IV: 197; V: 29, VII: 61, IX: 104.
Graves, Clotilde, VI: 156.
Graves Family (literary tradition), XVIII: 2.
Graves, [Rev.] James, XVI: 7.

Graves, O. L., IV: 205,
Graves, [Capt]. Robert (*Over the Brasier*), VIII: 17; IX: 56.
Gray, Edmund Dwyer XX: 15.
Gray, G. J., IV: 65.
Gray, Henry, IX: 1311.
Greacan, Nathaniel, IV: 290.
Greacen, Robert & Valentine Iremonger (*Contemporary Irish Poetry*), XXXI: 46.
Great Blasket, The, XI: 67
Great Contemporaries (Essays by Various Hands), XXIII: 55.
Great Irish Book Collectors & Collections—VII: 1, 21, 38, 59, 89 107, 180; (Thomas Willis) X: 5; (Sir John T. Gilbert), X: 56; (Dr. R. R. Madden) X: 82; XII: 99-101.
Great Irishmen in War and Politics & *Green and Gold* (both Felix Lavery), XII: 85.
Green, A. E. (*Fragments*), XI: 115.
Green, Alice Stopford [Mrs. J. R. Green], I: 48, 133, II: 158, III: 211, IV: 137, V: 7, X: 14, XIV: 46, XV: 23, 60, 64, XVII: 51; (*The Old Irish World*) III: 211.
Green, George Arthur (Obit.), XIII: 20-21.
Green-covered Monthly, The, IV: 111.
Greene, Alex., XIV: 58.
Greene, George A., XIII: 11, 20, 39.
Greene, Henry Plunket, (*From Blue Danube to Shannon*) XXIII: 27; (*Charles Villiers Stanford*) XXIII: 96.
Greene, Plunket, VIII: 47, 110.
Greenough, [Dr.] C. N., (Defoe's *Review*), XXI: 123.
Greer, Henry, VI: 6.
Greer, James, V: 45.
Gregg, Fortescue, XVII: 2.

Gregory, [Lady] Augusta, II: 155, III: 211, IV: 178; 190, 194, V: 125, VIII: 19, XI: 8; (*Kiltartan Poetry Book*) XI: 133; 135, XII: 84, 119; (*My First Play*) XVIII: 149.
Gregory, Padraic, III: 187, IV: 194, V: 16; ("Two Love Songs") V: 42; 140, 205, VI: 11 22; (*Love Sonnets*) VI: 60; VIII: 130, IX: 79, XI: 98; ("A Song Unsung") XII: 6; (Some Contemporary Irish Poets) XII: 71; (*Complete Collected Ballads*) XXIV: 45.
Greig, J. Y. T. (*Thackeray: A Reconsideration*), XXXI: 117.
Grey Feet of the Wind (Cathal O'Byrne), IX: 34.
Greys, (Dublin Engravers), III: 91.
Grierson, [Mrs.] Constantia, II: 136, 161, 179.
Griffard, Stanley Rees (*Irish Election Law*), XXXII: 39.
Griffin, Gerald [novelist], I: 168, II: 17; (Griffin MSS transcribed), XIX: 69.
Griffin, Gerald [translator] (*Gabriele d'Annunzio*), XXIV: 93.
Griffin, Martin Ignatius Laurence (Obit.), III: 101, 115.
Griffith, Amyas, I: 136, 154, VII: 186; (Amyas Griffith's Press) XVII: 11.
Griffith, Arthur [Art Ó Gríóbhtha], VI: 82, 100, VII: 160, XIV: 28; (*Griffith and his Times*) XIV: 29; XVII: 83, 107.
Griffith, Henry, I: 77.
Grimshaw, Beatrice, V: 57.
Grinne, Mhaol, XXVI: 60.
Grogan, L., VI: 133.
Grose, D. C., II: 151.
Grose, [Capt.] Francis, XXX: 56.
Grosjean, Paul, XXXII: 114.

Group of Nation-Builders (Patrick M. MacSweeney), V: 66, XVI: 13.
Grove's Dictionary of Music, II: 85, 86.
Guardian and Constitutional Advocate, XVII: 2.
Gu de tha mi leughadh? (Aonghas Mac Mhatbain), XXXI: 39-42.
Guests of The Nation (Frank O'Connor), XIX: 179.
Guide to Books for Social Students and Workers (Alfred Rahilly), VII: 186.
Guide to Books on Ireland, (Fr. Brown's proposal), I: 81, 102; ("Reader's Guide"), II: 57, 161, 181, 198; III: 150.
Guide to Irish Genealogical Collections, A [*Analecta Hibernica, VII*] (Seamus Pender), XXIV: 70.
Guide to Monasterboice (R.A.S. Macalister), XXX: 70.
Guinan, John, (*The Cuckoo's Nest*) XXI: 47; (Obit.) XXX: 11-12.
Guiney, Louise Imogen, (Obit.) XII: 89.
Guinness Family, The, VIII: 117.
Guinness, Bryan [Lord Moyne] (*A Fugue of Cinderellas*), XXXII: 149.
Guinness, Henry S., VIII: 89, XVI: 19, 22, 53.
Guinness, [Dr.] Henry Grattan (Obit.), II: 8.
"G.W.K.", III: 173.
Gwynn, Aubrey (Burke's presentation copy to Mary Shackleton), XXIX: 84.
Gwynn, Denis, VI: 184, XII: 71, 108, 118, XIV: 44, 48, XV: 61; (*Edward Martyn and the Irish Revival*) XVIII: 176; (*Memories of Tom Kettle*) XXII: 71; (*The

O'Gorman Mahon) XXIII: 18; (*The Life and Death of Roger Casement*) XXIV: 120; (*The Vatican and War in Europe*) XXVII: 287; (*Young Ireland and 1848*) XXXI: 68.

Gwynn, [Dr.] John (The Book of Armagh), VI: 48.

Gwynn, Stephen, (*Collected Poems*) XIX: 155; (*Burgundy*) XXIII: 18; (*Captain Scott*) XXII: [70l]; (*Claude Monet and His Garden*) XXII: 74; (*The Charm of Ireland*) XXII: 122; (*Mungo Park and the Niger*) XXIII: 26; (*Ireland in Ten Days*) XXIII: 98; (*Happy Fisherman, The*) XXIV: 138; (*Oliver Goldsmith*) XXIV: 138; (*Irish Literature and Drama*) XXV: 16; (*River to River: A Fisterman's Pilgrimage*) XXVI: 21; (*Scattering Branches*) XXVII: 262; (*The Book of Armagh*) XXIX: 77; (*Aftermath*) XXX: 70. (Sundry), I: 8, 30, 58, 62, 112, II: 90, 96, 124, IV: 111, 132, VI: 184, VII: 99, XI: 27, 44, 59, XII: 108, XIII: 93, 98, XIV: 11, 32, XV: 16, 28, 51, XXVI: 43, 45.

H

Hackett, Francis, X: 62; (*Story of the Irish Nation*) XV: 30, 54; (*Francis I*) XXIII: 26.

Hackett, James Dominick, XIII: 155; (*The Normans in Ireland*) XX: 14; XXI: 20; (*Home Sweet Home*) XXIV: 15; (*The Sunburst*), XXIV: 63.

Hackett, Florence, XIV: 103.

Hae, Ristéard de (*Clár Litridheacht na Nua-Ghaedhilge*), XXVI: 25.

Haes, Ger. M. J. (*Tobar Mhuire*), XXV: 112.

Hailstorms (unusual), XIX: 37.

Haliburton, Judge, IV: 173.

Haliday, Charles, VII: 121; (Pamphlet collection) VII: 121.

Haliday, William, XVII: 6; (Irish-language revivalist) XXI: 20, XXVI: 104.

Hall, Samuel Carter, III: 96.

Hall, [Mrs.] Samuel Carter [Anna Maria], II: 149.

Halliday, Bernard, II: 197.

Hallow-E'en and Poems of the War (W. M. Letts), VIII: 107.

Halpine, Charles Graham (pseud. "Miles O'Reilly"), XXXII: 65, 88, 139; (Abraham Lincoln) XXXII: 65; 88, 139.

Halsbury, Lord, XIII: 113.

Haly, James, XXI: 66.

Hamilton, Cicely (*Modern Ireland*), XXIV: 48.

Hamilton, [Miss] C. J. (Obit.) XXIII: 83.

Hamilton, Edwin, III: 107, (Obit.) XI: 15.

Hamilton, [Lord] Ernest (*Irish Rebellion of 1641*), XII: 119.

Hamilton, F. B. (Matthew Butler) XXIX: 81.

Hamilton, [Lord] Frederick, XI: 58, XIII: 57.

Hamilton, G. Rostrevor (*The Search for Lonliness and Other Verses*), IX: 62.

Hamilton, [Lord] George VIII: 19.

Hamilton, Gustavus Everard (*An Account of the Honourable Society of King's Inns*), VII: 30.

Hamilton, James, VI: 190.

Hamilton, Joseph, XVII: 90, XX: 61, XX: 113, XXI: 134, XXII: 39, 66.

Hamilton, [Sir] W. R., II: 149.

Hamilton, William, VII: 121.

Hamilton, William Tighe, IV: 16.
Hamlet (A Dublin discovery), X: 81.
Hammond, Cyril (*Adventures in the Revolution and under the Consulate*), XVII: 67-68.
Hammond, J. L. (*Gladstone and the Irish Nation*), XXVI: 119.
Hamper of Humour, A ("Liam"), IV: 157.
Hanan, Mrs., II: 2.
Hancock, W. Neilson, XII: 53.
Handbook of Celtic Ornament, A (John G. Merne), XIX: 128.
Handbook of Kerry (Rev. H. L. L. Denny), XIV: 43.
Handy Book about Books (John Power), I: 4.
Hanley, [Rev.] Elly ("The Coolan"), XVIII: 24.
Hanna, James William, III: 137, IV: 92.
Hannay, [Canon] James Owen, V: 7, 18, 45; VII: 134; XII: 119, XIII: 89, 99, 179, XIV: 70. See also George Birmingham.
Hannon, W. B. (*Quaint Irish Bygones*) VIII: 66.
Hanrahan's Daughter (Patrick Purcell), XXIX: 24.
Hansard, John (Waterford Printer), XIX: 95.
Hansard, Joseph, XV: 42.
Hansard's Paliamentary Debates, XX: 49.
Happy Fisherman, The (Stephen Gwynn), XXIV: 138.
Hardebeck, Carl, (*Fuinn Fiadha Fuinidh*), XXV: 117.
Harden, [Rev.] Ralph William (Obit.), VI: 131.
Harder, Hermann (*Irische Hein, Kehr*), XXXI: 112.
Hardiman, James, (Irish MSS) III: 172; XVI: 28, 45, XXIII: 72.
Harding, Edward, IV: 176.

Harding, George, VI: 48.
Hardy, [Rev.] Edward John (Obit.), XII: 69.
Hardy, Francis, XXX: 126.
Hardy, Philip Dixon (printer), II: 150.
Hare, (*The Trial of Burke and Hare*), XIII: 34.
Hargadon, M. A. (*A Lovely Home*), VII: 31.
Harley, Robert, Hon., II: 13.
'Harp of Erin', VI: 101,
Harp, The, X: 43, 71, XVI: 67, 71, XVII: 22-23,79.
Harpers, see *Irish Harpers and Pipers*.
Harris, Frank (ed. periodicals), XVIII: 131, XIX: 107.
Harris MSS, XXVI: 112.
Harris, Nugent, XIV: 48.
Harris, S. M. (pseud. "Athene"), V: 11.
Harris, Walter, (Harris's Down) II: 12; (Ware's *History of the Bishops of Ireland*) XXXII: 39.
Harrison, Frederick, XIII: 84.
Harrison, [Capt.] Henry (*Parnell Vindicated*) XVIII: 154; (*Parnell, Joseph Chamberlain and Mr. Gavin*) XXVI: 65; (*Ulster and the British Empire*) XXVII: 180.
Hart, Henry, II: 8.
Hart, [Sir] Robert, I: 9, III: 39.
Harty, Hamilton (*Five Irish Poems*), XXVI: 117.
Harvard University Library, II: 12, 35.
Harvey, John (*Dublin*), XXXI: 94.
Harvey, [Rev.] William, XII: 111.
"Harvest, 1914" (Jane Barlow), VI: 46.
Harwood, Philip, I: 93, 108.
Haslette, John, II: 198.
Haslip, Joan, (*Parnell*) 23. XXV; (*Portrait of Pamela*) XXVII:

239.
Haughton, Samuel, XIII: 82.
Haverty, Patrick, XVII: 103-104.
Haviland, M. D., II: 14.
Hawkesworth, John, III: 137.
Haydn, Joseph (*Dictionary of Dates*), X: 3.
Haydon, Eric (*Rosanna*), XXI: 21.
Hayes, Edward, X: 68.
Hayes, [Sir] George, I: 91.
Hayes, [Sir] H. B., III: 215, IV: 73, 161, V: 202.
Hayes, James, I: 118, 146, 167, II: 88, 151, IV: 32, VII: 119, XI: 61.
Hayes, Richard J. ("*Irlande à Jamais*"), XIX: 139; (Secret Service during the 1803 Insurrection) XX: 113; (*Irish Swordsmen of France*) XXIII: 52; (*The Last Invasion of Ireland*) XXVI: 18; (*Old Irish Links with France*). XXVIII: 72,
Hayes, [Dr.] Thomas, IV: 197.
Hayman, [Rev.] Samuel, X: 36.
Hayward, Richard, (*Where the River Shannon Flows*) XXVII: 261; (*The Corrib Country*) XXIX: 44; (*Belfast Through the Ages*) XXXII: 44.
Hazlitt (of Bandon), V: 61. 201.
Hazlitt, William (Irish extraction), XVIII: 132.
Headlam, Cuthbert (*Knights Reluctant*), XXII: 123.
Healy, [Archbishop] John, IX: 111.
Healy, Cahir, XXXII: 149.
Healy, James J. (*Life and Times of Charles J. Kickham*), VII: 30.
Healy, T. M., VIII: 47, XIII: 82, XVI: 27; (Bibliography of) XIX: 36; (*Loyalty Plus Murder*) XIX: 36; (*Why Ireland is Not Free*) XIX: 36; (*hy There is an Irish Land Question*) XIX: 36.

Hearn, Lafcadio (I. & P. D. Perkin), XIX: 19; (J. S. Crone) XIX: 137.
Hearth Money Records, III: 117.
Hedge Schools, II: 131; ("Hedge" Schoolmasters in Ireland, 1824-34), XVII: 11.
Heimskringla or Lives of the Norse Kings, XX: 95.
Hemans, [Mrs.] Felicia, IV: 99.
Hempton, John, VII: 118.
Hempton, Mossom, IV: 91.
Henchy, Patrick (Librarian, N.L.I.), XXXII: 107.
Henderson, Henry, I: 109.
Henderson, John, VI: 6.
Henebry, [Rev.] Richard, XVI: 120; (*Dr. Henebry's Handbook of Irish Music*), XVII: 54.
Henley, Theodore, C., IV: 196.
Hennig, John, (Dublin-printed travel-book on Germany) XXXI: 131; XXXII: 16, 37, 39, 68, 84, 102, 112; XXX: 54, 55; (German Script in Irish Printing) XXX: 89-91; (Dutch Publications Relating to Ireland) XXX: 114; (Swift in Switzerland) XXX: 114; (German Publications Relating to Ireland) XXXI: 13, 87; (Schottenkloster of St. James, Ratisbon) XXXI: 79; (German Literature on Napper Tandy) XXXI: 108, 109.
Henry Quinn, M. D. (T. Percy C. Kirkpatrick), XI: 98.
Henry, Françoise, (*Early Christian Irish Art*), XXXII: 113, 114; (*Irish Art in the Early Christian Period*) XXVII: 283; (*La Scripture Irlandaise pendant les premiers XII Siècles de l'Ere Christienne*) XXI: 70.
Henry, [Dr.] James, VIII: 18.
Henry, James Maxwell (*A New Fundamentalism*), XXII: 96.

Henry, R. M. (*The Evolution of Sinn Féin*), XI: 132, 139.
Henry, Sam (McSparran's *Norman de Borgos*), XXII: 66; (Memoirs of Alexander Ross), XXII: 66.
Hepburn, David, III: 119, 138.
Herbert, Dorothy, XVII: 140.
Herbert, Jean (*Escape the River, and The Magnolia Flower*), XXXI: 119.
Herbert, Robert (18th c. Limerick Printing Venture), XXVIII: 104-12; (Bibliography of Michael Hogan) XXVII: 276; (Richard Bulkeley, Limerick poet) XXIX: 79; (*Limerick Printers and Printing*) XXIX, 120.
Herbison, David, II: 149.
Hermathena (T.C.D.), VI: 119.
Heron, [Rev.] James, IX: 140.
Heron, William, II: 58, 76.
Hessens Irisches Lexicon (Seamus Caomhnach, Rudolf Hertz et al), XXIV: 17, 119, XXII: 145.
Hewn of the Rock (Diarmuid Murphy), XXII: 75.
Hibernia, X: 93, 110.
Hibernia Dominicana (Thomas De Burgo), IX: 121, XIV: 116, 136, 143, XV: 23, XVI: 5, 66, 117, XVII: 9, XXII: 38, 67, XXVII: 259.
Hibernian Journal, XIX: 90-91.
Hibernian Magazine (Walker), XVIII: 57.
Hibernian Musical Review, IV: 14.
Hickey, Elizabeth (*The Legend of Tara*), XXXII: 70.
Hickey, Emily, IV: 153, 214, VI: 111, XIII: 141, XIV: 138.
Hickey, James, XVII: 118.
Hickey, Michael, VI: 77.
Hickey, [Rev.] William, IV: 34, V: 98, 220, VI: 13, 32, 102, X: 67,
XI: 65, 128.
Hickie (Bookseller), IV: 126.
Hiffernan, [Dr.] Paul, (List of Works) XIX: 19; (Note on Life and Writings) XIX: 11.
Higgins, F. R. (*The Gap of Brightness*), XXVII: 263.
Higgins, Paul, see Ó Huiginn, Pól.
Higginstown, Co. Westmeath, XXVI: 86.
Highways and Byways in the Western Highlands (Seton Gordon), XXIV: 18.
Higinbotham family, VIII: 139.
Hilditch, Neville (*In Praise of Ireland*), XXXII: 24.
Hill, Arthur, (Obit.), XII: 142.
Hill, [Rev.] George, III: 156, VII: 69.
Hillsborough, ("Hillsborough Club") IX: 110; (Hillsboro Library Sale) XV: 6.
Hillsiders (Seamus O'Kelly), XIII: 60.
Hinkson, H. A., VI: 59; (Obit.) X: 72.
Hinkson, Pamela, XVI: 26; (*The Light on Ireland*) XXIII: 153.
Hinton, Edward M., XXVI: 66, 67, 92.
Historical Ballad Poetry of Ireland (J. Brown), III: 168.
Historical Manuscripts Commission, see Manuscript Commisson.
Histories (civil, ecclesiastical & political)—(*History of N. S. Presbyterian Church*) VI: 79; (*History of the Bishops*) II: 3; (*History of the Irish State*) XV: 60; (materials for history of Dunlavin), XVII: 61; (*History of the Times*) XXIII: 123; *History of Ireland in 18th Century* (W. E. H. Lecky), I: 17.
History and Antiquities of Inis

Cealtra, The (Prof. R. A. S. Macalister) VIII: 11.
History (local)—(*History of Dublin*) II: 6(*History of Magherafelt*) IX: 34; (*History of Enniscorthy*) XII: 64; *History of Enniskillen*) XII: 63-65; (*History of Galway*) XVI: 28; (*History of Howth*) XVII: 15; (*History of Kilkenny*) XVII: 15
History of Minterburn and Town of Caledon John J. Marshall), XIV: 31.
History of Steevens' Hospital, The (T. P. C. Kirkpatrick), XIV:107.
History of the Diocese of Ferns (W. H. Gratten Flood), VII: 185.
History of the Pigeon House (Colm Ó Lochlainn), XXVI: 84.
History of 1847 Famine, I: 26, 88.
Hitchcock, Fr., V: 216.
Hoare, Dorothy M. (*The Works of Morris and Yeats in Relation to Early Saga Literature*), XXV: 112.
Hobson, C. I. (Obit.), XIII: 146.
Hodges & Figgis, (Booksellers), XVIII: 14.
Hodgkin's Irish MSS, XX: 138.
Hoey, Christopher Clinton, III: 192.
Hoey, William, IX: 130, 139.
Hogan, C. B. (*Shakespeare in the Theatre, 1701-1750*), XXXII: 7.
"Hogan, David" [pseud. of Frank Gallagher], see Gallagher, Frank.
Hogan, [Rev.] Edmund (*Onomasticon Goedilicum*), IV: 8, IX: 64; (Obit.) XII: 6; XXI: 43.
Hogan, James (*Modern Ireland in the European System*), XII: 45.
Hogan, John (sculptor), II: 17.
Hogan, [Rev.] John F. (Obit.), X: 95; XV: 6.

Hogan, Michael ("Bard of Thomond"), XIII: 144; (Bibliography of) XXVII: 276, XXVIII: 135.
Hogg, R. M., VI: 152, VIII: 18.
Hoist, A. Roland (*Deirdre En De Zonen Van Usnach*), XXXI: 90.
Holberg, Ludvig (*Introduction to Universal History*), XXXII: 38.
Holbrook, Jackson (*The Anatomy of Bibliomania*), XXXI: 115.
Holland, Denis, VI: 46, VIII: 67.
Holland, J. C. (Obit.), XIII: 146.
Holloway, Joseph, IV: 92, V: 69, VI: 80, 190, X: 59, XI: 118; (The Late Joseph Holloway), XXIII: 15, 93.
Hollywood Cemetery (Liam O'Flaherty), XXIV: 22.
Holmes, Robert, I: 168.
Holiday in Dublin (Roy Genders), XXXI: 48.
Holy Ireland (Nora Hoult), XXIV: 22.
Homas, Ralph, I: 2, 46, 77.
Home is the Hero (Walter Macken), XXXII: 48.
Home Life in Ireland (Robert Lynd), II: 25.
Home Rule Movement, The (Michael MacDonagh), XI: 97.
Home Sweet Home (James Hackett), XXIV: 15.
"Home Thoughts" (P. J. O'Reilly), VI: 14.
Homespun Yarns While the Kettle and Cricket Sing (Rev. T. A. Fitzgerald), V: 200.
Hone, Joseph Maunsell, IV: 8, VII: 74, 160, XII: 15, XIII: 44, 149, 152, 179; (with Mario Rossi, *Bishop Berkeley*) XIX: 158; (*W. B. Yeats*) XXIX: 47; (*The Moores of Moore Hall*) XXVII: 191; (*The Life of George Moore*) XXIV: 143.

The Irish Book Lover 279

Honest Printer, XXVII: 209.
Hope, Henry, XIV: 78.
Hope, Luke Mullen, III: 115.
"Hop't She", (query about the song), VIII: 68.
Hore, Herbert F., XXVIII: 6, 27.
Horgan, [Fr.] Matthew, XVI: 4, 5.
Horgan, John J. (*Parnell to Pearse*), XXXI: 22.
Horner, John, XI: 14.
Hospital Libraries (Library Association on), XIX: 130.
Hoult, Nora (*Holy Ireland*), XXIV: 22.
Hounds of Banba (Daniel Corkery), XII: 82
House of Cards (Alice Curtayne), XXVII: 285.
House of Commons, XIV: 62.
House of Gladness (Kay O'Kelly), XIV: 90.
Houston, Edward, XVII: 143.
How the Bissets Came, XXIII: 36.
Howard, L. G. Redmond, VIII: 35.
Howard-Jones, J., V: 51.
Howe, Gerald (*Retrospection of Dorothea Herbert*), XVII: 140.
Howitt, Mary, II: 170.
Howth and its Owners, VIII: 136.
Howth (materials for a history of), XVII: 15.
"H.T.", I, 57, 112, 124.
"Huberto" (The Ghost of Dunboy Castle), XXI: 99.
Hudson, Henry, XVI: 33.
Hudson, W. E., II: 187.
Hue and Cry (*Pigott's Directory*), XIX: 90-91.
Huggins, H. C. (*Roadside Fancies*), X: 15.
Huggins, Lady, VI: 153.
Hugh Bryan—The Autobiography of an Irish Rebel (Rev. Samuel Anderson), X: 67.
Hughes, Herbert, XIV: 26.
Hughes, Tom ("Tom Brown"), XXXII: 32.
Hull, [Prof.] Edward, IX: 62.
Hull, Eleanor, II: 42, 194, IV: 86, 185, 203, VI: 3, 37, 89, 162, VII: 41, 81, 173, VIII: 37, 61, 79, XIII: 98, XV: 9; (Obit.) XXIII: 82.
Hull, [Rev.] J. D. (*The Lake and Other Poems*), III: 82, 103.
Humanitas, XVIII: 63.
Human Nature, This (Charles Duff), XVIII: 177.
Humour of Ireland (Charles L. Graves), VII: 61.
Humphreys, A. L., X: 107.
Hundred Years Ago, A, XII: 51.
Hunger, The, (Mildred Darby) I: 133, 150.
Hungry Grass, The (Donagh MacDonagh), XXX: 119.
Hunt, B. (*The Folk Tales of Brefny*), IV: 122.
Hunter, Arthur, VII: 14.
Hunter's Dublin Chronicle; or, Universal Journal, XII: 104-106.
Hussey, Walter (Thomas Ewing, "Ode to..."), XVIII: 67.
Hutch, [Archdeacon] William, IX: 16.
Huth Library, IX: 57.
Hutton, Annie (Irish Mediæval Translations from the Classics), II: 147.
Hyacinth Halvey (Lady Gregory), XVIII: 51.
Hyacinthe O'Gara (Rev. George Brittaine), I: 153, 171, XI: 14.
Hyde, [Rev.] Arthur (sermon) XXXI: 76.
Hyde, Douglas, III: 7, VII: 62, (*The Conquests of Charlemagne*) XI: 60; (*Legends of Saints and Sinners*), VII: 62.
Hynes, Michael J. (*The Mission of Rinuccini*), XX: 144.

I

I.B.L., see *Irish Book Lover*.
I Knock at the Door (Seán O'Casey), XXVI: 96.
I Will Go Back (Patrick MacGill), IV: 21.
Iberno-Celtic Society, XVI: 117.
Idman, N., V: 149, VI: 8.
"If I Should Die Tonight" (in Richard Haggard's *Jess*), XII: 80, 107.
"If this Book..." (jingle), XXIX: 92.
Image, The (Lady Gregory), IV: 190.
"Imaginary Lover, The", (Anon.) XXXI: 58.
Imitatio Christi [Imitation of Christ], (Dublin printing) XVII: 118; XXVII: 183, 280.
Imithe (Dán), XXXII: 25.
In Clay and in Bronze (Brinsley MacNamara), XXVII: 231.
In Dark and Evil Days (Francis Sheehy Skeffington), VIII: 86.
In Emmet's Day (trans. Isabel Garahan), XIX: 64.
In Galway (Ethel Rolt Wheeler), IV: 118.
In Land of Youth (James Stephens), XIV: 140.
In Mr. Knox's Country (Somerville & Ross), VII: 29.
In Old Belfast (L. R. Crescent), XIV: 141.
In Times of Peril (Linda Kearns), XIV: 29.
In Vinculis—With the Irish in Frongoch (W.J. Brennan Whitmore), IX: 80.
Incunabula in Ireland, VI: 144.
Independent Irish Parliament, XIII: 14.
Independent Irishman, The (Rare Dublin Periodical), XII: 104.

Indexes, Indexers and Books—(Indexing) II: 6, 73; (The Index Society) II: 7; (Index to periodicals) XIII: 110; (Indexes, Indexers and Books) XXIII: 2; (indexes to *I.B.L.*) XXIII: 4, 129; (An Irish-American Lexicographer) XXIII: 91; (American Reference Works) XXIII: 94; (*Sgéala o'n Domhan Thiar*) XXIII: 106; (Irish Classical Dictionary) XXIII: 117; (Pedigrees in preparation) XXIII: 130; (Obit.) XXIV: 1; (Suggestions for a Phrase Dictionary) XXIV: 2; (*Piers Plowman and Ireland*) XXIV: 3
Industry in Ireland, II: 147.
Informers, (pamphlet), VIII: 18.
Ingram, John Kells, XVII: 63-117.
Iniscarra, XVI: 5.
Inis-Eoghain and its Crosses, (F. R. Bigger) VII: 136.
Inisfail, (Magazine) XX: 66.
Initial Letters, III: 59.
Innishowen VIII: 140
Innisheeny (George Birmingham), XII: 65.
Inishfallen Fare Thee Well (Seán O'Casey), XXXI: 44.
Inniskilling Dragoons (records) I: 18.
Innocent III (Pope), II: 4.
Inscrutable Lovers, The (Alexander MacFarlan), XI: 82.
"Inspiration" (Francis J. McSwiggan), IX: 81.
Instructions of King Cormac—The Irish Solomon (Alfred Perceval Graves), VI: 121.
Insula Sanctorum (author), XX: 140,
Insula Sanctorum [Isle of Saints] XXI: 20.
Insurrection (Liam O'Flaherty), XXXI: 117.

The Irish Book Lover 281

Insurrection in Dublin (James Stephens), VIII: 64.
Insurrection of 1798, III: 197.
Insurrection of 1803, III: 72, 102; XXVIII: 44.
Insurrections (James Stephens), I: 19.
International Index of Catholic Biographies, XXIV: 48.
Invincibles (Dublin street ballads on), XXXI: 2.
Iomarbhagh na Bhfileadh: The contention of the Bards, (ed., [Rev.] L. McKenna) XII: 63.
Ireland, (Ireland and Louvain) XI: 63; (MSS relating to), IV: 64; (query on rivers), XIII: 139; (Ireland and Secret Printing), I: 27, 150.
Ireland (Dr. Von Julius Pokorny), XI: 84.
Ireland: A Study in Nationalism (Francis Hackett), X: 62.
Ireland: A Song of Hope (Padraic Gregory), IX: 79.
Ireland Among the Nations (Basil Clancy), XXX: 118.
Ireland and France (Alfred Dunquel), VIII: 39.
Ireland and the Early Church (J. M. Flood), XII: 82.
Ireland and the Imperial Conference (F. S. Oliver), VIII: 135.
Ireland and the Irish (Charles Duff), XXXII: 44.
Ireland and the Knights of Malta, XXVI: 137.
Ireland for Everyman (H. A. Piehler), XXVI: 69.
Ireland, France, and Prussia (John Mitchel), IX: 110.
Ireland Illustrated (periodical of 1844), XXXII: 15.
Ireland in London (periodical), IV: 11.
Ireland in the Last Fifty Years (Ernest Baker), VIII: 134.
Ireland in Travail (Joice M. Nankivell & Sydney Loch), XIV: 29.
Ireland, Its Humour and Pathos (Rev. J. Irwin Brown), I: 135.
Ireland: Its Saints and Scholars (J. M. Flood), IX: 84.
Ireland Over All, XVIII: 72.
Ireland Since Parnell (D. D. Sheehan), XIII: 31.
Ireland: The Rock Whence I was Hewn (Donn Byrne), XVII: 65.
Ireland Through Tudor Eyes (Edward M. Hinton), XXVI: 67.
Ireland Today, V: 65.
Ireland under the Normans, 1169-1216; and Do., 1216-1333 (Goddard Orpen), III: 55, XII: 23.
Ireland under the Stuarts (G. B. O'Connor), II: 9.
Ireland: Vital Hour (Arthur Lynch), VII: 114.
Ireland—What now? (A.W. & M.C. Brommage), XXVIII: 20.
Ireland, Michael, XIV: 26.
Ireland, Samuel James (Obit.), VIII: 92.
Ireland's Literary Renaissance (E. A. Boyd), VIII: 85.
Ireland's Vanishing Opportunity (J. W. Rolleston), XI: 13.
Ireland's Veils and Other Poems (Ethel Rolt-Wheeler), V: 49.
Irish Abroad, The (Elliot O'Donnell), VI: 165.
Irish Almanacs, see Almanacs.
Irish-American Lexicographer, see Hackett, J. D.
Irish and Highland Costume (Maj. H. F. McClintock), XXIII: 73.
Irish Annals., see Annals.
Irish Archaelogian Society, XVI: 117, XIX: 142; (origin of) XIX

165; XXI: 91.
Irish Art Union, XXIV: 84, 133; (pictures), XVI: 47.
Irish Athletics (bibliography of), XXI: 18, XXII: 109. See also Gaelic Athletic Association.
Irish at the Front, The (Michael MacDonagh), VII: 162.
Irish author in Calcutta (1788), XVII: 118.
Irish Authors (changes of names), XXIV: 130;
Irish Bar Sinister (Martin Francis Mahoney), VI: 62.
Irish Bible, VI: 202.
Irish Bibliography, Bibliographies, Bibliographers and the Irish Bibliographical Society, see under "B".
Irish Bibliographical Society, XIV: 61, 104.
Irish Biographical Dictionaries—(Irish National Biography) I: 35, 60, 77, 84, 153, IV: 80, 116; (Strickland, *Dictionary of Irish Artists*) V: 119; (*A Concise Dictionary of*) XVI: 127.
Irish Biography I: 35, 60, 77, 84, 153, II: 58; (*A Concise Dictionary of Irish Biography*) XVI: 127.
Irish Book Advertiser, XII: 24, 48.
Irish Book Lover (duplicate copies) XXI: 26; (list of plates) XVI: 36, XXXII: 66; (Note on the First Fifteen Vols.) XVI: 34-36; complete sets) XXIV: 85.
"Irish Book Lovers"(Stephen Gwynn), IV: 132.
Irish Bookman, The, X: 87, XI: 10, 47.
Irish Books—XIV: 135; (at Cambridge University) IV: 17; (*The Hundred Best*) XVII: 74; (*The Hundred Rarest*) XVII: 74; (captured by American Warship,

1781) XVIII: 145; (MS copies of books in Ireland), XXIV: 98; ('Not so common') XXXII: 75.
Irish Books and Irish People (Stephen Gwynn), XI: 59.
Irish Brigade, (in France) II: 114; VI: 54, XIII: 68, 111.
Irish Bulletin, XVIII: 70.
Irish Campanology, XVIII: 144.
Irish-Canadian Poets, IX: 75.
Irish Capuchins, XIII: 91.
Irish Castles, XIX: 113.
Irish Castle Library, XXI: 20.
Irish Catechism, (O'Reilly's *Irish Catechism*) XVIII: 170, XIX: 25; (O'Kenny's *Galway Catechism*) XIX: 100, 124;
Irish Centenaries, X: 35, X: 35-38.
Irish Chap Books, II: 12, 19, 33, 35, 110, 129.
Irish Characters in Boys' Books (P. S. O'Hegarty), XXXII: 26-32.
Irish Charm, An XXIX: 134.
Irish Chiefs: or The Harp of Erin (Earl of Buchan) VI: 170.
Irish Chronicle, VI: 13.
Irish Churches and Monastic Buildings (Harold G. Leask), XXXII: 111.
Irish College (Waterford), IV:77.
Irish Commonwealth, The ("Dalta"), X: 87, XII: 14.
Irish Commune: The History of Ralahine, An (after E. T. Craig), XII: 38.
Irish Conspiracies, II: 9.
Irish Constitution, The (A.W. & M.C. Brommage), XXVIII: 20.
"Irish Country Song" (Padraic Colum), IV: 63.
Irish County Histories, IX: 61.
Irish Deaths (recorded in *Walker's Hibernian Magazine of 1806*) XVIII: 58.
Irish Dictionaries—(*Smaller Irish-*

English Dictionary) II: 11; (Crab's Irish Dictionary) XVI: 88; (O'Conway's Irish Dictionary) XVII: 131; (Valencey's Irish Dictionary) XXI: 131; (Irish Classical Dictionary) XXIII: 117; (Suggestions for a Phrase Dictionary) XXIV: 2.
Irish Digest (Edward M. Hinton), XXVI: 92, XXVII: 190, 288; (review) XXVIII: 24.
Irish Drama and Dramatists, IV: 37.
Irish Drama, The (Andrew E. Malone), XVII: 70-71.
Irish Dramatists of Past Twenty-five Years, XVIII: 2.
Irish Drinking Song in French, XXVII: 232.
Irish Drolleries (J. J. Moran), I: 106.
Irish Eclogues, VII: 93.
Irish edition, XXXI: 70.
Irish Election Law (Stanley Lees Griffard), XXXII: 39.
"Irish Emigrant, The" (Lady Dufferin), XXI: 64.
Irish emigrants, (before 1860) XVI: 48; XIV: 73, XVII: 130.
Irish Epics, Old, II: 19.
Irish Examiner, The, XVII: 50.
Irish Exhortation, VI: 62.
Irish Exiles, III: 13.
Irish Fairy Tales, IV: 108; XII: 109; XII: 65-66.
Irish Fairy Tales (James Stephens), XII: 65-66.
Irish Family History, VI: 116.
Irish farce, an (title wanted), XI: 118, (*The Irish Valet*) 137.
Irish Farmer's Journal, XIX: 90-91.
Irish Felon, The (ed. John Martin), XVII: 50.
Irish fiddle makers, XVII: 116.

"Irish Fisherman's Prayer, An" (Cathal O'Byrne), XIX: 22.
Irish Folk-History Plays (Lady Gregory), III: 211.
Irish Folk Song Journal, XII: 109.
Irish Folk Song Society, XII: 46.
Irish Friend, The (periodical), VIII: 68.
Irish funeral entries, IV: 82.
Irish Gentleman: George Henry Moore, An, (Col. Maurice Moore) V: 31.
Irish Geography: The Bulletin of the Geographical Society of Ireland, XXX: 140, XXXI: 110, XXXII: 115.
Irish Ghost Stories, see *True Irish Ghost Stories*.
Irish Grammar, (Grammar and Dictionary) III: 194; (O'Donovan's Irish Grammar; T.C.D.), XVII: 19; (need for Irish Historical Grammar), XVIII: 65.
Irish Graves, XIII: 20.
Irish Genealogy, XXVI: 68.
Irish Harp Society of Dublin foundation of), XVIII: 54.
Irish Harp, The (ed. Michael Joseph McCann), XVI: 67.
Irish Harpers and Pipers, XVI: 47.
Irish Harpers' Programme in 1821, XXI: 36.
Irish Heroes in Red War (Alice M. Peppard Cooke), VII: 50.
Irish Historical Library (William Nicholson), XVI: 11.
Irish Historical Society in the USA, see American Irish Historical Society.
Irish Historical Studies, XXVI: 66, XXVII: 281, XXIX: 22, XXX: 24, 117, 140, XXXII: 115.
Irish History for Young Readers (Rev. H. Kingsmill Moore), V:

(Rev. H. Kingsmill Moore), V: 182.
Irish History, (Bibliographies) XIII: 73; (*A Sketch of Irish History*) XXI: 43.
Irish Ideals in Poetry and Drama, II: 79.
Irish Impressions (Sir Lees Knowles), XI: 12.
Irish Index, XIV: 124.
Irish Ironies ("An Philibin"), XVIII: 181.
Irish Inscriptions in Co. Meath, XXIV: 124.
Irish Institute—1811, The, XXVIII: 56.
Irish Interest books, see Bibliographies (half-yearly).
Irish Labour Movement (W. P. Ryan), XI: 12.
Irish language—("The Speche of an Irishe man in the yere 1542"), XVI: 80-81; (Children's Books in Irish) XVI: 47-48; (poem of Louth bard on Irish language) XVII: 21-22; (interesting defence of Irish language) XVII: 16; (Last Irish language speakers of Leinster) XX: 41, 122, XXII: 12; (Irish language magazines) XX: 66, 115, 140; (Irish language movement, Boston) XIX: 88; (Last Irish language speakers) XXI: 11; (Irish language in Couny Kilkenny) XXI: 65; (O'Kane's Notes on the Irish Language) XXI: 92; Irish Language Societies) XXII: 90; (Irish-Speaking Booksellers in Dublin) XXIV: 111; (Irish language in T.C.D.) XXIV: 14; (Irish language in America) XXVI: 38; (Irish language in *Dublin College Magazine*, 1880s) XXVI: 37; (An Irish Language Revivalist) XXVI: 104; (Irish language in Kilkenny, 1822) XXVII: 209; (Irish language in Co. Galway, 1870s) XXX: 78-79; (Irish language in London, 1773) XXXI: 32. Also (Irish [language]) XIII: 150.
Irish Learned Societies, X: 109, XI: 30.
Irish Learning, XXVII: 146, 177.
Irish Libraries—XXI: 65; (survey of), XXIV: 62.
Irish Literary and Musical Studies, V: 87.
Irish Literary Gazette, X: 42, 69.
Irish Literary Revival, VII: 189.
Irish Literary Society (reviews of sessions)—II: 79, 96, 113, 131, 147, 165, 184, III: 87, 104, 120, 140, 146, 149, 164, 184, 207, IV: 8, 27, 49, 65, 85, 89, 118, 137, 153, 169, 171, 202, V: 12, 83, 104. 125, 139, 161, 175, 194. 212, VI: 23, 57, 71, 96, 110, 128, 151, 162, 200, VIII: 61, 79, 109, IX: 54, 131, X: 22, 84, XI: 42, 56, 100, 115, 138, XII: 37, 47, 71, 87, 112-115, 139-140, XIII: 19, 67, 90, 116, 141, 167, XIV: 23, 48, 62, 78, 93, 144, XV: 8, 27, 38, XVI: 84, XVII: 123-124, XIX: 163, XVIII: 35, XVIII: 154, XXX: 91.
Irish Literature in English (a list), XVIII: 172.
Irish Literature, XIII: 157, 167; (memorials to the pioneers), XVII: 25.
"Irish Love Song, An" (Katherine Tynan), XXIX: 41.
Irish Magazine, The (c.1833-44), XXIX: 15; XXXII: 15.
Irish Manuscripts—(Old), II: 154; III: 155, IV: 174, VI: 13, 24, 153, VII: 75; (at Lambeth) XIII:

The Irish Book Lover 285

96; (British Museum Catalogue) XVI: 2; (St. Kieran's Coll., Kilkenny) XVI: 50-51; (destruction of), XVII: 18, XVII: 118, XVII: 125, XVIII: 30; (of M. Fauriel) XVIII: 25; (in Rome) XVIII: 49, 79; (sought by Fr. O'Flanagan), XIX: 69; (at Inishowen) XIX: 73; (Egerton MS) XX: 42; (of Cheltenham, now N.L.I.) XX: 114; (in Diocesan Library) XXII: 1; (of Arthur Brownlow) XXII: 18; (in Sheffield) XXII: 91; (in Marsh's Library) XXIII: 73; (O'Donovan letters on) XXVI: 79; (The Ambrosian Codex) XXVI: 108; (MS copies of *Meditationes Vitae Christi*) XXVII: 208; (sold in London) XXX: 92; (in Vatican) XXXII: 61.
Irish Manuscripts Commission (Publications), XXI: 48, 49, XXVII: 283. Medicine— (Irish Medical MSS), XXI: 73; (O'Sheil medical family), XXX: 50, 51, XXXI: 128.
Irish Memories (Sommerville & Ross), IX: 107.
Irish Miniatures facsimiles (Library of St. Gall), XXXII: 93.
Irish Minstrels and Musicians (Capt. Francis O'Neill), V: 183.
Irish Monasticism: Origins and Early Development (Rev. John Ryan), XIX: 127.
Irish Monthly (ed. Fr. Matthew Russell), IV: 42.
Irish Morgans, IV: 191.
Irish Music—(MS Collections) XVI: 33, 34; (Dr. Henebry's work on), XVI: 120; in London) XVII: 32; XVII: 54, XIX: 33; (Breton commentary on) XXVII: 168; (New York) XXIX: 109; (Goodman Collection) XXXII: 40, 137.
Irish Place-names, see Place-names.
Irish Nationalism and British Democracy (Elbert Strauss), XXXII: 19.
Irish National Tradition (Alice Stopford Green), XIV: 46.
Irish Nationality (Mrs. J. R. Green), II: 158.
Irish Newspapers in 1788, XXXII: 65.
Irish Novels, VIII: 88, XII: 112; (New Irish Novelists) IV: 187; (Irish Novelists) VI: 179, XIII: 105.
Irish on the Somme, The (Martin MacDonagh), IX: 33.
Irish Orators and Oratory (Thomas Kettle), VII: 62.
Irish *Ordo*, (earliest) XV: 8, 42.
Irish Paliament, II: 111, 127, 190; IV: 125; (Old Irish Parliament) VI: 80, 208.
Irish Paper Making, I: 159.
Irish Peer on the Continent, An (ed. Thomas U. Sadleir), XII: 61-63.
Irish Penny Journal, XXXII: 15.
Irish Penny Magazine (J. G. Rhynehart), II: 151, XXXI: 105, XXXII: 15.
Irish People (War Special 16 July 1922), XVIII: 72.
Irish Periodical in England, XVI: 71.
Irish Plays and Playwrights (Cornelius Weygandt), IV: 157.
Irish Presbyterian Magazines— Past and Present (A. A. Campbell), XI: 26.
Irish Presbyterianism in Two Centuries (ed. J. W. Kernohan), III: 75.
"Irish Priest, An" (*A Manual of Catholic Action*), XXII: 23.

Irish Printing, see Printing.
Irish Prophecies (*Prophecies of Columcille*) XVIII: 171.
Irish Pseudonyms, I: 121.
Irish Public Records (Destruction in Four Courts), XVIII: 73.
Irish Publisher's Reminiscences, IX: 69, 98,123.
Irish Rebellion of 1916, VIII: 18.
Irish Refugees at Paris (c.1728), XXXII: 37.
Irish Review, II: 145, VI: 76, XIV: 93.
Irish Rushlight, The, III: 115.
Irish bird-watching sanctuary, XXXII: 92.
Irish scholars and teachers—(18th c. Irish professors) XXI: 137, XXII: 65, 143, XXIV: 41; (Irish Scholars in 1853) XXVII: 256; (Irish students in England, 1303) XVIII: 59; (Irish scholars in Dublin, c.1720) XXVII: 208; (J. G. O'Keeffe's work in Irish scholarship) XXVI: 27; (Irish professors & students at Prague, 1689-90) XXXI: 82.
Irish Scientific Bibliography (Praeger's *Botany*), XVIII: 143.
Irish Scribe, The Last, XXVIII: 134.
Irish Sermons—(in Dublin, 1780) XXII: 11; (Pamphlet of 1860 sermon) XIX: 144.
Irish Sketches (F. E. Woodwright), VI: 185.
Irish Society, An, XVI: 126.
Irish Society, VII: 41, 67, 95, 129, 155.
Irish Song Books, II: 34, 81, 111.
Irish Songs and Poems (William Allingham) III: 76.
Irish speakers, see Irish language.
Irish Statesman, XII: 14, XIV: 5, 20, 37, 52, 67; (publication ceases) XVIII: 34.

Irish subjects in French books (1801-1900), XVI: 42-43, 59-61, 127.
Irish Syllabic Poetry 1200-1600 (Elasnor Knott), XVI: 127.
Irish Texts, XXII: 77.
Irish Texts Societies, The, II: 11, 41, III: 7, 202, IV: 4, VII: 8, XV: 21, XXIV: 64.
Irish Times, The (Irish-interest articles listed) XVIII: 103, 4.
Irish Tradition, see Society of Irish Tradition
Irish Tribune, II: 172.
Irish Tricolour, XXVII: 159.
Irish Type [or fonts]—(Evolution of) XIV: 81; (Monotype Corporation on) XVII: 38; (Description of type) XVIII: 17; (Type in *Lucerna fidelium*) XVIII: 17; "Figgins" Type, XIX: 78; (Sadlier Type Foundry) XX: 40; (Irish v. Roman Characters) XX: 56-57; (account of Talbot B. Reed) XX: 94; (Louvain Irish Type) XX: 103; (Petrie's Gaelic Type) XXVII: 161, XXIX: 89; (Beautiful types) XXIX: 138; (Earlist Gaelic type in Cork), XXXII: 144.
Irish Unionism (James Winder Good), XII: 45.
Irish Utopia, An (J. H. Edge), VII: 72.
Irish Visions of the Other World, (St. John D. Seymour), XIX: 28.
Irish Wars: A Military History of Ireland from the Norse Invasion to 1798, The, (J. J. O'Connell) XII: 38-40.
Irish Witchcraft and Demonology (St. John D. Seymour), V: 66.
Irish World (on Thomas Mooney), XIX: 76.
Irish Writers' Rewards, XIII: 29.

Irish Writing (ed. David marcus), XXXII: 95.
Irishman and His Family, An (Maud Wynne), XXV: 67.
Irishman, The (Blyth Oliver), XII: 66.
Irishmen All (George Birmingham), V: 101.
Irishmen in the American Civil War, XXIX: 139.
Irishmen like P.R., (Brommage, A.W. & M.C.) XXVIII: 20.
Irisleabhar na Gaedhilge, XXII: 103, 125, 127.
"*Irlande à jamais*" (Camille le Mercier d'Erm), XIX: 139.
Irrelagh, X: 92.
Irvine, Alexander, V: 145, VIII: 132, XIII: 19, 31.
Irvine, [Dr.] G. M. (*The Lion's Whelp*), II: 57.
Irvine, Herbert (*The Wondrous Cross*) XXVII: 288.
Ivernian Society of Cork, I: 59; (Journal of) XX: 66, 140.
Irwin, [Rev.] Clarke H., VI: 164.
Irwin, Edward, III: 13.
Irwin, T. C., VI: 210, XXII: 41.
Irwin, Thomas P. (*Benson's Flying Column*), XXIV: 21.
Island of the Mighty, The (Padraic Colum) XV: 46.
Itinerant Poet, An (Patrick O'Kelly), XXIII: 42-45.
Ivernian Society of Cork, I: 59; (*Ivernian Journal*) XX: 140, XXV: 62, XVI: 4.

J

Jackson, Andrew, XIII: 96.
Jackson, Kenneth (*Studies in Celtic Nature Poetry*), XXIV: 138.
Jackson, [Mrs.] John, II: 48.
Jackson, T. A. (*Ireland, Her Own*), XXX: 142.
Jacob, Rosamond (*Rise of the United Irishmen*), XXV: 117.
Jail Journal (John Mitchel), II: 145, 164, 181.
James & Co. [publisher], V: 221.
James, Andrew (pseud. of James Andrew Strahan), XVIII: 37.
James, Henry (*A Small Boy and Others*), IV: 192.
James the Third [the Old Pretender], III: 155.
Jamestown, Co. Leitrim, XXVII: 242.
Jaspert, Willem (*Ireland*), XXVII: 164.
"J.D.H" (Benjamin Franklin's Visit to Ireland), XVIII: 145.
"J.D.N.", XIII: 172, 178.
"J. De L.", III: 21, V: 82, VI: 117, VIII: 140, IX: 35, 138.
Jebb, [Dr.] John [Protestant Bishop of Limerick], IV: 107.
Jebb, Horsley, II: 42.
Jeffreys, Letitia Dorothea, XII: (Obit.) 43.
Jeffries, J. M. N (War Correspondent), XI: 77.
Jennings, I. R. B. (Obit.), XVI: 49.
Jennings, [Rev.] Brendan, (*The Two O'Hagans*) XXIII: 46; (*Michael Ó Cleirigh*) XXV: 17.
Jennings, [Rev.] John Andrew (Obit.), XIV: 16.
Jessop, George H. (*Where the Shamrock Grows*), II: 178; (Obit.) VI: 154.
"J.F.W.", II: 12.
"J.H.P.", II: 27.
"J.J.M.", I: 157.
Job, The (Ella MacMahon), V: 199.
Jocelyn, Robert, III: 108.
John Field of Dublin (W. H. Grattan Flood), XII: 108, 109.
John Keogh: The Pioneer of

Catholic Emancipation (Denis Gwynn), XVIII: 179.
John the Hermit and Other Poems (S. S. McCurry), XIV: 108.
"Johnny Armstrong's Last Good Night" (anon. ballad), V: 176, 222.
Johnson, Geoffrey (*The Ninth Wave*), XXX: 144.
Johnson, Lionel, II: 14, VII: 56.
Johnson, Samuel (Visit to Ireland), XXVI: 98.
Johnston, Denis, (*The Moon in the Yellow River*) XXI: 22; (*The Old Lady Says 'No'*) XXI: 22.
Johnston, Francis, (Architect), XXVIII: 115.
Johnston, James B. (*Place Names of Scotland*), XXIII: 24.
Johnston, Myrtle (*Laleen and Other Stories*), XXV: 110; (*The Rising*), XXVI: 118.
Johnston, [Rev.] William VII: 51.
Johnston, William (of Ballykilbeg), I: 5, 109.
Johnstone, [Rev.] T. M. (*Ulstermen: Their Fight for Fortune, Faith and Freedom*), V: 193.
Johnstown (printing in), VII: 164, 188.
Joly, Jaspar Robert, XII: 99.
Jones, Henry McNaughton (Obit.), X: 19; XV: 54.
Jones, Howard, V: 51.
Jones, Jack, XIV: 121.
Jones, John Fleming (auctioneer), XXVII: 230.
Jones, William, I: 157.
Jones, William Todd, IV: 73, 92, 106.
Jonnes, Moreau de (*Adventures in the Revolution and under the Consulate*), XVII: 67-68.
Jordon, [Sir] John, II: 56.
Jottings on Journals, VI: 180.

Journals—(*Journal of the Royal Society of Antiquaries of Ireland*), VII: 51; XXVIII: 20; XXVIII: 93; XXVIII: 136; XXIX: 23, 117; XXX: 23; XXVII: 214, 282; (*Journal of Celtic Studies*, Philadelphia) XXXII: 96; (*Journal of the Irish Folk Song Society*) XII: 108,109; (*Journal of the Ivernian Society*) XXV: 62; (*Journal of the Co. Louth Archaeological Society*) XXIX: 23, 142; XXX: 96; (*Journal of the American Irish Society*), XXVI: 67. [For journals and magazines with names *Journal of ... &c.*, see under individual titles.].
Journeys with Jerry (Alexis Roche), VII: 11.
Joy, Francis, I: 160.
Joyce, James, VI: 60; (*Portrait of the Artist*) VIII: 9; VIII: 113; X: 23; (*Exiles*) X: 46-47; (*Pomes Penyeach*) XXI: 117; XI: 95; XIII: 42, 149; (*Finnegans Wake*) XXVII: 165; ("Araby") XXXII: 107. [See also reference at XXXI: 47 (George Birmingham, *Irish Short Stories*).]
Joyce, Patrick Weston, II: 8, 25, 48, V: 125, 127, 202 [also III]; (*English As We Speak It in Ireland*) II: 25; (*The Origin of Irish Names of Places*) V: 125.
Joyce, Robert Dwyer, VII: 131.
Joyce, W. B., (Central Catholic Lirbrary) XVIII: 72; (Eight Irish Magazines) XX: 66.
Joynt, Ernest (*Histoire de l'Irlande*), XXIV: 116.
Joynt, J. W. (Celt and Maori), VI: 142-43; VIII: 132; XIV: 144.
Joynt, Maud, XV: 32.
"J.P.C.", XI: 85.

"J.R.B", XII: 12.
"J.S.", XIV: 5, 20, 32, 37, 52.
"J.S C.", see John S. Crone.
"J.S.H.", II: 76.
"Jude" (*Medicinal and Perfumery Plants of Ireland*), XXI: 94.
Judith Quinn (Conal O'Riordan), XXVI: 120.
Juring and Non-Juring Priests (Rev. John Brady), XXIX: 18.
"J.W.", II: 75.
"J.W.K.", II: 46, 60; VII: 116.

K

K., XI: 13.
Kane, Whitford (*Are We All Met?*), XIX: 150.
Katherine Frances Purdon (Susan L. Mitchell), XII: 79.
Kathleen Mavourneen (Anon. play) V: 69.
"Kathleen Mavourneen" (song), XIV: 39.
Kavanagh, [Dr.] George, XIV: 72.
Kavanagh, Michael, II: 195.,
Kavanagh, Patrick (*The Ploughman and Other Poems*), XXV: 45; (*Tarry Flynn*) XXXI: 48.
Kavanagh, [Rev.] Patrick Fidelis, (Obit.), X: 72.
Kavanagh, Rose, I: 45.
"Kay, D. L." [pseud. of D. L. Kelleher] (*The Glamour of Dublin*), X: 61, 87.
Keane, Augustus H., III: 134.
Keane, John F. (*On Blue Water*), I: 34.
Keane, Molly, see Farrell, M. J.
Kearns, Linda (*In Times of Peril*), XIV: 29.
Keating, Geoffrey, (*History of Ireland*) I: 26, 47, III: 125, 155; XIV: 63, XVII: 91, 116, 118, 143; (Genealogy) XIX: 89; (*Tri Biorgaoithe an Báis/The Three Shafts of Death*), XX: 20.
Keating, Joseph, VII: 78.
Keddy, Ursula (*Irland/Éire*), XXVII: 186.
Kee, John, IX: 63.
Keegan, John, II: 150.
Keenan, [Rev.] John Sproule, XXVII: 211.
Keeper of Swans, A (Patrick Purcell), XXIX: 144.
Keightley, [Sir] Samuel, III: 116.
Kelleher, D. L. ["D. L. Kay"], V: 179; (*In Cork's Own Town*) XI: 61, (*The Glamour of Cork*) 98; (*Ireland of the Welcomes*) XVII: 96.
Kelleher, Mary, XIII: 143.
Kelly, Dominic, XXXII: 17.
Kelly, J. Fitmaurice, XIV: 16.
Kelly, [Rev.] John, XI: 128.
Kelly, John [Westmeath poet], (MSS), XXXII: 40.
Kelly, Mary ["Eva" of the Nation] (Obit.), I: 163.
Kelly, Patrick (M. R. L. Kelly), XXX: 115.
Kelly, Richard J., (Dublin Book Binding) II: 152-53; (Later Loughrea Printing) II: 181; (Some Connaught Literary Men) VI: 1-3; (*Charles Joseph Kickham*) VI: 41; (*Louvain and its Irish Press*) VI: 105-06; (Thomas Dermody) VI: 129; (Printing in Tuam) XV: 7; (Notes on Provincial Printing) XV: 44-45; (Anthony Trollope and Ireland) XVIII: 48, 66, XIX: 110; (On the Fair of Ballinasloe) XIX: 59; (Sundry) III: 209, IV: 131; VI: 8, VII: 96, 104;
Kelly, Thomas (Loughrea printer), XIX: 172.
Kelly, Thomas Hughes (Library of), XXIII: 58.

Kelly, William Edward, XXII: 109, 144.
Kellys, The, and The MacDermots (Anthony Trollope), XVIII: 66.
Kelsey Papers, The, XVII: 109.
Kelso, Hamilton, Dr., XII: 67.
Keltic Journal, IV: 125, 147.
Kelvin, Lord, see Thomson, William.
Kenealy, Alexander Cockburn (Obit.), VII: 15.
Kenealy, Arabella, II: 106.
Kenealy, Edward Vaughan, XI: 3, 5.
Kenmare Manuscripts (ed. Edward MacLysaght), XXIX: 20.
Kennedy, Caroline (The Crystal), XXI: 93.
Kennedy, C. R., II: 176.
Kennedy, David, III: 154, VI: 152, 211, VIII: 89, XIII: 63.
Kennedy, Frances, VI: 139.
Kennedy, [Rev.] Geoffrey A. Studdert (pseud. "Woodbine Willy"), X: 104, XIII: 12, XIV: 14, XVII: 29.
Kennedy, G. M., XXVIII: 17.
Kennedy, J. Stewart, VI: 208.
Kennedy, James, XVII: 22-23, 79.
Kennedy, [Col.] John Pitt, X: 104.
Kennedy, Mathew (trans. The Spiritual Rose), XVIII: 141.
Kennedy, William, II: 169, 176, III: 61, 102, XII: 35.
Kenney, Francis, (The Sources for the Early History of Ireland, Vol. 1), XVIII: 62, 126.
Kenney, [Mrs.] Stockpoole (Carrow or Carryduff), III: 56; V: 11.
Kenny, James Francis, XX: 43.
Kensal Green, XIII: 20.
Kentworthy, [Lt.-Cmdr.] J. M. (Sailor, Statesman and Others), XXII: 21.
"Ken ye aught o' Captain Grose?"
(Maurice James Craig), XXX: 56-58.
Keogh, William Nicholas (Judge Keogh), IV: 210; IX: 55.
Keon, Miles Gerald, XIII: 81.
Keons, The, XIII: 139.
Kerney, Michael, XII: 112, 138.
Kernohan, Coulson, XIII: 85.
Kernohan, J. W., IV: 16; (Parish of Kilrea and Tamlaght O'Crilly) IV: 122, 145, VI: 198, IX: 110, X: 15, 68, XIII: 110.
Kerr, John, XI: 64, 86, XII: 42.
Kerry Cousins, XIV: 42.
Kerry—History of Kerry, I: 22, 168, II: 161, III: 9; (Co. Kerry) V: 218; (The Kerry Society) XIV: 12; (Handbook of Kerry) XIV: 43; (Kerry Evening Post) XIX: 90-91; (Kerry Western Herald) XIX: 90-91; (Kerry Tradition) XXXI: 118; See also Earl of Kerry [Sir William Petty, 1st Marquis of Lansdowne] XII: 61-63.
Kettle, (Thomas Michael, (ed. Irish Orators and Oratory)VII: 62; ("Rememberence" [of Lt. Thomas Kettle] by R. McDonnell)VIII: 34; (Obit.) VIII: 46; ("T. M. Kettle", by Cruise O'Brien) 72; IX: 88, XII: 71.
Kevin, Neil (No Applause in Church), XXXI: 45.
Kickham, Charles Joseph. [(pseud. Slievenamon"), II: 12, 27, 48; (The Priest and His People, pseud. "Slievnamon") III: 1; 30, 47, 103, 114, VI: 41, 76; (Life of) VII: 30; XI: 82, XII: 13, 38, 42; (Kickham's Novels) XXVI: 41.
Kidd, Benjamin, VIII: 69.
Kiely, Benedict, (The Cards of the Gambler) XXXII: 46; Kiely,

Benedict, (*Honey seems Bitter*) XXXII: 72.
Kiersey, Thomas, XII: 14; (Obit.), XXVII: 177; XXVII: 231; (Publisher), XXVIII: 43.
Kildare Place Society, XIV: 40.
Kilkeel, XIII: 34.
Kilkenny Chronicle, The, XVII: 79.
Kilkenny—(A Kilkenny Play Bill), II: 88, 111; VI: 118, VII: 116, 164; (*Nooks and Corners of the County of Kilkenny*) VII: 102, X: 92; (writers) XIV: 103, 125; (Irish poetry collected by Canon Carrigan in Kilkenny) XVIII: 144; (*Kilkenny Moderator*) XIX: 90-91; (Irish language in Kilkenny), XXI: 65; (A Kilkenny Printer's Will), XXIV: 40; (Irish in Kilkenny, 1822) XXVII: 209.
Kilkenny (printing in)—IV: 97, V: 138, XIX: 8, XX: 113; (18th c. printing in) XVI: 6-9, 40-41, 55-58; (19th c. printing in), XVI: 89-109; (17th c. printing in) XXI: 91.
Killamoy (M. Ó Conalláin S.P.), XXXI: 37.
Killanin, Lord (*Sir Godfrey Kneller and His Times*), XXXI: 16.
Killaroo and Oher Place Names (Fr. Paul Walsh), XXVIII: 98-103.
Killashee, Co. Longford, XXX: 6.
Killen, John Bryce (ed. *Northern Star*), VIII: 118.
Killilea, John (Matthew Butler), XXX: 35-37.
Killsmin, Lord, VII: 28.
Killyleagh Academy, I: 11.
Killylea, Co. Armagh (printing), XIV: 60.
Kilmore (printing in), XI: 136.
Kilronan, X: 68.
Kilrush Magazine, The, III: 62.
Kiltartan Poetry Book (Lady Gregory), XI: 133.
Kinane, [Rev.] Thomas (Obit.), V: 16.
Kindellons of Ballinakill, The (John Brady), XXX: 38-39.
King, J. (*History of Kerry*), II: 161.
King Among Carpenters (May Langrishe), XIV: 109.
King Edward VII and Some other Figures, (Ruaraidh Erskine), XXIV: 65.
King of the Beggars (Seán Ó Faoláin), XXVI: 71.
King, [Archbishop] William. IV: 9.
King, Ashe [see King, Richard Ashe].
King, Brian, VIII: 135.
King, [Sir] Charles Simeon, XII: (Obit.) 144.
King, Jeremiah, I: 22, 108, XIII: 137, XIV: 124, XVI: 68.
King, [Sir] Lucas, XV: (Obit.), 48, 55.
King, Richard Ashe, I: 97, VII: 45, 56, XII: 15, 134, XV: 39, XVI: 75, 84, XVII: 53.
King, [Rev.] Robert, V: 157.
King's County and Uí Failghe (origin of), XXVI: 50.
King v. Pepyat, XIX: 19.
Kinsale, VIII: 40.
History of Kinsale Florence O'Sullivan), VIII: 40.
Kiph, Owen, (see Ó Caoimh, Eoghan).
Kirkpatrick, James, XII: 112.
Kirkpatrick, Richard Carr, IX: 12.
Kirkpatrick, [Dr.] T. Percy C., (*Henry Quinn*) XI: 98; (*Edward Hill*) XII: 110; (*The Dublin Parmacopœias*) XIII: 156; (*The*

History of Dr. Steevens' Hospital, Dublin) XIV: 107; (*Notes on the Printers in Dublin During the 17th c.*) XVII: 113; (Dublin Printers during the 17th c.) XVIII: 20; (Sir Patrick Dun's Library), XVIII: 105-17; (*Life and Writings of Paul Hiffernan*) XIX: 11; (An Unrecorded Example of Drogheda Printing) XX: 39; (Samuel Mather and Joseph Ray) XX: 40; (Frankton's ornaments) XXI: 16; (Obit.) XXXII: 73, 74 [with port.]; Obituaries, XXXII: 73; (Sundry) IV: 13, XII: 115, XIII: 150, XIII: 167.
Kirkpatrick's *History of Orangeism*, IV: 124.
Kirkwood, Robert (engraver), XV: 63, XXX: 63.
Kirwan, [Dr.] Richard (Books captured by American Warship), XVIII: 145; XXXII: 86.
"Kitty of Coleraine" (song), VI: 167, 169, XV: 11.
Knife, The (Peadar O'Donnell), XVIII: 182.
Knight, Patrick, III: 193.
Knights of Malta and Ireland, XXVI: 137.
Knockinscreen Days (Jackson C. Clarke), V: 30.
Knocknagow (A Note on the Story), XXXII: 100.
Knott, Eleanor, X: 93, XVI: 127; (*Tromdamh Guaire*) XIX: 182; (*Togail Bruidne Da* Derga) XXV: 19; (on placename *Eadar*) XXXI: 56.
Knott, George E. (*Trial of Sir Roger Casement*), IX: 59.
Knott, [Dr.] John Freeman (Obit.), XII: 117.
Knowles, James Sheridan, II: 169.
Knowles, [Sir] Lee, XI: 12.

Knox, Collie (*It Might Have Been You*), XXVI: 90.
Knox, D. B., XV: 16.
Knox, E. V. ["Evoe"], XIV: 27.
Knox, E. F. Vesey, II: 79; (Obit.) XIII: 13.
Knox, Hubert, XIII: 137.
Knox, William M., X: 67, XI: 102, 135, XIV: 91, 111.
Knox's Letters, IV: 12t.
Kochskaemper, Von Max (*Herbergen der Neuen Jugend*), XXV: 113.
Kohl, J. G. (*Travels in Ireland*), II: 18.
Kottabos (T.C.D. magazine), VI: 71.
Küttner, Henry (*Briefe über Irland*), IV: 123.

L

Lá Bealtaine (Sinéad Ní Fhlannagáin), XXIV: 140.
Labour Bulletin (Literature of the Conflict), XVIII: 72.
Lacey, John, see George Darley.
Lacy, (American genealogy), XVII: 44, 81. See also de Lacy
Lady Morgan, see Sydney Owenson.
Lady of the Cromlech, The (Aodh de Blacam), XVIII: 94.
Lady of the Reef (Frank Frankfort Moore), VI: 148.
Laffan, [Dr.] Thomas, III: 100, 117, IX: 118.
Láimscríbhinn Sheaghain Gaillidhe, XX: 82, 83, 109, 132, 133; XXI: 54, 28-29, 76-78.
Lalor, James Fintan, (*James Fintan Lalor*) X: 63; (Papers in National Library) XXX: 84-86; (F. Carroll) XXXI: 129.
Lambert, Dorothy (*Strange Lover*), XXI: 93.

Lambeth Palace (Library of), V: 156; (Lambeth MSS), XIII: 96.
Lámh Fhada Dhubh, An, XXIII: 67.
Land of Italy, The (Jasper Moore) XXXI: 94, 120.
Land of Pat (Gertrude Griffiths), VIII: 135.
Land War of 1770 (James Matthews, intro. F. J. Bigger), I: 133.
Landreth, Helen, (*Dear Dark Head*) XXV: 106; (*The Pursuit of Robert Emmet*) XXXI: 17.
Lane, Denny, X: 37.
Lane, [Sir] Hugh Percy, VIII: 48; (Lane Pictures and Irish Printing) XXI: 40.
Lane, Timothy O'Neill, VI: 212.
Lane, Temple, (*Sinner Anthony*) XXI: 68; (*Battle of the Warrior*) XXVII: 285; (*House of my Pilgrimage*), XXVIII: 95.
Lang, W. J., (British and Irish Newspapers before 1801), XXII: 56, 102.
Langbridge, [Canon] Frederick, XIII: 146.
Langrishe, May (*King Among Carpenters*), XIV: 109.
Lansdowne Maps of the Down Survey (Sir William Petty), XII: 61-63 [recte Lansdowne].
Lanyon, Helen, (*Fairy Led and Other Verses*), VII: 100.
Laoighis Epitaph, XIX: 175.
Large, Dorothy M., (*Cloonagh*), XX: 48; (*Irish Airs*), 21; (*The Open Arms*) XXI: 68; (*A Cloney Carol*), XXIII: 156.
La Rochefoucauld, François (*Moral Maxims*), XXII: 2.
Larmine Collection., VI: 210.
Larmour, [Sir] Joseph, I: 8, II: 124.
Larne (printing in), IV: 91.

Last Independent Parliament of Ireland, IX: 136.
Last Irish Scribe, The XVI: 13-14.
Last Irish-Speakers of Leinster, XX: 122.
Last Songs (Francis Ledwidge), IX: 137.
Latimer, [Rev.] William Thomas, II: 13, III: 102, IV: 7, 17, 54, 73, 173, VI: 26, 132, 173; VII: 118, 162; (*A History of the Congregations in the Presbytery of Dungannon*), X: 14; XI: (Obit.) 15.
Latouche [or La Touche], (family) VIII: 117.
Latouche, James Digges, VIII: 1, XIII: 70.
La Transformation De La Géographie Politique De L'Irlande Au XVIIe Siecle (Sir William Petty), XIX: 64.
The Laughing Journey (Thomas Lennon), XXIII: 128.
Lavery, Felix (*Great Irishmen in War and Politics* and *Green and Gold*), XII: 85.
Lavery, John III: 12, IV: 31.
Lavery, [Sir] John (*The Life of a Painter*), XXVII: 262.
Lavery, Marion, XXI: 40.
"L.A.W.", II: 12.
Law, Arthur, IV: 176.
Law, Hugh, II: 165.
Law, James S., XIII: 36.
Lawless, [Hon.] Emily, V: 84; (with Shan Bullock, *Race of Castlebar*), V: 103, 165; 109, VII: 129, XXXII: 76.
Lawless, John (and P. B. Shelley), XVII: 2; (*The Compendium of the History of Ireland*) XVII: 3.
Lawlor, Dave (*Life and Struggles of an Irish Boy in America*) XXV: 18.
Lawlor, [Dr.] (T.C.D.), II: 3.

Lawlor, H. C. (*Dunluce Castle and the Route*), XI: 26.
Lawlor, Michael, III: 186.
Lawrence [Sir] Alexander in India, II: 113.
Lawrence, [Dr.] (Archbishop of Cashel), II: 1.
Lawrence, Peter (Dublin Bookseller, 1706), XVII: 47, 61.
Lawrence, W. J., I: 154, II: 111, III: 24, 29; (*Eighteenth Century Magazine of Music*) III: 76; 103, IV: 15, 33, 82, VI: 118, VII: 49, 193, VIII: 36, IX: 105; (Some Old Dublin Theatrical Journals) XIV: 115, 131.
"Lay of Oisin in the Land of Youth" (ed. Brian O'Looney), VIII: 139.
Lay of the Liffey, A (Eimhar O'Duffy), X: 46-47.
Lays and Legends of Thomond (Michael Hogan), XXVII: 205.
Lays and Legends of all Countries (W. J. Thoms), III: 63, VI: 45.
Leabhar Breac, An (John Patten), VII: 31.
Leabharlann, An (bibliographical journal), I: 31.
Leabhra nua Ghaedhilge, XVI: 82-83.
Leabharlanna Conndhae Na Gaillimhe (Co. Galway Libraries), XIX: 152.
Leader, The (influence of), XVIII: 34.
Leaflets, (Joseph H. Fowler), XXVI: 16.
Leaguer of Limerick, The (Patrick Creagh MacMahon) VII: 10.
Leahy, Maurice (*Anthology of Contemporary Catholic Poetry*), XIX: 151.
Learning in Ireland, XXX: 133-135.
Learning of Irish, The, XXX: 92.

Lea's *Ecclesiastical Registry*, IV: 211.
Leask, Harold G. (*Irish Castles*), XXVIII: 138; (*Irish Churches and Monastic Buildings*), XXXII: 111.
Leatham, Diana (*The Story of St. Brigid of Ireland*), XXXII: 119.
Leaves on the Wind (S. M. Crevequer), X: 46,47.
Leavys of Westmeath, XXVII: 174, 254.
Lecky, William Edward Hartpole, I: 17, 75, II: 87; (Mrs. Lecky) IV: 11; IV: 49, VIII: 132; (*Leaders of Public Opinion*), XXVI: 59.
"Lector" [pseud. of James Coleman], III: 46.
Lectures on Early Welsh Poetry, (Ifor Williams), XXIX: 24.
Ledestown Press, I: 69, IV: 98, XI: 116.
Ledwidge, Francis, V: 27-28, 137, VII: 92, VIII: 107, IX: 29, 32, 37, 55, 88, 104 137; XII: 27; XIII: 143.
Lee, [Sir] Sidney, IV: 117, 210, V: 3.
Leech, Henry Brougham, XI: 100, XII: (Obit.) 142.
Leech, John, IV: 46.
Le Fanu, Joseph Sheridan, IV: 210, 211, VIII: 30, 37; (bibliography) XVIII: 100, XXIV: 36.
Le Fanu, T. P. (*Memoirs of the Le Fanu Family*), XV: 14.
Lefanu, W. R. (*Seventy Years of Irish Life*), VI: 79.
Lefroy, [Dean] William, I: 43.
Legacy of Swift, The (Maurice J. Craig), XXXI: 69.
Legendary Stories of Carlingford (Michael George Crawford), VI: 11.

Legends of Saints and Sinners (Douglas Hyde), VII: 62.
Legends of the Lee (John Fitzgerald), V: 102.
Leinster Journal, XVI: 6, XIX: 90-91.
Leith-Sgéal—agus Ceathramha!, XXIV: 25.
Leitrim (in Anthony Trollope), XVIII: 46.
Lenihan, Maurice, II: 26, III: 92, 114; (*Williamite and Jacobite Wars,* with Robert Cane) XXVI: 58, 85.
Lennhoff, Eugen (*De Valera*), XXII: 94.
Lennon, Thomas (*The Laughing Journey*), XXIII: 128.
Lennox, P. J (*The Glories of Ireland,* with Joseph Dunn), VI: 149.
Lenox-Conyngham, Mina (*An Old Ulster House*), XXXI: 67.
Lenyon, Helen, VI: 212.
Leonard, J. P., XXVI: 114.
Lepper, John Heron, (*A Tory in Arms*) VIII: 58; IX: 32, XIII: 89, 96, XIV: 139.VIII: 58.
Leprechaun Booklets, XIII: 92.
Leprechaun of Kilmeen, The (Seamus O'Kelly), XI: 62.
Le Roux, Louis N. (*Tom Clarke*), XXIV: 142.
Leslie, [Rev.] Charles, IV: 9.
Leslie, [Rev.] J. B. (*Armagh Clergy and Parishes*), I: 172.
Leslie [Sir] Shane, I: 88, VII: 114, VIII: 20; (*End of a Chapter*) VIII: 38; IX: 56, XIV: 140; XVII: 74; (*Lough Derg*), XX: 117; (*The Oxford Movement*) XXII: 69; (*Poems and Ballads*) XXII: 72; .(*The Passing Chapter*) XXII: 123; (*The Script of Jonathan Swift and Other Essays*), XXIV: 6.

L'Estrange, [Rev.] Guy W. C., V: 6.
L'Estrange, Thomas, VII: 43.
Letter from London, XX: 122.
Letterkenny (Episcopal Library), VIII: 111.
Letts, [Miss] W. M., III: 8, 30, 73; ("Says She") III: 79; 79, 103, IV: 120; (*Songs from Leinster*) IV: 206, XXX: 119; (*Hallow-E'en and Poems of the War*) VIII: 107; (*St. Patrick, The Travelling Man*) XX: 96; (*Knockmaroon*) XXI: 115.
Lever, Charles James, III: 3, VIII: 63, IX: 138; (*A Rent in a Cloud*), XI: 23; XVII: 3; (Lever's MSS) XXIV: 15.
Levey, R. M., XIX: 23.
Levinge, Godfrey, IV: 112, 173.
Levins, William, XX: 19.
Levison, Wilhelm (*A Bibliography*), XXXI: 23.
Levy, John ["Capt. Prout"], XIV: 106.
Lewis, Frank R. (Dr. S. Madden, Dr. Johnson and Benjamin Franklin), XXVI: 98.
Lewis, Lorna (ed. *The Children's Holiday Book of Verse*), XXIV: 18.
"Lex" (Irish Exiles), III: 13.
Lexikon fuer Theologie und Kirche (eds. Michael Buchberger & Konrad Holler), XXIX: 45.
Lhuyds, Edward (Irish MSS), XXIX: 134.
L'influence des huguenots français en Irlande aux XVIIe et XVIIe sicles (Albert Carr), XXVI: 88.
Libraries, private—(Beaufoy Library), I: 4; (Whitley Stokes's Library) I: 119; (Library of Sir Francis Brady) I: 123; (Stamer Park Library) I: 146; (Bonaparte Library) II: 140; (Library of

Thomas Davis) V: 37, XXVII: 156, XXX: 40, 41, 69; XXXI: 66; (Charlemont [Caulfeild] Library) XIV: 121; (Francis Joseph Bigger Memorial Library) XVIII: 99; (Sir Patrick Dun's Library) XVIII: 17, 105-17, 160; (A Book from Swift's Library) XVIII: 158; (James Collins' Library) XIX: 25; (Jonathan Swift & Thomas Davis's Libraries) XIX: 58; (Redington Memorial Collection) XX: 141; (Library of Sir Bernard Burke) XXIII: 16; (Thomas Hughes Kelly's Library) XXIII: 58; (Libraries of Three Young Irelanders) XXVII: 156; (Thomas MacNevin) XXVII: 156; (Library of Seán Ó Floinn) XXVII: 210; (William Andrew Clark Memorial Library) XXXI, 19; (Dr. Plunket's Library) XXXII: 106. Also Pratt Library.

Libraries, public—(New Medical Library Association) I: 10; Lismore Cathedral Library, II: 2; (The Franciscan Library, Killiney) IV: 3, 21, XXVII: 182, 202; (Irish MSS. at Lambeth) V: 156, XIII: 96; (T.C.D. Library) VII: 153; (Letterkenny Episcopal Library) VIII: 111; (Huth Library) IX: 57; (Cork Library) XII: 80, 106, XIII: 33; (National Library of Ireland) XIII: 16; (Antrim Libraries) XIII: 47; (Libraries and the *Irish Book Lover*) XVI: 14-15; (Milltown Park Library) XVI: 37-39; (Library Association of Ireland/Cumann na Leabharlann) XVII: 73, 195-207; (boardroom designs for N.L.I.) XVIII: 25; (Catholic Central Library) XVIII: 72; (Bodleian: Irish Books & Periodicals) XVIII: 130; (Hospital Libraries) XIX: 130; (*Leabharlanna Conndhae Na Gaillimhe*/Co. Galway Libraries) XIX: 152; (St. Columb's College Library) XX: 138; (Youghal, An Old Library) XXI: 43; (Irish Libraries) XXI: 65; (Irish MSS in Libraries) XXIII: 17, 73; (Limavady Library) XIII: 35; (Irish MSS in Marsh's Library) XXIII: 73; (Survey of Irish Libraries) XXIV: 62; (American Irish Historical Society Library) XXIV: 112; (Irish MSS in Maynooth) XXIX: 93.

Library series—(The Parlour Library) II: 90, 133; (The Library of Ireland) XI: 91; (Every Irishman's Library) XI: 106; (Duffy's Library of Ireland) XII: 137.

Life and Letters of Stopford Brooke (L. P. Jacks), IX: 77.

Life in Old Dublin (James Collins), V: 32.

Life of Canon Sheehan (Fr. Francis Boyle), IX: 124.

Life and Struggles of an Irish Boy in America (D. Lawlor), XXV: 18.

Life of George Moore, The (Joseph M. Hone), XXIV: 143.

Light to the Blind, A (Jacobite Narrative of the War in Ireland), IX: 15.

Lightening Flash (Margaret O'Leary), XXVII: 191.

Lilburn, Richard, II: 76.

Limavady, (Records of Limavady) IV: 121; (printing in) XI: 102; (Limavady Library) XIII: 35.

Limerick—(printing in) III: 92, 114, 157, XVIII: 24, XXIII: 133;

(excursion to) IV: 203; (League of Limerick) VII: 10; (*Antiquities of Limerick*) VIII: 10; 16 (Irish poets and scholars in) XVI: 72, XXII: 68; (Insurrectionary leader in 1803) XVII: 81-81; (19th c. Limerick) 39, XVIII: 75, 101, 135, 163; (a bookseller-poet) XVIII: 58; (Bookseller, Flin or Flyn) XVIII: 58; (*Fallacious Queries*, printed in) XVIII: 24; 19th Century printing in) XX: 84, 85, 106-08, 124, XXI: 7-9, 30, 56, 78-80, XIX: 117-20, 134, 174; (White's *Annals of Limerick*) XVIII: 60; (*Advertiser*) XIX: 90-91; (*Chronicle*) XIX: 90-91; (*Evening* Post) XIX: 90-91; (*Limerick Journal*) XIX: 90-91; (West Limerick anthology) XXIV: 53, XXV: 10, 59; (George Rowland, Limerick printer) XXII: 7; (The first newspaper in) XXIV: 53; (Whole-day Auction in) XXIV: 127; (Arthur Thomas of Limerick) XXVI: 38; (18th c. printing in) XXVIII: 104-12; (*The Piper*) XXIX: 38; (a Limerick novel) XXXI: 104.

Linch, John Fitzjames, XIX: 37, 96.

Lincoln, Abraham, XXXII: 65, 88, 139.

Lind, Jenny (Irish visit), XXVI: 84.

Lindsay, Alex Hamilton, VIII: 67.

Lindsay, [Prof.] J. A., IX: 55.

Lindsay, Jack (*Medieval Latin Poets*), XXIII: 31.

Lindsay, Jane (*Wear the Green Willow*), XXIV: 22.

Lindsay, John, XXVIII: 134.

Lindsay, Robert, XVI: 11.

Linegar, Charles (Professor of Irish), XXXII: 42, 65, 93.

Linn, Henry (Belfast bookbinder), II:110.

Linn, [Capt.] Richard, I: 10, 73, 78, III: 43, IV: 146.

Lion's Whelp, The (G. M. Irvine), II: 57.

Lisburn (Old), VIII: 110; (printing in) VII: 90; (records of) XII: 137.

Lismore Cathedral Library, II: 2.

Literary, Debating and Dialect Societies of Great Britain, Ireland and France. 1953, (Geoffrey Handley Taylor) XXXII: 72.

Literary Forgeries in Irish, XXVII: 273.

Literary Inquirer, The, I: 1, 2.

Literary Relic of "Ninety-Eight", V: 43.

Literary Society, see Irish Literary Society.

Literature and Rebellion, VIII: 28.

Literature in Ireland (Thomas MacDonagh), VIII: 37.

Literature of the Conflict, 1922-23, XVII: 127-28; XVIII: 31, 69; ("M.G." on) 3, 31; (Frank Gallagher on), XVIII: 69; (F. S. Bourke on) XVIII: 31, 69; (Séamas Ó Maolchathail on) XVIII: 71.

Lithography in Ireland, XVI: 47.

Little, George A. (*Brendan the Navigator*) XXX: 21; (*Malachi Horan* Remembers) XXIX: 96.

Little, [Canon] Knox, IX: 105, 112.

Little, Philip Francis (*Thermopylae and Other Poems*), VII: 17.

Little White Roads (Hugh A. Macartan), VIII: 107.

Liturgy (French edition), IV: 93.

Lloyd, Clifford (Trollope's Capt. York Clayton based on) XVIII:

48; (ballad on) XVIII: 74.
Lloyd, D. Myrddin (*Sayings of Poor Richard*), XXVII: 180.
Lloyd George, David (*War Memories*), *V*, XXIV: 117.
Lloyd, Nora (*The Young May Moon*), XXIII: 103.
Lloyd, Seaghan [Séan], XXX: 49, 50.
Lloyd, Silvester, II, 12, XVI: 69-70.
Loch, Sydney, & Joice M. Nankivell (*Ireland in Travail*), XIV: 29.
Lóchrann na gCreidmheach, see *Lucerne Fidelium*, XVIII: 19.
Lóchrann, An (Eamonn Ó Mathghsmhna), XVI: 5.
Lockhart, J. G., IV: 27.
Loftie, [Rev.] William John, III: 11.
Loftus, [Rev.], IV: 57.
Logan, James, III: 99, XIV: 75, XV: 63.
Logue, [Cardinal] Michael, XVI: 23.
"Londeriados" (pseud. of John Hempton), VII: 118.
Londonderry—(*Londonderry Journal*) I: 108, 161; (*Londonderry in Three Centuries*) XIII: 110; (Londonderry Air, doubtful antiquity of) XVII: 98-99; (*Londonderry Journal*) XIX: 90-91. For Siege of Londonderry, see Siege of Derry.
Londonderry, Marchioness of, & H. Montgomery Hyde [eds.] (*Russian Journals of Martha and Catherine Wilmot*), XXII: 139.
Londubh an Chairn (Mr. & Mrs. Seamus Clandillon), XVI: 23.
Lonergan, Walter, VIII: 119.
Long Black Hand, The, (see *Lámh Fhada Dhubh, An*.)

Long Retreat, The (Arnold F. Graves), VII: 30.
Longain, Micheál Og, XVI: 4.
Longford, [Lady] Christine, (*Counry Places*) XX:96; (*A Biography of Dublin*) XXIV: 126; (*Printed Cotton*) XXIII: 97; (*Lord Edward*), XXVIII: 139.
Longford, Earl of [Edward Pakenham], (with Christine Longford) *The Oresteia of Aischylos*, XXI: 117; (*Yahoo*) XXIV: 6; (*More Poems from the Irish*) XXX: 20; (The *Dove in the Castle*) XXX: 46.
Longford, [Prof.] Joseph, XI: 45.
Loon, Hendrik Van (*The Home of Mankind*), XXI: 115.
"L.Ó.R." (ed. *Eochar na bhFlathas*), XIX: 125.
Lord Clandonnell (S. M. Christina), VI: 132.
Lord Edward (Katherine Tynan), VIII: 112, 125.
Lord, Patrick, XVII: 78, 120.
Lost Lawyer, The (George A. Birmingham), XIII: 89.
Lost Nightingale, The 1951, ("An Philibín"), XXXII: 24
Lough Fea Library, V: 23, 60.
Lough, Thomas, XIII: 147.
Loughrea—Loughreagh (printing in), II: 151, 181, XVII: 120; (Loughrea Records) VIII: 90; (*Loughrea Journal*) XIX: 172, XXI: 13.
Louth—(*Journal of the Louth Archaeological Society*) II: 91. VII: 72, IX: 11, XIV: 91, XXXII: 96; (poem in Irish by "Bard of Louth"), XVII: 21-22.
Louvain (College of St. Anthony), IV: 4; (printing in) VI: 37, 87, 105, 133; (Louvain-printed books of 17th c.) XVIII: 33; (ouvain Irish Type) X: 103;

(Louvain Grammarians) XXI: 107-109; (Louvain Irish Printing Press) XXXII: 36.
Love, Oscar, XXII: 13.
Love Songs of Connacht (Douglas Hyde), XXX: 125.
Love Sonnets (Padraic Gregory), VI: 60.
Lovely Home, A (M. A. Hargadon), VII: 31.
Lover, Samuel, II: 149, 151, III: 24, 70, 118, IV: 37.
Low, Charles R., IX: 139.
Lowry, Mary, IV: 193.
Loyalist, The, XXIII: 34.
Loyalty Plus Murder (T. M. Healy), XIX: 36
Luaighnigh, Liam (Obit.), XXVI: 26.
Lucas, E. V. (The Two Ladies'), VII: 127.
Lucerna Fidelium (Fr. Francis O'Molloy) XVIII: 5; 17.
Lucy, John (*There's a Devil in the Drum*), XXVI: 46.
Lugard, Lady [Flora Shaw], XVII. 4.
Luke, [W. B.] (More Memories of Dr. Crone), XXX: 26, 27.
Lurgan—(printing in) XIII: 54, 114, 1761 (*Lurgan Magazine*) XIII: 108; ("Lurgan Town", ballad) XXIX: 133.
Luttrell, [Col.] Henry (shooting of), XVII: 84-85.
Lynam, E. W., II: 184, VI: 75, VII: 129, XIV: 48, 81.
Lynam, [Col.] William Francis (Mick McQuaid, III: 4, 5, 6, 29, 47, 80; IV: 161; (*Darby The Dodger*) V: 51; (*Christ Church Faults*), XXVI: 16, XXVII: 249.
Lynass, B., VI: 81.
Lynch, [Col.] Arthur, V: 135; (*Ireland's Vital Hour*) VI: 14, 211, VII: 114; (shakespeare Found Out) XI: 24.
Lynch, [Judge] Charles, VI: 182.
Lynch, Diarmuid, (*The I.R.B. and the 1916 Rising*, ed. Florence O'Donoghue), XXXII: 151.
Lynch, Hannah (A Dublin Novelist), XXI: 133.
Lynch, J. H. (mason), XIV: 13.
Lynch, Patricia (*Fiddlers Quest*), XXVIII: 96; (*Long Ears*) XXIX: 24; (*The Mad O'Haras*) XXXI: 21.(*The Boy at the Swinging Lantern*) XXXII: 46.
Lynch, Patrick (*Patrick Lynch of County Down—Irish Scholar*), XVI: 70.
Lynch, P. J. (New Light on Lord Edward), IX: 21
Lynch, Stanislaus (*From Foal to Tally-Ho*) XXXI: 21.
Lynch, William, II: 12, 28.
Lynd, Robert ["Y.Y."], I: 31, (*Home Life in Ireland*) II: 25; IV: 68; V: 63; 203; VI: 136, 164, 186; VII: 28; XI: 55; XIII: 118, 157; XIV: 44, 56, XVI: 75; (*Rain Rain, Go to Spain*) XIX: 184; (*An Anthology of Essays*) XXI: 116.
Lynd, Sylvia (*The Enemies*), XXII: 147.
Lynegar, *see* Linegar, Charles.
Lynman, E. W. (The O'Flaherty Country), V: 194.
Lynn, Adam, III: 151.
Lynn, Robert J., XI: 44.
Lyons, Dean, IV: 57, 78, (*History of Erris*), XVIII: 174; XVIII: 278.
Lyons, George A., XIV: 29.
Lyons, John Charles, I: 6, IV: 98, 173.
Lyons, J. J. (O'Conway's MS Irish Dictionary), XVII: 131.
Lyrical Poems, V: 146.
Lysaght, Edward E. (*Irish*

Eclogues), VII: 93; (*The Gael*), XII: 18.
Lysaght, Sydney Royse (*My Tower in Desmond*), XV: 62.
Lyster, Thomas William, V: 49, 93, XI: 86.
Lyttle, W. G., III: 137; (*Daft Eddie, or The Smugglers of Strangford Lough*) VI: 41.
Lytton, Edith [pseud. of Emily Lawless], XXXII: 76.
Lytton, Lord [Edward Bulwer] (*O'Neill, or The Rebel*), II: 27.
Lytton, Rosina [Lady Lytton], (*Letters*), VI: 29.

M

Macadam, Robert Shipboy, XIII: 3.
Macafee, David Lyndsay, II: 68, 104.
McAleer, P. (*Townland Names of County Tyrone*), XXV: 70.
Macalister, Alexander, (Obit.) XI: 31.
Macalister, [Prof] R. A. S., VIII: 11, X: 88, XIII: 173, 174; (*History and Antiquities of Inis Cealtra*) VIII: 11. (*Tara*) XX: 22; (*The Secret Languages of Ireland*) XXV: 43; (*The Archaeology of Ireland*) XVI:37, XXXI: 92; (*Corpus Inscriptionum Insularum Celticarum*) XXIX: 141; (*Monasterboice*) XXX: 70.
Mac Amhlaoí, Pádraig ("Brighdín Deas ní Mháille"), XXII: 63.
McAnaspie, Thomas, II: 143.
Macaomh, An, VIII: 44.
Mac Aoidh, Tomás ("Amhrán Bádóra"), XXVI: 57.
Mhac an t-Saoi, Máire (*Margadh na Saoire*), XXXII: 147.
MacArdle, Dorothy (*The Irish Republic*), XXV: 116.
Macartan, Hugh A. (*Little White Roads*), VIII: 107.
MacArthur, William, II: 92, 124, 162, III: 1. 37, V: 34, 107, 167, VI: 32, 43, 45, 130, 134, 153, 170, 190, VII: 76, 101, 115, 117, 137 163 165, VIII: 83, IX: 61, 82, 102, X: 18, 69, 52, 113, XI: 14, 32, XIII: 35, 95, 118, 166.
Macaulay, Lord, IV: 9.
McAuliffe, Max Arthur (Obit.), IV: 195.
McAuliffe, J. J. (Ploughing by Horses' Tails) XXIX: 9.
McBean, G. N. B., VI: 152.
McBride, [Rev.] John, IV: 16.
MacBrien, Peter (*Poems*), XIV: 75; X: 46-47.
McBurney, William, II: 60, 73, XI: 124.
Mac Cába, Alasdair (*The Irish Year Book*), XXIV: 118.
MacCabe, [Lt. Col.] F. F., XI: 28.
McCabe, Joseph (Irish Men of Letters), XII: 10.
McCall, John, III: 128.
McCall, Patrick John (*Irish Fire-Side Songs*), III: 150; X: (Obit.) 86, 93.
McCall, R. A., VII: 97 112.
MacCall, Seamus (*Gods in Motley*) XXIII: 151; (*And So Began the Irish Nation*) XX: 46.
McCallin, William, XII: 135.
McCalmont's Press, IV: 91.
McCance, Finlay, X: 12.
McCance, Stouppe, V: 129, VI: 129, VII: 7, 108, XI: 48, XII: 19.
McCann, Michael Joseph, XVI: 67, XXIII: 48.
Mac Carrthaigh, Micheal, XVII: 53.
MacCartan, Hugh A., VIII: 107, X: 107, XII: 136.
McCartan, Patrick (*With de

Valeria in America), XX: 116.
MacCarthy [also McCarthy], Denis Florence, (A Centenary Sketch) VIII: 121; IX: 14, XX: 86, XXXII: 50; (Library of) XX: 86-91, XXVII: 156.
McCarthy, J. Bernard, XI: 115; (*Playboy of the Seven Worlds*) XXIX: 96; (*The Shadow of the Rose*) XI: 115.
McCarthy, J. F., XV: 24.
McCarthy, Justin, I: 172, II: 8, 146, III: 29, 99, 181, 186, 212, 215, IV: 47, 170.
McCarthy, Justin Huntly, I: 120.
MacCarthy, Samuel Trant, XIII: 180, XIV: 42, 43, XV: 14.
MacCarthys of Munster, XIV: 42.
McCarvill, Mary (*Rhymer's Wake*) XIX: 147.
Mac Cathmhaoil, Seosamh, see Joseph Campbell.
Mac Cerbaill, Diarmuid, (A Story of), XXVIII: 75.
Mac Coitir, Tadhg, ("Failbhe Fionn") XVIII: 88; (his pseud.) XXVII: 212.
McCollum, [Rev.] Randal, XIII: 18.
Mac Coluim, Fíonán, X: 13, XVI: 120; (on J. G. O'Keeffe) XXVI: 26; XXXII: 121.
McComb, William, VI: 7.
MacConroy, Florence, VI: 105.
MacCooey, Art (MSS written and destroyed by), XVIII: 30.
McCoy, G. A. Hayes (*Scots Mercenary Forces in Ireland*) XXVI: 19.
MacCoy, [Rev.] Edward, III: 63, IV: 131, XVII: 84.
Mac Craith, Donnchadh ("Amrán ó Inse an Rinnce"), XIX: 141.
Mac Craith, [an t-Ath.] M. (*Cinnlae Imhlaoibh Uí Shúilleabháin*), XXV: 49.

Mac Craith, Padraig, XIV: 42, 77, XVII: 4, 78, 144.
Mac Craith, Seán, XVII: 18, XIX: 141, XXI: 133; (Obit.), XXI: 3; (J. C. Mangan, Wm. Smith O'Brien and Stephens MSS) XVIII: 173; (Achill Printing) XIX: 96, 101.
McCready, [Rev.] Christopher Teeling (Obit.), V: 105; XVI: 77.
McCreery, John (Irish Music), XXI: 90.
McCrossan, J. L. (Some Notes on Dublin City Maps), XXVI: 2.
McCrudden, Mena (*Songs of the Glen*), XV: 47
Mac Cruitín, Aindréis (*Danta*), XXIV: 17.
McClelland, [Baron] James, I: 78.
McClintock Dix, E. R., see under Dix, McClintock, E. R.
McClintock, [Major] H. F. (*Irish and Highland Costume*), XXIII: 73.
McClure, Canon, VI: 147.
McClure, S. S. (*My Autobiography*), VI: 75.
McCullagh, T., I: 44.
McCurry, Samuel S. (*The Smell of the Turf*), IV: 123; (*The Ballads of Ballytumulty*) XIII: 90; (Ulster Ballads) XII: 99, 143; (*John the Hermit and Other Poems*) XIV: 108; XV: 27.
"MacD.", XIII: 144.
MacDermot, Frank (*Theobald Wolfe Tone*), XXVII: 187.
MacDermot, or the Irish Chieftain (John Agg), XII: 21.
"MacDermot, or The Irish Fortune Hunter" (John Durant de Breval), VIII: 57.
MacDermot, [Dr]. Phillip, XVI: 66, XXI: 45, XXIV: 30, XXXII: 50.

McDermott, M., III: 154, 173.
MacDermott, Martin, XIII: 6.
Mac Dermott, Máire (trans. Françoise Henry, *Early Christian Irish Art*), XXXII: 113, 114.
MacDermott, N., XXXII: 117.
MacDermott, William Robert, (Obit.), X: 20.
MacDonagh, Donagh (with Niall Sheridan, *Twenty Poems*), XXII: 147; (*Poems from Ireland*) XXIX: 143; (*Happy as Larry*) XXX: 46 (*The Hungry Grass*) XXX: 119.
MacDonagh, Frank, III: 94, 114, IV: 211, V: 23, 148, VI: 188, 206, VII: 32, 34, IX: 13, 36, XIII: 29, XVI: 26, 84.
MacDonagh, John, VIII: 42.
MacDonagh, John P., (Obit.), XXIV: 107.
MacDonagh, Michael, VI: 81, 209, VII: 143, 162, IX: 33, XI: 97, XIII: 144, XIV: 62, XV: 30, XVI: 26, 112; (Michael Hogan) XVIII: 36; (*The Home Rule Movement*) XI: 97.
MacDonagh, MSS., XIII: 66.
McDonagh, Patrick A. (*Shamrock Leaves*), XXIV: 65
MacDonagh, Thomas, II: 107, V: 146, VII: 192, VIII: 21, 29, 37, IX: 128, XIII: 132, 155; (*Literature in Ireland*) VIII: 37; (Poems) by XIII: 155.
MacDonald, [Rev.] Walter, XI: 83, (Obit.) 138, XV: 61.
McDonnell and the Norman de Borgos (Archibald McSparran) XXIII: 94.
MacDonnell, John de Courcy, VII: 142.
McDonnell, Eneas, X: 92.
MacDonnell, J. Francis Carlin [or McDonnell], VI: 192, VII: 75, 138, VIII: 18, IX: 135.

McDonnell, Randal [or MacDonnell], IV: 199, V: 70, 80, 99, 128, 191, VI: 39, 54, 93, 178; ("Sarah Curran") VII: 26; VIII: 34, X: 90, (*My Sword for Sarsfield*) XII: 108,109; ("The Dreamer"), IV: 199; ("For Motherland"), VI: 39. ("Remembrance of Lieutenant Thomas Kettle"), VIII: 34.
McDonnell, Robert (*Irish Nationality in 1870 by a Protestant Celt*), VII: 101, 136.
MacDonnell, [Capt.] Sorley, XXII: 81, 143.
MacEnery, Marcus (A 17th c. Anglo-Irish Library), XXX: 30; (*Ploughing by the Tail*), XXIX: 39.
MacEntee, John Francis ("The Tramp"), VIII: 129, IX: 129.
McFadden, [Canon] James, VIII: 143.
McFarlan, Alexander [also MacFarlan], XI: 82; (*The Inscrutable Lovers*) XI: 82.
McFarland, Alfred, III: 8, 22, 118, XXXII: 93.
MacFayden, Dugald, III: 119, 138.
Mac Fhinn, Pádraig Eric, (Ar laimhsgríbhinnibh Gaedhilg i gCathair na Roimhe) XVIII: 49; (Pól Ó Huiginn) XIX: 98.
Mac Firbhisigh [or MacFirbiss], Dubhaltach, (Genealogies) III: 107, 152; (Maynooth MS) XXIV: 38; (ancestry) XXVII: 221.
Mac Gamhradhan, Tomás (*Book of the O'Conor Don*), II: 174.
McGann, Francis, XXVI: 29.
McGarrity, Joseph (*Celtic Moods and Memories*), XXVII: 216.
Mac Gearailt, [An tAth.] Uilliam, XXIV: 105, 134, XXV: 57.
McGee, [Lt.Col.] James, X: 67.

McGee, Thomas D'Arcy, XV: 33, 53, 54.
MacGeoghegan's History, XXVIII: 89.
MacGill, Patrick ["The Navvy Poet"] (*Gleanings From a Navvy's Scrapbook*), III: 41; (Autobiographical Note) 71; 96, 100, 133, 146, 169, 196, IV: 21, 106, 141, V: 164, 179, VI: 40, 147, 187, VII: 18, 55, 98, 143, VIII: 84, 132; (*The Brown Brethren*) IX: 33, XI: 9, 47, 81, 111, XII: 35, 139; ("Going Home") III: 145; (*Songs of Donegal*) XII: 83-86; (*The Glen of Carra*) XXIII: 53; (*The Rat Pit*) VI: 147.
MacGill, [Mrs.], Patrick (The Rose of Glenconnell), VIII: 132, IX: 31.
McGlashan and Gill (Dublin Publishers 1856-1872), XXVIII: 66.
MacGinley, P. T. (ed. *The Donegal Christmas Annual*), XXXII: 76.
McGovern, J. B., I: 46, II: 59, 93; (The O'Conor Don's Book) II: 174-75, III: 7; 82; (Historian of Limerick) III: 114; (Dublin Debating Society) IV: 209; (John Tafe as a Dantist) V: 95-97; VI: 191; The Irish Blue Stocking) VI: 207; VIII: 89, X: 92.
McGovern, [Rev.] J.J. (Obit.), V: 219.
MacGrath Genealogy, XXII: 144.
McGrath, Helen, XXX: 65.
MacGrath, Kevin, XXXI: 35, 63; (Irish Professors and Students at Prague) 82; XXXI: 98, 100; XXXII: 12.
"McGrath, Terence" [pseud. of Sir Henry Arthur Blake], XVIII: 121.
McGreavy, Thomas, (*Poems*), XXII: 95.
MacGregor, Alasdair Alpin, (*Searching the Hebrides with a Camera*), XXIV: 19; (*The Peat Fire Flame*), XXVI: 68.
MacGregor, John James, XV: 48.
M'Gauran, Hugh ("Plearáca na Ruarcach"), XVI: 45.
MacGusty, J., (Private Press), XVIII: 25.
McGuinness, Charles, (*Nomad*), XXIII: 102.
MacHale, [Archbishop] John, II: 145; IV: 57, 78, 132.
McHenry, James, XIII: 16.
McHugh, Mary F., (*Thalassa*) XIX: 126; (*The Bud of Spring*) XX: 47.
McHugh, Roger J. (*Henry Gratan*), XXIV: 89.
McIlroy, Archibald, VI: 192.
McIvor, Dr., VI: 135.
McKay, [Prof.] Robert (*Potato Diseases*), XXXII: 116; (*Tomato Diseases*) XXXI: 116; R. McK), XXXII: 20.
Mackay, J., (*Ten Islands and Ireland*) XII: 62; (*Forestry in Ireland*) XXII: 151.
MacKay, Wallis, III: 91.
Mackay, William, Joseph & Wallis, XI: 53, 54.
McKee, Mrs., XII: 106.
Macken, Walter, (*Mungo's Mansion*) XXX: 47; (*I am Alone*) XXXI: 95; (*Home is the Hero*) XXXII: 48; (*Sunset on the Window Panes*) XXXII: 119; (*The Bagman*) XXXII: 22.
McKenna, [Rev. Mother] Augustine [or MacKenna], VI: 30. VII: 34.
MacKenna, Stephen, XIII: 112.
MacKenzie, Andrew, III: 197.

Mackenzie, Compton (*Literature in My Time*), XXII: 19.
Mackenzie, [Dr.] R. S., II: 171.
MacKenzie, Shelton, VII: 97.
Mackenzie, Thomas, IX: 35.
McKinstry, Robert, VI: 169, VII: 75; (Celt and Saxons), XI: 84-85.
McKnight, [Dr.] James, (*Letters*) X: 15, IX: 62, 110.
McKowen, James (*Sailor with Banjo: Entertainment in Rhyme and Song*), IX: 10.
MacLaren, Hamish, XVII: 140.
MacLaughlin, D., (*Maggie M'Fadden's Breach of Prime Case*), X: 46,47.
McLaughlin, James (*Inishowen*), VII: 136, VIII: 140.
MacLiammóir, Micheál, (*Oidceanna Síde*), XIII: 171; (*Put Money in thy Purse*), XXXII: 45.
McLees, William Hubert, XXIII: 91.
MacLeod, Catriona (*Robert Emmet*), XXIV: 24.
MacLeod, D. J. (ed., Samuel Johnson, *A Description of the Western Islands of Scotland*), XXIII: 25.
Maclise, Daniel (painter), I: 151, II: 46, IV: 28.
Mac Lochlainn, Alfred, XXXII: 65, 142.
McLoughlin, [Rev.] James, IV: 22.
MacLysaght, Edward (on Thomas Arthur, Bishop of Limerick), XXVI: 38.
MacMahon, Bryan, (*The Lion Tamer*) XXXI: 18; (*Children of the Rainbow*) XXXII: 47; (*Red Petticoat and Other Stories, The*), XXXII: 119.
MacMahon, Ella (*Job, The*) V: 199.
MacMahon, Marshal, IX: 138.
MacMahon, Patrick Creagh (*The Leaguer of Limerick*), VII: 10.
MacMahon, Thornton, V: 201, 220.
MacMahon, W. H. (*An Amended Spirit of the Nation*), XIV: 118.
McManus, Anna Johnston, X: 11.
MacManus, Francis, (*After the Flight*) XXVI: 116; (*Candle for the Proud*) XXIV: 142; (*Pedlar's Pack*) XXIX: 144; (*Watergate*) XXIX: 24; (*Stand and Give Challenge*) XXIII: 53; (*The Wild Garden*) XXVIII: 22; (*Flow on, Lovely River*) XXVIII: 94.
MacManus, Henry, VI: 39.
MacManus, M. J. [also *Mc*Manus], XX: 86; (Unexplored Fields in Irish Bibliography) XXII: 33-37, XXIV: 36, 53, 75, XXIX: 26; (Swift pamphlet) XXX: 52-54; (*Rackrent Hall and other poems*), XXVIII: 96; (Appreciation) XXIX: 26; (Elegy) XXXII: 3; (Goldsmith) XVIII: 167; ("*Quoi dono ... libellum*" (elegy for) XXXII: 3.
MacManus, Seamus, V: 180; (*The Bold Heroes of Hungry Hill*) XXXII: 48.
Mac Mhathain, Aonghas (Gu de tha mi leughadh?), XXXI: 39.
McMonagle, Alexander, (Obit.), XI: 10.
McMullan, [Prof.] S. J., XIV: 11.
MacMunn, [Dr.] C. A., VI: 40.
McNally, Leonard, I: 135, XII: 52; (Irish Studies) XXIX: 114.
MacNamara, B. M., III: 13, 31, 33, 60.
MacNamara, Brinsley [pseud. of John Weldon], XIII: 57, XIV: 25, X: 104, XXXII: 21; (*In Clay*

and in Bronze) XXVII: 231; (Margaret Gillian) XXII: 148; XXVIII: 43.
MacNamara, Donough Ruadh [also Red Donough], II: 26, XV: 53.
McNamara, John (a collector of Irish MSS), XXI: 57, XXII: 10, 67, 90, XXIII: 117.
Macnaughten-Jones, Dr., II: 142.
MacNeice, Louis (Holes in the Sky), XXX: 143.
McNeill, Charles (Rawlinson MSS), XIX: 60.
MacNeill, Eoin, (Phases of Irish History) XI: 46; (Neglect of his Works in Irish Schools), XVIII: 65; (Early Irish Laws and Institutions) XXIII: 79; (St. Patrick) XXIII: 103; (Bronnadh na Feil Scribhinne ar) XXVII: 217.
McNeill, [Maj.] H. C., X: 104.
MacNeill, John Gordon Swift, IX: 109.
MacNevin, Thomas, IV: 210; (Library of) XXVII: 156; (The Nation) XXXI: 98.
McNeill, [Rev.] W., (His Reverance Listens Again), XXII: 20.
MacNevin, William James (family of), XVIII: 122.
MacOireachtaigh, Mícheál, The Placename 'Eadar', XXXI: 33.
McParlan, James, V: 52.
Mac Partholán, Aodhagáin, XXXII: 61, 101.
Mac Piarais, Padraig, XIV: 117.
McQuaid, L. P., III: 11.
McQuaid, Mick, III: 4, 46.
McQuilland, Louis J. [also MacQuilland], VI: 183. 199, VII: 183. VIII: 20, 41, XII: 139.
MacRory, [Cardinal] Joseph (The New Testament and Divorce)
XXIII: 120.
MacRory's Duncairn Press, I: 7, 25, 91.
Mac Ruaidhrí, M. ("Pádraic Daéd"), XXX: 44.
McSkimmin, S., I: 48, 134, 153, II: 149, 196, VI: 85. 98, 112, 132.
McSparran, Archibald, XXII: 52, 66; (McDonnell and the Norman de Borgos) XXIII: 94.
Mac Suibhne, Maolmordha, XXVII: 266.
Mac Suibhne, Pádraic [Mac Sweeney, Patrick M.], (Group of Nation-Builders) V: 66, XVI: 13, (Obit.) XXIII: 133.
MacSweeney, [Rev.] Eugene J., XVII: 16.
McSwiggan, Francis J. ("Inspiration!"), IX: 81.
MacSwiney, Terence J., XIII: 31; XII: (Obit.) 70, 86.
MacSwiney, Marquess, XIII: 174.
McTeague, P. (Bentley's Miscellany), V: 201.
MacTeerney, M. C. (Volume of Poems), VI: 209.
Mac Tighearnain, Eoin, XXXII: 93
Mac Tomais, Peadar, (Days and Destinies) XI: 26, XII: 9.
Mac Uidir, Connor, II: 160.
MacWilliam, A., XIII: 65, 95, 119; XIV: 60, 76.
McWilliams, Hugh, III: 154.
Mabbott, [Dr.] T. O., XIV: 127.
Madan, Falconer (Irish Descent), XII: 60, XVIII: 130.
Madden, [Dr.] Richard Robert, IV: 27, 109, VI: 29, VIII: 20, X: 82; (United Irishmen: Their Lives and Times) XII: 19, 83-86, XVII: 56, 104; XIII: 29, XVIII: 171; (Manuscript) XV: 1;

(indebted to Luke Cullen) XVII: 56; (lack of interest in Irish) Madden, Samuel (visit to Ireland with Dr. Johnson & Benjamin Franklin), XXVI: 98.
Maeleachlainn na nUirsgeal (15th c. Irish bard), XXVI: 86.
"Maelmire" (*Shamrockiana*), XVIII: 32.
Maffett, [Rev.] R. S., I: 39, 47, 59, 121, II: 6, 65, III: 201, VI: 17, VII: 7, 12, 47, 91, 139, 164, IX: 7, 60, X: 30, XI: 117, XIV: 44.
MaGabrin [Mac Gabhráin], Seán (MSS of), XIX: 98.
Magazines—(Rare Magazines) VIII: 25; (provincial magazines), XIV: 20. See also Newspapers. .
Magee, [Archbishop] William Connor, IV: 209, XIII: 80.
Mageean, Nicholas (informer), XXXII: 142.
Magees (of Belfast & Dublin), VIII: 35.
Mageoghegan, Antony (Bishop of Clonmacnois), XXVII: 205.
Mageoghegan, Conall, (Description of Hailstorm) XIX: 38; XX: 75; (Conall Mageoghegan's Neighbour-hood) XXI: 4-7. Also (Two Mageoghegans), XX: 75.
Magennis, Bernard, II: 123.
Magennis, Peter (Bard of Derrygonnelly), II: 123.
Maggie M'Fadden's Breach of Prime Case: An Ulster Comedy in Two Acts (D. MacLaughlin), X: 46,47.
Magic Glasses, The (E. Duffin), XXIV: 45.
Magill, [Rev.] Robert, XI: 48.
Maginn, Charles A., VIII: 133.
Maginn, [Dr.] William, I: 133, 148, II: 106, 139, III: 4, 96, VI: 29, IV: 117, 52, VIII: 127, 133, XI: 3; (*Ten Tales*) XXII: 3.

(*Blackwood's* Magazine), XXVI: 73.
Maginn, [Rev.] C. A., XXII: 3.
Magistrate Everyone Knows, The, (Editorial Commentary), XIX: 92.
"Maglone, Barney" [pseud. of Robert Arthur Wilson], I: 161, XII: 75.
Magnus, [Sir] Phillip (*Edmund Burke*), XXVII: 188.
Maguire Clan, The, II: 132.
Maguire Miller, [Dr.] II: 132.
Maguire, Thomas Miller, XII: (Obit.) 70.
Maguires and Irish Learning, The, XXVII: 146, 177.
Maguires of Fermanagh, VI: 32; (Maguires and Irish Learning) XXVII: 146, 177.
Mahaffy, [Prof.] John Pentland, V: 30, VI: 95, X: (Obit.) 112; XIII: 9; XV: 40.
Mahoney, [Fr.] Francis, III: 3, 4, XII: 132, XX: 74.
Mahoney, Frank, III: 324.
Mahony, Sylvester, [see Prout, Fr.].
Maidir linn Féin, XXIX: 2.
Maighdean an tSoluis/TheMaiden of Light (Feargus MacRoigh), V: 103.
Mainistir na gCapuis Éirennaigh, XXIV: 108.
Mainly Victorian (Stuart M. Ellis), XV: 47.
"Máire" [pseud of Seamus Ó Grianna], (*Thiari dTír Chonaill*) XXVII: 235.
Maitland, W. H. (*History of Magherafelt*), IX: 34.
"Major Muskerry" [pseud. of William Dowe], VII: 34, 54.
Majoribanks, Edward (*The Life of Lord Carson*), XX: 116.
Malachi's Daughter: An

Historical Drama of the Ninth Century (T. W. Kerrigan), X: 46,47.
Malet, Dr. (Librarian, RIA), II: 4.
Malleson, Constance (*The Coming Back*), XXI: 46.
Mallon, John, II: 9.
Malone, Andrew E., XVII: 66; (*The Irish Drama*) 70-71; 111.
"Malone, Carroll", II: 60, 73, XI: 124.
Malone, Robert, III: 57.
Maloney, William J. (*The Forged Casement Diaries*), XXIV: 120.
Manchester Martyrs, I: 10.
Mangan, James Clarence, II: 137, 143, 149, 150, 151, 187, IV: 26, 168; VI: 61, 79, 137, 146; XVII: 51; (MS autobiography), XVIII: 173; (Smith O'Brien & James Stephens) XVIII: 173; (his age complex) XXXII: 133; ("Dream of MacDonnell Claragh") XXXII: 134-36.
Mangan, Henry, XXII: 116, XXIX: 27. 137; (ed., *Poems of of Alice Milligan*) XXXII: 94.
Mangin, [Rev.] Edward (1772-1853), XXXI: 28.
Mankind at the Watershed (W. S. Armour), XXIV: 141.
Mansergh, Nicholas (*The Irish Free State, Its Government and Politics*), XXII: 149; (*The Government of Northern Ireland*) XXV: 65; (*Ireland in the Age of Reform and Revolution*) XXVIII: 45.
Mant na Mulchan, XXIV: 64, 87.
Manuscripts—(Old Irish MSS) II: 154; (Historical MSS Commission) III: 9; (Ormonde MSS) III: 91 ; (Irish MSS) III: 155, VII: 75; (Hardiman's Irish MSS) III: 172; (The Wodow MS) IV: 16; (MSS relating to Ireland) IV: 64; (Life of St. Fechin) IV: 124; (Irish MSS) IV: 174; (Roch MSS) VI: 61; (Cathach MS) VII: 8; (Rinucinni MSS) VII: 75, 134; (D'Alton's MSS) VII: 101, 116, 138, 187; (Pinkerton MSS) VII: 138; (O'Morain's MSS) XIII: 35; (MacDonagh, MSS) XIII: 66; (Antrim MSS) XIII: 94; (Irish MSS at Lambeth) XIII: 96; (Rawlinson MSS) XV: 60, XIX: 60; (Thompson MSS) XIV: 61; ("Union, The' MS of) XIV: 106; (Irish MSS in British Museum.Catalogue of) XVI: 2; (MS Collections of Irish Music) XVI: 33, 34; (Irish MS in St. Kieran's College, Kilkenny, An) XVI: 50-51; (Destruction of Irish MSS in Cahirciveen, Rome &c.) XVII: 118, 125, XVIII: 30, 88; (Luke Cullen's MSS) XVII: 56-57; (John Sullivan's Irish MSS) XVII: 139; (MS of Charles Dickens) XVIII: 3; (Irish MSS of M. Fauriel) XVIII: 25; (MSS of Art MacCooey) XVIII: 30; (Irish MSS in Rome) XVIII: 49, 79; (MS Life of St. Patrick) XVIII: 72; (MSS owned by John O'Mahony) XVIII: 80; (MSS of Seán Ó Mathghamhna) XVIII: 80ff., XIX: 98; (O'Mahony's Keating MS) XVIII: 144; (MS Autobiography of James Mangan) XVIII: 173; (MS History of Erris) XVIII: 174; (General Vallancey's Irish MSS) XVIII: 89; (MSS of James Stephens) XVIII: 146, 173; (J. C. Mangan, W. S. O'Brien & James Stephens' MSS) XVIII 173; (MSS of James Boswell in Malahide Castle) XVIII [q.p.];

(of *Críoch Deigheanach Don Duine*) XIX: 8; (O'Laverty MSS) XIX: 27; (Rawlinson MSS) XIX: 66; (17th c. Irish MS at Innishowen) XIX: 93; (MS of Aodh Mac Gabhrain) XIX: 98; (John McNamara: Collector of Irish MSS) XXI: 57, XXII: 10, 67, 90, XXIII: 117; (Irish MSS in Sheffield) XXII: 91; (Charles Lever's MSS) XXIV: 15; (Arthur Brownlow and his MSS) XXIV: 26, 78, 133; (MS of Mac Firbhisigh at Maynooth) XXIV: 38; (MSS of the Four Masters) XXIV: 81; (MS Copies of Irish Books) XXIV: 98; (Catalogue of Irish MSS in the Royal Irish Academy) XXV: 41; Irish MS and O'Donovan Letters) XXVI: 79, 137; (MSS transcribed by O'Curry) XXVI: 110; (Catalogue of MSS in Walter Harris MS) XXVI: 112; (MSS in Franciscan Library) XXVII: 4, 202; (Place Names in MS 23D17) XXVII: 157; (MS of [Rev.] Bernard Callan) XXVII: 160; (Irish MS copies of *Meditationes Vitae Christi*) XXVII: 208; (Work of Irish MSS Commission) XXVII: 283; (MSS repaired by Miss Kennedy) XXVIII: 17-18; (Irish MSS held by Edward Lhuyd) XXIX: 134; (Irish MSS sold in London) XXX: 92; (Medical MSS) XXX: 42, 67; (G. B. Shaw: Gift of Early MSS to Dublin) XXX: 18; (MSS of Peadar Ó Doirnín) XXXI: 6; (Desmond Murray, Medical MSS) XXXI: 14; (Chester Beatty MSS Collection) XXXII: 105; (Illuminated Western MSS at Trinity College, Dublin) XXXII: 105; (Irish MSS in Vatican) XXXII: 61; (MSS of John Kelly) XXXII: 40; (MSS in Plunket's Library) XXXII: 106; (Irish MSS in British Museum) XXXII: 109.
Manuscript Commission—II: 24, 125; III: 9; (publications) XXI: 48, 49, XXVII: 283.
Manuscripts and Record Society of Ireland, XI: 80, XXXII: 40;
Maolmórdha Mac Suibhne, XXVII: 266.
Maps—(Map-Printers in Dublin) XVII: 78, 144; (Dublin City) XXVI: 2.
Marbhna Pádhruic (phonetic copy), XXII: 89.
"Marcus", (*Mrs. Flynn and Mrs. Quinn*) II: 27
Marcus (Florence Davidson), XXII: 71.
Marcus, David (*To Next Year in Jerusalem*), XXXII: 95.
Margin, [Rev.] Edwin (memoir of his father), XXXI: 122.
Marginalia (Edward Berwick), XXX: 126, 128.
Markievicz, [Countess] Constance (*Prison Letters*), XXIII: 19.
Marlay Letters, The, (R. Warwick Bond), XXV: 72.
Marlow, Thomas, VIII: 43.
Married in May (Margaret T. Pender), XI: 134.
Marshall, John J., I: 11, II: 34, 60, 94, 171, III: 62, 194, IV: 36, V: 58, 221, VII: 46, 51 116, 135, IX: 13, 62, 63, XII: 31, 35, (*The Annals of Aughnacloy, The*) XII: 63-65; XIII: 108, XIV: 31, 59, 101; (*Benburb: Its Battlefields and Histories*) XIV: 124; XVII: 69; (*The Orange Bibliography*) XXV: 87.

Marsh's Library, I: 31, VI: 91, 108, X: 42, XXIII: 17, 73.
Marsland, G., XIV: 59.
Martin, Cecil P. (*Prehistoric Man in Ireland*), XXIV: 88.
Martin, Dick, XIV: 27.
Martin Family Cup, XXIV: 13, 31.
Martin, James, XXVIII: 18.
Martin, Jane (Obit.), VIII: 92.
Martin, John, II: 171, XVII: 50; (Diary in Belfast Record Office), XXXII: 142.
Martin, [Mrs]. John, V: 7.
Martin, Mary Letitia ["Princess of Connemara"], XIV: 27.
Martin, Robert Montgomery, III: 82.
Martin, Violet, VII: 120, 127; see also Somerville & Ross.
Martin, William Todd, VII: 120.
Martin, [Col.] William Gregory Wood, II: 21.
Martyn, Edward, (*The Dream Physician*) X: 46-47; XIV: 16, 73;
Marward, Janet, XXIV: 99.
Mary Mansfield, or Ireland Ten Years Since, (from *The Irish Union Magazine*) XIII: 178.
Masai, F. (*Essai sur les origins de la miniature dite Irlandais*), XXX: 139, 140.
Masefield, John (ties with Ireland), XVIII: 69.
Masefield, Muriel (*Women Novelists*), XXII: 150.
Mason, Stuart, VII: 53.
Mason, Thomas H. (*The Islands of Ireland*), XXV: 16.
Mason, William Monck, VII: 125.
Massey, Nassau, III: 190.
Massingham, H. G. (*An Englishman's Year*), XXXI: 43.
Mather, Samuel and Joseph Ray, XX: 40.
Mathew, [Fr.] Theobald (Centenary), XXVI: 40.
Mathew, Frank, XIV: 143.
Mathew, [Sir] James Charles, XV: 32, 48.
Mathghamhna, Eamonn, XVI: 5.
Matthews, Elkin, XIII: 114.
Matthews, James (*Land War of 1770*), I: 133.
Maturin, Chales Robert, III: 70, 102, XII: 34, XIV: 12.
Maturin, Fr., VI: 211.
Maunsel & Co. [publishers], VII: 18, 55, 78.
"Maureen" (Randall McDonnell), VI: 178, XI: 81.
Maxwell, Constantia, II: 145, 160, XIII: 111; (*Dublin under the Georges*), XXIV: 136; (*Country and Town in Ireland Under the Georges*) XXVII: 284.
Maxwell, Henry (*Ulster Was Right*), XXII: 140.
Maxwell, William Hamilton, I: 110, 122, 152, VII: 9; *Wild Sports of the West* (W. H. Maxwell), VII: 61; VII 69, XVII: 63.
May Eve, or the Tinker of Ballinatray (E. Temple Thurston), XV: 14.
May, Robert, VI: 57, IX: 10.
Mayes, William, IV: 73.
Mayne, Ethel Colburn, XII: 87.
Mayne, Reid, XVII: 62.
Mayne, Rutherford, (*The Troth*) I: 112; (*Bridgehead*) XXVII: 167.
Mayne, T. E., II: 10.
Mayne, W. Erskine, III: 47.
Maynooth—(*A Maynooth Professor*) XV: 61; (MS. of Mac Firbhisigh) XXIV: 38; (Catholic Record Society of Maynooth) XVII: 49.
Mayo (John O'Donovan's Ordinance Survey Letters), XIX: 96.

Mayo Constitution (Castlebar), XIX: 90-91.
"M.C.S.", II: 96, XI: 130, 132, 148.
Meade, Lizabeth Thomasina, VI: 81.
Meagher family (two members), XXI: 10.
Meagher, James Anthony, XXXII: 144.
Meagher, John Francis (*Annals ... of Carrick-on-Suir*), XIV: 109, 141, XXI: 10, 132, XXII: 38.
Meagher, Thomas Francis ["Meagher of the Sword"], III: 20, VII: 160, VIII: 140; (*Personal Recollections*) X: 110, XI: 65.
Meagher, William, XXI: 10, 112.
Measgra Mhichil Uí Cleirigh, XXIX: 140.
Meath—(History of the Diocese) XVII: 49; (Fragments of Meath History) XXI: 124; (Four Masters 1450) XXIV: 56; (An Irish Inscription in Co. Meath) XXIV: 124; (Meath before the Famine) XXX: 68, 69.
Medical Family of O'Sheil, XXX: 50.
Medical Manuscripts (Desmond Murray), XXXI: 14.
Meditationes Vitae Christi, XXVII: 208.
Meehan, Denis (*Window on Maynooth*) XXXI: 96.
Meehan, [Fr.] Charles Patrick, II: 129, 187; (Rev. Meehan, O.P.) IV: 23, 25, 71.
Meehan, J. F., IV: 50.
Mé féin agus an Cinnlae (Séamus Ó Casaide), XXVI: 32.
Megaw, W. R. (*Carragloon*), XXIII: 100.
Mela Mór in Co. Kilkenny (Pól Breathnach), XXVI: 138.

Melmoth the Wanderer (C. R. Maturin), XII: 34.
Melo, Helen de (Genealogy of Mrs., McGrath), XXII: 144.
"M.E.M.", VII: 53.
Memento of '48, III: 20.
Memoir of Lieut. Finlay McClance, X: 12.
Memoranda Gadelica, XIX: 166.
Memories of Connemara (Douglas Thompson), XXXII: 149.
Memories of Mountjoy (Sean Milroy), IX: 81.
"Memory, A" (L. A. G. Strong), XIII: 179.
Men and Memories: Recollections of William Rothenstein (Willaim Rothenstein), XIX: 103.
Men of '48, IV: 31.
"Menenius", I: 136.
Menken, Adah, XIII: 86.
Mercier, Richard Edward (Obit.), V: 106.
Mere Trifle! A, (longest words), XXVIII: 92.
Meredith, George, I: 18.
Merne, John G. (*A Handbook of Celtic Ornament*), XIX: 128.
Merriman, Brian (or Bryan Merryman), III: 13, 31, 33, 60, 64, 152; (Poet, Philomath and Flax Sower) XXV: 103; (*Midnight Court*, US edition) XVII: 117; (*Cúirt an Mheadhon-Oidhche*) XXX: 8-11.
"Merry Andrew" [pseud.] I: 133, 150; XXX: 48.
Meyer, Kuno, II: 14, 88, 126, 154, 174, 175, 198, XI: 35.
Meynell, Mrs., IX: 56.
"M.G." (on Literature of the Conflict, 1922-23), XVIII: 3, 31.
Mic Fhirbhisigh, Leacán, XXVII: 210.
"Mick McQuaid" (in *The Shamrock*), III: 4, 46.

Michael Hogan's *Lays and Legends of Thomond*, XXVII: 205.
Microscope, The, III: 9.
Middle Years, The (Katharine Tynan), VIII: 85.
Midnight Court, The, see *Cúirt Mean Oidche* and Merriman, Brian.
Milesian Magazine, XVII: 2, 23.
"Miles O'Reilly", see Halpine, Charles Graham.
Military Poet in Birr, A, XXVII: 231.
Mill in the North, The, Patricia, O'Connor, XXVI: 46.
"Mill, The" (James H. Cousins), VI: 187.
Miller, Ruddick (*The Ulster Book*) XVII: 75; (*Stirabout from an Ulster Pot*) XVIII: 37.
Milligan, Alice, (Mrs. Milligan) V: 180; (*The Daughter of Donagh*) XI: 134; XI: 141; (with W. H., *The Dynamite Drummer*) XII: 36; (Obituary) XXXII: 63; (*Poems*) XXXII: 94.
Milligan, Seaton F. VII: 191.
Millin, S. Shannon, XI: 115, 141, XII: 16.
Milltown Park Library, XVI: 37-39.
Milroy, Sean, IX: 81.
Milton's *Comus*, XI: 86.
Minchin, George M., V:
Mind You, I've Said Nothing (Honor Tracy), XXXII: 72.
Minnie's Bishop and Other Stories (George Birmingham), VI: 204.
Minstrel of Erin, The (Terence O'Hanlon), XVIII: 150.
Minstrelsy of Ireland, The (Alfred Moffat), XXVII: 234.
Mirror in the Dusk (Brinsley MacNamara), XIII: 89.
Miscellany (18th c.), XII: 114.

Miscellany of Irish Proverbs, A (ed. T. F. O'Rahilly) XIV: 46.
Misconceptions ("Saracen"), XIII: 171.
Misfit: An Autobiography (J. R. White), XVIII: 125.
Misprints from Epitaph, XVIII: 143.
"Miss Eleanor", III: 184, 194, 195, 202.
Miss Gascoigne (Katherine Tynan), X: 46,47.
Miss Rudd and Some Lovers (Eimar O'Duffy), XIV: 73.
Missing—(Missing Books) XI: 136; (Missing Irish MS) XXVII: 60; (Missing MS [of] Matthew Butler) XXIX: 11; Missing translation of *Imitation of Christ*) XXVII: 233.
Mitchel, John, II: 74, 89, 145, 164, 171, 172, III: 27; (*Life of Aodh O'Neil*) IV: 161; (*The Adventurer*) IV: 161; (Mitchel's books) V: 136; VI: 31; (a short biography) VII: 57, 86 95. VII: 74; (Bibliography) VII: 86; ("Gleanings") VII: 139; IX: 84; (*Ireland, France, and Prussia*) IX: 110; XIII: 42, 83; XVII: 50, 63; (A Rare Item) XXVIII: 68.
Mitchell, Justin, XII: 83.
Mitchell, Susan, VIII: 87, XII: 13, 79.
Mitchell, [Mrs.] T., VII: 139.
Mitchelbourne, [Col.] John, I: 158, II: 13.
Mitford, Miss, III: 18.
"M.J.G.", IX: 110.
"M.J.J.", I: 157.
"M.M.M.E.", VII: 53.
"Modereen-a-rua/The Red Fox" (Irish Hunting Song), VI: 129.
Modern Anglo-Irish Verse (ed. Padraic Gregory), VI: 11.
Modern Ireland in the European

Padraic Gregory), VI: 11.
Modern Ireland in the European System (James Hogan), XII: 45.
Moffat, Alfred (*The Minstrelsy of Ireland*), XXVII: 234.
Mollan, [Mrs.] H. C. [Helen Cromie], I: 155.
Molloy, James Lynam, II: 68, 85, 112.
Molloy, Maura, XIV: 124.
"Molly Astore" (George Ogle), VIII: 18, 42.
Moloney, D. (Skibbereen printer), XIX: 60.
Molony, J. Chartres (*The Tragic Comedians*), XXIII: 23.
Molyneux, William [Elder brother of Sir Thomas] (*Case of Ireland*), V: 116; (Manuscripts) XII: 40; XXXII: 86.
Moments with all the best Amateurs (smallest Irish periodical), XIV: 141.
Monaghan—VII: 137; (*The Spiritual Rose*) XVIII: 141; (Monaghan for 200 Years) XIII: 5; (Monaghan in 18th Century) VII: 64; (Two Old Monaghan Journals) X: 30, XI: 29, XXVIII: 80; (printing in Monaghan) IV: 200, V: 2, 26, X: 34, 55).
Monahan, [Canon] Peter, XVII: 17, 78.
Monahan, Michael, VII: 10.
Monastery of Saint Mochaoi of Nendrum (H. C. Lawlor), XV: 58.
Monck, William Henry Stanley, VII: 16.
Monotype Corporation (on Gaelic type), XVII: 38.
Mons, VI: 132.
Montague, C. E. (*A Hind Let Loose*), I: 148.
Montégut, Emile (*John Mitchell: A Study in Irish Nationalism*),

VII: 74.
"Montez, Lola" (stage name of Rose Gilbert), X: 36.
Montgomery, Henry Riddell, I: 100, 101, IX: 71-72.
Montgomery, James (Ulster poet), XII: 3, 41.
Montgomery, J. W. ["The Bard of Bailieborough"] (Obit.), III: 42, 82.
Montgomery, Mrs. (*Angels and Symbols*), II: 178.
Montgomery, William (Description of Ards Penninsula), XX: 28.
Montgomerys of Ballyleek, V: 220.
Month, The (Irish issue) XXXII: 150.
Monthly Museum, VI: 44.
Monthly Visitor and Friend of Ireland, III: 216.
Montiaghisms (William Lutton), XIV: 31.
Monuments Eblanæ (hand-pinted sketches of Dublin), XXV: 58.
Monypenny, W. F.,
Monypenny, William Flavelle (biography of Beaconsfield) II: 31; (Obit.) IV: 85; (Ireland and Home Rule) 146.
Moody, T. W. (*Thomas Davis*), XXX: 20.
Mooney, [Fr.] Canice, (Missing Irish MS) XXVII: 60; XVII 181, 233; (*Meditationes Vitae Christi*) XXVII: 208; (MS. of Rev. Bernard Callan) XXVII: 160; (Fr. Philip Ó Conaill) XXVII: 181; (Franciscan Library MS) XXVII: 4, 202; Franciscan Library Acquisitions) XXVII: 182; (Missing trans. of *Imitatio Christi*) XXVII: 233; (Mummers', Play) XXVII: 270; (Yeats and "The Sally Gardens")

XXXI: 86.
Mooney, Thomas, X: 70, 109, XI: 24, XVII: 43, XIX: 76; (date of death) XVIII: 31.
Moore, Augustus M., II: 103.
Moore, Frankfort, I: 57, II: 44, 76, 89, V: 164, 182, 211, VI: 5. 148, XII: 16, XIX: 70.
Moore, [Mrs.] G. M. [pseud. "E. M. Lauderdale] (Obit.), VII: 142.
Moore, George Henry [politician], V: 31.
Moore, George [novelist], II: 198; II: 198; IV: 13; V: 144, 150, 179, 203.; VI: 40. 95; VII: 96 191; VIII: 87; VIII: 87; XVII: 99; (Arnold Bennett) XXIII: 131; (Charles Morgan, *Epitaph on George Moore*) XXIV: 20; (Hone's Life of Moore) XXIV: 143.
Moore, [Sir] John (burial), V: 3.
Moore, Kingsmill, V: 182.
Moore, [Mrs.] L. F. (*Spring Songs and Other Verses*), X: 15.
Moore, Norman, [Sir], II: 99, VI: 185, VIII: 78, X: 104, XXIV: 14.
Moore, Thomas, II: 142, III: 162, IV: 28, 32, 47, 163; (early verses) X: 111; (Mrs. Moore) XI: 23, 112; XII: 23, XIII: 30, 103; XV: 49; XVII: 3, 4; (contrib. to *Edinburgh Review*) XVIII: 3; (and the Irish Language) XX: 57; (and Robert Emmet) XXII: 8; (*Captain Rock in Rome*), XXXII: 40, 92.
Moore's Melodies and the Paper Maker, XXVIII: 88.
Moran, D. P., see *Leader, The*.
Moran, [Cardinal] Francis Patrick, III: 36.
Moran, J. J. (*Irish Drolleries*), I: 106.
Moran, John, see Ó Modhráin, Seán.
Mordant, [Capt.] Nicholas, XXIII: 134.
More, Jasper (*The Land of Italy*), XXXI: 94, 120.
More Pricks than Kicks (Samuel Beckett), XXII: 96.
Morgan, Charles (*Epitaph on George Moore*), XXIV: 20.
Morgan, Lady [Sydney Owenson], III: 69, 143, 161; (the Irish Morgans) IV: 191; V: 148; (the father of), XXII: 79; XIII: 104, XV: 30.
Moriarty, Edward Aubrey, IV: 123, VI: 45.
Moriarty, Mrs., XIV: 107.
Morison, Stanley (*The English Newspaper*), XX:72.
Morisy, John [or Morrisey], see Young, Townsend.
Morley, Christopher (*Parnassus on Wheels*) XXXII: 46.
Morni: An Irish Bardic Story in Three Cantos (Richard Benson), VII: 76.
Morning Post, XIII: 87.
Morris, Henry, see Ó Muirgheasa, Énrí.
Morrissey (Edmund Downey), XIV: 140.
Morrow, George, XIV: 27.
Morrow, H. L. (ed. *John O'London's Weekly*), XVI: 75-76.
Morrow, Norman, V: 123.
Mors et Vita (Shan F. Bullock), XIV: 89.
Morton and Black (*All Square with Fate*), XXI: 21.
Morton, J. B. (*The New Ireland*), XXVI: 44.
Morton, H. V. (*In Search of Ireland*), XIX: 68.
Morton, May (*Sing to the Spinning*

Wheel), XXXII: 118.
Mosada (W. B. Yeats), XV: 54.
Mosher, T. B. (*A Little Book for John O'Mahoney's Friends*), I: 75.
Mosney: A Meath Place Name (Rev. John Brady), XXIX: 19.
Moss, Bernard Hugh, XXXII: 89; 92;107.
Moth and the Star, The ("An Philibín"), XXVI: 45.
Mould, [Dr.] Daphne D. C. Pochin (*Irish Pilgrimage*) XXXII: 110.
Moult, Thomas (ed., *The Best Poems of 1936*), XXV: 45.
Mount Mellaray, VI: 23.
Mount Music (E. Œ. Somerville & Martin Ross), XI: 112.
Mount Trenchard Private Press, IX: 7.
Mountainy Singer, The (Joseph Campbell), I: 28.
Mountjoy, Desmond, II: 10.
Moyne, Lord [Walter Edward Guinness], XXII: 38.
"M.P.", III: 63, 81, 103, VII: 15, 34.
"M.R." ("The Eddystone Lighthouse"), VI: 13.
"M.R.S.", V: 61.
Mrs. Martin's Man (St. John Ervine), VI: 99.
Mr. Wildridge of the Bank (Lynn C. Doyle), VIII: 59.
MS & MSS, see Manuscripts
Mud and Purple (Seamus O'Sullivan), IX: 54.
Museum, The, (18th c. literary periodical) XXII: 40-41.
Mulcahy, [Dr.] Denis Dowling, I: 169, II: 58, 95, IV: 55.
Mulcahy, Timothy (Clonmel book-lover, Obit.), XXIV: 84.
Mulchrone, K., ed., *Bethu Patraic*, XXVII: 214.
Mulgan, [Rev.] Mason, X: 18.

Mulhall, Patrick, XIV: 141.
Mulholland, Rosa, XIII: 21.
Mullain, Sean, XXIII: 107.
Mullan, William, VI: 6, 25.
Mullanphy, Brian, and Canon O'Hanlon, XX: 16.
Mullen, Pat (*Man of Aran*) XXIII: 49; (*Irish Tales*), XXVI: 95.
Mullin, [Dr.] James, XI: 86; XIII: 59.
Mullingar (printing in), II: 120, IV: 112, VI: 127, 140, 160.
Mulvany, William Thomas, VII: 183.
Mummers—(Christmas Ryhmes and) XVI: 126; (of County Wexford), XVII: 59-61, XXXII: 103; (series in *Ireland's Own*) XVIII: 173; (Article in the Yorkshire Press on) XX: 18; (description of Fingal) XX: 91; (R. J. E. Tiddy, *The Mummers' Play*) XXVII: 270.
Munro, Alida, (ed. *Recent Poetry 1923-33*), XXII: 72.
"Munro, C. K." (*The Rumour*), XIV: 11.
Munro, Henry (extant likeness), XXXII: 142.
Munro, Neil, (*The Poetry of*, intro. John Buchan) XIX: 181; (*The Brave Days, The Looker On*), XXII: 75.
Munster Telegraph, XV: 48.
Munster Twilight, A (Daniel Corkery), VIII: 138.
Murphy, Alison Barstow (*Every Which Way in Ireland*), XVIII: 178.
Murphy, Bernadette (*The Unwilling Player*), XXIII: 80.
Murphy, [Bishop] John (A Book Loving Bishop), II: 17-19; III: 179, 212, IV: VII: 1, 48, 52, 122; XVI: 4. 27.
Murphy, Diarmuid (*Hewn of the*

Rock), XXII: 75.
Murphy, Francis Stack, XIV: 77.
Murphy, Gerard, (*Tales from Ireland*) XXX: 96; XXXII: 65.
Murphy, Hazel (*Himself*), XX: 48; (*The Travelling People*), XXII: 152.
Murphy, John, XIII: 118.
Murphy, K. M. (*Poems*), XX: 119.
Murphy, M. A., VII: 142.
Murphy, Michael J. (*At Slieve Gullion's Foot*), XXVIII: 138.
Murphy, Nicholas P. (Obit.), V: 220.
Murphy, William, III: 213, XII: 42; (Obit.) XXIV: 107.
Murray, Daly, II: 62.
Murray, Desmond (Medical MSS), XXXI: 14; XXXII: 113.
Murray, [Dr.] John O'Kane Irish American Writer), V: 97.
Murray, John, IV: 19.
Murray, John Fisher, II: 187.
Murray, [Fr.] Laurence P. (*Omeath Co. Louth*), VII: 73; (*History of the Parish of Creggan—Seventeenth and Eighteenth Centuries*) XXVIII: 69; (*County Louth Archaeological Journal*) XXVIII: 136.
Murray, M. J. G., II: 128.
Murray, Robert H. (*Revolutionary Ireland*), II: 189; IV: 104.
Murray, Thomas Cornelius (*Michaelmas Eve*) XX:142; (*Maurice Hart*) XXII: 147; (*A Stag at Bay*) XXII: 147; (*Spring Horizon*) XXV: 113.
Murry, Desmond (An Irish Charm), XXIX: 134.
Murtagh, James Behan, XXII: 109.
Muse, The (organ of Dublin Writers' Club), XVIII: 138.
Museum, The (18th c. Cork magazine), XXII: 40.

Musgrove, P. J., (*A Socialist and War 1914-16*), XXVIII: 47.
Musical Epitaphs in Ireland (request for), XXXII: 142.
Muskenry, Major, VII: 34, 54.
Mulvany, C. P[elham] (*The History of the North-West [Canadian] Rebellion of 1885*), XI: 107.
My Ireland: Songs and Simple Rhymes (Francis Carlin). X: 46,47.
My Irish Friends (Mrs. William O'Brien), XXVI: 89.
My Lady of the Chimney Corner (Alexander Irvine), V: 145.
My Sword for Sarsfield (Randal McDonnell), XII: 108,109.
My Talks with Dean Spanley (Lord Dunsany), XXV: 17.
My Tower in Desmond (Sydney Royse Lysaght), XV: 62.
Myths and Legends of the Irish Race (T. W. Rolleston), III: 74.

N

Na Buideil Draoidheachta (Mrs. de Velera), XXIV: 140.
Naas (printing), VII: 6.
Nally, Lilian Mary, (*A Knapsack of Dreams*), XXIII: 30.
Nangle, [Rev.] Edward, II: 65, 66.
Nankivell Joice M. & Sydney Loch (*Ireland in Travail*), XIV: 29.
Nation, The, I: 62.
Nation: (War Issue, 1922), XVIII: 31.
National Being, The (Æ), VIII: 66.
National Economic Recovery (Anon.), XXIII: 121.
National Gallery of Ireland (portrait in), XVIII: 45.
National Library (also New Irish Library), V: 160.

National Library of Ireland, see Libraries (public).
National Literary Society, VII: 67, 131; 153, VIII: 84, VI: 111, 200.
National Literary Society of Dublin, I: 63.
National Museum Report, XXI: 26.
National Review, The, XI: 21.
National School System (opposition to Irish language), XX: 65.
National Student, The, XVIII: 52.
National Univiversity of Ireland Club, London, XXXII: 92.
National Volunteer, VI: 75.
Nationality, (War Issue, 1923), XVIII: 31.
Navan Printing, VI: 31.
"Navvy Poet, The" [psud. of Patrick MacGill], see MacGill, Patrick.
Neagh, Lough, III: 81, 193.
Neale W. G., VI: 48, VII: 138.
Neale, John and William, XXXII: 145.
Nedley, Dr., XIII: 8.
Neil, Crawford, VIII: 84.
Neill, Patrick, VI: 157, 159.
Neilson, "Dr.", XII: 68.
Neilson, William, XIII: 78.
Neligan, Harry, VI: 100.
Neligan, [Dr.] William Chadwick, VII: 21, 98.
Nelligan, Emile, II: 41.
Nelson (publishers), XXX: 144.
"Nemo", (on Patrick Stanton & Bud Sullivan), XVIII: 143.
Nendrum monastery, XV: 58.
Nesbitt, R., VII: 138.
"Nescio", (Swift's Knowledge of Greek), XIX: 25.
Nevin, May (*Over the Hills*), XXIV: 23.
New Evening Post, The, XII: 104-106.
New Invasion, (Winefride Nolan), XXXII: 71.
New Ireland Review, II: 125.
New Irish Journal, 1842, XXXII: 15.
New Irish Library (see also National Library), V: 160.
"New Lights of Askeaton, The", XXI: 102, XXII: 11.
New Novels, XII: 65-66.
New Querist, The (Anon.), XXII: 145.
New Review, Political, Philosophical and Literary, The, XXVIII: 130.
New Ross (history of), XVIII: 98.
Newbery's Irish Accidence 1562-63 (Séamus Ó Casaide), XVI: 61.
"Newman, A" [pseud. of Herbert Pim] (*The Pessimist*), V: 163; (*Philosophical Development Among the Irish*) VII: 119; (*The Irishman*) 133; VII: 134.
Newman, [Cardinal] Henry, II: 87; (*The Idea of a Liberal Education*), XXXII: 45.
Newport, Lord, III: 108.
"Newriensis" (*Historical Sketch of Newry*), VII: 115.
Newry—(Printing), I: 160, 11, V: 201, VI: 17; (*Historical Sketch*) VII: 115; XVII: 142; (Liter-ary Distinction) XVII: 62-64.
Newry Telegraph, XIX: 90-91.
Newsome, James Clarence (Obit.), V: 106.
Newspapers—(First Irish Papers) IV: 61, 97; (Old Newspapers) XVII: 55, 78; (Newspaper in German Printed in Dublin) XVIII: 88; (Newspapers of Ireland in 1819) XIX: 90-91; (British and Irish before 1801) XXII: 56, 102; (First Limerick Newspaper) XXIV: 53. (Newspapers in 1788) XXXII: 65.

Newsted, III: 193, IV: 15.
Newtownards Chronicle, II: 30.
Newtownards (printing), XII: 101.
Newtowncrommelin Press, II: 12, 28.
Ní Bhroin, Máire (Obit.), XIX: 1.
Ni Dhochartaigh, Brighid (*Cainnt Choitcheannta o'n Gheadhealtacht*) XIII: 172.
Ní Dhomhnaill, [Máire] (Red Hugh's Sister), XXVI: 105.
Ní Dhubhgbail, Máire (David Comyn, Language Movement Pioneer), XXXI: 4.
Nic Neill, Ida (*Cú na gCleas*), VI: 78.
Nice Distinctions: A Tale (Miss Driscoll), XXX: 44.
Nicholls, [Mrs.] A. B., VI: 163.
Nicholson, William, (Bishop of Derry), XVI: 11.
Nicoll, [Sir] Robertson, VIII: 141.
Night Nurse, The (James Johnston Abraham), IV: 187.
Night of the Big Wind, (description by Michael Burke), XVII: 130, 131; (account by Michael Burke), XVIII: 77.
'Ninety Eight [Rebellion of 1798], VII: 15; (leaflets) XXVI: 16, 115; (a novel) XXXI: 105.
Ninth Music Book (John Gay and the Ballad Opera), XXXII: 145.
Noble, Margaret, III: 77, VI: 119, 129.
Nochera, Don Jayme, XXVI: 113, 135, XXVII: 159.
Nolan, Winefride (*Exiles Come Home*), XXXII: 120; *The New Invasion*, 1953, XXXII: 71.
Non-Juring Priests in 1714, XXV: 99.
Noonan, John D., V: 39, VII: 12, XI: 63, 84, 116, XII: 22, 137; (Davis's Library) XXX: 40-41; XXX: 69.

Nooth, Charlotte, VI: 170.
Norman de Burgos, XXIII: 94,
Norman Surnames, Pól Breathnach, XXVII: 173.
Normans in Ireland, XXII: 14.
"Norreys Connell" [pseud. of Conal O'Riordan), XI: 115.
"North Antrim" (*An Antrim Keepsake*), XXII: 70.
North East Corner, The (J. Heron Lepper) IX: 32.
North, John (notes of will), XVII: 64.
Northern Herald, The, XII: 138.
Northern Patriot (monthly), XXXII: 63.
Northern Whig, XIV: 28.
Norton, [Mrs.] Caroline. I: 64.
Norway, [Mrs.] Hamilton VIII: 20.
Norway Man, The (Joseph O'Connor), XXXI: 95.
Note on Ballad on Clifford Lloyd, (see Lloyd, Clifford).
Note on Domhnall O'Fearachair, (see O'Fearachair, Domhnall).
Note on Graiseberry, Printer, (see Graiseberry).
Note on Dr. Keating, (see Keating, Dr.).
Note on the Life and Writings of Paul Hiffernan, (see Hiffernan, Paul).
Notes and Queries, XIX: 25, 58, 95, 124, 142, 175, XX: 15, 41, 61, 92-94, 113, 137, XXI: 18, 42, 64, 89, 135, XXII: 11, 38, 64, 89, 114, 142, XXIII: 14-17, 46-48, 72, 92-95, 116-117, 147, XXVIII: 18-19, 43-44, 66-69, 87-92, 133-135.
Notes on Children's Games - L. H. Daiken. XXVIII: 117-119.
Notes on Provincial Printing, see Printing.
Notes on the Irish Language Columns of *The Shamrock*, (see

Shamrock).
Notes on Two Mageoghegans, (see Mageoghegan)
Notices of New Books, X: 12, 62, 63, 91, XII: 16-18, 38-40, 61-63, 83-86, 108-109, 112, 134-135, XV: 12, 30, 60, 46.
Novel Business, This (editorial), XXIV: 121.
Novels on Ireland, XXIV: 97.
Novelists' Names Wanted, XII: 41.
"Níl sé in a Lá" (Irish Song), XX: 115.
"Nubhar", II: 112.
Nugent of Corbetstown (Rev. John Brady), XXIX: 90.
Nugent, [Fr.] Francis (Ludwig Bieler), XXX: 98, 99.
Nugent, [Fr.] Robert S.J., (Rev. John Brady), XXIX: 17; XXX: 100-102.
Numbering of Dublin Houses, XXI: 65, 137.
"Nun of Kenmare", VI: 133.
Nutt, Alfred, I: 166.

O

Ó Aodha, Séamus (An Dara Óir Chiste), XIX: 184.
O'Baggot, James, XVII: 81-82; (Obit.), XVIII: 19.
Obituaries, see under individual names.
O'Boyle, Michael (*The Western Rover*), XX: 137.
O'Brennan, K. (on Alice Furlong), XXX: 105-106.
O'Brennan, [Dr.] Martin Andrew, XVII: 4.
Ó Briain, [An t-Ath.] Pól, XXVI: 63.
Ó Briain, [Bean] Chruis (also Ui Bhriain),(Cló scribhnedireacht i gCursai Gnátha), XXVI: 92.

Ó Briain, Feilim, (Franciscan texts), XVIII: 87; (The Louvain Grammarians), XXI: 107-09.
O'Brien, Barry, II: 156, IX: 106, 112, 113, XIII: 30, XVII: 74.
O'Brien, Charlotte Grace, I: 21, 89.
O'Brien, Conor (*Two Boys Go Sailing*), XXIV: 139; (*Runaways*) XXVIII: 138
O'Brien, Cruise, VIII: 72.
O'Brien, Dierdre, (*Lover's Folly*) XXI: 68; (*Many Roads in Heaven*) XXIII: 128.
O'Brien, Donough (*History of the O'Briens*), XXXI: 120.
O'Brien, [Dr.] (*Economic History of Ireland in the 17th c.*), XII: 10
O'Brien, E. J. (ed. *Short Stories of 1937*), XXVI: 23.
O'Brien, Eris (*The Foundation of Australia*), XXVI: 20.
O'Brien, Fitzjames, XI: 32.
O'Brien, F., [Rev.], XVII: 57.
O'Brien, George (*The Four Green Fields*), XXV: 24.
O'Brien, Georgiana (ed. *The Reminiscences of Lord O'Brien Chief Justice of Ireland*), VIII: 48, 138.
O'Brien, [Rev.] John F. X., S.J. (Obit.), XI: 95.
O'Brien, Kate (*The Ante-Room*) XXII: 120; (*Pray for the Wanderer*) XXVI: 69.
O'Brien, Nellie, XII: 13.
O'Brien, [Lord] Peter, VI: 63, VIII: 48, 138.
O'Brien, P. J. (*Will Rogers*), XXV: 44.
O'Brien, Seamus, XI: 61.
O'Brien, W. J. (The Irish Literary Revival), VII: 189.
O'Brien, William Smith [Young Irelander], I: 118, III: 20, 24; VI: 117, XVII: 51; (Papers), XVIII:

173.
O'Brien, William [politician] II: 44, 70, 71, III: 5, 57, IV: 17, XIII: 180; (Life of) XVI: 112; XII: 17.
O'Brien, [Mrs.] William (*My Irish Friends*), XXVI: 89.
O'Briens (*Memoir of the O'Briens*), XIII: 65.
Ó Broin, León, XVI: 83.
Ó Broin, Pádraig, XXXII: 141.
Ó Brollachan, P., VI: 133.
O'Byrne, Cathal, VII: 33; (*Grey Feet of the Wind*) IX: 34; ("An Irish Fisherman's Prayer") XIX: 22; (*The Burthen*), XXI: 23; (*The Returned Swank*), XXI: 23; (*The Gaelic Source of the Bronte Genius*) XXII: 46.
O'Byrne, Dermot, X: 61, XI: 61.
O'Bryne, Owen (St. Evin), III: 63; (Rev. Edward MacCoy) IV: 132-33; VII: 137 139.
Ó Cadhain, Máirtín (*Báinne Dhubh na Féile*), XVI: 30.
Ó Cadhla, Cormac (Stáid an Lucht Saothair), XXII: 146.
O'Callaghan, Edmund Bailey (An Irish American Writer), IV: 101.
O'Callaghan, John Cornelius, IV: 8.
Ó Caoimh, Eoghan, XX: 65.
Ó Caomhinaigh, Seamus (*Humanitas*), XVIII: 96.
Ó Cearbhalláin, Toirbdeallach (Turlough O'Carolan), see Carolan, Turlough.
Ó Casaide, Séamus [also Séamus Uí Casaide, O'Casaide], (An Seanchaidhe Muimhneach) XII: 11; (Sean O'Casey) XIV: 72, 144, XV: 16, 30, XVI: 67, 109-111; (R. M. Levey) XIX: 23; (James Stephens) XIX: 25, 97, XX: 15; (O'Reilly's *Irish Catechism*) XIX: 25; (Bonaventura O'Connor) XIX: 59; (Skibbereen Publication) XIX: 60; (Rev. H. Quinn) XIX: 60, 97; (Barry, Anna Marie) XIX: 61; (*Pléaráca na Ruacach*) XIX: 61; (*Castle Martyr*) XIX: 62; (printing in Drogheda) XIX: 78; Crioch Deigheanach Don Duine (Séamus Ó Casaide), XIX: 80; (Origin of the Boston Pilo-Celtic Society) XIX: 88; (The Keetings and the Sheehys) XIX: 89; (Irish Newspapers, 1819) XIX: 90; (Athlone Printing) XIX: 95, XXIII: 93; (Bonmahon Printing) XIX: 95; (Rev. Bernard Callan) XIX: 97; (Ó Mathgamhna MS) XIX: 97; (Ma Gabhran MSS) XIX: 98; (O'Kenny's *Irish Catechism*) XIX: 100, 124; (Thomas Abbott) XIX: 100; (Irish-speaking Dublin Booksellers) XIX: 111, 140; (*Amhrán ó Innse an Rinnce*) XIX: 141; (Irish Archeological Society) XIX: 142, 165, XXI: 91; (E.G. Finnerty) XIX: 143; (Laoghis Epitaph) XIX: 175; (Dr. J. O'Reardon) XIX: 177, XX: 64; (James Emmet) XIX: 177; (Country Postbag) XX: 9; (John Carey) XX: 15; (Dean Lynches) XX: 16, 62, XXI: 20; (Peadar Ó Doirnín) XX: 17, 52; (Capt. William Levins) XX: 19; (Cumha Mná an Tabhairne) XX: 34; (An Bharuntacht) XX: 37; (printing in Enniscorthy) XX: 43; (Seán Ó Faoláin of Kilkenny) XX: 43, 114, XXI: 91; (FitzJames O'Brien) XX: 44; (Irish v. Roman characters) XX: 56; (Sean Clarach and Liam Dall Ó hIfearnáin) XX: 58; (Joseph Haly) XX: 61, XXI: 114, XXII:

39, 66; (Dublin Booksellers) XX: 62; (Eoghan Ó Caoimh) XX: 65; (National School Opposition to Irish) XX: 65 (*Láimhscribhinn Sheaghain Gaillidhe*) XX: 82; (Fingal Mummers) XX: 91; (George Smith) XX: 92, XXII: 16; (Celtic Times and Irish Athletics) XX: 93; (Charles Scott, MS) XX: 93; (Proinsias Ó Maolmhuidh) XX: 94; (Talbot B. Reed and Irish Type Fonts) XX: 94; (Charter of the Philo-Celtic Society of Philadelphia) XX: 111; (Printing in Achill) XX: 114, XXII: 103; ("Níl sé in a Lá") XX: 114; (Coryat's Crudities) XX: 138; (Hodgkin's MS) XX: 138; (Réamonn Ó Conaill) XX: 138; (St. Columb's College, Derry) XX: 138; (Tomás Ó Doirnín) XX: 139; (*Banba, An Gaodhal, Journal of the Ivernian Society*) XX:140; (Seán MacCraith) XXI: 3; (Lough Fea Library) XXI: 13; (Some Owners of Irish MSS) XXI: 19; (David Fitzgerald) XXI: 19; (T. A. Emmet and Irish Language) XXI: 19; (Irish Castle Library) XXI: 20; (Dr. Whitley Stokes) XXI: 20; (Irish Language in Belfast and Co. Down) XXI: 23; (Irish Harpers' Programme, 1821) XXI: 36; (Phillip Barron) XXI: 42; (Rev. Edmund Hogan, S.J.) XXI: 43; (*Sketch of Irish History*) XXI: 43; (Old Youghal Library) XXI: 43;(Auctioneer's Hammer) XXI: 44; (Irish Poem in *Frazer's Magazine*) XXI: 45; (Dr. Philip MacDermott) XXI: 45; (Uilliam Ua hEaghra) XXI: 45; (John McNamara.) XXI: 57, XXII: 10, XXIII: 117; (Ormond Ploughman) XXI: 64; (James Haly) XXI: 66; (Old Almanac) XXI: 81; (Swift, Auction Catalogue) XXI: 85; (printing in 17th c. Cork) XXI: 90; (John McCreery) XXI: 90; (Donlevy's *Irish Catechism*) XXI: 91; (17th c. printing in Kilkenny) XXI: 91; (O'Kane's Notes on Irish) XXI: 93; ("New Lights of Askeaton") XXI: 102; (*Western Rover*) XXI: 111; (Last Irish Speakers) XXI: 111; (O'Reilly Family) XXI: 111; (Dr. John O'Fergus) XXI: 112; (Uilliam Ó Meachair) XXI: 112; (Irish MSS in 1806, IV) XXI: 127; (Vallencey's *Irish Dictionary*) XXI: 131; (John Francis Meagher) XXI: 132; (O'Baggot of Ballingarry) XXI: 135; (James Petre) XXI: 136, XXII: 42; (Michael Ignatius Dugan) XXI: 136; (The Book of Lecan) XXI: 136; (Séamus Ó Scoireadh) XXI: 137; (18th c. Irish Professors) XXI: 137, XXII: 65, 143; (Old Limerick Printer) XXII: 7; (Thomas Moore & Robert Emmet) XXII: 8; (Portraits of Carolan) XXII: 9; (Irish Sermon in Dublin, 1780) XXII: 11; (Triglot's *Celtic Dictionary*) XXII: 12; (*Ireland's Dirge*) XXII: 14; (printing in Clonmel) XXII: 14; (Seán Ó Dreada) XXII:15; (O'Kelly, Itinerant Poet) XXII: 16; (*The Psalter of Cashell*) XXII: 39, 91; (Old Cashel Magazine) XXII: 39, 91; (Cashel Chapter Library) XXIII: 40; (*The Musæum*) *X*XII: 40; (Fleix O'Gallagher) XXII: 40; (*Pé in Éirinn I*) XXII: 40; (T. C. Irwin) XXII: 41;

Wilson) XXII: 57; (Skeffington Gibbon) XXII: 58; (An Sutach 'sa Mhathair) XXII: 65; (Chevalier O'Gorman) XXII: 66; (O'Reilly Pedigree) XXII: 67, 114; (*Bibliotheca Putlandia*) XXII: 68; (Irish Poets of Limerick) XXII: 68; (Mrs. O'Rooney's Sketches) XXII: 68, 91; (Irish Language Societies) XXII: 90; (*Iris na Gaedhilge*) XXII: 103; (Bibliography of Irish Athletics) XXII: 109; (Irish Book Collectors, II) XXII: 109; (John Casey, Mathematician) XXII: 113; (*Cruise of the Daring*) XXII: 115; (James Weale) XXII: 117; (The Two Patrick Lynches) XXII: 118; (Waterford Bardic Sessions) XXII: 133; (Peadar Dubh Ó Dálaigh) XXII: 141, XXIII: 93; (*An Bad Beag glasí*) XXII: 144; (Michael Joseph McCann) XXIII: 48; (Risteárd Ó Cronghaile, *An Lámh Fhada Dhubh*) XXIII: 71; (James Hardiman) XXIII: 72; (Brian O'Looney) XXIII: 73; (Early Dublin Song Books) XXIII: 92; (Irish Bibliography) XXIII: 95; (Tomás Ó hAitheirne) XXIII: 95; (Poet of the Lee) XXIII: 107; (O'Kelly Patrick, The Eudoxologist) XXIII: 116; (printing in Limerick) XXIII: 133; (*Beirt Ghaedheal fuair Bás thar Sáile*) XXIII: 146; (Patrick O'Kelly, translator of Mac Geoghegan) XXVIII: 84-86; (*Ad'imthigh uainn an Oadh lá d'Aibreán*) XXIX: 11; (Matthew Butler) XXIX: 26; (Unrecorded Irish Book, 1716) XXVIII: 131-33. Further articles and reviews by, I: 34, 47, 59, 62, 85, II: 6, 12, 28, 62, 129,141,182,194, III: 13, 23, 25, 35, 63, 80, 115, 129, 141, 153, 155, 172, IV: 15, 53, 59, 80, 126, 145, V: 13, 14, 106, 20, VI: 13, 19, 46, 63, 102, 116, 117, 136, 151, 164, 170, 188; VII: 13, 32 52, 53 101, 102 137, 142 163, 164, 187, VIII: 17, 18, 43, 87, 111, 139, IX: 9, 15 28, 74, X: 13, 42, 66, 91, 109, XI: 30, 64, 65, 103, 117, 118, 136, XII: 21, 22, 40, 67, 140, XIII: 16, 35, XIV: 30, 75, 76, 93, 107, XV: 8, XVI: 2, 5, 22, 14, 23, 25, 34. 39, 45, 47-48, 51, 61, 66, 68, 70-73, 81, 112, 116-120, 125-127, XVII: 1, 6, 8-9, 11, 14-17, 19-20, 22-23, 32, 37, 44, 54, 59, 61, 71, 77-79, 82-83, 85, 90-91, 93, 102, 113, 115-121, 129, 131, 136, XVIII: 110, XXIV: 6, XXIX: 25, 26, 27, XXVII: XXXII: 104.

O'Casaide, Tomas, XIII: 18.

O'Casey, Sean (*The Silver Tassle*), XVI: 67, 109-111; (*Englische Studeen*) XVIII: 74; (*The Flying Wasp*) XXV: 70; (*I Knock at the Door*) XXVI: 96; (*Within the Gates*) XXII: 92; (*Purple Dust*) XXVIII: 71; (*Inishfallen Fare Thee Well*) XXXI: 44; (*Sunset and Evening Star*) XXXII: 118.

Ó Ceallaigh, Séamus (John O'Donovan & Irish MSS), XXVI: 137.

Ó Ceallaig, [An tAth.] Tomás (*Caol na nOilean*), XX: 21.

Ó Cearnaigh, Nicholas (Edition of *Columcille's Prophecies*), XVIII: 171.

Ó Céilleachair, Séamus, (*An Taistealaí*) XXX: 121; (*Páid*), XXXI: 1; XXXII: 25.

Ó Cianáin, Cuchonnacht, XVII: 119.

O'Cianain, Adam, VI: 191.
O'Ciarghusa, Seán, XVI: 83.
Ó Ciosáin, Tadhg (Obit.), XXIII: 146.
Ó Cleirigh, Cuchoigcriche (Pól Breathnach), XXIII: 60; (Will of), XXIV: 87; XXVIII: 135.
Ó Cleirigh family of Tir Conaill (Fr. Paul Walsh), XXVI: 140.
Ó Cleirigh, Tomas, (Seodini Cuimhne), XXVII: 163.
O'Clery, Arthur [also Ua Cleirigh], VI: 191, 206.
O'Clery, Helen (*Sparks Fly*), XXXI: 21.
O'Clery, John, XXX: 42, 43.
O'Clery, Keyes, IV: 213.
O'Clery, Michael, IV: 4, 21.
Ó Coindealbain, Seán, XIII: 33.
Ó Coindialbháin, Padhg, XVI: 45.
Ó Conaill, Peadar Rua, XVI: 48.
Ó Conaill, Peadar [also Peter/P. O'Connell, or Peadar/P. Ó Conaill], VIII: 6, XIV: 93, XVI: 72, 119; (literary patron) XVII: 71; (Stephen Cooke) XX: 92; (Some Plunkett Inscriptions) XXX: 16; (The Scully Diary) XXX: 110-111; XXX: 114; XXXII: 40.
Ó Conaill, [Fr.] Philip O.F.M., XXVII: 181.
Ó Conaill, [An tAth.] Réamonn, XX: 138.
Ó Conaire, Pádraic, XII: 135, XIII: 43, 91, XVI: 74-75, 82, XVII: 141, 142; (articles in *Samhain*), XVIII: 123; (*The Woman at the Window*) XX: 20; (*Scothscéalta*), XXXII: 148.
Ó Conaire, [Canónac] Mícheál (*Amhrán ó Oileán Cliara*), XXVI: 30.
Ó Conalláin, [Fr.] M., (Killashee, Co. Longford) XXX: 19; (Killamoy) XXXI: 37.

Ó Conchubhair, Padraic (The Irish tricolour), XXVII: 159.
"O'Connell and Biddy Moriarty" (from *Anecdotes of Irish Wit and Humour*), III: 154.
O'Connell Five Hundred Years Ago!, An, XVI: 116.
O'Connell, Daniel (edited paper on), XVIII: 172; III: 3, 92.
"O'Connell, Edmund", (pseud. of William Halliday).
O'Connell, F. W. (*An t-Europach*), XVIII: 66.
O'Connell, J. J., XII: 39; (*The Irish Wars: A Military History of Ireland* [...]), XII: 38-40.
O'Connell, [Rev.] John (*Saint Thomas More*), XXIV: 68.
O'Connell, Peter (see Ó Conaill, Peadar).
O'Connell, Philip, XX: 63, 113; XXVIII: 12; (Bernard Nulty), XXXI: 107.
O'Connell, William, III: 4, 11.
O'Connor, Batt. (*With Michael Collins in the Fight for Irish Independence*), XVIII: 61.
O'Connor, Dermod, III: 125, 155, XVI: 10-11, XVII: 143.
O'Connor, Frank [pseudonym of Michael O'Donovan] (*Guests of the Nation*), XIX: 179; (*The Saint and Mary Kate*) XX:69 (*Bones of Contention*) XXIV: 70; (*Three Old Brothers and Other Poems*) XXV: 65; (*The Fountain of Magic*) XXVI: 144.
O'Connor, [Maj.] G. B. (*Stuart Ireland—Catholic and Puritan*), II: 9, XIII: 40
O'Connor, Joseph, (*The Norway man*), XXXI: 95.
O'Connor, Laurence (Rebel Schoolmaster), XXVI: 61.
O'Connor, Norreys Jephson [also O'Conor] (*Celtic Memories and*

O'Connor, Norreys Jephson [also O'Conor] (*Celtic Memories and Other Pems*), V: 68; IX: 137; (*The Early Irish Fairies, and Fairyland*), XII: 108-109; (*Songs of the Celtic Past*), XII: 108-109.
O'Connor, Patricia, (*The Mill in the North*), XXVI: 46.
O'Connor, Patrick Eugene, XXX: 18, 19, 44.
O'Connor, Richard (scribe), XXI: 52, 112.
O'Connor, S. (on John Banin), XXIX: 19.
O'Connor, T. P., V: 215, VIII: 79, XIII: 83, XIV: 26, XVII: 122-123; (Pat O'Rourke), XVIII: 120.
O'Connor, Thomas, (Ordnance Survey), XXV: 81.
O'Connor, V. L. (*A Book of Caricatures*), VII: 50.
O'Conor, [Rev.] Charles (*Rerum Hibernicarum Scriptores Veteres*), XXXII: 106.
O'Conor, Norris Jephson, see O'Connor, Norreys Jephson.
O'Conor, [Rev.] Willaim Anderson, XII: 53.
O'Conway, Matthew, XVII: 131.
Ó Criomhthain, Tomás [Thomas O'Crohan], (*Seanchas an Oileán Tiar*) XXXII: 148; (*The Islandman*) XXIII: 49.
Ó Croleus, Florentius, XXV: 105.
Ó Cronghaile, Risteárd, (*An Lámh Fhada Dhubh*), XXIII: 70.
Ó Cuív, Brian, XXXII: 33; (*Cath Muighe Tuireadh*) XXX: 24; (Peadar Ó Doirnin, MS) XXXI: 6; (Art Ó Laere) XXXI: 38.
Ó Cuív, Shán (Prós na hAoise Seo), XXIII: 103.
O'Curry, Anthony, XVII: 126-127.

O'Curry, Eugene, II: 187, III: 107, IV: 22, 23, 58, 78, 174, VIII: 7, XVI: 13, 17, XVII: 126, 127, 129, XX: 66, XXXII: 41; (MSS. transcribed by), XXVI: 110; (Signature), XXX: 18, 19, 44; ("The Pearl of the Snowy Breast"), XXXII: 137.
O'Curry, Gerald, IV: 188.
Ó Dálaigh, Peadar Dubh, XXIII: 93, XXIV: 110; (Enri Ó Muirgheasa), XXII: 6, XXII: 114; (Séamus Ó Casaide), XXII: 141; (genealogical note), XXV: 51, 58.
Ó Dálaigh, Seán (Song from MSS), XX: 58.
O'Daly, Edmund E., (*History of the O'Dalys*), XXVI: 43.
O'Daly, John, XIV: 65, 110; XXVI: 135; (Scholar and Bookseller), XXVI: 135; (Celtic Society), XXIX: 12.
O'Daly, P. J., (Irish Language in Boston), XIX: 88.
Ó Dhíosca, Una Bean, [also Uí Dhíosca], (*Cailin na Gruaige Duinne*), XXII: 99.
Ó Dighe, Seán, XXIV: 86.
Ó Direáin, Peadar, XVI: 82.
O'Doherty, Kevin Izod, I: 163, II: 171.
O'Doherty, [Mrs.] K. I., I: 163.
Ó Doirnín, Peadar [Peter O'Dornin] (The Bard of Louth) XVII: 21-22, 92; XX: 17, 52. (MSS) XVIII: 30; (*The Independent Man*) XVIII: 170; (Brian Ó Cuiv on MS of) XXXI: 6.
Ó Doirnín, Tomás, XX: 17; (Book of Ballymote), XX: 139
Ó Domhnaill, Aodh Ruadh, (Life), XXV: 102.
Ó Domhnalláin, Padraic, XVI: 82.
Ó Donnabháin, Séamus, (J. J.

Callanan) XVII: 108-09; 128, 140; (A Current Commentary), XVIII: 17, 51, 73, 103.

Ó Donnchadha, Tadhg ["Torna"], XVI: 4; (Fion Gearmaineach) XVIII: 151; (Leabhar Cloinne Aodha Buidhe) XIX: 183; (Filidheacht Fiannaigheachta) XXII: 99; (*Fionn ag Caoineadh*) XXVII: 169; (Clódóir I gCorcaigh) XXX: 49, 50.

"O'Donnell Abu", XXIII: 48; (Royal Kent Bugle) XXVI: 85-86.

O'Donnell, Edward, VII: 27.

O'Donnell, Elliot, VI: 165.

O'Donnell, Frank J. H., I: 89, 133, II: 184, VIII: 69; (*The Dawn Mist*), XIV: 30.

O'Donnell, Hugh, (16th cent. MSS), XIX: 73.

O'Donnell, John Francis, III: 91.

O'Donnell, Peadar (*Adrigoole*), XVII: 110, 111; (*The Knife*) XVIII: 182; (*The Gates Flew Open*) XX:46; (*Wrack*) XXII: 47; (*Salud: An Irishman in Spain*) XXV: 67.

O'Donoghue Papers, The, XII: 102, 126-128, XIII: 6, 25, 52,132, XIV: 70.

O'Donoghue, Alec, II: 104.

O'Donoghue, David James [D. J. O'Donoghue], I: 57; (Henry Montgomery) I: 101; (Irish Pseudonyms) I: 121; (John Rutherford) I: 171; (Daniel Maclise) II: 46; (C. J. Kickham) II: 48, III: 1; (Mulcahy's Irish Biographical Dictionary) II: 59; (Indexes) II: 73; (William McBurney) II: 74; (Zim-mer Library) II 102-03; (Belfast Bookbinder) II: 110; (Poets who have passed away) II: 123; (Young Ireland Press) II: 161; (Biblio-graphy of W.B Yeats) II: 162; (Constantia Grierson) II: 179; (The Author of "Mick Mc-Quaid") III: 5-7; (David Brindon) III: 27; (*Poets of Ireland*) III: 29, III: 188, IV: 11, 35, V: 81; (*D.N.B.*) IV: 33; (Dublin Direct-ories) IV: 34; (*John O'Leary and His Friends*) V: 80; (Authors Wanted) VI: 12, 103; (James Byers) VI: 46; (Dublin University Magazine) VI: 81; (*Essays Literary & Historical* by Thomas Davis) VI: 113; (William A. Roddy) VI: 114; (Dr. Thomas Antisell) VI: 118-19; (*The Cork Magazine*) VI: 125-27, 169; (Irish Novelists) VI: 179-80; (Eugene Geary) VI: 191; ("Thaumaturgus") VI: 209-10; (W. H. S. Monck) VII: 16; (Mother Augustine McKenna) VII: 34; (Duffy's *Fireside Magazine*) VII: 46-47; (Daniel Casey) VII: 53; ("Major Muskerry") VII: 54; (C. McC. Tenison) VII: 77; (Davis Charles Bell) VII: 103; (Capt. V. D. Shortt) VII: 104; (John De Courcy MacDonnell) VII: 142; (*The West Briton*) VII: 188; (Thomas H. Wright) VII: 191; (Michael Doheny) VIII: 19; (Literature and the Late Rebellion) VIII: 28; (George Coffey) VIII: 46; (*The Dublin and London Magazine*) VIII: 53-56; (John Denvir) VIII: 91; (M. P. Hickey) VIII: 114; (James Bryce Killen) VIII: 118; (Obituary) IX: 5-7, 10; 66, (O'Donoghue Family Fund) IX: 89, 103, X: 20; (Edward Evans) X: 58; (Reliques of D. J. O'D.) X: 100; (Carroll Malone) XI:

124; (Mrs. D. J. O'Donoghue) XV: 41; (Sundry) II: 93, 143, 149, 150, 151, III: 24, V: 90, VI: 96, 169-70, VII: 136, 163, IX: 135, X: 81, XI: 39, XXVI: 112.
O'Donoghue, Florence, see under Diarmuid Lynch.
O'Donoghue, John, X: 71, XI: 63.
O'Donoghue, Tadgh, XII: 131.
O'Donovan, Gerald (*Father Ralph*), IV: 188; XIII: 91, 106.
O'Donovan, Jeremiah, XVII: 130, 131; (Washington Bookseller), XVIII: 30.
O'Donovan, [Dr.] John [also J. Donovan], I: 31; (Supplement), VII: 163; (Books), VII: 164; VIII: 87, IX: 15; X: 58; (Belfast Lectures), XVIII: 59; XVI: 13, 17, 27, 50,73, XVII: 6, 16, 19, 130; (Ordinance Survey Letters from Mayo), XIX: 96; XX: 66, 92; (slips in *Four Masters*) XXV: 100; XXIV: 110; (Dr. Todd) XXVII: 101, XXVII: 161, 179; (Annals) XXVII: 179, 43; (John O'Clery) XXX: 43; (O'Donovan & Irish MSS) XXVI: 137; (Family) XXVII: 207, XXIX: 17; (Colonel Larcom) XXIX: 122; (Denis Florence McCarthy) XXXII: 50; (Genealogy) XXXII: 53; XXX: 42, 43. See also O'Donovan, Dr [John], II: 149, 150, 187; III: 7, IV: 184
O'Donovan Rossa, Jeremiah, VII: 15; (Mrs. O'Donovan Rossa) VIII: 70; XIII: 140; XVII: 130.
Ó Dreada, Seán, XVI: 5, XXII: 15.
Ó Dubhgaill, Maolsheachlain, ("An Ciarraigheach Malluithe"), XXXI: 134.
O'Duffy, Eimar (*Bricriu's Feast*), XI: 25; (*A College Chorus*) XI: 62; (*The Wasted Island*) XI: 82;
(*Miss Rudd and Some Lovers*) XIV: 73; (*Life and Money*), XX:23; (*Asses in Clover*), XXI: 120; (Obit.), XXIII: 83; (Plays), XXVI: 60, 114.
O'Duffy, R. J. (*Historic Graves in Glasnevin Cemetery*), VII: 36, 50.
Ó Duigenan, David, (Scribe), XX: 4.
Ó hEódhasa, Giolla Brighde [or Bonabhentura, Bonaventura], XVII: 133; (Transcription of Verse Preface in *Teagasg Criosdaidhe*), XVIII: 1.
Ó Faircheallaigh, Seán, XVI: 13-14, 34.
O'Faoláin, Eileen (*The King of the Cats*), XXVIII: 95.
Ó Faoláin, Liam, reference to, XX: 34.
Ó Faoláin, Seán [also Sean O'Faolain], (*A Nest of Simple Folk*), XXI: 143; (*Constance Markovicz*), XXII: 138; (*Bird Alone*), XXIV: 96; (*A Purse of Coppers*, XXV: 110; (*She Had to Do Something*), XXVI: 93; (*Silver Branch, The*), XXVI: 144; (*The Short Story*), XXXI: 18.
Ó Faoláin, Seán [namesakes]—(of Kilkenny) XX: 43, 114; (fl.1763) XXI: 91; (fl824), XXVI: 39.
O'Farrell, Irish Piper I804, XVII: 37, 61.
O'Farrell, T. T., (A Loughrea Printer), XIX: 109; (*The Loughrea Journal*), XIX: 172.
O'Farrelly, Agnes, (*Out of the Depths*), XIII: 155.
Ó Fearachair, Domhnal, (Life), XVIII: 156.
O'Fergus, [Dr.] John, XXI: 112.
Office of Holy Week, III: 138,

154. Ó Fionnagain, Donnchadh, XVI: 5.
O'Flaherty Country, The, V: 194.
O'Flaherty, Liam, XVII: 96, XIV: 14; (*The Puritan*), XX: 24; (*Skerrett*), XX: 118; (*Hollywood Cemetery*), XXIV: 22; (*Famine*), XXV: 22; (*Short Stories*), XXVI: 22; (*Insurrection*), XXXI: 117.
O'Flaherty, John T., VI: 187.
O'Flaherty, Tom, (*Aranmen All*), XXII: 151.
Ó Flannghaile, Tomás (1846-1916), XXVIII: 68.
Ó Floinn, Críostóir, (*An t-Iolar Dubh*), XXXII: 147.
Ó Floinn, Seán (Irish Magazines), XX: 115; (William & John Meagher) XXI: 10; (*IBL* Duplicates) XXI: 26; (Finds in Waterford) XXII: 31; (John F. Meagher) XXII: 38; (A Booklover) XXIV: 84; (Thomas Kiersey) XXVII: 177; (Books) XXVII: 210; (A Poet) XXIX: 136.
Ó Foghludha, R., (*Cois na Ruachtaighe*), XXVI: 140.
Ógáin, Róis Ní, (*Duanaire Gaedhilge*), XVIII: 64.
Ó Gallachuir, Séamus Ruadh, XVII: 103.
O'Gallagher, Felix, (Mathematician), XXII: 40, XXIV: 4I, XXVI: 39.
O'Gara, Fergal, (Rev. John Brady), XXIX: 78.
O'Gara, Hyacinth, I: 153, 171, XI: 14.
Ó Gealacáin, Peadar [also Peter Galligan], XXIV: 42, 61, 109; XVII. 10, 23, 102; (Patron), XXVI: 36; (Almanacs), XXVI: 80.

Ogilvie, George, XIV: 75.
Ó Giobuin, Pól, (Sheamus Ó Caomhánaigh), XVIII: 127.
O'Gorman, Chevalier, XXII: 11, 66.
t-Oglach, An XVIII: 72.
O'Grady, Standish, James [Viscount Guillamore] X: 23; XII: 60; XVIII: 94; (Bibliography) XVIII: 94.
O'Grady, Standish Hayes, III: 34, VII: 77, 81, 95, 96, 139; XI: 76; XII: 60; XVI: 49.
O'Grady, S. C. (son of Standish James O'Grady), XIX: 2.
Ó Gríobhtha, Art, see Griffith, Arthur.
O'Hagan, John, II: 187, VI: 43.
O'Hagan, [Lord] Thomas, VI: 205, XIII: 36, XVII: 63.
O'Hagans, The Two [Henry & Seán], XXIII: 46.
Ó hAitheirne, Tomás, XXIII: 95.
O'Halloran, Silvester, XXXII: 87.
O'Halloran, T. P., V: 184, VI: 189.
O'Hanlon, [Canon] John, IV: 25, XIII: 79, XVII: 15, 16, XX: 16.
O'Hanlon, Redmond, V: 68.
O'Hanlon, Terence (*The Minstrel of Erin*), XVIII: 150.
O'Hanluain, Henry, V: 69.
Ó h-Aodha, Tomás (*The Hills of Clare and Other Verses*), XXIII: 125.
O'Hara, Anthony, XXXII: 87.
O'Hara, M. M., VI: 212.
O'Hara, Valentine, XIII: 142.
O'Hara, William, (see Haliday), XXI: 45, XXVI: 104
O'Harney, Thomas, IV: 78.
O'Hart, John, XVII: 135; (*Irish Pedigrees*), XVIII: 53.
O'Hea, John Fergus, III: 90, 106, 107.
Ó h-Eodhasa, Bonabhentura

[Giolla Brighde], see O'Hussey, Bonaventura.
O'Hegarty, Patrick Sarsfield, (*The Shamrock*) XXV: 31.
(Bibliography of Standish James O'Grady) XVIII: 94; (Eimar O'Duffy's Plays) XXVI: 60; (An Unrecorded Private Press) XXVII: 259; (Some Association Books of Irish Interest) XXX: 74-78; (Irish in Co. Galway in the 1870s) XXX: 78-79; (Stopford Brooke on Ireland) XXX: 109-10; (T. W. Rolleston on Ireland in 1884) XXX: 112; (Dublin Street Ballads about the Invincibles) XXXI: 2; (An Electioneering Bill of Former Days) XXXI: 8; (Books of Irish Interest) XXXI: 50; (Petrus Borel's *Madame Putiphar*) XXXI: 74; (An Irish Sensational Novel of Limerick) XXXI: 104; (A 'Ninety-Eight Novel) XXXI: 105; (Obit.) XXXII: 97; (Sundry) III: 27, IV: 93, VI: 117, VIII: 44, IX: 126, XIV: 78, 117, XXX: 2, 41, 43, 44, 61, 67, 74-79, 108-10, 112, 113; XXXII: 4, 15, 19, 26, 75, 78; XXXII: 100.
Ó Heidhin, Tomás, (Ui Chronghaile agus *An Lámh Fhada Dhub*), XXIII: 70.
O'Hiccada, U., II: 27.
O'Hickey, Ben, (*From Prison Cells*), XIX: 139.
O'Hickey, [Rev.] Michael Patrick (Obit.), VIII: 92, 114, 118, XV: 62.
O'Hickey, Thomas, IV: 78.
Ó Hogáin, S., (A Chara na n Órd n-Eólglan), XXXI: 121.
Ó h-Uaithnin, Seán, (Féile Thiobóid), XXXI: 25.
Ó hUiginn, [An t-Ath.] Pól, [or Paul Higgins], XVII: 132, XXII: 118; (Burial Place of) XVIII: 85, 143, 144; XXX: 15.
Ó Huiginn, Tadhg Dall, XX: 115; (A Limerick link with) XXI: 33-35.XXIV: 14, XXV: 84, XXI: 33, 107; (Unpublished Poem) XXIII: 5, 117..
O'Hussey, Bonaventure [Giolla Brighde Ó hEódhasa], XVII: 183; (*Teagasg Criosdaidhe*) XVIII: 89, XVIII: 1; (Obit. and Poem) XVIII: 55; (Correction of Error) XVIII: 89; (*Catechism*) XVIII: 175.
Oidiopus I gColon, (Padraig de Brun), XVIII: 62.
Oidceanna Side, (Michael Mac Liamhoir), XIII: 171.
Oidhche na Gaoithe Moire, XVII: 130; XVIII: 77, 170.
Óige Handbook, An, 1934, XXII: 44.
O'Kane, [Sir] Robert (Notes on the Irish Language), XXI: 92
O'Kearney, Nicholas, XI: 64, XII: 111.
O'Keefe [O'Keeffe], John G. (*Adventures of Siuibhne Geilt*), IV: 183; X: 59, XXVI: 26, 27, 28; (*Buile Shuibhne*) XIX: 182. (Obit.) XXVI: 26; (Irish scholarship of) XXVI: 27.
O'Kelly, Francis, XVI: 22, 32, 54, 79, XXI: 66; (Quarto volume, 1726) XXIII: 47; (Youghal Bookbinder) XVIII: 173; (18th c.Dublin Bookbinders) XXIV: 10.
O'Kelly, J. J., VIII: 82, 114, IX: 13, 61.
O'Kelly, Kay, XIV: 90.
O'Kelly, Patrick [poet], XXII: 16, XXIII: 42, 116.
O'Kelly, Patrick (translator of MacGeoghegan), XXVIII: 84-

86; (An Historian of the Rebellion of 1798) XXVIII: 37;
O'Kelly, Seamus, IX: 54, XI: 59, 62, XIII: 60; (*The Golden Barque*) XI: 59; (*The Leprechaun of Kilmeen*) XI: 62. *Hillsiders* XIII: 60.
O'Kenny, [Nicolaus Antoninus] (*Galway Catechism*), XIX: 100, 124.
O'Kirby's of Munster, XXVI: 12.
Old Dublin Almanac, An, see Almanacs.
Old Ballad Re-sung, An, XXIII: 115.
Old Ballymena (John Weir), II: 42
"Old Contributor, An", X: 110.
Old Cork, XIV: 27.
Old Fashioned Verses and Sketches, (Rosamund Praeger), XXX: 120.
Old Galway (M. D. O'Sullivan), XXIX: 23.
Old Irish Kings, III: 193, 214.
Old Irish Life (Josephine M. Callwell), III: 133;
Old Irish Tales, VIII: 89, 140.
Old Irish World, The (Alice Stopford Green), III: 211.
"Old John Boon" (*Victorians, Edwardians and Georgians*), XVI: 68.
Old Lisburn, VIII: 110.
Old Moore's Almanacs, XVIII 156.
"Old Times", VI: 150.
Olden, Balder (*Sir Roger Casement*), XXI: 142.
Oldham, Charles Hubert, V: 9.
Old Ulster House, An (Mina Lenox-Conyngham), XXXI: 67.
Ó Laere, Art, [also Art O'Leary], XXXI: 84, 100
O'Laverty, (Irish MSS), XIX: 27.
O'Leary, Con, XIV: 120, 144;(*The Hillside Man*), XXI: 69; (*A Wayfarer in Ireland*), XXIII: 123.
O'Leary, Ellen, XII: 103.XIV: 106.
O'Leary, John, XI: 39, XIII: 25, 32, XV: 4; (Keating's MS), XVIII: 144; (W. B. Yeats) XXVII: 245.
O'Leary, Margaret, (*Lightening Flash*), XXVII: 191.
O'Leary, [Rev.] P., XI: (Obit.) 118, 120.
O'Leary, Patrick, IV: 160.
O'Leary, William (Poems), XVII: 18.
'Olive Branch in Ireland, An', II: 71.
Oliver, F. S. (*Ireland and the Imperial Conference*), VIII: 135.
O'Loan, [Rev.]Daniel, III: 101.
O'Longan, P. C., IX: 36.
Ó Longáin, Mícheál Óg (*Saoghal An Duine*), XXX: 25.
O'Looney, Brian, XVII: 20, XXIII: 73.
O'Loughran, [Rev.] Robert, X: 91.
"Ó Lochlainn i bhFeirg" (Seán Ó h-Uaithnín), XXXI: 49.
Ó Lochlainn, Colm [Colm O'Lochlainn] (Wail of the Candleman) XII: 40; XVI: 16, 24, 63, 85, 87, 126; XVII: 18, 112, 121, 141; (Type used in *Lucerna Fidelium*) XVIII: 16; (Books in Preparation) XXIII: 1; (Indexes to *I.B.L.*) XXIII: 4, 129; (Tadhg Dall Ó Huiginn, unpub. poem) XXIII: 5, 17; (Edward Lloyd) XXIII: 13; (Victor O'D. Power) XXIII: 15; Géag dhe Chloinn Shuibhne ar lár) XXIII: 33; (Saothar na Seanchaí) XXIII: 81; (*Studies*) XXIII: 57; (Giotaí Gaedhilge san *I.B.L.*) XXIII: 105; (Old ballad resung) XXIII: 115;

XXIV: 6; (Tadhg Dall Ó Huiginn) 14; (*Leith-sgéal—agus Ceathramha!*) 25; (editorials) 73, 97-98, 121; (Irish Art Unions) 84; (editorials) XXV: 1, 25, 49, 73; (Irish language) 14-15; (Ordnance Survey letters) 39; XXVI: 108; (Pope Pius XI) XXVI: 97; (MS transcribed by O'Curry) XXVI: 110, 116; (on Jayme Nochera) XXVI: 113, 135; (Cead Foghla thug Torna) XXVI: 121; (Cathal Brugha's Election Poster) XXVI: 138; (*Tobar Fiorghlan Gaedhilge*) XXVII: 185; (*A Chuisle na h-Eigse, eirigh suas*) XXVII: 241; XXIX: 33; (Ár gCreach is ár gCár) XXVIII: 97; (Ancient Trade Signs) XXIX: 99; XXX: 41, 42, 43, 44, 64, 65, 69; (Gaelic Society of London in 1840) XXX: 80-84; 87-88; (Dean Swift) 113-114; (Battle of Carrickshock) XXXI: 26; (Samuel Ferguson and John T. Gilbert) 123-125; XXXII: 8; ("The Battle of Carrickshock") 26-27; (placenames) 57; (reviews) 109-10, 120; (*Irishmen of Learning*) 111; (farewell) XXXII: 152.

Ó Luaighnigh, Liam, XXVI: 26.

Ó Madaoin, P. L. (An Irish Inscription in Co. Meath), XXIV: 124.

O'Madden, P., XVII: 96.

Omagh (printing), VII: 7, 46.

O'Mahoney, John, I: 75.

O'Mahony, Edmund [Eamonn Ó Mathghamhna] XVI: 5.

O'Mahony, John [Seán O'Mathghamhna], XVII: 80; (C. Ó Síonáinn on) XVIII: 43; (*DNB* article) XVIII: 43; (Keating MSS) XVIII: 144; (unpublished biography) XVIII: 45; (photostatic copy of signature) XVIII: 174.

O'Mahony, Michael (Obit.), XXIV: 107.

O'Mahony, Nora Tynan (*Fields of Heaven*), VII: 11.

O'Mahony, [Rev.] Timothy J., VIII: 143.

O'Maille, Michael, III: 134.

Ó Máille, Tomás [or Thomas O'Malley], I: 31, XVI: 45; (Micheál MhacSuibhne) XXIII: 75.

O'Malley, Ernie (*Rebellion in Ireland*), XXVII: 187.

O'Malley, Thomas [see Ó Máille, Tomás].

O'Malley, William, (*Glancing Back*), XXI: 140.

Ó Maolchathail, Séamas (Literature of the Civil War), XVIII: 71.

Ó Maolmhuaidh [of Fir Ciall] (The Four Masters, 1454), XXIV: 31.

Ó Maonaigh, Cainneach, see Canice, [Rev.]

Ó Mathghamhna, Seán [also John O'Mahony], XVIII: 43.

Omeath Co. Louth, (Rev. L. Murray), VII: 73.

O'Meara, John (Giraldus, *Topography of Ireland*), XXXII: 23.

Ó Miléadha, Pádraig (An Fiannaidhe Fáin), XXII: 100.

Omniana, The Autobiography of an Irish Octogenerian, (J. F. Fuller), VIII: 16, XI: 97.

Ó Modhrain, Seán, XVII: 76-77.

O'Mohony, John, XVII: 118.

O'Molloy, [Fr.] Francis, IV: 59, XVIII: 10; (*Lucerna Fidelium*), XVIII: 5.

O'Molloy, [Capt.] Green, XXIII: 134, XXV: 26-31.

O'Morain's MSS, XIII: 35.
Ó Morchadha, [Fr.] Domhnall, XXI: 28, 54, 76, 100, 101, 102, 128, XXIV: 112; XXIII: (Obit.)146.
O'More, Kathleen, VI: 190.
Ó Muirgheasa, Énrí [also Henry Morris], (*The Dirge of Erin*) XIII: 3, XXII: 14; XVII: 10, 13, 17, 102, XIX: 27; (Tadhg Dall Ó hUiginn) XIX: 27, XXV: 84; (Amhráin na Midhe) XXII: 43; (*Bolg an tSolathar*) XXII: 143; (Peadar Dubh Ó Dálaigh) XXII: 6, 114; (*New Lights of Askeaton*) XXII: 11; (Leo Casey's Poems) XXII: 13; (Dhá Chéad de Cheoltaibh Uladh) XXIII: 19.
Ó Mulláin, Seán, (Leeside poet), XXIII: 107.
Ó Murchadha, Gearóid, (poet), XXX: 102-104, 129-132.
On Another Man's Wound (Ernie O'Malley), XXV: 14.
On Our Hill (Annette Barlee), XXVIII: 96.
One Hundred and Fifty Years of Publishing, XXX: 144.
One Tailteann Week, XIV: 124.
One Unfaithfulness of Naoise, The, (Moirin A Cheavasa)XVIII: 184.
Ó Neachtain's, Tadhg (home of), XXXI: 106.
O'Neale, [Sir] Turlogh, XXII: 118.
O'Neil: A Play, VI: 80.
O'Neil, or The Rebel (Lord Lytton), II: 27.
O'Neil, Miss (Lady Becher), III: 4.
O'Neil, S., VI: 61.
O'Neill, Brian (*The War for the Land in Ireland*), XXII: 148.
O'Neill Claimants in Dublin, XXVIII: 133.

O'Neill, Eoghan, XIX: 5.
O'Neill, Eugene, (*Ah! Wilderness*), XXIII: 21; (*Days Without End*), XXIII: 21.
O'Neill, [Capt.] Francis (Irish music collector), V: 183, IX: 34, XVI: 33; XXIX: 2.
O'Neill, [Rev.] George, XI: 83, 129.
O'Neill, [Dr.] Henry, V: 220.
O'Neill, James J., VI: 123, 145, XII: 14, 39.
O'Neill, Joseph (*Land Under England*), XXIII: 127; (*Wind from the North*) XXIII: 127; (*Day of Wrath*) XXIV: 1.
O'Neill, Moira ["Mrs. Skeine"], V: 185, VI: 13, XVI: 26.
O'Neill, Peggy, XIII: 143.
Ó Néill, Séamus (Tonn Tuile), XXX: 117.
O'Neill, S., VI: 61.
Ó Néill, Toirrdhealbhach Luineach, XXIII: 14
O'Neill, Thomas P., (on "God Save Ireland"), XXIX: 130-32; XXX: 40, 84-86.
O'Phean's Epitaphs, XX: 114.
O'Rahilly, The [Michael Joseph O'Rahilly], XVI: 63.
O'Rahilly, Thomas Francis, IV: 175, V: 124, VII: 75, 104, VIII: 6, 65, XIV: 46, XV: 51; (*The Two Patricks*) XXIX: 22; (*Gadelica*) IV: 143; (Obit.) XXXII: 64.
Ó Raithbheartaigh, T., (Maighistrí san Fhilidheacht), XXII: 124.
Ó Raithille, Tomás XVII: 13, 91, 3; (*Samhain*) XVIII: 123; (Irish Dialects) XX: 45; (Literary Forgeries in Irish) XXVII: 273.
Orange Society [Order]—II: 47, 60, (History) II: 75; 76, 94, IV:164; (The Orange Minstrel) IV: 163; (Songs) V: 149;

Orangeman, The, VII: 185; (Bibliography), XXV: 2, 85.
Ordnance Survey, (Letter reproduced) XVIII: 77; (authors) XXV:13, 39, 81; XXV: 39.
'Ordo' (*Directorium sive Ordo Divini Offici Recitandi Sacrique*) XIV: 132; (Ireland) XXIII: 73.
O'Reardon, [Dr.] John (from *Freeman's Journal*), XVI: 72, 119; (Obit.) XX: 64.
O'Reilly, Andrew, IV: 73, XIII: 62.
O'Reilly, Bernard, XXXII: 87.
O'Reilly, Edward, IX: 45.
O'Reilly, Fr. (Franciscan Library), IV: 3, 22.
O'Reilly family (Obit.), XX: 127, XXI: 111; (O'Reilly Genealogies) XXIII: 85l; XXII: 114
O'Reilly, [Dr.] Farrell (*Irish Catechism*), XVIII: 170; XIX: 25.
O'Reilly, [Rev.] James (poet), XXVI: 113.
O'Reilly, John Boyle, I: 132.
O'Reilly, Michael. IV: 78.
"O'Reilly, Miles", see Halpine, Charles Graham.
O'Reilly, [L'Abbe] Patrice John ("Home Thoughts"), VI: 14; ("Old Times") VI: 150; XXV: 103.
Orgel, Vera (*A New View of the Plays of Racine*), XXX: 142.
Ó Riain, [An tAth.] Eóin, (Bronnadh na Féil), XXVII: 217.
Ó Riain, [An tAth.] Maitiú, XXVII: 145, 193.
Origin of Grail Legend (A. C. L. Brown), XXIX: 43.
"Original Night, An" (Frank Fahy), XIV: 23.
O'Riordan, Conal [pseud. F. Norreys Connell], III: 150, XII: 65, XIII: 107, XV: 9, XVI: 3; (*Napolean Passes*) XXI: 70; (*Soldier's Wife*) XXIII: 56; (*Judith Quinn*) XXVI: 120.
O'Riordan, [Dr.] John, XIX: 177.
O'Riordan, Monsignor (Irish College, Rome), VI: 131.
Ó Ríordáin, Seán P., (*Antiquities of the Irish Countryside*) XXXII: 71; (*Tara: The Monuments on the Hill*) XXXII: 116.
Ormond Ploughman, The (Thomas Abbot), XIX: 100, XXI: 64.
Ormonde MSS, III: 9.
Ormsby, [Prof.] Robert, II: 87.
O'Rorke, Alderman, XXV: 40, 64.
O'Rorke, [Rev. Dr.] Terence [also O'Rourke], XXV: 40, 64.
O'Rourke, Dean, II: 21.
O'Rourke Family History, XVII: 14, 21, XXV: 104.
O'Rourke's Feast, XVI: 45, XIX: 61, 97.
Orpen, Goddard H., III: 55, XVIII: 98; (*Ireland under the Normans, 1169-1216*) III: 55; (*Ireland under the Normans, 1216-1333*) XII: 23; (Library) XVIII: 98.
Orpen, [Sir] William, XIII: 112.
Orrery, Earl of—(John Boyle) IV: 47; (Roger Boyle) XIII: 9.
O'Ryan, William P. (*The Plough and the Cross*), II: 56.
Oscar Wilde: Plays, Prose Writings and Poems (Hesketh Pearson), XIX: 63.
Ó Scoireadh, Séamus, XXI: 137.
Ó Seagdha, Risteard (Cuma Mná an Tabairne), XX: 34.
Ó Searcaigh, Séamus (*Cú na gCleas*), VI: 78; (Nua Sgribhneáirí na Gaedhilge) XXII: 24, XXIV: 17.
O'Shaughnessy, Arthur, VI: 104, 136.
O'Shaughnessy, Richard M. (R.

M. Levy), XIX: 23.
O'Shea, D. A., III: 13, VIII: 90, IX: 15.
O'Shea, John, A., VII: 98, IX: 85.
O'Shea, Michael C., XXX: 8-11.
O'Shiel, F. Carroll (medical family), XXXI: 128, XXX: 50.
O'Sheil, Kevin, XII: 83.
Ó Siochhfhradha, M. [pseud. "An Seabhac"] (*Stair Sheanchas Eireann*), XXII: 146; (*Eachtra Thaidhg Mhic Céin*) XXIII: 30.
Ó S[ionainn], C. (on Seán O'Mathghamhna), XVIII: 43.
Ó Suileabháin, Muiris (*Twenty Years a-Growing*), XXIII: 50
Ó Súilleabháin, Amhlaoibh [Humphrey O'Sullivan] (MS Diary), XXII: 101; XXVII: 6, 258; (Cinnlae) XXVI: 32.
Ó Súilleabháin, Domhnal (also D. J. O'Sullivan) XI: 137, XVI: 23, 24, 33, 70.
Ó Súileabháin, Eoghan Ruadh ("An Ciarruigheach Malluithe"), XXIX: 73, 97; XXXI: 134.
Ó Súilleabháin, Proinsias, XXXII: 49.
O'Sullivan, [Fr.] Daniel, IV: 78.
O'Sullivan, Florence, VIII: 40.
O'Sullivan, M. D., (*Old Galway*), XXIX: 23.
O'Sullivan, Owen Roe, XV: 52.
O'Sullivan, [Rev.] P. P. (Obit.), X: 45, 46.
O'Sullivan, Seamus, VI: 48; (*Mud and Purple*) IX: 54; IX: 54, X: 46; (*The Rosses and other Poems*) X: 46-47; (*Collected Poems*) XXVIII: 21; (*Essays and Recollections*) XXIX: 95; (*The Rose and Bottle*) XXX: 47; (Elegy on M. J. McManus) XXXII: 3.
O'Sullivan, Tadhg, III: 25.
O'Sullivan, Timothy, II: 26.

O'Sullivan, Vincent, (*Aspects of Wilde*), XXIV: 94.
O'Sullivan's *Pious Miscellany*, I: 129.
"Ossian", VIII: 139.
Otaheite Language in Dublin, XXXII: 144.
Ó Tighearna[idh], Séamus, XXI: 101, 129.
Ó Tuathail, Eamonn (Irish Language in County Kilkenny) XXI: 65; (Bennett Family, Forkhill) XXII: 32; (Northern MS) XXII: 54; (Wicklow MS) XXII: 88; (Toirrdhealbhach Luineach Ó Néill) XXIII: 14; (Arthur Brownlow MSS) XXIV: 26; (Ulster Booklet) XXVI: 122.
O'Toole, Edward ('Mummers' in *Ireland's Own*), XVIII: 173.
O'Toole, John, XXXII: 141.
O'Toomey, John, XV: 52.
Otway, Caesar, II: 149, VI: 190.
Oulton, [Dr.] J. E. L. (*Cathedral Church of St. Patrick*), XXVII: 237; (*The Credal Statements of St. Patrick*) XXVIII: 140.
Our Irish Theatre (Lady Gregory), V: 125.
Our Welcome (editorial), I: 26.
"Ourselves Alone", see Sinn Féin.
Ouseley, Frederick Arthur Gore, VI: 1, 146.
Ouseley, Gideon [Methodist preacher], VI: 1.
Out of Doors Book, *The* (ed. Arthur Stanley), XXII: 74.
Out of the Depths (Agnes Farrelly), XIII: 155.
Over Here (Helen Duffin), IX: 137.
Over the Brasier (Robert Graves), VIII: 17.
Owen, D.J., VIII: 112.
Owenson, Robert (father of Lady Morgan), XXII: 79.

Owenson, Sydney (Lady Morgan), III: 69, 143, 161, V: 148, XIII: 104, XV: 30.

P

"P.", X: 70.
Pacata Hibernia, XXVIII: 104.
Paddy's Resource (Francis Joseph Bigger), XIII: 126.
"Paddy-the-Cope" [pseud. of Patrick Gallagher], (*My Story*), XXVI: 144; (Cahir Healy on) XXXII: 149.
Page of Irish History [...] *University College, Dublin, 1883-1909* (Rev Henry Browne, S.J.), XVIII: 90
Page, Mrs., II: 8.
Paintings of Jan Vermeer, The (with an introduction by Thomas Bodkin), XXVIII: 70.
Pair of Idols, A (Stewart Caven), XI: 133.
Pakenham, [Gen.] Edward Michael, VI: 188.
Pakenham, Frank [Lord Longford] (*Peace by Ordeal*), XXIII: 119.
Palatine Settlements in Ireland (J. G. Rhynehart), XXXI: 133.
Palmer, Herbert (*The Rowing Angler*), XXI: 118.
Palmer, William, VI: 32.
Palmer, W. F. (*The Complete Hill Walker*), XXIII: 102.
Palov ("A Book Lover's Song"), V: 29.
Pamphlets—(of Thomas Davis) I: 105; ("Fidelis" Irish pamphlet) IV: 144; (Parcel of) V: 158; (Haliday Pamphlets) VII: 121; (*Informers*) VIII: 18; (Prose and Poetry) X: 13-15; (*Young Ireland* pamphlets) XVIII: 86; (*Why Ireland is Not Free* [and] *Why There is an Irish Land Question* by T. M. Healy) XIX: 36; (J. F. Fowler, sermon) XIX: 144; (Cork-printed pamphlets) XXII: 26; (Swift pamphlet) XXX: 52-54;
Panter, G. W. (*Dublin Street Cries*), XIV: 141.
Pápa Gaedhealach (Pope Pius XI), XXVI: 97.
Papal Brigade of 1860, V: 167.
Paper Making, XIX: 124.
Parish of Kilrea and Tamlaght O'Crilly (J. W. Kernohan), IV: 122.
Parish Register Society, III: 14.
Parliament, Back Lane, see Back Lane Parliament.
Parliament, The Irish, II: 127; (Old Irish Parliament) VI: 80, 208.
Parliamentary Party, History of, I: 133.
Parlour Library, the, II: 90, 133.
Parmiter, G. de C. (*Roger Casement*), XXIV: 120.
Parnell (St. John Ervine), XV: 60.
Parnell, Anna, III: 57.
Parnell, Charles Stewart, III: 12; (Mrs. Parnell [Kitty O'Shea]) V: 69, 214, XIII: 44; V: 186, 198, VII: 192, VIII: 15, XIII: 11, XIV: 62.
Parnell, John Henry, VI: 14; VIII: 15.
Parnell, W. Hayes, XIII: 79.
Parnellite, The (Matthew Butler), XXIX: 19.
Pars Vérna, XXVII: 280.
Parson Annaly (Richard Sinclair Brook), XIII: 65.
Parsons, E. B. (*Tales of Tara*), XXII: 92.
Pastoral Annals (Rev. J. Spenser Fox), VII: 17.
Paterson's Irish Song Book (ed. Redmond Friel), XXXII: 146.
Patman, [Rev.] Philip O'Carroll,

II: 12, 28.
Patriot (Dublin paper) XIX: 90-91.
Patterson, R. Stewart, IX: 80, X: 17, 68.
Paul Pry in Derry: or Literary Pioneer (ed. "Arthur O'Harrow"), VIII: 57.
Peace and War (Eamon de Valera), XXIX: 143.
Pearl of the White Breast (melody and words), XXXII: 137.
Pearse, Patrick Henry, VIII: 21, 29, 44, 72; (*Patrick H. Pearse*, by "Coilín") VIII: 135, IX: 9, 128; (*Patrick H. Pearse: Storyteller*) XI: 61.
Pechell, G. M. (*De Valera*), XXVII: 189.
Peddie, R.A., I: 86, III: 53, 55, IV: 32.
Peden, Andrew, VII: 167.
"Pedigree" [Davis] (brother of Thomas Davis), XXXII: 12.
Pedigrees in Preparation, XXIV: 14.
Pedlar's Pack (Francis MacManus), XXIX: 144.
Pedlar's Way, The (Alicia Sheridan), X: 63.
Peel [Sir] Robert, VII: 117; (The Peel Pamphlets), VII: 118, VIII: 44, XIII: 176.
Peep-o-Day Boys v Defenders, IV: 123.
Peeps into Pamphlets, XI: 99, XV: 43.
Peeps into Periodicals, XIII: 61, 92.
Pé in Eirinn í, XXII: 40
"Peigín Leitirmóir", XXVII: 212.
Pellizzi, Camillo (*English Drama*), XXIV: 2.
Pen Portraits, X: 23, 24.
Penal Days (Catholic Writers), XVII: 78.

Pender, [Mrs.] Margaret T., (Obit.) XI: 119; XI 134, XIII: 15.
Pender, Seamus (*Guide to Irish Genealogical Collections*), XXIV: 70.
Penhaligon, Tom (*The Impossible Irish*), XXIII: 154.
Pennefather, Frederick William (Obit.), XII: 143.
Penny Journal, II: 149, XXXII: 15.
Penny Magazine (J. G. Rhynehart), II: 151, XXXI: 105, XXXII: 15.
Penny News Pamphlets, XVIII: 71.
Penrose, [Mrs.] H. H., III: 169; (*Burnt Flax*) V: 164.
People of Our Class, Boyd's Shop (St. John Ervine), XXV: 69.
Pepper, George (*Pepper's History of Ireland*), XVII: 42-43.
Pepyat, Jeremiah [bookseller], XIX: 82.
Percy, [Sir] James, XIII: 12, XVI: 76.
Periodicals of the 18th c., I: 39, 71, 108.
Perrott, James (*The Chronicle of Ireland*), XXII: 25.
Perry, Janet. V: 12, VI: 106.
Perry, Jennie ("The Wee Ould Wean"), IV: 152.
Perry, John (Obit.), XII: 43, 67.
Perry, Miss, VI: 106.
Personal Paragraphs, XII: 118-120.
Pertwee, Guy, VI: 204.
Pessimist, The ("A. Newman"), V: 163.
Peter Porcupine [William Cobbett] (Marjorie Bowen), XXIV: 93.
Petrie, George, (*Ecclesiastical Architecture of Ireland*), I: 87; II: 75, 149, 150, 155, 182, VI:

The Irish Book Lover 335

150, XVI: 13, 17, 33, XVII: 6, 30, 99; (Petrie's Gaelic Type) XXVII: 161, XXIX: 89.
Petrie, James, XXI: 136, XXII: 42, XXIV: 61.
Petrus Borel's Novel *Madame Putiphar* (P. S. O'Hegarty), XXXI: 74.
Petty, [Sir] William [Marquis of Lansdowne], I: 45, 70, IV: 103; (*Lansdowne Maps of the Down Survey*) XII: 61-63; (*Noms de Lieux Irlandais dans l'oeuvre géographique de Sir W. Petty*) XIX: 64; XXXII: 85. See also Down Survey.
Phases of Irish History (Eoin MacNeill), XI: 46.
Phelim the Blind and Other Verses (Annie M. Pike), VI: 41.
"Philibín, An" [pseud. of John Hackett Pollock], (*Irish Ironies*) XVIII: 181; (*The Valley of the Wild Swans*) XX: 143; (*Peter and Paul*) XXII: 20; *William Butler Yeats*) XXIII: 97; (*The Fourth Wise Man*) XXIV: 22; (*The Moth and the* Star) XXVI: 45; (*Grass of Parnassus*) XXIV: 119; (*Wild Honey*) XXIX: 24; (*The Lost Nightingale*) XXXII: 24.
Philip Barron's Irish College (Waterford), IV: 77.
Phillipps, [Sir] Thomas, III: 10.
Phillips, [Mrs.] Olga (Charles Lever MSS), XXIV: 15.
Philo-Celtic Society of Boston, XIX: 88.
Philo-Celtic Society of Philadelphia (Charter of), XX: 111.
Piatt, Don, XX: 122, XXI: 111, XXII, 12, XXIII: 40.
Piehler, H. A. (*Ireland for Everyman*), XXVI: 69.

Pienne, Peter de (Waterford printer), XXIV: 75.
Piercetown, Co. Westmeath (Rev. John Brady), XXIX: 114.
Piers Plowman and Ireland, XXIV: 3.
Pigeon House (history), XXV: 84, (Fort) XXVII: 182.
Piggott, H. E. (*Songs that Made History*), XXV: 108.
Pigot, John Edward, II: 149, 187.
Pigott, Richard, VIII: 105, XI: 21.
Pirate publishers (18th c.), II: 156; III: 46, 60.
"Pike, Alexander", II: 26.
Pike, Annie M., VI: 41.
Pilgrim's Progress (Irish trans.), XVI: 118.
Pilgrimage and Other Poems (Austin Clarke), XVII: 66.
Pilkington, [Col.] Henry Lionel (Obit.), V: 161.
Pilkington [Laetitia & Matthew], IV: 50.
Pillar Box, The (Robert Kirkwood), XV: 63.
Pim, Herbert [pseud. A. Newman"], VII: 29, 78, 119, IX: 53, 80; XI: 9, 14.
Pinkerton MSS, VII: 138.
Pirate publishing (in the 18th c.) II: 156; III: 46, 60.
Pirates of the Spring, The (Forrest Reid), XII: 35-36.
Pius XI (Pápa Gaedhealach), XXVI: 97.
"P.J.", XXXII: 67.
"P.J.H." (on Fr. Francis Brown), XVIII: 144.
Place-names—(Joyce, *Origin of Irish Names of Places*) V: 125; (Some Names of Co. Westmeath) VII: 64; (*Place Names and Antiquities of S. E. Cork*) X: 88; (Johnston, *Place Names of Scotland*) XXIII: 24;

(Another Place Name in Westmeath) XXVIII: 54-56; (Some Place Names in MS 23D17) XXVII: 157; (a supposed placename) XXVII: 179; (Hogan, *Onomasticon Goidelicum*) XXVII: 179; (Eleanor Knott on Eadar [Howth]) XXXI: 56; (Port Airchinnigh—Airchinneach—Portrunny) XXXII: 55.
Place of the Lion, The (Charles Williams), XXXII: 47.
Plantation of Ulster—II: 9; (Plantation of Co. Tyrone and Co Londonderry) X: 14; (*The Planter's Progress*) XIII: 32; (*The Victims of 1615*) XIX: 36.
Playboy of the Western World, The (J.M. Synge), IV: 7.
Plays for Earth and Air (Lord Dunsany), XXV: 111.
Plea for Local History, A, ("F. R.")., XXX: 40.
Plearaca na Ruarcach (Hugh M'Gauran), XVI: 45.
Plomer, Henry R., I: 17, 28, 151, II: 30, III: 110, 127, XVI: 11.
Plough and the Cross, The (William P. O'Ryan), II: 56.
Ploughing by Horses' Tails (Rev. John Brady), XXIX: 40.
Plunket family, (genealogies) XXV: 50, XXVI: 16, 17; (Some Plunket Inscriptions) XXX: 16.
Plunket, Blessed Oliver [now Saint] (the family of), XXIV: 44, XXIX: 135.
Plunket, Dr., XXXII: 106.
Plunkett, [Count] George, IV: 8, VI: 95, XIII: 39, XVI: 127; (A Note on the Orange Bibliography), XXV: 89.
Plunkett, Geraldine, X: 15.
Plunkett, Joseph Mary, VIII: 21, 30; (*Poems*) IX: 33; IX 128,

(Mrs. Joseph Plunkett [Grace Gifford]) XI: 62; XXXII: 57.
Plunkett, Richard (or Pluncead, Riostard; sometimes Plunket), III: 80; XVII: 13-14, 115.
Plunkett, [Sir] Horace, IV: 154.
Plus ça change ...! (Colm Ó Lochlainn), XXX: 87-88.
"P. M." (on Patrick Byrne), XVIII: 146.
Poblacht na hEireann, XVIII: 31, 70.
"P.ÓC." (on Reilly's *Irish Catechism*), XVIII: 170.
Poe, Edgar Allen, II: 80.
Poems and Hymns, XII: 67.
Poems and Translations (Robin Flower), XIX: 183.
Poems from Ireland (Donagh MacDonagh), XXIX: 143.
Poems of Eva Gore-Booth (ed. Esther Roper), XVIII: 182.
Poems of the Irish Republican Brotherhood (Padraic Colum), VIII: 65.
Poems on Dermot MacMurrough, XXXI: 106.
Poems, Plays and Prose (J.S.C.) XII: 9-10.
Poet, Philomath and Sower, (Brian Merriman) XXV: 103.
Poet of the Lee, A (Séamus Ó Casaide), XIX: 107.
Poetry Ireland (ed, David Marcus), XXXII: 95; XXXII: 45.
Poets of Ireland, The (D. J. O'Donoghue), III: 188, IV: 11, 35, XXVI: 112.
Poets, Past and Present, X: 89.
Pokorney, Julius, XI: 84.
Pollock-Holmes Letters (ed. Mary de Wolfe Howe), XXIX: 21.
Pollock, John Hackett, see "Philibín, An" [pseud].
Pomes Penyeach (James Joyce),

XXII: 13, 46.
Poor Richard (an Irish version), XXIV: 135; XXVI: 40; XXVII: 180.
Poore, Lady (*Reccollections of an Admiral's Wife*), VII: 165.
Poortenaar, Jan (*The Art of the Book and Its Illustration*), XXIV: 19.
Pope, Alexander, II: 129.
Popular Pennyworths, Old, II: 149.
Popular Rhymes and Sayings of Ireland (J. J. Marshall), XV: 43.
Port Airchinnigh (Airchinneach, Portrunny), XXXII: 55.
Portadown (printing in), VII: 123, 164.
Portarlington (printing in), XI: 117.
Porter, [Fr.] Francis, (as Irish scholar), XVIII: 11.
Porter, [Rev.] James, IV: 17, XIII: 126.
Portláirge agus Menévia, XXIV: 73.
Portrait of the Artist as a Young Man (James Joyce), VIII: 113.
Post Bag, The [Irish Book Lover], (Miscellaneous Notes), X: 17, 18, 4, 65, 91, XIII: 16, 37, 66, 95, 174, XII: 19,40, XV: 7, 24, 42, 53. XII: 67, 86, 110-111, 137.
Post Boy, XVI: 11.
Postgate, R. W. (*Robert Emmet*), XX: 94.
Poulter, F.W., XIII: 97, 118, 166.
Pound, Ezra, VI: 163; (*The A.B.C. of Reading*) XXXII: 23.
Povey, K., (John Salmon) XXV: 63; (printing in Coleraine), XXVII: 178.
Powell, Humphrey, IV: 108, 107.
Powell, S., IV: 107.
Powell, William, VI: 135, VII: 34.

Power, Arthur, (*From the Old Waterford House*) XXVIII: 46; (The Rotunda Hospital), XXX: 72.
Power, [Dr.] D'Arcy, IV: 5.
Power, James R. (*Home Sweet Home*), XXIV: 15.
Power, John, I: 1, 22; (*Handy Book about Books*), I: 4; III: 74.
Power, O'Connor, X: 86.
Power, [Rev. Prof.] Patrick, X: 88, XIV: 60, 132; (*The Ogham Stones*) XXI: 120; (John Fleming, Irish Scribe and Scholar) XXV: 77; *Waterford and Lismore*, XXVI: 42; (Irish MS and O'Donovan Letters) XXVI: 137.
Power, Victor O'D. (Obit), XXIII: 15.
Praeger, Robert Lloyd, (Bibliography of Irish Botany) VI: 104, 165; (*Irish Topographical Botany*) XVIII: 143; *Beyond Soundings*) XVIII: 178; (*The Botanist in Ireland*) XXIII: 51; (*The Way that I Went*) XXV: 120; (*A Populous Solitude*) XXVIII: 24.
Praeger, Rosamund (*Old Fashioned Verses and Sketches*), XXX: 120.
Prague, (Irishmen in) III: 209.
Pratt Library (Baltimore), VII: 189.
Prayers of the Gael, VII: 71.
Prehistoric Ireland (Joseph Raftery), XXXII: 22.
Prehistoric Man in Ireland (Cecil P. Martin), XXIV: 88.
Preliminary Survey of the Ancient Monuments of Northern Ireland, A (ed. D. A. Chart), XXVII: 260.
Prendergast, John Patrick, XV: 1.
Presbyterian Historical Society, I:

169.
Press, The [Dublin United Irishmen], VII: 13, 55.
Press at Brookfield (Co. Down), XVII: 19.
Press Cuttings (Irish Book Lover), III: 76, 121, 139, XIV: 14, 32, 64, 79, 95, 112, 128, XV: 16, 64.
Pressick, George, I: 16, 122.
Preston, George, XIX: 5.
Pretty Pair of Ruffians, A (Pól Breathnach), XXIII: 134-141.
Previte-Orton, C. W. (ed. *Cambridge Medieval History*, with Z. N. Brooke), XXV: 18.
Prévost (*Dean of Coleraine*), XXXII: 37.
Price, Cecil, XXXII: 107.
Price, Liam (Place Name of Co. Wicklow), XXIX: 143.
Prichett, V.S. (*The Spanish Virgin*), XVIII: 148.
"Pride of Sligo Town, The" [song], XXVI: 29, 136.
"Priest and His People, The" (Charles Kickham), III: 1.
Prim, John George Augustus, XIII: 174.
Principles of Freedom (Terence MacSwiney), XIII: 31.
Principles of Psychology (Colonel Arthur Lynch), XII: [q.p]
Printers [alphabetically]— (Thomas Browne) XII: 20, XVI: 15, XXXII: 8-11, 59; (Bull) IV: 53; (John Chambers) XXVII: 234; (Cornelius Carter) XVII: 84-85, 119; (Zachariae Conzatti) XVIII: 123; 18 (Peter Cooney) XXIV: 64; (Edmund Finn) XXIV: 40; (John Francton) III: 59, 109; (D. Graiseberry) XVIII: 24; (D. Moloney) XIX: 60; (Peter de Pienne) XXIV: 75; (Myles Swinney, letter founder) XVII: 93; (White) XXX: 37.

Printers (in Dublin)—(Dickson Family) XVII: 45-47; (Maps printers) XVII: 78, 144; (Depositions by) XVII: 33-35; (17th c. Dublin Printers) XVII: 12, 113, XVIII: 20; (Dublin Music Printers and Sellers) XVIII: 26ff.; (Zacharia Conzatti) XVIII: 123; (English Financial Records) XXVIII: 112-15;
Printers (Provincial)—(Armagh) XVII: 2, 4; (Provincial printers in 1819) XVI: 121-25; (Catalogue of early Belfast printing) XVII: 52; (Drogheda) XVII: 120; (Loughrea) XVII: 120; (Sligo) XVII: 120; (Loughrea) XVII: 120; (Skibbereen) XIX: 60; (Kilkenny) XXIV: 40; (Waterford Printer) XXIV: 75; (Limerick) XXIX: 120
Printers & printing (sundry)— (Printing in Ireland) I: 13, 168; (Bibliography of), II: 4, 23, 51, 66, 84, 101, 120, 151, 186, III: 51, 177, 200; (Private Printing) II: 45, 46, 62; (Irish Bible) II: 109; (Printing Title Pages) III: 33, 78, 129; (Local Printing) III: 9; (Irish Towns) VII: 110; (Irish Ballad Printers) XIV: 88; (Technical Aspects of Gaelic Printing) XVI: 62-63, 85-87; (Plays printed in Ireland before 1701) XVII: 36-37; (Maps printers, Dublin) XVII: 78, 144; (Bossuet's *Exposition* Printed in Rome, 1675) XVIII: 10; ("Irish Ballads and Their Printers) XVIII: 19; (Printers, Booksellers and Book-binders who died in 1806) XVIII: 57; price of printing in 1808) XX: 35; (Printing and the Lane Pictures) XXI: 40; (Law as to Printing in Ireland before the Act of Union)

XXII: 110-13; (MS copies of Printed Books in Irish) XXIV: 98; (Honest Printer) XXVII: 209; (Merry Andrew: My Friend the Printer) XXX: 48; (Ballade of a Quinsical Printer) XXX: 132; (Printing on Irish Printing Press in Louvain, Kevin McGrath) XXXII: 36. Also (sundry) IV: 53, 71, 90, 93, 107, 108, 141. See also Catalogues.

Printing (alphabetically by location)—(Achill), II: 65, 110, VI: 104, 116; (Armagh) I: 160, IV: 83, XIV: 7, 55, XVII: 4; (Artane, Co. Dublin) XXVII: 259; (Athlone) II: 84, VI: 106, 136; (Athy) XVII: 58-59; (Ballinasloe) VII: 6; (Ballinrobe) XVII: 9, 93; (Ballyclare) V: 129. 167, 185, VII: 33; (Ballymena) XII: 128,129, 130, XIII: 67, 95; (Ballyshannon) XVII: 101-102; (Baltimore) VII: 189; (Banbridge) XVII: 7; (Belfast) IV: 15, VI: 157, 159, 187, 209, XI: 102, XIII: 176; (Birr or Parsonstown(III: [?]; (Bluebell, Co. Dublin) XXVII: 212; (Bonmahon) I: 97, 121, II: 47, VI: 209; (Boyle) VII: 24; (Brookfield) XVII: 19; (Cabra, Co. Dublin) XXVII: 210; (Carlow, III: 25, VII: 6, XI: 75, 94, 109, 126, XII: 11-12; (Carrick) III: 36, 60, IV: 161; (Carrickfergus) II: 196, VII: 186; (Carrick-on-Suir) VIII: 139; (Cashel) VI: 194, XI: 103; (Castlebar) IX: 47; (Cavan) I: 83, IV: 165, XI: 6, 22, 40; (Charlestown) V: 6; (Clare) XI: 104; (Clonmel) III: 78, IV: 42, 72, XXIV: 135, XXVI: 39; (Coleraine) XXIV: 15, XXVII: 178; (Cookstown) XVII: 137-138; (Cork) III: 129, IV: 129, 125, VII: 45; (Derry) III: 112, IV: 91, XVII: 92; (Donaghadee) VII: 46; (Drogheda) IV: 1, VI: 116; (Dublin) IV: 32, 53, 71, 90, 93, 107. 108, 141 [see also Printers in Dublin]; (Duncairn) I: 7, 25, 91; (Dundalk) V: 46. 58, 78, VIII: 123, IX: 4; (Dungannon) IV: 188, VIII: 75, 100; (Dungarvan) XIV: 67; (Enniscorthy, XIV: 83, 111, XVII: 138-139, XXVI: 64; (Enniskillen) II: 186, III: 80, V: 147, VII: 3 32, 47; (Fermoy) XIII: 76, 175; (Galway, II: 50, IV: 59, IX: 190, X: 9-10, XIV: 76; (Glenmore) XIV: 110; (Gorey) XIV: 100; (Greenisland) VII: 7; (Johnstown) VII: 164, 188; (Kilkenny) IV: 97, V: 138, XVI: 6-9, 40-41, 55-58. 89-109, XVII: 20; (Killylea) XIV: 60; (Kilmore) XI: 136; (Kilrush) IX: 73; (Larne) IV: 91; (Ledeston) I: 69, IV: 98; (Letterkenny) XII: 31; (Limavady) XI: 102, XII: 78; (Limerick) XIX: 117-120, 134, 174, XX: 84, 85, 106-108, 124, XXI: 7-9, 30-32, 56, 78-80; (Limerick and Ennis) III: 157; (Lisburn) VII: 90; (Longford) XII: 53-54; (Loughrea) II: 151, 181, VI: 175; (Louvain) VI: 37; (Lurgan) XIII: 54, 114, 17; (Monaghan) IV: 200, X: 34, 55; (Monaghan) X: 34, 55; (Mullingar) II: 120, VI: 127, 140, 160; (Mullingar [Ouilean]) IV: 112; (Naas) VII: 6; (Navan) VI: 31; (Newry) III: 12, V: 201, VI: 17, VII: 7, XVII: 142; (Newtownards) XII: 101; (Newtowncrommelin) II: 12, 28;

(Omagh) VII: 7, 46; (Portadown) VII: 123; (Portarlington) XI: 117; (Rosanna) III: 141, IV: 16, 54, VIII: 17; (Roundwood [Tochar], Co. Wicklow), I: 37, 59, 61, , III: 142, 199, IV: 53, XXIV: 41; (Sligo) II: 21, VI: 52, 69, 89, VII: 47, VIII: 115; (Strabane) IV: 48, 114, 134, VII: 68, 91, IX: 60; (Thomastown) XVII: 102; (Tralee) IV: 147, X: 79, X: 80; (Trim) I: 63, 77, 107; (Tuam) II: 101, 145, VII: 40, 91, XV: 7; (Co. Tyrone) XXIV: 55; (Waterford) I: 117, IV: 53, 97, VII: 170, XXVI: 128, XXIV: 75, XXVII: 149, 183; (Wexford) XXVII: 250; (Wicklow [see also Roundwood]) XXVI: 58; (Youghal) IV: 4. See also Presses.

Printing Presses—(Achill Press) II: 65, 110, III: 29, 38, VI: 104, 116, XIX: 101, XX: 114, XXII: 103; (Amyas Griffith's Press) XVII: 11; (Bonmahon Press) I: 97, 121, II: 47, XIX: 95, XXXII: 79; (Brookfield, Co. Down) XVII: 19; (Caledon Private Press) IX: 5; (Cambridge University Press) XX: 95; (Carogh Orphanage Private Press) IX: 7; (Carrickfergus Press) II: 196; (Cashel Private Press) IX: 8; (Cecil Press, Co. Tyrone) XXIV: 55; (Columba Press) XXXII: 57, 58; (Cuala Press) XI: 119; (Curzon St., Mayfair), IV: 112; (Donemana Private Press) IX: 8, 63; (Dublin University Press) II: 3, 163, IV: 32, XXIII: 13, 97; (Duncairn Press) I: 7, 25, 91; (Gortin Private Press) IX: 8, 60; (Larkfield Press, Kimmage) XXXII: 57, 58. (Ledestown Press) I: 69, IV: 98, XI: 116; (MacGusty's Press), XVIII: 25; (McCalmont's Press) IV: 91; (Mount Trenchard Private Press) IX: 7; (Newtowncrommelin Press) II: 12, 28; (Riccardi Press) XXX: 67; (Rosanna Press) III: 141, IV: 16, 54, V: 130; VIII: 17; (Roundwood Press) I: 37, 59, 61, III: 142, 199; (Singleton's Press) I: 116; (Synge's Private Press) IX: 7; (Talbot Press), IX: 52, X: 60, XII: 82; (Thomas Browne's Three Candles Press) XXXII: 8, 59; (Colm Ó Lochlainn's Three Candle Press), XII: 40, XVI: 15; University Presses, II: 8; (Young Ireland Press) II: 137, 161, 162, 171. Also (New Private Press) V: 6; (Suppression of Nationalist Press) VI: 116; (An Unrecorded Private Press) XXVII: 259, and (sundry) XI: 85, 116, 135, XIV: 52, 67.

Prison Letters of Countess Markievicz, XXIII: 19.

Prior, Thomas (books by and relating to), XXXII: 2.

Proclamations (donated to U.C.D.), XXIII: 108, 144.

Prophecies of Pastorini ("Pastorini" [pseud. of Charles Walmsley]), IX: 61.

Prout, [Rev.] André (Watergrasshill), XVIII: 86.

"Prout, Fr." [pseud. Sylvester Mahony], III: 3, 4; (birthplace) XVIII: 86.

Provinces of Ireland, XIII: 153; (Bibliography) XX: 74;

Psalter of Cashel, The (Séamus Ó Casaide) XXII, 39, 91.

Pseudonyms, I: 121.

Pseudo-Irish Songs (Colm Ó Lochlainn), XXXI: 12.

Psychology and Mystical Experience (John F. Howley), XII: 23.
Psyche (Mrs. Tighe), III: 141, 172.
Public Avenger or The Theatrical Chronicle, The, (Rare Dublin Periodical), XII: 104-106.
Public Prompter and Irish Journal, The, XII: 104-106.
Publishing and publishers—Publishers—(Dublin Publishers in 1720) II: 93, 112; (Simms and McIntyre) II: 133; (Pirate Publishers) II: 156, III: 46, 60; (Irish Publisher's Reminiscences) IX: 69, 98,123; (James Duffy, publisher) XVIII: 9, 168-69; (Decay of Publishing in Ireland) XVIII: 97; (Thomas Kiersey) XXVII: 177; (Publishers of O'Donovan's Four Masters) XXIV: 110; (Publications) XXX: 2; (Nelson publisher) XXX: 144.
Punch, XIV: 27.
Punchersgrange (Co. Kildare), XXVII: 178.
Purcell, Anna, XV: 63.
Purcell, Patrick (*Hanrahan's Daughter*) XXIX: 24; (*Fiddler's Green*) XXXI: 95; (*A Keeper of Swans*) XXIX: 144.
Purcell, [Dr.] Richard J., XVI: 48.
Purcell, Theobald. A., VI: 137; (and Arthur O'Clery) VI: 206.
Purdon, [Miss] K. F. (*The Folk of Furry Farm*), V: 165; (*Candle and Crib*) VI: 114.
Purser, [Dr.] Louis C., VII: 153.
Purser, Sean (*A Troth Replighted*), XXXII: 46.
Put Money in thy Purse (Micheál MacLiammóir), XXXII: 45.
Pyne, Michael, X: 66.

Q

Quaint Irish Bygones (W. B. Hannon), VIII: 66.
Quarterly Bibliography, see under *Irish Book Lover*.
Quiggin, [Prof.] Edward Crosby, II: 154, 174; III: 7; (*Poems from the Book of the Dean of Lismore*, ed. with J. Fraser), XXV: 109.
Quigley, [Rev.] Hugh (*The Cross of Shamrock*), IV: 34; (*The Highlands of Scotland*) XXV: 16.
Quinn, John, XIV: 22, 104, 122.
Quinn, [Dr.] Henry, XI: 98.
Quirke, Henry (Obit.), VIII: 143.
Quirke, [Capt.] A. J. (*Forged, Anonymous, and Suspect Documents*), XIX: 63.
Quirke, William M. (*Recollection of A Violinist*), VI: 60.
"*Quoi dono ... libellum*" (elegy for M. J. McManus), XXXII: 3.

R

Race of Castlebar (Emily Lawless & Shan Bullock), V: 103, 165.
Racing Calendar, XIX: 90.
Radcliffe, Mrs. (Mary Longfield), XII: 34.
"Radiant Boy, The", VII: 15, 55.
Raftery, Gerald (*Adolescent*), XXVI: 63.
Raftery, Joseph (*Prehistoric Ireland*), XXXII: 22.
Rahilly, Alfred (*A Guide to Books for Social Students and Workers*), VII: 186.
Rain, Rain, Go To Spain (Robert Lynd), XIX: 184.
Rambles in Ireland (Robert Lynd), IV: 68.
Ramsay, Robert W. (*Henry*

Cromwell), XXIII: 77.
Rankin, [Rev.] (*The Christian's Guide*), XI: 65.
Raphael, [Sister] Mary, V: 198, 215.
Rapid Reviews, XII: 130-131.
Rare Dublin Periodicals, XI: 65; XII: 104-06 (*Censor or Covent Garden Journal*; *Dublin Mercury*; *Dublin Spectator*; *Hunter's Dublin Chronicle*; *Evening Chronicle*; *Flying Post*; *Independent Irishman*; *Weekly Oracle, or Universal Library*).
Rare Ulster Booklet, XXVI: 122.
Rare Waterford Printed Book (1647) and its Printer, A, Peter de Pienne, XXIV: 75.
Rat Pit, The (Patrick MacGill) VI: 147.
"Rath na Bliana Orainn—1948" (Brian Ó hUiginn), XXX: 73.
Rathangan, Castledermot, and Athy, VII: 163.
"Rathkyle, M. A." [pseud.] (*Farewell to Garrymore*), XI: 62.
Rathlin Catechism, The (Dr. Francis Hutchinson), XI: 14, 65.
Rathmore, Lord [David Plunkett], IV: 209, XI: (Obit.) 31.
Rattray, R. S. (*The Leopard Priestess*), XXIII: 50.
Rawlinson MSS, XV: 60.
Ray, Joseph (and Samuel Mather), XX: 40, 54.
Ráiste, Tomas de (Fr. Domhnall Ó Morchadha's Books), XXIV: 64.
"R.C.R.", I: 75.
"R.D." (Graveyard at George's Hill, Dublin), XVIII: 175.
Rea, John, IV: 13, 37.
"Reachtaire" (Literary Distinction—A Topographical Inquiry), XVII: 62-63 117.
Reade, Charles, XIV: 73.

Reader's Guide to Irish Fiction, see *Guide to Books on Ireland* (Fr. Stephen Brown).
Real Ireland (C. H. Bretherton), XVII: 75.
"Réamhradh agus Colophon" (Bonabhentura Uí Eodhasa), XVII: 133, 134.
Reardon, Conor (*Shake Hands with the Devil*), XXII: 99.
Reardon, [Dr.] Simon, XVII: 71.
Rebel Irishwomen (R. M. Fox), XXIV: 48.
Rebel Schoolmaster, A, XXVIII: 92.
Rebellion of 1642 [Irish Rebellion], II: 43, 49, 72, 118, 125, 127, 141.
Rebellion of 1798—IV: 17; (Ballad Version of) XVII: 118.
Rebellion of 1916, VIII: 12, 13, 14, 16; (*Irish Rebellion of 1916*), 18; VIII: 47.
Rebels: True Man and Traitor, The (M. MCD. Bodkin), XIII: 154.
Reciter's Treasury of Prose and Verse (eds. A. P. Graves & G Pertwee), VI: 204.
Recollection of a Violinist (William M. Quirke), VI: 60.
Recollections of a Collegian (George Darley), XXXII: 75.
Recollections of an Irish Doctor (Lombe Atthill), II: 177.
Recollections of an Old Book Lover, I: 130, 146, II: 87.
Recollections of Commons, XIV: 62.
Record Society, The, II: 7.
Recorder: Bulletin of The American Irish Historical Society, The, XIX: 152.
"Red Flag, The" (James Connell), XIV: 45.
Red Hand of Ulster (George A.

Birmingham), IV: 32.
Red Hugh's Sister [Mary] (Pól Breathnach), XXVI: 105.
Redington Memorial Collection [Catalogue] (Galway Library), XX: 141.
Red Owen ("Dermot O'Byrne" [pseud. of Arnold Bax]), XI: 46.
Red Petticoat and Other Stories, The (Bryan MacMahon), XXXII: 119.
Reddin, Mary G. VIII: 120.
Redmond, John Edward, I: 119, 132, 172; IX: 113, 133, XX: 98.
Redmond-Howard, VIII: 35.
Redmond's Vindication (Rev. Robert O'Loughran), X: 91.
Reed, James, VI: 7.
Reed, Talbot B. (Irish Type-fonts), XX: 94.
Reeves, Boleyne, I: 46.
Reeves, [Bishop] William, II: 42, 97, 182; XVI: 17; *Ecclesiastical Antiquities*, XXVI: 64..
Reference to in *Calendar of State Papers*, (see *State Papers, Calendar of*).
Reference to Work on Irish Campanology, XVIII: 144.
Reformer, The (Edmund Burke), VIII: 68.
Register of the Proiry of the B.V.M. at Tristernagh (ed. Miss M. V. Clarke), XXVIII: 137.
Registry of Deeds, The, XX: 55.
Reid, Benjamin, VII: 46.
Reid, Forrest, III: 98, IV: 68, VI: 96, (*W. B. Yeats*) VII: 113; (*The Pirates of the Spring*) XII: 35-36; (*Uncle Stephen*), XIX: 180; (*Brian Westby*) XXII: 92; (*The Retreat*) XXIV: 67. Also XI: 140.
Reid, James Seaton, II: 10.
Reid, [Dr.] Thomas, IV: 5.
Reid, [Capt.] Thomas Mayne, I: 155, IV: 47.
Reidy, Donal A., (*Spanish State Papers relating to Ireland*) XXI: 42; (*St. Brendan in History and Literature*), XXXI: 19.
Reilly, James Myles, III: 214.
Reilly's Dublin News-Letter, I: 41.
Reincarnations (James Stephens), IX: 137.
Reliques of Irish Poetry (Hugh M'Gauran), XVI: 45.
"Remembrance of Lieutenant Thomas Kettle" (Randal McDonnell), VIII: 34.
Reminiscences of an Eastern Tour (J. A. Whelan), XVIII: 146.
Reminiscences of Lord O'Brien of Kilfenora (Georgina O'Brien), VIII: 138.
Renehan's *Bishops*, XV: 25, 95, XVI: 87.
Rent in a Cloud, A (Charles Lever), XI: 23.
Rentoul-Esler, [Mrs.] Erminda, V: 83, VI: 110, VIII: 132; (Obit.) XIV: 112.
Rentoul, [Prof.] J. Lawrence ["Gervais Gage"] (*From Far Lands: Poems of North and South*), VI: 131; (*At the Sign of the Sword*) VII: 162; (*At Vancouver's Well*) IX: 79.
Rentoul, [Judge] James Alexander, XII: 88; (*Stray Thoughts and Memories*) XIII: 14.
Renwick, W. L. (ed. *Spenser's View of the Present State of Ireland*), XXII: 124.
Repair of Manuscripts, XXVIII: 17.
Repealer, The, IX: 28.
Reprints (Dublin), II: 128.
Republican War Bulletin 1922-23, XVIII: 31.
Rerum Hibernicarum Scriptores Veteres (Charles O'Conor),

XXXII: 106.
"R.E.S.", IX: 15.
Responsibilities (W. B. Yeats), VIII: 60.
Retaliator, The, XI: 29.
Retreat, The (Forrest Reid), XXIV: 67.
Retrospection of Dorothea Herbert (Gerald Howe), XVII: 140.
Reult, An (Irish magazine) XX: 66.
Reveries over Childhood and Youth (W. B. Yeats), VIII: 60.
Reviews by Diarmud Coffey, Georóid Ó Murchadha, J. J. Hayes, P. C. Trimble, M Ní N., Sean, and etc., XXII: 19-24.
Reviews by—(Prof. Liddell, M. Lavery, Pól Mac Giobin, P. C. Trimble, J. K., et al.) XXI: 139-144; (P. C. T., M. L., D. B., V. B., Colm [Ó Lochlainn], J. J. H.) XXII: 69-76; (Stephen Gwynn, Prof. Trench, George. O'Brien, P. C. Trimble, et al.) XXI: 115. (Reviews sundry others) IV: 11, 32, 51, 68, 88, 112, 141, 157, 172, 193; 206, [...] XX: 20, 45, 67, 94-96, 116, 141-44, XXI: 46-48, 68, 93-96, XXII: 43-48, XXII: 92-100, 119-24, 145-52, XXIII: 18-32, 49-56, 74-80 96-104, 118-28, 149-56, XXVIII: 20-24, 45-48, 69-72, 93-96, 136-40.
Revolution Tracts and Broadsides, IV: 190.
Revolutionary Ireland (Robert H. Murray), II: 189.
Revolutionist The (Terence J. MacSwiney), V: 200.
Reward of Irish Writers, XIII: 29.
Reynolds, H. Fitzgerald, VIII: 115, XIII: 140.
"R.G.M.", XIX: 78.
Rhyme and Reason (C. H. Bretherton), XIV: 74.
Rhynehart, J. G. (Two Little-known Books), XXXI: 34; (*Irish Penny Magazine*) XXXI: 105; (Ballytubber and the Pedlars) XXXI: 106; (Palatine Settlements in Ireland) XXXI: 133.
Rhys, Ernest, XVII: 15, 28 (*Letters from Limbo*) XXV: 65.
Rhys, Grace, XVII: 27, 28.
R.I.C in Literature, XII: 7, 29-31.
Riccardi Press Booklet, A, XXX: 67.
Richardson, James Nicholson, XIII: 59, 71.
Richardson, P. B., Loughrea Printer, XV: 109.
Rickard, [Mrs.] Victor [pseud. "Marjorie Dovie"] (*The Story of the Munsters*), VII: 73, 103; XII: 33, 112.
Riddall, [Dean] Walter (Obit.), V: 128.
Riddell, Alex, II: 47; (*The Ulster Calendar of Persons and Events*) II: 91.
Riddell, [Mrs.] J. H. [Miss Charlotte Cowan], XI: 51, 52.
Riddell, Patrick, XXX: 27-29.
Ridgeway, [Prof.] William, II: 19; VI: 26.
Riley, J. Whitcomb, XIV: 57.
Rinuccini, [Cardinal] Giovanni Battista, II: 104; (MSS) VII: 75, 134.
Rival Confederate Generals, The (Pól Ó Breathnach), XV: 5.
River to River: A Fisterman's Pilgrimage (Stephen Gwynn), XXVI: 21.
Rivers of Ireland, XIII: 139.
Rivoallan, A. (*L'Irlande*), XXII: 119.
"R.K.B.", IX: 61.
Roberts, D. Kilham (*Titles to Fame*), XXV: 507.

Roberts, Earl [Frederick], VI: 82.
Roberts, H. I. K. *Nana: Memory of an Old Nurse*), XXIV: 65.
Roberts, Michael (ed., *Faber Book of Modern* Verse), XXIV: 90.
Roberts, William, VIII: 43, XII: 132.
Robertson, James D. (*The Dream of Life*), XXIII: 25.
Robin Ernest William Flower (H. I. Bell), XXXI: 18.
Robinson, John, VIII: 116.
Robinson, Joseph, IV: 200.
Robinson, Lennox, VI: 155, IX: 89; (*White-headed Boy*) XI: 135; XIV: 93; (*Crabbed Youth and Age: A Little Comedy*) XIV: 124; XV: 31; (*Ever the Twain*) XIX: 30; (*Brian Cooper*) XX: 47; (*Is Life Worth Living?*) XXII: 23; (*More Plays*) XXIV: 24; (*The Irish Theatre*) XXVII: 264; (*Palette and Plough*) XXXI: 16.
Robinson, M., V: 167.
Robinson, Nugent, III: 105, 135, 191.
Robinson, William (Obit.), XXIII: 83.
Roch MSS, VI: 61.
Rouchefoucauld, see La Rochefoucauld, François.
Roche, Alexis, VI: 75 136, 211, VII: 11.
Roche, [Rev.] James (of Macroom), XXVI: 59.
Roche, Mary F. (*Leaves and Blossoms from Our Lady's Garden*), XXIV: 66.
Roche, Regina Maria (*The Children of the Abbey*), XI: 117.
Roche, Thomas (Early Dublin printing), III: 181, XXIV: 44.
Rocque's *Index* and *Plan* (to Dublin), XVI: 77, 78.
Roddy, William A. (Obit.), VI: 114.
Roddy the Rover and his Aunt Louisa (Aodh de Blácam), XXII: 97.
Roe, Peter, IV: 77.
Roger Casement (G. de C. Parmiter), XXIV: 120.
Rogers, [Dr.] J. Guinness, III: 43.
Rogue's Memoirs, A (Augustine Birrell), VIII: 105.
"Roisin Dubh", XX: 93.
Róiste, Tomás de, (the Irish Language) XXI: 92; (*Maurhin Phadrick*) XXII: 89; (Louis Marie de Cormenin), XXIII: 95.
"R.O'K.", XI: 118.
Rokeby, William (the *DNB* Corrected), XXVIII: 19.
Rolleston, Thomas William Hazen, II: 42, III: 74, 165, 186, IV: 153, 202, V: 153, 169, VI: 27, 49, 65, VII: 61, 78, IX: 93; (*Ireland's Vanishing Opportunity*) XI: 13; XII: 31; (Obit.) XII 81; (Mrs. Rolleston) XII: 106; XII: 139, XIII: 34; (Rolleston on Ireland in 1884) XXX: 112.
Rolt, L. T. C. (*Green and Silver*), XXXI: 109.
Rolt-Wheeler, Ethel, IV: 118, 168, V: 83; (*Romance of Irish Heroines*) V: 126; XI: 56.
Roman Almanack, The, XXVIII: 91.
Romanian Songs and Ballads (R. Stewart Patterson), IX: 80.
Romantic Inishowen (H. P. Swan), XXX: 71.
Ronan, James, IV: 125, 147.
Ronan, [Rev.] Myles, (*Christ Church Cathedral*; *Guide to Glendaloch*) XXIII: 80.
Ronayne, M. Christine VIII: 120.
Ronayne, Rev., (of St. Jarleth's, Tuam), IV: 57.

Rooney, Philip (*All Out to Win*), XXIV: 23 (*Red Sky at Dawn*), XXVI: 94.
Rooney, Teresa J., III: 42.
Rope, [Rev.] H. E. G. (*Fisher and More*), XXIII: 104
"R.O'R.", I: 62, III: 29, 47, 81, 139.
Rorke, Alexander (The O'Rorkes), XXV: 104.
"Rory of the Hill" (ballad), III: 2.
Ros, Amanda McKitterick, XII: 57; (*Delina Delaney*) XXIII: 126.
"Rós Geal Dubh" (song), XX: 93.
Rosanna Press, The, III: 141, IV: 16, 54, V: 130; (printing)VIII: 17.
Rosapenna, III: 27, 47.
Rose and De Rupe [pseuds. of Miss Kirwin (Rose) and Francis Maria Roche (De Rupe)], IV: 14.
Rose and Bottle, The (Seumas O'Sullivan), XXX: 47.
Rose Forbes (George Buchanan), XXV: 48.
Ross, Adrian ("A Goliardic Rime"), XXXI: 36.
Ross, Alexander (*Memoirs of Alexander Ross*), XXII: 66.
Ross, Francis, X: 68.
Ross, [Sir] John, XIV: 47; (*Years of my Pilgrimage*) XV: 13.
Ross, Martin, see Somerville & Ross
Rosses and Other Poems, The (Seaumus O'Sullivan), X: 46-47.
Rossi, Mario M. (ed. *Swift: or the Egotist* with Joseph M. Hone), XXIV: 6.
Roth, Bernard (*Coins of Danish Kings of Ireland*) II: 107.
Rothenstein, William (*Men and Memories: Recollections*), XIX: 103.
Rotten Ropes, XXIX: 113.
Round Table, The, XIV: 124.
Roundwood Press, The, I: 37, 59, 61, III: 142, 199; (printing) IV: 43, XXIV: 41.
Rowan, Hamilton, I: 135, XVII: 3.
Rowland, George (Limerick Printer) XXII: 7.
Rowley, Richard, IX: 109.
Royal Academical Institution, I: 172.
Royal College of Physicians in Ireland (as publisher), XVIII: 507.
Royal Dublin Society, (The 1731-1941), XXVIII: 60.
Royal Hibernian Tales, (Reference to by Thackeray), XVIII: 174.
Royal Irish Academy, The, II: 4, 81, 90, 98, III: 149, IV: 174, VIII: 35, IX: 50, XIII: 58, XX: 149.
Royal Irish Constabulary, see "R.I.C.".
Royal Kent Bugle and O'Donnell Abu, XXVI: 85.
Royal Society of Antiquaries of Ireland (*Journal of*) XXII: 120, XXIV: 47, XXIV: 113, XXXII: 151.
"R.S.M", IV: 54.
Rushlight, The (Joseph Campbell), III: 115.
Russell, Charles [Lord Killowen], I: 28, II: 89, XVII: 63.
Russell, Charles C. (*The People and Language of Ulster*), II: 107; (*The Ulsterman*) XIV: 13.
Russell, Charles E. (*Bare Hands and Stone Walls*), XXII: 148.
Russell, [Rev.] Charles William (contributor to *Edinburgh Review*), XVIII: 3.
Russell, [Sir] Edward, VIII: 83.
Russell, Elbert (*History of*

Quakerism), XXIX: 46.
Russell, George ("Æ"), I: 92; IV: 20, 31; (*Dublin Debating Society*) IV: 209; V: 109, 203, VII: 37; VIII: 66; XIII: 41; (His Influence on Thought in Ireland) XVIII: 34; (*Song and its Foundations*) XX: 68; XII: 13, 118; (*The House of the Titans*) XXIII: 54; (*Selected Poems*) 155.
Russell, [Lord] John, IV: 48.
Russell, [Fr.] Matthew, I: 45, II: 8, III: 24, IV: 41, 62, 88.
Russell, R. L., (*The Child and his Pencil*) XXIV: 46; (*Adventures in a Country School*) XXIV: 46.
Russell, Thomas, XIII: 37.
Russell, [Sir] William H., I: 29, II: 108, 126, 130, XII: 52.
Ruth, R. B. A.,VIII: 140.
Rutherford, Mark, IV: 157.
Rutherford, James C. (*An Ards Farmer*), IV: 208.
Rutherford, John, I: 93, 109, 136, 141.
Ruttledge, [Miss] A. K. (*Dream Mists*), III: 40.
Ryan, [Rev.]Abram J., XI: 128.
Ryan, Darby, V: 200; VI: 135.
Ryan, Desmond, XV: 13; (*The Invincible Army: A Story of Michael Collins*) XX: 118; (*St. Eustace and the Albatross*) XXIII: 126; (*Unique Dictato*) XXV: 23; (*The Phoenix Flame*) XXVI: 20; (*Ireland, Whose Ireland?*) XXVII: 215.
Ryan, Frederick, IV: 196. 198, XIII: 115.
Ryan, [Rev.] Thomas F., XVI: 37.
Ryan, William Patrick (*The Irish Labour Movement*), XI: 12; XIII: 13, 19; (*Poets in Paradise*) XVIII: 93.
Rynne, Stephen (*Green Fields*), XXVI: 47, XXX: 95.

S

Sadleir, John (in fiction), XI: 81, 102.
Sadleir, [Mrs.] Mary Anne, XII: 53.
Sadler Type Foundry, XX: 40.
Sadlier, Michael (on *Dublin University Magazine*), XV: 28, XXV: 61, XXVII: 215.
Sadlier, Thomas Ulick, VI: 203, VII: 52; (ed. *Alumni Dublinensis* with G. D. Burtchaell) XIV: 123.
"Sailm Daibid", (Psalms in Gaelic) IV: 51.
Sairseal agus Dill (publisher), XXXII: 147.
Sale Catalogues, see Book Sales.
Salkeld, Blanaid (*The Fox's Covert*), XXIII: 125.
Salmon, John, XXV: 14, 63.
Salud (Peadar O'Donnell), XXV: 67.
Samhain (W. B. Yeats), XVIII: 123.
Sampson, Donat (Obit.), VI: 114.
Sampson, William, II: 49, XIV: 57.
Samuel Forde: An Irish Artist, (Henry Mangan) XXIX: 137.
Sandy Chronicle, The, VIII: 84.
Sandys, Edwin XVIII: 123.
"Saoghal an Duine" (Mícheál Óg Ó Longáin), XXX: 25.
Saothar Gan Tairbhe, XXX: 98.
Saothar na Seanchaí, XXIII:81
"Sapper" [pseud. of Maj. H. C. McNeill), X: 104.
"Saracen" [psued.] (*Misconceptions*), XIII: 171.
"Sarah Curran" (Randall McDonnell), VII: 26.
Saroyan, William (*The Bicycle*

Rider on Beverley Hills), XXXII: 47.
Sarr, Kenneth (*Somewhere to the Sea*), XXIV: 70.
Sarsfield, Patrick (*Sarsfield's Letters*), XV: 9; (*Patrick Sarsfield*) XXIII: 56.
Sassoon, Siegfried (*Sherston's Progress*), XXV: 71.
Saunders' News-Letter, XIX: 90, 91.
Saunders, [Dr.] Fred W., XXV: 64; (Irish Language Revivalists), XXVI: 104; (Obit.) XXX: 14.
Saunders, [Dr.] George, IV: 175.
Savage, John, VI: 80; (John O'Mahony), XVIII: 43.
Savage-Armstrong, G. F., XI: 115.
"Sax Rohmer" [pseud. of Arthur Sarsfield-Ward], XII: 33.
Sayings of Poor Richard (D. M. Lloyd) XXIV: 135; XXVI: 40; XXVII: 180.
Sayle, Charles, II: 175, VIII: 101, XIII: 116.
"Says She" (W. M. Letts), III: 79.
Scandanavian Relations, XIV: 74.
Scarriffhollis, (a supposed placename) XXVII: 179.
Sceilg, *Rudhraigheacht*, XXIII: 151.
Scéim agus Ceistiúchán le h-aghaidh Stair Paráiste, XVII: 113.
Schmitz fifwerbler Der Pessimisimus Bei ... Jonathan Swift [et al.] (G. Van den Bergh), XXXI: 114.
"Scholemaster, The" (Anon.), XXX: 135.
School for Scandal, The (R. B. Sheridan), XVII: 3, 4.
Schoolmaster of Esker, The XXIV: 86.
Schoolmaster's Magazine, XIII: 63.
Schoolmasters of Ireland in 1824 and 1834, XVII: 11.
Schottenkloster of St. James, Ratisbon, XXXI: 79.
Schultze, J. H. (*Grossbritanniert und Irland*), XXXII: 112.
Scott, Charles Kennedy (*Madrigal Singing*), XX: 71.
Scott, Charles (his MSS), XX: 93.
Scott, D. McCance, IV: 35.
Scott, G. D. (*The Stones of Bray*), V: 145.
Scott, [Maj.] John, XXXII: 144.
Scott, Samuel, XI: 86.
Scott, [Rev.] T. H. M., II: 48, 112.
Scott, [Sir] Walter, II: 13.
Scott-James, R. A. (*Englishman in Ireland*), II: 106.
Scots Book, The (Ronald Macdonald Douglas), XXIV: 18.
Scrap Book, Our, IV: 126, 178, XIII: 43.
Scribe of the Book of Clannaboy, XIX: 165.
Scribes (Irish), XVI: 4-5; XVI: 13-14.
Scribhinne ar Éoin Mac Néill, XXVII: 217.
Scriptorium (eds. F. Lyna & C. Gasper), XXX: 93, 116.
Scully Diary, The, 1776-1814 [John Scully], (P. O'Connell), XXX: 110-111.
"Seabhac, An", see Ó Siochfhradha, Pádraig.
Seacome, John, IV: 106.
Seadna: An Dara Chuid (Fr. Peadar Ua Laoghaire), XXXII: 78.
Séaghda, Pádraig (see 'Conan Maol'). XVI: 44-45.
Seago, Edward (*Sons of Sawdust*), XXIII: 78.
Seamus Beg: The Rocky Road to Dublin (James Stephens), VII:

94.
Seán Clárach agus Liam Dall cct. (Séamus Ó Casaide), XX: 58-59.
"Sean Gall" [also Sean or Shaun Ghall, pseud.] I: 25, 85; XIII: 73, XIV: 29.
Seanchaidhe Muimhneadh, An, XX: 11.
Second Chronicle of Jails (Darrell Figgis), XI: 61.
Secret Hill, The (Ruth & Celia Duffin), V: 126.
Secret History of Fenian Conspiracy (John Rutherford), I: 136, 141, 147.
Secret Instructions to Military Officers (Columba Press, Dublin), XXXII: 58.
Secret Printing in Ireland, I: 27, 116, 150, 169.
Secret Service during the 1803 Insurrectionary period, XX: 13.
Sedley, Lionel, X: 43.
Sé Fáth mo Bhuartha (Colm Ó Lochlainn), XXVI: 1.
Seigne, J. W. (*A Bird Watcher's Notebook*), XIX: 29.
Selected Bibliography of Literature Relating to Nursery Rhyme Reform, A (Geoffrey Handley-Taylor), XXXII: 44.
Selected Poems (Herbert M. Pim), IX: 80.
"Senex", XII: 41.
Sentinel, (Londonderry) XVII: 109.
Separatist (war weekly, 1922), XVIII: 72.
Sermon by Rev. Arthur Hyde, XXXI: 76.
Septs of Muintear Ghallchubhair (Pól Breathnach), XXVII: 194.
Seton, Lady, XIII: 67.
Seton, Malcolm C., I: 136, V: 202, VI: 202, VIII: 89.
Seventeen Ninety-Eight Leaflets, XXVI: 16, 115.
Seventeenth Century German Catalogue of Irish Books, XXXII: 102.
Seventeenth-Century Advertisement Printed in Dublin, XVIII: 122.
Seventy Years of Irish Life (W. R. Lefanu), VI: 79.
Seymour, Edward (*Christ Church Cathedral*), XXII: 2.
Seymour, James A., III: 63.
Seymour, St. John D. (*Irish Witchcraft and Demonology*), V: 66; 90, VI: 100, XVII: 112; (*Irish Visions of the Other World*) XIX:28.
Sgáthán Spioradálta [trans. of *Specchio spirituale del principio e fine della vita umana*] (Angelo Elli), XXIV: 51.
Sgéal Brónach thar Tuinn, XXIV: 1,
Sgéal Chathail Bhrugha, XXIII: 144-146.
Sgéala ó Cathair na gCeó, see John S. Crone.
Sgéul fá Bheatha agus pháis ár d-Tighearna agus ár Slánuigh-theóra, Íosa Críost (Riobárd Ua Cionga), XXVI: 122.
Shackleton, [Sir] Ernest, XIII: 136, 147.
Shaded Lights (W. A. Duffy), XIV: 46.
Shadow of the Rose, The (J. Bernard McCarthy), XI: 115.
Shakespeare, William, (Shakespeare Portrait) VIII: 116; (and Ireland) XIII: 142, XV: 56; (A Dublin Statue) XV: 23-24; (Irish editions of) XXXII: 4; (*Shakespeare in the Theatre*), XXXII: 7.
Shamrock, The, III: 4, XXV: 31; (Bibliography of) XXI: 37-40.

Shamrockiana ("Maelmire"), XVIII: 32.
Shamrog, The (rare Cork newspaper), V: 13.
Shan van Vocht (eds. Miss Milligan & Eithne Carbery) XXXII: 63.
"Shan Van Vocht" (Sydney R. Lysaght), V: 220, VI: 147.
Shanachie, The, XI: 10.
Shane, Elizabeth, XIV: 47; (*Collected Poems*), XXX: 94.
"Shane" [a Cork poet], VII: 163.
Shanks, James, IV: 208.
Sharman-Crawford, Mabel, III: 152.
Shaw, C. M. (*Bernard's Brethren*), XXVII: 167.
Shaw, Flora, XVII: 4.
Shaw, [Rev.] Francis (ed. *The Dream of Óengus*), XXIII: 76.
Shaw, George Bernard, VI: 96, XIV: 122, XVII: 2; (*The Political Madhouse in America and Nearer Home*) XXI: 119; (*Prefaces*) XXII: 145; (Arnold Bennett) XVIII: 131. (Gift of early MSS to Dublin) XXX: 18.
Shaw, Henry, XIII: 95.
Shaw, Rose (*Carleton's Country*), XVIII: 150.
Shaw, Thomas J., II: 75; V: 107, VI: 14.
Shaw, William, IV: 207, V: 49, 222, VI: 21.
Shaw, [Mrs.] W. F., IX: 140.
She Had to Do Something (Seán Ó Faoláin), XXVI: 93.
Shea, John A., VI: 170.
Shearer, [Dr.] Alex, VIII: 43.
Shearman, [Fr.] John Francis, XVII: 15.
Shearman, Hugh (*Anglo-Irish Relations*), XXX: 138-139.
Sheaves of Revolt (Maeve Canavagh), VIII: 34.

Sheed and Ward [publishers], (*The Irish Way*) XX: 95; (*A Second Anthology*) XXIII: 27.
Sheehan, [Canon] Patrick, V: 62; (*The Graves at Kilmorna*) VI: 148; [Sheehan, Bp.] VII: 76, 180; IX: 124; (*Sermons*, ed. M. J. Phelan) XII: 108-09; XII: 110.
Sheehan, [Capt.] D. D. (*Ireland Since Parnell*), XIII: 31.
Sheehy, [Fr.] Eugene, VII: 95.
Sheehy, Michael (*Divided We Stand*) XXXII: 117.
Sheehy-Skeffington, Francis, VIII: 20; (*In Dark and Evil Days*) VIII: 86.
Sheehy's Relationship to the Keatings, XIX: 89.
Sheil, Richard Lalor, III: 92, XIII: 29.
Shelbourne, The (Elizabeth Bowen), XXXII: 45.
Shelley, Percy Bysshe, II: 176; XVII: 2; (*Compendium of the History of Ireland*) XVII: 3; (*Shelley, Goodwin and their Circle*) XXXII: 24.
Sheridan, Alicia (*The Pedlar's Way*), X: 46-47.
Sheridan, Richard Brinsley, I: 64; (Biographies and Portraits) XVI: 48, 68, 88; XVII: 3, 4, 17, XX: 27; (Letters to be published) XXXII: 107.
Sheridan, John Desmond (*Vanishing Spring*), XXIV: 23; (*Here's Their Memory*) XXVIII: 95.
Sheridan, Niall (ed. *Twenty Poems* with Donagh MacDonagh), XXII: 147.
Shinrone Conspiracy The, III: 93.
Shirley, Evelyn Phillip, V: 23.
Shore, [Rev.] Thomas Teignmouth, III: 101.
Shore, W. Teignmouth, XIII: 116.

The Irish Book Lover 351

Short Annals—(*History of Port of Belfast*) VIII: 112; (*of Tirconaill*) (Pól Breathnach) XXII: 104-109, XXIV: 13; (*Fir Manach*) XXIII: 7-9; (*of Leinster*) XXIV: 58, 87.

Short Bibliography of Irish History (Constantia Maxwell), XIII: 111.

Short Stories (Liam O'Flaherty), XXVI: 22.

Short Story, The (Seán O'Faoláin), XXXI: 18.

Shorter, Clement K., II: 89; IX: 56.

Shorter, Dora Sigerson, IX: 86, 87, 104, 117.

Shortt, [Capt.] Vere Dawson, VII: 104.

Shrines of Colman of Lynn, see Colman.

Shrovetide and Inid (Pól Breathnach) XXVI: 106; (Rev. Paul Walsh) XXVIII: 34-36.

Sidney, [Sir] Henry, XIX: 96.

Siege—(of Derry) II: 13, 48, 189; II: 74; (of Limerick) IV: 9; (of Cork) VIII: 34.

Sigerson, George, IV: 31, V: 75, VI: 94, VII: 131, IX: 136, XII: 13, XIII: 180; (Obit.) XV: 17, 22.

Sign of the Three Candles, XVI: 15, 27, XXXII: 8.

Signs (old Dublin), XXXII: 8-11, 59.

Silva Gadelica (reprinting of), XVIII: 3.

Silver Branch, The (Seán Ó Faoláin), XXVI: 144.

Silver Tassie, The (Sean O'Casey), XVI: 67, 109-111.

Simington, Robert C. (*The Civil Survey, A.D. 1654-56: Donegal, Londonderry and Tyrone*), XXV: 68; (*The Civil Survey*) XXVIII: 140; (*The Civil Survey, A.D. 1654-1656: Wexford*) XXXII: 115.

Simms and McIntyre (publishers), II: 133.

Simms, Samuel (Select Bibliography of Orange Society), XXIII: 72, XXV: 2.

Simple Guide to Irish Genealogy (Rev. Wallace Clare), XXVI: 68.

Simpson, Adam Boyd, XXVIII: 114.

Sinclair, C. E. R. (*Problem Island*), XXXI: 119.

Sing to the Spinning Wheel (May Morton), XXXII: 118.

Singer and Other Plays, The (Padraic Pearse), X: 46-47.

Singing Men at Cashel, The (Austin Clarke), XXIV: 65.

Singleton's Press, I: 116.

Sinn Féin—(*Ourselves Alone in Ulster*) X: 14; (*The Evolution of Sinn Fein*) XI: 13, XV: 8; (origin of name) XXXII: 107.

Siota sa Mháthair, An, XXIV: 134, XXV: 14.

Sir Richard Grenville (J. H. Bushnell), XXIV: 143.

Sirr, [Dr.] D'Arcy, II: 10, 36.

Sirr, Harry, II: 10, 36, 159, IV: 108.

Sirr, [Maj.] Henry Charles, II: 36, 37.

Sixpenny Magazine (E. R. McC Dix), XIX: 101.

Sjoestedt, Marie-Louise (*Gods and Heroes of the Celts*), XXXI: 110.

Skeffington, Francis Sheehy, see Sheehy-Skeffington, Francis.

Skeffington, Gibbon (in the Goldsmith Country), XXII: 58.

Skelton, Phillip, II: 25; (*Life of*), VI: 185.

Sketches of North and West (Mary R. Wilson), V: 30.
Skibbereen (printing in), XIX: 60.
Skrine, F. H., II: 114, VI: 96, VIII: 109, XIII: 68, 111.
Skrine, [Mrs.] Nesta (see Moira O'Neill). VI: 13, XVI. 26.
Slater, Patrick (*The Yellow Briar*), XXIII: 28.
"Slievegallion" (*Lays and Legends of the North of Ireland*), III: 119, 138.
"Slievenamon", see Kickham, Charles.
Sligo—(printing in Sligo), II: 21, VII: 47, 139, VIII: 115; (Sligo Magazine Race) VI: 56; (a Sligo printer) XVII: 120; (*Sligo Journal*) XIX: 90-91.
"Sliocht Tuire Thomáis Mhic Mhathúna" (Micheál Coimín), XXXI: 101, 102.
Sloan, [Rev.] Isaac, XI: 137.
Sloane, Alexander, XXVI: 39.
Smaointe Beatha Chríost (ed. Rev. Canice Mooney), XXIX: 140.
"S.M.", XII: 42.
"S.M.E.", VII: 55.
Smellie, John (*Shipbuilding and Repairing in Dublin*), XXIV: 66.
Smillie, Bob, XIV: 121.
Smith, George, XX: 92, XXI: 66, XXII: 16, XXVI: 38.
Smith, Joseph Huband, XXVI: 62.
Smith, Robert, VIII: 67.
Smith O'Brien, William, XVII: 51; (with J. C. Mangan & James Stephens) XVIII: 173.
Smithson, Annie M. P., XIII: 60, (*Traveller's Toy*) XVIII: 178; (*Leaves of Myrtle*) XX: 67; (*The Light of Other Days*) XXII: 48; (*The Marriage of Nurse Harding*) XXIV: 46; (*Wicklow Heather*) XXVI: 94.
Smugglers (Irish), VI: 152.

Smyth, J. A., VI: 153.
Smyth, [Rev.] John, V: 33.
Smyth, J. de Lacy, VIII: 39; (booklist) XVIII: 172; (Swift's Library) XIX: 58; (Thomas Davis) XIX: 58.
Smyth, Luke (of Damma, Co. Kilkenny), XXXII: 91.
Smyth, Nathalie Bouligny (*Poems*), XIV: 47.
Smyth, P. J., XIV: 128; (*Waterford Citizen*) XXX: 48.
Smyth, T. S. (*Postal History*), XXVIII: 23.
Smyth, [Rev.] William S., III: 190.
Smythe, Albert Ernest Stafford, IX: 8 ,76; (*Garden of the Sun*) XIV: 108.
Smythe, Joseph, I: 159.
Snell, Ralph M. (Irish papermakers in USA), XIX: 124.
"Snowflakes, The", (*Poetry Review*), XXXII: 45.
Society of Irish Tradition, XI: 61.
Society of United Irishmen, see United Irishmen
Soldier Songs, VIII: 64.
Some Ethical Questions of Peace and War (Rev. Walter MacDonald), XI: 83.
Some Gaelic Poets, XV: 51.
Some Interesting Finds, VI: 159, XI: 63.
Some Irish Ballads and their Printers, XVIII: 19.
Some Irish Men of Letters— (Joseph McCabe) XII: 10; (Dr. O'Brien) XII: 11.
Some Missing Books, I: 34, 59.
Somerville & Ross (Edith Somerville & Violet Martin], (*In Mr. Knox's Country*) VII: 29; VII: 127, IX: 107; (*An Incorruptible Irishman*) XXI: 71; (*The Smile and the Tear*)

XXII: 20.
Somerville, [Admiral] Boyle Townshend (*Will Mariner*), XXIV: 137.
Sometime in Ireland: A Recollection (Anon.), XVII: 99.
Son of Learning, The (Austin Clarke), XVII: 113-114.
Song Books (Early Dublin), XXIII: 92.
Song Books (Irish), II: 34, 81, 11. 163, 177.
Song Wanted, XI: 137.
"Songs Erin Sings, The" (A. P. Graves), I: 132.
Songs from Leinster (W. M. Letts), IV: 206.
Songs from the Clay (James Stephens), VI: 167.
Songs from the Heart (Albert C. White), VI: 167.
Songs of Donegal (Patrick MacGill), XII: 83-86.
Songs of Erin (Geoffrey Marsland), XIV: 59.
Songs of Myself (Whitman), II: 107.
Songs of Peace (Francis Lidwedge), VIII: 107.
Songs of the Celtic Past (N. J. O'Connor), IX: 137.
Songs of the Fields (Francis Lidwedge), VII: 92.
Songs of the Glen (mena McCrudden), XV: 47.
Songs of the Open Road (L. J. McQuilland), VIII: 41.
Songs that Made History (H. E. Piggott), XXV: 108.
Songs (love), V: 42.
Sons of the Sea Kings W. H. & Alice Milligan), V: 199.
"Sorrow of Loneliness" (Randall McDonnell), V: 70.
Souls of Poor Folk (Alexander Irvine), XIII: 31.

Sources for the Early History of Ireland (James F. Kenney), XVIII: 126.
Southern Patriot, The, XI: 103.
Southey, Robert, II: 149; (Southey and Emmet) XI: 118, 137.
Spanish Raggle-Taggle (Walter Starkie), XXIV: 144.
Spanish State Papers Relating to Ireland, XX: 100, XXI: 42.
Speaight, Robert (*The Unbroken Heart*), XXVI: 114.
Speche of an Irishe Man in the Yere 1542 (Séamus Ó Casaide), XVI: 80, 81.
Speers, Thomas, XII: 42.
Spenser, Edmund (*A View of the Present State of Ireland*), II: 59.
"Speranza", see Wilde, Lady Francesca.
Spielmann, M. H., VIII: 116.
Spindler, Capt. Karl (*The Mystery of the Casement Ship*), XXIII: 119.
Spirit of the Nation, The, II: 187, XIV: 118, XXV: 40.
Spiritual Rose (trans. Mathew Kennedy), XVIII: 141.
Sports on Irish Bogs (Horsley Jebb), II: 42.
Spring Days (George Moore), IV: 13.
"S.R.E.", IX: 15.
St. Brigid, see *Story of St. Bridget of Ireland, The*.
St. Colman of Lynn (shrine), XXVII: 200.
St. Columb's College Library, XX: 138.
St. Fechin (MS. life of), IV: 124.
St. John, [Dr.] James, XXIV: 61, 87.
St. Kieran's College, Kilkenny (An Irish MS in), XVI: 50-51.
St. Macartan's Hymn, XIII: 18, 35, 95.

St. Patrick—(MS Life in Irish, Catholic Central Library) XVIII: 72; (Mrs. Concannon) XIX: 178; (W. M. Letts) XX: 96; (Rev. J. H. Bernard & J. E. L. Oulton) XXVII: 237.
St. Thomas' Abbey (Register of), XXV: 14, 40, 103.
St. Thomas More (Sir John O'Connell), XXIV: 68.
St. Ursula's Annual, VIII: 63.
Stacpoole, Henry de Vere, I: 32, 74; Stackpoole (*Garryowen*) I: 106, 167, 172, V: 179, VII: 17, XI: 57, XII: 119.
Stamer Park Library, I: 146.
Standard, The, VII: 159, 190.
Stanford, [Sir] Charles Villiers, XIV: 79; (Harry Plunket Greene) XVIII: 17.
Stanley, Arthur (ed. *The Out of Doors Book*), XXII: 74.
Stannus, Bartholomew Teeling, I: 109.
Stanton, Patrick (trans. *Life of St. Finbarr*), XVIII: 143.
Staples, Ponsonby, VII: 133.
Stapleton, [Brig.] Walter, V: 148.
Stapleton, William, XIII: 66. (on Rev. James White), XVIII: 60.
Starkie, [Dr.] Walter (*Raggle-Taggle*), XXI: 72, XXIII: 98; (*Spanish Raggle-Taggle*) XXIII: 29; (*Don Gypsy*) XXIV: 95, XXVI: 91.
Starkie, William Joseph Miles, XII: (Obit.) 43.
Starry Threshhold, The (Alan Downey), VIII: 108.
State Policy in Irish Education, VIII: 66.
Stationer to his Majesty in Ireland, XIX: 82.
Statistical and Social Inquiry Society of Ireland, The (S. Shannon Millen), XII: 16.

Staunton, Michael, III: 137.
Steele, Robert, III: 24.
Steenson, W. J. (*Apple Blossom, The, and Other Poems*), XIV: 46.
Stephens, James [Fenian] (MS of *History of Fenianism*), XVIII: 146; (MS *Memoirs*) XVIII: 173, XIX: 25, XIX: 58, 97; (with Edmund Dwyer Gray), XX: 15.
Stephens, James, (*Insurrections*) I: 19; (*The Charwoman's Daughter*) III: 169; (*The Crock of Gold*) IV: 68, V: 108; (A Readers Portrait) IV: 95; (Pen and Ink Sketch) V: 123; (*The Demi-Gods*) VI: 78; (*Songs from the Clay*) VI: 167; (*The Rocky Road To Dublin*) VII: 36; (*Dunphy's Corner*) VII: 95; ("Spring in Ireland, 1916") VIII: 15; (*Insurrection in Dublin*) VIII: 47, VIII: 64; (*The Táin*) XII: 13; (*Irish Fairy Tales*) XII: 66; (*Arthur Griffith: Journalist and Statesman*) XIV: 28; (*In Land of Youth*) XIV: 140; (*Etched in Moonlight*) XVI: 27; (*Strict Joy*) XIX: 146; (*Fionn der Held*), XXV: 118; (Sundry) VI:163, XV: 64, XXXI: 130.
Stephen's Green, XXX: 88.
Stern, Laurence, (*Life of Laurence Sterne*) I: 88; V: 99.
Stevens, John (*Journal*), IV: 104.
Stevenson, Burton E., VII: 17.
Stevenson, [Sir] John, IX: 50, XI: 14, 113.
Stewart, [Rev.] D., I: 11, V: 135.
Stewart, James, II: 60.
Stockley, W. F. P. (*Essays in Irish Biography*), XXII: 98.
Stockwell, La Tourette, XVII: 95; (Example of 17th c. Dublin printing) XVIII: 122; (Appreciation) XXIV: 122; (*Dublin*

Theatres and Theatre Customs) XXVII: 166.
Stoker, Bram, III: 73, 171.
Stokes, Whitley, I: 119; (Library of)
Stolen Waters (T. M. Healy), XIX: 36.
Stones of Bray (G. D. Scott), V: 145.
Stoney, [Dr.] George Johnstone, III: 11.
Storey, George, IV: 9.
Story of a Toiler's Life (James Mullin), XIII: 59.
Story of the Bagpipe (W. H. G. Flood), III: 99.
Story of Diarmaid Mac Cerbaill, A (Fr. Paul Walsh), XXVIII: 74-80.
Story of the Irish Nation, The (Francis Hackett) XV: 30.
Story of Iveleary, The (Sean Ó Coindealbain), XIII: 33.
Story of St. Brigid of Ireland, The (Diana Leatham), XXXII: 119.
Story of St. Nicholas' Collegiate Church Galway, The (Rev. J. Fleetwood Berry), V: 87.
Story of St Patrick for Boys and Girls, The (Rev. M. H. Gaffney), XIX: 153.
Story of the Irish Society,The (John Betts), V: 10.
Story of the Munsters, The (Mrs. Victor Rickard) VII: 73.
Story Teller's Holiday A (George Moore), X: 46-47.
Stott, Thomas, XII: 4; ("Hafiz") XII: 123-26; XIII: 17.
Stoye, Johannes (*Irland frei von England*), XXVI: 89.
Strabane—(*Strabane Magazine*) III: 144; (printing in) IV: 48, 114, 134, VII: 68, 91; (*Strabane Morning* Post) XIX: 90-91.
Strahan, James Andrew, I: 33, XI: 24, 43, 58, 95, 111, 129, XII: 32, 34, 60, 61, 81; (Obit.), XVIII: 37.
Strahan, [Dr.] Sam, I: 33.
Straight and Crooked (James H. Cousins), VI: 186.
Straight Talk [1922], XVIII: 31.
"Stranger Minstrel, The" (William Watson), XIII: 58.
Strauss, E. (*Irish Nationalism and British Democracy*), XXXII: 19.
Stray Thoughts and Memories (James A. Rentoul), XIII: 14.
Street & Seymour, XXII: 2.
Street Ballads on Irish Boxers, XXVIII: 91.
Street, George (*Christ Church Cathedral*), XXII: 2.
Strickland, Walter G., IV: 16, V: 51, 119.
Strong, Leonard Alfred George, XIII: 179; (*The Garden*) XIX: 67; (*King Richard's Land*) XXII: 70; (*Corporal Tune*) XXII: 95; (*Mr. Sheridan's Umbrella*) XXIII: 153; (*The Last Enemy*) XXIV: 116; (*The Seven Arms*) XXIII: 101; (*The Swift Shadow*) XXV: 111; (*They Went to the Island*) XXVII: 287.
Stronge, E. M., 195.
Stuart Ireland—Catholic and Puritan (G. B. O'Connor), II: 9.
Stuart, Francis [Henry F. Stuart], XIV: 25; (*The Coloured Dome*) XX: 119; (*Glory*), XXI: 144.
Stuart, [Dr.] James (Historian of Armagh), XVII: 2.
Stuart, T. P., XI: 6.
Stubbs, J. W., XIII: 83.
Studdert-Kennedy, G. A., ("Woodbine Willie" [poem]) XIV: 14.
Studies (journal), XXIII: 77, 92.
Studies in Early Irish Law (Rodolf Thurneysen), XXIV: 66.

Study in Starlight, A (Randall McDonnell) X: 90.
Stukeley, [Sir] Thomas, XIII: 141.
Suaitheantas Uí Lochlainn Boirne, XXXI: 75.
Sugar Beet Diseases in Ireland (Robert McKay), XXXII: 69.
Sullivan, Alex Martin, III: 89, 106, 107.
Sullivan, [Sir] Edward, VI: 29; (*The Book of Kells*), XII: 108, 109.
Sullivan, Joseph, XXVI: 39.
Sullivan, John (Irish MSS), XVII: 139.
Sullivan, Timothy Daniel, III: 91, 107, V: 173; (*History of England*) XVIII: 95; (*Story of England*) XVIII: 143.
Sullivan, W. K., XIII: 82; (with O'Looney, ed. *Táin Bo Cualnge*) XVII: 20.
Summe of Intelligence (Early Dublin Journal), VIII: 52.
Sunburst, The (James Hackett), XXIII: 148, XXIV: 63.
Sunset and Evening Star (Seán O'Casey), XXXII: 118.
Sunset on the Window Panes (Walter Macken), XXXII: 119.
Suppression of Nationalist Press, VI: 116.
Surnames in Ireland (Edward MacLysaght), XIV: 58.
Survey of Irish Libraries, XXIV: 62.
"Sutach 'sa Mháthair, An", XXII: 65.
Sutherland, Donald (*Gertrude Stein*), XXXII: 22.
Swan, H. P. (*Geographical Society of Ireland, The*), XXX: 45 140; (*Romantic Inishowen*) XXX: 71.
Swan, Percival (*'Twixt Foyle and Swilly*), XXXI: 91.
Swanlinbar (Maitiú de Buitléir on), XXX: 114; (P. Ó Conail on) XXX: 114.
"S.W.B.", X:43.
Sweeney, Myles, IV: 160.
Sweet County Down, XV: 58.
"Sweet Portaferry", XXIII: 115.
Swift, Jonathan [Dean Swift], II: 47, 91, 129, 156, III: 12, 84, IV: 47, 49, 50, XII: 107, 133; XIII: 44, 86, XVII: 12, 27, 100; (Almanac annotated by) XVIII: 18; (System of Marking Notable Passages in Margins) XVIII: 138; (A Book from his Library) XVIII: 158; (MS Catalogue of Swift's Books in his own Handwriting) XVIII: 160; (Printed Sale Catalogue of Dean Swift's Books) XVIII: 161; XIX: 25, 58, 61; (Williams, *Dean Swifts' Library*), XX: 141; (Auction Catalogue) XXI: 64; (Priced copy of Swift's Auction Catalogue) XXI: 85-87; (Recent Books: *Gulliver's Travels*, ed. Hayward, & *Drapier's Letters*, ed. Davis) XXIV: 6; (An Unrecorded Item) XXX: 52-54; (*Swift in Switzerland*) XXX: 54-55; (Source-book for *A Tale of a Tub*), XXXI: 58.
Swinburne, Algernon Charles, I: 10.
Swinney, Myles (letter founder), XVII: 93.
Sword of Justice, The (Gore-Booth, Eva), X: 46-47.
Synass, Benjamin, VI: 81.
Synge and the Irish Theatre (Maurice Bourgeois), V: 85.
Synge, [Archbishop] Edward, IV: 172.
Synge, J. M. (*Collected Poems*), II: 14; (*Collected Works*) II: 44, III: 187; (Obit.) II: 125, 197; II: 155, 158, III: 2, 14, 24, 31, 132,

The Irish Book Lover 357

(*The Playboy*) IV: 7-8, 128, 198; (*John Millington Synge*) 70; IV: 127, 155, 170, V: 108, 144 (*J. M. Synge: A Few Personal Recollections*) VI: 154; (Synge's Private Press) IX: 7, XIV: 110; (Synge's Sources) IX: 126, XIII: 37; (L. A. G. Strong: "A Memory") XIII: 179; (in the O'Donoghue papers) XIV: 71; (*Plays*) XXI: 71; (*Synge and Anglo-Irish Literature*) XIX: 102.

T

Taaffe, [Rev.] Denis, XVII: 506.
Tabuteau, B. M., XII: 107.
Taffe, John, V: 73, 95; (*Adelais*) 208; XIII: 104.
Taggart, Moses, II: 92.
Tailteann Week, XIV: 120, 138.
Táin Bo Cuailnge, XVII: 20.
Taistealaí, An (Séamus Ó Céilleachair), XXX: 121.
Talbot Press Publications, IX: 52, X: 60, XII: 82.
Tale of a Tub, A (Source for), XXXI: 58.
Tales from Ireland (Gerard Murphy),X: 96; XXXII: 65.
Tales My Father Told (Una Ní Cathill), XXIX: 144.
Tales of Tipperary (C. J. Kickham), XII: 38-40.
Tamerlane (Nicolas Row), XXIV: 86.
Tara: The Monuments on the Hill, (Sean P. Ó Ríordáin), XXXII: 116.
Tarry Flynn (Patrick Kavanagh), XXXI: 48.
Tarpey, William Kingsley, III: 57.
"Tasman", II: 75, 164, 181.
Taylor, Alexander O'Driscoll (Obit.), I: 150.

Taylor, Fanny, IV: 39.
Taylor, Geoffrey Handley (*Literary, Debating and Dialect Societies of Great Britain, Ireland and France*), XXXII: 72.
T.C.D., see Trinity College, Dublin.
"T.D.", VII: 92.
Teach i n-Áirde (Mrs. De Velera), XXIV: 140.
Teagasg Criosdaidhe (Bonaventura O'Hussey), XVIII: 89.
Teeling, Bartholomew John (Obit.), XII: 118.
Teerink, Herman (Swift's *A Tale of a Tub*), XXXI: 58.
Tegart, K. F. (*Castle Bran*), XXVI: 22.
Teggart, Moses. V: 203.
Tempest, Harry G., II: 1; (*Tempest's Annual*), XI: 100, XXVIII: 23; XXVII: 116, XV: 43.
Tempest, William, IX: 105, XV: 43.
Temple, The, XII: 87.
Ten Islands and Ireland (J. Mackay), XII: 61-63.
Tenison, Charles McCarthy, VII: 77.
Tennyson, Alfred [Lord], II: 10.
Tercentenary of Irish Presbyterianism, V: 50.
Terny-Athlone Herald, IV: 179.
Tevlin, James, XXI: 89, XXVI: 82.
"T.H.", 57, 112, 124.
Thackeray, Elias, III: 194.
Thackeray, William Makepeace, I: 158; (*Irish Sketch Book*) II: 139, 192; III: 3, 70, 96; IV: 28, 29; (Thackeray and Patrick Kennedy) V: 33.
"Thank you, Mr. Editor" (Helen McGrath), XXX: 65.

Thaumaturgus (Anon.), VI: 209, VII: 34, 54.
Theatricals, XIII: 16.
These Professors! (P.D.), XXX: 17.
"They had no Poet" (John Henry Titus), XXXI: 15, 103.
Things Past Redress (Augustine Birrell)., XXV: 72
This Criticism, XXIX: 3.
This is Ireland: Connacht and the City of Galway (Richard Hayward), XXXII: 23.
Thomas Andrews, Shipbuilder (Shan Bullock), IV: 105.
Thomas, [Dr.] Daniel, XVII: 16.
Thomas, Ralph, II: 47, 70, 87, 105.
Thomastown (printing in), XVII: 102.
Thompson MSS, XIV: 61.
Thompson, Douglas ("Memories of Connemara"), XXXII: 149.
Thompson, Mary, VII: 143.
Thompson, Miss, XIV: 61.
Thompson, Robert Hely ["Robert Blake"] VIII: 14, 144.
Thompson, S. T. (A Belfast Book Auction), XXIV: 28.
Thompson, William Marcus [journalist], VII: 190.
Thomson, Hugh, IV: 193; VI: 59; VII: 99, (Obit.) XI: 131.
Thomson, William [Baron Kelvin], I: 30, 90.
Thorndike, Lynn (*A History of Magic and Experimental Science*), XXIX: 21.
Three Blind Bards, V: 221.
Three Candle Press, The (Colm Ó Lochlainn), XII: 40, XVI: 15.
"Three Candles Press" (Thomas Browne), XXXII: 8, 59.
"Three Candlesticks", XIV: 142.
Three Gaelic Pioneers (Máire Ní Dhúbhghaill), XXVIII: 14.

Three Irish Scribes, XVI: 4-5.
Three Irishmen I Knew (Ralph Thomas), II: 68, 85, 104.
Three Kerry Families, XIV: 43.
Three Northern Novels, XII: 35-36.
Three Notable Novels, X: 40-41.
Three Old Brothers and Other Poems (Frank O'Connor), XXV: 65.
Three Rock Road, The (H. A. Doak), XI: 12.
Threshold of Quiet (Daniel Corkery), IX: 52.
Thrift, Gertrude, VIII: 90, 117.
Thurston, E. Temple, IX: 12; XV: 14.
Thurston, Katherine Cecil, III: 42, 73, 84.
Tierney, Michael, XI: 62.
Tighe, Mary, III: 141, 172, XII: 138.
Times, The, IV: 151; (Irish Number) XI: 41.
"Timothy", III: 81.
Tinker Boy (Patricia Lynch), XXXII: 120.
Tinker's Hollow (F. E. Crichton), IV: 69.
Tinsley's Magazine, VIII: 73, 97.
Tiny Magazine, A (*Moments with ... Amateurs*), XIV: 141.
Tipperary's Annual, II: 72.
Tipperary's Families, III: 117.
Tippermessan, Co. Meath (Pól Breathnach), XXVI: 15.
Tír Dhá Scrios, An, (Oliver Goldsmith in trans.), XXXII: 49.
Tirconaill Annals, XXII: 104, XXIV: 143.
Title-pages (facsimiles), III: 33, 78.
To Denis (Mrs. E. C. O'Sullivan), V: 181.
To Hold as 'Twere (Mrs. Joseph Plunkett), XI: 62.

To Next Year in Jerusalem (David Marcus), XXXII: 95.
"To William Watson" (Randall McDonnell), V: 128.
"To Untidiness" (Anon.), XXXI: 81.
Tóchar (Roundwood) Printing, XXIV: 41.
Todd, [Dr.] John H. (and John O'Donovan), XXVII: 161.
Todhunter, John, VIII: 70, IX: 93.
Tóibín, Nioclás, XVI: 83.
Tóibín, Sean, X: 13.
Tóibín, Tomas (*Cúirt Éigse Chorcaighe*), XXIX: 1.
Toirrdhealbhach Luineach (Ó Néill-Éamonn Ó Tuathail, XXIII: 14.
Tom Clarke (Le Roux, Louis N.), XXIV: 142.
Tom Creagan (Dermot Barry), XIX: 149.
Tom Moore and The Crokers, XV: 49.
Tomassini, [Fra] Anselmo (*Irish Saints in Italy*), XXVI: 18.
Tone, Theobald Wolfe, III: 194, 213; IV: 209; XIV: 57; XXIII: 47.
Toner, [Rev.] Dr., XVI: 27.
Tongue of the Gael, The, XV: 25.
Topical Play of Ninety-Eight, A (J. O. Bartley), XXVIII: 57-60
Topographer, The (John Gough), XIII: 35, 64.
Topographical Trio, A, X: 88, XII: 63.
Torna, see Ó Donnchadha, Tadhg.
Torney, Henry C. S., VIII: 139.
Torrens, W. M., XII: 103.
Toryes (methods of suppression in Ireland), XIX: 133.
Tory in Arms, A (John Lepper), VIII: 58.
Toulouse-Lantrec, Henri de (*Hunting with 'The Fox'*),
XXXI: 70.
Towards The Republic (Aodh de Blacam), X: 91.
Town Wall Fortifications, VI: 30.
Townlands, III: 27.
Tracy, Honor (*Mind you, I've Said Nothing*), XXXII: 72.
Tracy, Thomas Stanley, XXXII: 17.
Trail of the Black and Tans ("The Hurler on the Ditch"), XIII: 110.
Trainer, John P., II: 123, VII: 163.
Tralee (printing in), IV: 149, XII: 110.
"Tramp, The" (J. F. MacEntee), VIII: 129.
Transactions of the Cambridge Bibliographical Society, XXXI: 112.
"Transatlantic" (pseud. of Thomas Mooney), XVIII: 31, XXVIII: 36.
Trant Family (S. T. MacCarthy), XV: 14.
Translations from the Irish, III: 131.
Travel Book on Germany published in Dublin (John Hennig), XXXI: 131.
Travelling in Ireland (Charles Bianconi), XXIX: 34.
Treasure of the Mountain, The (Fr. M. Bodkin), XXV: 48.
Treasures New and Old, XIV: 75.
Trench, C. E., XXVIII: 43.
Trench, Frederic FitzCurrie (*Music of Thought*), XXIII: 125.
Trench, [Miss] M. Chenevix, I: 104.
Trench, W. F., XVII: 35; (*Tom Moore*), XXII: 138; (recent books on Swift), XXIV: 6.
Trench, William Stewart, XI: 13.
Trevelyan, G. M. (*The Mingling of the Races*), XXII: 150.
Trial of Sir Roger Casement (ed.

George E. Knott), IX: 59.
Tribune, The Irish, II: 171.
Tribune, The, V: 82, VI: 32, 46, VII: 54, IX: 14.
Tricolour (modern Irish flag), XXVII: 159.
Trim—(printing in) I: 63, 77, 107); VIII: 9.
Trimble, Delmege, V: 14.
Trimble, Joan (*Buttermilk Point Reel*), XXVI: 117.
Trimble, P. C. ["P.C.T."], XVII: 66, 67, 11, 114, 119, 142; XIX: 31, 112; ("This Novel Business") XXIV: 121.
Trinity College, Dublin [T.C.D.; Dublin University]—II: 3, 8; (Dublin University Press) II: 3, 163, IV: 32, XXIII: 13, 97; (Bicentenary Celebrations) IV: 10.; (Medical Teaching at) IV: 13; (*T.C.D. Miscellany*) X: 93; (MS. of O'Donovan's Irish Grammar) XVII: 19; (Irish in T.C.D.) XXIV: 14; (Friends of the Library of T.C.D.) XXX: 112; (Exhibition of Illuminated Western MSS) XXXII: 105.
Tristram, Henry (*The Idea of a Liberal Education—A Selection from the works of Newman*), XXXII: 45.
"Triúr ar Lár" (Aindrias Ó Muimhneacháin), XXVIII: 49.
Trollope, Anthony, VI: 115, 116, XIV: 80, XV: 28; (Trollope and Ireland) XVIII: 46; (*The Kellys and the O'Kellys, The Mac Dermots*) XVIII: 66; (Trollope in Ireland) XIX: 110.
Tromhamh Guaire (Eleanor Knott) XIX: 182.
Troth, The (Rutherford Mayne), I: 112.
Troth Replighted, A (Sean Purser), XXXII: 46.

Trotter, John Bernard, I: 41, 59, 85.
Trotter, [Capt.] Lionel, III: 190.
True Irish Ghost Stories (St. John D. Seymour & Harry L. Neligan), V: 90, VI: 100.
True Patriotism, XXVIII: 57.
Truth [1922 issue], XVIII: 72.
Truth About Ulster (F. Frankfort Moore), V: 182.
Tuam—(Archbishop John) II:145; (*Tuam Gazette*) XIX: 90-91; (printing in) VII: 40, 91; XV: 7.
Tuite, James, I: 46, 71; II: 6, 120; VIII: 61, 117.
Tulloch, Jessie, IV: 195.
Tumbling in the Hay (Oliver St. Gogarty), XXVI: 116.
Turkington, [Miss] S., VI: 104.
Turner's Commonplace Books, XXI: 137.
Twain, Mark, IX: 13.
Twenty-five Years Reminiscences (Katharine Tynan), V: 86.
Two Belfast Gaels, XIII: 3.
Two Boys Go Sailing (Conor O'Brien), XXIV: 139.
Two Centuries of Life in Down, XI: 113.
Two Irish Novels (L. M. Foster & Mary McCarvill), XIX: 147.
"Two Ladies, The", VII: 127.
Two Little-Known Books on Irish Life, XXXI: 84.
"Two Love Songs" (Padraic Gregory), V: 42.
Two Plays (Sean O'Casey), XV: 30.
Tymms, Ralph (*Doubles in Literary Psychology*), XXXI: 46.
Tynan, Katherine, IV: 66, 128, 198; (*Twenty-five Years Reminiscences*) V: 86; VIII: 47, 48, 85, 112; IX: 104; (*Miss Gascoigne*) X: 46,47; (*The*

Years of the Shadow) XI: 11; X: 15; (*Bithas' Wonderful Year*) XIII: 17; (*Collected Poems*) XVIII: 80; (*An International Marriage*) XXII: 22; XII: 32; XIII: 44, 172.
Tyndall, [Prof.] John, III: 135; XII: 52.
Type—(Louvain Irish) XX: 103; (Sadler's foundry Dublin) XX: 40; (Reed's account of Irish fonts) XX: 94.
Typo, X: 68.
Typographical Gazetteer, II: 1; XIV: 30, 52, 60.
Tyrone—(Bibliography of) I: 43; (printing in) IX: 8, 60; (An Interesting Book) I: 11; (Earl of Tyrone) XXI: 138; (The Cecil Press) XXIV: 55.
Tyrrell, [Fr.] George, I: 31.
Tyrrell, Robert Yelverton, VI: 55, 71.

U

Ua Laoghaire, [An t-Ath.] Peadar, XXXII: 78.
Ua Maelechlainn (Kings of Meath), XXIX: 37.
Ua (or Uí) Casaide, Séamus, see Ó Casaide, Séamus
U'Calegon, 15.
Uí Eanna (O'Kirby's of Munster), XXVI: 12.
Uí Failghe and Origin of King's County, XXVI: 50.
Uilleann Pipes, XVI: 46-47.
Ulster—(Ulster Dialect) I: 11, 79; (Ulster Plantation) II: 9; (People & Language of) I: 11, II: 107; (*Ulster As It Is*) I: 91; (*Ulster Journal*) I: 153; (The Ulster Calendar) II: 91; (Ulster Literary Theatre) II: 165; (Weaver Poets) II: 148; (Rural Rhymsters) IV: 91; (*Ulster Folk Lore*) V: 65; (Famous Ulstermen) V: 9, 193; (in Song) V: 75; (*From Ulster's Hills*) V: 101; (*The Ulsterman*) V: 164, 193, XIV 13, 164; XVII: 13; (*Truth About Ulster*) V: 182; (An Ulster Village) VI: 106; (Song Books) VII: 108; (*The Ulster Scot*) V: 192, XIV: 101; (Printers and Poets) VI: 20; (*Ulsterman for Ireland*) IX: 84; (*Ulster and Ireland*) XI: 45; (*Ulster-Songs and Ballads*) XI: 98; (An Ulster Folk Song) XI: 130; (*An Ulster Childhood*) XII: 88; (*Ulster Fireside Tales*) XII: 135; (Ballads) XIII: 143; (*The Ulsterman*) XIV: 13; (*Ulster in X-Rays*) XIV: 75; (*Ulster Review*) XIV: 106; (*Ulster Repository*) XV: 11; (*Ulster Antiquities*) XV: 43; (*The Ulster Book*) XVII: 75; (*Stirabout from an Ulster Pot*) XVIII 37; (The Great Fraud of Ulster) XIX: 36; (*Ulster Chronicle*) XIX: 90-91; (*The Birth of Ulster*) XXIV: 95; (*Ulster Journal of Archaeology*) XXVI: 66; (a rare booklet) XXVI: 122; (*Ulster Journal of Archaeology*) XXVI: 66; (*Ulster and the British Empire*) XXVII: 180; (*An Old Ulster House* by Mina Lenox-Conyngham) XXXI: 67.
Uncle Stephen (Forrest Reid), XIX: 180.
Unfinished Books, VII: 175.
Union Magazine, VI: 138.
Union Pipes, XVI: 46-47.
Union Star, The, VIII: 89.
Union Tracts, VIII: 138.
Union, The (MS of) XIV: 106.
United Irishman—(Dublin) XVII: 3, XXXII: 77; XVII: 50, 56; (*Lives and Times*) XII: 83-86;

XII, 104, 144, XXXII: 121-28.
United Irishman, The, II: 172, XII: 83.
Universal Emancipation, XVII: 3.
Universal Journal, The, XII: 104-106.
University College, Dublin [U.C.D.]—(*L&H 1855-1955*) XXXII: 148; (*Story of University College, Dublin, 1883-1909*) XIV: 90.
University Journalist, XII: 104-06.
University Magazine, IV: 161, 173, 211.
University Presses, II: 8.
Unknown Immortals, IX: 53.
Unrecorded Irish Book of 1716, An, XXVIII: 131.
Unrecorded Private Press, XXVII: 259.
"Unsung Song, An" (Padric Gregory), XII: 6.
Upper Fews, XIV: 5.
Up the, Rebels! (George A. Birmingham), XI: 99.
Urlin, R. Denny, I: 44.
Ursuline nun, V: 220.
Ussher, [Archbishop] James, II: 3, 36.
Ussher, R. J. (Obit.), V: 85.
Ustermen: Their Fight for Fortune, Faith and Freedom (Rev. T. M. Johnstone)V: 193.

V

Valera, de, see de Valera.
Vallancey, [General] Charles (sale of Irish MSS), XVIII: 89; (Irish Dictionary) XXI: 131.
"Valley of the Roe, The" ("J.F."), XIII: 69.
Van den Bergh, G. (*Pessimisimus Bei ... Jonathan Swift*), XXXI: 114.
Vanessa and Her Correspondence with Jonathan Swift (A. M. Freeman), XII: 136.
"Vanessa" (Jonathan Swift's), I: 74.
Van Hamel, [Prof.] A. G. (Obit.), XXX: 34.
Vanishing Spring, (J. D. Sheridan), XXIV: 23.
Various Versifiers, XV: 63.
Vatican Catalogue, XVI: 46.
Vaudeville Magazine, XVII: 2.
Vendryes, J. (*Études Celtiques*), XXV: 115.
Ventry Harbour (battle), IV: 212, V: 52.
Vere, Aubrey de, XXIV: 42.
Vesey, Mrs. [Elizabeth], VI: 176-77.
Veronica, [Sister] St., XXXII: 93.
Verses Grave and Gladsome (James Logan), XV: 63.
Viceroys of Ireland, The (Sir John Gilbert), V: 12.
Viceroy's Post-Bag, The (Michael MacDonagh), II: 10.
Vicissitudes of an Anglo-Irish Family (Philip H. Bagenal), XV: 31.
Victory of Sinn Fein (P. S. O'Hegarty), XV: 15.
Village Plays (M. E. Dobbs), XII: 134.
Vindiciarum Catholicorum Hibernia (Fr. John Callaghan) II: 104, 129.
Violin Makers (Irish and British), XVII: 1, 56.
Visons and Beliefs in the West of Ireland (Lady Gregory), XII: 84.
Vocations (Gerald O'Donovan), XIII: 91.
"Voice of Insurgency, A" (Maeve Cavanagh), VIII: 108.
Voice of Ireland (ed. W. G. Fitzgerald), XV: 12.
Volunteer Sermon, XII: 19.

Volunteers of 1782, VI: 123, 144.
Volunteers of 1798, IV: 92, 108, 145.
Von Dewall, Wolf (*Die Insel der Heiligen*), XXII: 152.
von Pokorney, Julius, see Pokorny, Julius, XI: 84.
Vorster, Elias, I: 157.

W

Waddell, Helen V: 143; (*Beasts and Saints*) XXIII: 79; (*Medieval Latin Lyrics*) XXI: 139; (*Peter Abelard*) XXI: 95; (*The Desert Fathers*) XXV: 16; (*The Wandering Scholars*) XXI: 139; (*Sing a Song of Children*) XXIV: 45; (*Wandering Scholars and Medieval Latin Lyrics*) XVIII: 4.
Wadding, Luke, IV: 22, 24, XVI: 50.
Wail of the Candleman, XII: 40.
Waiting (Gerald O'Donovan), V: 199.
Waldman, Milton (*Elizabeth*), XXII: 60.
Waldron's Sale, 91,
Wales [periodical], XXVI: 140.
Walk of a Queen, The (Linda Kearns), XIV: 29.
Walker's *Hibernian Magazine*, 1806 (Irish deaths), XVIII: 57.
Wall, Bernard (ed. *The Changing World* with Marrya Harari), XXX: 120.
Wall, C. W., (*Mountaineering in Ireland*), XXVII: 192.
Wallace, Vincent, III: 209, IV: 40, 52.
Walled Gardens (T. B. Rudmose-Brown), X: 46.
Walsh or Callaghan?, II: 104, 129.
Walsh, A. (*Scandanavian Relations with Ireland*), XIV: 74.

Walsh, A. T. (*Casey of the I.R.A.*), XIV: 30.
Walsh, Edward, II: 149, III: 1, 30, 192, 213.
Walsh, James (*The Islan' Man*), XVIII: 51.
Walsh, J. C., (*The Lament for John MacWalter Walsh*), XXII: 43.
Walsh, Louis J., XII: 118, XIII: 98; *John Mitchel*, XXIII: 29.
Walsh, Maurice, (*Sons of the Swordmaker*) XXVI: 70; (*Green Rushes*) XXIII: 156.; (*Son of Apple*) XXX: 96; (*Trouble in the Glen*) XXXI: 119.
Walsh, Michael, (*The Heart Remembers Morning*), XX: 21.
Walsh, Miss, XI: 135.
Walsh, Monsignor (Biography of Archbishop Walsh), XVI: 27.
Walsh, [Fr.] Paul [Pól Breathnach], III: 104, VII: 32, 64, XIII: 38, XXVI: 61, 140; (Bonaventure O'Hussey) XVIII: 55; (Battle of Cluain Tiobraid) XXI: 103-06; (Earls of Tyrone and Tyrconnell) XXII: 4; (The Will and Family of Hugh O'Neill) XXVI: 140; (Ó Cleirigh family of Tir Conaill) XXVI: 140; (Addresses to Tibbot na Long) XXVIII: 2; (*Catalogue of Irish Manuscripts in Maynooth College Library*) XXIX: 93; (Shrovetide and Inid) XXVIII: 34-36; (Another Place Name in Westmeath) XXVIII: 54-56; (Historian) XXVIII: 50-53; (Collected Works), XXVIII: 133; (*Irish Men of Learning*) XXXI: 112; (Sundry articles and reviews) XXV: 26, 37, 50, 99, 100, 102. See also under Breathnach, Pól.
Walsh, [Rev.] Robert, VIII: 120.

Walsh, Thomas (Obit.), XXVII: 275.
Walsh, [Archbishop] William John, (Obit.), XII: 142-143; XIII: 38, XVI: 27.
Walter, J.F., II: 149.
"Walter Luin", XX: 12.
Wandering Scholars (Helen Waddell), XVIII: 4.
Ward, Francis A., XXXII: 88, 139.
Ward, Hugh, IV: 4, 21.
Ward, Isaac W., VII: 118; VIII: 62.
Ward, John, II: 135, III: 151.
Ward, Katherine, XII: 41.
Wardell, Professor, IV: 191.
Wardle, R. M., (William Maginn and *Blackwood's* Magazine), XXVI: 73.
Ware, Robert, IX: 100.
Ware, [Sir] James, II: 11, XXXII: 39.
Ware's *Annals* Annotated, XXVIII: 69.
Ware's Works (Record Price in Dublin for), XVI: 71-72.
Warren, Robert, VII: 120.
Warwick, Archibald, IV: 17.
Was it the Dean? XXX: 113-114.
Wasted Island, The (Eimar O'Duffy), XI: 82.
Waterford—(Start of Waterford) VI: 10; (Almanac printed in, 1646) XVIII: 38; (Bardic Sessions) XXII: 133; (Christian Brother Poet) XXIX: 136; (during Civil War) IV: 89; ("Finds" in County Farmhouses) XXII: 31; (Waterford Glass) VI: 119; (Histories of) XIV: 142, XXII: 64; (Parochial History) IV: 121; (printing in) XXVII: 149, 183; (Peter de Pienne, printer) XXIV: 75; (in 1914) VI: 11; (Early Printing in) I: 117; (Guide to) I: 168; (Waterford's "Magna Carta"), X: 54.
Waterford Newspapers and Journals—(*Waterford and Lismore*) XXVI: 42; (*Waterford Archaeological Journal*) VI: 114, XVI: 12, 49, XVII: 5, 6, 83; (*Waterford Chronicle*) XVII: 5, XIX: 90-91; (*Waterford Citizen*) XVIII: 133, XXX: 48; (*Waterford Evening Packet*) XIX: 90-91; (*Waterford Export List*) XIX: 90-91; (*Waterford Flying Post*) XXIX: 18; (*Waterford Freeman*) XXIX: 91; (*Waterford Mail*) XVIII: 133; (*Waterford Mirror*) XIX: 90-91; (*Waterford Spectator*) XVIII: 133; (Govt. printing in newspapers) XXXI: 12.
Waters, Abbe, V: 34.
Watson, [Sir] William, IV: 170, XIII: 57.
Watson, W. J., (*Scottish Verse from the Book of the Dean of Lismore*), XXV: 109.
Way that I Went, The (R. Lloyd Praeger), XXV: 120.
"Wayfarers" (Randall McDonnell), V: 80, IX: 54.
"W.C.R.", III: 138.
Weale, W. H. James, II: 12, 29, 46, 61, XXII: 117, VII: 48.
Weale, W. M., VII: 48.
Weaver Poets of Ulster, The, II: 148.
Webb, Alfred (*Compendium*), I: 35, 46, 60, 84.
"Wee auld Wean, The" (Jennie Perry), IV: 152.
Week in the West, A., XI: 7.
Weekly Freeman's Journal, XIX: 90-91.
Weekly Magazine and Literary Review (1779), XVII: 74-75.
Weekly Miscellany, The, 10 January, 1733-34. (Rare Dublin

Periodicals), XII: 104-106.
Weekly Oracle: or Universal Library, The, XII: 104-106.
Weekly Selector (Sligo), VI: 56.
Weir, John (*Old Ballymena*), II: 42
Weldon, James, XIV: 25.
Weldon, Robert, VI: 47.
Wellington, Duke of [Arthur Wellesley], II: 38, IV: 48.
Wells, Warre B., XII: 13.
Welsh, Charles, II: 12.
Wesley College Quarterly, XXVI: 37.
West Briton, The, VIII: 17.
West, [Sir] Algernon, IV: 210.
West, William, IV: 36.
Western Illuminated Manuscripts, XXXII: 105.
Western Rover, The (Thomas W. O'Boyle), XX: 137, XXI: 111.
Westmeath—(*Westmeath Journal*) XIX: 90-91; (Westmeath Leavys) XXVII: 174, 254; (Earl of Westmeath) XXII: 74.
Westropp, Thomas Johnson, (*Antiquities of Limerick and its Neighbour-hood*) VIII: 10; VIII 36, 135.
Wexford—(The War in), I: 107, 149, 170; (Antiquities of) II: 107, 127, 129; (*The Wexford Insurgent*) IV: 160; (printing in) XII: 67, 110; (Mummers) XVII: 59-61, XXXII: 103; (Works on) XVIII: 98; (*Wexford Herald*) XIX: 90-91; (Tradition in) XXVI: 7; (Printing in the 19th c.) XXVII: 250; (9th c. printing in) XXVII: 250; (The Civil Survey of County Wexford) XXXII: 115; (Works on), XVIII: 98.
Weygandt, Cornelius, IV: 157.
"W.H.D.", X: 70.
Whale and the Grasshopper, The (Seumas O'Brian), XI: 61.

What Shakespeare Knew About Ireland (Sir. D. P. Barton), XV: 56.
What Sinn Fein Stands For (A. De Blacam), XIII: 87.
What's in a Format, XXXI: 15.
Wheatley, Henry B., II: 7.
Wheeler, Ethel Rolt II: 79; (*In Galway*), IV: 118, VI: 178.
Wheeler, H. A. (*The Dublin City Churches of the Church of Ireland* & M. J. Craig), XXXI: 115.
Whelan [Dr.] J. (*Loose Leaves from a Doctor's Diary*), II: 24.
Whelan, J. A., IV: 14; XVIII: 146.
Whibley, Charles, VIII: 127.
White, Albert C. (*Songs from the Heart*), VI: 167; VII: 23, 74.
White, [Sir] George, VI: 154, VII: 17.
White, [Rev.] Harry Vere (*Children of St. Columba*), V: 218; (*Bishop Jeb of Limerick*), XV: 15.
White, James (ed. *My Clonmel scrap-Book*), I: 74.
White, [Rev.] James, XIV: 123; (*Annals of the City and Diocese of Limerick*) XVII: 144; XVIII: 60.
White, [Capt.] J. R. (*Misfit: An Autobiography*), XVIII: 125.
White, John Davis, VI: 193, VII: 32.
White, Newport B., VI: 108, XX: 19, 54, 113; (Irish Libraries) XXI: 65; (Elizabethan Dublin Printing) XXI: 113; (Irish Manuscripts in Marsh's Library) XXIII: 73; (The Register of St. Thomas' Abbey) XXV: 40, 103.
White (Printer), XXX: 37.
White, Vere, XV: 15.
White-headed Boy, The (Lennox Robinson), XI: 135.

Whitmore, W. J. Brennan ("In Vinculis"), IX: 80.
Whitla, [Sir] William, XIII: 180.
Whitty, Edward Michael, VI: 45.
Whitty, Michael James, VIII: 53, 83.
Whitty, [Miss] St. John, XV: 11.
Why Ireland is Not Free [and] *Why There is an Irish Land Question* (T. M. Healy), XIX: 36.
"Why Liquor of Life" (in French), XXVII: 232.
Wickham, William, III: 72, 102.
Wicklow—(A Wicklow MS) XXII: 88; (printing in), XXVI: 58.
Wild Geese (Irish exiles), XXXII: 37.
Wild Geese, The (Brigid Boland), XXVI: 69.
Wild Honey ("An Philibín"), XXIX: 24.
Wild Sports of the West (W. H. Maxwell), VII: 61.
Wild Swans at Coole, The (W. B. Yeats), X: 90.
Wilde, [Lady] Francesca ["Speranza"], II: 178, XII: 126, XX: 60, 74.
Wilde, Oscar, II: 178, IV: 7, 85, VI: 1, VII: 53; (Bibliography) VII: 151; XI: 139, XII: 126; (*Plays, Prose, Writings, Poems*) XIX: 63.
Wilde, [Sir] William, R. (The Writings of) VI: 1, XXV: 61; (*The Beauties of the Boyne*) XXXI: 71.
Wilkins, [Rev.] George, XI: 87.
Wilkinson, James, IV: 36.
Wilkinson, Henry Spenser (*Thirty Five Years*), XXI: 140.
Will and Family of Hugh O'Neill, The (Rev. P.Walsh), XXVI: 140.
Will Calenders, I: 89.

Will Rogers (P. J. O'Brien), XXV: 44.
William Andrew Clark Memorial Library (*Report*), XXXI: 19.
William Brawders (Matthew Butler), XXIX: 30.
Williamite Wars, The, IV: 8, 56, 72; (*Jacobite and Williamite Wars*) XXVI: 58, 85.
Williams, Barney, IV: 92.
Williams, Charles, IX: 13; (*The Place of the Lion*), XXXII: 47.
Williams, Harold (*Dean Swifts' Library*), XX: 141.
Williams, Ifor (*Lectures on Early Welsh Poetry*), XXIX: 24.
Williams, Richard Dalton, II: 171, 178.
Williamson, Benedict (*How to Build a Church*), XXIII: 23.
Williamson, Benjamin, VII: 168.
Willis, [Dr.] Thomas, XI: 30.
Wills, Freeman Crofts, VI: 2, 8.
Wills, [Rev.] James, II: 149, VI: 2.
Wills, William Gordon, VI: 2.
Wilmot, Martha and Catherine (*Russian Journals of*), XXII:139.
Wilson Croker Collection, III: 143, 160, 212.
Wilson, Charles Henry, II: 182, IV: 55, VII: 187, XXII: 57.
Wilson, Charles, M., VII: 134.
Wilson, Edward Daniel Joseph, V: 15, 18, VI: 155.
Wilson, Florence M., (*The Coming of the Earls*), X: 62-63.
Wilson, John G. H, V:185.
Wilson, Peter, XVI: 19, 22, 52, 53.
Wilson, Philip, IV: 70, XIII: 141, XV: 27.
Wilson, Robert Arthur [pseud. "Barney Maglone"], XII: 75-77.
Wilson, Robin N. D. (*Equinox*), XXV: 119.
Wilson, T. G., (The Writings of

Sir William Wilde), XXV: 61.
Wilson, W., XXXII: 144.
Wind upon the Heath A, Murray, Nora, J. X: 46-47.
Windele, John, XVI: 4, 28; (Windele's Cork) II: 72.
Windle, [Sir] Bertram C. A., III: 116, XVII: 8.
"Winter Queen, The" (W. F. T. Butler), VIII: 137.
Winthorp, F. (*Callaghan*), XIII: 15.
With Every Year (Catherine Gaskin), XXXI: 47.
With the Dublin Brigade (Charles Dalton), XVIII: 61.
With Michael Collins in the Fight for Irish Independence (Batt. O'Connor), XVIII: 61.
With the Irish in Frognoch (W. J. Brennan Whitmore), IX: 80.
Witherow, Thomas, XIV: 133.
"W.J.L.", II: 26, 106, 111, 130, 143.
"W.L.G.", III: 116.
"W.L.M.", II: 76.
"W.M.", II: 61, 82, 95,
Wodrow MS, The, IV: 16.
Wogan, Pat, I: 157.
Woke, Rev., V: 13, 212.
Wolfe, [Rev.] Charles, Notes and Queries on, XVIII: 172; (Epitaph), XIV: 77; V: 4
Wolseley, [Lord] Garnet Joseph, IV: 160, 174.
Woman at the Window, The (Padraic Ó Conaire) XIII: 91.
Women Poets (Irish), II: 165.
Wood, Herbert, III: 14.
"Woodbine Willie", see Kennedy, Geoffrey C. Studdert.
Woodburn, [Rev.] James B., V: 192.
Wooden Book, A, XIII: 13.
Wood-Martin, William Gregory, IX: 87.

Woods, Edward, IV: 14.
Woods, James, (Obit.) VIII: 92.
Woodward, [Dr.] Richard, IX: 24.
Word and the World (Kevin Faller), XXXI: 10.
Word for Ireland, A (T. M. Healy), XIX: 36.
Wordsworth, William, (*Wordsworth in Scotland*), XXXII: 146.
Workers' Republic, XVIII: 71.
Works on Wexford, XVIII: 98.
World, The, XIV: 38.
World's Paper Trade Review, I: 159.
Worm Turneth, The, ("Auctor"), XXXI: 54.
Worth, Edward, I: 128.
Worthies of Thomond (ed. Robert Herbert), XXIX: 142.
Woulfe, [Fr.] Patrick, XI: 78.
"W.P.C.", II: 29.
Wrack and Other Stories (Arnold Bax), X: 61
Wright, [Dr.] Hagberg, I: 106.
Wright, [Prof] Percival, I: 155.
Wright, R. H., VII: 9.
Wright, Thomas H. (Obit.) VII: 191.
Wright, [Rev.] W. Ball, IV: 196.
Writings on the Walls (Conall Cearnach), VII: 162.
Wulff, Winifred (*The Cure for Sprain throughout the Ages*), XXIV: 129-30.
Wyndham, Horace (*Victorian Paradise*), XXIII: 27.
Wynne, Jake (*Ugly Brew*), XXIV: 91.
Wynne, Maud (*An Irishman and His Family*), XXV: 67.
Wyse, W. C. Bonaparte, XXXII: 17.

X

"X.Y.Z.", VI: 45

Y

Year-Book of Agricultural Co-operation, 1936 (ed. Horace Plunkett Foundation) XXV: 46.
Years of my Pilgrimage, The (Rt. Hon. Sir John Ross), XV: 13.
Years of the Shadow, The (Katharine Tynan), XI: 11.
Yeats, Jack B., III: 98, XIII: 147; (Sligo) XVIII: 95; (*Apparitions*) XXI: 139; (*Sailing, Sailing Swiftly*) XXII: 94; (*The Amaranthers*) XXIV: 67.
Yeats, John B. (*Essays Irish and American*), X: 12.
Yeats, William Butler, (Civil List Pension) II: 142; (Bibliography) II:162; (*The Land of Heart's Desire*) III: 210; (Synge and *The Playboy*) IV: 7; (Irish Literary Society) IV: 202, V: 100, V: 215, VI: 77, 130, VII 184, 192; (American Visit) V: 9; (*Yeats, Lady Gregory and Synge*) V: 122; (*Memory Harbour*)VI: 63; (Hone, *W. B. Yeats*) VII: 160, XXIX: 47; 111; (Forrest Reid, *W. B. Yeats*) VII: 113, VI: 96; ("Mosada") VIII: 13; 59, 62; (*Responsibilities*) VIII: 47, 60; (*The Sphere*) IX: 32; (marriage) IX: 57; (Mr. Yeats, by Himself and Others) XI: 15; (allusion to) XI: 58; (*Eight Poems*) XII: 16; (*Irish Poets of Today*) XII: 141; (Four Years, 1887-1891) XIII: 13, 34; (*Recollections*) XIII: 45; (*Poems Written in Discouragement*) XIII: 83; (*Thoughts Upon the Present State of the World*) XIII: 92; (Univerity of Aberdeen protest) XIII: 152; (Nobel Prize) XIV: 10-11; (*Plays and Controversies*) XIV: 64; (*Essays*) XIV: 89; (Yeats Exhibition) XIV: 128; (*Reveries over Childhood and Youth*) VIII: 60; (*Wild Swans of Coole*) X: 90; (*Essays*) XIV: 89; ("Confessions") XV: 19; XV: 47, 54; (Encouragement to John Masefield) XVIII: 154; (*Samhain*) XVIII: 123; (*The Winding Stair*) XXII: 72; (*Collected Plays*) XXIII: 54; (Arnold Bennett) XVIII: 131. (Yeats and O'Leary) XXVII: 245; (*Last Poems and Plays*) XXVII: 238; (Yeats at High School, Dublin) XXX: 3; (*The Man and the Masks*) XXXI: 94; ("The Sally Gardens") XXXI: 133; (*The Identity of Yeats*) XXXII: 117; (*Autobiographies*) XXXII: 117.
'Yellow-Back' (earliest specimen in Belfast), XVIII: 67.
Yellow Book of Lecan, The, XX: 115.
Yorkshire Celtic Studies, XXVII: 286.
Youghal, (printing in) IV: 24; (a Youghal bookbinder) XVIII: 173; (Old Library) XXI: 43..
Young, Ella (*Celtic Wonder Tales*), XV: 32.
Young, Filson, IV: 51, IX: 31, XIII: 85.
Young Ireland—(Press, 1848) II: 137, 161, 162, 171; (Movement) VI: 13; (Relic) VIII: 140, IX: 35; (*Young Ireland*, Pamphlets) XVIII: 86; (Libraries of Young Irelanders) XXVII: 156; (Young Ireland and Sinn Féin) XXXII: 107.
Young, Lewis, VIII: 88.
"Young McCance" [Samuel McCance], IV: 34.
Young, Townsend ["J.E.B." and pseudo. of John Morrisey], XIV: 127, XX: 66.

Younge, Marianne, VIII: 144.

Z

Zimmer, Heinrich, II: 40, 102.
"Zozimus" (Michael Moran), III: 89, 105, XIV: 86, XXVI: 16, 58.

The *Irish Book Lover* and Its Critics
Bruce Stewart

I

In a recent book on Irish literary journals Frank Shovlin calls attention to Terence Brown's remark that periodicals are 'social facts, just as potato crops, tractors and new industries are'.[1] In his seminal work *Ireland: A Social and Cultural History* (1985) where this observation is to be found, Brown makes extensive use of just such sources to illustrate his argument. Shovlin's examination of six specific journals—*The Irish Statesman, The Dublin Magazine, Ireland To-Day, The Bell, Envoy*, and *Rann*—traces the aspirations and opinions of their editors as well as the constraints under which they laboured. It is necessary to admit at this point that not one reference is made to the object of the present compilation in either work. This is perhaps excusable on the grounds that *The Irish Book Lover* was less a literary organ than a bibliographical newsletter. Neither a venue for poetry or fiction excepting only verses addressed by one contributor to another, a few translations and a number of 'undiscovered' poems, it contains nothing that an editor might covet for an anthology of Irish literature. Nor does it contain any exercises in extended criticism: only short reviews and 'notices' of newly-published works with some information about plots and characters and often questionable judgements on their literary merits. In this respect it was to be superseded by Stephen Brown's *Ireland in Fiction* (1919) and the continuation of that work by Desmond Clarke (1985).[2] At the same time, its two hundred and forty-nine numbers issued between 1909 and 1957 constitute a run of an 'almost impossible length' for any Irish literary journal—as Nicholas Allen tells us in his introduction to the present volume—and arguably summon our attention on that account alone.[3]

If longevity is one reason why *The Irish Book Lover* should be reprinted, the prospect of its shedding light on the role of bookmen in the twentieth-century Irish nation-building is another. It is particularly

---

[1] Frank Shovlin, *The Irish Literary Periodical 1923-1958* (Clarendon Press 2003), p.11.
[2] See Stephen Brown, S.J., *Ireland in Fiction: A Guide to Irish Novels, Tales, Romances and Folklore* (Dublin: Maunsel 1919) and Desmond Clarke, *Do.* [Pt. 2] (Cork: Royal Carbery 1985).
[3] See p.15, *supra*.

strange to find it largely overlooked considering the number of contributors who clearly saw themselves as standing in direct line of descent from the scholarly crew of the Royal Irish Academy and the Ordnance Commission in the centuries before. Many were themselves members of the Royal Society of Antiquaries of Ireland, others of the Bibliographical Society of Ireland. The venerable literary names bandied in these pages—Cambrensis, Keating and O'Molloy, Sir James Ware, Sylvester Lloyd and Charles Vallancey and John O'Donovan— are those who also feature in the older staples of Irish studies such as Russell Alspach's *Irish Poetry from the English Invasion to 1798* (1957) and more recent works such as Joep Leerssen's *Mere Irish and Fíor Ghael* (1986) and Michael Cronin's *Translating Ireland* (1996). *The Irish Book Lover* has a strong North-South profile, with an Ulster presence made up of men like F. J. Bigger who cut considerable figures in their day. The Gaelic-revival element is pronounced at all stages with Irish names and titles prominent in the title page and index. A strong clerical influence is maintained by contributors such as Fr. Paul Walsh (otherwise Pól Breathnach), Edmund Hogan, S.J., Rev. John Brady, and Fr. Stephen Brown, all of whom brought a somewhat pietistic and patriotic note to their philological, onomastic and bibliophilic studies. As such they are representative of the intellectual *zeitgeist* of their Irish moment—a moment that admitted little room for the agnostic semiologies of today.

Aside from any consideration of content, it is possible to defend *The Irish Book Lover* on the grounds that the characteristic form of attention exhibited in its pages anticipates the 'book-history' method as a means of constructing a materialist version of cultural history. (The terms book production, book circulation, and book reception are the key to the mysteries of this method.) In this sense, the thirty-two volumes of *The Irish Book Lover* are a precursor of the five-volume "History of the Book in Ireland" currently reaching completion under the joint editorship of Robert Welch and Brian Walker. At the same time the actual contents of *The Irish Book Lover* make a very real claim on our attention inasmuch as its green-clad volumes comprise a quite unique corpus of information about the Irish book trade, as well as a rich source of information about the booksellers and collectors, bookmen and authors in every period. The attraction of the series is not confined to dry-as-dust memorials to dead scholars either. A set of notices on the 1916 leaders printed in the double-issue for August and September, for example, offers a striking insight into the mixed feelings that stirred in the breasts of literary folk during the weeks and months immediately after the Easter Rising. Reviewing eye-witness accounts hot from the press presented opportunities to express editorial opinions—or, more exactly, to produce the medley of conscious and unconscious reactions that characterise these intriguing articles. While speaking of the 'terrible outbreak that drenched the streets of Dublin in blood during the Black Easter' in a review of John H. Boyle's *A Brief History of the Revolt and Its Suppression* (1916), the editor adverts to the 'unfortunate leaders'. That the phrase so clearly echoes the 'unfortunate Mr. Emmet' of an earlier rebellion indicates the frame of reference to which the new events were at first assimilated.[4] We may safely infer that the review was written by John Crone, the founding editor, because the phrase 'unfortunate leaders' also crops up in "Editor's Gossip" where he notes the rising price for books by the dead leaders a little earlier in the same issue.[5] Therein he also notices an essay on "The Secret Constitution of Shinn Fane" written for the *English Review* by a certain Major Stuart Stephens who claims to have had prior knowledge of the planned rebellion. Our editor adds 'Sic' to the misspelt title, and not a word more.

It was in the course of reviewing James Stephens's *Insurrection in Dublin* for the issue spanning winter 1916–17 that Crone struck the note—neither adulation nor anathema—that best illustrates the journal's reaction to the Easter Rising:

> The utter unexpectedness of the whole thing, the popular feeling varying with each speaker, the hopelessness of the attempt, and the numerous 'effective' incidents, are all portrayed with the skill of the practised writer, and oh! the pity of it.[6]

Only an exclamation about 'a terrible attack on John Redmond!' in Stephens's book reveals the fault-line that might divide one contributor to The *Irish Book Lover* from another since this involves the question whether Redmond had sent the Irish Volunteers to 'needless death' in France (to borrow Yeats's phrase) and, with it, the corresponding question of the rights and wrongs of physical-force republicanism at home. In Crone's sentence, 'terrible' is used in its etymological rather than its demotic sense—closer, in fact, to Yeats's 'terrible beauty' than to facile condemnation. The moderate nationalist of Redmond's parliamentary party was but a year away from electoral annihilation at the

---

[4] 'Notices of New Books', *The Irish Book Lover*, Vol. VIII, Nos. 1 & 2 (Aug. & Sept. 1916), 16 [Henceforth *IBL*].
[5] 'Editor's Gossip', *IBL* (Aug. & Sept. 1916), 12.
[6] 'Notices of New Books', *IBL* (Dec. & Jan. 1916–17), 64

time of writing. It is possible that Crone's coverage of 1916 met with some dissent among readers back in Dublin. If so, the only indication is a longish note by D. J. O'Donoghue in the following volume that offers a fuller listing of the leaders' published works while identifying Thomas MacDonagh as 'beyond question the most distinguished of the insurgents'.[7] A shorter communication from P. S. O'Hegarty adds further titles with bibliographical aplomb and notable reserve about other aspects of the matter, especially considering that he himself was a member of the Irish Republican Brotherhood and would later endorse the Anglo-Irish Treaty as a member of the Supreme Council.[8]

II

Omission from scholarly indexes is not the worst that *The Irish Book Lover* has to face in the way of critical disparagement. Take for instance the charges laid against it by Gerry Smyth when he writes that the 'bookman's approach' adopted by Colm Ó Lochlainn—the third and last editor—was 'completely divorced from issues of analysis or explication or "literary criticism" in any of its contemporary forms'.

> [D]espite the Irish interest to be hunted down in each text, its value as a commodity is not influenced by questions about the relationship between culture and nation.[9]

This elastic inference enables us to view *The Irish Book Lover* under Ó Lochlainn's management as 'a politically quietistic rejoinder to those writer-critics wishing to make criticism a powerful interventionary weapon in current debates'.[10] A defect of just that kind may well be identified in issues for 1929 and 1930 where a bibliographical strand is introduced under the heading "Literature of the Conflict" signifying, at the outset, books about the Civil War. Willing contributions from Frank Gallagher and others led Ó Lochlainn to moot a wider bracket commencing with the Irish Volunteers in 1913 and this he proposed to call "The Literature of Revolt".[11] Is this a quietistic rejoinder intended to

---

[7] D. J. O'Donoghue, 'Literature and the Late Rebellion', *IBL* (Oct. & Nov. 1916), 28. O'Donoghue had taken up his post as librarian of University College, Dublin, seven years earlier.

[8] 'Post Bag', *IBL*, Vol. VIII, Nos. 3 & 4 (Oct. & Nov. 1916), 44.

[9] Gerry Smyth, *Decolonisation and Criticism: The Construction of Irish Literature* (London: Pluto Press 1998), pp.126-27. He writes specifically of Colm Ó Lochlainn, the third and final editor of the journal.

[10] Ibid., p.127.

[11] 'Literature of the Conflict', *IBL* (May & June 1930), 69ff.

dampen down political debate? In adopting a posture of bookish objectivity, Ó Lochlainn is possibly attempting to turn persistent division into a matter for cultural reflection—surely more pacificist than quietistic in intent. Perhaps it ought to have been otherwise, given the imperative summons of the ideal republic; but there remains a danger of being led by our own determination to see literary theory as the chief vehicle of social change to overlook the actual conditions of critical discourse in the Ireland of the day—a complex ecology of allegiances and beliefs, enthusiasms and constraints. (An apparent confusion between *contemporary* and *current* in the foregoing may be a symptom of just this problem.)

Even allowing that *The Irish Book Lover* was mainly about books in their material aspect—and, issue by issue, it certainly was—it was also pervasively informed by a nationalist conception of the world of letters without which no such journal could have been conceived (or not, at least, with the word 'Irish' in the title). Dr. John S. Crone, its founder and an Ulster Protestant, was notionally non-political but nevertheless an effectual transmitter of the ecumenical spirit of Young Ireland. This he had in common with Francis Joseph Bigger, the Belfast solicitor, amateur archaeologist, and Gaelic-revivalist whom Sir Shane Leslie described as 'a Protestant with Franciscan leanings' in his novel *Doomsland*, where he models for MacNeill.[12] In his posthumous tribute to Crone, P. S. O'Hegarty begins by confessing his own overriding interest in 'the Irish Ireland movement' before offering this account of the older man: 'He took no interest at all in Irish politics, beyond being a good Irishman, and I never knew, nor cared to know, where he stood upon politics.'[13] An element of exoneration is apparent in those words: if not an active Republican at least Crone was not a Unionist. It was not, however, difficult to determine where he stood on politics since he served for many years in senior political posts on the Willesden Urban District and Middlesex County Councils. In 1918 he stood as a Liberal candidate for Parliament in Willesden West, losing to Charles Pickham.[14] At the death of Parnell his standing in Liberal circles had been such that the train made a stop at Willesden to allow him to place a wreathe on the Home Rule leader's coffin. In 1925 his Irish language

---

[12] See "F. J. Bigger" in PGIL EIRData [www.pgil-eirdata.org]. Bigger's archaeological digs gave rise to the expression 'well and truly biggered' among Northern Irish archaeologists.

[13] P. S. Hegarty, 'Some Memories of Dr. Crone', in *IBL* (Oct. 1946), 1ff.

[14] I am grateful to my friend and colleague Brian Keogh, Esq., for researching this information.

sympathies led him to prefix the *Irish Book Lover* title of the fifteenth volume—the last he edited—with an Irish translation: *An Leabhar Chara Gaodhlach*. All that he lacked, then, to rank as a true patriot in P. S. O'Hegarty's eyes, was membership of the Sinn Féin Party.

At the close of his *eulogium*, O'Hegarty recalls a final encounter with Crone that offers positive information regarding the latter's ultimate position:

> The last time I saw him was to meet him in College Green accidentally ten years ago, and to spend fifteen happy moments with him. He said to me then, what F. A. Fahy and W. P. Ryan had said not so long before in almost the same place, that it was most heartening and most wonderful to see how much the Treaty had changed Ireland for the better. We did not see it here, we were too close to it. But the London Irishman sees it.

Here is surely an example of the mechanism that Benedict Anderson has spoken of in a famous phrase about 'imagined communities'[15]—in this case, a community of bookmen that draws together the cheerful, judicious figure of Dr. Crone along with the songster Fahy and the literary journalist Ryan (two leading lights of the Irish literary movement in London prior to 1894) as witnesses to the success of Saorstát Éireann. That Crone said something to allay anxieties of the author of *The Victory of Sinn Féin: How It Won It, and How It Used It* (1924) is undeniable; how those words revolved in his own mind before he gifted O'Hegarty with them is as uncertain as anything else about the mentality of a man imbued with a particoloured blend of Irishness and Britishness.[16] Yet, if any ambiguity surrounds the national outlook of John S. Crone, there is less of that about Séamus Ó Casaide and Colm Ó Lochlainn, the later editors of *The Irish Book Lover* (respectively from 1928 and 1930). The difference here can perhaps be measured in terms of a distinction Seamus Deane has drawn between two variant kinds of cultural nationalism: that of *adherence* and that of *separation*.[17] The former is a subaltern outlook that puts the heritage of the colonised group at the disposal of the dominant culture in return for some measure of 'parity of esteem' (a process theorised by Matthew Arnold in his 1865 "Lectures on Celtic Literature"), The latter consists

---

[15] See Benedict Anderson, *Imagined Communities: Reflections on the Origin and Spread of Nationalism* [rev. edn.] (London: Verso 1991), p.7.

[16] P. S. O'Hegarty, *The Victory of Sinn Féin: How it Won It and How It Used It* [Modern Ireland in the Making Ser.] (Dublin: Talbot Press; London: Simpkin, Marshall, Hamilton, Kent 1924).

[17] See Seamus Deane, *Heroic Styles: The Tradition of an Idea* (Derry: Field Day Co. 1984), p.7.

in a rejection of the imperial centre and its authority, at first by cultural but ultimately by harsher measures resulting in political freedom. The successive editorships of *The Irish Book Lover* straddle the divide between these two attitudes, with Dr. Crone standing on one side and Séamus Ó Casaide on the other.

Some consideration of the cultural niche into which *The Irish Book Lover* was inserted may be useful here. Though first published in 1910, Crone's journal was the outcome of an awakening of interest in Irish books which arguably began when, in October 1884, Henry Bradshaw gave a lecture at Trinity College, Dublin, calling on Irish book lovers and librarians to commence collecting information about printing presses in Ireland. Bradshaw, Keeper of Rare Books at Cambridge University Library and often spoken of as the 'father of modern bibliography', was the son of Ulster-born parents whose first enthusiasm for his subject was inspired by contact with a substantial collection of Irish books in his father's home. This enthusiasm he communicated to men such as Ernest Reginald McClintock Dix who would form the earliest cohort of contributions to *The Irish Book Lover*—and hence it is that Dix reproduces the *Freeman's Journal* account of Bradshaw's speech at Trinity in his own contribution to the first issue of the new journal: 'The great object', Bradhaw had declared, 'was to get at those sources of information which were subsidiary to the writing of history; and this was more essential than ever at present, when the study of History was being more than ever placed on a scientific or, at all events, a methodical basis'.[18] At his death in 1886 the books that Bradshaw received from his father and substantially augmented were left to Cambridge University Library where they still form the nucleus of the Irish Collection. A first volume of the 1,340-page catalogue published by C. E. Sayle was greeted by *The Irish Book Lover* as a great event in May 1910.[19]

For Dix, writing on Bradshaw the year before, the manner of his passing away, as his biographer Prothero narrates it, was worth recalling:

> On the morning of the 11th February, 1886, he was found dead 'sitting in his arm chair, at the table in his inner room, a little Irish book, closed, lay on the table in front of him.' The ruling passion strong in

---

[18] E. R. McClintock Dix, "Henry Bradshaw on Printing in Ireland", *IBL* (Aug. 1909), 13f.
[19] A second volume appeared in 1916.

death.[20]

That ruling passion had of course been Irish books, but it did not make him an Irish nationalist. Dix, his Irish counterpart whom Crone called 'the most accomplished Irish bibliographer of the present day',[21] presumably reached an accommodation with nationalist Ireland, as did his Alexandra-College educated wife.[22] When it came to nominating the 'father of Irish bibliography', however, Crone turns to John Power, a Cork-born non-practising civil engineer who had single-handedly produced several issues of *The Irish Literary Enquirer* in London during 1865-66. Later on he edited a newspaper in Panama before his health collapsed, returning to England to die in 1872. As Nicholas Allen tells us (and this selection shows) Crone inteviewed officials at the British Library who remembered 'a tall, thin, gray man with a bad cough' and nothing more.[23]

III

The survival of *The Irish Book Lover* for forty-eight years is chiefly attributable to an amicable transfer of ownership under circumstances documented in the first issue for 1928. As the incoming editor, Séamus Ó Casaide, wrote: 'Owing to his continued exile from Éire, Doctor Crone found himself unable to retain the editorship of *The Irish Book Lover* and it is now re-established under a new editor with the full approval and the very welcome assistance of its predecessor.'[24] This may be taken as meaning that no editor residing in the British metropolis could hope to conduct a lively Irish journal after Ireland ceased to be the political province it had been when the journal was established—or, in other terms, that the shift from adherence to separation needed to be marked by a corresponding change of editor. It seems clear that Dr. Crone was happy to 'give back' the journal to its rightful owners now that the question of sovereignty of Ireland had been resolved in favour of a native government. In that spirit he started his "Sgéala ó Chathair na gCéo" column, which was to run for many

---

[20] Dix, op. cit., idem.
[21] Crone, Idem.
[22] J. S. Crone, "Foreword", *IBL* (Aug. 1909), 1. (The title is given as 'foreward' both in the body of the article and in the index.)
[23] Dix's wife Úna—née Elizabeth Rachel Leech—wrote novels in Irish for An Gúm as "Brenda". See the Boston College Exhibition "Art of the Free State" [online at www.bc.edu/libraries/centers/burns/exhibits/virtual/bk covers/.
[24] Séamus Ó Casaide, 'Editorial', *IBL* (Jan. & Feb. 1928), 1.

years, with this gracious thought:

> In the first place, allow me to offer you my best wishes and hearty congratulations on your assuming the editorial control of a new series of *The Irish Book Lover*. May you never find a thorn in the cushion of your editorial chair, your occupancy of it be as long and happy as mine was, your contributors as able and generous, and your subscribers as loyal.[25]

In the very year that Ó Casaide removed *The Irish Book Lover* to Dublin, John Crone published his own *Concise Dictionary of Irish Biography*—the fruit of an extended strand in early issues addressing the need for a full-scale reference work along the lines of the British *Dictionary of National Biography*, the latter having occasioned some disgruntlement in Ireland on account of its omissions as well as its pervasively imperialist assumptions.[26] Crone dedicated his reference work to James McNeill, the second Governor-General of the Free State, adorning it with an epigraph that echoes the Virgilian motto of the RDS: '*Quae regio in terris nostri non plena lab-oris*'. His preface similarly reflects a widely-held preoccupation with the statistical prominence of distinguished Irishmen abroad—many of course as servants of the British Empire. Two of Crone's own sons were army officers, one an O.B.E. in India, another a port authority in Australia, while a third served as librarian to the Royal Geographical Society.[27]

One clue to Crone's unruffled friendship with the *gaelgóir* editors who succeeded him can be found in the way he responded to the violence into which Ireland descended during 1919-23. Far from putting a break on publication, these events appear to have galvanised the editor into formulating a definite interpretation of modern Irish literary history based on the role played by the Anglo-Irish revivalists which still resonates in the classrooms of today. Here the method—as so often with this journal—was to copy an article that had appeared elsewhere, in this instance a review of *Irish Poets Today*, an anthology edited by Lettice D'Oyley Walters in 1921.[28] It may be guessed that the original,

---

[25] J. S. Crone, 'Sgéala ó Chathair na gCeó', *IBL* (Jan. & Feb. 1928), 2 [i.e., 'Report from the City of Fog'].

[26] See John S. Crone, *A Concise Dictionary of Irish Biography* (Dublin: Talbot Press 1928).

[27] See "In Memoriam John Smyth Crone, 1858-1945", Vol. XXX, No. 1 (Oct. 1946), 1.

[28] Lettice D'Oyley Walters, *Irish Poets of Today: An Anthology* (London: T. Fisher Unwin 1921), 127pp. In the more recent "Missing Persons" volume, Eoin MacNeill was given as 'leader of the extremists'.

which appeared in the *Saturday Review*, was written by Robert Lynd, a fellow-Ulsterman and close associate of Dr. Crone who used his columnist's position as "Y.Y." of the *Spectator* to criticise the British management of Ireland—as he pointedly did in the wake of the 1916 executions with a pamphlet comparing the 1916 leaders to English patriots repulsing the invading Hun should Germany ever land on British soil.[29]

Lynd begins by pondering how a country which had produced the Celtic-Twilight poems gathered in the anthology under consideration could have reached its present pass—a question which implies the redundancy of that anthology or at least the inaccuracy of the time-line in its title. 'A few years ago Ireland seemed to be the greatest dreamer among nations', he writes.

> From all that we have come in half-a-dozen years to battle, murder and sudden death [...] The strings of the harp are broken, or their sound cannot be heard because of the roar of bomb or machine-gun.[30]

He first seeks an explanation in the inevitable swing of the pendulum 'back from dream to action', a change that 'brought Ireland rapidly from its achievement of spiritual independence to a fierce struggle for economic and political freedom'. Digging deeper, he comes to see the Anglo-Irish writers as precursors, even revolutionaries in their own unconscious way—though, like Moses, they will never enter the promised land. At this point our reviewer begins to 'speculate' about cultural causes and political effects, asking

> whether the imprisonment of Standish O'Grady, Yeats, Hyde, "Æ", Lady Gregory, and other pioneers of the Gaelic mood in Anglo-Irish literature, once they showed tendencies to revert to ancestor worship, might not have made it unnecessary to have five thousand young Irishmen in prison today?

And, finally:

> How much of all that dream went into the insurrection, how much of all that poetry comforts the hearts of the outlawed members of the Republican Army, trysting among the mountains and rocks, and in the starry nights, we may know perhaps when some of them later write their memories.[31]

It is against this background that we may best construe W. B. Yeats's

---

[29] *If the German Conquered England* (Dub/London: Maunsel 1917).
[30] "Irish Poetry" [extract from *Saturday Review*], IBL, (Oct. 1921), 27
[31] Idem.

rhetorical question: 'Did that play of mine send out certain men the English shot?'—which Paul Muldoon has revised to read: 'If Willie Yeats had saved his pencil lead / Would certain men have stayed in bed?'[32] Stephen Gwynn (a contributor often mentioned in these pages) had the same thought when, returning from the first night of *Cathleen Ni Houlihan*, he asked his journal 'if such plays should be produced unless one was prepared to go out to shoot and be shot.'[33]

IV

While rarely 'interventionist' in the sense that post-colonial critics use the term, nor even 'literary critical' in a contemporary sense aligned with Eliot or Empson or ourselves, reviewers for *The Irish Book Lover* held definite views about the proper conduct of Irish literature that often precluded writers that we ourselves most admire. So it was with James Joyce and Liam O'Flaherty, whose realism seemed to them repulsive and disgraceful in comparison with such improving works as Mrs. Thomas Concannon's *Defenders of the Ford* (1931). Here is a book whose 'record of the heroism, uprightness, and patriotism of Ireland's youth is a wonderful one' and which ought therefore to be 'placed in the hands of our boys at an impressionable age'.[34] Similarly, the editor himself prefers D. P. Moran's *The Leader* to George Russell's *Irish Statesman*, as the notice marking the passing of the latter in April 1930 clearly shows. Russell was previously lauded in a cutting from *The Nat-ion* which Crone had reprinted in 1921. This underscored Æ's services to Ireland in recognising the 'national value of those poets, scholars and essayists who began to infuse a new spirit into their nation about thirty years ago.'[35] By contrast, when the *Statesman* collapsed a decade later we are tepidly told that its 'passing [...] will be regretted by many who were *not* "constant readers"' [italics mine]— meaning presumably Colm Ó Lochlainn and his associates at *The Irish Book Lover*.[36]

If the tone of encomium is notably reserved, the reason for this soon emerges: ever a 'fearless champion of free speech [...] in a country

---

[32] Quoted by Fintan O'Toole, reviewing Nicholas Grene, *The Politics of Irish Drama*, in *The Irish Times*, Weekend Section (11 March 2000).

[33] Quoted in Peter Costello, *The Heart Grown Brutal: The Irish Revolution in Literature from Parnell to the Death of Yeats, 1891-1939* (Gill & Macmillan 1977), p.4.

[34] *IBL* (March & April 1931), p.64.

[35] 'Pen Portraits' [extract from *The Nation*], *IBL* (Oct. 1921), 41.

[36] Colm Ó Lochlainn, 'Editorial', *IBL* (March & April 1930), 34.

where freedom is more spoken of than understood', Russell had the added handicap that he lacked 'understanding of the Irish language or Gaelic cultural activities' and hence 'opened his columns to the vapourings of self-styled authorities whose right to fulminate was strenuously denied by many who listened eagerly to Æ's doctrine on economics and literature'. At this point the editor inserts an equally long notice on *The Leader* on no other pretext than that he hopes the deficit will be made up by the more worthy organ:

> And now almost alone among the weeklies stands *The Leader*, still independent, still edited by the veteran D. P. Moran. Is it too much to hope that *The Leader*'s message—economic and National—will once more find a welcome in the minds of those Irishmen who set their country's good above the clash of contemporary political endeavour? *The Philosophy of Irish Ireland* after thirty years still rings true, and the walls of Jericho have not yet 'come atumbling down'. The re-Gaelicising of Ireland connotes the revitalising of Irish life. In the Church, in the schools, in commerce, and in sport there is a broad field for National work. If *The Leader* leads will Ireland follow?[37]

It was but a short step from this position to full support for the Censorship Act of 1929 of which Nicholas Allen writes in his introduction to the present volume.[38] In October 1930 Colm Ó Lochlainn noted with approval the likelihood that the Northern Irish state would emulate the measures instituted in the south.[39] When, in another place, Séamus Ó Donnabháin says, 'it may be that an Irish author will one day attain to the doubtful distinction of being included in a subsequent list', he is speaking harshly of modern Irish writers rather than the Irish censors.[40]

From our standpoint Joyce, O'Flaherty and Beckett and all those others who trespassed against the straightened moral principles and *politesse* of Free-State Ireland eventually won the day. Yet, however cylopean the censors' view may seem in retrospect, it nevertheless reflected the dominant ethos and the intellectual climate of contemporary Ireland. Positive hostility to the atheistic bent of non-Irish intellectuals was an essential—if not defining—part of it. Nor was this confined to the clergy or their literary myrmidons at the Catholic Truth Society

---

[37] Idem.
[38] See p.13, *supra*.
[39] [Colm Ó Lochlainn], "A Current Commentary", Vol. XVIII, No. 5 (Sept. & Oct. 1930),
[40] Séamus Ó Donnabháin, 'A Current Commentary', in *IBL* (May & June 1930), pp.3-4.

against whom Ó Lochlainn once raised the cudgel. Prominent among those on board *The Irish Book Lover* who actively disputed the claims of socialism in Ireland was P. S. O'Hegarty and his critique of Seán O'Casey is certainly one of the representative texts of the period.[41] In reviewing a volume of O'Casey's autobiography, he writes of the exiled dramatist:

> He can have Big Ben, and the lights of London, and the Red Flag—he is curiously irritated about the Red Flag and the refusal of Irishmen to adopt it as their flag—and we will keep the three [Dublin] plays. And we shall always have a corner in our hearts, not for the man he thinks he is, nor for the man he would like to be, but for the man he was.[42]

Similar remarks about Peadar O'Donnell's weakness for 'Spanish anarchism' keenly suggest reasons why today's readers might find *The Irish Book Lover* less appealing than several other Irish journals of the period.[43] This hardly warrants overlooking its significance as the revealing 'social fact' that it is; for if the latter pages are overly-endowed with the parochial virtues of newly-independent Ireland, they are faithful to the dominant humour of the day. In the wake of those revolutions in ideas and manners which separate us from that era—and more so, perhaps, from the Edwardian era in which its first contributors were writing—it is worth emphasising its continuing utility as a source-book for Irish studies and an inspiration to Irish book lovers of today.

---

[41] 'A Dramatist of New Born Ireland', a similar piece first published in *Northern American Review* (1927), was reprinted in as in Ronald Ayling, ed., *Sean O'Casey: Modern Judgements* (1969), pp.60-67.
[42] Review of *Inishfallen, Fare Thee Well*, in *IBL* (June 1949), p.44.
[43] Review of Peadar O'Donnell, *Salud!*, in *IBL* (March & April 1937), p.67.

The Irish Book Lover
Appendix I
Chronology of Issues

VOLUME 1

I: 1 (Aug. 1909)
I: 2 (Sept. 1909)
I: 3 (Oct. 1909)
I:4 (Nov. 1909)
I: 5 (Dec. 1909)
I: 6 (Jan. 1910)
I: 7 (Feb. 1910)
I: 8 (March 1910)
I: 9 (April 1910)
I: 10 (May 1910)
I: 11 (June 1910)
I: 1 2 (July 1910)

VOLUME 2

II: 1 (Aug. 1910)
II: 2 (Sept. 1910)
2. 3 (Oct. 1910)
II: 4 (Nov. 1910)
II: 5 (Dec. 1910)
II: 6 (Jan. 1911)
II: 7 (Feb. 1911)
II: 8 (March 1911)
II: 9 (April 1911)
II: 10 (May 1911)
II: 11 (June 1911)
II: 12 (July 1911)

VOLUME 3

III: 1 (Aug. 1911)
III: 2 (Sept. 1911)
III: 3 (Oct. 1911)
III: 4 (Nov. 1911)
III: 5 (Dec. 1911)
III: 6 (Jan. 1912)
III: 7 (Feb. 1912)
III: 8 (March 1912)
III: 9 (April 1912)
III: 10 (May 1912)
III: 11 (June 1912)
III: 12 (July 1912)

VOLUME 4

IV: 1 (Aug. 1912)
IV: 2 (Sept. 1912)
IV: 3 (Oct. 1912)
IV: 4 (Nov. 1912)
IV: 5 (Dec. 1912)
IV: 6 (Jan. 1913)
IV: 7 (Feb. 1913)
IV: 8 (March 1913)
IV: 9 (April 1913)
IV: 10 (May 1913)
IV: 11 (June 1913)
IV: 12 (July 1913)

VOLUME 5

V: 1 (July 1913)
V: 2 (Sept. 1913)
V: 3 (Oct. 1913)
V: 4 (Nov. 1913)
V: 5 (Dec. 1913)
V: 6 (Jan. 1914)
V: 7 (Feb. 1914)
V: 8 (March 1914)
V: 9 (April 1914)
V: 10 (May 1914)
V: 11 (June 1914)
V: 12 (July 1914)

VOLUME 6

VI: 1 (Aug. 1914)
VI: 2 (Sept. 1914)

VI: 3 (Oct. 1914)
VI: 4 (Nov. 1914)
VI: 5 (Dec. 1914)
VI: 6 (Jan. 1915)
VI: 7 (Feb. 1915)
VI: 8 (March 1915)
VI: 9 (April 1915)
VI: 10 (May 1915)
VI: 11 (June 1915)
VI: 12 (July 1915)

VOLUME 7
VII: 1 (Aug. 1915)
VII: 2 (Sept. 1915)
VII: 3 (Oct. 1915)
VII: 4 (Nov. 1915)
VII: 5 (Dec. 1915)
VII: 6 (Jan. 1916)
VII: 7-8 (Feb./March 1916)
VII: 9-10 (April/May 1916)
VII: 11-12 (June/July 1916)

VOLUME 8
VIII: 1-2 (Aug./Sept. 1916)
VIII: 3-4 (Oct./Nov. 1916)
VIII: 5-6 (Dec.-Jan. 1916-17)
VIII: 7-8 (Feb./March1917)
VIII: 9-10 (April/May 1917)
VIII: 11-12 (Jun/July 1917)

VOLUME 9
IX: 1-2 (Aug./Sept. 1917)
IX: 3-4 (Oct./Nov. 1917)
IX: 5-6 (Dec./Jan. 1917-18)
IX: 7-8 (Feb./March 1918)
IX: 9-10 (April/May 1918)IX: 11-12 (June/July 1919)

VOLUME 10
X: 1-2 (Aug./Sept. 1918)
X: 3-5 (Oct./Dec. 1918)
X: 6-8 (Jan./March 1919)
X: 9-10 (April/May 1919)
X: 11-12 (June/July 1919)

VOLUME 11
XI: 1-2 (Aug./Sept. 1919)
XI: 3-4 (Oct./Nov. 1919)
XI: 5 (Dec. 1919)
XI: 6-7 (Jan./Feb. 1920)
XI: 8-9 (March/April 1920)
XI: 10 (May 1920)
XI: 11-12 (June/July 1920)

VOLUME 12
XII: 1-2 (Aug./Sept. 1920)
XII: 3-4 (Oct./Nov. 1920)
XII: 5 (Dec. 1920)
XII: 6-7 (Jan./Feb. 1921)
XII: 7-8 (March/April 1921)
XII: 9-11 (May/July 1921)

VOLUME 13
XIII: 1-2 (Aug./Sept. 1921)
XIII: 3 (Oct. 1921)
XIII: 4 (Nov. 1921)
XIII: 5 (Dec. 1921)
XIII: 6 (Jan. 1922)
XIII: 7-8 (Feb./March 1922)
XIII: 9-10 (April/May 1922)

VOLUME 14
XIV: 1 (Jan. 1924)
XIV: 2 (Feb. 1924.)
XIV: 3 (March 1924)
XIV: 4 (April 1924)
XIV: 5 (May 1924)
XIV: 6 (June 1924)
XIV: 7-8 (July/Aug. 1924)
XIV: 9-10 (Sept./Oct. 1924)
XIV: 11-12 (Nov. /Dec. 1924)

VOLUME 15
XV: 1 (Jan. 1925)

The Irish Book Lover

XV: 2 (April 1925)
XV: 3 (June 1925)
XV: 4 (Oct. 1925)

VOLUME 16
XVI: 1 (Jan./Feb. 1928)
XVI: 2 (March/April 1928)
XVI: 3 (June/July 1928)
XVI: 4-6 July/Dec. 1928)

VOLUME 17
XVII: 1 (Jan./Feb. 1929)
XVII: 2 (March/April 1929)
XVII: 3 (May/June 1929)
XVII: 4 (July/Aug. 1929)
XVII: 5 (Sept./Oct. 1929)
XVII: 6 (Nov. /Dec. 1929)

VOLUME 18
XVIII: 1 (Jan./Feb. 1930)
XVIII: 2 (March/April 1930)
XVIII: 3 (May/June 1930)
XVIII: 4 (July/Aug. 1930)
XVIII: 5 (Sept./Oct. 1930)
XVIII: 6 (Nov./Dec. 1930)

VOLUME 19
XIX: 1 (Jan./Feb. 1931)
XIX: 2 (March/April 1931)
XIX: 3 (May/June 1931)
XIX: 4 (July/Aug. 1931)
XIX: 5 (Sept./Oct. 1931)
XIX: 6 (Nov./Dec. 1931)

VOLUME 20
XX: 1 (Jan./Feb. 1932)
XX: 2 (March/April 1932)
XX: 3 (May/June 1932)
XX: 4 (July/Aug. 1932)
XX: 5 (Sept./Oct. 1932)
XX: 6 (Nov./Dec. 1932)

VOLUME 21
XXI: 1 (Jan./Feb. 1933)
XXI: 2 (March/April 1933)
XXI: 3 (May/June 1933)
XXI: 4 (July/Aug. 1933)
XXI: 5 (Sept./Oct. 1933)
XXI: 6 (Nov./Dec. 1933)

VOLUME 22
XXII: 1 (Jan./Feb. 1934)
XXII: 2 (March/April 1934)
XXII: 3 (May/June 1934)
XXII: 4 (July/Aug. 1934)
XXII: 5 (Sept./Oct.1934)
XXII: 6 (Nov./Dec. 1934)

VOLUME 23
XXIII: 1 (Jan./Feb. 1935)
XXIII: 2 (March/April 1935)
XXIII: 3 (May/June 1935)
XXIII: 4 (July/Aug. 1935)
XXIII: 5 (Sept./Oct. 1935)
XXIII: 6 (Nov./Dec. 1935)

VOLUME 24
XXIV: 1 (Jan./Feb. 1936)
XXIV: 2 (March/April 1936)
XXIV: 3 (May/June 1936)
XXIV: 4 (July/Aug. 1936)
XXIV: 5 (Sept./Oct. 1936)
XXIV: 6 (Nov./Dec. 1936)

VOLUME 25
XXV: 1 (Jan./Feb. 1937)
XXV: 2 (March/April 1937)
XXV: 3 (May/June 1937)
XXV: 4-6 (July-Dec. 1937)

VOLUME 26
XXVI: 1 (July/Aug. 1938)
XXVI: 2 (Sept./Oct. 1938)
XXVI: 3 (Nov./Dec. 1938)

XXVI: 4 (Jan./Feb. 1939)
XXVI: 5 (May 1939)
XXVI: 6 (Sept. 1939)

VOLUME 27
XXVII: 1 (Jan. 1940)
XXVII: 2 (March 1940)
XXVII: 3 (May 1940)
XXVII: 4 (July 1940)
XXVII: 5 (Nov. 1940)
XXVII: 6 (Feb. 1941)

VOLUME 28
XXVIII: 1 (April 1941)
XXVIII: 2 (June 1941)
XXVIII: 3 (Sept. 1941)
XXVIII: 4 (Feb. 1942)
XXVIII: 5-6 (May 1942)

VOLUME 29
XXIX: 1 (May 1943)
XXIX: 2 (March 1944)
XXIX: 3 (Dec. 1944)
XXIX: 4 (March 1945)
XXIX: 5 (June 1945)
XXIX: 6 (Nov. 1945)

VOLUME 30
XXX: 1 (Oct. 1946)
XXX: 2 (Feb. 1947)
XXX: 3 (Nov. 1947)
XXX: 4 (Jan. 1948)
XXX: 5 (May 1948)
XXX: 6 (Nov. 1948)

VOLUME 31
XXXI: 1 (March 1949)
XXXI: 2 (June 1949)
XXXI: 3 (Oct. 1949)
XXXI: 4 (April 1950)
XXXI: 5 (Feb. 1951)
XXXI: 6 (Nov. 1951)

VOLUME 32
XXXII: 1 (June 1952)
XXXII: 2 (July 1953)
XXXII: 3 (March 1954)
XXXII: 4 (Jan. 1955)
XXXII: 5 (July 1956)
XXXII: 6 (Sept. 1957)

The Princess Grace Irish Library (Monaco)
"The Irish Book Lover"
a symposium on
Irish Booklore Past, Present & Future
4th-7th October 2002

THE PARTICIPANTS

Nicholas Allen (Irish Government Fellow/DIT)
Brendan Barrington (Editor/*Dublin Review*)
Anthony Farrell (Publisher/The Lilliput Press)
Pauline Ferrie (Editor, *The Irish Emigrant* online)
Tony Farmar (Publisher/Former Chairman of Cló)
Anthony Hutton (Univ. of Ulster/EyeSpy)
Clare Hutton (Univ. of London)
Máire Kennedy (Dublin City Libraries)
Des Kenny (Kennys' Bookshop/Galway)
Nicholas Lee (Librarian/Birmingham UL)
Maurice Harmon (EIRData Adviser/UCD emeritus)
Christina Mahony (Catholic University of America)
Siobháin O'Rafferty (Librarian/Royal Irish Academy)
Colin Smythe (Publisher & Bibliographer)
Caroline Walsh (Literary Ed./*The Irish Times*.)

THE PROGRAMME

FRIDAY 4TH
5.00-7.00: Arrival & Greetings
8.00: Welcoming Dinner

SATURDAY 5TH
9.30-10.30: Keynote lecture
Nicholas Allen: "*The Irish Book Lover* (1909-1957)"
11.00-12.00: Participation & Response
12:30 – Lunch
2.30-3.30: Keynote lecture
Clare Hutton: "Chapters of Moral History: Failing to Publish *Dubliners*"

3.30-4.00 – Afternoon tea
4.00-5.00: Round-table Agenda
8.00 Ireland Fund of Monaco Gala Dinner

SUNDAY 6TH
9.30 10.30: Keynote Lecture
Christina Hunt Mahony: "Irish Studies in North America"
11.00-12.00: Participation and Response
12:30 – Lunch
2.30-3.30: Keynote Lecture
Bruce Stewart & Anthony Hutton:
"PGIL *EIRData*—Serving Irish Studies Online"

3.30-4.00 - Afternoon tea
4.00-5.00: Round-table Agenda
8.00: Farewell Dinner